REBELLION AND VIOLENCE IN ISLAMIC LAW

Khaled Abou El Fadl's book represents the first systematic examination of the idea and treatment of political resistance and rebellion in Islamic law. Premodern jurists produced an extensive and sophisticated discourse on the legality of rebellion and the treatment due to rebels under Islamic law. The book examines the emergence and development of these discourses from the eighth to the fifteenth centuries, and considers juristic responses to the various terror-inducing strategies employed by rebels including assassination, stealth attacks, and rape. The study demonstrates how Muslim jurists went about restructuring several competing doctrinal sources in order to construct a highly technical discourse on rebellion. It also points to the ways in which they negotiated language, historical events, and religious doctrine to arrive at certain legal positions. Many of these rulings have been developed in response to challenges in Islam's history and have come to influence contemporary Islamic practices. This is an important and challenging book which sheds light on Islamic law and premodern attitudes to dissidence and violence.

KHALED ABOU EL FADL is an Acting Professor at the University of California Los Angeles School of Law. His publications include *Speaking in God's Name: Islamic Law, Authority and Women* (2001).

REBELLION AND VIOLENCE IN ISLAMIC LAW

KHALED ABOU EL FADL

University of California Los Angeles School of Law

CAMBRIDGE
UNIVERSITY PRESS

CAMBRIDGE UNIVERSITY PRESS
Cambridge, New York, Melbourne, Madrid, Cape Town, Singapore, São Paulo

Cambridge University Press
The Edinburgh Building, Cambridge CB2 2RU, UK

Published in the United States of America by Cambridge University Press, New York

www.cambridge.org
Information on this title: www.cambridge.org/9780521793117

First published 2001
Reprinted 2002, 2003
This digitally printed first paperback version 2006

A catalogue record for this publication is available from the British Library

Library of Congress Cataloguing in Publication data
Abou El Fadl, Khaled, 1963–
Rebellion and violence in Islamic law / by Khaled Abou El Fadl.
p. cm.
Includes bibliographical references and index.
ISBN 0 521 79311 4 (hardback)
1. Islamic law. 2. Insurgency – Islamic countries. 3. Terrorism – Islamic countries.
I. Title. LAW
340.5′9 – dc21 2001025743

ISBN-13 978-0-521-79311-7 hardback
ISBN-10 0-521-79311-4 hardback

ISBN-13 978-0-521-03057-1 paperback
ISBN-10 0-521-03057-9 paperback

To my father, Medhat Abou El Fadl
To my mother, Afaf El-Nimr
For enduring so much, for patiently waiting,
And for tolerating rebellion.

Contents

Preface and acknowledgments

About ten years ago, this book started out as an exploration into the subject of political violence and terrorism in the modern Islamic world. I was particularly interested in the contemporary juristic treatments of rebellion and irregular warfare. At the conceptual level, the idea that the state ought to have a monopoly over the use of force against its foes appeared to me to be profoundly unreasonable. It seemed confounding that a fairly small armed elite is empowered to use force against some people (usually dissidents) in the name of all the people (the faceless masses). The many theories of representation and delegation of authority failed to make this proposition more coherent. At the same time, the idea that all individuals and groups in society should be armed and empowered to inflict damage upon each other did not make better sense. Therefore, I was interested in examining the ways in which the so-called guards of justice and order, namely the institutions of law, negotiated the resolution of conflicts in situations where order is frustrated and justice is challenged. After spending a couple of years reading on the issue, I became thoroughly bored. As far as the secondary literature was concerned, the cause of my boredom was not the lack of exciting books, essays, and otherwise learned treatises. What induced my boredom was that the methodologies and conclusions of many commentators were far more predictable than the dynamics and objectives of the movements they studied. Many of the commentators seemed to take an event or a set of events, and generalize about the past, present, and future. They seemed to think that the past inevitably led to the present, and that the present inevitably heralds the future. Many commentators spoke of long-established traditions of quietism, passivity, and acceptance of brutality. Since the subject of politically motivated violence and terrorism aroused strong feelings for all concerned, the field was ripe for result-oriented investigations, and sweeping generalizations that aimed to uphold or undermine one cause or another. Unfortunately, I found that by examining the social and institutional position of a particular commentator, I could easily predict the conclusions of the commentator, and whom that commentator will brand as a terrorist, victim, or hero. As far as the primary sources were concerned, the full and unmitigated co-optation of the processes and mechanisms of Islamic law by the modern state made the contemporary discourses quite dull. The contemporary Islamic discourse often appeared of a singular focus – the interests of the collectivity must prevail over individual interests, and rebels are the agents of sedition and chaos.

Several historians and political scientists argued that the stagnation of Muslim juristic discourses on issues related to political violence was a natural product of the historical processes of the Islamic political and legal experience. According to these authorities, Islamic law had played a consistently conservative legitimating role as far as the powers and functions of the state were concerned. And, thus, several prominent scholars concluded that Islam does not have and never has had a law of rebellion or a discourse on irregular warfare. For reasons explored in the book, I doubted that very much. For one, the premodern Islamic juristic heritage, unlike the contemporary legal practice, has always proved creative, inventive, and rich. As a result, I started an enthralling nine-year journey into the historical juristic discourses on methods of armed rebellion, terror, and other acts of defiance and destruction. The most fascinating part of this research has been the subtleties of the premodern juristic discourse. By carefully examining the particulars of the linguistic practice of the juristic discourse – the micro-discourses so to speak – I uncovered a highly symbolic, negotiative, and, at times, puzzling discourse. The shifts in legal doctrine were expressed in the most unassuming and technical fashion – texts that appeared to adhere to precedent were actually materially restructuring the field, and jurists who announced that they were reinventing the law turned out to adhere to precedent.

Ultimately, my plans were transformed, and I left the contemporary setting for what I believe to be a far more intellectually satisfying investigation. This is not a form of antiquarianism, but perhaps the traditional role that Muslim jurists played as mediators between the state and the God-fearing masses, and perhaps the epistemology and processes that permitted a semi-autonomous existence for the Islamic juristic culture, have now vanished. I consider this field to be too undeveloped for any firm conclusions, but I think it is reasonable to say that the premodern juristic culture hoped to limit the monopoly of the state over the use of force in ways that are inconceivable today. If the past serves as a source of inspiration and ideas, the juristic debates described in this book may have a renewed life, and may be transformed into normativities that influence the way contemporary Muslim culture thinks about political violence and terrorism.

As noted, this work focuses on the details of the juristic discourses and traces their various permutations and transformations over the course of several centuries. There is no alternative but to share with the reader those details, and as a result, at some points this book will have a discursive quality to it. I regret that this is inevitable considering that this book would be pointless unless the reader is given a near first-hand experience in the mechanics and practices of the text. The shifts and transformations in the legal doctrine are subtle and elusive, and this not only requires a careful reading, but also a precise and fastidious presentation. This book was written both to challenge some long-held assumptions about the dynamics of the Islamic juristic discourses and as a reference source on the law of rebellion in Islam.

A few mundane remarks are necessary. Since this work was done over a number of years, I was often forced to use several editions of the same work. For instance, some editions that I used in Princeton or Austin might no longer have been available to me in Los Angeles. Therefore, the bibliography and footnotes might cite different editions of the same work. In addition, I have consulted a large number of works that I did not cite. Unfortunately, because of concerns over the size of this book, I did not include these works in the bibliography. I apologize to these authors who influenced my thinking over the years, but whom I could not cite for any specific proposition or information. Again, because of concerns over size, I dispensed with the practice of giving the full reference the first time a book is cited. All citations in the footnotes are in short form. The reader is kindly asked to look in the works cited section for a full reference.

For aesthetic reasons, I have decided to ignore the *tashdid* at the beginning of transliterated words. In my view, a word starting with a double "s", for example, looks awkward. I have placed the *hamza* only before the name Ubbi to facilitate pronunciation. Again, to help pronunciation, the *ta' marbuta* was represented with an "h" at the end of a word only for the word *bughāh*. Otherwise, I omitted the *ta' marbuta* in transliteration. In citing jurists, I have used the name that commonly identifies a particular jurist, which may or may not be a jurist's proper last name. Furthermore, often the way to pronounce a jurist's last name or *kunya* is somewhat of a mystery. Sometimes the printed books do not include the correct pronunciation either. I have investigated the proper pronunciation of the names of jurists, and reflected the results of my research in the transliteration. Without doubt, my research has not been perfect and there will be some unintended mistakes, and for that I apologize. I have also included the death dates of jurists in the main text or footnotes where I thought that identifying the era of a jurist is pertinent to the argument. At times, I repeat the date of death when reminding the reader that such a date is of particular relevance.

Over the years, I have accumulated such an enormous debt of gratitude that I fear that I will never be able to repay it. First and foremost, I thank Professor Hossein Modarressi, my thesis advisor at Princeton, mentor, and inspiration. I owe everything to him, and the value of his guidance has been immeasurable in all my work. He is truly a boundless fountain of knowledge, and I regret that this book will not reflect his level of depth and exactitude. At Princeton, I had the privilege of working with a group of inspiring scholars. I thank Professors Abraham Udovitch, Andras Hamori, Carl Brown, and Richard Falk for their feedback and valuable insights. My special thanks to Professor Michael Cook who is the living embodiment of what a true scholar and teacher should be. He is never impressed unless two-thirds of a page is taken up by learned citations. Most of the pages of this book will disappoint him, but there are few in the scholarly world that can match his learning and fortitude. My heartfelt gratitude to my colleagues at the UCLA School of Law for their support. Two years of the research and rewriting for this book was accomplished in the friendly environment of the law school. Rick Abel, Stephen Bainbridge, Stephen Gardbaum, Carole Goldberg, Steve Munzer, Randy Peerenboom, Clyde Spillenger, Richard Steinberg, and Steve Yeazell have all provided valuable feedback or advised me in the publication process. I also thank Robert Goldstein and Jon Varat for providing me with the financial support that enabled me to complete this book. My deep gratitude to the UCLA School of Law library and its personnel for their unfailingly competent assistance. The personnel in the library have promptly obtained sources for me from all over the country.

I am honored to have had the competent assistance of several truly dedicated and gifted students. Anver Emon, Hisham Mahmoud, Mairaj Syed, and Jihad Turk have gone beyond the call of duty in helping with the numerous tasks associated with producing this work. At times, their commitment to this work surpassed mine, and I pray that they will in due time be blessed with equally inspiring students of their own.

The anonymous readers of Cambridge University Press provided very helpful comments and this work is all the better for it. The copy-editor of this volume, Mary Starkey, is the best I have worked with, and I am very grateful to her. I thank Naheed Fakoor and Cherif, my son, for helping to create a pleasant and supportive environment in which I could work. My deeply felt gratitude to Grace, my wife, for reading and editing this book, and for her selfless and unfailing support.

Introduction

DISCOURSING ON REBELLION

One of the most important issues confronting Islamic law today is how to balance the obligation to obey God against the fact that God's will is represented by human beings. In Islamic thought, God is the authoritative source of law, but what is the balance between God's authoritativeness and the potential for human authoritarianism? From an institutional and social point of view, God's will could be represented by a variety of political or social realities including an absolute ruler, a court, a body of clergy, an ingrained bureaucracy, a well-established social practice, or even the unchallenged assertions of the head of a household. From a doctrinal and, perhaps, dogmatic perspective, God's will is represented primarily by the ruler and jurists who are considered God's special agents on the earth. While Muslims in general, arguably, are God's viceroys on this earth (*khulafāʾ fī al-arḍ*), it is rulers and jurists who traditionally have enjoyed the power to speak for the divine law. Doctrinally, both rulers and jurists, to different extents, are empowered to construct and represent the divine will in Islam.[1] This creates a dichotomy between the roles, interests, and aims of rulers and Muslim jurists. Inherent to this dichotomy is an implicit form of negotiation – a power sharing or, at times, competition.

The negotiative dynamic between rulers and jurists in Islamic history has produced a complex and rich doctrinal discourse which, at least as understood and constructed by the juristic culture, has been recorded in Islamic legal sources. An integral part of this negotiative discourse is the law of rebellion in Islam. This juristic discourse deals with the moral and legal position of those who rebel against the political authority of the state, and addresses the treatment that should be afforded to such rebels. Importantly, these juristic discourses carry considerable normative weight

[1] On this issue, see Abou El Fadl, *Speaking*.

in the contemporary age and, therefore, they may exercise a powerful prescriptive influence on how oppositions, rebellions, and, in fact, armed struggles of any sort are understood and treated in the modern Islamic world.

The purpose of this study is to examine the Islamic law of rebellion. This stated purpose, however, needs to be qualified in certain significant respects. Joseph Schacht has described Islamic law as a case of "jurists' law."[2] By this, Schacht meant that Islamic law has developed through a process of theoretical, juristic discourse. Without endorsing Schacht's views on the history or nature of Islamic law, this study will focus on the Islamic juristic discourses on rebellion rather than the Islamic or Muslim law of rebellion.[3] Conceptually, one should distinguish between juristic discourses, Islamic law, and Muslim law. In order for one to speak of the Islamic law, as opposed to the Muslim law or juristic law, of rebellion, one would need to point to a set of authoritative or canonical rules that apply to a specific behavior that is identified as rebellion. Essentially, one would need to point to a set of legal standards that define an act of rebellion, and thus indicate when the canonical rules would come into force. This study, however, goes beyond explicating the doctrinal rules that apply to the treatment of rebels. Muslim juristic discourses incorporate the rules of Islamic law, but also engage in a rhetorical dynamic through which the jurists adjudicate, advocate, protest, and aspire for certain goals.

An investigation into the Muslim law, as opposed to Islamic law, of rebellion would need to engage in several inquiries which are not the primary focus of this study. Such an investigation would need to focus on the positive legal enactments in various periods of Islamic history that identified an act of rebellion, and that responded to those accused

2 Schacht, *Introduction*, 5. Schacht states: "Islamic law represents an extreme case of 'jurists' law'; it was created and developed by private specialists; legal science, and not the state, plays the part of a legislator, and scholarly handbooks have the force of law." Schacht, however, overstates his case. Several recent studies indicate that the role of the state in the development of Islamic law is far more complex than Schacht assumes: Jackson, *Islamic*, esp. 185–224; Fadel, "Adjudication," esp. 2–120; Melchert, *Formation*, esp. 200; Zaman, *Religion*.

3 Relying on the fact that Islamic law developed through a process of juristic discourses, Schacht reaches the conclusion that Islamic law represents a unique phenomenon of legal science: Schacht, *Introduction*, 210. He further argues that Islamic law is perhaps not law at all, as if the concept of law did not exist in Islam: ibid., 200. I take serious issue with Schacht's conclusion that Islamic law is simply a juristic discourse, but not law. I also take issue with his contention that Islamic law is a unique phenomenon of legal science, but not a legal system. Besides being ahistorical, Schacht's view relies on a very limited and strict positivist definition of law. As Alan Watson and I demonstrate, a jurists' law is hardly a phenomenon unique to Islamic law. See Abou El Fadl and Watson, "Fox," esp. 28–9.

of such an act. It would also need to address the way in which the political and legal order actually dealt with those who chose to challenge or disobey its imposed system of order within specific historical contexts. Therefore, one would have to address the actual treatment of rebels and rebellion in different stages of Islamic history.[4] Furthermore, one would have to examine closely the process by which these legal practices were justified in terms of an Islamic frame of reference, and hence can be considered part of the Islamic legal heritage.[5] While this approach has obvious merits, it is rather limiting because it would have to be qualified by specific historical and social practices. Therefore, one would have to speak, for instance, of the Umayyad law of rebellion or the Ottoman law of rebellion. This study, however, focuses on the intellectual history of the law of rebellion as understood and constructed by the jurists. Muslim juristic discourses do selectively incorporate and creatively reconstruct the legal practices of society. Therefore, it is necessary to contextualize these discourses within certain historical events, and to examine these discourses in light of a historical continuum. Nevertheless, the issue of the actual legal practices on rebellion requires numerous other and more specific socio-historical studies.

The primary focus of this study will be the debates among Muslim jurists on the idea of rebellion, and on the way a rebel was understood, constructed, or deconstructed. We are not only interested in the various positive enactments or legal rules that Muslim jurists argued should apply to rebels, but also in the value or moral judgments that Muslim jurists passed on the act of rebelling. Hence, for example, we are not only interested in whether Muslim jurists thought a rebel should be executed, but also whether they thought that a rebel was committing a sinful act or, *a priori*, whether they thought that a crime was being committed at all. Fundamentally, we are interested in the dynamics of the juristic process, and more specifically, we are interested in the process by which Muslim jurists approached the doctrinal sources and selectively reconstructed the sources in response to political and social dynamics. We will focus on the way Muslim jurists negotiated law and power through the medium of language, and responded to their understanding of political and social demands through a variety of creative acts.

[4] To what extent one can consider historical or, for that matter, contemporary state practices to be "Islamic" is open to debate. Nevertheless, the Muslim legal system as represented by Muslim legal practices, and not just the juristic discourse, has been ignored for too long.

[5] Of course, regardless of the frame of reference, these practices may still be considered a part of the Muslim, as opposed to the Islamic, legal heritage.

In this context, we are using the word "rebellion" in its most general sense; it means the act of resisting or defying the authority of those in power. There is a broad array of acts that could qualify as acts of rebellion. On the one hand, rebellion could be an act of passive non-compliance with the orders of those in power, or on the other hand, it could be an act of armed insurrection. A rebellion could take the form of a counter-culture that seeks an alternative mode of social expression, or it could take the form of an assassination attempt against a famous religious or political figure. But beyond the issue of the means or form that a rebellion may take, there is also the issue of the target of a rebellion. A rebellion could be directed against a social or political institution. Alternatively, it could be directed against the religious authority of the *ʿulamāʾ* (the jurists) or the idea of God. Often it is extremely difficult to distinguish between one form of rebellion and another. For instance, it is not always possible to distinguish between heresy, treason, sedition, revolt, and an act of political opposition. Frequently, the line drawn between one and the other does not necessarily relate to the nature of the act, but rather is a matter of degree. The difference, for example, between an act of sedition and an act of treason will depend on the context and circumstances of such an act, and on the constructed normative values that guide the differentiation. Therefore, often the distinction created between one and the other is quite arbitrary in nature.

This study does not attempt to create a theoretical construct distinguishing one act from another, and then attempt to fit Islamic legal discourses within the framework of that theoretical construct. Rather, it attempts to understand and make sense of the legal categories and distinctions made by Muslim jurists, and then reach certain conclusions about the nature of these juristic discourses. I am interested not only in what these juristic discourses were trying to achieve politically and socially, but also in what they can tell us about the premodern Muslim juristic culture. For example, as discussed later, one of the often-reached conclusions about Muslim legal history is that Muslim jurists were realists and quietists. Muslim jurists, it is often argued, traded in an extreme form of political idealism for an equally extreme form of political pragmatism, and in doing so have advocated politically passive or quietist positions. This study will challenge these generalizations.

This study, however, does not simply aim to reach an ultimate judgment about the role of political pragmatism in Islamic juristic discourses. More importantly, it is interested in tracing the way language, historical events, and religious doctrines are co-opted, constructed, or channeled to reach certain legal positions. For example, the word used by Muslim jurists to describe an act of rebellion is *baghy*. The word comes from the root word *baghā*, which in its various forms could mean: (1) to desire or seek something; (2) to fornicate or cause corruption; or (3) to envy or commit injustice.[6] The process by which this term was co-opted and used in Islamic juristic discourses is not only useful for understanding how rebels were perceived or understood, but it is also important for understanding the creative process by which Islamic law expresses a legal development. Put differently, the methodology used by Muslim jurists in constructing and arguing for an Islamic law of rebellion is extremely probative in understanding the process by which Islamic law changes and develops. In fact, the failure to pay careful attention to the linguistic practices, or the terminology and the specific methods by which Muslim jurists discoursed on Islamic law, I believe, is largely responsible for the view that Islamic law has remained static and unchanging since the fourth/tenth century.[7] In the area of the law of rebellion, Muslim juristic discourses continued to develop and change within the paradigm or framework constructed by Muslim jurists themselves for discoursing on the subject.

This study traces the development of Islamic legal discourses on rebellion by relying on original sources spanning from the second AH/eighth CE to the fourteenth/twentieth centuries. Nonetheless, its main focus is the development of the legal discourse from its incipient years to the eleventh/seventeenth centuries. I argue that the law of rebellion, as a systematic and coherent body of discourse, in all probability developed in the late second/eighth century and continued to be restated, rearticulated, and reconstructed within the same framework until the eleventh/seventeenth century. With the advent of the age of colonialism and modernity, the discourses on rebellion, but not necessarily the law of rebellion, were co-opted by Muslim activists and underwent major reconstructions. In the modern age, the classical juristic rules that deal with the treatment of rebels have been, to a large extent, ignored. Nonetheless, there has been a reconstructed debate on waging *jihād* against unjust rulers, but this matter deserves a separate study.[8] This study focuses on

6 Ibn Manẓūr, *Lisān*, 1:321–3.

7 Schacht and others have argued that Islamic law ceased to develop from the end of the third/ninth or the beginning of the fourth/tenth centuries: Schacht, *Introduction*, 70–1; Anderson, *Law*, 7; Coulson, *A History*, 81. This view has been ably challenged by the work of several scholars: Udovitch, *Partnership*; Johansen, *Islamic*; Hallaq, "Gate," Hallaq, "Model." See also Abou El Fadl, "Islamic"; Abou El Fadl, "Tax."

8 For an excellent introduction to the topic of *jihād* against unjust or corrupt rulers, see Peters, *Islam*, esp. 39–165.

the juristic discourses on *aḥkām al-khawārij wa al-bughāh* (the law relating to rebels) and on *aḥkām al-ḥirāba* (the law relating to bandits and brigands).[9] The difference between brigands and rebels will be explored later. *Aḥkām al-ridda wa al-zandaqa* – the laws of apostasy and heresy, although they overlap in certain important respects with the law of rebellion, require a separate treatment.[10] Finally, although I have consulted the major sources in both Sunnī and non-Sunnī traditions, the main focus of this study will be on the Sunnī schools of thought.

In addition to being a work on intellectual history, this is a book of legal theory. I am interested in what I have called the linguistic practice of the juristic culture, the way that a juristic culture negotiates power primarily through the use of language, and the way a juristic culture talks to and about political power. As I emphasize in this book, linguistic technique is the primary means by which a juristic culture attempts to direct and negotiate power, and it does so through a series of creative and symbolic acts.

The plan for this book is as follows: First, I will go through the tedious, but necessary, process of surveying the largely inadequate scholarship produced to date on the issue of rebellion and Islamic law. As will become apparent, I propose an entirely different approach to this field of study. I will lay the foundations for this book by positioning it within a legal conceptual framework that I believe is necessary for understanding the juristic discourses in this field. In order to emphasize the creative and negotiative process by which these discourses developed, I will analyze in some detail the conflicting doctrinal foundations that have been coopted and deployed in the discourses on rebellion. Next, I will analyze the development of the juristic discourse through three main points of development. The first part will deal with the birth of the discourse and its continuation up to the fourth/tenth century. The second part will deal with the developed debates in the fifth/eleventh century. The third part will deal with the continuation and revision of the debates after the Mongol invasions and the destruction of the caliphate in 656/1258. The final part of the book will focus on analyzing the implications of the

9 Some scholars have invited me to adopt the word "terrorism" as a faithful translation of the term *ḥirāba*. I decline to do so largely because I believe this to be an anachronism. Terrorism, as a concept, accompanied the emergence of the notions of political crime and national liberation in the modern age. As I argue later, *ḥirāba* does share many similarities with contemporary conceptions of terrorism, but in order to preserve the historical flavor of this work, I have used the terms bandits and brigands as synonymous with *ḥirāba*.

10 For an insightful study on the ways that accusations of heresy and rebellion overlap, see Fierro, "Heresy."

process by which this field developed for our understanding of the dynamics of Islamic law. I will also trace the development of the discourses on rebellion in the contemporary age, primarily as a means of exploring the potential of pre-modern discourses for the modern age.

CHAPTER 1

Modern scholarship and reorienting the approach to rebellion

ISLAMIC REBELLION IN MODERN SCHOLARSHIP

Aḥkām al-bughāh, or the juristic discourses on rebellion, have received very little attention in both non-Muslim and Muslim modern scholarship. Nevertheless, there has been no shortage of statements about the absence of a right to rebellion in Islamic legal discourses. Most commentators have tended to focus on the history of Islamic discourses on the caliphate, and then deduced from this history the Islamic position on rebellion. Very little attention has been given to the specific juristic tradition from which *aḥkām al-bughāh* arose, or to the specific legal paradigm upon which Muslim jurists relied. Contemporary commentators have tended to treat Muslim juridical pronouncements on the duty of obedience to those in power as if they are a genre of political thought or theory. The legal culture that provided these jurists with the terms of their discourse, and that imposed modes of thought and expression, has been largely ignored.[1]

In its most basic formulation, the accepted thesis is that Muslim jurists moved from the absolute realm of political idealism to an absolute realm of political realism. Muslim jurists insisted on strict qualifications for the position of caliph, and insisted that the caliphate only be assumed through a proper *ʿaqd* (contract) and *bayʿa* (pledge of allegiance). The caliph had to be pious and just, and had to enforce the *Sharīʿa*.[2] Importantly, only a single, just *imām* may represent the *khilāfa* and the *umma*. If

[1] Al-Azmeh (*Muslim*, 171) recognizes the specifically legalistic nature of the juristic theories of the caliphate. However, as will be noted, when it comes to juristic discourses on rebellion, al-Azmeh himself fails to heed his own warning against ignoring the legalistic nature of Islamic juristic discourses. Enayat (*Modern*, 4) notes that pre-modern Islamic political thought was always subsumed under some other discipline. Rosenthal (*Political*, 31) notes that pre-modern Muslim jurists were not political philosophers, and that politics as a discipline did not interest them. But he does not take account of the specific legal culture of Muslim jurists.

[2] On the traditional qualifications demanded of the caliph, see Gibb, "Constitutional," 6–14.

the caliph is neither legitimate nor just, the *umma* may remove him and replace him with another.

These requirements and qualifications were a pious ideal which perhaps was never realized. According to H. A. R. Gibb, in response to the Khawārij's anarchy and fanatical revolts, the jurists were increasingly forced to deprecate the right of rebellion against an unjust *imām*.[3] The two civil wars in early Islam and the constant rebellions in the first two centuries pressured Muslim jurists to emphasize the duty of obedience to the ruler, whether just or unjust, and to engage in endless polemics about the evils of rebellion and anarchy. In other words, Muslim jurists reacted by going to the other extreme – from an extreme of idealism to an extreme of realism.[4]

The power and influence of the ᶜAbbāsid caliphate steadily decreased throughout the third/ninth century. By the fifth/eleventh century, it had been reduced to virtual impotence. According to Gibb, the first theoretical and systematic compromise was a pious invention by the Shāfiᶜī jurist al-Māwardī (d. 450/1058) as he attempted to defend the caliphate against the Buwayhid warlords and the Fātimids ruling Cairo. Under certain conditions, al-Māwardī recognized the legitimacy of usurpation as a means of coming to power in the provinces. Al-Māwardī argued that the usurper, by pledging allegiance to the caliph and complying with certain conditions, became the caliph's agent.[5] Effectively, al-Māwardī had created a legal fiction of sorts:[6] under certain circumstances a usurper could become the caliph's agent even if the caliph had no real power to restrain or direct his agent. Gibb insists that al-Māwardī had opened the door for the eventual supremacy

3 Ibid., 6. 4 Ibid., 15.

5 Ibid., 18–19; Gibb, "al-Māwardī's"; Watt, *Islamic*, 101–2; Lambton, "Changing," 55. Al-Azmeh (*Muslim*, 169) argues that systematic, juristic statements on the caliphate were a fifth/eleventh-century innovation by al-Māwardī and Abū Yaᶜlā.

6 In this context, Rosenthal (*Political*, 30–1) states:

> What appears to us as pious fraud, as born of political expediency, as condoning aggression and brute force must be set against the overriding principle ruling the guardians and interpreters of Muslim law: to preserve the unity of the Muslim community under the authority of the *khalīfa* whose religious aura increased in proportion to the decrease of his effective power and authority.

Evidently, Rosenthal is not aware of the quite common use of legal fictions in Islamic and non-Islamic legal systems. I would argue that Muslim jurists were not necessarily preserving the unity of community. Rather, they were doing what was, by training and habit, dictated by their legal culture; that is, resolving conflict and maintaining order. See below on the function of law and the roles of jurists.

of political expediency over legal order. I will quote Gibb at length because it is important to demonstrate the tenor of his argument on this point. Gibb states:

> It must be supposed that in his zeal to find some arguments by which at least the show of legality could be maintained, al-Māwardī did not realize that he had undermined the foundations of all law. Necessity and expediency may indeed be respectable principles, but only when they are not invoked to justify disregard of the law. It is true that he seeks to limit them to this case, but to admit them at all was the thin end of the wedge. Already the whole structure of the juristic theory of the caliphate was beginning to crumble, and it was not long before the continued application of these principles brought it crashing to the ground.[7]

Gibb argues that Muslim political theory increasingly became an after-the-fact rationalization of actual historical practices, as Muslim jurists ignored any moral imperatives and focused solely on the element of power.[8] Muslim jurists not only sanctioned the authority of those who usurped power, but also made obedience to them a moral and legal, as well as religious, obligation. Thus, according to Gibb, the belief was fostered "that rebellion is the most heinous of crimes, and this doctrine came to be consecrated in the juristic maxim, 'Sixty years of tyranny are better than an hour of civil strife.' "[9]

The Seljuks gained control of Baghdād in 447/1055, shortly before al-Māwardī's death. The next main figure usually mentioned in this context is the Shāfiʿī jurist Abū Ḥāmid al-Ghazālī (d. 505/1111).[10] Al-Ghazālī wished to reconcile the temporal powers of the sulṭānate to the religious authority of the caliph. The caliph would officially confer the title of sulṭān upon sovereign princes in the temporal field. Hence, al-Ghazālī went further in legitimating usurpation as a lawful means of gaining power. According to Ann Lambton, he was preoccupied with the threat of internal disturbances (*fitan*), and the dangers posed by the Bāṭinī movement to Sunnī Islam. He was far less concerned with the danger posed by the external threat of the Crusades.[11] Al-Ghazālī placed

[7] Gibb, "al-Māwardī's," 164. Mikhail (*Politics*, 43) criticizes Gibb's overly dramatic presentation of al-Māwardī but seems to accept Gibb's basic conclusions.

[8] Gibb, "al-Māwardī's," 162; Lambton, *State*, 84.

[9] Gibb, "Constitutional," 15. Enayat (*Modern*, 12) lends his support to this argument in stating: "Acknowledging the necessity of strong government . . . is one thing; justifying tyranny in the name of religion is another. The price of medieval flexibility was to sanctify the latter position, which soon became the ruling political doctrine among the majority of Muslims of all sects."

[10] Imām al-Ḥaramayn al-Juwaynī (d. 478/1085), al-Ghazālī's teacher, frequently receives honorable mention in this context. See Lambton, *State*, 104–5; Mikhail, *Politics*, 50. I deal with al-Juwaynī's views later.

[11] Lambton, *State*, 109.

an undue emphasis on the duty to obey those in power, even if unjust or impious. Al-Ghazālī's rather infamous statement is usually quoted in this context:

> An evil-doing and barbarous sulṭān, so long as he is supported by military force, so that he can only with difficulty be deposed and that the attempt to depose him would create unendurable civil strife, must of necessity be left in possession and obedience must be rendered to him, exactly as obedience is required to be rendered to those who are placed in command... We consider, then, that the caliphate is contractually assumed by that member of the ᶜAbbāsid house who is charged with its functions, and that the office of government (*wilāya*) in the various lands is validly executed by the sulṭāns who profess allegiance to the caliph... For if we were to decide that all *wilāyāt* are now null and void, all institutions of public welfare would also be absolutely null and void... Nay, but the *wilāya* in these days is a consequence solely of military power, and whosoever he may be to whom the holder of military power professes his allegiance, that person is the caliph. And whosoever exercises independent authority, while he shows allegiance to the caliph by mentioning his name in the *khuṭba* and on the coinage, he is a sulṭān, whose orders and judgments are executed in the several parts of the earth by a valid *wilāya*.[12]

After explaining that these concessions are involuntary but necessary, al-Ghazālī then asks rhetorically:

> Which is the better part, that we should declare that the *qāḍīs* are divested of their functions, that all the *wilāyāt* are invalid, that no marriages can be legally contracted, that all executive actions in all parts of the earth are null and void, and to allow that the whole creation is living in sin – or to recognize that the *imāma* is held by a valid contract, and that all executive acts and jurisdictions are valid, given the circumstances as they are and the necessity of these times?[13]

The Mongol invasion finally destroyed the ᶜAbbāsid caliphate in 656/1258, but by then all vestiges of political legitimacy had disappeared. According to the prevailing scholarly view, Muslim jurists were willing to accept raw power, without anything further, as grounds for political legitimacy. The next often-discussed figure is the Syrian Shāfiᶜī jurist Ibn Jamāᶜa (d. 733/1332–3).[14] Born in Ḥalab, he later moved to Jerusalem and lived the majority of his adult life as a judge in Mamlūk

[12] Quoted in Gibb, "Constitutional," 19. This passage is also quoted in Lambton, *State*, 116–17. See also Rosenthal, *Political*, 42.

[13] Quoted in Gibb, "Constitutional," 19–20. Laoust (*La Politique*, 88) argues that al-Ghazālī incorporated both the caliphate and sulṭānate in a mixed theory of the *imāma*.

[14] See Mikhail, *Politics*, 28; Lambton, *State*, 138–51; Rosenthal, *Political*, 43–51. Gibb incorrectly identifies Ibn Jamāᶜa as a Ḥanafī: "Constitutional," 23.

Egypt.[15] Ibn Jamāʿa equates power with legality and, according to Gibb, he abandons law in favor of secular absolutism.[16] A much-quoted statement by him is the following:

When the *imāma* is thus contractually assumed by one person in virtue of his military power and conquest, and there subsequently rises up another who overcomes the first by his might and his armies, then the first is deposed and the second becomes *imām*, on the grounds which we have already stated, namely, the well-being and unity of the Muslims.[17]

The reproduction of these long quotations is justified by the fact that these statements have had a pervasive influence on the way political authority was analyzed in Islamic history, particularly as it pertains to the issue of quietism and activism. With Ibn Jamāʿa, the journey from political idealism to realism, with a few exceptions, had become complete.[18] Order and stability became the primary concern; neither legitimacy nor justice mattered.

Admittedly, I do not find this view of the history of Islamic political thought, despite its wide acceptance, to be convincing. But for our purposes, this is not the material issue. Rather, the material issue is that this view has resulted in certain conclusions about the right to rebellion and the treatment of rebels in Islamic jurisprudence, which are largely inaccurate. For example, Gibb concludes that Muslim jurists ultimately adopted quietism and rejected any right to rebel against an unjust *imām*.[19] Lambton agrees and adds that neither Sunnī nor Shīʿī jurists discussed the issue of rebellion at any length.[20] According to Lambton, the problem of tyranny presented a practical as well as a theoretical problem, and "in the conflict between ideal and practice, it came to be recognized that tyranny prevailed."[21]

Hanna Mikhail is critical of Gibb's conclusions regarding the stark realism of Muslim jurists. Mikhail argues that although Muslim jurists accepted the political reality, they continued to insist that Muslim rulers

[15] The Mamlūk dynasty flourished in Egypt between 648/1250 and 922/1517.

[16] Gibb, "Constitutional," 23.

[17] Quoted in ibid.

[18] Ibn Taymiyya, for example, insists on the ideal of *Sharīʿa* but ignores the question of the *khilāfa* altogether: see Rosenthal, *Political*, 51–61.

[19] Gibb, "Constitutional," 6, 15.

[20] Lambton, *State*, 261–3.

[21] Ibid., 313. Marlow (*Hierarchy*, 40–1) argues that quietism was eventually endorsed by Sunnī and Shīʿī jurists. Cook ("Activism," 21–2) argues that the activist heritage reflects the importance of tribal society in Islamic history. With the demobilization of tribal armies and large-scale conversions to Islam, Muslim masses who had no hope of partaking in the political process emerged. The result was political quietism.

strive towards certain ideals. Mikhail notes, for example, that both al-Māwardī and Ibn Jamāʿa continued to insist that a ruler fulfill the requirements of religion and justice.[22] But, ultimately, he concurs in the judgment that Muslim jurists became quietists – demanding absolute obedience to unjust rulers and forbidding rebellion.[23] In fact, Mikhail concludes that in the eighth/fourteenth century, Abū Ḥayyān (d. 754/1353–4) "stands out as a voice in the wilderness" when he argues that force may be used against an unjust ruler.[24]

Fazlur Rahman, consistent with the prevailing scholarship, argues that there is no law of rebellion in Islam. Whatever activist tendencies might have existed in early Islam became extinct as the Murji'a's quietist doctrine of non-judgment became widespread. According to Rahman, Muslim jurists rationalized any political reality that might have confronted them, and forbade any rebellions against an established ruler.[25] Bernard Lewis, however, notes that both the quietist and rebellious traditions are old and deeply rooted in Islam. He argues that the quietist–authoritarian and the activist–rebellious traditions competed throughout early Islamic history.[26] It was only with much reluctance and difficulty that Muslim jurists accepted the necessity of obedience to tyranny.[27] Ultimately, complete quietism was accepted.[28]

Riḍwān al-Sayyid seems to agree with this basic assessment. He argues that there were two distinct trends concerning the caliphate: a law-based trend and a realism-based trend. The law-based trend insisted on the caliphate being contracted by a proper contract and *bayʿa* (pledge of allegiance given to the ruler), while the realism-based trend accepted the rule of the usurper. According to al-Sayyid, Abū ʿAbd Allāh al-Ḥalīmī (d. 403/1012–13) was the last representative of the law-based trend. Al-Ḥalīmī refused to recognize the legitimacy of the usurper, and argued

[22] Mikhail, *Politics*, 28. [23] Ibid., xxxii, 16, 38, 50.

[24] Ibid., 50. Mikhail further concludes that since the eleventh/seventeenth century, most theological works either held that (1) between injustice and rebellion, Muslims must choose the lesser evil, or (2) rebellion is always the greater evil. Mikhail does not seem to distinguish between theological and legal works. Furthermore, he does not seem to give adequate weight to the significance of this equation.

[25] Rahman, "Law," 1–10; also see Sonn, "Irregular," 133–8. Cook ("Activism," 15–23) argues that the Murji'a started out as an activist creed and subsequently evolved towards quietism.

[26] Lewis, *Political*, 92. Also see pp. 101–2 where Lewis reproduces the infamous quotes from al-Ghazālī and Ibn Jamāʿa. Somewhat inconsistently, Lewis asserts that the duty of obedience to *legitimate* authority is a religious obligation, and that disobedience is a sin as well as a crime at ibid., 91.

[27] Ibid., 100; Lewis, *Islam*, 290. [28] Lewis, *Islam*, 314.

that only a caliph who came to power through a proper contract should be recognized as the legitimate ruler even if he lacked effective political power. The legal acts (such as adjudicating cases or collecting taxes) performed by usurpers, al-Ḥalīmī contended, were recognized only in one situation. If a usurper controlled one of the provinces, and the just caliph was weak and unable to impose his authority, then the legal acts of the usurper could be recognized. However, according to al-Ḥalīmī the usurper would remain illegitimate; legitimacy could only be granted to the ruler who came to power through legal means. Al-Sayyid, however, argues that the realism-based trend became dominant, and juridical quietism became the norm.[29]

Integral to the quietism thesis is the argument that through the course of Islamic history temporal authority split from religious authority: The Sunnī caliph lost his religious authority to the jurists, and his political authority to the sulṭāns.[30] Presumably, Muslim jurists concerned themselves with the administration of religious law and left secular concerns to those in power. Therefore, as long as Muslim jurists could be recognized as the guardians of religious law, they were willing to ignore issues concerning political justice and even to lend support to unjust rulers. Patricia Crone puts it nicely: "Intellectually, it is the very totality of the disjunction between the exponents of state and religion that explains why the relationship between the two could come to be seen even by the medieval Muslims as a symbiosis: once the divorce was finalized, there was nothing to obstruct an improvement in the relationship between the divorcees."[31]

Recently, Muhammad Zaman challenged this simple dichotomy between the religious authority of the jurists and the political authority of the rulers. Zaman argues that the *ᶜulamāʾ* (jurists) existed in a cooperative relationship in which they shared religious and political authority. This cooperative relationship existed before the *miḥna* (inquisition), which was instituted in 218/833 by the ᶜAbbāsid caliph al-Ma'mūn. According to Zaman, the *miḥna* was an attempt by the rulers to challenge the authority of the *ᶜulamāʾ*, and to claim a certain degree of religious competence. But the challenge ultimately failed. Post-*miḥna*, a certain degree of tension and

[29] Al-Sayyid, *al-Ummah*, 136–43. I will argue that the issue of recognizing the legal acts of the usurper needs to be completely reexamined.

[30] Crone and Hinds, *God's*, 19. Crone and Hinds, however, argue that this is not the way things began. They argue that the early Umayyad caliphs did enjoy considerable religious authority.

[31] Crone, *Slaves*, 88.

conflict continued to exist between the *ʿulamāʾ* and the authorities, but it was cooperation, patronage, and the sharing of religious and political authority that became the earmark of the relationship between the *ʿulamāʾ* and the rulers. In other words, no real separation between politics and religion ever took place, at least during the early ʿAbbāsid period.[32] The *ʿulamāʾ* for the most part supported the rulers and, in return, the rulers were willing to grant the *ʿulamāʾ* some political privilege. Partly because of this relationship of patronage, or because of political repression, the *ʿulamāʾ*, from the early ʿAbbāsid period, became political quietists as they completely excluded the option of rebellion against rulers.[33]

Aziz al-Azmeh recently published a powerful challenge to the whole framework from which the issue of authority and legitimacy in Islamic history is approached. Al-Azmeh argues that much of the contemporary discourse on premodern Islamic thought is, among other things, ahistorical.[34] Muslim juristic discourses on the *imāma*, he contends, cannot be understood in terms of realism or idealism. Muslim jurists were neither idealistic nor realistic, but simply and thoroughly legalistic.[35] Muslim jurists and theologians were functioning under what al-Azmeh calls the historical absolutist imperative. The absolutist imperative arises from the anthropology and conceptions of power of the age.[36] Pursuant to this historical imperative, it was not entirely surprising that the caliphs would be perceived and discoursed upon as mini-gods, beyond good or evil.[37] The emphasis of early writers was on order and the need to obey the ruler, who was often portrayed as a shepherd taking care of his sheep. These conceptions of power were Islamized through the works of Muslim jurisprudence and the sanctification of Islamicity.[38] Al-Azmeh argues that it was never the case that politics became secular and devoid of religious influence. Rather, with al-Māwardī, there was an attempt to create a reliance on the *ʿulamāʾ* as a corporate group.[39] In due time, the *ʿulamāʾ* created a corporate religious logic on which politics could find, legitimate, and even judge itself.[40] By the time of Ibn Jamāʿa, there is a representation of the "*ʿulamāʾ* as an autonomous corporate group capable of standing in for political power in the regulation of public affairs in the absence of a convincing king."[41] However, correlative with this development was an insistence by the jurists on the idea of obedience

[32] Zaman, *Religion*, 81–2, 105–6. [33] Ibid., 49, 76, 78, 81–2, 98.
[34] Al-Azmeh, *Muslim*, 74. [35] Ibid., 171.
[36] Ibid., 115–53. [37] Ibid., 77. [38] Ibid., 100–1.
[39] Ibid., 106–7. [40] Ibid., 104. [41] Ibid., 103.

to those in authority, and that disorder was worse than injustice. Although the jurists might have denied the rulers titles such as *khalīfat Allāh* (the caliph of God), the status and function of ruling was perceived and discoursed upon with a high degree of devotional sanctification. Put differently, obeying the ruler was considered a part of obeying God. The only limitation or condition imposed was largely theoretical – the ruler cannot be obeyed if he orders something contrary to the divine command. But even this limitation was, at times, "ruled out as a disobedience of disobedience."[42] In al-Azmeh's colorful language: "In all, the rhetorical and visual assimilation of the caliph to prophecy, to divinity, to a charismatic line, and his conception in terms of inviolability, incommensurability, ineffability, and sheer potency, produced a critical mass creative of a sublime and holy authoritarianism, one which flows in the social and imaginary-conceptual capillaries of Muslim political traditions."[43]

Integral to al-Azmeh's argument is that Muslim jurists did not start out with a political ideal that degenerated into coarse opportunism. Rather, Muslim jurists worked under a historical absolutist imperative that produced a certain practice, which was then systematized from historical practice into juristic form. Therefore, al-Azmeh asserts: "The imperative of absolutism was also the *leitmotif* behind the universal aversion to the idea of contesting a ruling power. Sedition in Muslim law books is a legal offense of great consequence, attendant upon which is a particularly rigorous statutory penalty (*ḥadd*)."[44] But he adds: "That Māwardī and other jurists did not propose a legal theory for sedition is unsurprising and does not imply, as modern Western scholarship generally assumes, the opportunistic legalization of injustice."[45]

Al-Azmeh is correct in criticizing most contemporary works for not taking the historical context sufficiently into consideration. Furthermore, al-Azmeh's basic argument about the existence of a historical absolutist imperative is sound. But one problem with al-Azmeh's argument is that he does not closely examine Islamic legal texts and, thus concludes that sedition in Islamic law is a grave crime punishable by a *ḥadd*.[46] By sedition, one can only assume that he means rebellion or perhaps

[42] Ibid., 123. Al-Azmeh argues that, ultimately, the inconsistency between the absolute duty to obey the ruler and God was never resolved in Islamic discourses. The theoretical possibility of disobedience to the ruler was left open, but with much ambiguity.

[43] Ibid., 162. [44] Ibid., 173. [45] Ibid., 174.

[46] Al-Azmeh, for example, states: "It is the opinion of the vast majority of jurists that sedition, whatever its cause and even when directed against a miscreant or maleficent ruler, is illegitimate" (ibid., 108).

insurrection. But when we examine Islamic legal sources, we will find that this is not an accurate description of the juristic discourses. How should one then analyze this fact? One option, and the option that I suspect al-Azmeh would prefer, is to say that this fact is inapposite; Muslims jurists were writing thoroughly legalistic works, and technical legalistic questions of legitimacy were largely irrelevant to the socio-historical dynamics of society.[47] However, if one makes this argument, then one cannot cite the supposed absence of discourses on sedition as evidence for the supremacy of the absolutist imperative. More fundamentally, when one argues that legalistic questions were irrelevant, it is not quite clear what one means by this claim of irrelevance. If one claims that legalistic distinctions and discourses did not influence the historical, social, or political practices of Muslims, that is quite possible. But this is an empirical claim that needs to be examined within the confines of a specific historical period and place. If, on the other hand, one claims that the legalistic distinctions made by jurists were irrelevant to the way the juridical culture understood or dealt with power, this argument hardly makes any sense.[48]

Al-Azmeh warns that legal works by Muslim jurists must be read within the specific genre to which they belong – they must be read as books of law and not as political theory.[49] He also argues that Muslim legal works systematized past practice in juristic form.[50] But al-Azmeh does not sufficiently recognize the role of legal culture. Legal works do not simply appropriate reality and then systematize it.[51] Jurists also work within a legal paradigm that might be called, to modify a phrase, the "legal imperative." This legal imperative, by the very nature of law, as will be discussed below, favors order and stability. But order and stability is the framework from which law begins, and then aspires to achieve certain social and

[47] See ibid., 165, where al-Azmeh argues that legalistic discussions on the legitimacy of Marwān b. al-Ḥakam or ʿAbd Allāh b. al-Zubayr remained without doctrinal, dogmatic, or political consequence. Al-Azmeh also argues that although al-Māwardī, for example, stated preferences for certain positions, "there is no implication that these were in any way binding on the caliph, who had the same capacity for legal decision as does a judge" (ibid., 170).

[48] The failure to carefully examine the legal sources allows al-Azmeh to argue that shortly after al-Māwardī compulsion became a legitimate means of appointment to power on a par with other means of appointment: ibid., 172–3. In reality, as discussed later, compulsion as a means to power became recognized long before al-Māwardī.

[49] Ibid., 170. [50] Ibid., 173.

[51] Al-Azmeh makes the rather sweeping claim that all jurists at all times and places are realists: ibid., 170. I agree that a successful jurist needs to be a realist to a certain extent, but that is quite different from claiming that all jurists are realists. Jurists also work within a specifically legal culture that incorporates precedent as well as social, political, and religious goals. In his "Islamic," 250–61, al-Azmeh makes a convincing case that Islamic law was not simply theory, but that Muslim jurists appropriated reality. But it is a gross simplification to conclude from this that all jurists are realists.

political goals. If, as al-Azmeh seems to argue, Muslim jurists responded to a historical reality and an imperative of absolutism and nothing else, then we can hardly make sense of *aḥkām al-bughāh* as a discourse.

I do not wish to overstate my case; as stated above, al-Azmeh provides a very useful paradigm by which we can understand conceptions of power and authority in premodern Islam. As al-Azmeh demonstrates, arguments by contemporary scholars about quietism and a mythical journey from idealism to realism are ahistorical. Importantly, however, they also make very little sense in terms of how law works, and they fail to explain the continued existence of *aḥkām al-bughāh*. But al-Azmeh's thesis fails on that account as well. I agree with al-Azmeh that it is surprising to find jurists condoning sedition or rebellion. But it is surprising not only because of an absolutist imperative, but because the crude advocacy of rebellion or sedition is quite contrary to the tendencies of law and the role of jurists – or what I called the juristic imperative.

Despite al-Azmeh's criticisms of Gibb, Lambton, and others, he ultimately endorses the argument that Muslim jurists forbade rebellion and demanded absolute obedience to those in power. Al-Azmeh historicizes the accepted scholarly view, but he does not disagree with its basic conclusions. Aside from the argument about the absolutist imperative, I have three main criticisms of al-Azmeh's thesis, and of what I have called the accepted view in contemporary scholarship. The first criticism is terminological, the second is theoretical, and the third is theological.

First, as discussed above, the accepted view argues that Muslim jurists became quietist rather than activist. Nonetheless, the terminology of activism or quietism is extremely unhelpful, and only serves to obfuscate and obscure the role of jurists and the functions of law. It is never clear what is meant by quietism or activism, or in what sense modern commentators are using them. For example, if a jurist advocates disobedience to the law, is he being activist or lawless? If a jurist advocates passive non-compliance with what he considers to be an illegal order, is he being activist or is he advocating an individualized and subjective notion of justice? If a jurist leaves open the possibility of rebellion by arguing that one should rebel only if that is the lesser evil, is that a lawless or quietist argument? One cannot intelligibly start to answer these questions until one first defines the legal framework within which a jurist is acting. Quietism and activism are inherently relative and subjective terms, and they acquire a concrete meaning only from within a specific context.[52]

[52] For example, the activism of a soldier could be the use of force. The activism of a jurist could be the issuing of decisions that are unhelpful to the government.

The second criticism flows naturally from the first. The accepted view maintains that Muslim jurists had become quietist because they had accepted the legitimacy of the usurper and forbade rebelling against anyone coming to power, regardless of the means by which they acquired power. But if one argues that power could legitimately be obtained by usurpation, the necessary implication is that usurpers could be legitimate. In other words, if the act of usurpation could create political legitimacy, then the attempt to achieve this legitimacy is not necessarily reprehensible. Or, to put it differently, if those who are in power are perceived, in an ideal sense, to have an absolute moral claim to power, then those who rebel cannot be perceived to have any legitimacy. But if those who are in power are perceived to have a functional claim to power, that cannot preempt the moral claim of those who rebel against them. If, for example, a jurist claims that a usurper must, of necessity, be obeyed, the jurist is conceding a functional or practical legitimacy to the usurper. But this means that the usurper's claim to power is relative because it arises out of simple necessity. The necessary implication is that a challenger to the usurper's power may also have a relative claim to legitimacy. In other words, as a matter of logic, if one recognizes the legitimacy of usurpation, one also implicitly recognizes the functional legitimacy of rebellion. This point demonstrates the extent to which the language of quietism versus activism is unhelpful. Pursuant to the logic above, recognizing the legitimacy of a usurper could be an activist stance.

Third, besides the existence of a historical and legal imperative, there is also a theological imperative. The accepted view fails to take account of the early and late debates on early civil wars and rebellions in Islam. As discussed later, some of the most esteemed religious figures in Islam rebelled against those who were in power. ʿĀʾisha bint Abī Bakr (d. 58/678), Ṭalḥa b. ʿUbayd Allāh (d. 36/656), and al-Zubayr b. al-ʿAwwām (d. 36/656) rebelled against ʿAlī b. Abī Ṭālib (d. 40/661); al-Ḥusayn b. ʿAlī (d. 61/680) and others rebelled against the Umayyads. These rebellions created a theological imperative. Since Sunnī Muslims insisted on affirming the moral worth of all the Companions of the Prophet, if one maintains that armed rebellion against those in power is sinful, perhaps the conclusion that some of the Companions were iniquitous would be inescapable. Therefore, if one were to hold that all rebellions against unjust rulers are a sin, these theological and legal precedents either had to be explained away or distinguished. As we will see, the precedents of rebellions led by Companions played a powerful and complex role in the discourses on rebellion. Most of the legal discourses on these precedents took place in the field of *aḥkām al-bughāh*. Nevertheless, as we will see, the precedents were discussed not simply to defend the moral worth of all the Companions, but to co-opt and employ these precedents in a normative and prescriptive fashion. Of course, there are also many largely apologetic discussions on the early rebellions in theological works and in books written on *fitan*. But in contrast to these apologetic theological works, the legitimacy of a usurper or a rebel and the normative value of the early civil wars and rebellions are discussed at length in the discourses on *aḥkām al-bughāh*.[53] It is in this field that we find that the precedents of the Companions were deployed in order to generate theological and legal imperatives on rebellion.

I am not arguing that, when it comes to understanding how Muslim jurists responded to issues of power and political authority, the only relevant discourse is that which is found in *aḥkām al-bughāh*. Rather, *aḥkām al-bughāh* is simply one part, yet certainly a very crucial part, of the total framework that informs our understanding of how Muslim jurists understood and dealt with issues of power and authority. As noted above, *aḥkām al-bughāh* has received very limited attention in modern scholarship.[54] Some contemporary scholars have discussed or incorporated aspects of this field into their writings without being fully aware that they were dealing with a specific genre of legal discourse.[55] Some have dealt with the field as a specific discourse, but committed many technical errors or failed to

[53] I do not want to understate the value of these apologetic works, however. Like many legal treatments of political issues in situations of crises, legal discourses often provide a method of restoring the "psychic balance" of society. Many of the works on *fitan* written by jurists were specifically aimed at mending a serious rift in the Muslim psychology. I borrowed the phrase "psychic balance" from Christenson, *Political*, 4.

[54] Joel Kraemer has written a very helpful introduction to this and other related issues: see Kraemer, "Apostates." Also see Abou El Fadl, "*Ahkam*," 149–79. Khadduri, *War* has a short section (77–80) on fighting the *bāghī* and on highway robbers.

[55] Mikhail (*Politics*, 23), for example, quotes a rather typical passage from *aḥkām al-bughāh* on recognizing the legal acts of usurpers, but does not otherwise draw attention to this field of law. He treats the passage as if it is unique to al-Māwardī, and concludes that the passage aims to "accommodate to the ᶜAbbāsid caliphate a variety of dissident groups" such as the Shīᶜīs and Fāṭimids. Al-Sayyid (*al-Ummah*, 138–9) seems to treat the issue of recognizing the legitimacy of legal acts performed in the jurisdiction of a usurper as a fifth/eleventh-century development, and as part of the realism-based trend, as opposed to the law-based trend, in Islamic discourses. As we will see, this issue is a common part of the discourses on the *bughāh*, and is a fairly early development. Lewis (*Political*, 81–2) discusses the law of rebellion in Islam. In his *Islam*, after a short discussion on *aḥkām al-bughāh*, Lewis concludes: "It is clear that what the jurists have in mind is not an attempt to overthrow the regime but merely to withdraw from it and establish an independent state within a certain territory. In a word, their concern is not with revolution, but with secession" (p. 318). I will argue that this is not accurate.

take account of the progressive development of the juristic discourse.[56] Works by contemporary Muslim lawyers have tended to explore the implications of the field as it relates to the doctrine of political crimes.[57] There have been few works on the related topics of terrorism and political dissent in Islamic law. But these works do not get beyond unhelpful polemics and are seriously handicapped by an inability to use original sources.[58]

As discussed later, *aḥkām al-bughāh* has rather clear implications for contemporary discourses on political dissent and terrorism. In fact, perhaps no intelligible discussion can take place on these issues without incorporating *aḥkām al-bughāh* into the analysis. Yet one must be careful not to confuse the views and debates of professional Muslim jurists with some grand metaphysical reality called Islam. Many contemporary works tend to equate the institutionalized views of jurists with the greater reality of Islam. Besides being essentialist, these works do not make methodological sense. The juridical discourses are only a part of the reality of Islam. Furthermore, these discourses reflect the institutional, ideological, and sociological role of the jurists, and are very much a product of their specific historical contexts.

Muslims jurists responded to a variety of historical and sociological contexts and demands. In the field of rebellion, Muslim jurists also responded to theological demands, e.g. how does one declare rebellion to be a crime without suggesting that some of the most esteemed Companions of the Prophet were criminals? Significantly, however, they also worked within an inherited legal culture that imposed its own logic and language. Muslim jurists literally invented the field of *aḥkām al-bughāh* by reconstructing and emphasizing certain theological precedents and

56 Hamidullah, *Muslim*, 178–87; his treatment is generally accurate but he confuses Ḥanafī doctrines with the doctrines of other schools. Furthermore, he does not discuss the progressive development of the law; Mohammad Kamali (*Freedom*, 183–206) discusses the topic at length, but his treatment is full of inconsistencies and inaccuracies. For example, he confuses the legal doctrine of giving permission to fight the rebels with a legal rule decreeing the death sentence for an act of rebellion. He assumes that because it is legally permissible to fight the rebels, then it also means that they may be executed: see esp. 198. Bahnasī (*Madkhal*, 95) makes the same error.

57 See Abū al-Faḍl, "Jarīma," 69; Sanad, *Naẓariyyāt*; ᶜŪdah, *al-Tashrīᶜ*, I:100–9, II:671–705. Abū Zahra (*al-Jarīma*, 148–9) deals with political crimes under the topic of *ḥirāba*. See, on contemporary treatments, Abou El Fadl, "Political Crime." Al-Jamīlī, in his two-volume work on the subject, *Aḥkām*, does not get beyond mass reproduction of long quotes from original sources.

58 For example, see Schwartz, "International"; Arzt, "Heroes." A few studies have been done on the related topic of apostasy in Islamic law. Peters and De Vries, "Apostasy" is a solid study. Zwemer, *Law*, and Bercher, "L'apostasie," are religiously motivated and not very helpful.

deemphasizing others.[59] Muslim jurists invented the field for both theological and political reasons. Once the corporate identity of the jurists developed and a body of precedents and legal discourses were firmly established, Muslim jurists labored under what might be termed a legal imperative, or the logic of law. By corporate identity, I mean a social body unified by a common linguistic practice, a sense of hierarchy, and a basic frame of reference; and vested in a shared set of symbolism signifying legitimacy. A corporate identity does not mean the sharing of exactly the same set of interests, but it does mean the sharing of a common sense of conditions for legitimacy, purpose, and destiny. Jurists as a corporate entity come to speak a common language and employ a shared set of symbolism signifying meaning and purpose. Corporate entities will produce indicators of status and value, and will often produce a jargon or technical language that becomes the symbol of inclusion and personal legitimacy. The jargon or technical language and the way it is deployed and developed is what I have called the linguistic practice of jurists. This linguistic practice is founded on a language of specialization, and it is the perception of specialization that plays an important role in the ability of the legal culture to authenticate and legitimate the acts of others.[60] In order for a researcher to understand what a juristic culture is doing, the researcher needs to analyze carefully the technicalities of the jargon and communication of that culture. By carefully scrutinizing this linguistic practice, we will discover that Muslim jurists generated an exceedingly subtle and sophisticated discourse on rebellion. Essentially, like all good legal minds, Muslim jurists affirmed a general legal principle: those in power must be obeyed. But they went on to riddle the field with qualifications, exceptions, and provisos so as to render the general principles quite complicated,[61] and to elicit the classic legal response to many legal issues – "It depends."

corporate identity breeds legal imp.

[59] The issue of whether Muslim jurists invented the precedents, as opposed to picking and choosing from a variety of circulating precedents in order to invent a field of law, is entirely uninteresting. The type of reconstructive or revisionist work that Schacht and others have done and do with Islamic law is not consistent with the way law develops. See Schacht, *Origins*; Calder, *Studies*. For a technical critique of Schacht, see al-Azami, *On Schacht's*. Rahman, *Islamic*, Hasan, *Early*, and Dutton, *Origins*, outline a more convincing methodology than that which is employed by Schacht and Calder. It is certainly true that jurists are painfully dependent on precedent and authority. However, while they may reorganize, and selectively emphasize and deemphasize certain precedents over others, they do not usually invent them.

[60] See Kirchheimer, *Political*, 13.

[61] Interestingly, Bernard Lewis seems to see this process in the reverse. He states, "In time, the duty of disobedience was hedged around with restrictions and qualifications and was in effect forgotten in the general acceptance, in theory as well as in practice, of the most complete quietism" (Lewis, *Islam*, 314).

Before turning to *aḥkām al-bughāh*, I will address the issue of the function of law. As discussed above, an analysis of juristic discourses on rebellion or insurrection cannot be performed without first making explicit the assumptions about law and legal culture that inform the analysis. Furthermore, this discussion is crucial for establishing our understanding of the legal context in which Muslim jurists constructed their discourses. In fact, it is not possible to evaluate properly the juristic discourses on rebellion without gaining an appreciation for the legal logic and paradigms that direct the determinations of jurists. In addition, as alluded to earlier, analyzing the issue of juristic quietism and activism is incomprehensible unless we take account of the specific nature of juristic cultures.

THE FUNCTION OF LAW AND THE ROLE OF JURISTS

One of the basic and most essential functions of law is to resolve conflicts and maintain order. Perpetuation of order is in the nature of law. The very idea of law is about defining privileges, rights, or limits, and resolving disputes or competing claims to an asserted privilege or limit by the imposition of order.[62] Law could have various goals or aspirations, and the dynamics of law could reflect a variety of values and processes. It could aspire to achieve justice or channel social behavior, or serve certain economic classes or interests.[63] But this does not necessarily negate the idea that law aspires to resolve conflicts and uphold stability and order. Of course, there have been innumerable theories dealing with the nature and function of law arising from rationalist and empiricist epistemologies. Such theories have relied on a wealth of moral, historical, and social insights.[64] For example, Lon Fuller has argued that law is purposive human activity because it relies on the collaborative articulation of

[62] Watson, *Nature*, 41. Watson, however, goes on to argue that the essential feature of law is the existence of a *process*. The essential function of the process is to resolve actual or potential disputes with the specific object of inhibiting further unregulated conflict. Hence, it is the process that distinguishes law from simple aspirations or rules. According to Watson, law is about a process; the process is about resolving conflict and establishing order (ibid., 40). For our purposes, we need not reach the issue of process or the essential function of such a process. However, my point is more simple; achieving and maintaining order and stability is one of the main functions of law. Friedrich (*Philosophy*, 206–14) argues that justice and order are co-dependent; one cannot be realized without the other. But this is a normative argument. The point of this argument is that order should not be put before justice because ultimately order itself is threatened by the lack of justice. This is probably true, but it is difficult to imagine a law, unless it is a moral law, that consists of justice but not order.

[63] See Watson, *Nature*, 9.

[64] See generally, Murphy and Coleman, *Philosophy*; Kelly, *Short*, 301–454.

shared purposes. Law, according to Fuller, has an inner morality which relies on what he calls the principles of procedural natural law.[65] John Finnis, on the other hand, has argued that reasonable laws must serve "basic human goods" such as life, health, knowledge, and sociability. Unreasonable laws violate basic human goods in either individual or social life by contravening what Finnis calls "modes of responsibility."[66] Some jurists from the positivist tradition advocated the rather simplistic notion that the purpose of law is to maximize the public good[67] or that law is the command of the sovereign backed by the threat of sanction.[68] Furthermore, several theorists, relying on sociological

[65] Fuller, *Morality*. Fuller's principles are: (1) generality; (2) promulgation; (3) prospective legal operation; (4) intelligibility and clarity; (5) avoidance of contradictions; (6) avoidance of impossible demands; (7) constancy in time; and (8) congruence between official action and declared rules. Also, from the natural law tradition, Philip Selznick argues that law relies on the principle of legality which is contrary to arbitrariness. The aim of a legal system is to reduce such arbitrariness which of necessity exists in positive law. Scientific inquiry about the proper ends and values can produce a scientific, but not necessarily eternal, natural law. See Selznick, *Moral*; Selznick and Nonet, *Law and Society*; Selznick, Nonet, and Vollmer, *Law, Society*. Morris Raphael Cohen, another author from the natural law tradition, argues that law expounds rules that serve as norms. Such norms command obedience and control conduct. They must be studied as normative jurisprudence, and normative jurisprudence depends on ethics. See Cohen, *Law*; Cohen, *Reason*; Cohen, *Faith*. On classical natural law theory, see d'Entreves, *Natural*. Heinrich A. Rommen wrote a very interesting, and rather unusual, history of positivism and natural law. He strongly attacked the historical and philosophical role of positivism. Rommen argued that law performs many functions such as teaching civic values, rendering justice, preserving order, and promoting social harmony. Law is a peremptory command which excludes certain options from the realm of individual choice. However, law does not consist merely of facts induced by force, but also by principles of obligation, discoverable by experience and reason. See Rommen, *Natural*.

[66] Finnis argues that the first principle of natural morality is the principle that one ought to choose, and to will those, and only those, possibilities whose willing is compatible with integral human fulfillment. In other words, one ought not to will those possibilities that are incompatible with integral human fulfillment. This abstract first principle is given content through intermediate principles (modes of responsibility). Examples of intermediate principles are: (1) do unto others as you would have done unto you; (2) that one should not answer injury with injury, even when one could do so fairly; or (3) that one should not commit evil in the hope of achieving good. A law that contravenes these intermediate principles would be unreasonable. See Finnis, *Natural*; also see Finnis, Boyle, and Grisez, *Nuclear*.

[67] Bentham, *Limits*; Bentham, *Laws*.

[68] John Austin, relying on the idea of the pedigree of law, argues that law is a command from the sovereign that obliges a person to act because of the threat of sanction. Austin also argues that law is habitually obeyed. See Austin, *Lectures*; Austin, *Province*. From a different philosophical basis, Hans Kelsen argues that law is a normative science, consisting of a hierarchy of norms backed up by the threat of a sanction. Each norm derives from a superior norm until one reaches the *Grundnorm*. The *Grundnorm* is the initial hypothesis of the law which is not derived from a higher norm. See Kelsen, *Pure*. In a much more sophisticated positivist theory, H. L. A. Hart challenges Austin's theory of the sovereign. Hart argues that law consists of primary and secondary rules. Primary rules are duties without a system of priority or application. Secondary rules cure the inconsistencies of primary rules and consist of rules of recognition, rules of change, and rules of adjudication. See Hart, *Concept*.

perspectives, focused on the social dynamics of law. For example, Roscoe Pound argued that law is the product of the conflict and balancing of interests in society. The essential task of law, Pound argued, is social engineering in order to achieve particular social results.[69] Several theoretical approaches, most notably from within the movement of American realism, focused on the process by which law resolves controversies and conflicts, and thus tended to understand law as a means to social ends.[70]

None of the theories mentioned above is necessarily inconsistent with the idea that one of the essential functions of law is to resolve conflict and impose order. For one, none of the roles mentioned above is reachable without the imposition and perpetuation of a system of order.[71] Second, as Alan Watson recognizes, this is a minimalist argument: the minimum function of law is the resolution of conflict and the maintenance of order.[72] This minimum function could then be utilized to achieve justice or channel behavior or any other alternative. However, unlike Watson, I am not arguing that the resolution of conflict and the establishment of order is always and invariably the function of law. Law could and does have many direct functions that vary in response to social and institutional dynamics. Furthermore, as argued later, often the role of law is symbolic; in other words it can communicate values and

[69] Pound, *Social*; Pound, *Introduction*, 47. Pound argues that the process of law engages in a "fiction of interpretation in order to maintain the general security," *Introduction*, 49. Pound's point is that the legal process does not simply and mechanically apply fixed rules to human conduct, but engages in a creative and complex process of social engineering. Other sociological perspectives include Rudolph Von Jhering, Eugen Ehrlich, Leon Duguit, and others. Von Jhering argues that law depends on coercion, norms, and purpose, and is the product of social life as supported by the power of the state. The purpose of law is to secure the conditions for social life. On Von Jhering, see Kelly, *Short*, 332–3. Ehrlich argues that law is produced by social facts or forces operating in society which exist in the conviction of people. The source of most norms is society, and not the state. The center of gravity of legal development is society, and not legislation or courts: see Ehrlich, *Fundamental*. Leon Duguit, claiming to rely on a scientific positivist method, argues that law is produced by objective conditions of social solidarity, and that the function of law is to promote social solidarity. On Duguit, see Kelly, *Short*, 355–6. For other authors who argue that law is the product of binding social facts or that law is determined by social welfare, see Ross, *Law*. On Alf Ross, Vilhelm Lundstedt, and Karl Olivecrona, see Kelly, *Short*, 369–71.

[70] Gray, *Nature*; Llewellyn, *Bramble*; Llewellyn, *Common*; Frank, *Law*.

[71] For instance, John Finnis argues that law is a necessary condition of morality because basic human goods cannot be realized without coordinating between many people. Finnis contends that law is necessary to deal with what he calls "co-ordination problems." See Finnis, *Natural*. Whether or not one adopts Finnis's specific categories, I would argue that most lawyers would tend to believe that coordination, conflict resolution, or order is necessary for any substantive vision of justice. Notice, for example, the solemnity, decorum, and order imposed in contemporary courts of law. The assumption is that the imposition of these structures is necessary for the administration of justice.

[72] Watson, *Nature*, 8.

legitimate power structures or social practices.[73] I am also not arguing that the juridical resolution of conflicts is objective or devoid of social or political values. In fact, the simple fact that legal systems can maintain the appearance of impartiality and objectivity plays a powerful stabilizing role in legitimating and authenticating traditional power structures.[74] My argument is that the values of order, stability, and conflict resolution are strongly ingrained in a legal culture. A legal system does not easily endorse a state of anarchy or the potential for instability. In response to intense social or political demands, a legal system might legitimate a certain degree of instability or disorder. But even in doing so, the legal system affirms its own legitimacy, and the legitimacy of the ultimate value of legality, order, and stability.[75] Ultimately, the tendency of a juridical culture to favor order and stability is consistent with the pursuit of particular norms and goals. In essence, it is exactly because law performs social and political functions that it needs to affirm the norms of order and stability.

Even if, as is the case with Islamic law, the law aspires to fulfill divine commands, this merely serves to complicate the analysis, but it does not materially alter it. If the law aspires to fulfill a divine command, this means that the imperative of temporal order might, at times, be challenged because of an imagined or perceived divine order. But, as a general matter, divine law does not dictate anarchy. In fact, divine law seeks to resolve conflicts and maintain order, but it does so pursuant to a particular frame of reference and hierarchy of commands. Perhaps divine law sanctifies the demand for justice, but it does not negate the need for order as a necessary condition of legality. Jurists, even if working

even divine law necessitates order

[73] See Abel, "Redirecting," 803, 817–26. MacCormick (*Legal*, 233–9), concedes that law does embody values and that these values are expressed in the statements of the principles of a legal system.

[74] For instance, see Kirchheimer, *Political*, 6. Legal determinations often rely on the appearance of impartiality – the appearance of rendering "a decision not merely serving the needs and pressures of the moment, but capable of finding a wider and less transient adherence; a skillfully rationalized decision able to withstand a dispassionate scrutiny of its motivations" (ibid., 424).

[75] For instance, over certain hotly contested issues, courts might recognize a limited right to civil disobedience, or confronted by widespread rioting, courts might hand down lenient sentences. Furthermore, a government, under certain circumstances, might grant clemency to political foes. See ibid., 389–418. Nonetheless, as Kirchheimer demonstrates, systems of justice are thoroughly challenged by political cases. Often a legal system deviates from its asserted normative values and regular procedures when confronted by a political case in which there is political or social pressure, or perceived pressure. Courts will often succumb to such pressures by producing swift convictions and imposing harsh penalties, but in doing so, they also threaten to undermine the appearance of impartiality and their own legitimacy. See ibid., 46–172, 419–31.

under a so-called "religious system of law," will be concerned with issues of order, conflict resolution, and stability. They may demand that this order be just, or that it would comply with the divine command, but they can hardly be expected to advocate lawlessness or anarchy.

Muslim jurists frequently repeat the formula that a ruler succeeds the Prophet in guarding the religion and regulating the affairs of this world (*ḥirāsat al-dīn wa siyāsat al-dunyā*).[76] *Dīn* (religion) and *dunyā* (temporal worldly affairs) are not necessarily in conflict or inconsistent with each other. The *imām* is charged with the implementation of the *Sharīᶜa*, and the *Sharīᶜa* guards both the temporal and the non-temporal. In this context, most Muslim jurists contend that the very purpose and function of the *Sharīᶜa* is to fulfill the interests and welfare of the people in worldly life and the Hereafter (*taḥqīq maṣāliḥ al-ᶜibād fī al-maᶜāsh wa al-maᶜād*). They usually go on to elaborate that the values that the *Sharīᶜa* aims to safeguard are divided into what are regarded as necessities (*ḍarūriyyāt*), needs (*ḥājiyyāt*), and luxuries (*taḥsīniyyāt*, also referred to as *kamāliyyāt*). All *Sharīᶜa* laws are aimed, or ought to be aimed, at fulfilling these values in order of importance – first, the necessities, then the needs, and then the luxuries. The five core or necessary values of *Sharīᶜa*, according to the jurists, are the preservation and protection of religion, life, lineage, property, and intellect (some also add honor). From a normative perspective, any system implementing Islamic law is obligated to pursue and serve those values.[77] The question becomes: Do these values take precedence over any other value, including order and stability? Do these values set the standard for legality so that if they are not being fulfilled there is no justification for being concerned with order and stability? Not surprisingly, Muslim jurists argue that order and stability are primary functional values, without which it would not be possible to fulfill any other value. From a pragmatic and functional perspective, order and stability and the avoidance of *fitan* (disorder and turbulent social and political circumstances) are prerequisites for the pursuit of higher moral values. Consequently, when Muslim jurists specify the duties and functions of the *imām*, they first list the duty of protecting the orthodox religion. The second and third duties are concerned with preserving order and resolving conflict. The second duty is to implement

76 See, for example, al-Māwardī, *al-Aḥkām*, 5; Ibn Jamāᶜa, *Taḥrīr*, 48; al-Mālaqī, *al-Shuhub*, 56.

77 Al-Āmidī, *al-Iḥkām*, III:270–3; al-Ghazālī, *al-Mustaṣfā*, I:286–90; Ibn Qayyim al-Jawziyya, *Aᶜlām* (Cairo), III:5; al-Qarāfī, *Sharḥ*, 391–3; al-Rāzī, *al-Maḥṣūl* V:172–4; al-Shāṭibī, *al-Muwāfaqāt*, II:4–9; al-Maḥmaṣānī, *Falsafat*, 199–200; Abū Zahra, *Uṣūl*, 289–301.

the law as to litigants, and to resolve conflicts so that justice may prevail. The third duty is to keep the peace and guarantee security so that people may safely go about their affairs.[78] This concern with order and stability is neither unusual nor excessive. Rather, it is fundamental to the function of law and the role of jurists.

Nevertheless, what if the rule of law is challenged with a rebellion? As Watson states, "Violent rebellion is not a stable condition; a situation at rest without unlawful violence will be sought; and the force that emerges as the strongest, whether the existing government, a new government of a different type, or a compromise, will want acquiescence in its legal rules."[79] The tendency of a system of law, and the profession of lawyers, will be to gravitate towards a state of stability and order again. It is likely that a juristic culture will not relish being forced to break with its routine legalistic activities, and being compelled to take a position on controversial political issues. Nevertheless, the juristic culture will seek to uphold the principle of legality, which often assumes the existence of stability and order.[80] Yet, as Otto Kirchheimer asserts, "The concept of legality . . . is not supposed to perpetuate the right of resistance, but instead make it superfluous."[81] In most circumstances, the issue is not whether the cause of the rebel is defensible or just; rather, the issue is that the rebel's thought process draws him into the sphere of illegality.[82] When it comes to rebels espousing a cause, this sphere is one that often attempts to distinguish between rules of law and the rule of law. This ultimately poses a serious challenge to the very source from which the juristic culture obtains its legitimacy and authenticity. The loftiness of legalism and the apparent detachment of the legal process often invite even jurists to confuse and lapse the rules of law with the rule of law. Confronting this challenge, in most cases, instead of aligning themselves with the so-called just or good party, jurists will fall upon the safeguard of order and stability, which is presumed to be the foundation of legality.[83] So, for instance, if rebels prevail over a certain territory, or simply overthrow the government but are subsequently defeated, contracts or marriages concluded under the rebel regime might very well be recognized. This recognition is neither a compromise of an ideal nor an opportunistic catering to power. It

[78] See, for example, al-Māwardī, *al-Aḥkām*, 18; Abū Yaʿlā, *al-Aḥkām*, 27. Also see Ibn Taymiyya, *al-Siyāsa*, 138–9; Ibn Jamāʿa, *Taḥrīr*, 48–9.

[79] Watson, *Nature*, 76. [80] Kirchheimer, *Political*, 423.

[81] Kirchheimer, "Legality," 46. [82] Ibid., 54. [83] Ibid.

is simply an attempt to resolve conflict and reestablish order, an attempt that is dictated by the very logic and function of law. Hence, when Muslim jurists argue that the adjudications and legal acts of rebels must be recognized, they are not, as some contemporary scholars assume, being opportunistic or exhibiting a realistic, as opposed to a legalistic, trend.[84] Rather, perhaps in the interests of legality, they are reestablishing order and minimizing disorder.[85]

The argument thus far has been about proclivities or tendencies – jurists have a proclivity towards order and stability, and towards precedent and continuity.[86] This tendency is well captured in the legal maxim *stare decisis et non quieta movere*.[87] This is especially so among jurists who are a part of a corporate reality or a legal system. There is no doubt that Muslim jurists were a part of a corporate reality that was concerned with, among other things, order and stability. Even if Muslim jurists did attempt to maintain a certain degree of distance from those in power, they still represented the *Sharīʿa* which, as a corporate legal system, imposed its own imperative of order and justice.[88]

The question, however, is what happens to the Islamic legal principle that a human being should not be obeyed if it entails disobeying God? This question is not different from the one dealt with in the natural law or even positive law tradition. From the perspective of natural law, one can pose the question in the following way: What happens if one believes a legal rule to be contrary to natural law? Alternatively, from the perspective of positive law, one can pose the question thus: What should one do if one believes the law to be immoral? One

[84] See Mikhail, *Politics*, 23; al-Sayyid, *al-Ummah*, 138–9.

[85] In fact, as we will see, this is exactly what Muslim jurists say they are doing by recognizing the legal acts of rebels.

[86] This is reflected in the jurisprudential concepts of *qiyās* (rule by analogy) and *istiṣḥāb* (the presumption of continuity). *Qiyās* and *istiṣḥāb* share many of the qualities of rule by precedent or *stare decisis*. Both concepts reflect a desire for consistency, predictability, and order. On *qiyās* and *istiṣḥāb*, see Kamali, *Principles*, 202, 297–308; Mahmasani, *Philosophy*, 90ff. See also Cross and Harris, *Precedent*, 206.

[87] "To abide by precedent and not to unsettle things which are settled." Another legal maxim provides that *maxime paci sunt contraria vis et injuria* ("The greatest threat to peace are force and wrong").

[88] See Makdisi, *Rise*, for a review of the complex institutions of legal learning in Islamic history. See Zaman, *Religion*, 78–81, for a discussion on the reluctance of the *ʿulamāʾ* to accept judicial positions. See Crone and Hinds, *God's*, 93–4, on the conflict between the *ʿulamāʾ* and the caliphs over religious authority. Apart from the distance that a legal culture is able to maintain for itself, it is often in the interest of a government to concede to legal institutions a degree of "space" that, relatively speaking, is independent. This might be more conducive to maintaining the appearance of the impartiality of law. See Kirchheimer, *Political*, 425–6.

option is to refuse to obey an immoral rule. One can argue that the rule is not law at all (natural law), or that the law is unjust and, therefore, bad. As we will see, several Muslim jurists insisted on this option, and argued that an unjust ruler is illegitimate. In fact, they argued that an unjust ruler is the real rebel, and not those who refuse to yield to injustice.

The other option is to weigh the evils of compliance and disobedience. Under this option, when a rule is immoral, then, as succinctly stated by Watson, the obligation to obey the law is reduced to two questions: "First, what effect – and there need not be any – will disobedience have upon order? Secondly, if order will be affected by the disobedience, is order in this particular instance a good thing, or does it have such moral or social worth that its preservation outweighs the harm committed by the . . . immoral act?"[89] It makes no sense to describe this position as either opportunistic or quietist. It is quite conceivable that the amount of harm that would result from rebelling against an immoral order would, in itself, be immoral. Alternatively, an order could be so immoral that the possibility of compliance cannot be entertained.[90] Fundamentally, the balance of social or moral evils doctrine leaves open the possibility of disobedience or rebellion. In other words, it does not preclude disobedience or rebellion because order and stability are not the only relevant moral considerations. As we will see, several Muslim jurists adopted this position as well.

CONCLUSION

To sum up, the dichotomy between quietism or activism is incoherent. Muslim juridical discourses must not only be considered in light of historical imperatives alone. Careful attention must be given to the logic of law that Muslim jurists, and all jurists who function within a legal system, labor under. As stated above, given the fact that order is one of the main functions of law, and that the culture of lawyers creates a proclivity

[89] Watson, *Nature*, 128. Watson, who is a positivist, although not in the Austinian sense, seems to argue that if a law is morally very wrong, then one must not obey the law. If the law is morally neutral or marginally wrong, then one must engage in the type of balancing act he outlines. It is not clear why he only addresses these two situations – of a law that is morally very wrong or marginally wrong. It would seem that there is quite a gap between these two points of the moral spectrum.

[90] For example, the majority of Muslim jurists have argued that a person should not comply with an illegal command if it means killing a person or persons: see Abou El Fadl, "Common." Shīʿī scholars have held that *taqiyya* (dissemblance) is not permitted if it involves the killing of innocent people: see Murwārīd, ed., *Mawsūʿa*, IX:15, 56, 106–7, 165, 191, 220, 240, 269, 275.

towards favoring stability and the reestablishment of order and legality, it is not at all surprising that Muslim jurists would demand obedience to the law or a government. The surprising fact, and the fact that needs to be analyzed, is why many jurists permitted rebellion at all. This analysis is exactly what will occupy us for the rest of this study.

language of "what's not surprising"
↓
I don't care what's surprising — the question remains: is the proclivity toward stability and order good? Seems too conservative to permit decades of violence to avoid civil strife

I appreciated arg about legitimating usurpation amounts to legitimating rebellion, but it just doesn't square. People are bound to irrationally compartmentalize and so allow the former but oppose the latter. (Or accept only in retrospect.) In either way, seems like a dangerous culture.

CHAPTER 2

The doctrinal foundations of the laws of rebellion

THE ORIGINS OF THE DISCOURSE

According to Muslim jurists, other than fighting the unbelievers, there are three types of combat (*qitāl*): (1) fighting apostates (*murtaddūn*); (2) fighting brigands (*muḥāribūn*); and (3) fighting rebels (*bughāh*).[1] Apostates may be killed unless they repent,[2] and brigands and highway robbers may be killed, crucified, have a hand and foot amputated, or banished; however, rebels may not be killed, tortured, or imprisoned. Apostasy and brigandage are very serious crimes and are punished harshly. Insurrection or rebellion is not a crime and is treated leniently. A *bāghī* (rebel) may not be executed, crucified, or tortured. In Islamic discourses, the word for brigandage is *muḥāraba*, which means to contest, to disobey, or to fight.[3] By itself, the word is value-neutral; it does not necessarily connote something illegal or immoral. The word for rebellion is *baghy* and, as noted earlier, it means to demand or to exceed the limits or to commit injustice.[4] The word is *not* value-neutral, yet Muslim sources consistently state that the term, in law, does not connote censure or blame (*laysa bi ismi dhamm*).[5] However, certain jurists insist that *baghy* is an offense that results in the greatest corruption (*aʿẓamu al-jināyāti mafsadatan*) because it results in the destruction of life and property.[6] Furthermore, several jurists assert that the law of rebellion, in particular, is so significant that the

[1] For example, see al-Māwardī, *al-Aḥkām*, 69.

[2] Of course, many contemporary Muslims have opposed the execution of the apostate, and pointed out that the tradition is based on insufficient evidence. Khadduri, *Islamic*, 238; El Awa, *Punishment*, 49–56, 61–2; Shaltūt, *al-Islām*, 280–1.

[3] Ibn Manẓūr, *Lisān*, II:816; al-Rāzī, *Unmūdhaj*, 117.

[4] Al-Māwardī, for example, says that *baghy* means to use force to demand that which one does not have a right to claim (*al-taʿaddī bi al-quwwati ilā ṭalabi mā laysa bi mustaḥaqqin*): al-Māwardī, *al-Ḥāwī*, XIII:97.

[5] See, for example, al-Makkī, *Fayḍ*, II:303; al-Jamal, *Ḥāshiya*, V:113; Ibn Ḥajar al-Haytamī, *Fatḥ*, II:294; al-Shirbīnī, *Mughnī*, IV:124. As discussed later, many jurists state that *baghy* is not a sin. See, for example, al-Ramlī, *Fatāwā*, IV:19; al-Maqbiliyyi, *al-Manār*, II:484.

[6] Al-Ṣāwī, *Bulgha*, II:414.

sole reason the Companions of the Prophet fought each other is so that they would teach Muslims *aḥkām al-bughāh*.[7] Other jurists, such as Ibn ᶜĀbidīn (d. 1252/1836–7), state that the offense of *baghy* rarely occurs.[8]

These seemingly paradoxical positions point to the complex origin and context of *aḥkām al-bughāh*. The dynamics of these discourses reflect a complex matrix of theological and political motivations. The juristic discourses utilized and heavily relied on the theological debates about the civil wars between the Prophet's Companions, but they also served important political and historical functions. The terminology, and many of the debates, indicate that Muslim jurists were attempting to make history and politics consistent with theology. In doing so, however, they were also reconstructing theology according to the categories of law. Law was the negotiating instrument between history, theology, and politics. Furthermore, these juristic debates became the vehicle by which jurists provided commentary on various forms of dissent. One form of dissent could be declared an apostasy or brigandage while another could be declared a *baghy*. In each situation, the legal, and perhaps the symbolic, results are very different. These discourses were the vehicle by which the jurists regularly commented on the legitimacy of the rebellions of, among many others, al-Ḥusayn b. ᶜAlī (d. 61/680), ᶜAbd Allāh Ibn al-Zubayr (d. 73/692), and Muḥammad Ibn ᶜAbd Allāh al-Nafs al-Zakiyya (d. 145/762). Furthermore, the jurists discussed responses to the Umayyads, Qarāmiṭa, Fāṭimids, and Khawārij, as well as others. Muslim jurists balanced functionalist considerations against theological and moral imperatives, and constructed a highly technical and symbolic discourse.

In order to construct their discourse, Muslim jurists co-opted, constructed, and reconstructed doctrinal and historical precedents. This process, and it is a process, must be understood through a historical continuum. As noted earlier, we will discuss this historical continuum by tracing the main points of development and re-formulation. Nevertheless, before tracing the various points of the debates, it is important to lay the proper foundation by reviewing the doctrinal precedents that were co-opted, and that were brought into the service of the legal arguments. It is also important to review the historical context out of which the juristic debates were born. Through this, we will observe the formation of a sacred history with doctrinal significance. Most importantly, we

[7] See, for example, Ibn al-ᶜArabī, *Kitāb*, II:593–4; Ibn al-ᶜArabī, *Aḥkām*, IV:1720, 1722; al-Qurṭubī, *al-Jāmiᶜ* (1987), XVI:319.

[8] Ibn ᶜĀbidīn, *Ḥāshiya*, VI:410. Also see al-Ṭaḥṭāwī, *Ḥāshiya*, II:493.

will discuss the process by which the juristic culture creatively negotiated its context and constructed a historical narrative authenticating its normative positions.

THE DOCTRINAL SOURCES

There are two main sources cited for the law of rebellion in Islam: ᶜAlī b. Abī Ṭālib (d. 40/661) and the Qurʾān.[9] According to numerous sources, when it comes to Muslims fighting each other, ᶜAlī is the example and the teacher (*ᶜAlī al-qudwa wa al-muᶜallim*).[10] The main points cited as precedent are that: (1) ᶜAlī refused to attack the rebels, particularly the Khawārij, before he was attacked first; and (2) he spared the lives and property of the prisoners, the wounded, and the fugitive in the Battle of the Camel in 36/656.[11] He refused to take any of the women or children captive, and pardoned his enemies.[12] After the Battle of the Camel, ᶜAlī ordered that no property would be kept as booty, and that whoever

[9] The conduct of Abū Bakr, the first caliph (d. 13/634), ᶜUmar b. al-Khaṭṭāb, the second caliph (d. 23/644), ᶜUthmān b. ᶜAffān, the third caliph, (d. 35/656), and the Umayyad caliph ᶜUmar b. ᶜAbd al-ᶜAziz (d. 101/720) is, at times, cited as well. For example, see al-Māwardī, *al-Ḥāwī*, XIII:101, 106; Ibn Qudāma, *al-Mughnī*, X:52; Ibn ᶜAbd al-Barr, *al-Tamhīd* (1982), XXIII:338; Abū Yaᶜlā, *al-Aḥkām*, 56. However, the main reliance is on ᶜAlī. ᶜUthmān and ᶜUmar b. ᶜAbd al-ᶜAzīz, in particular, are cited only for very specific points of law, for example, whether a killed loyalist should be washed before burial.

[10] For example, see al-Simnānī, *Rawḍa*, II:1214; al-Makkī, *Manāqib*, 345; al-Marghīnānī, *al-Hidāya*, II:171. Al-ᶜAynī (*al-Bināya*, VI:735) asserts that if it had not been for ᶜAlī, we would not know how to conduct warfare among *ahl al-qibla*. The same point is made in al-Baghawī, *Sharḥ*, VI:169–70. Al-Māwardī (*al-Ḥāwī*, XIII:104, 121) asserts that Muslims followed the practice of ᶜAlī (*wa ᶜalayhā ᶜamila al-Muslimūna*); the Shīᶜī Muḥammad Ḥasan al-Najafī (*Jawāhir*, XXI:335) states that ᶜAlī's example left its impact upon people (*wa qad raʾaytum āthāra dhālika huwa dhā sāʾir fī al-nās*); also see al-Ḥurr al-ᶜĀmilī, *Wasāʾil*, XI:58–9. ᶜAlī is reported to have wondered, "If I would not have come to the people, who would have applied this conduct to them (*law ghibtu ᶜan al-nāsi man kāna yasīru fīhim bi hādhihi al-sīra*)?": al-Ṣanᶜānī, *al-Muṣannaf*, X:124.

[11] The Battle of the Camel (*waqᶜat al-jamal*) took place near Baṣra between the forces of the Prophet's wife ᶜĀʾisha bint Abī Bakr (d. 58/678), Ṭalḥa b. ᶜUbayd Allāh (d. 36/656), and al-Zubayr b. al-ᶜAwwām (d. 36/656) and the forces of ᶜAlī. ᶜĀʾisha was defeated, and Ṭalḥa and al-Zubayr were killed.

[12] Ibn Qutayba (attrib.), *al-Imāma*, 77–8; Ibn Ḥajar al-ᶜAsqalānī, *Fatḥ*, XIV:559. Al-Ṭabarī (*Taʾrīkh*, IV:581) notes that the Khawārij were unhappy about ᶜAlī's clemency. Al-Bayhaqī (*al-Sunan*, VIII:181) mentions a report in which ᶜAlī's soldiers are distressed by the command not to pursue their defeated enemy (*fa-shaqqa ᶜalaynā dhālik*). Ibn al-Athīr (*al-Kāmil*, III:130) reports that the consensus, among all of the combatants in the Battle of the Camel, was to spare the lives of the fugitive, wounded, and prisoner, and not to enslave people or confiscate property. But he also reports that ᶜAlī issued specific commands to that effect in the Battle of the Camel, and in the Battle of Ṣiffīn (37/657): ibid., 140, 175. Ibn al-Wardī (*Taʾrīkh*, I:150) reports that in the Battle of Ṣiffīn, ᶜAlī commanded his forces not to initiate the fighting, not to pursue the fugitive, not to seize property, and not to molest women. Al-Asadī (*al-Fitnah*, 157, 181) reports that *ahl al-Kūfa* believed that the lives of the wounded, fugitive, and prisoner should be spared, and that this was ᶜAlī's regular conduct. The above source also reports that both sides at Ṣiffīn agreed on these terms of conduct.

recognized their property should retrieve it. In an incident often cited in legal sources, ᶜAlī's soldiers were cooking a meal in a pot they had found, when a man from ᶜĀ'isha's defeated forces recognized the pot as his own. When the man demanded his pot back, ᶜAlī's soldiers asked him to wait until they finished cooking the food. However, the man refused to wait, spilled the food onto the ground, took his pot, and left.[13] Obviously, the story is designed to illustrate the uncompromising sanctification of the rebel's property.[14]

The accuracy of these historical accounts is not the point.[15] Rather, the significant fact is that Muslim jurists co-opted these reports and constructed them into precedents for their discourse on rebellion. Conflicting reports about ᶜAlī's conduct were largely ignored or interpreted in such a fashion so that they would have a limited effect,[16] or be explained away.[17] The conduct of ᶜĀ'isha bint Abī Bakr (d. 58/678), ᶜUthmān

[13] Ibn Qudāma, *al-Mughnī*, x:65; al-ᶜĀmilī, *Ghāyat*, i:502; al-Suyūrī, *al-Tanqīḥ*, i:574.

[14] Ibn Abī al-Ḥadīd, *Sharḥ*, iv:25–6. Ibid., i:247–8, notes that ᶜAlī followed the example of the Prophet when the latter conquered Mecca in 8/630. The same point is made by al-Najafī (*Jawāhir*, xxi:350) and al-Suyūrī (*al-Tanqīḥ*, i:574). Often, Shīᶜī sources that compare ᶜAlī's conduct to the case of Mecca wish to imply that the rebels against ᶜAlī were not actually Muslim, but that ᶜAlī opted to follow the Prophet's behavior simply as a matter of discretion (*ta 'assī*). In other words, their argument has a sectarian orientation. See al-Tustarī, *Iḥqāq*, xvii:170–1, 279–80, 281, for reports attributed to the Prophet stating that those who rebelled against ᶜAlī should be killed as unbelievers (*kuffār*). I address this point later. Sunnī sources such as al-Shīrāzī, *al-Muhadhdhab*, ii:283, argue that ᶜAlī's conduct with the Khawārij followed the example of the Prophet in dealing with the hypocrites of Medina. See also, al-Māwardī, *al-Ḥāwī*, xiii:118. The same point is made by Ibn Qudāma, *al-Mughnī*, x:60.

[15] Jaᶜīṭ (*al-Fitnah*, 231) argues persuasively that the reports of ᶜAlī's clemency are historically accurate.

[16] For conflicting reports on ᶜAlī's conduct, particularly in the Battle of Ṣiffīn (37/657), see al-Bayhaqī, *Maᶜrifa*, vi:283; al-Najafī, *Jawāhir*, xxi:328. Al-Jaṣṣāṣ (*Aḥkām*, iii:402) reports that ᶜAlī killed a prisoner in the Battle of the Camel. The same is reported by al-Nuᶜmān (*Daᶜā'im*, i:393–4). Al-Jamal (*Ḥāshiya*, v:117) asserts that ᶜAlī executed the Khawārij; the same point is made in al-Ramlī, *Nihāya*, vii:407. Ibn Mufliḥ (*Kitāb*, vi:163) argues that ᶜAlī took the property found in the Khawārij camp because they usurped much more than that from Muslims. It is reported that in 38/658 Jāriyya b. Qudāmah al-Saᶜdī, ᶜAlī's agent, crucified and burned ᶜAmr b. al-Ḥaḍramī, Muᶜāwiya's agent, who was sent to Baṣra to agitate against ᶜAlī. Some reports say that Ibn al-Ḥaḍramī was surrounded in a home and burned, i.e. he was not crucified: al-Ṭabarī, *Ta'rīkh*, v:57–8; Ibn Ḥajar al-ᶜAsqalānī, *Fatḥ*, xiv:522; al-Qasṭalānī, *Irshād*, x:179–80; see also the discussion of this incident in Ibn Abī al-Ḥadīd, *Sharḥ*, iv:52–3. Al-Nafrāwī (*al-Fawākih*, ii:218) reports that ᶜAlī burned the heretics (*al-zanādiqa*). Al-Nuᶜmān (*Daᶜā'im*, ii:475) reports that ᶜAlī crucified a *muḥārib* alive for three days. Kraemer ("Apostates," 47) asserts that ᶜAlī took captive the Banū Nājiya. Ibn al-Athīr and others report that only those who did not convert back to Islam were taken captive. See Ibn al-Athīr, *al-Kāmil*, iii:239; al-Ṭabarī, *Ta'rīkh*, v:65; Abū Yūsuf, *Kitāb*, 67.

[17] In an interesting report, a man complained to ᶜAlī b. al-Ḥusayn Zayn al-ᶜĀbidīn that ᶜAlī b. Abī Ṭālib, in Baṣra, did not follow the Prophet's example, when the Prophet conquered Mecca. ᶜAlī b. al-Ḥusayn became upset and said that ᶜAlī did, in fact, follow the Prophet's example. ᶜAlī gave his commander written orders not to kill the wounded, prisoners, or vanquished, and not to enslave a Muslim, but the commander did not read the orders until after the fighting started: al-Ṭūsī, *Tahdhīb*, vi:154–5. On this report see, al-Majlisī, *Malādh*, ix:411.

b. ʿAffān (d. 35/656), or Muʿāwiya b. Abī Sufyān (d. 60/680), for the most part, was excluded or not cited.[18] The process of selecting legal precedent, bolstering its credibility, and consolidating its authoritativeness was pursued by several means. For instance, Muslim jurists often cite a report in which an Umayyad caliph is made to acknowledge ʿAlī's precedent as a historical fact. It is reported that Marwān b. al-Ḥakam (d. 65/685) told ʿAlī b. al-Ḥusayn (Zayn al-ʿĀbidīn) (d. 95/713): "I have never seen one more generous in victory than your father. When we were defeated in the day of the Camel [Battle of the Camel], his [ʿAlī's] caller shouted, do not pursue anyone who is retreating and do not kill the wounded."[19] In fact, a *ḥadīth* attributed to the Prophet was put into circulation confirming ʿAlī's clemency as God's direct command. According to this report, the Prophet asked Ibn Masʿūd (d. 33/653) whether he was aware of God's command as to the *bughāh*. Ibn Masʿūd replied that God and His Prophet know best. The Prophet then declared that the wounded, the captive, or the fugitive should not be killed.[20]

[18] For example, ʿUthmān is reported to have written to order his governor in Egypt to execute, amputate, and crucify the rebels who laid siege to his home, but this precedent is not cited: see Ibn Khayyāṭ, *Taʾrīkh*, I:146; Jaʿīt, *al-Fitnah*, 114, and for Muʿāwiya's precedent, ibid., 90. ʿĀʾisha's faction is reported to have massacred 600 men suspected of taking part in ʿUthmān's assassination. This precedent is never cited: ibid., 152; also see al-Ṭabarī, *Taʾrīkh*, IV:547–8. Qays b. Saʿd b. ʿUbāda, al-Ḥasan's governor over Egypt, made peace with Muʿāwiya, and abdicated his position on the condition that all liabilities for blood or property be forgiven. This precedent is very rarely cited by legal sources. For the incident, see al-Ṣanʿānī, *al-Muṣannaf*, V:462. ʿAmr b. al-ʿĀṣ, Muʿāwiya's partisan, had Muḥammad b. Abī Bakr al-Ṣiddīq, ʿAlī's governor-designate for Egypt, either executed or burned alive inside the corpse of a dead donkey in 38/658: Ibn Khayyāṭ, *Taʾrīkh*, I:174–5. See the discussion of this incident in Ibn Rushd I, *al-Bayān*, XVII:559, where ʿAmr says that he simply followed the orders of Muʿāwiya.

[19] Al-Bayhaqī, *al-Sunan*, VIII:181; al-Bayhaqī, *Maʿrifa*, VI:282; al-Zaylaʿī, *Tabyīn*, III:295; al-Shawkānī, *Nayl*, VII:169; Ibn Mufliḥ, *al-Mubdiʿ*, XI:162; al-Shāfiʿī, *al-Umm*, IV:216. The version reported in al-Nawawī, *al-Majmūʿ*, XIX:203, states, "I have not seen one more generous with us than your father." See Abū Yūsuf, *Kitāb*, 214, where Hārūn al-Rashīd (149/766–193/809), the fifth ʿAbbāsid caliph, asked about how war against fellow Muslims should be conducted. Al-Makkī (*Manāqib*, 184) reports that the ʿAbbāsid caliph al-Manṣūr (d. 158/775) called upon Abū Ḥanīfa (d. 150/767) to ask him about the rules of conduct in fighting fellow Muslims, and Abū Ḥanīfa cited ʿAlī's precedent. For non-Sunnī sources see al-Ṣanʿānī, *Kitāb*, IV:330. The Shīʿī al-Ṭūsī (*Tahdhīb*, VI:155) reports that Marwān b. al-Ḥakam, "may God curse him," said that when "ʿAlī defeated us at Baṣra, he returned to people their property. Whoever presented proof, he returned [his property] to him. Whoever did not have proof, [ʿAlī] took the oath from him and returned his property" (the curse could be an addition by the copyist). On Zayn al-ʿĀbidīn, see Modarressi, *Crisis*, 4–6.

[20] Al-Shawkānī, *Nayl*, VII:169; al-Zarkashī, *Sharḥ*, VI:226; Ibn Qudāma, *al-Kāfī*, IV:148. Al-Bayhaqī (*al-Sunan*, VIII:182) notes that the *ḥadīth* is weak; Ibn al-Humām (*Sharḥ*, VI:98) also notes that the *ḥadīth* is problematic. In al-Shaybānī and Ibn Ḍuwayyān, *al-Muʿtamad*, II:443, the same is noted. Also see al-Dimashqī, *Kifāya*, 493 (editor's note that both the Prophet's *ḥadīth* and the report about Marwān are weak).

ʿAlī purportedly was acting in compliance with this divine command.[21]

Importantly, authentication of the discourse was sought from the Qurʾān as well. Two specific verses became integral to the discourse. Both verses address rebellion only indirectly. The reports about the occasions for their revelation were not directly related to issues of rebellion either. We will discuss the verse on *baghy* first.

THE BAGHY VERSE

The word *baghā* occurs in the Constitution of Medina (*wathīqat al-Madīna*); it is used in the sense of transgression – the believers are to cooperate against those who transgress or commit injustice (*ʿalā man baghā minhum*).[22] The word is used in a non-technical fashion to signify that all Muslims will cooperate against any unjust or offending party. Nevertheless, despite its apparent significance, this precedent is hardly ever cited in Islamic legal sources. Rather, it is the Qurʾānic verse on the subject that is cited in nearly every discourse on rebellion. The verse states the following:

> If two parties among the believers fight each other, then make peace between them. But if one of them transgresses (*baghat*) against the other, then fight, all of you, against the one that transgresses until it complies with the command of God. But if it complies, then make peace between the two parties with justice and be fair, for God loves those who are fair and just. The believers are but a single brotherhood. So reconcile your two [contending] brothers, and fear God so that you will receive His mercy.[23]

Significantly, the verse uses the word *baghat* which, in this context, means to transgress or treat unfairly.[24] This verse became commonly known as *āyat al-baghy* or the verse on *baghy*. We will later address the reports on

21 The Umayyad caliph ʿUmar b. ʿAbd al-ʿAzīz wrote to his governor in Kūfa instructing that in fighting the Ḥarūriyya the governor should not slaughter a woman or child, execute a prisoner, pursue a fugitive, or kill the wounded. Ibn ʿAbd al-ʿAzīz justified these instructions by quoting the Qurʾān (2:190) to the effect that doing otherwise would be a transgression and an injustice: Ibn al-Jawzī, *Sīra*, 95–6.

22 See al-Sayyid, *al-Ummah*, 54; also see Watt, *Islamic*, 131.

23 Qurʾān 49:9–10. I have consulted ʿAlī, trans. *Meaning*; however, I translated from the original Arabic.

24 The Qurʾān typically uses the word *baghy* to mean transgression or injustice. For instance: "Say: God has forbidden shameful deeds, whether open or secret; sins and transgression (*baghy*) against truth or rights; assigning partners to God, for which God hath given no authority; and saying things about God of which you have no knowledge" (7:33). Also see 2:90; 2:173; 2:213; 3:19; 6:145; 6:146; 10:23; 10:90; 16:90; 42:14; 42:39; 45:17; 96:115. The Qurʾān also uses the term to mean sexual transgression: see 19:20; 19:28; 24:33.

how the Companions understood and debated this verse.[25] For now, it is important to note that the verse addresses a conflict between two seemingly equal parties. The only thing that seems to distinguish one party from the other is the offense of committing transgression. However, there is no elaboration in the verse as to the nature of the transgression. The transgression could possibly be the act of resorting to violence or the decision to refuse reconciliation or to continue fighting despite attempts at reconciliation. Importantly, however, the verse does not seem to address a situation in which there is a hierarchy of authority. In other words, it does not seem to address a situation in which a person revolts against a superior or in which one rebels against an established government.

The reported reasons for the revelation of this verse are rather curious. There are many different reports on why this verse was revealed.[26] In one report, a woman from the Anṣār, identified only as Umm Zayd, was forbidden by her husband to visit her parents. When the woman insisted on visiting her family, the husband imprisoned her. Consequently, her family and his family quarreled and continued to fight until the verse was revealed.[27] Another report states that the Prophet was riding a donkey and passed by ᶜAbd Allāh b. Ubayy b. Salūl of al-Khazraj (known as the head of the hypocrites). When the Prophet's donkey defecated, Ibn Ubayy plugged his nose and yelled out: "Take your donkey away; its odor has offended us!" ᶜAbd Allāh b. Rawāḥa of al-Aws, who was standing nearby, was angered and yelled back: "The Prophet's donkey smells better than you and your father." The supporters of each started arguing, and the argument descended into fighting in which fists and shoes were used. Some versions of this report add that the Prophet interceded to stop the fighting but the parties were not open to reconciliation (*fa-karihū dhālik*), and so the verse was revealed.[28] Some reports add that weapons were

[25] For example, as discussed later, there are reports in which ᶜĀ'isha, ᶜAbd Allāh b. ᶜUmar, and others lament the fact that this verse has been ignored or misapplied.

[26] These types of reports are called the occasions for revelation, or *asbāb al-nuzūl*.

[27] Al-Suyūṭī, *al-Durr*, VI:99; al-Ālūsī, *Rūḥ*, XXVI:151. A slightly different version appears in al-Suddī, *Tafsīr*, 442; he reports that there was some problem between the woman and her husband, so he imprisoned her. Consequently, their families fought each other but the Prophet intervened and reconciled them. It seems that this report emerged early on because al-Suddī died in 128/745. This report does not appear in Muqātil, "Tafsīr," 74/II:163. Muqātil died in 150/767.

[28] Al-Ālūsī, *Rūḥ*, V:330; al-Ṭabarī, *Jāmiᶜ*, XXV:82; Ibn Kathīr, *Tafsīr*, IV:222; al-Thaᶜālibī, *al-Jawāhir*, IV:188. Abū Ḥayyān (*Tafsīr*, II(2):979) states only that the Prophet was on his way to visit an ill companion when Ibn Ubayy verbally assaulted him. Al-Nasafī (*Tafsīr*, III:1678) adds to the story in the text above: "The urine of the Prophet's donkey smells better than your musk." Substantially, the same report is in Muqātil, "Tafsīr" 74/II:163 except that the fight breaks out after the Prophet leaves. The early *tafsīr* of ᶜAbd al-Razzāq al-Ṣanᶜānī (d. 211/826) reports that

used in the fighting.[29] A variant of this story involves Muslims and non-Muslims. The same facts about the Prophet's donkey and Ibn Ubayy's displeasure with the donkey's odor are presented. However, in this version, the incident is said to have taken place before the Battle of Badr (2/624). Ibn Ubayy was sitting with unbelievers and Jews when the Prophet came to invite them to Islam. Ibn Ubayy rudely told the Prophet not to disturb their social event, and that the Prophet should wait at home where those who wished to listen might seek him. After Ibn Rawāḥa retorted by inviting the Prophet to come talk to him and declaring that he would be more than happy to listen to the Prophet preach, Muslims, Jews, and unbelievers quarreled with each other until the Prophet intervened.[30] In yet another report, the reason for revelation is said to be very different. In this version, two men from the Anṣār fought. Because one of the men belonged to a powerful clan, he proclaimed that if need be, the dispute would be settled by force, but the other man insisted that they should go to the Prophet for mediation. They continued to argue until they fought, using their hands and shoes.[31]

These reports might represent various trends in early Islam that sought to establish the authoritativeness of the Prophet's role. However, none of them relates directly to the issue of rebellion or insurrection. The tenuous relationship between the verses on *baghy* and the law of rebellion, as discussed later, is noted by several, particularly Shīʿī, scholars.[32] Even Sunnī jurists frequently point out that the term *baghy* used in

two Muslim groups fought using their hands and shoes, so the verse was revealed: al-Ṣanʿānī, *Tafsīr*, II:188. Some reports simply state, without further elaboration, that two tribes from the Anṣār fought and so the verse was revealed: see al-Rāwandī, *Fiqh*, I:372. Other reports simply state that the verse was revealed when the ʿAws and Khazraj fought: see Ibn al-Murtaḍā, *Tafsīr*, V:50; al-Bayḍāwī, *Anwār*, V:88. One report involves murder. According to this report, Sumayr killed Ḥāṭib, and then the ʿAws and Khazraj fought because of this incident: al-Qurṭubī, *al-Jāmiʿ* (1952), XVI:316–17.

29 Al-Ṭabrisī, *Majmaʿ*, VI:88. The significance of the point about the use of weaponry is that some of ʿAlī's detractors argued that weaponry should never be used in inter-Muslim fighting. Relying on the reports stating that the Anṣār used their hands and shoes, they argued that only hands, and perhaps sticks or rocks, may be used. The point of this report is to criticize ʿAlī's use of weaponry against fellow Muslims. See al-Ṭabarī, *Jāmiʿ*, XXV:82; al-Jaṣṣāṣ, *Aḥkām*, III:400.

30 Al-Ṣāwī, *Ḥāshiya*, IV:110–11.

31 Some versions of the report are careful to note that no weapons were used: al-Suyūṭī, *al-Durr*, VI:99; al-Jaṣṣāṣ, *Aḥkām*, III:399; al-Māwardī, *al-Nukat*, V:330; al-Ṣanʿānī, *Tafsīr*, II:188. Al-Ṭabarī (*Jāmiʿ*, XXV:81–2) also reports that, as a general matter, the verse was revealed because parties would fight, and the Prophet would invite them to an arbitration, but they would refuse.

32 For example, see al-Suyūrī, *Kanz*, I:386, who notes that the *bughāh* in the verse are not necessarily the *bughāh* addressed by the jurists. The late Shīʿī jurist al-Ṭabāṭabāʾī (*al-Mīzān*, XVIII:320) notes that considering the reports on the occasions for revelation, it is not clear why the verse applies to rebellion. Al-Bayhaqī (*al-Sunan*, VI:278–9) points out that the implications of the verse are not clear.

ordinary language is different from the technical meaning given to it in law.[33]

The historical, but not necessarily the legal, connection between the *baghy* verse and rebellion was made through the problem of *fitna*. By *fitna*, we mean the civil strife that exploded at the time of the assassination of ᶜUthmān, and the ensuing warfare between ᶜAlī and his opponents.[34] There are several reports, not necessarily all Shīᶜī, that assert that this verse was revealed to address the *fitna* between the Companions of the Prophet. According to these reports, upon the revelation of this verse, the Prophet informed one of his esteemed Companions, ᶜAmmār b. Yāsir (d. 37/657), that he (ᶜAmmār) would be killed by the unjust group (*al-firqa* or *al-fiʾa al-bāghiya*).[35] ᶜAmmār was a long-time partisan of ᶜAlī, and was killed fighting Muᶜāwiya in the Battle of Ṣiffīn.[36] The implication of this report was that Muᶜāwiya, being the *bāghī* – the unjust or aggressor – should have been fought, and that ᶜAlī should have been supported.[37]

33 For example, al-ᶜAynī, *al-Bināya*, VI:735; al-Zaylaᶜī, *Tabyīn*, III:293. As noted above, the Qurʾān uses the term in its common sense, which means transgression or exceeding the bounds.

34 On the dynamics and meaning of the rebellion that resulted in the murder of the caliph ᶜUthmān see Madelung, *Succession*, 78–140; Hinds, "Murder"; Hawting, "Significance."

35 Al-Kiyā al-Harrāsī, *Aḥkām*, IV:382. Al-Jaṣṣāṣ (*Aḥkām*, III:400) argues that the ᶜAmmār *ḥadīth* is so firmly established in the Islamic tradition that even Muᶜāwiya could not deny its authenticity. Muᶜāwiya is reported to have argued that he did not kill ᶜAmmār. Rather, those who killed ᶜAmmār were the ones who brought him to battle and "threw him upon our spears," i.e. ᶜAlī and his followers are themselves responsible: al-Bayhaqī, *al-Sunan*, VIII:189. Ibn al-ᶜArabī (*Aḥkām*, IV:1717) reports that the verse was revealed to address the Khawārij. Ibn ᶜArabī (*Tafsīr*, II:519–20) asserts that ᶜAmmār fought Muᶜāwiya so that people would know that Muᶜāwiya was the *bāghī*; but there is some question as to the real author of this work. Al-Ḥurr al-ᶜĀmilī (*Wasāʾil*, XI:17) reports that when the verse was revealed, the Prophet predicted that ᶜAlī would fight pursuant to a sound interpretation, in the same fashion that the Prophet fought pursuant to a sound revelation; see also Ibn al-Murtaḍā, *Tafsīr*, V:50–1. A large number of reports assert that the Prophet said that ᶜAlī was going to be killed by the unjust party, and that ᶜAlī would fight to uphold the rightful cause while ᶜAlī's opponents would be the wrongful party: al-Hindī, *Kanz*, XI:613–16; al-Bayhaqī, *al-Sunan*, VIII:189; al-Nasāʾī, *Kitāb*, 134–49. See Tustarī, *Iḥqāq*, XVII:100, 166–7, 169, 349 for a list of the reports that occur in Sunnī sources.

36 See Reckendorf, "ᶜAmmār," in *EI2*, II:448. Also found in *EI1*, II:333–4.

37 It is this implication that motivated Ibn Taymiyya to raise doubts about the authenticity of that *ḥadīth*. Ibn Taymiyya also argues that even if the *ḥadīth* were authentic the expression *al-firqa al-bāghiyah* used in the *ḥadīth* meant the group that sought (*tabghī*) redress for ᶜUthmān's blood, but not the unjust or transgressing group. But even if the *ḥadīth* is referring to the unjust group, then it meant to condemn the specific combatants who actually committed the killing, not Muᶜāwiya. Ibn Taymiyya also adds that Muᶜāwiya and his supporter ᶜAmr b. al-ᶜĀṣ disapproved of ᶜAmmār's death: Ibn Taymiyya, *al-Fatāwā*, III:456, 458. As noted earlier, there is a vast amount of apologetic literature discussing the issue of the *fitna* between the Companions, and vindicating all the Companions including ᶜAlī and Muᶜāwiya. Many sources assert that ᶜAlī was the true *imām* and that Muᶜāwiya was a *bāghī*: see for example Ibn al-ᶜArabī, *Aḥkām*, IV:1717; Ibn Rushd I, *al-Bayān*, XVI:361, XVIII:175–7; al-Wazīr, *al-ᶜAwāṣim*, VIII:20–1, 82; al-Kāsānī, *Badāʾiᶜ*, VII:140. We will have an occasion to discuss many of the arguments of this genre of literature in the context of reviewing the positions of various jurists.

Contextually, the existence of this report is hardly surprising. The verse on *baghy* seems to have played a substantial role in the early polemics in the *fitna* between the Companions of the Prophet. The caliphs ᶜUthmān and Muᶜāwiya were accused of being *bughāh* by their detractors.[38] Furthermore, the Khawārij accused ᶜAlī of ignoring the injunctions of the verse by accepting the arbitration (*taḥkīm*) with Muᶜāwiya.[39] In fact, it seems that the accusations of *baghy* and being a *bāghī* were freely traded between the supporters of ᶜAlī and his opponents.[40] Perhaps the most interesting aspect of these polemics is the genre of reports in which ᶜĀ'isha, ᶜAbd Allāh b. ᶜUmar, and even Muᶜāwiya lament the fact that the verse on *baghy* had been neglected and ignored.

ᶜAbd Allāh b. ᶜUmar (d. 73/693) had remained strictly neutral during the political turmoils of his time.[41] He is reported to have refused to join ᶜAlī or any of the rebellions after ᶜAlī's death. In the Battle of Ḥarra in 63/683[42] between the Medinese and Yazīd (d. 64/683), he is reported to have said, "We are with whoever wins (*naḥnu maᶜa man ghalab*)."[43] It does appear that Ibn ᶜUmar adapted well to living under the Umayyads, and that he had even gained their trust. For instance, after defeating ᶜAbd Allāh b. al-Zubayr (d. 73/692) in Mecca, the caliph ᶜAbd al-Malik b. Marwān (d. 86/705) is said to have commanded al-Ḥajjāj (d. 95/714), the Irāqi governor, to lead a convoy of pilgrims to Mecca. Importantly, the caliph also instructed al-Ḥajjāj to defer to Ibn ᶜUmar on all matters relating to the rites of pilgrimage.[44] Nevertheless, despite Ibn ᶜUmar's apparent cooperation with the Umayyads, he is quoted as saying,

[38] Al-Warjalānī, *al-ᶜAdl*, II:44–5; al-Wazīr, *al-ᶜAwāṣim*, VIII:82; Jaᶜīṭ, *al-Fitnah*, 210–13.

[39] Al-Yaᶜqūbī, *Ta'rīkh*, II:191–2; al-Ashᶜarī, *Maqālāt*, II:141.

[40] Al-Ṣanᶜānī, *al-Muṣannaf*, X:122; al-Amīnī, *al-Ghadīr*, X:291, 320, 325, 342. The Muᶜtazilī al-Bayhaqī (*Risāla*, 98) calls Muᶜāwiya *bāghin ḍāll*. For the polemics between ᶜAlī and Muᶜāwiya, see Ibn Abī al-Ḥadīd, *Sharḥ*, IV:13–26. See Ibn al-Murtaḍā, *Kitāb*, VI:379, for Karrāmiyya's view that al-Ḥusayn b. ᶜAlī (d. 61/680) was a *bāghī*. On the Karrāmiyya, see al-Shahrastānī, *al-Milal*, I:124–31; Margoliouth, "Karrāmīya." See also al-Ṭabarī, *Ta'rīkh*, V:138, where Muᶜāwiya's opponents are called *bughāh*.

In an interesting report that demonstrates the complex subtleties and negotiative nature of this discourse, Muᶜāwiya reportedly ordered al-Aḥnaf b. Qays to curse ᶜAlī; al-Aḥnaf refused to do so. Instead, he cursed whichever party committed *baghy* (*al-fi'a al-bāghiya*). This implies that Muᶜāwiya was the transgressing and unjust party: Ibn Khallikān, *Wafayāt*, II:505. Also see Ibn al-Wardī, *Ta'rīkh*, I:168.

[41] See Zettersteen, "ᶜAbd Allāh ibn ᶜUmar"; Vaglieri, "ᶜAbd Allāh ibn ᶜUmar."

[42] See al-'Ubbī, *Sharḥ*, VI:558–61.

[43] Ibn Jamāᶜa, *Taḥrīr*, 55. When asked, if two rulers fight, with whom should people pray *jumᶜa*, he is reported to have said, "With whoever wins (*maᶜa man ghalab*)": Abū Yaᶜlā, *al-Aḥkām*, 22. Ibn ᶜUmar figures prominently in the anti-*fitna* traditions. He is often quoted as counseling against disobedience or rebellion. See al-Nawawī, *al-Majmūᶜ*, XIX:190; al-Bayhaqī, *al-Sunan*, VIII:192–3; al-Qasṭalānī, *Irshād*, X:199; Al-ᶜAynī, *ᶜUmda*, XXIV:209. Ibn ᶜUmar is also reported to have opposed Ibn al-Zubayr's rebellion: for example, see al-'Ubbī, *Sharḥ*, VI:557, 563–4.

[44] Ibn Taymiyya, *Minhāj*, II:255.

"Nothing has pained me as much as the fact that I have not fought against the *bāghiya* group (*al-firqa al-bāghiya*) as God has commanded me to do."[45] However, there is no agreement as to what Ibn ʿUmar meant by this statement. According to one report, Ibn ʿUmar sincerely regretted not fighting on ʿAlī's side against all of ʿAlī's foes.[46] It is also reported that Ibn ʿUmar was assassinated with a poisoned spear upon the orders of al-Ḥajjāj. However, in another report, Ibn ʿUmar was asked which of the groups he considered to be *bāghiya*; he said that it was Ibn al-Zubayr because Ibn al-Zubayr violated his oath of allegiance to the Umayyads.[47] In yet another report, when al-Ḥajjāj defeated Mecca, Ibn ʿUmar asserted that he did not know the just from the unjust party (*al-bāghiya min al-mabghī ʿalayhā*), but if he did, no one would surpass him in upholding the commands of the verse. In other words, if only he could ascertain whether al-Ḥajjāj or the rebels of Mecca were right, he would not hesitate to join the fight.[48] In all probability, more than anything else, the various versions simply display the allegiances of the transmitters of the reports.

In a different genre of reports ʿĀʾisha, the Prophet's wife and one of the rebels against ʿAlī, lamented that the whole nation (*umma*) had neglected or ignored the verse.[49] Nonetheless, while, arguably, the report refers to the *fitna* at the time of ʿAlī, it is not at all clear what is intended by the statement.[50] Ibn Rushd I (d. 520/1122), for example, struggles with the

45 Al-Suyūṭī, *al-Durr*, VI:99.

46 Al-Ālūsī, *Rūḥ*, XXVI:151; al-Zamakhsharī, *al-Kashshāf*, IV:11. In fact, it is reported that on his deathbed Ibn ʿUmar said that he regretted nothing more than not supporting ʿAlī. However, it is also reported that al-Ḥajjāj visited Ibn ʿUmar on his deathbed: Ibn Mufliḥ, *Kitāb*, VI:153–4. In al-ʿAynī, *ʿUmda*, XXIV:192, Ibn ʿUmar expresses the same regret, but cites a promise given to his father as the reason for not being able to support ʿAlī. See also Ibn Abī Shayba, *al-Muṣannaf*, VIII:723, where Ibn ʿUmar (incorrectly printed in the source as Ibn ʿAmr) informs Muʿāwiya that he was on his side, but cited his father as the reason for his inability to fight. Interestingly, there is a report that ʿAmr b. al-ʿĀṣ joined Muʿāwiya because ʿAmr's father ordered him to, and he had to obey his father: Ibn Rushd I, *al-Bayān*, XVII:240–3. Al-Qāḍī Nuʿmān reported that ʿAlī cut off Ibn ʿUmar's financial grant because of his failure to support him (ʿAlī). Ibn ʿUmar then told ʿAlī that he regretted nothing more than not supporting him. After ʿAlī's son al-Ḥasan interceded on Ibn ʿUmar's behalf, his grant was restored: al-Nuʿmān, *Daʿāʾim*, I:391–2.

47 Al-Bayhaqī, *al-Sunan*, VIII:172; Ibn Ḥajar al-ʿAsqalānī, *Fatḥ*, XIV:577.

48 Al-Suyūṭī, *al-Durr*, VI:99.

49 Al-Bayhaqī, *al-Sunan*, VIII:173. Al-Amīnī (*al-Ghadīr*, X:275) takes a "stab" at ʿĀʾisha by asserting that she herself was one of the people who ignored the verse by rebelling against ʿAlī.

50 Arguably, the report refers to the killing of ʿUthmān, and to the fact that ʿĀʾisha believed that ʿAlī's caliphate was illegitimate because, in her view, it developed from this murder. Therefore, ʿĀʾisha is lamenting the fact that people failed to support or protect ʿUthmān. However, Muslim jurists, including Ibn Rushd I, give this tradition a much broader meaning. In some reports, ʿĀʾisha appears critical of Muʿāwiya. For instance, in one such report, after hearing of the terrible fate that befell Muḥammad b. Abī Bakr (see below for the incident), ʿĀʾisha proclaims

meaning of the report centuries after its circulation.[51] However, his interpretation, as argued later, reflects a developed position indicative of his own era. In an even more ambiguous report, after ᶜAlī's death, Muᶜāwiya chides Saᶜd b. Abī Waqqāṣ (d. 50/670–1 or 55/674–5)[52] for failing to comply with the verse during the *fitna*. Muᶜāwiya tells Saᶜd, "You were not among those who reconciled between the fighting factions, nor did you fight the iniquitous party [as the verse commands]." Saᶜd replies, "Yes, I regret not fighting against the iniquitous party!"[53] The question becomes: Is Saᶜd apologizing for not fighting ᶜAlī, Muᶜāwiya, ᶜĀʾisha, or the Khawārij? It is quite possible that the report intends to blame Saᶜd for his silence during the revolt against ᶜUthmān. In other words, Muᶜāwiya could be criticizing Saᶜd for his failure to defend ᶜUthmān against the revolt that ultimately led to ᶜUthmān's murder.[54] Importantly, however, Saᶜd's report is discussed by Sunnī jurists in the context of addressing the rebellions against ᶜAlī, and not the rebellion against ᶜUthmān.

The historicity, or lack thereof, of these reports is not the point. The point is that these reports provide clues as to how a verse that could possibly have been revealed to address a domestic dispute or a street brawl became co-opted and reconstructed to serve as the basis for a juristic discourse on rebellion. Early Muslims saw a connection or nexus between the verse and the tribulations plaguing the Companions. The terminology of the Qurʾān was, in turn, co-opted and applied to this specific historical setting. A debate raged on as to whether a certain faction or another was intended by the term "*bāghiya*," or whether reconciliation or fighting was necessary. Some even argued that ᶜAlī should not have fought any of those who rebelled against him, and should have followed ᶜUthmān's example in sitting passively at home and allowing himself to be killed.[55]

that what Muᶜāwiya did to Muḥammad was not going to deter her from speaking the truth: al-ʾUbbī, *Sharḥ*, VI:513. The implication is that she would speak the truth against Muᶜāwiya and his faction despite their cruelty to their opponents. No elaboration is provided on this report, and it seems that after ᶜĀʾisha was defeated in the Battle of the Camel, she lived a quiet, apolitical life except, perhaps, for an incident when al-Ḥasan, ᶜAlī's son, died. On ᶜĀʾisha, see Seligsohn, "ᶜĀʾisha"; Watt, "ᶜĀʾisha Bint Abī Bakr"; Spellberg, *Politics*.

51 Ibn Rushd I, *al-Bayān*, XVI:359–60.

52 Saᶜd was one of the Prophet's close companions. He refused to support either ᶜAlī or Muᶜāwiya and withdrew to his estate in al-ᶜAqīq. See Zettersteen, "Saᶜd"; Hawting, "Saᶜd," 696–7.

53 Ibn al-ᶜArabī, *Aḥkām*, VI:1719; al-Qurṭubī, *al-Jāmiᶜ* (1952), XVI:319.

54 It is unlikely that the report meant the Khawārij, since it seems that in early Islam they were referred to as *al-firqa al-māriqa* and not *al-firqa al-bāghiya*. Furthermore, both Muᶜāwiya and Saᶜd were not in the vicinity of Kūfa at the time of the rebellion by the Khawārij.

55 Ibn Qāsim, *Ḥāshiya*, VII:386; al-Buhūtī, *Kashshāf*, VI:155–6.; Ibn Mufliḥ, *al-Mubdiᶜ*, IX:155; Ibn al-ᶜArabī, *Aḥkām*, IV:1717. Ibn Kathīr (*Tafsīr*, II:53–4) reports that Abū Hurayra tried to

But this debate became the platform on which the discourse on rebellion was established. As pointed out earlier, some jurists went so far as to say that the sole reason God made the Companions fight each other was to teach Muslims the law of rebellion. Fundamentally, the discourse on the fighting between the Companions of the Prophet was a discourse on theology, on rehabilitating the Prophet's legacy, and on establishing the basis of the Islamic creed. For Sunnī Muslims in particular, the primary concern was to preserve or salvage the credibility of all the Companions despite the quarreling and fighting.[56] This involved an intricate process of creative apologetics in which it was argued, among other things, that all the Companions were correct to a certain extent, but ᶜAlī was more correct than the others. The Companions were all exercising an *ijtihād* (independent judgment), and all would be rewarded by God. However, ᶜAlī's position was, ultimately, more justified than those of any of his opponents. All of the Companions would, in the end, go to heaven.[57] Alternatively, an argument was constructed that one must not judge who from among the Companions was wrong or right, therefore one must abstain from judgment and leave the matter to God to sort out at the end.[58]

Whatever the merits of the apologetics, the historical memory of the early warfare between the Companions produced a strong tradition of what can be called anti-*fitna* (civil strife) literature. *Fitna* was associated early on with anarchy and chaos (*al-haraj*) or corruption (*al-ifsād fī al-arḍ*), and was condemned in this genre of literature in the strongest terms.[59] The duty of a Muslim during a *fitna*, according to the tradition, is to abstain or refrain from participating, and to avoid supporting civil turmoil or strife.[60] Therefore, it is argued that the Companions who refused to

defend ᶜUthmān but ᶜUthmān refused his help, telling him that whoever kills one person, it is as if he has killed humanity. This is in reference to the Qur'ānic verse 5:32. The Shīᶜī source al-Ṭūsī (*al-Mabsūṭ*, VII:279) mentions that ᶜUthmān had 400 armed slaves. He commanded them not to defend him, and in fact offered to free any slave who would put down his weapon. See the Shīᶜī Abū Mikhnaf (d. 157/773), *Nuṣūṣ*, I:86–7, who reports the same.

56 For example, see al-Ashᶜarī, *Maqālāt*, II:145–7; al-Baghdādī, *al-Farq*, 280–1; and al-Yamanī, *ᶜAqā'id*, I:95–213, for his passionate defense of Abū Bakr, ᶜUmar, ᶜUthmān, ᶜAlī, ᶜĀ'isha, Ṭalḥa, and Zubayr. Also see al-Hindī, *Kanz*, XI:525–647.

57 For example, see Ibn Abī Shayba, *al-Muṣannaf*, VIII:722–3; Ibn al-ᶜArabī, *Aḥkām*, IV:1718, 1719; Ibn al-Humām, *Sharḥ*, VI:97.

58 For the various views, see al-Ashᶜarī, *Maqālāt*, II:140–2, 145–6. For the various views from a Shīᶜī perspective, see al-Mufīd, *Awā'il*, 42–4; also see al-Murtaḍā, *al-Intiṣār*, 232, for criticism of what he describes as the *ahl al-ḥadīth* position. (In this context *ahl al-ḥadīth* means the Sunnīs.) For criticism from a Muᶜtazilī perspective, see al-Bayhaqī, *Risāla*, 98.

59 Al-Sayyid, *Mafāhīm*, 40–1; al-Muqrī, *al-Sunan*, I:211–40; Ibn Abī al-Ḥadīd, *Sharḥ*, X:47.

60 The terminology usually used is *ittiqā'* or *iᶜtizāl al-fitna* or *al-iᶜrāḍ ᶜan mā shajara baynahum*. This genre of literature is quite extensive. See, for example, Ibn Ḥammād, *Kitāb*, 78–99, 103–9; al-Muqrī, *al-Sunan*, I:211–360, II:363–80, esp. I:355–60, II:363–72; Ibn Kathīr, *al-Nihāya*, I:11–18, 36–7; Ibn Abī Shayba, *al-Muṣannaf*, VIII:590–649; al-Bukhārī, *Ṣaḥīḥ* (Dār Iḥyā' al-Turāth

participate and who refused to support either ʿAlī or his opponents were not blameworthy.[61] It is important to note, however, that this was not a unitary discourse. In other words, this was not a discourse of political pacificity alone, for after all, ʿAlī, ʿĀ'isha, and their supporters did take part in the civil war, and their credibility had to be upheld as well. For the most part, the *fitna* discourse served to restore what I called earlier the "psychic balance" of the Muslim nation by providing a means of explaining, justifying, and reconciling the conflicting positions of the Companions of the Prophet in the early civil wars.

Nevertheless, there is a tension in the *fitna* discourse between the fear of civil strife and the historical precedent of political activism. Precedents for both political pacificity and activism existed in Islamic history. The tension, however, was created because of the theological need to uphold the credibility of the Companions who adopted diametrically opposed positions on the use of force against fellow Muslims. The tension and the attempt to resolve it are well demonstrated in a passage by Ibn Rushd I. In commenting on the report that ʿĀ'isha lamented the fact that people ignored the verse on *baghy*, he states:

> By this statement ʿĀ'isha meant to ascribe fault to the Companions who refused to become involved in the wars that took place between them, and who abstained and refused to be with one side against the other. ʿĀ'isha believed that it was their duty to attempt to reconcile between the contending parties, and if they were unable to effect a reconciliation, then they should have joined the forces of the party *they believed* to be in the right, as the verse requires them to do. [However], it should be noted that those who refused to join either side did so as to stay on the side of safety and certainty because they could not ascertain who was right and who was wrong. Hence it was incumbent upon them to abstain from becoming involved because it is not permitted for a Muslim to kill another while acting on speculative belief rather than certainty. Likewise, it was incumbent upon those who did fight to do so because *they believed* that to be right, pursuant to their own *ijtihād* on the matter. Consequently, each of them is praiseworthy for what they have done. The killer and the killed are in Heaven, and this is what every Muslim should believe as to the conflict that befell the Companions. [emphasis added][62]

Ibn Rushd I then goes on to argue that it would be improper to claim that every *mujtahid* is correct, and to believe that all the parties are equally right

al-ʿArabī), IV:221–33; Ibn Ḥajar al-ʿAsqalānī, *Fatḥ*, XIV:524; Ibn Rushd I, *al-Bayān*, XVII:240–3. Most of the *fitan* reports are documented in al-Hindī, *Kanz*, XI:107–365. For a work on *fitan* from a Shīʿī perspective, see Ibn Ṭāwūs, *al-Malāḥim*.

[61] See citations in the previous note and Amḥazūn, *Taḥqīq*, II:169–83; Ibn Abī Shayba, *al-Muṣannaf*, VIII:622–34; al-Zarkashī, *Sharḥ*, VI:220–1.

[62] Ibn Rushd I, *al-Bayān*, XVI:360.

or equally wrong in order to avoid taking a position. Rather, one must assertively decide who is right or wrong. Sunnīs, Ibn Rushd I argues, believe that ʿAlī was right and so he would be rewarded twice in the Hereafter, and the rebels were wrong, and so they would be rewarded once. Therefore, while ʿAlī was ultimately the just party, his opponents are not blameworthy.[63]

According to this argument, all the Companions would end up in heaven. Nonetheless, the relevant question is: What happens to Muslims who follow their example, years or centuries later? Could rebels in later episodes of Islamic history be considered to be in error, but not blameworthy, because they followed the example of ʿĀʾisha or Muʿāwiya? In other words, perhaps the *fitna* literature resolves the theological problem of upholding the credibility of all the Companions, but it does not necessarily resolve the legal issue of how to discourse on or treat rebels after the age of the Companions.

The nexus between the theological solution and the legal implications is exemplified in an exchange that reportedly took place between Abū Mūsā al-Ashʿarī (d. 42/662–3) and ʿAbd Allāh b. Masʿūd (d. 33/653).[64] An unidentified man asks al-Ashʿarī about the wars taking place between the Companions. The man asks, "What if I take my sword and, seeking the pleasure of Allāh, strike with it whomever I wish?" Al-Ashʿarī responds, "You have a right to do so (*laka dhālik*)." Ibn Masʿūd, who overhears the conversation, cautions al-Ashʿarī, "Be careful with what you say, many will rebel in this *ummah*, all of them seeking the pleasure of Allāh, and none of them will find it."[65] Two trends are represented in this report: the theological (one has a right to act on his belief and support whichever Companion one believes to be right), and the legal (an individualized subjective standard for the use of force could lead to lawlessness). There is a theological or moral imperative to act on one's beliefs, but

[63] Ibid., 361, XVIII:175–7. The issue of being rewarded twice or once refers to a *ḥadīth* attributed to the Prophet. According to this tradition, whoever performs *ijtihād* will be rewarded. If they are right, they will be rewarded twice. If they are wrong, they will be rewarded once. On this tradition, see al-Jarrāḥī, *Kashf*, I:66–8; al-Suyūṭī, *Ikhtilāf*, 21–39.

[64] There are contradictory reports on the dates of death for both individuals. According to one report, Abū Mūsā died in 52/672. Ibn Masʿūd is reported to have died in 32/652–3. See Gibb and Kramers, eds., *Shorter*, 47, 150.

[65] See the discussion in Ibn Rushd I, *al-Bayān*, XVIII:288. Ibn Masʿūd died during the caliphate of ʿUthmān, before the civil war between the Companions. Abū Mūsā al-Ashʿarī was one of the judges in the arbitration (*taḥkīm*) between ʿAlī and Muʿāwiya. He was ʿAlī's representative, and he was either tricked by ʿAmr b. al-ʿĀṣ or he deserted ʿAlī and failed to represent his claims fairly. Because of these facts, this report is most certainly apocryphal. On al-Ashʿarī, see Ibn Saʿd, *al-Ṭabaqāt*, IV:105–16. On Ibn Masʿūd, see ibid., III:150–8. Also see Vaglieri, "al-Ashʿarī"; Vadet, "Ibn Masʿūd," 873–5.

there is the ever-present risk that strife and lawlessness would become widespread. The report poses the tension between the two trends, but does not resolve it.

On the one hand, the *fitan* literature emphasized an imperative of abstaining from civil discord and fractitious conduct. But as Abū Jaᶜfar al-Ṭabarī (d. 310/923) is reported to have argued, "If in every discord between two factions, one has the duty to escape and stay close to home (*luzūm al-manāzil*), no divine law would be upheld, and no injustice would be negated."[66] On the other hand, if one advocates an unmitigated duty to uphold what one believes to be right and just, the risk becomes widespread lawlessness or chaos. Both trends are well represented in the theological tradition. In the Sunnī tradition, most of the debates take place in the context of discourses attempting to defend or rehabilitate the credibility of the Prophet's Companions. These debates, with their various trends and tensions, became the foundation on which the law of rebellion was established. The juristic discourses on rebellion moved from the realm of theological apologetics to the realm of legalities in which the primary concern was the function of law and the construction of order. Before commencing on a description of the juristic debates on rebellion, we must first introduce the second Qurʾānic passage that is central to this field.

THE *ḤIRĀBA* VERSE

The second Qurʾānic verse relevant to this field is the following:

> The punishment of those who wage war (*yuḥāribūn*) against God and His Prophet, and strive to cause corruption on the earth (*yasᶜawna fī al-arḍi fasādan*) is that they be killed or crucified[67] or have a hand and foot cut off from opposite ends or be exiled in the land. That is their disgrace in this world and they will receive a heavy punishment in the Hereafter. Except for those who repent before you are able to capture them. In that case, know that God is most-forgiving and merciful.[68]

This is often referred to as *āyat al-ḥirāba* or the *ḥirāba* verse. Unlike the *baghy* verse, the attendant consequences to the act described are very

[66] Al-Qurṭubī, *al-Jāmiᶜ* (1952), XVI:317.

[67] In Arabic, crucifixion (*ṣalb*) does not mean placing on a cross or the driving of nails through the hands or feet. As the term is used in the Qurʾān and in Islamic law, it simply means tying and hanging someone on the bark of a tree (*yurbaṭ fī jizᶜi al-nakhla*). Nailing someone to a cross would be considered heretical in Islamic theology. See al-Qanūjī, *al-Rawḍa*, II:415, 417.

[68] Qurʾān 5:33–4.

severe. The possible punishments are execution, crucifixion, severance of limbs, or exile. Nonetheless, on the face of it, it is not clear what would bring these punishments into effect. Theoretically, the language "cause corruption on the earth" could be applied to a wide range of activities including anything from writing heretical poetry to raping and pillaging.[69] Significantly, the language of the verse lends itself to use in the political field, and could easily be applied to rebellion or sedition.[70] If, as Crone and Hinds argue, the Umayyad and other caliphs saw themselves as the representatives of God and the Prophet (*khulafā' Allāh*), then arguably one who fought against them would be fighting against God as well, and would deserve the severe punishments dictated in the verse.[71]

Conceptually, however, this verse might apply to those in power as well. In other words, the verse does not necessarily have to be read so that it applies only to those who rebel against an established government. Rather, it could also be read to mean that those in power could possibly be the corrupters of the earth. As will be seen, Muslim jurists insisted that this verse does not apply to rebels, and co-opted this verse to their discourse on highway robbers and brigands. By doing so, they argued that the harsh penalties dictated in the verse should not be applied to rebels, but should be applied to highway robbers and brigands. As we will see later, some jurists argued that even if the sulṭān and his supporters usurp property and terrorize people, then they should be treated as brigands.[72] The co-optation of the verse in this fashion, as will be demonstrated, took centuries.

The Qur'ān repeatedly condemns those who cause corruption on the earth,[73] and in one verse, it associates *fitna* with corruption on the earth.[74] But the verse quoted above is the only verse in which earthly punishments are dictated for an offense that relates to corruption on earth. The cited occasions for the revelation of this verse are as contradictory

69 This is so in legal theory, but the Qur'ān limits corruption on the earth to the destruction of property, such as crops or, perhaps, the economic system, and the destruction of lives (*ihlāk al-ḥarth wa al-nasl*). See Qur'ān 2:205. The Qur'ānic concept of corruption appears to be specific and limited although in Muslim practice it has been used rather expansively.

70 Interestingly, the famous translator of the Qur'ān, ᶜAbdullah Yūsuf ᶜAlī, assumes that the verse applies to sedition and treason: ᶜAlī, *Meaning*, 257.

71 Crone and Hinds, *God's*, 24–42, 80–96.

72 For example, see Ibn Ḥazm, *al-Muḥallā*, XII:283. Also see al-Wazīr, *al-ᶜAwāṣim*, VIII:15, where he describes Yazīd I b. Muᶜāwiya (r. 60–4/680–3) as the equivalent of a *qāṭiᶜ al-ṭarīq* (brigand).

73 For example, see Qur'ān 2:11, 2:27, 2:60, 2:205, 5:32, 5:64, 7:56, 7:85, 11:85, 13:25, 18:94, 26:152, 26:183, 28:77, 30:41, 38:28, 40:26, 47:22. The expression "corruption on earth" is also found in the *fitan* literature: see note 60.

74 Qur'ān 8:73.

and ambiguous as the verse on *baghy*. Furthermore, it seems that in the early centuries of Islam, Muslim scholars could not agree on who was the intended subject of the verse.

The first set of reports are very general. In these reports, a group of scriptuaries (*ahl al-kitāb*) purportedly had an unspecified covenant with the Prophet, but they broke the covenant and caused corruption on the earth, so the verse was revealed. The second set of reports provide that the tribe of Hilāl b. ᶜŪwaymir[75] entered into a reciprocal treaty with the Prophet not to attack any group that passed by Hilāl heading towards the Prophet. However, when a group from Banū Kināna passed by seeking to join the Prophet, Hilāl's tribe attacked, killing the men and stealing their property. The verse was then revealed. Importantly, some reports add that the Prophet was given a choice in dealing with them: he could select any of the penalties spelled out in the verse, including banishing them.[76] In a third set of reports, it is argued that the verse was revealed to address a group of polytheists who attacked Muslims, caused corruption on the earth, and then fled to non-Muslim territory before they could be captured.[77] A fourth set of reports asserts, without further elaboration, that the verse was revealed to address the Israelites (Banū Isrā'īl).[78] A fifth report asserts that the verse was revealed to address the Ḥarūriyya (the early Khawārij).[79]

The final report, and the one that espoused the most controversy, asserts that a group of men from the tribe of ᶜUrayna[80] adopted Islam and came to Medina in poor health. They complained to the Prophet that they were a people of the desert and, therefore, were unable to live in Medina. The Prophet sent with them camels so that they could,

75 Also known as Abū Burda: see Ibn al-Jawzī, *Zād*, II:344. Also reported as Abū Barza al-Aslamī: see al-Rāzī, *al-Tafsīr*, XI:169; Ibn Manẓūr, *Lisān*, II:816.

76 Al-Suyūṭī, *al-Durr*, II:307; al-Jaṣṣāṣ, *Aḥkām*, II:407; Ibn al-Jawzī, *Zād*, II:343; al-Ṭabarī, *Jāmiᶜ*, V:132.

77 Al-Suyūṭī, *al-Durr*, II:307; Ibn Kathīr, *Tafsīr*, II:55, 59; Ibn al-Jawzī, *Zād*, II:344; al-Ṭabarī, *Jāmiᶜ*, V:133; al-Rāwandī, *Fiqh*, I:366; al-Ṭabrīsī, *Majmaᶜ*, II:82. Ibn al-ᶜArabī (*Aḥkām*, II:594–5) argues that this is the most convincing occasion for revelation.

78 Al-Rāzī, *al-Tafsīr*, XI:169. Al-Ṭabarī (*Jāmiᶜ*, V:134–5), argues that the most convincing opinion is that it was revealed concerning the Israelites. However, he argues that that does not necessarily mean that the verse should not apply to Muslims. Ibn al-ᶜArabī (*Aḥkām*, II:595) denies that it was revealed concerning the Israelites.

79 Al-Suyūṭī, *al-Durr*, II:305; Ibn Kathīr, *Tafsīr*, II:55.

80 According to one report, ᶜUrayna was from Bahrain: Ibn Kathīr, *Tafsīr*, II:55–6. Some sources report that they were from ᶜUkal: al-Nasā'ī, *Tafsīr*, I:434–5. Some reports assert that they were both from ᶜUkal and ᶜUrayna or Bujayla and ᶜUrayna while other reports assert that they were from Banū Fazāra or Banū Salīm: see al-Suyūṭī, *al-Durr*, II:305; Ibn Kathīr, *Tafsīr*, II:56–7; al-Thaᶜālibī, *al-Jawāhir*, I:459. Shīᶜī sources report that the men were from Banū Ḍabba: see al-Kulaynī, *al-Furūᶜ*, VII:245; al-Ṭūsī, *Tahdhīb* X:135; al-Ḥurr al-ᶜĀmilī, *Wasā'il*, XVIII:535.

pursuant to their bedouin practice, drink the camels' milk and urine and regain their health. The Prophet also sent with them a Nubian shepherd boy known as Yasār.[81] The men stayed in a place called Liqāḥa (about six miles from Medina) until they recovered their health. The men then apostatized and tortured the shepherd boy by severing his limbs, inserting thorns in his eyes, and then crucifying him. They stole the camels and fled. After seizing them, the Prophet severed their hands and feet from opposite ends, blinded and crucified them, and then left them to die in the desert.[82] According to some reports, after killing them, the Prophet also burned their corpses.[83]

The debates around this particular report focused on whether the revelation of the verse meant to abrogate or reprimand the Prophet for what he did to the men from ᶜUrayna. It was argued that because mutilation (*muthla*) was prohibited in Islam, God reprimanded (*ᶜātaba*) the Prophet for blinding the men from ᶜUrayna, and for leaving them to die in the desert. Some reports assert that the prohibition against *muthla* came after, and not before, this incident. Therefore, God did not reprimand the Prophet but abrogated what the Prophet had done, and specified the proper legal penalties when an offender betrays and causes corruption in the earth. Some sources argued that neither abrogation nor reprimand was applicable because the Prophet blinded the men as retaliation for blinding the shepherd boy, and hence no mutilation was involved. Still other reports argue that the Prophet only intended to blind them, but before he was able to do so God revealed the verse and, therefore the Prophet refrained from any form of retaliation not specified in the verse.[84] Interestingly, some reports resolve the matter

81 Al-Ṣāwī, *Ḥāshiya*, I:280.

82 Al-Rāzī, *al-Tafsīr*, XI:169; Ibn Kathīr, *Tafsīr*, II:55–7; Ibn al-Jawzī, *Zād*, II:343; al-Zamakhsharī, *al-Kashshāf*, I:335; al-Ṭabrīsī, *Majmaᶜ*, II:82–4; Ibn Ḥajar al-ᶜAsqalānī, *Fatḥ*, XIV:66–9. This is the only occasion for revelation reported in the early works of Muqātil (d. 150/767), "Tafsīr," 74/II:98, and al-Suddī (d. 128/745), *Tafsīr*, 227. The incident is reported to have taken place in 6/627. On the incident, see Ibn al-Jawzī, *al-Muntaẓam*, III:263–4. Ibn Saᶜd (*al-Ṭabaqāt*, II:93) reports that Yasār was not sent with them. Rather, after ᶜUrayna stole the camels, Yasār chased after them. They captured him, however, severed his limbs, and stuck thorns in his tongue and eyes until he died. Ibn al-Athīr (*al-Kāmil*, II:94) mentions the incident in passing; he does not give any of the details. Al-Thawrī, who died 161/777, does not mention any of the occasions of revelation in his *Tafsīr*. Several commentators maintain that the Prophet never crucified or blinded anyone. (See notes below.)

83 Ibn Kathīr, *Tafsīr*, II:57; al-Ṭabarī, *Jāmiᶜ*, V:133; al-Rāwandī, *Fiqh*, I:366.

84 Al-Suyūṭī, *al-Durr*, II:305–6; Ibn Kathīr, *Tafsīr*, II:56–7; al-Jaṣṣāṣ, *Aḥkām*, II:407–8; al-Ṣāwī, *Ḥāshiya*, I:280; al-Ālūsī, *Rūḥ*, VI:121–2; al-Ṭabarī, *Jāmiᶜ*, V:134–5; al-Kiyā al-Harrāsī, *Aḥkām*, III:65; Ibn al-ᶜArabī, *Aḥkām*, II:594; al-Qurṭubī, *al-Jāmiᶜ* (1952), VI:149–50; al-Thaᶜālibī, *al-Jawāhir*, I:459; al-Rāwandī, *Fiqh*, I:366. Al-Zaylaᶜī (*Tabyīn*, III:237) and Ibn al-Humām (*Sharḥ*, V:408–9) assert that the Prophet never crucified anyone. Ibn Ḥazm (*al-Muḥallā*, XII:285–8)

in the form of a *ḥadīth*. According to these reports, when the incident with ᶜUrayna took place, the Prophet asked the angel Jibrīl about the proper course of action. Jibrīl then revealed the verse to the Prophet, and specified that those who steal should be amputated from opposite ends, those who murder should be killed, and those who kill and rape should be crucified. The Prophet punished the offenders accordingly, and did not blind any of them.[85]

Early Muslim commentators also disagreed on who was the intended subject of the verse on *ḥirāba*. Three main positions were advocated. The verse, it was argued, either applied to polytheists or apostates who waged war on Muslims, or to Muslims who committed highway robbery (*qaṭᶜ al-ṭarīq*). The latter position was eventually adopted by the vast majority of Muslim jurists. Many of the opinions were related to the specific occasion of revelation argued by the particular commentator. However, the emerging, and eventually dominant, legal opinion was that even if the verse was revealed with regard to polytheists or apostates, it was intended to apply to Muslims who commit an act of brigandage or highway robbery. In other words, even if the revelation of the verse was occasioned by the behavior of a certain group of polytheists or apostates, as a legal matter, the sanctions specified in the verse are to be applied to Muslims and not to polytheists or apostates.[86] In doing so, Muslim jurists

argues vehemently that the ᶜUrayna tradition is authentic, but what the Prophet did to them does not even have the semblance of *muthla*. Shīᶜī sources usually do not mention blinding. Al-Ṭabāṭabāʾī (*al-Mīzān*, v:330–1) mentions the various positions, but is keen to point out that none of the reports that were narrated by *ahl al-bayt* contain the blinding incident. The author's point is that the blinding report is a fabrication. See the following Shīᶜī sources: al-Ḥurr al-ᶜĀmilī, *Wasāʾil*, xviii:535; al-Kulaynī, *al-Furūᶜ*, vii:245, which do not mention the blinding; Ibn al-Murtaḍā, *Tafsīr*, ii:31, which does not mention the blinding or the crucifying.

85 Ibn Kathīr, *Tafsīr*, ii:58; al-Māwardī, *al-Nukat*, ii:33; al-Ṭabāṭabāʾī, *al-Mīzān*, v:333. Al- Kāsānī (*Badāʾiᶜ*, vii:94) and Ibn al-Humām (*Sharḥ*, v:407), mention that the Jibrīl *ḥadīth* occurred over the Abū Burda incident. A version of this *ḥadīth* is reported without the angel Jibrīl's involvement. This version mentions that after the Prophet captured the men from ᶜUrayna, he considered the matter, and then decided to amputate the limbs of whoever stole property; execute whoever committed murder: and crucify whoever stole and committed murder: al-Suddī, *Tafsīr*, 227. There is also a *ḥadīth* reported from ᶜĀʾisha in which she says the Prophet said: "The blood of a Muslim cannot be shed except for three reasons: adultery, murder, and a man who has apostated and fought Muslims (*kharaja min al-Islāmi fa-ḥārab*). He must be killed, crucified, or banished in the earth." See al-Suyūṭī, *al-Durr*, ii:306; al-Jaṣṣāṣ, *Aḥkām*, ii:409.

86 Al-Rāzī, *al-Tafsīr*, xi:169–70; al-Kiyā al-Harrāsī, *Aḥkām*, iii:64; al-Ālūsī, *Rūḥ*, vi:121; al-Ṭabrīsī, *Majmaᶜ*, ii:82; al-ᶜAynī, *ᶜUmda*, xxiii:284–6; al-ʾUbbī, *Sharḥ*, vi:93, 98. Ibn Ḥajar al-ᶜAsqalānī (*Fatḥ*, xiv:66) notes that the practice of Muslims proved that the verse was applicable to Muslim brigands. Al-Jaṣṣāṣ (*Aḥkām*, ii:407–8) argues that the opinion of late jurists was that the verse applied to apostates, but he rebuts this view and argues that the verse applies to Muslims. The author died in 370/980–1, and it is difficult to understand what he means by late jurists. The evidence is that the view that the verse applied to apostates emerged quite early. In all probability, however, al-Jaṣṣāṣ is referring to Ḥanafī jurists who emerged after the

argued that the punishments of execution, amputation from opposite ends, crucifixion, or banishment, as the verse specifies, are reserved for brigands or highway robbers. Concurrently, as we will demonstrate, a separate legal category was created for rebels who, according to the constructed discourse, were not to receive the same treatment, and were to be distinguished from the subjects of the *ḥirāba* verse.

This should be understood within the context of a rather complex historical practice. Banditry or brigandage played a social role in early Islamic history.[87] Islamic legal and historical sources are replete with references to violence caused by banditry. Furthermore, it is important to note that some of the groups that rebelled for ostensibly political or religious reasons, such as the Khawārij, especially the Azāriqa, and the Qarāmiṭa, used methods that are difficult to differentiate from common acts of banditry. These groups often slaughtered indiscriminately, raped, and usurped property.[88] As discussed later, Muslim jurists attempted to create legal categories that distinguished between rebels who spread terror and destruction and rebels who used less destructive means.

The ᶜUrayna incident and the language of the *ḥirāba* verse seem to have been more consistent with the actual historical practice in the Umayyad and early ᶜAbbāsid periods than the carefully structured discourses of the jurists would lead us to believe. I am not claiming that there is a causal connection between the *ḥirāba* verse and the historical practice. Rather, the language and the penalties of the *ḥirāba* verse were co-opted

formative generation of the Ḥanafī school (c. 250 and on). See also the discussion in Ibn Rushd I, *al-Muqaddamāt*, III:227–30; Ibn Rushd II, *Bidāya*, II:454–5. Al-Simnānī (*Rawḍa*, II:1327) mentions that some argued that the verse itself was abrogated because it was conditioned on "those who fight the Prophet" (*wa ḥukmuhā al-yawma zāʾilun . . . wa annahā mansūkhatun wa sharṭuhā ghayru mawjūd*). After the death of the Prophet, that condition cannot exist. (It is not entirely clear whether al-Simnānī is asserting that the verse itself had been abrogated [*naskh*] or whether he is arguing that the normative ruling established by the verse is now abrogated [*bāṭilu al-ḥukmi bi zawāli al-mawḍūᶜ*].)

87 "Serfs" or "serf-like" individuals who could not pay their taxes or debts often became bandits: see Lewis, *Islam*, 308. It is likely that banditry continued to play an important social role throughout Islamic history. See Barkey, *Bandits*, esp. 152–6, 240, on the political and social role of banditry in the Ottoman administration. Barkey argues that the Ottoman administration did not distinguish between bandits and rebels, and that the state often negotiated with and co-opted bandits. This is by no means unique to Islamic history. On the role of banditry in the Roman Empire, see MacMullen, *Enemies*, esp. 211–18. Also see Laven, "Banditry," 221–48.

88 Watt, *Formative*, 20–2; Watt, *Islamic*, 55–6. See a description of the indiscriminate slaughter committed by the Azāriqa in al-Ṭabarī, *Taʾrīkh*, VI:373. On the Azāriqa, see al-Shahrastānī, *al-Milal*, I:137–41; and Rubinacci, "Azāriḳa." On the Qarāmiṭa, see Kennedy, *Prophet*, 186, 193–4; Madelung, "Ḳarmaṭī," 660–5; and Bianqus, "Autonomous," 87, 106–8. The Qarāmiṭa attacked *ḥajj* convoys, and in 317/930 they sacked Mecca and removed the revered Black Stone. See the description of this event in al-Ṭabarī, *Taʾrīkh*, XI:464, and Ibn Kathīr, *al-Bidāya*, XI:171–4. Also see al-ʾUbbī, *Sharḥ*, VI:556.

and imitated in historical practice. This, of course, could mean that the ᶜUrayna incident was an early Umayyad invention intended to sanction the way the Umayyads dealt with their political foes. In fact, as discussed below, the infamous Umayyad governor al-Ḥajjāj reportedly would cite the *ḥirāba* verse in defending his often ruthless policies against rebels. The juristic discourse frequently intimated that the measures cited in the *ḥirāba* verse were rarely used except against the most vicious bandits. However, as discussed below, amputations from opposite ends and crucifixions were primarily used against political opponents, and it is very likely that the ᶜUrayna incident is not historical, but simply a political invention.

The accusation of causing corruption on the earth was used frequently between political opponents in Islamic history. Early on, the execution by Muᶜāwiya of the Companion al-Ḥujr b. ᶜAdī al-Kindī and his supporters in 51/671, and the slaughter of al-Ḥusayn b. ᶜAlī and many members of the family of the Prophet in 61/680 during the reign of Yazīd I, left a lasting impression on the collective memory of the jurists. Muᶜāwiya is said to have ordered that one of al-Ḥujr's supporters be buried alive. The heads of al-Ḥusayn and his supporters were severed and paraded.[89] In the same year, there were summary executions of several Khawārij, and in one case the same year, a Khārijī was tortured with the sanctions identified in the *ḥirāba* verse: his feet and hands were amputated and then he was crucified.[90] Eventually, it became common practice for the Umayyads and early ᶜAbbāsids to execute rebels and mutilate their bodies. Frequently, limbs from opposite ends would be severed, the corpse would be crucified, and, at times, burned. It was also common practice to sever the head and send it to the ruler as a trophy.[91] In some cases, opponents were taken captive and sold into slavery.[92]

89 For the execution of al-Ḥujr and his supporters, see al-Ṭabarī, *Taʾrīkh*, V:141–2, and Ibn al-Athīr, *al-Kāmil*, III:336. For the slaughter of al-Ḥusayn, see al-Ṭabarī, *Taʾrīkh*, V:202–37; Ibn al-Athīr, *al-Kāmil*, III:428–44; and Ibn Aᶜtham, *al-Futūḥ*, III:114–52. Also see the Shīᶜī Abū Mikhnaf (d. 157/773) (*Nuṣūṣ*, I:491–3, 497–8), who notes that the heads of the rebels were sent to ᶜUbayd Allāh b. Ziyād, and that the property of the rebels was looted, even the cloth off womens' backs. Ḥusayn's head was hung (*ṣulib*) on a door.

90 See Ibn al-Athīr, *al-Kāmil*, III:444–5.

91 For gory details of the torture and mutilation methods used against rebels and others in Islamic history see the multi-volume al-Shaljī, *Mawsūᶜa*.

92 The following is a demonstrative, and not exhaustive, list of some of the treatment afforded to rebels: al-Ṭabarī, *Taʾrīkh*, V:159 (ᶜUbayd Allāh b. IV Ziyād, Muᶜāwiya's governor, severs the limbs of a Khārijī in 58/677 and kills his daughter); Ibn al-Athīr, *al-Kāmil*, IV:343–4 (heads severed and Muslims enslaved during the reign of Yazīd b. ᶜAbd al-Malik, 102/720); ibid., 455 (Zayd b. ᶜAlī killed, crucified, and burned in 122/739 during the reign of Hishām b. ᶜAbd al-Malik). See the description of the Zayd b. ᶜAlī incident by Ibn al-Jawzī (*al-Muntaẓam*, VII:211–12),

The point, of course, is not to make an essentialist assessment of early Muslim practices.[93] Nonetheless, it is important to note that these violent practices did, in fact, exist and hence formed part of the cumulative heritage that was available to Muslim jurists as they constructed their legal discourses. Muslim jurists were well aware of these practices, and often selectively referred to them in the context of creating separate legal categories between rebels and bandits.[94] Importantly, what Muslim jurists omitted or dismissed from the historical record is as significant as what they included. For example, it is reported that when Ibn Muljim

who says it took place in 121 AH; also see al-Ṭabarī (*Taʾrīkh*, VII:96), who says that his corpse was crucified in 123 AH; Ibn al-Jawzī, *al-Muntaẓam*, VII:248 (the torture and killing of Khālid al-Qasrī, client of the Umayyads, in 126/743); ibid., VII:266 (the parading of the severed head of a Khārijī in 128/745); al-Ṭabarī, *Taʾrīkh*, VII:171–2, 187 (the killing and crucifixion of al-Ḥārith b. Surayj and al-Karamānī, who was crucified with a fish, in 128/745). Crucifying people with animals as an act of humiliation was a common practice in premodern times, see below. Also see al-Ṭabarī, *Taʾrīkh*, VII:164–5 (the massacre of rebels and execution of prisoners, bombardment with mangonels, and the severing of the genitals and noses of rebels in 127/744); ibid., 175 (Marwān b. Muḥammad severs the hand, foot, and tongue of an agent suspected of sympathizing with the Khawārij in 128/745). Incidents described in al-Masʿūdī, *Murūj*, include: II:102 (severing the head of al-Ashʿath and carrying it to al-Ḥajjāj), 167 (crucifixion of Yaḥyā b. Zayd; al-Ṭabarī [*Taʾrīkh*, VII:116] also reports that his hand and foot were severed), 194 (execution and crucifixion of Umayyads by Abū al-ʿAbbās al-Ṣaffāḥ), 241 (killing of ʿAbd Allāh b. ʿAlī and a slave girl by al-Manṣūr; placing them in a room and then demolishing it so that it looked like an accident), 258–9 (killing of al-Ḥusayn b. ʿAlī b. al-Ḥasan and execution of many of his supporters), 346 (execution and crucifixion of Abū al-Sarāyā), 352–3 (execution and crucifixion of Ibn ʿĀʾisha, grandson of Ibrāhīm al-Imām), 372 (crucifixion and burning of al-Afshīn), etc. Ibn Abī Shayba (*al-Muṣannaf*, VIII:625–6) reports that Ibn al-Zubayr was crucified with a cat in a mosque and that Ibn ʿUmar uttered words sympathetic to Ibn al-Zubayr. Al-Ashʿarī (*Maqālāt*, I:150–66) has a long list of ʿAlid rebels during the time of the Umayyads and ʿAbbāsids; he notes that most of them were killed, and some crucified after death. Al-Jāḥiẓ ("Risāla fī al-Nābita," 244–5) accuses the Umayyads of corruption on the earth and of crucifying their opponents. See al-Wazīr, *al-ʿAwāṣim*, VIII:158, for a discussion of the crucifixion of Zayd b. ʿAlī in 122/740.

93 There are many examples of amnesty or tolerance. For instance, in 117/735, a group of rebels agreed to surrender on the condition of being given amnesty. They were granted the request: al-Ṭabarī, *Taʾrīkh*, VII:54. In 82/701, ʿAbd al-Malik offered the people of Irāq the removal of al-Ḥajjāj if they would not support Ibn al-Ashʿath's rebellion: ibid., VI:486, also see p. 489 for a release of prisoners. However, Ibn al-Athīr (*al-Kāmil*, IV:203) says that al-Ḥajjāj killed 11,000 people when he tricked them with an offer of amnesty. Once they surrendered, he killed them. It seems that the ʿAbbāsids adopted a benevolent policy towards rebels from the same ruling family (i.e. the ʿAbbāsids), at least until the caliphate of al-Maʾmūn (d. 218/833); See Lassner, *Islamic*, 113.

94 Al-Gharnāṭī (*Qawānīn*, 456) notes that al-Ḥajjāj killed and crucified ʿAbd Allāh b. al-Zubayr. He also notes that the Umayyad caliph ʿAbd al-Malik b. Marwān killed all who opposed him. Al-Saʿdī (*Qāmūs* VIII:355) claims that all rebels before the reign of the Umayyad caliph ʿUmar b. ʿAbd al-ʿAzīz suffered amputation from opposite ends and were blinded. Al-ʾUbbī (*Sharḥ*, VI:535) discusses al-Ashʿath's rebellion and his death. Ibn Farḥūn (*Tabṣira*, II:192) mentions the crucifixion of a man accused of being a heretic (*zindīq*). One of the points that the Khārijī Abū Ḥamza al-Mukhtār b. ʿAwf mentions against the Umayyad caliph Marwān b. Muḥammad is that he blinded his opponents and cut off their hands and feet: see Crone and Hinds, *God's*, 132.

assassinated ᶜAlī, ᶜAlī's dying testament was that Ibn Muljim should not be tortured or mutilated. Nonetheless, some historical reports claim that Ibn Muljim's hands and feet were amputated, his eyes were blinded, and then he was killed and burned.[95] Similarly, according to some reports, al-Burak, the man who made a failed attempt on Muᶜāwiya's life, had his hand and foot amputated from opposite ends, and eventually was killed and crucified.[96] Muslim jurists, however, as discussed later, do not cite or rely on these reports. They only mention that ᶜAlī ordered that Ibn Muljim not be tortured or mutilated, and then discuss whether Ibn Muljim should be treated as a rebel. In other words, the Ibn Muljim incident becomes channeled into a technical discourse on the necessary legal criteria for someone to qualify as a *bāghī*. What Muslim jurists presented in their legal discourses, as often happens in legal discourses, is a highly sanitized and cleansed version of historical practice in order to advocate a particular view of law and order.

Early reports indicate that the distinction between a bandit and a rebel was not as clear and precise as it eventually became in the constructed discourse of the jurists. In these early reports, the language and symbolism of the *ḥirāba* verse are used in a context sufficiently ambiguous to be possibly applicable to rebels. One report, for example, asserts that the sulṭān is the avenger of blood for whoever fights religion and causes corruption on the earth.[97] What this means is that the relatives of the victim of the crime, who are normally the avengers of blood, do not decide the fate of the offender; the ruler becomes the avenger of blood, and he decides the offender's fate. Notably, the report does not mention highway

[95] Al-Masᶜūdī, *Murūj*, I:609. Ibn al-Athīr (*al-Kāmil*, III:258) reports that the people (*al-ᶜāmma*) burned him, but does not mention the amputation or blinding. Ibn al-Jawzī (*al-Muntaẓam*, V:175) reports that it was ᶜAlī who told his family to kill and burn Ibn Muljim. Ibn al-Jawzī (*Talbīs*, 130) says Ibn Muljim's hands and feet were amputated and his eyes were burned with a hot rod. Ibn al-Wardī (*Ta'rīkh*, I:155) does not report ᶜAlī's testament concerning Ibn Muljim. He does report that ᶜAbd Allāh b. Jaᶜfar amputated Ibn Muljim's hand and foot, cut his tongue off, blinded him, and then had the corpse burned. Ibn Aᶜtham (*al-Futūḥ*, II:281, 284) asserts that while ᶜAlī was on his deathbed, he told his sons to execute Ibn Muljim only if he (ᶜAlī) should die. However, ᶜAlī was keen to protect Ibn Muljim from molestation, and would often ask if he had been fed. When ᶜAlī died, al-Ḥasan executed Ibn Muljim without mutilating him, but ᶜAlī's supporters tore Ibn Muljim's corpse to pieces.

[96] Ibn al-Athīr, *al-Kāmil*, III:259. Al-Masᶜūdī (*Murūj*, I:611) reports that he was either killed or was released after he promised to kill ᶜAlī.

[97] Al-Ṣanᶜānī, *al-Muṣannaf*, X:111–12; Ibn Abī Shayba, *al-Muṣannaf*, VII:605. Different versions of this report are attributed to ᶜUmar b. al-Khaṭṭāb, the second caliph, or to the Umayyad caliph ᶜUmar b. ᶜAbd al-ᶜAzīz. ᶜUmar b. ᶜAbd al-ᶜAzīz ordered his governor in Kūfa not to fight rebels unless they shed blood and cause corruption on the earth. He also offered to debate them before fighting: Ibn al-Athīr, *al-Kāmil*, IV:317. Debating before fighting was reportedly the habit of ᶜAlī as well. This became a part of the rules of conduct with the *bughāh*.

robbery; it only talks of those who fight religion and cause corruption, an obvious reference to the *ḥirāba* verse. However, Muslim jurists, as will be discussed, interpreted this report so that it only applied to highway robbers and bandits, but not to rebels.

It is quite clear that there was quite a bit of overlap between the *ḥirāba* and *baghy* verses in the first centuries of Islam. For example, some of the early reports argued that ᶜAlī fought those who caused corruption on the earth or that the opponents of ᶜAlī were *muḥāribūn* in the sense in which the verse used these expressions.[98] The language, symbolism, and boundaries of the two categories were often diluted and mixed, not just in historical practice, but in legal discourse as well. For instance, after the defeat of Zayd b. ᶜAlī in 122/740, the governor of Irāq, Yūsuf b. ᶜUmar al-Thaqafī, is reported to have given a speech accusing the Kūfans of *baghy* and of fighting God and His Prophet. The symbolism of fighting God and His Prophet is derived from the *ḥirāba* verse.[99] Furthermore, early Muslim juristic authorities often mixed the symbolism of the two categories when they discussed the Khawārij and their terror-oriented methods. A number of reports, for instance, state that ᶜAlī fought the Ḥarūriyya (later known as the Khawārij) only after they terrorized the roadways.[100] As noted above, a set of reports claimed that the *ḥirāba* verse was revealed to address the early Khawārij (*al-Ḥarūriyya*).[101] In fact, some late Muslim jurists, in certain contexts, lapsed the categories of *baghy* and *ḥirāba* together.[102] But, as will be shown, for the most part, the two categories became separate and distinct, and even the Khawārij were declared to be rebels, entitled to the treatment given to the *bughāh*, and not bandits.

The laws of *ḥirāba*, in their basic form as constructed by the jurists, maintained that if a highway robber kills, he *must* be killed; if he usurps property and kills, he is to be killed and crucified;[103] if he usurps property

98 ᶜAlī is reported to have told the Khawārij that he would not fight them until they started causing corruption on the earth: Ibn Ḥajar al-ᶜAsqalānī, *Fatḥ*, XIV:288. Some sources state that ᶜAlī fought those who caused corruption on the earth: see al-Kāsānī, *Badāʾiᶜ*, VII:140. Other reports state that those who fight the clients of God (*awliyāʾ Allāh*) have committed *ḥirāba* against God. See al-Nasafī, *Tafsīr*, I:394–5; al-Rāzī, *al-Tafsīr*, XI:117.

99 Abū Mikhnaf, *Nuṣūṣ*, II:373.

100 Ibn Abī Zayd, *al-Nawādir*, XIV:541.

101 Early reports often refer to the early Khawārij as highway bandits: see al-Ṣanᶜānī, *al-Muṣannaf*, X:117.

102 Some late Sunnī jurists state that those who fought ᶜAlī are *muḥāribūn* pursuant to the verse, but go on to argue that the penalties specified by the verse apply only to highway robbers: see al-Jaṣṣāṣ, *Aḥkām*, II:406. Also see Ibn Ḥazm, *al-Muḥallā*, XII:281–3, who gives a very broad definition of *ḥirāba*.

103 As noted earlier, crucifixion meant the hanging or tying of a person or corpse to the bark of a tree. It did not mean nailing or placing someone on a cross.

alone, he is to have limbs amputated from opposite ends; and if he terrorizes but does not kill and does not usurp property, he is to be exiled or banished. If the highway robber repents before being captured, he is to be pardoned.[104] Importantly, this basic structure is called *tartīb*; a basic proportionality is established between the crime and punishment. This contrasts with a methodology of *takhyīr* in which discretion is given to the ruler to apply whichever punishment the ruler sees fit. So, for example, even if a highway robber does nothing more than terrorize caravans, but does not kill or usurp property, he may still be killed, have limbs amputated, or be crucified. In a *takhyīr* scenario, the ruler possesses a considerable amount of power and discretion; no proportionality between the offense and the punishment needs to exist. For easy reference, we will call this the *tartīb* versus *takhyīr* debate.

As argued above, it is rather clear that the Umayyads, in the first century of Islam, applied, or at least used, the dogmatic symbolism of the *ḥirāba* verse against their political opponents. The use of crucifixion against political opponents, who were often indistinguishable from brigands or bandits, is by no means unique to the Islamic tradition. The Romans did not distinguish between bandits or rebels, and often punished either or both by crucifixion and impaling.[105] Nevertheless, in trying to find an Islamic grounding for their policies, the Umayyads must have found the *ḥirāba* verse to be quite convenient. Furthermore, there is some evidence that suggests that the Umayyads and the early ᶜAbbāsids advocated the doctrine of *takhyīr*, according to which no proportionality needs to exist between an alleged offense and the penalty.[106] It appears that it was the Kūfans and al-Shāfiᶜī

104 There are many varieties of this basic structure which will be discussed later.

105 See Kraemer, "Apostates," 68–9; Jackson, *Theft*, 33–5. For the ruling of the *Mishneh Torah*, see Maimonides, *Code*, 138–50. Also see MacMullen, *Enemies*, 218; Schisas, *Offenses*, 3–15. On political crimes and blinding, amputations, burying alive, burning, hanging with dogs, torture, and quartering, see Schild, "History," 129–30, 134, 140–8. But see Bauman, *Crime*, 24, 81 for clemency and humanitarian positions. Anglo-Saxon law punished murder, treason, arson, manifest theft, and assaults upon homes with execution: see Hudson, *Formation*, 78. The *Leges Henrici* assigned several pleas as belonging to the king alone. Among such pleas were breach of the king's peace, unfaithfulness or treason, despising or speaking badly of the king, arson, assault on the king's highway, rape, and abduction: Downer, trans., *Leges*, 108. Under Glanvill, the killing or betrayal of the king, the breach of the king's peace, homicide, arson, robbery, rape, and forgery were all treated as a special category of crimes punishable by death or the cutting off of limbs. See Hudson, *The Formation*, 161.

106 According to some reports, early Shīᶜī jurists upheld the doctrine of *takhyīr* out of *taqiyya* (dissimulation adopted for personal safety or the safety of others): see al-Ḥurr al-ᶜĀmilī, *Wasāʾil*, XVIII:536; al-Ṭūsī, *al-Istibṣār*, IV:257. Ibn al-Murtaḍā (*Kitāb*, VI:199–200) notes that some early jurists adopted the position of absolute *takhyīr* according to which the ruler can choose any punishment regardless of the nature of the crime. He says, however, that absolute *takhyīr* is unjust. Most of the reports in al-Ḥurr al-ᶜĀmilī, *Wasāʾil*, XVIII:532–7, adopt *tartīb*. On some of the *tartīb* reports, however, see al-Majlisī, *Malādh*, XVI:260, 268.

(d. 204/819–20) who adopted and argued for the *tartīb* option.[107] This is consistent with the position, which we argue later, that the Kūfans and al-Shāfiᶜī played key roles in developing the law of rebellion in Islam.

In order to establish the law of banditry and distinguish it from the law of rebellion, Muslim jurists sought to ground their discourse in the authority of reports. These reports gave the distinct impression that not only the Rightly Guided Caliphs ᶜUmar and ᶜAlī but also the Umayyads recognized the law of banditry as a distinct legal field. These reports can be seen as counter-traditions to Umayyad practice. In one report, the Umayyad caliph ᶜAbd al-Malik b. Marwān (r. 65/685–86/705)[108] wrote to Anas b. Mālik (d. 93/712), a Companion of the Prophet, asking him about the *ḥirāba* verse. Anas wrote back informing him that when the ᶜUrayna incident took place, the Prophet asked Jibrīl about God's judgment in the matter. Jibrīl informed the Prophet that whoever terrorized people and usurped property should have his hand and foot amputated from opposite ends; whoever terrorized people and committed murder should be killed; and whoever terrorized people and committed rape should be crucified. Another version states that the Prophet asked Jibrīl about the punishment of those who committed the crime of *ḥirāba*, and Jibrīl gave the same response as above.[109] Note that the *tartīb* position is now articulated as God's will, communicated through Jibrīl.[110] Another narrative creates a negative nexus between the *ḥirāba* verse and the Umayyad administration. Al-Ḥajjāj (d. 95/714), the Umayyad governor of Kūfa, is reported to have asked Anas b. Mālik about the *ḥirāba* verse, and Anas told him about what the Prophet did to ᶜUrayna.

[107] Ibn Ḥajar al-ᶜAsqalānī, *Fatḥ*, xiv:67. It is reported that during the reign of the ᶜAbbāsid caliph al-Muᶜtaṣim (r. 218/833–227/842), a group of bandits were seized after attacking a caravan going to *ḥajj*. Al-Muᶜtaṣim gathered a group of jurists, among them the ninth ᶜAlid *imām*, Abū Jaᶜfar Muḥammad b. ᶜAlī al-Riḍā (d. 220/835), and asked what the punishment should be. After citing the verse on *ḥirāba*, all the jurists advised that the caliph had absolute discretion (*takhyīr*). Abū Jaᶜfar, however, said that the jurists were wrong and advised that the rule of God is *tartīb*. If the bandits terrorized people without anything further, they were to be banished by being placed in jail. If they terrorized and killed, they were to be killed. If they terrorized, killed, and usurped property, their limbs were to be amputated from opposite ends and they should be crucified. According to the report, al-Muᶜtaṣim implemented Abū Jaᶜfar's advice on the matter: al-Ḥurr al-ᶜĀmilī, *Wasāʾil*, xviii:535–6.

[108] It should be recalled that during ᶜAbd al-Malik's reign, Ibn al-Zubayr was crucified, and the infamous governor of Irāq, al-Ḥajjāj, was appointed.

[109] Al-Suyūṭī, *al-Durr*, ii:305; Ibn Kathīr, *Tafsīr*, ii:56, 58; al-Māwardī, *al-Nukat*, ii:33; al-Ṭabarī, *Jāmiᶜ*, v:134.

[110] This report was not accepted by everyone. For example, the jurist Mālik b. Anas (d. 179/795) is reported to have adopted either an unlimited *takhyīr* position (see Ibn Ḥajar al-ᶜAsqalānī, *Fatḥ*, xiv:67) or a somewhat limited *takhyīr* position (see Saḥnūn, *al-Mudawwana*, iv:428). Mālik b. Anas, *al-Muwaṭṭaʾ*, does not have this report or many of the other reports on *ḥirāba*.

Al-Ḥajjāj would thereafter proclaim in his sermons: "Anas b. Mālik has told me that the Prophet amputated the limbs of people and blinded them, and you claim that I apply cruel punishments to you?" Anas b. Mālik remarks that he wished that he (Anas) would have died before telling al-Ḥajjāj of the ᶜUrayna incident.[111] There are conflicting reports about whether Anas lived a politically active life, and whether he supported rebellions against the Umayyads. Reportedly, at one point, he was punished and humiliated by al-Ḥajjāj for his political activity.[112] At any case, it is doubtful that Anas b. Mālik would have been indiscreet enough to tell al-Ḥajjāj about the ᶜUrayna incident. Rather, the likelihood is that, as stated earlier, the ᶜUrayna incident is an Umayyad invention, and that this report attributed to Anas was a counter-tradition alerting its audience to the dangers inherent in the ᶜUrayna precedent.

In an anti-crucifixion tradition, Mālik b. Anas (d. 179/795), the jurist, is asked about crucifixion as a punishment. He responds that he has not heard of anyone who has applied this penalty except for ᶜAbd al-Malik b. Marwān, who crucified a man named al-Ḥārith.[113] The impression given in this report is that crucifixion is an almost unheard-of penalty.[114] By implication, crucifixion is identified as unusual and, perhaps, contrary to the inherited practice. In another report about yet another Umayyad caliph, ᶜUmar b. ᶜAbd al-ᶜAzīz (r. 99/717–101/720), the harsh aspects of the *ḥirāba* verse are deemphasized. ᶜUmar's governor wrote to him stating that he had captured a group of robbers. The governor quoted the *ḥirāba* verse but omitted the part in the verse that referred to banishment

[111] Al-Zamakhsharī, *Rabīᶜ*, III:315. In another version, al-Ḥajjāj asks Anas to tell him about the harshest penalty the Prophet ever exacted. Anas told him about the ᶜUrayna incident. Al-Ḥajjāj used to tell people, "The Prophet amputated the hands and feet of people, and left them to die in the desert," and he would cite this incident in justifying his own cruel policies. Anas would often say that he never regretted anything as much as he regretted telling al-Ḥajjāj about this incident: Ibn Kathīr, *Tafsīr*, II:55–6; al-Zarkashī, *Sharḥ*, VI:361. However, it is also reported that Anas said that fighting bandits is better than fighting the Romans: Ibn Farḥūn, *Tabṣira*, II:185.

[112] See Gibb and Kramers, eds., *Shorter*, 43. Also see below.

[113] Saḥnūn, *al-Mudawwana*, IV:428. Al-Ḥārith al-Mutanabbī al-Kadhdhāb claimed to be a prophet and seems to have gathered a large following. He was crucified and killed in Jerusalem in 79/698: see Ibn al-Jawzī, *al-Muntaẓam*, VI:204–10; Ibn Kathīr, *al-Bidāya*, IX:29–31. As discussed above, several people had been crucified before this incident, including Ibn al-Zubayr who was crucified in 73/692. Of course, because al-Ḥārith was considered a heretic, this could be read as a pro-Umayyad tradition. In other words, it could be interpreted as giving credit to the Umayyads for being the first to properly protect religion. I do not believe this interpretation is persuasive because the tradition simply mentions al-Ḥārith without any derogatory identification such as *al-kadhdhāb* (the liar).

There is a report that ᶜAlī hung a man on the bark of a tree for banditry. See al-Nuᶜmān, *Daᶜāʾim*, II:475; al-Ṣadūq, *Kitāb*, IV:68; al-Kulaynī, *al-Furūᶜ*, VII:246; al-Ṭūsī, *Tahdhīb*, X:135.

[114] Perhaps Mālik was referring to the Christian concept of nailing to a cross. However, the historical accounts are not clear as to how al-Ḥārith was crucified.

(*nafy*), therefore implying that the robbers should be killed, crucified, or suffer amputation, but not be banished or exiled. ʿUmar wrote back to his governor, chiding him for the omission, and said, "Do not alter things [according to your whim]. Have you dedicated yourself to killing and crucifying people? . . . If you get my letter, banish the robbers to Shaghab."[115] In a widely cited report, it is asserted that ʿAlī pardoned a bandit who repented and asked for a guarantee of safe conduct before being captured.[116] Similar reports claim the same for ʿUthmān, Muʿāwiya, and even al-Ḥajjāj.[117] ʿAlī is also reported to have banished bandits from Kūfa to Baṣra.[118]

The point is not that all of these reports are necessarily apocryphal or that there was no authentic Islamic practice in the first century of Islam. Authenticity and the formation of the authoritative, however, is a creative and constructive process of selection, co-optation, and direction. Principles and precedents are selected, co-opted, and channeled towards certain results. Legal reasoning is both creative and selective, at least until it becomes encumbered by the cumulative and progressive weight of precedent. As the corporate structure of law and jurists becomes more formed, and as precedent and legal rulings accumulate, the creative process becomes more constrained and burdened. Even then, the creative legal process does not necessarily slow or come to a full stop. Rather, the legal process finds a more disciplined and limited method to articulate creativity and development. This usually takes place through the art of distinguishing one precedent from another, or arguing that a former rule or precedent is inapposite to a contemporary case.

[115] Al-Ṭabarī, *Jāmiʿ*, V:141; another report says that the robbers were Coptic Christians. Another version emphasizes that the robbers had terrorized people, but they did not steal nor kill anyone; yet the governor wanted to amputate their limbs or kill them. ʿUmar chided the governor and told him to banish them instead: al-Bājī, *al-Muntaqā*, VII:169, 171; Ibn Abī Zayd, *al-Nawādir*, XVII:465. It should be noted that some reports indicate that bandits were simply banished to the outskirts of the inhabited towns.

[116] Al-Suyūṭī, *al-Durr*, II:307; Ibn Kathīr, *Tafsīr*, II:59; al-Ālūsī, *Rūḥ*, VI:121; Ibn Abī Shayba, *al-Muṣannaf*, VII:603; al-Zamakhsharī, *al-Kashshāf*, I:336; al-Ṭabāṭabāʾī, *al-Mīzān*, V:332; Abū Ḥayyān, *Tafsīr*, I:577; al-Qurṭubī, *al-Jāmiʿ* (1952), VI:155; al-Kāsānī, *Badāʾiʿ*, VII:96; al-Sarakhsī, *al-Mabsūṭ*, IX:204; Ibn Ḥanbal, *Masāʾil*, 430. The name of the bandit is al-Ḥārith b. Badr. Ibn Ḥazm claims that al-Ḥārith was ʿAlī's enemy and used to malign him: Ibn Ḥazm, *al-Muḥallā*, XII:274. This raises the question of whether al-Ḥārith was a political opponent.

[117] Ibn Kathīr, *Tafsīr*, II:59–60 (for ʿUthmān and Muʿāwiya); al-Ṭabarī, *Jāmiʿ*, V:143–4 (for ʿAlī, ʿUthmān, and Muʿāwiya); also see p. 146 where it is claimed that al-Ḥajjāj knew the technicalities of the law of banditry and the rules of repentance from such an offense.

[118] Al-Ṭūsī, *Tahdhīb*, X:133; al-Ḥurr al-ʿĀmilī, *Wasāʾil*, XVIII:533.

CONCLUSION

As we demonstrated, two verses from the Qur'ān were candidates for selection and co-optation.[119] The reports surrounding these verses are complex and conflicting. Furthermore, they reflect a tension between various trends in early Islam. It is logical to assume that the Umayyads and early ʿAbbāsids would have wanted to co-opt the *ḥirāba* verse and use it against their political foes, and some of the evidence does point in this direction. As argued earlier, the function of law and the role of jurists tend to emphasize the need for order and stability. Furthermore, the terror-based and indiscriminate methods of some rebellious groups, such as the Khawārij, emphasized the need for security and stability. Yet there are also certain contravening considerations. The Qur'ān does command Muslims to enjoin the good and forbid the evil,[120] which could imply a duty to resist injustice. Furthermore, some of the most notable figures in Islamic history rebelled against those in power.[121] The Umayyads and ʿAbbāsids came to power through rebellions as well. Significantly, Muslim jurists, for a variety of reasons discussed later, had an interest in mitigating the cruelty by which rebels were treated. These diverse elements and considerations motivated Muslim jurists, when it came to dealing with fellow Muslims, to create two categories of discourse, one concerned with rebels and the other concerned with bandits. We will now address some of the historical circumstances that led to the development of these categories of discourse.

[119] I am not arguing that these were the only possible verses that could have been selected and co-opted. For example, there are reports that al-Bāqir, Ibn ʿAbbās, ʿAmmār, and ʿAlī said that some of the Qur'ānic verses on fighting the hypocrites (9:73) and apostasy (5:54) were revealed to address the *bughāh* of the Battle of Baṣra: see al-Suyūrī, *Kanz*, 1:387–8.

[120] For example, Qur'ān 3:104, 9:112. These verses and the reports surrounding them require a separate study.

[121] For example, al-Ṣanʿānī (*Kitab*, IV:8) lists among the notables the rebellions of al-Ḥusayn (d. 61/680), Ibn al-Ashʿath (d. 82/701), Zayd b. ʿAlī (d. 122/740), and Muḥammad b. ʿAbd Allāh (al-Nafs al-Zakiyya) (d. 145/762). See Modarressi, *Crisis*, 6, on Sunnī support.

CHAPTER 3

The historical context and the creative response

THE EARLY CONTEXT AND IBN TAYMIYYA'S CLAIMS

Ibn Taymiyya (d. 728/1327–8) accused the *fuqahāʾ* (jurists) of Kūfa[1] and al-Shāfiᶜī (d. 204/819–20) of inventing *aḥkām al-bughāh*. They did so, he claimed, because they wished to defend ᶜAlī; and so they argued that it was incumbent upon ᶜAlī to fight those who rebelled against him; and that it was incumbent upon Muslims to support ᶜAlī against the rebels. But they carried this beyond the legacy of ᶜAlī, and transformed their position into a legal principle (*qāᶜida fiqhiyya*). According to this legal principle, they declared whomever they wished to be the just ruler (*al-ᶜādil*), and those who opposed him to be the rebels (*al-bughāh*). Then they argued that it was necessary to support the just ruler by fighting against those who rebelled against him. The truth of the matter, Ibn Taymiyya argued, is that nothing had been reported from the Prophet about fighting rebels except for one fabricated *ḥadīth*.[2] None of the books of *ḥadīth* refer to fighting rebels; rather, they only refer to fighting the Khawārij and the apostates. These jurists, Ibn Taymiyya contended, confused *fitna* wars with the *bughāh* wars, and equated fighting the Khawārij and the hypocrites, which is proper, with fighting unjust rulers, which is improper. Effectively, these jurists opened the door for all types of people to rebel while believing that they were seeking the establishment of justice. The reality, however, is that these rebels spread corruption and caused more damage than good.[3] Even if people believed that they were enjoining the

[1] By Kūfa, Ibn Taymiyya probably meant the pre-Ḥanafī jurists of the city such as Ibrāhīm al-Nakhaᶜī, Shārik, etc. The jurists of Kūfa eventually developed into the Ḥanafī school of law. See, on the Kūfa school and its development, Melchert, *Formation*, 32–8.

[2] This is the *ḥadīth* discussed above in the context of the revelation of the *baghy* verse.

[3] Ibn Taymiyya, *Majmūᶜ al-Fatāwā*, IV:440–1, 444, 450–2; the author also says that followers of Aḥmad b. Ḥanbal (d. 241/855) and Abū Ḥanīfa (d. 150/767) contributed to this invention. Also see Ibn Taymiyya, *Minhāj*, II:233, 244. Al-Nawawī (*al-Majmūᶜ*, I:9) says that al-Shāfiᶜī was the first to write on *qitāl ahl al-baghy* (fighting the rebels).

good and forbidding the evil when they rebelled, they were only doing more harm than good.[4]

We will return to Ibn Taymiyya's arguments later, but for now it is important to note that he saw wars between Muslims within a dichotomous paradigm: theological wars versus political wars. Theological wars are fought against *ahl al-ahwāʾ* or *bidaᶜ* (people of heretical beliefs), such as the Khawārij. Political wars are fought against opponents over political power. Political wars are a *fitna* and prohibited by God. Theological wars are *bughāh* wars, and are legal and even recommended.[5] Ibn Taymiyya's basic point is that Muslims should refrain from getting involved in political wars.

Ibn Taymiyya was correct in suspecting that the jurists of Kūfa and al-Shāfiᶜī were responsible for the development of a legal discourse – a discourse which Ibn Taymiyya considered to be unfortunate. But, as he seems to have realized, his argument for a dichotomy between the war of *fitna*, as he defined it, and the war of *baghy* is as much of an invention as is the discourse of his opponents. He argued that *aḥkām al-bughāh* was invented when, among other things, the Ḥanbalī jurist al-Khiraqī (d. 334/945–6) relied on or borrowed from the Shāfiᶜī jurist al-Muzanī (d. 264/877–8), and al-Muzanī relied on the Ḥanafī jurist Muḥammad b. al-Ḥasan al-Shaybānī (d. 189/804).[6] It is entirely reasonable to suspect that the discourse developed through a process of juristic borrowing. In fact, law often develops through a process of borrowing or

4 Ibn Taymiyya, *Minhāj*, II:243.

5 Ibn Taymiyya includes ᶜAlī's wars against Muᶜāwiya and ᶜĀʾisha, and the war between the ᶜAbbāsids al-Amīn (d. 198/813) and al-Maʾmūn (d. 218/833) as part of the *fitna* wars. He also argues that the rebellions of al-Ḥusayn b. ᶜAlī, Ibn al-Zubayr, Zayd b. ᶜAlī, Muḥammad b. ᶜAlī al-Imām (the initiator of the ᶜAbbāsid *daᶜwa*), and the rebellion of the ᶜAbbāsid client Abū Muslim (d. 137/754) against the last Umayyad caliph, Marwān b. Muḥammad (al-Ḥimār), were all a *fitna*. See Ibn Taymiyya, *Minhāj*, II:233, 241–3, 245–6; and his *Majmūᶜ al-Fatāwā*, IV:450–2. Ibn Taymiyya also maintains that the fighting referred to in the *baghy* verse is a third type of fighting that is unrelated to the other two types of war: see his *Minhāj*, II:233. Elsewhere, Ibn Taymiyya talks about the sinfulness of those who fight out of tribalism and blind solidarity (*ᶜaṣabiyya wa daᶜwā jāhiliyya*) such as the Syrian tribes of Qays and Yaman. He implies that this is different from those who fight over power or kingship as is the case in the wars of *fitna*. See Ibn Taymiyya, *al-Siyāsa*, 70, 83. Qays and Yaman fought a very bloody battle in Marj Rāhiṭ in 65/684. The Yamanis won, and provided the basis for the rule of the Umayyad caliph Marwān b. al-Ḥakam, who died in 65/685. The feud between the two tribes, however, continued for centuries. See, on these two tribes, Crone, "Were."

The war between al-Amīn and al-Maʾmūn lasted roughly from 193/809 until al-Maʾmūn entered Baghdād in 204/819. Interestingly, Kennedy (*Prophet*, 152), in commenting on this war, remarks: "The fighting, once begun, was increasingly difficult to stop, and *bāb al-fitnah*, the gate of civil strife, once opened, proved very difficult to close."

6 Ibn Taymiyya, *Majmūᶜ al-Fatāwā*, IV:450–1.

transplanting, but this does not make the legal discourse artificial or any less authentic.[7]

What Ibn Taymiyya seems to concede is that this so-called invention spread and became widely accepted and, in fact, had an impact on the way people understood and reacted to authority. But, as we will demonstrate later, his own position involved a reconstruction of Islamic history no less creative or inventive than the process adopted by the jurists he criticizes. Furthermore, the discourses of the jurists who developed *aḥkām al-bughāh* were as motivated by their historical context as Ibn Taymiyya was motivated by his own. In a significant passage, Ibn Taymiyya criticizes those who fail to distinguish between fighting the Khawārij and the *bughāh*, and then he states:

> This is why you will find that many from this group [i.e. those who do not recognize the distinction] become involved in the whimsies of the kings and governors. They command people to fight on the side [of the kings and governors] basing themselves on the argument that they [the kings and governors] are the just party (*ahl al-ᶜadl*) and that those who fight them are the unjust party (*al-bughāh*). In doing so, they are just like the fanatics who adhere [blindly] to certain jurists, theologians or [Ṣūfī] masters, and whimsically claim that they are right and their opponents are wrong . . . This is widespread among the scholars of the *ummah*, and its laity, rulers and soldiers.[8]

In this passage, Ibn Taymiyya criticizes *aḥkām al-bughāh* because it is used by some to solicit support for those in power. In other words, the argument that it was imperative to support ʿAlī against those who rebelled against him is now used against the rebels of Ibn Taymiyya's age. But, as stated above, Ibn Taymiyya also blamed *aḥkām al-bughāh* for encouraging insurrection and rebellion. Whether Ibn Taymiyya was aware of the paradoxical nature of his argument is open to conjecture. Nonetheless, this paradox points to the highly contextual nature of his arguments, and to the fact that his criticisms of the early jurists are an anachronism. Furthermore, Ibn Taymiyya ignored the fact that *aḥkām al-bughāh* is not just concerned with determining who can be designated as a *bāghī*, but is much more concerned with how those so designated are to be treated. As we noted earlier, many Muslim jurists insist that the term *baghy*, in its legal context, does not imply blame (*laysa ism dhamm*). Furthermore, as noted earlier, those who are designated as

[7] Watson, *Legal*, 21–30, 95–101. For the specific culture of law and the implications for the development of law, see Watson, *Evolution*, 115–19.

[8] Ibn Taymiyya, *Majmūᶜ al-Fatāwā*, IV:452.

bughāh cannot be executed, tortured, imprisoned, or have their property confiscated. These various factors or elements make Ibn Taymiyya's narrative on the purpose and history of *aḥkām al-bughāh* problematic, and lead us to restate the question: Why was the discourse on rebellion initiated?

Ibn Taymiyya reports that the traditionist Yaḥyā b. Maᶜīn (d. 233/848) complained to Aḥmad b. Ḥanbal (d. 241/855) about the fact that al-Shāfiᶜī cited or relied on the conduct of ᶜAlī with the *bughāh*. By doing so, Yaḥyā complained, he was making some Companions of the Prophet, such as Ṭalḥa and al-Zubayr, *bughāh*, which Yaḥyā contended is highly improper. Ibn Ḥanbal is reported to have answered: "Woe unto you! What else could he [al-Shāfiᶜī] do in this context?"[9] The report uses the word *bughāh* here in its non-technical and non-legal sense; it is using the word in its linguistic sense, which means the unjust. The report could have two possible distinct interpretations. It could mean that al-Shāfiᶜī was referring to an already existing discourse by ᶜAlī on the *bughāh* and that, by doing so, al-Shāfiᶜī was supporting ᶜAlī and maligning Ṭalḥa and al-Zubayr. Alternatively, it could mean that al-Shāfiᶜī, by citing ᶜAlī's conduct, was taking part in a discourse that was novel and troubling. The first interpretation would blame al-Shāfiᶜī for not exercising appropriate discretion in failing to censor an already existing discourse initiated by ᶜAlī. The second interpretation would blame al-Shāfiᶜī for taking part in creating a discourse that had not previously existed. Both interpretations are ahistorical and make little sense.[10] Nevertheless, the report points to an unresolved theological tension in the discourses on the *bughāh*. As we discussed earlier, the *aḥkām al-bughāh* discourse has serious implications for the debate on the credibility and merit of some of the Prophet's Companions. Furthermore, as we discuss later, much of the discourse on the *bughāh* revolved around whether individuals after the time of the Companions of the Prophet were *bughāh* or not. In this sense, part of the discourse was about the legitimacy of the Umayyad or ᶜAbbāsid dynasties. Nonetheless, this does not explain why the citing of ᶜAlī's

[9] Ibid., IV:438. Ibn Taymiyya interprets Ibn Ḥanbal's response to mean: Who else from among the rightly guided Companions could al-Shāfiᶜī cite or rely upon? This report defends al-Shāfiᶜī's discourse by making Ibn Ḥanbal agree with him. The report is probably apocryphal or, at least, the Ibn Ḥanbal response part of it, since, considering Ibn Ḥanbal's political and theological positions, it is very unlikely that Ibn Ḥanbal would have agreed with al-Shāfiᶜī's narrative on *aḥkām al-bughāh*. See Ibn al-Jawzī, *Manāqib*, 214.

[10] As noted above, al-Nawawī (*al-Majmūᶜ*, I:9) claims that al-Shāfiᶜī wrote a chapter on *qitāl ahl al-baghy*. This does not mean that al-Shāfiᶜī invented the discourse. It only means that he was the first, or among the first, to restate an already existing discourse into a systematic legal field.

conduct, more than a hundred years after the fact, would pose a problem or tension worth circulating a report about.[11]

Part of the response can be gleaned from some of the Shīᶜī discourses on ᶜAlī's conduct. Several Shīᶜī sources, in attempting to explain ᶜAlī's benevolent conduct towards his enemies, note that his conduct was better for his party than anything under the sun (*khayrun li shīᶜatihi min mā ṭalaᶜat ᶜalayhi al-shams*).[12] ᶜAlī knew, it is argued, that he would have a party of followers (*li-annahu kāna yaᶜlamu annahu sayakūna lahu shīᶜa*), and that an unjust government would prevail.[13] He also knew that if he did not follow a benevolent policy towards his opponents, then his party would suffer untold hardships from their opponents (*la-laqiyat shīᶜatuhu min al-nāsi balāʾan ᶜaẓīmā*).[14] If ᶜAlī had held his opponents captive or confiscated their properties, then people would have done the same to his followers. Effectively, it is argued that ᶜAlī set a precedent that was followed, to an extent, by Muslims after him, and that the beneficiaries of this precedent were ᶜAlī's followers. The reports also claim that anyone who examines history will see proof of the truth of this assertion, i.e. that ᶜAlī's followers benefited from his precedent.[15] Muḥammad Ḥasan al-Najafī (d. 1266/1850) also notes that ᶜAlī wanted to set the precedent so that all who came after him would be judged by that standard. Hence, if anyone did not follow ᶜAlī's example, it would be known that he/she exceeded the limits and committed injustice.[16]

In all probability, this discourse is not historical, but this is largely inapposite. Most of the statements of the jurists above seem to be focused on the contention that ᶜAlī's conduct prevented Sunnī Muslims from enslaving Shīᶜīs and, in fact, it does seem that for the most part Sunnīs did not sell captive rebels into slavery.[17] More importantly, the Shīᶜī reports

[11] I am not using the expression "circulating a report" here to mean inventing and then spreading a report. I am using the expression to mean selecting, remembering, preserving, and spreading a report. The idea of invention or the lack of it, as stated earlier, is not interesting. The mere fact that a report was remembered and preserved, whether it was invented or not, is the material issue.

[12] Al-Ḥurr al-ᶜĀmilī, *Wasāʾil*, XI:56–7. [13] Ibid., XI:58–9.

[14] Ibid., XI:59. [15] Ibid., XI:56–9; al-Ṭūsī, *Tahdhīb*, VI:154, 155.

[16] Al-Najafī, *Jawāhir*, XXI:330, 335. This author, and the authors above, also note that the *qāʾim* (awaited messiah) does not need to follow ᶜAlī's example when he appears from occultation.

[17] See Abū Mikhnaf, *Nuṣūṣ*, I:500, for a debate between Yazīd and the women of al-Ḥusayn's family on this issue resulting in the family's non-enslavement. For incidents where this did not hold true, see Ibn al-Athīr, *al-Kāmil*, IV:344, for the enslavement of rebels in the rebellion of Yazīd b. al-Muhallab in 102/720–1. Ibn Khayyāṭ (*Taʾrīkh*, II:368, 370) reports the enslavement of Muslims in al-Maghrib in 122 and 124 AH. Also see *Akhbār*, 47–8, for the enslavement of

point to the possibility that ʿAlī's conduct was used by Muslim jurists as a means of articulating criticism against the conduct of the Umayyads and early ʿAbbāsids. We have already argued that ʿAlī's conduct was constructed by the collective memory of Muslims and, particularly, by the jurists. Sunnī (especially the Shāfiʿī) sources are more one-sided about the portrayal of ʿAlī's conduct than are their Shīʿī counterparts. In other words, they are more unequivocal about asserting ʿAlī's benevolent conduct than are Shīʿī sources. To argue that ʿAlī's conduct was constructed does not mean that I am arguing it was invented. Construction is a selective process of remembering and emphasizing, not inventing. The question then is: What was the point of this construction? It would stand to reason that early Muslim jurists developed the discourse as a critical leverage against those in power in the first centuries of Islam. This is especially so when we consider the role played by many jurists in the rebellions of early Islam.

As discussed later, late Sunnī sources often insist that al-Ḥusayn b. ʿAlī did not commit a sin by rebelling against Yazīd b. Muʿāwiya.[18] This, however, is hardly surprising considering the infamy that Yazīd enjoys in Islamic history.[19] However, as we will see later, many late Sunnī sources express sympathy with ʿAlid contenders to Umayyad and ʿAbbāsid caliphs. For example, al-Dhahabī (d. 748/1374) asserts that al-Ḥasan (d. 49/669), al-Ḥusayn (d. 61/680), Zayn al-ʿĀbidīn (d. 95/713), and his son al-Bāqir (d. 114/733) were all qualified to be caliphs. Al-Dhahabī goes on to state that al-Bāqir's son, Jaʿfar al-Ṣādiq (d. 148/765), was more worthy of the caliphate than al-Manṣūr (r. 137/754–159/775), and al-Ṣādiq's son, Mūsā al-Kāẓim (d. 183/799), was more worthy of the caliphate than was Hārūn al-Rashīd (r. 170/786–193/809).[20] This is demonstrative of the impact of the legacy of the family of the Prophet and their descendants (*ahl al-bayt*) on the collective conscience of subsequent

Muslims, who included Arabs, in Muslim Spain in 124/742. In a masterful study, Blankinship (*End*, 221) comments on this incident by asserting that the enslavement of Muslims was contrary to received and accepted practice, and that Islamic sources expressed outrage at the incident. There are later examples of enslavement of rebels in Transoxania from the tenth to the twelfth centuries AH.

[18] For example, al-Dardīr, *al-Sharḥ*, printed with al-Ṣawī, *Bulgha*, II:414; al-Dusūqī, *Ḥāshiya*, II:298. Also see al-Wazīr, *al-ʿAwāṣim*, VIII:63. Al-Dhahabī (*Siyar*, IV:38) refers to him as the martyr, and says that God withdrew His blessings from Yazīd because he killed al-Ḥusayn.

[19] As discussed later, Ibn Taymiyya attempted to rehabilitate Yazīd's reputation in Islamic history by reinterpreting many of the offenses attributed to him.

[20] Al-Dhahabī goes on to praise other members of the ʿAlids, and criticize the Shīʿī doctrine of occultation: al-Dhahabī, *Siyar*, XIII:120–2. See Modarressi, *Crisis*, 6. Al-Dhahabī also asserts that Zayd b. ʿAlī died a martyr: al-Dhahabī, *Siyar*, V:391.

Muslims. It is also demonstrative of the problematic basis of the legitimacy of the Umayyad and ᶜAbbāsid caliphates. Importantly, moreover, it reflects the impact of the precedents set by some of the early jurists in supporting, or at least sympathizing with, rebellions in early Islam.

THE EARLY REBELLIONS AND THE JURISTS

Al-Ḥusayn b. ᶜAlī, the Prophet's grandson, was killed in the Battle of Karbalā' in 61/680 after rebelling against the Umayyads. While one cannot claim that this was a major rebellion, the moral impact of the incident far outweighed its political consequences.[21] Many Sunnī jurists strongly sympathized with al-Ḥusayn and lamented his martyrdom.[22] However, among the many early rebellions, ᶜAbd Allāh b. al-Zubayr's rebellion in Mecca was particularly serious, and posed a formidable challenge to the Umayyads.[23] Because Ibn al-Zubayr's rebellion seemed to be based on a Qurayshī claim to power, it occupies an ambiguous position in the discourses of Muslim jurists. As we will see later, Muslim jurists disagree on whether his rebellion was based on tribalism (*ᶜaṣabiyya*) or a legitimate claim to power.[24] However, it is reported that Anas b. Mālik said that Ibn al-Zubayr had a more legitimate claim to power than Marwān or his son, ᶜAbd al-Malik.[25] Apparently, Anas accepted Ibn al-Zubayr's caliphate and was appointed by Ibn al-Zubayr to lead prayer in Baṣra.[26] Furthermore, Abū Bakr al-Zuhrī (d. 124/741), whose father supported Ibn al-Zubayr, played a crucial role in the development of the reports on the treatment due to rebels.[27] Al-Zuhrī reconciled himself to

[21] See Shaban, *Islamic 1*, 91.

[22] Abū Mikhnaf, *Nuṣūṣ*, I:401. For example, Sunnī historical sources dedicate a relatively large amount of space to this incident, and narrate its particulars in great detail. See Ibn al-Athīr, *al- Kāmil*, III:407–44; Ibn Kathīr, *al-Bidāya*, VIII:152–214; Ibn al-Jawzī, *al- Muntaẓam*, V:335–48; al-Ṭabarī, *Ta'rīkh*, V:176–236; Ibn Aᶜtham, *al-Futūḥ*, III:71–155.

[23] On Ibn al-Zubayr's rebellion, see Hodgson, *Classical*, 219–23; Kennedy, *Prophet*, 89–98; Gibb, "ᶜAbd Allāh b. al-Zubayr."

[24] For example, see Ibn Ḥajar al-ᶜAsqalānī, *Fatḥ*, XIV:309, 573–4, 577–8, and al- 'Ubbī, *Sharḥ*, VI:561–2, 564.

[25] See al-'Ubbī, *Sharḥ*, VI:567, who also reports that when the Medinan jurist Saᶜīd b. al-Musayyab (d. 94/713) refused to give his *bayᶜa* to Ibn al-Zubayr, he was flogged. He was flogged again when he refused to give his *bayᶜa* to al-Walīd b. Marwān. For a discussion of this issue, see Ibn al-Jawzī, *al-Muntaẓam*, VI:322. Reportedly, Ibn al-Zubayr threatened to burn ᶜAbd Allāh b. al-ᶜAbbās and Muḥammad b. al-Ḥanafiyya if they did not give him their *bayᶜa*. Ibn al-Zubayr also imprisoned Ibn al-Ḥanafiyya: see Ibn Khallikān, *Wafayāt*, IV:172; al-Masᶜūdī, *Murūj*, II:59; Ibn Aᶜtham, *al-Futūḥ*, III:273–81.

[26] Al-Ḥajjāj punished Anas for supporting Ibn al-Zubayr. See al-Dhahabī, *Siyar*, III:402; Ibn Khayyāṭ, *Ta'rīkh*, I:255.

[27] For example, see al-Ṣanᶜānī, *al-Muṣannaf*, X:120–1.

the Umayyads but he also transmitted material unfavorable to them.[28] Although al-Zuhrī accepted the reality of power in his age, consistent with the logic of jurists, he remained sufficiently detached and focused on the technicalities of the treatment of rebels that were intentionally unhelpful to the Umayyads.[29]

In 63/683, Medina rebelled against Yazīd b. Muʿāwiya, which led to the infamous Battle of Ḥarra. After the siege of Medina, Muslim b. ʿUqbah, pursuant to Yazīd's orders, raped and pillaged the city for three days. Importantly, many religious scholars were killed when they took part in the rebellion.[30] The Syrian forces then headed to Mecca seeking to defeat Ibn al-Zubayr.[31] During the siege, Yazīd died and the siege was lifted, but not before Mecca was bombarded with mangonels and the Kaʿba was burned.[32] In 65/684, a movement known as al-Tawwābūn (the repentants) marched out of Kūfa seeking to avenge the killing of the Prophet's grandson, al-Ḥusayn. The Syrians, however, defeated them without much difficulty.[33] But in 66/685, Kūfa, which remained loyal

[28] See Watt, *Formative*, 70; also see al-Dhahabī, *Siyar*, V:329, where ʿAbd al-Malik b. Marwān taunts al-Zuhrī about his father's past. ʿAbd al-Malik tells al-Zuhrī, "Your father was a man of *fitan* (*kāna abūka la-naʿ ʿāran fī al-fitan*)." Al-Zuhrī then asked the caliph to forget and forgive the past.

[29] The relationship between al-Zuhrī and the Umayyads has been the subject of much scholarly debate. Ignaz Goldziher and Michael Lecker argued that al-Zuhrī accepted and cooperated with the Umayyads without reserve. Abdul Aziz Duri, Fouad Sezgin, and Khālid ʿAthāmina have challenged this proposition and argued that al-Zuhrī's relations with the Umayyads were far more complex. See Lecker, "Biographical"; Duri, *Rise*, 117–18; ʿAthāmina, "Ulamaʾ." I do not find the evidence cited by Goldziher and Lecker persuasive. In any case, I think the importance of this issue has been highly exaggerated. A jurist could cooperate with those in power and still negotiate power in a variety of complex ways. In fact, al-Zuhrī could have been far more effective as a critic or negotiator while working within the system than choosing to reject and rebel against the political system.

[30] See Ibn Taymiyya, *Minhāj*, II:241; al-ʾUbbī, *Sharḥ*, VI:529–30; al-Qasṭalānī, *Irshād*, X:199; Ibn al-Wardī, *Taʾrīkh*, I:165; Abū Mikhnaf, *Nuṣūṣ*, II:16–17. For a description of the raping and pillaging, and the religious notables who were killed, see al-Masʿūdī, *Murūj*, II:54–5; Ibn Kathīr, *al-Bidāya*, VIII:223–7; Ibn al-Jawzī, *al-Muntaẓam*, VI:14–16; Ibn al-Athīr, *al-Kāmil*, III:456–62; al-Ṭabarī, *Taʾrīkh*, V:246–50; Ibn Aʿtham, *al-Futūḥ*, III:181–91. Al-Shiblī (*Iḥkām*, 230–1) claims so many Companions of the Prophet were killed in Medina that even the jinn cried. See also Abū Mikhnaf, *Nuṣūṣ*, II:19.

[31] For the bombardment of Mecca and the burning of the Kaʿba, see al-Masʿūdī, *Murūj*, II:55–6; Ibn al-Kathīr, *al-Bidāya*, VIII:228; Ibn al-Jawzī, *al-Muntaẓam*, VI:22; Ibn al-Athīr, *al-Kāmil*, III:464; al-Ṭabarī, *Taʾrīkh*, V:251–2; Ibn al-Wardī, *Taʾrīkh*, I:165; Ibn Aʿtham, *al-Futūḥ*, III:185. As noted by the sources above, some reports attempted to clear the Syrian forces from the responsibility of burning the Kaʿba.

[32] Ibn al-Jawzī, *al-Muntaẓam*, VI:35–7; Ibn al-Athīr, *al-Kāmil*, IV:3–12; Abū Mikhnaf, *Nuṣūṣ*, II:42–9; Shaban, *Islamic I*, 93–5.

[33] Ibn al-Jawzī, *al-Muntaẓam*, VI:28–9. Al-Mukhtār executed some individuals who were implicated in al-Ḥusayn's death: see al-Masʿūdī, *Murūj*, II:58; Ibn al-Athīr, *al-Kāmil*, IV:27–49. Ibn Aʿtham (*al-Futūḥ*, III:270, 291–2) reports that al-Mukhtār tortured and mutilated many people accused of being involved in al-Ḥusayn's death. Reportedly, he severed their hands and feet, cut off

to the ʿAlid cause, rebelled under the leadership of al-Mukhtār b. Abī ʿUbayd who proclaimed Muḥammad b. al-Ḥanafiyya (d. 81/700) as the awaited Mahdī, and vowed to avenge the killing of al-Ḥusayn.[34] Al-Mukhtar's rebellion, however, lasted for two years and never extended beyond Kūfa.[35] He was betrayed by the *ashrāf* (notables) of Kūfa, and was killed in 67/687 by the forces of his competitor Ibn al-Zubayr. Importantly, many prominent scholars gave their oath of allegiance to Ibn al-Zubayr, and he effectively controlled Hijāz, Irāq, and Egypt.[36] After the Umayyad Marwānids were able to re-consolidate their power, ʿAbd al-Malik recaptured Egypt and Kūfa from Ibn al-Zubayr and directed al-Ḥajjāj b. Yūsuf to besiege Mecca. Once again, Mecca was bombarded with mangonels, and water and food were cut off from the city in 73/792.[37] Several notable individuals, including Ibn al-Zubayr himself, were killed in the siege. [38]

A considerable number of jurists were involved in a rebellion led by ʿAbd al-Raḥmān b. al-Ashʿath against the Umayyads.[39] Nonetheless, in

their lips, tongues, ears or noses, blinded them, burned them, or had them flogged to death. Abū Mikhnaf (*Nuṣūṣ*, II:119, 124–7, 134, 136–7, 140–54) reports that al-Mukhtār guaranteed the safety of everyone except those who were directly involved in al-Ḥusayn's murder: of those he executed some, burned some alive, had a few skinned alive, and severed and hung their heads. Also see Ibn al-Wardī, *Taʾrīkh*, I:168. On al-Mukhtār see Hawting, "Al-Mukhtār."

34 Some sources insist that al-Mukhtār was a fraud, and that he even conspired to have al-Ḥusayn surrendered to the Umayyads. See Ibn Kathīr, *al-Bidāya*, VIII:252–3.

35 Ibn al-Jawzī, *al-Muntaẓam*, VI:64–6; Ibn al-Athīr, *al-Kāmil*, IV:64–72; al-Ṭabarī, *Taʾrīkh*, VI: 359–70; Ibn Aʿtham, *al-Futūḥ*, III:326–7. Reportedly, 7,000 of al-Mukhtār's supporters were executed: see Ibn al-Wardī, *Taʾrīkh*, I:168. This number is probably exaggerated, although it was not uncommon for the victorious party to eliminate the entire camp of the defeated. For more on al-Mukhtār and various assessments of the impact and meaning of his rebellion, see Kennedy, *Prophet*, 95–6; Hodgson, *Classical*, 222; Shaban, *Islamic 1*, 94–6; Marin-Guzman, *Popular*, 63–5.

36 Ibn Kathīr, *al-Bidāya*, VIII:242–3. As noted above, one of them was Anas b. Mālik. Ibn Kathīr notes that before Ibn al-Zubayr was able to consolidate his power, there were many *fitan* and various types of *bughāh* who fought each other: see p. 250. In Abū Mikhnaf, *Nuṣūṣ*, II:33, it is reported that the opponents of the Syrians considered the Syrians Muslims, and prohibited looting of their property.

37 See Ibn Kathīr, *al-Bidāya*, VIII:334–5; al-Ṭabarī, *Taʾrīkh*, VI:406; Ibn al-Wardī, *Taʾrīkh*, I:169; Ibn Aʿtham, *al-Futūḥ*, III:386–7.

38 Ibn Kathīr, *al-Bidāya*, VIII:350–4. Ibn Kathīr held Ibn al-Zubayr in high esteem. He repeats the invocation "May God be pleased with him," and calls him *amīr al-muʾminīn*. It makes sense that Ibn Kathīr would praise Ibn al-Zubayr because Ibn al-Zubayr was hostile to ʿAlī, and Ibn Kathīr was rather unsympathetic to ʿAlī's cause. But also see Ibn al-Jawzī, *al-Muntaẓam*, VI:124–7, 137–41. Ibn al-Athīr (*al-Kāmil*, IV:121–9) calls him a caliph and speaks of his virtues. He also notes that Ibn al-Zubayr was crucified with a dog or fish after he was killed: ibid., 127. Ibn al-Wardī (*Taʾrīkh*, I:169) reports that Ibn al-Zubayr was pious. Ibn Aʿtham (*al-Futūḥ*, III:389) reports that Ibn al-Zubayr was crucified after he was killed.

39 Al-ʾUbbī, *Sharḥ*, VI:533–8; Ibn Taymiyya, *Minhāj*, II:241. Among the jurists were Saʿīd b. Jubayr (d. 95/714), al-Shaʿbī (d. 103/721), Ibn Abī Laylā (d. 148/765), Dharr b. al-Ḥamdānī (d. 82/701), and even the Prophet's Companion Anas b. Mālik (d. 93/712). See Ibn al-Jawzī, *Manāqib*, 422–3 for a list of jurists punished.

many ways, Ibn al-Ashʿath was not an ideal candidate to lead a rebellion. He had betrayed al-Mukhtār, and for a period of time became a partisan of the Umayyads. Nonetheless, he was supported in Baṣra and Kūfa, especially by the piety-minded al-Qurrāʾ, an esteemed class of Qurʾānic reciters and students.[40] In 81/701, Ibn al-Ashʿath was defeated by al-Ḥajjāj in the Battle of Dīr al-Jamājim, and considerable slaughter ensued.[41] Many jurists were killed either in battle or shortly after.[42] Al-Ḥajjāj punished some jurists, such as Anas b. Mālik;[43] pardoned some, such as al-Shaʿbī;[44] and executed some, such as Saʿīd b. al-Jubayr.[45] According to one report, al-Ḥajjāj had Anas brought before him, and said: "You foul person, you roam in *fitan*. Once you support ʿAlī, then you support Ibn al-Zubayr, and then you support al-Ashʿath. By God, I will strike you like a tree is struck down." Although Anas managed to escape, he was eventually apprehended and beaten.[46]

Some jurists such as Ṭalq b. Ḥabīb (d. 100/718) and al-Ḥasan al-Baṣrī (d. 110/728) are reported to have vehemently opposed getting involved in the rebellion. Al-Baṣrī is reported to have argued that "al-Ḥajjāj is God's punishment; do not [attempt] to repel God's punishment with your own hands, but repel it with prayer and supplication." Similarly, Ṭalq b. Ḥabīb would say, "Fight the *fitna* with piety."[47] Al-Baṣrī, who became a prominent figure in the *bughāh* discourse, also opposed a Baṣran rebellion under the leadership of Yazīd b. al-Muhallab against the Umayyads. Ibn al-Muhallab was killed in the rebellion, and a number of the rebels were

[40] The Qurrāʾ accused the Umayyads of causing the death of ritual prayer (*imātat al-ṣalāh*), and their battle cry was "avenge the prayers" (*yā thārāt al-ṣalāh*). See Hawting, *First*, 70. On the Qurrāʾ, see Nagel, "Ḳurrāʾ"; Juynboll, "Qurrāʾ"; Juynboll, "Qurʾān."

[41] See, on the event generally, al-Ṭabarī, *Taʾrīkh*, VI:485–8, 491–504; Ibn Aʿtham, *al-Futūḥ*, IV:84–115; Kennedy, *Prophet*, 101; Marin-Guzman, *Popular*, 30. In Abū Mikhnaf, *Nuṣūṣ*, II:313–21, 403, the heads of Ibn al-Ashʿath and the members of his family were sent to al-Ḥajjāj. Reportedly, al-Ḥajjāj would not accept the repentance of a Kūfan rebel without the rebel first confessing that by joining the rebellion he had become an unbeliever (*kāfir*). Anyone refusing to make the admission was executed.

[42] Ibn Kathīr, *al-Bidāya*, IX:55; Ibn al-Athīr, *al-Kāmil*, IV:213–17; Abū Mikhnaf, *Nuṣūṣ*, II:405.

[43] Al-ʾUbbī, *Sharḥ*, VI:535.

[44] Ibn Kathīr, *al-Bidāya*, IX:52–3; Ibn al-Jawzī, *al-Muntaẓam*, VI:248–9; Ibn al-Athīr, *al-Kāmil*, IV:221.

[45] See Ibn Kathīr, *al-Bidāya*, IX:101–3; al-Ṭabarī, *Taʾrīkh*, VI:556–8; Ibn al-Jawzī, *al-Muntaẓam*, VI:318; Ibn al-Athīr, *al-Kāmil*, IV:280–1; Ibn al-Wardī, *Taʾrīkh*, I:170–1. Saʿīd was executed for his participation in the rebellion, although he was killed more than ten years after the fact. The execution of Saʿīd is lamented by Muslim sources. See, for instance, Ibn Aʿtham, *al-Futūḥ*, IV:115–22.

[46] See al-Dhahabī, *Siyar*, III:402, 404. According to some reports, because of Anas's highly revered status, ʿAbd al-Malik ordered al-Ḥajjāj to apologize to Anas.

[47] Ibn Taymiyya, *Minhāj*, II:241. Al-Ḥasan is reported to have cursed al-Ḥajjāj to his face, but then retracted when his life was threatened: Ibn al-Jawzī, *al-Muntaẓam*, VI:250.

executed in 102/720.[48] However, it seems that al-Baṣrī did not oppose Ibn al-Muhallab just out of a general aversion to rebellion. Rather, he considered him to be indistinguishable from the Umayyad despots. When asked if he excused or forgave the corruption of the Umayyads, he is reported to have said that he did not, but that he considered both the Umayyads and Ibn al-Muhallab to be corrupt, and wished that the earth would swallow all of them together.[49]

Zayd b. ᶜAlī, another member of the Prophet's family, rebelled against the Umayyads in Kūfa in 122/740, but was easily defeated, killed, and crucified. His son Yaḥyā was executed after a short-lived rebellion in 125/742. While these seem to have been relatively minor rebellions without the involvement of many jurists, the moral impact of the killing of these descendants of the Prophet was considerable.[50] One notable jurist who is reported to have supported Zayd b. ᶜAli's rebellion is Abū Ḥanīfa (d. 150/767), the founder of the Ḥanafī school of thought. The reports on Abū Ḥanīfa's exact relationship to Zayd's rebellion are contradictory. All of the reports concur that he sympathized with Zayd's revolt but disagree on the reason that he was not able to join the actual fighting. According to one report, Zayd asked Abū Ḥanīfa for his *bayᶜa*; Abū Ḥanīfa said that if he did not know that people would betray Zayd and allow him to be killed, he (Abū Ḥanīfa) would have joined Zayd. Abū Ḥanīfa, however, supported Zayd with a considerable sum of money.

48 Ibn al-Athīr, *al-Kāmil*, IV:342–3; Ibn Aᶜtham, *al-Futūḥ*, IV:242–58. Ibn al-Wardī (*Ta'rīkh*, I:173–4) praises Ibn al-Muhallab and his family. See, generally on the rebellion, Kennedy, *Prophet*, 107–8. On the significance and popularity of this rebellion, see Marin-Guzman, *Popular*, 32–3. On Ibn al-Muhallab's family, see Hawting, *First*, 73–6.

49 Ibn Khallikān, *Wafayāt*, VI:304. Abū Mikhnaf (*Nuṣūṣ*, II:345, 349–50) reports that al-Baṣrī used to curse the Umayyads, and also used to discourage people from joining Ibn al-Muhallab's rebellion. In Ibn al-Jawzī, *al-Muntaẓam*, VII:68, al-Baṣrī mocks the idea that Ibn al-Muhallab is calling for the observance of the Qur'ān and *Sunna*, and observes that until recently Ibn al-Muhallab had been serving the Umayyads, and supporting their corrupt behavior. Al-Baṣrī also makes it clear that he held the Umayyads responsible for pillaging Medina, killing the Prophet's family, and destroying the Kaᶜba. For the polemics between Ibn al-Muhallab and al-Baṣrī, see al-Ṭabarī, *Ta'rīkh*, VI:609. In al-Ṭabarī, al-Baṣrī is reported, as a matter of principle, to be opposed to Muslims killing each other.

50 On these events, see Ibn Kathīr, *al-Bidāya*, IX:342–4, X:6–7; Ibn al-Athīr, *al-Kāmil*, IV:452–6, 471–2; Ibn al-Jawzī, *al-Muntaẓam*, VII:218–19, 243–4; Ibn Aᶜtham, *al-Futūḥ*, IV:313–25; Ibn al-Wardī, *Ta'rīkh*, I:175. Both individuals were crucified, then burned, and prisoners from the rebellion were executed. Abū Mikhnaf (*Nuṣūṣ*, II:371–3) reports that Zayd b. ᶜAlī's body was buried and hidden in a river when Yūsuf b. ᶜUmar, the Umayyad governor, dug it out, mutilated the body, and hung it. He also reports that Yūsuf b. ᶜUmar al-Thaqafī stood at the podium of the mosque in Kūfa and declared to the Kūfans that they were a people of *baghy* and that every one of them waged war against God and His Prophet. Yūsuf proclaimed that were it not for the caliph's orders, he would have executed all of them and enslaved their women.

According to another report, Abū Ḥanīfa was unable to join Zayd because of an illness, and in yet another version, Abū Ḥanīfa was unable to join the revolt because he was responsible for many trusts. Abū Ḥanīfa asked the jurist Ibn Abī Laylā (d. 148/765) to take over the responsibility of the trusts, but Ibn Abī Laylā refused. Unable to find anyone who would take responsibility for the trusts, Abū Ḥanīfa had no choice but to not join the battle, but whenever he would recall the death of Zayd, he would cry.[51] Certainly these reports are, for the most part, ahistorical but it would not be surprising if Abū Ḥanīfa did, in fact, sympathize with Zayd's rebellion but refrained from a public endorsement because he was sure that it would fail. A few years later, Yazīd b. Hubayra, the avid Qaysī supporter of the Marwānids, ordered Abū Ḥanīfa to assume a judicial position in Kūfa. This would have been a valuable symbolic gesture in favor of the legitimacy of the Umayyads. Abū Ḥanīfa refused to do so and, as a result, was tortured. According to some reports, it was a fellow jurist, the same Ibn Abī Layla referred to above, who recommended that Abū Ḥanīfa receive four hundred lashes.[52]

The legitimacy of the Umayyads, by this time, had become very problematic as they increasingly relied on brute force to suppress rebellion and maintain their power.[53] In 127/744, the Umayyad Marwān b. Muḥammad (al-Ḥimār) overthrew Ibrāhīm b. al-Walīd (r. 126/744–127/744) and took power, but was immediately faced with widespread rebellions by the Khawārij, among them the rebellions of al-Ḍaḥḥāk b. Qays and Abū Ḥamza al-Khārijī. Both rebellions were fairly serious: al-Ḍaḥḥāk managed to occupy Mosul, and Abū Ḥamza occupied Medina for a period of time before they were defeated and killed.[54] Furthermore, a serious rebellion, known as the Jaʿfarī rebellion, was launched from Kūfa by ʿAbd Allāh b. Muʿāwiya, a descendant of Jaʿfar, ʿAlī b. Abī Ṭālib's brother. The rebellion was supported by various parties, and it spread to Persia before it was crushed in 130/748. ʿAbd Allāh escaped,

[51] See al-Makkī, *Manāqib*, 267. It is also reported that Abū Ḥanīfa would claim that the people of Syria (i.e. the Umayyads and their sympathizers) did not like him because if he had been alive in earlier days, he would have joined ʿAlī against Muʿāwiya, and the people of *ḥadīth* did not like him because of his love for *ahl al-bayt*: ibid., 275, 344.

[52] Ibid., 306–7. Also see Ibn Kathīr, *al-Bidāya*, X:110.

[53] See Blankinship, *End*, 21, 191; Shaban, *Islamic 1*, 144, 168. On these events as precursors to the ʿAbbāsid revolution, see Lassner, *Islamic*, 89.

[54] Al-Ṭabarī, *Taʾrīkh*, VII:174–5, 188–9; Ibn Kathīr, *al-Bidāya*, X:35; Ibn al-Jawzī, *al-Muntaẓam*, VII:266, 277–8; Ibn al-Athīr, *al-Kāmil*, V:12–14, 21–2, 39–40. Numerous rebellions by the Khawārij took place in the years preceding the fall of the Umayyads: see Marin-Guzman, *Popular*, 67.

but he was eventually seized and killed by Abū Muslim, the partisan and architect of the ᶜAbbāsid revolution.[55]

By the end of the Umayyad period, only the family of the Prophet could supply the necessary basis for legitimacy.[56] None of the ᶜAlid revolts had succeeded in overthrowing the Umayyads, but the ᶜAlids' cause continued to enjoy a high degree of popularity, particularly in Kūfa. However, it was the ᶜAbbāsids who successfully spread their propaganda in Khurāsān, and who were able to overthrow the Umayyads.[57] The ᶜAbbāsid revolution was officially started by Abū Muslim in the Khurāsānī capital, Marv, in 130/748.[58] When the Umayyads became aware that Abū Muslim was courting Ibrāhīm al-Imām, a descendant of ᶜAlī's brother ᶜAbd Allāh, they executed Ibrāhīm in 132/749.[59] In the same year, however, the Khurāsānīs were able to capture Kūfa from the Umayyads, and the issue of who should become the spiritual leader of the ᶜAbbāsids presented itself. Compared to the ᶜAlids, the ᶜAbbāsids' claim to legitimacy was problematic. The ᶜAbbāsids were descended from al-ᶜAbbās, the Prophet's uncle, whose conversion to Islam was doubtful.[60] According to some reports, certain members of the ᶜAbbāsid movement, such as Abū Salma al-Khallāl in Kūfa, wished to offer the leadership of the ᶜAbbāsids to the ᶜAlid branch of the family, but these attempts failed.[61] Instead,

55 Al-Ṭabarī, *Ta'rīkh*, VII:187–8; Ibn Kathīr, *al-Bidāya*, X:35–6; Ibn al-Athīr, *al-Kāmil*, V:36–8. Also see Lassner, *Islamic*, 97.

56 Kennedy, *Prophet*, 116. Also see Hawting, *First*, 104–18. For a lengthy study of the social and moral impact of the ᶜAlid rebellions, see al-Ḥasanī, *al-Intifāḍāt*.

57 See Marin-Guzman, *Popular*, 92; Sharon, *Black*, 51–4. On the role of ᶜAbbāsid leadership in Kūfa, see Lassner, *Islamic*, 86–7. On the Khurāsānīs, see Hawting, *First*, 105–7.

58 On the gradual and prolonged process that resulted in the ᶜAbbāsid revolution, see Lassner, *Islamic*; Marin-Guzman, *Popular*; Sharon, *Black*; Sharon, *Revolt*.

59 There are also other reports as to what exactly happened to Ibrāhīm al-Imām. A common report is that a letter from Ibrāhīm to Abū Muslim encouraging him to slaughter the Umayyads was intercepted. Ibrāhīm was imprisoned for a period and then killed in prison. Another report, which Ibn Kathīr considers to be the most authentic, is that Marwān heard that Abū Muslim and his followers referred to Ibrāhīm as the caliph, so he ordered his execution. See Ibn Kathīr, *al-Bidāya*, X:41–2; al-Ṭabarī, *Ta'rīkh*, VII:219–20; Ibn al-Jawzī, *al-Muntaẓam*, VII:266, 277–8; Ibn al-Athīr, *al-Kāmil*, V:72–3; al-Masᶜūdī, *Murūj*, II:192–3.

60 See, on this issue, Kennedy, *Prophet*, 124–7. In order to address the problem of legitimacy, the ᶜAbbāsids invented various traditions that connected them either to the ᶜAlid branch or to the Prophet. In one tradition, it is claimed that Abū Hāshim (d. 98/716), a descendant of ᶜAlī, on his deathbed transferred the ᶜAlid right to rule to Muḥammad b. ᶜAlī b. al-ᶜAbbās. In the second tradition, it is claimed that the Prophet gave descendants of al-ᶜAbbās the right to rule: see al-Ṭabarī, *Ta'rīkh*, VII:212. On these and other ᶜAbbāsid apologetics, see Lassner, *Islamic*, 3–36; Lassner, *Shaping*, 60–1.

61 Ibn Kathīr, *al-Bidāya*, X:42. Among those to whom leadership was allegedly offered was Jaᶜfar al-Ṣādiq (d. 148/765): Modarressi, *Crisis*, 7; Shaban, *Islamic I*, 186–7. On Jaᶜfar al-Ṣādiq, see Hodgson, "Djaᶜfar al-Ṣādiḳ."

Ibrāhīm's brother, Abū al-ʿAbbās (known as al-Ṣaffāḥ) was given the oath of allegiance in Kūfa and declared a caliph by his party. Although the ʿAbbāsid revolution seems to have been quite popular, if Marwān had been able to defeat Abū al-ʿAbbās, this too would have gone down in history as yet another failed rebellion. However, the outnumbered ʿAbbāsids defeated the Qaysī supporters of Marwān in the Battle of Zāb (132/750), and this effectively brought an end to the Umayyad dynasty.[62]

Significantly, the ʿAbbāsids, like the Umayyads, came to power through a usurpation or a revolt.[63] Yet, for the most part, their caliphate was accepted by the jurists. This point cannot be overemphasized; the idea of a revolt as a means to power was neither alien nor abhorrent to Muslim jurists. Furthermore, the precedents available to Muslim jurists did not necessitate that a rebel be considered a traitor or malevolent person. This does not mean that the jurists necessarily counseled or encouraged rebellion. Rather, the precedents of early Islamic history did not, of necessity, create a legal culture in which rebels were unequivocally despised or condemned. The major difference, however, between the Umayyad period and the early ʿAbbāsid era was that the corporate identity of jurists and their culture had become more developed and distinct. The *ʿulamāʾ* were developing a jurisprudential corpus over which they could speak authoritatively. This gave them a vested interest in the institutions of law and order, but it also permitted them a certain degree of distance from the institutions of politics and power. I will return to this point again later.

Shortly after coming to power, the ʿAbbāsids started a massive massacre of the Marwānid family and the crucifixion of some of its members.[64] After a violent power struggle, Abū Jaʿfar al-Manṣūr (r. 137/754–159/775) became the second ʿAbbāsid caliph, only to encounter a serious rebellion by members of the ʿAlid family.[65] In 145/762, Muḥammad b. ʿAbd Allāh b. al-Ḥasan, known as al-Nafs al-Zakiyya,

[62] Hawting, *First*, 115–18. [63] See Lassner, *Islamic*, 7.

[64] On the unprecedented scale of the massacre, see ibid., 136–7; Marin-Guzman, *Popular*, 100–1; Zaman, *Religion*, 72–3; Ibn Qutayba, *al-Imāma*, 145–8; Ibn al-Athīr, *al-Kāmil*, V:78–9; al-Masʿūdī, *Murūj*, II:194–5. Apparently, this was the first time the extermination of an entire clan was attempted.

[65] There were other rebellions as well: ʿAbd Allāh b. ʿAlī, al-Manṣūr's uncle, revolted but was defeated by Abū Muslim. Al-Manṣūr imprisoned ʿAbd Allāh and later had him killed. Al-Manṣūr also killed Abū Muslim. These events are analyzed in Lassner, *Shaping*, 39–57. On the killing of Abū Muslim, see al-Masʿūdī, *Murūj*, II:230–2; on the killing of ʿAbd Allāh, see ibid., II:241–2. Al-Masʿūdī reports that the jurist Ibn Abī Laylā approved of the killing of ʿAbd Allāh while the jurist Ibn Shubruma advised against it.

"the pure soul," for his piety, rebelled in Medina and his brother, Ibrāhīm, rebelled in Baṣra. The ʿAbbāsids were aware of the plotting of the rebellion and kept Kūfa, the traditional base of ʿAlid support, under careful watch. Ultimately, the rebellions, through the use of Syrian and Khurāsānī troops, were crushed and al-Nafs al-Zakiyya and his brother were killed.[66] Nonetheless, the rebellions are notable because of their popularity, particularly among the jurists.[67] Some jurists seemed to have joined the fighting, but many, such as Abū Ḥanīfa, ʿAbd Allāh b. Abī Sabra, and Mālik b. Anas, lent only financial or moral support.[68]

Mālik b. Anas, the famous founder of the Mālikī school, was asked about the legality of giving the *bayʿa* to al-Nafs al-Zakiyya. He responded that it was legal because the *bayʿa* given to the caliph al-Manṣūr was obtained under duress and therefore was invalid. Effectively, Mālik suggested that it was legal to join the rebellion. Interestingly, however, Mālik seems to have stayed home and did not take part in the actual fighting.[69] Moreover, it is reported that after the rebellion, Mālik isolated himself and allegedly refused to attend any public gatherings until he died.[70] Nevertheless, al-Manṣūr's cousin, who was Medina's governor, had Mālik beaten and flogged for his views on duress and, possibly, for supporting the rebellion.[71]

The fate of another jurist, Abū Ḥanīfa, was the subject of various reports, with most of the disagreement focusing on whether he was

66 See Kennedy, *Prophet*, 132–3. Also see Lassner's detailed treatment of the mechanics of the rebellion in *Shaping*, 69–79.

67 Al-Iṣfahānī (*Maqātil* 359) claims that all the jurists joined the rebellion. Ibn al-Wardī (*Taʾrīkh*, I:186) claims that 4,000 jurists supported the rebellion. This number is most probably exaggerated. See also Ibn Taymiyya, *Minhāj*, II:243. Al-Masʿūdī (*Murūj*, II:233) notes that many principalities gave their *bayʿa* to al-Nafs al-Zakiyya. He also notes that in trying to convince the Khurāsānīs to fight the rebels, al-Manṣūr referred to Kūfa as a place of *fitan* and strife (ibid., 237–8).

68 See al-Iṣfahānī, *Maqātil*, 283, 361, 364–5. On Ibn Abī Sabra, see Wakīʿ, *Akhbār*, I:201. Zaman (*Religion*, 73–5) argues that several jurists refrained from getting involved in the rebellion. This is certainly true. See Ibn Saʿd, *al-Ṭabaqāt*, VII:264, for an ʿAbd Allāh b. ʿAwn b. Arṭabān who locked himself up at home and refused to get involved. Also see Wakīʿ, *Akhbār*, I:196–7. Jaʿfar al-Ṣādiq also refrained from joining the revolt. See Modarressi, *Crisis*, 8. But this does not mean the rebellion was not popular among jurists.

69 Ibn Kathīr, *al-Bidāya*, X:86; al-Ṭabarī, *Taʾrīkh*, VII:281; Ibn al-Jawzī, *al-Muntaẓam*, VIII:64.

70 Ibn Kathīr, *al-Bidāya*, X:180. The authenticity of this report is doubtful. Ibn al-Athīr (*al- Kāmil*, IX:45) reports that he isolated himself at home until al-Nafs al-Zakiyya was killed.

71 There is some disagreement as to why he was punished. According to one report, he was asked whether a divorce pronounced under duress was valid. He said it was not, and as a result was flogged. It is also reported that those who were envious of him conveyed his views on duress and divorce to the governor, and thus he was flogged. See al-Dhahabī, *Siyar*, VIII:79–80; Ibn al-Jawzī, *al-Muntaẓam*, IX:44; Ibn al-Wardī, *Taʾrīkh*, I:196. A jurist's views on duress and divorce had serious political implications. The pivotal issue was the legality of acts performed under coercion because such acts could include a coerced *bayʿa* or an oath of allegiance to a ruler. See Abū al-Fidāʾ, *al-Mukhtaṣar*, I:316–17, who is explicit about this point.

poisoned or tortured to death. Reportedly, Abū Ḥanīfa was very vocal in support of Ibrāhīm's rebellion and continued to speak favorably of Ibrāhīm even after the rebellion ended, and so al-Manṣūr had Abū Ḥanīfa poisoned. Other reports provide that al-Manṣūr never forgave Abū Ḥanīfa for his position on the rebellions. As proof of his loyalty, al-Manṣūr ordered Abū Ḥanīfa to accept a judicial position, but when he refused, al-Manṣūr had him imprisoned and tortured to death.[72] Some reports even claim that al-Manṣūr had Abū Ḥanīfa crucified, and had a dog buried with him.[73]

In what is definitely an apocryphal tradition, the caliph al-Manṣūr requested the presence of Abū Ḥanīfa. When Abū Ḥanīfa arrived, he found Ibn Abī Laylā, the judge of Kūfa, and Ibn Shubruma, the judge of Baghdād, present with the caliph. Al-Manṣūr asked Abū Ḥanīfa about the liability of the rebellious Khawārij for the life and property they destroyed. Abū Ḥanīfa responded by saying, "Ask the two judges first." One of the judges said they were liable, and the other said they were not. Abū Ḥanīfa said they are both wrong; rather, the Khawārij are liable only for what they destroyed before they commenced their rebellion. But they are not liable for what they destroyed *in the course* of their rebellion. Reportedly, at that point, al-Manṣūr had to acknowledge Abū Ḥanīfa's juristic proficiency and superior knowledge.[74] While it is quite plausible that Abū Ḥanīfa played a role in the development of the law of rebellion, this report is too staged to warrant any credibility. Furthermore, the position reportedly articulated by Abū Ḥanīfa, as discussed later, is too precise and developed to be historical. Nonetheless, it is a good representation of the developing interest in the law of rebellion and its authentication. Despite Abū Ḥanīfa's personal history, and perhaps because of his personal history,[75] reports were circulated claiming that he advised people to refrain from getting involved in *al-fitna*.[76] Yet other reports have Abū Ḥanīfa saying that if he had lived at the time of ʿAlī,

72 In some reports, Abū Ḥanīfa eventually accepted the judicial position as a result of the torture, but died a few days later. Other reports claim that after the rebellion, al-Manṣūr wished to test Abū Ḥanīfa's loyalty. He sent a man to ask Abū Ḥanīfa if it was legal to obey the caliph if the caliph ordered the killing of an innocent victim. Abū Ḥanīfa gave a negative response, so al-Manṣūr had Abū Ḥanīfa poisoned. Most of the reports are in al-Makkī, *Manāqib*, 299–305. Ibn al-Jawzī (*al-Muntaẓam*, VIII:143) obviously did not approve of Abū Ḥanīfa because he took the trouble to point out the many occasions where Abū Ḥanīfa contravened the Prophet's *Sunna*. Nonetheless, Ibn al-Jawzī reproduces many of the reports. Al-Dhahabī (*Siyar*, VI:401–3) mentions most of the reports and calls Abū Ḥanīfa the martyr. Ibn al-Wardī (*Taʾrīkh*, I:188) reports that Abū Ḥanīfa died in prison.

73 Al-Makkī, *Manāqib*, 304–5. 74 Ibid., 184.

75 See, on his life, Gibb and Kramers, eds., *Shorter*, 9–10.

76 Al-ʿAynī, *al-Bināya*, VI:740; al-Sarakhsī, *al-Mabsūṭ*, X:124.

he would have fought on ʿAlī's side.[77] These reports can only be seen as manifestations of the rising interest in the debate on the status of rebels and the law of rebellion.

A report that perhaps better reflects the status of the developing discourse on the law of rebellion occurs in the context of the polemics between al-Manṣūr and al-Nafs al-Zakiyya. Al-Manṣūr wrote to al-Nafs al-Zakiyya citing the *ḥirāba* verse, and threatened to have al-Nafs al-Zakiyya killed, crucified, or to amputate his limbs in accordance with the specifications of the verse. However, again pursuant to the verse, al-Manṣūr promised to pardon al-Nafs al-Zakiyya, his family, and followers if he would quit the rebellion before being captured. Al-Manṣūr also promised to grant him money and property and to release all the ʿAlids in prison. Al-Nafs al-Zakiyya responded by saying that the ʿAlids had a greater right to rule than the ʿAbbāsids, and promised to forgive al-Manṣūr and pardon him for the crimes he had committed, except for the *ḥudūd* of God or any right that belonged to a Muslim or *dhimmī*. Al-Nafs al-Zakiyya also noted that al-Manṣūr's promises were worthless since he had betrayed his own followers, such as Abū Muslim and al-Manṣūr's uncle.[78] Ultimately, al-Manṣūr was unable to enforce his threat because al-Nafs al-Zakiyya died in battle, but there are reports that his corpse and the corpses of his followers were crucified.[79] Significantly, at one point when Ibrāhīm, al-Nafs al-Zakiyya's brother, had the upper hand in battle over al-Manṣūr, then Ibrāhīm, consistent with ʿAlī's conduct, ordered his troops not to pursue the fugitive.[80] Notably, however, al-Manṣūr considered al-Nafs al-Zakiyya a *muḥārib* deserving of the treatment specified in the Qurʾānic verse. Evidently, both the *ḥirāba* verse and the conduct of ʿAlī were being employed and manipulated in the polemics of the political arena. As noted earlier, these precedents became central in the development of *aḥkām al-bughāh*.

The tension raised by the above-mentioned rebellions, and by the problem of how to perceive or deal with rebels, is well illustrated in a report about Muḥammad b. ʿImrān al-Ṭalḥī, the judge of Medina at the time of al-Manṣūr. Ibn ʿImrān failed to join the rebellion of al-Nafs al-Zakiyya. When the rebellion was defeated, al-Manṣūr ordered his agents in Medina to arrest anyone suspected of supporting the rebellion

[77] Al-Makkī, *Manāqib*, 275, 345.
[78] Ibn Kathīr, *al-Bidāya*, x:87–8; Ibn al-Jawzī, *al-Muntaẓam*, viii:64–5; Ibn al-Athīr, *al-Kāmil*, v:151–2; al-Ṭabarī, *Taʾrīkh*, vii:284–5.
[79] Ibn al-Jawzī, *al-Muntaẓam*, viii:68; Ibn al-Athīr, *al-Kāmil*, v:161.
[80] Al-Ṭabarī, *Taʾrīkh*, vii:325.

(*amara bi aṣḥābihi yultaqaṭūna fī kulli wajhin*). Nonetheless, the arrest of political opponents was hardly a scientific process, so there was a sense of general fear and insecurity. Ibn ᶜImrān, the judge, overcome by terror, would pray: "May others be arrested and not me (*Allāhumma ḥawālaynā wa lā ᶜalaynā*)."[81] The jurist ᶜAbd Allāh b. ᶜAbd al-ᶜAzīz al-ᶜUmarī, who joined the rebellion with his sons, would comment, "Have you seen anyone more ignorant than this judge? He prays for harm to befall Muslims!"[82] There was no suggestion of rancor or hate on the part of Ibn ᶜImrān against the rebels, only fear for his personal security. On the other hand, those being harmed were perceived as fellow Muslims, and an unmitigated desire to distance oneself from them was seen as a sign of ignorance and lack of piety. It was exactly these dynamics that played themselves out in the articulation of the discourse on rebellion.

After al-Manṣūr, tribal and Khawārijī rebellions continued to plague the reign of his successor al-Mahdī (r. 158/775–169/785). Al-Mahdī followed a policy of reconciliation with the ᶜAlids, releasing them from prison and offering them financial grants.[83] His reign was relatively peaceful with minimal ᶜAlid opposition.[84] In 167/783, he initiated an inquisition directed mostly, but not exclusively, at those who advocated Manichaean doctrines (the *zanādiqa*).[85] Nonetheless, several ᶜAlid sympathizers were accused of heresy and killed.[86] Interestingly, al-Mahdī dealt with some rebels in a fashion reminiscent of the verse on *ḥirāba*,[87] and although upon coming to power he granted a general amnesty to all

[81] The literal meaning of the phrase is: "God, may such or such fall around us and not on us." The statement was allegedly made by the Prophet when the people of Medina suffered from persistent heavy rains. Reportedly, the Prophet prayed that the rain would fall around Medina and not on Medina.

[82] Wakīᶜ, *Akhbār*, I:196–7.

[83] Al-Yaᶜqūbī, *Taʾrīkh*, II:394; Kennedy, *Prophet*, 137; Shaban, *Islamic I*, 21.

[84] The ᶜAlid ᶜĪsā b. Zayd b. ᶜAlī attempted to organize a rebellion against al-Mahdī without much success. He went into hiding until he died. Al-Mahdī reportedly also had the ᶜAlid ᶜAlī b. al-ᶜAbbās b. al-Ḥasan imprisoned and then poisoned for suspected seditious activity. See al-Iṣfahānī, *Maqātil*, 403–4, 405–28. On Sufyān al-Thawrī's opposition to al-Mahdī, see below.

[85] Al-Ṭabarī, *Taʾrīkh*, VIII:409; Ibn Kathīr, *al-Bidāya*, X:153; al-Yaᶜqūbī, *Taʾrīkh*, II:400; Ibn al-Wardī, *Taʾrīkh*, I:191–3. Ibn al-Jawzī (*al-Muntaẓam*, VIII:235) reports that in 163/779 al-Mahdī had several people accused of heresy killed and crucified. On this inquisition, see Ibrahim, "Religious." On the thought and historical role of the *zanādiqa*, see Chokr, *Zandaqa*.

[86] Ibrahim, "Religious," 56. Ibrahim demonstrates that the inquisition was brought about because of a changing socio-political culture. It was also used against political opponents who were summarily killed.

[87] For example, in 160/776, Yūsuf b. Ibrāhīm rebelled in Khurāsān; his hands and feet were amputated and he was crucified: see Ibn al-Jawzī, *al-Muntaẓam*, VIII:235; al-Yaᶜqūbī, *Taʾrīkh*, II:397.

political prisoners, he exempted from this amnesty those who "caused corruption on the earth."[88]

It was not until the reign of al-Hādī (r. 169/785–170/786) that there was another serious ᶜAlid rebellion. Al-Hādī had followed a hardline policy towards the ᶜAlids, cutting off their allowances and keeping them under close surveillance. According to some sources, this policy was the reason the ᶜAlid al-Ḥusayn b. ᶜAlī, Ṣāḥib al-Fakhkh, rebelled in Medina in 169/786.[89] But his rebellion was short-lived and he was trapped and killed on his way to Mecca.[90] Sunnī sources report that the caliph, al-Hādī, did not approve of the killing of this ᶜAlid – if true, probably because he realized that this would generate more propaganda against the ᶜAbbāsids.[91] Nonetheless, the relative paucity of the support for his rebellion[92] is an indication that the ᶜAbbāsids had succeeded in consolidating their power base, and in integrating many jurists within the institutions of government.[93] Many prominent jurists such as Layth b. Saᶜd (d. 175/791), Sharīk al-Nakhaᶜī (d. 187/803), al-Qāḍī Abū Yūsuf (d. 183/799), and Muḥammad b. al-Ḥasan al-Shaybānī (d. 189/804) accepted judicial positions while others enjoyed the patronage of the caliph.[94] This was especially true during the reign of the fifth ᶜAbbāsid caliph, Hārūn al-Rashīd (r. 170/786–193/809).

Hārūn al-Rashīd came to power through a *coup d'état* arranged by his supporters from the Barmakid family. His supporters were even suspected of having poisoned the previous caliph. There were several serious rebellions during his reign, such as the Khārijī rebellion in Ḥijāz by Walīd b. Ṭarīf (in 178/794) and the tribal rebellion in Samarqand by Rāfiᶜ b. Layth (in 189/804). Nevertheless, his reign enjoyed considerable stability, and it was the last period in which central Muslim territory from North Africa to the Sind in the east was united under the control of a caliph.[95] Hārūn al-Rashīd, however, remained apprehensive about ᶜAlid contenders, and although many jurists served in his administration, his relationship with some of the most prominent jurists remained problematic. For example, in the short-lived rebellion of al-Ḥusayn b. ᶜAlī, Ṣāḥib al-Fakhkh, one of the ᶜAlids' supporters was Yaḥyā b. ᶜAbd Allāh

88 Ibn al-Jawzī, *al-Muntaẓam*, VIII:227; Ibn Kathīr, *al-Bidāya*, X:133.
89 Al-Yaᶜqūbī, *Taʾrīkh*, II:404.
90 Ibn Khayyāṭ, *Taʾrīkh*, II:478; al-Masᶜūdī, *Murūj*, II:258–9.
91 One hundred rebel heads were severed and displayed, but al-Hādī was upset when the head of al-Ḥusayn b. ᶜAlī was brought to him. Ibn al-Jawzī, *al-Muntaẓam*, VIII:310; Ibn al-Athīr, *al-Kāmil*, V:268; Ibn al-Wardī, *Taʾrīkh*, I:193–4; Abū al-Fidāʾ, *al-Mukhtaṣar*, I:311–12.
92 Al-Yaᶜqūbī (*Taʾrīkh*, II:405) reports that only 500 people fought with this ᶜAlid.
93 Kennedy, *Prophet*, 140.
94 See, on this point, Zaman, *Religion*, 147–66.
95 Kennedy, *Prophet*, 141–8.

why is the corpus of the jurists even accepted – it's clear it's super biased

b. al-Ḥasan (later known as al-Daylamī) who escaped to the mountains of Daylam near the Caspian Sea when ᶜAlī was killed. Al-Daylamī seems to have been quite popular and many people in Mecca, Medina, Irāq, Yemen, and Egypt gave him their allegiance. Several jurists, even before Hārūn al-Rashīd came to power, had either sympathized with or pledged their allegiance to al-Daylamī. Among these jurists was the founder of the Shāfiᶜī school, Muḥammad b. Idrīs al-Shāfiᶜī (d. 204/819–20).[96] Evidently, al-Daylamī's popularity distressed Hārūn al-Rashīd considerably, so he persuaded al-Daylamī to leave his hideout in the mountains by issuing him a guarantee of safe conduct. Al-Daylamī arrived in Baghdād and is said to have been allowed to visit Medina and pay off al-Ḥusayn b. ᶜAlī's debts.[97]

Before long, Hārūn al-Rashīd started conspiring to have al-Daylamī killed. He accused al-Daylamī of treason and of continuing to agitate against him in Baghdād and Medina.[98] Therefore, al-Rashīd argued that al-Daylamī's guarantee of safe conduct was invalid, and that he (al-Rashīd) was not obliged to honor it. Importantly, Hārūn al-Rashīd sought the support of the prominent jurists of his time for this rather unusual position. He reportedly asked several jurists about whether it was legal to violate the guarantee of safe conduct. Some jurists insisted that it was not legal, while others obliged the caliph, and still others refused to respond.[99] Among the jurists asked was al-Shaybānī, the famous student of Abū Ḥanīfa. Al-Shaybānī insisted that the guarantee of safe conduct was legally binding, and could not be revoked. Hārūn al-Rashīd, however, continued to argue with al-Shaybānī, but to no avail. In debating al-Rashīd, at one point, al-Shaybānī reportedly commented, "What if [the man] was a *muḥārib* and he repented, wouldn't he be safe then?"[100]

It is difficult to understand the exact sense in which the word *muḥārib* is used in this context. However, at a minimum, al-Shaybānī distinguished between al-Daylamī and a fighter or, perhaps, a bandit. Al-Shaybānī could be arguing that al-Daylamī, at one time, was a *muḥārib* who had now repented and so could not be molested, or alternatively he could be

[96] Ibn al-ᶜImād, *Shadharāt*, I:338. On the revolt of Yaḥyā, see Ibn Sahl, *Akhbār*.
[97] Ibn al-ᶜImād, *Shadharāt*, I:339.
[98] On the conspiracy to have al-Daylamī killed, see al-Iṣfahānī, *Maqātil*, 471–9.
[99] Ibn al-ᶜImād, *Shadharāt*, I:339; al-Iṣfahānī (*Maqātil*, 479–80) reports that the jurist Mālik b. Anas was among the jurists consulted on the matter. Mālik said the guarantee of safe conduct could not be revoked.
[100] Ibn al-Jawzī, *al-Muntaẓam*, IX:16–7; Ibn al-Athīr, *al-Kāmil*, V:291; al-Ṭabarī, *Taʾrīkh*, VIII:450. Also see the discussion in Wakīᶜ, *Akhbār*, I:249, which is somewhat different than the above sources.

arguing that al-Daylamī fell in a legal category separate and apart from that of a *muḥārib*.[101] Furthermore, al-Shaybānī could also be arguing that even under the worst of circumstances, if al-Daylamī was a *muḥārib*, his repentance would still be accepted and the promises given to him would be honored. In any event, Hārūn al-Rashīd was not convinced, and he solicited the views of the chief judge of Raqqa, Abū al-Bakhtarī Wahb b. Wahb (d. 200/815).[102] Obliging the caliph, Abū al-Bakhtarī immediately declared the guarantee of safe conduct invalid. Hārūn al-Rashīd proclaimed, "You are the chief judge, and so you are more knowledgeable [than al-Shaybānī]." The paper on which the guarantee was written was torn up and it is reported that Abū al-Bakhtarī spat on it. Al-Daylamī was then seized and killed in 176/793.[103]

As might be expected, Abū al-Bakhtarī was generously rewarded for his loyalty, and in 192/807 he was made the governor and the judge of Medina. All the judges who declared the safe conduct valid were reportedly dismissed, and al-Shaybānī was banned from issuing legal opinions for a period of time.[104] But al-Shaybānī managed to regain the caliph's favor, and was appointed to the position of a judge in Raqqa in 180/796.[105] He was dismissed in 187/803, reportedly because of lingering distrust as a result of the Daylamī affair. However, in 189/804, he was ordered by Hārūn al-Rashīd to accompany him on an expedition to suppress a rebellion in Samarqand by Rāfiᶜ b. Layth, a grandson of the last Umayyad governor of the province. Ironically, al-Shaybānī died on the way in Rayy.[106]

Even if al-Shaybānī regained the caliph's favor, it does not necessarily mean that he became a representative of the interests of the state. It only meant that he now had a vested interest, but not a singular interest, in the

[101] I am not at all discounting the likelihood that al-Shaybānī never uttered this statement. Rather, it was later attributed to him to demonstrate his keen knowledge of law as compared to the caliph's ignorance.

[102] On Abū al-Bakhtarī, see al-Ziriklī, *al-Aᶜlām*, VIII:126.

[103] Ibn al-Jawzī, *al-Muntaẓam*, IX:16–17; Ibn al-Athīr, *al-Kāmil*, V:291; al-Ṭabarī, *Taʾrīkh*, VIII:450. On different versions of how al-Daylamī was killed, see al-Iṣfahānī, *Maqātil*, 481–2; Ibn al-ᶜImād, *Shadharāt*, I:339. Some reports say he was starved or strangled to death in prison while other reports claim he was tortured to death. Ibn al-Wardī (*Taʾrīkh*, I:195) and Abū al-Fidāʾ (*al-Mukhtaṣar*, I:315) report that al-Rashīd treated al-Daylamī well, and then had him imprisoned. Al-Daylamī then died in prison. Interestingly, there are many traditions that are derogatory of Abū al-Bakhtarī. Some reports call him the "lying judge" while others say that he was detested by the jurists and the laity. Most of the reports focus on Abū al-Bakhtarī's desire to gain favor with the ᶜAbbāsids: see Wakīᶜ, *Akhbār*, I:252–3.

[104] Al-Iṣfahānī, *Maqātil*, 480. On Abū al-Bakhtarī also see Wakīᶜ, *Akhbār*, I:243–4.

[105] Reportedly, al-Shaybānī was not happy about this appointment.

[106] Ibn Saᶜd, *al-Ṭabaqāt*, VII:336–7. See also Gibb and Kramers, eds., *Shorter*, 518–19; Khadduri, trans., *Islamic Law*, 32–5.

institutions of the state. In all likelihood, al- Shaybānī was not an ᶜAlid sympathizer, and the reason for his position on the Daylamī affair had little to do with al-Daylamī himself. Al-Shaybānī was a representative of the emerging conception of law and order, but even more, he was a representative of a developing legal culture with its own logic and corporate interests. However, this legal culture was neither cohesive nor uniform.[107] Some of its prominent members were, in fact, ᶜAlid sympathizers, or at least not partisans of the ᶜAbbāsids and their administration.[108] One of the most prominent jurists who seems to fall in this category is al-Shāfiᶜī.

As mentioned above, al-Shāfiᶜī reportedly gave his allegiance to al-Daylamī, and in fact, al-Shāfiᶜī was suspected of *tashayyuᶜ* or of being a secret Shīᶜī sympathizer.[109] For a jurist as influential as was al-Shāfiᶜī, he managed to keep a considerable distance from public office. Nonetheless, probably as a test of his loyalty, Hārūn al-Rashīd ordered al-Shāfiᶜī to take office in Najrān, Yemen.[110] Before long, in 187/803 or 189/804, he was arrested with nine ᶜAlids and brought in chains before al-Rashīd in Raqqa while, reportedly, al-Shaybānī was present. Despite their vehement denials that they were plotting against al-Rashīd and, in the case of one of the accused, denials that they were even loyal to the ᶜAlids, al-Rashīd ordered the execution of the nine. Reportedly, al-Shaybānī stood silent, and neither condoned nor opposed the executions. However, al-Shaybānī did intervene to stop the execution of a fellow jurist, and al-Shāfiᶜī's life was spared. Interestingly, al-Shāfiᶜī defended himself by arguing that he was just a jurist, and had nothing to do with the ᶜAlids. The import of al-Shāfiᶜī's defense seems to have been that as a jurist he is unlikely to be involved in such political intrigues.[111]

[107] I deal with the nature of the emerging juristic culture later.

[108] Even if a particular jurist was not an ᶜAlid sympathizer, as noted above, the members of the family of the Prophet, at least in the first two centuries of Islam, continued to carry considerable moral weight. For example, Jaᶜfar al-Ṣādiq (d. 148/765) was highly revered until his death: see Modarressi, *Crisis*, 6–7; also see Ibn al-Jawzī, *Ṣifa*, 1:496–502. Al-Iṣfahānī (*Maqātil*, 464) reports that Mālik b. Anas used to respect al-Daylamī, and that when al-Daylamī entered the presence of Mālik, Mālik would stand up and seat al-Daylamī next to him.

[109] Al-Dhahabī, *Siyar*, x:58. The author vehemently denies this accusation. Reportedly, al-Shāfiᶜī said that as a child, he dreamt of ᶜAlī b. Abī Ṭālib. In the dream, ᶜAlī gave al-Shāfiᶜī his ring, which is a symbolic act of adoration and support. See Abū al-Fidāʾ, *al-Mukhtaṣar*, 1:334.

[110] Ibn Kathīr, *al-Bidāya*, v:263. See also Gibb and Kramers, eds., *Shorter*, 512–13.

[111] Ibn al-ᶜImād, *Shadharāt*, 1:323; according to one report, the caliph did not know that al-Shāfiᶜī was one of the apprehended suspects, and once al-Shaybānī verified that it was, in fact, al-Shāfiᶜī who stood before him, the caliph released him immediately. This is very unlikely, and in all probability the account was embellished to emphasize al-Shāfiᶜī's esteemed position. In a different report, it was al-Shaybānī and Abū Yūsuf who conspired to get al-Shāfiᶜī into trouble. They told the caliph that al-Shāfiᶜī was an ᶜAlid sympathizer and that he even considered himself qualified to be a caliph. Al-Dhahabī (*Siyar*, x:78) alludes to this report but refuses to

Nevertheless, al-Shāfiᶜī is reported to have said that the reason he was arrested was because he criticized the governor of Yemen, who was a tyrant, and opposed the tyrant's injustices.[112] In any case, after the incident, al-Shāfiᶜī moved to Egypt, away from the center of politics in Irāq, and remained there until he died.

The caliph al-Rashīd remained worried about ᶜAlid sympathies and imprisoned or assassinated several members of the ᶜAlid family.[113] Most notably, he arrested Mūsā b. Jaᶜfar al-Kāẓim, the seventh Shīᶜī *imām*, in Medina, imprisoned him in Irāq, and eventually had him killed in 183/799[114] Al-Kāẓim was highly respected in his time and even later, Sunnī, sources mention him with considerable admiration and reverence.[115] Nevertheless, al-Rashīd's policy continued until his death.[116] The events that ensued from the time of his death and leading up

discuss it because, he says, it is a shameless lie. Of course, Abū Yūsuf could not have been involved in the incident because he was dead at the time (he died 183/799). The likelihood is that the report is a product of the later polemics between the Ḥanafī and Shāfiᶜī schools of thought, and that it was intended as anti-Ḥanafī propaganda. Other reports maintain that al-Shaybānī and al-Shāfiᶜī were good friends, and that al-Shaybānī used to lend or give books to al-Shāfiᶜī, a sign of great admiration in the legal culture. These various reports are in Ibn al-ᶜImād, *Shadharāt*, I:323. Ibn Aᶜtham (*al-Futūḥ*, IV:403–8) asserts that al-Rashīd had never heard of al-Shāfiᶜī when al-Shaybānī nominated him to take the position in Yemen. Al-Rashīd interviewed al-Shāfiᶜī who claimed to be knowledgeable in, among other things, law, medicine, and astronomy. Al-Shāfiᶜī then proceeded to give advice to al-Rashīd with such eloquence until al-Rāshīd burst into tears and, as a result, al-Rashīd appointed al-Shāfiᶜī to the post in Yemen. When al-Rashīd heard that al-Shāfiᶜī was supporting an ᶜAlid rebel, he became enraged and insisted on killing al-Shāfiᶜī (Ibn Aᶜtham comments that the accusation against al-Shāfiᶜī was simply untrue). In any case, al-Shaybānī interceded on behalf of al-Shāfiᶜī, arguing that if al-Rashīd killed al-Shāfiᶜī, people would most likely think that he (al-Shaybānī) was responsible for the execution. But al-Rashīd would not hear of it, and blamed al-Shaybānī for nominating al-Shāfiᶜī to the post in Yemen in the first place. When al-Shāfiᶜī was brought before al-Rashīd, al-Rashīd angrily interrogated him. Al-Shāfiᶜī defended himself by stating that everyone knew that the ᶜAlids expected the whole world to be their slaves, and it was highly implausible that he, a Qurayshī, would support an ᶜAlid. Al-Rashīd was impressed by this logic, and pardoned al-Shāfiᶜī. However, al-Rashīd insisted that before he did so, al-Shaybānī must get al-Shāfiᶜī to admit that a commitment made under duress is binding. Initially, al-Shāfiᶜī resisted, but eventually he gave in. Reportedly, al-Rashīd commanded al-Shāfiᶜī not to release people from commitments made under duress, and al-Shāfiᶜī responded, "Your order is my command." This report is too staged to be authentic.

112 Al-Ṣafadī, *Kitāb*, II:174.

113 See al-Iṣfahānī, *Maqātil*, 487–506; he lists eight prominent members.

114 Ibid., 499–505; Ibn al-Wardī, *Ta'rīkh*, I:197–8; Modarressi, *Crisis*, 10. Al-Masᶜūdī (*Murūj*, II:280) says he was killed in 186 AH.

115 For example, see Ibn Khallikān, *Wafayāt*, V:308–10; Ibn al-Jawzī, *Ṣifa*, II:508–10; Ibn al-Wardī, *Ta'rīkh*, I:197–8; Abū al-Fidā', *al-Mukhtaṣar*, I:318–19.

116 In 187 AH al-Rashīd also put to death his longtime minister Jaᶜfar b. Yaḥyā of the Barmakids. Reportedly, al-Rashīd executed him because, among other reasons, Jaᶜfar released the ᶜAlid Yaḥyā b. ᶜAbd Allāh b. al-Ḥasan from prison. The Barmakid family was becoming powerful and al-Rashīd feared that they would ally themselves with the ᶜAlids. Al-Rashīd hung Jaᶜfar's corpse on one bridge and his head on another in Baghdād. After a year or more, al-Rashīd had the body brought down and burned: Abū al-Fidā', *al-Mukhtaṣar*, I:319–21.

to the designation of ᶜAlī b. Mūsā al-Riḍā (d. 203/818), the eighth Shīᶜī *imām*, as heir apparent by the caliph al-Ma'mūn (r. 198/813–218/833), proved to be very significant for the development of the discourse on rebellion.

One of al-Rashīd's sons, al-Amīn (r. 193/809–198/813), became caliph immediately after his father's death. Before long, al-Ma'mūn, the governor of Khurāsān and al-Amīn's brother, rebelled. The resulting civil war was extremely violent, and led to the siege of Baghdād in 196/812. Al-Amīn armed the commoners of the city, often referred to as the *ᶜayyārūn* (vagabonds), and street-to-street fighting ensued; Baghdād was also blockaded and bombarded with mangonels. Even after al-Amīn was killed, fighting continued, and al-Ma'mūn was not able to enter Baghdād until 204/819.[117] During the chaos of these years, one of the most significant ᶜAlid rebellions broke out in Kūfa in 199/815. The bloody civil war resulted in a general state of insecurity and chaos.[118] According to some sources, a rumor spread that al-Faḍl b. Sahl, al-Ma'mūn's close advisor and military leader who was later killed by the caliph in 202/817,[119] had imprisoned al-Ma'mūn, and was the one in actual control. This encouraged some members of the ᶜAlid family to make another bid for power.[120] The rebellion was declared in the name of the pious ᶜAlid Muḥammad b. Ibrāhīm, known as Ibn Ṭabāṭabā, but its effective leader was Abū al-Sarāyā. The rebellion spread from Kūfa to Baṣra, Mecca, Medina, and Yemen, and reportedly, even the people of Syria were willing to give their allegiance to Ibn Ṭabāṭabā.[121] Abū al-Sarāyā was a former soldier who seemed to be in the habit of turning to banditry when he was not properly paid a salary.[122] It is not clear whether he or Ibn Ṭabāṭabā initiated the rebellion, yet in any case, Ibn Ṭabāṭabā died shortly after the rebellion started. The reason for Ibn Ṭabāṭabā's death is the subject of significant disagreement. When Abū al-Sarāyā defeated the ᶜAbbāsid partisan Zuhayr b. al-Musayyab, he

117 See Kennedy, *Prophet*, 148–52.

118 As a symptom of the chaos highway robbery and banditry spread, especially around Baghdād. Reportedly, many women and children were sold into slavery. See Abū al-Fidā', *al-Mukhtaṣar*, I:328.

119 Ibid., I:330.

120 Ibn al-Athīr, *al-Kāmil*, V:416; Ibn al-Jawzī, *al-Muntaẓam*, X:73–4; al-Ṭabarī, *Ta'rīkh*, VIII:590–1.

121 Al-Iṣfahānī, *Maqātil*, 534. The report about the people of Syria and their willingness to join the rebellion is doubtful. Nonetheless, the rebellion was quite widespread: see Ibn Qutayba, *al-Maᶜārif*, 387; Ibn Kathīr, *al-Bidāya*, X:255; al-Masᶜūdī, *Murūj*, II:345–6. It is reported that the rebels in Kūfa minted coins with their own markings. See al-Ṭabarī, *Ta'rīkh*, VIII:591.

122 Ibn al-Athīr, *al-Kāmil*, V:416; al-Ṭabarī, *Ta'rīkh*, VIII:592; Ibn Qutayba, *al-Maᶜārif*, 387. On the demand for salaries by soldiers and rebellion, see Kennedy, *Prophet*, 153.

reportedly slaughtered most of his soldiers, and captured weaponry, livestock, and much money. The amount of loot taken was considerable, and according to Sunnī sources, Ibn Ṭabāṭabā did not give Abū al-Sarāyā a fair share. Upset by the incident, and realizing that Ibn Ṭabāṭabā was in effective control, Abū al-Sarāyā had Ibn Ṭabāṭabā poisoned, and replaced him with someone whom Sunnī sources describe as a rebellious or insolent kid (*ghulām amrad*), Muḥammad b. Muḥammad b. Zayd.[123] Abū al-Faraj al-Iṣfahānī (d. 356/966) reports a very different version which reflects the influence of *aḥkām al-bughāh*. According to this version, Abū al-Sarāyā looted the camp of his enemy and divided the spoils of war. Ibn Ṭabāṭabā was already very ill, and when Abū al-Sarāyā came to him after the battle, he found Ibn Ṭabāṭabā very upset. Ibn Ṭabāṭabā condemned Abū al-Sarāyā's behavior and said, "You had no right to fight them without warning them first, and you had no right to take anything from [the enemy] other than their weaponry." Abū al-Sarāyā admitted his error, blamed the fervor of war, and promised never to repeat this conduct again.[124] It is quite possible that Ibn Ṭabāṭabā was, in fact, unhappy with Abū al-Sarāyā's conduct, but the language reported in this version is too tailored after the technical style of *aḥkām al-bughāh* to be historical. Significantly, however, the symbolism of ᶜAlī's conduct, as cast and presented by *aḥkām al-bughāh*, had sufficiently permeated the political polemics.

Interestingly, Sunnī sources insist that the ᶜAlid rebels dealt with the areas they conquered in a shameful fashion, and that this cost them the support of the people and contributed to their defeat. According to these reports, the ᶜAlid Ibrāhīm b. Mūsā became known as al-Jazzār (the butcher) because of the number of people that he killed in Yemen. He is also reported to have usurped much property and to have taken women captive. The ᶜAlid Ḥusayn b. Ḥasan al-Afṭas reportedly committed rape, usurped property, and even set up an area of torture known as the "House of Torture." Zayd b. Mūsā b. Jaᶜfar became known as Zayd al-Nār (Zayd of fire) because of all the ᶜAbbāsids and their properties he had burned in

[123] Ibn al-ᶜImād, *Shadharāt*, I:356; Ibn al-Jawzī, *al-Muntaẓam*, X:74; Ibn Qutayba, *al-Maᶜārif*, 388; Ibn al-Wardī, *Taʾrīkh*, I:202-3. In some reports it is not clear whether Ibn Ṭabāṭabā refused to distribute the loot at all or refused to give Abū al-Sarāyā a share. In either case, the people accepted Ibn Ṭabāṭabā's decision, and this motivated Abū al-Sarāyā to poison him. See al-Ṭabarī, *Taʾrīkh*, VIII:591; Ibn al-Athīr, *al-Kāmil*, V:417. Ibn Aᶜtham (*al-Futūḥ*, IV:448) states that al-Maʾmūn killed Ibn Ṭabāṭabā, but this is most likely a copyist's error.

[124] Al-Iṣfahānī, *Maqātil*, 534. This source also claims that Ibn Ṭabāṭabā died of natural causes and that Muḥammad b. Muḥammad was chosen by the ᶜAlid family: ibid., 532-3. Al-Yaᶜqūbī (*Taʾrīkh*, II:445) asserts that it was Abū al-Sarāyā who appointed Muḥammad b. Muḥammad.

Baṣra. When the ᶜAbbāsids defeated Abū al-Sarāyā in Kūfa and Baṣra, and the ᶜAlids realized that they had lost popular support in Mecca and Medina, they approached Muḥammad b. Jaᶜfar, who was highly respected and who had refrained from engaging in any of the abuses committed, and asked him to become their leader. After considerable pressure, he accepted and received the *bayᶜa* from the people of Mecca. Reportedly, he was nothing more than a figurehead, and the abuses in the areas under ᶜAlid control continued, which caused further deterioration in their popular support. In a few months, the ᶜAlids were defeated by al-Maʾmūn's forces, and Muḥammad b. Jaᶜfar was brought before a large audience in Mecca. He admitted that he was overcome by the temptations of *fitna*, abdicated his claim to the caliphate, and confessed the error of his ways.[125] He was allowed to die in peace; most of the rebels were killed in battle; and Abū al-Sarāyā was killed, mutilated, and then crucified.[126]

These events must have left a powerful and lasting impact on al-Maʾmūn. His reign had been engulfed in a serious civil war and a widespread ᶜAlid rebellion. Furthermore, the corporate culture of jurists had developed to the point of posing a serious threat to the caliph's authority as a law maker and executor. The juristic culture had developed a corpus of jurisprudence consisting of principles, opinions, and precedent that required a considerable degree of training and competence to master. It appears that al-Maʾmūn had fancied himself a *faqīh* (jurist) or an intellectual of sorts, and would make himself available to debate jurists on Tuesdays. In this context, when asked why he chose to stay in power, he is reported to have answered that he learned that whenever he neglected this role (the role of a caliph), chaos and civil discord spread (*thumma naẓartu fa-raʾaytu annī matā takhallaytu ᶜan al-Muslimīn . . . ghalaba*

[125] Al-Ṭabarī, *Taʾrīkh*, VIII:594–6; Ibn Kathīr, *al-Bidāya*, X:256–8; Ibn al-Jawzī, *al-Muntaẓam*, X:76, 84; Ibn al-Athīr, *al-Kāmil*, V:421-2. Al-Masᶜūdī (*Murūj*, II:346) says that Muḥammad b. Jaᶜfar called himself *amīr al-muʾminīn*, and that no one else from the ᶜAlids had ever adopted this title, before or afterwards (the ᶜAlids reserved this title for ᶜAlī himself). Al-Iṣfahānī (*Maqātil*, 534) mentions the legacy of Zayd al-Nār but omits the rest. Earlier, he implies that the alleged abuses are fabrications: see ibid., 518. However, see al-Yaᶜqūbī, *Taʾrīkh*, II:449, who records some of Zayd b. Mūsā's abuses. Ibn al-Wardī (*Taʾrīkh*, I:203) and Abū al-Fidāʾ (*al-Mukhtaṣar*, I:327) assert that Ibrāhīm b. Mūsā was called "the butcher" because of the number of people he slaughtered or enslaved.

[126] Al-Ṭabarī, *Taʾrīkh*, VIII:594; Ibn Kathīr, *al-Bidāya*, X:257; Ibn al-Athīr, *al-Kāmil*, V:421; al-Masᶜūdī, *Murūj*, II:347; Ibn al-ᶜImād, *Shadharāt*, I:358. The fact that Muḥammad b. Jaᶜfar died suddenly might mean that he was assassinated: see Ibn al-ᶜImād, *Shadharāt*, II:7; however, see Ibn al-Jawzī, *al-Muntaẓam*, X:121, who says that he died because he did too much for one day. See Ibn Qutayba, *al-Maᶜārif*, 389, who implies that Muḥammad b. Jaᶜfar and his family were killed.

al-harj wa al-fitna). He also claimed that he had no desire to rule but simply filled the void until someone else was found upon whom Muslims could agree. If they did, he would promptly abdicate his position.[127] Even if the report was highly exaggerated, it betrays a sense of insecurity and tentativeness about his reign and its legitimacy. But it also conveys a sense of detachment and objective distance that is more fitting for the culture of jurists, not caliphs.[128]

In 201/817, in order to remedy this sense of insecurity, al-Maʾmūn took a very daring step; he named the eighth Shīʿī *imām*, ʿAlī b. Mūsā al-Riḍā (d. 203/818), who was a highly honored scholar in his time, as his heir apparent.[129] He also married his daughter to al-Riḍā; ordered soldiers and state officials to wear green, the color of the ʿAlids, as opposed to black, the color of the ʿAbbāsids; and minted coins in al-Riḍā's name.[130] This was designed to bolster his position *vis-à-vis* the religious scholars, and strengthen his political legitimacy as well.[131] However, this development alarmed the ʿAbbāsid family which reacted by leading a rebellion in Baghdād, and naming Ibrāhīm b. al-Mahdī as the new caliph.[132] In 203/818, al-Riḍā died under mysterious circumstances,

[127] Al-Masʿūdī, *Murūj*, II:341. Al-Atābakī (*al-Nujūm*, II:225) says that al-Maʾmūn was educated in religious sciences and mastered Ḥanafī jurisprudence. Ibn al-ʿImād (*Shadharāt*, II:39) says that the caliph made many contributions to scholarship.

[128] See al-Yaʿqūbī, *Taʾrīkh*, II:468, where al-Maʾmūn demonstrates his competence over technical points of law, and chides the jurists for their failure to understand or apply technical rules of procedure. Zaman (*Religion*, 111–12) notes that al-Maʾmūn seemed to claim for himself the type of authority that a Sunnī jurist claims.

[129] Modarressi, *Crisis*, 11; Kennedy, *Prophet* 153–4. ʿAlī al-Riḍā had reportedly chided his brother Zayd b. Mūsā for his conduct towards the people of Baṣra. This pleased al-Maʾmūn and he commented, "This is how the family of the Prophet should behave." See Ibn al-ʿImād, *Shadharāt*, II:6; Ibn Khallikān, *Wafayāt*, III:271.

[130] Al-Yaʿqūbī, *Taʾrīkh*, II:448; Ibn al-ʿImād, *Shadharāt*, II:2; al-Masʿūdī, *Murūj*, II:347; Ibn Khallikān, *Wafayāt*, III:270; Ibn al-Athīr, *al-Kāmil*, V:431–2; Ibn al-Jawzī, *al-Muntaẓam*, X:93–4.

[131] It is possible, as some have argued, that al-Maʾmūn genuinely held a certain affinity to Shīʿism, and was not simply opportunistic in his policies. See, for example, Sourdel, "La politique." But even if true, this does not mean that this was the sole motivation for his policies. Al-Maʾmūn had to figure out a way to balance competing political and religious interests, all with their own separate demands and burdens. Among the many considerations was the prevalent reverence given to the family of the Prophet and their descendants. The painful events that surrounded Abū al-Sarāyā's rebellion must have somewhat weakened the popularity of the ʿAlid cause; it is not clear how much actual leverage al-Maʾmūn gained from his close association with al-Riḍā. Furthermore, assuming that al-Maʾmūn was sincere in his ʿAlid sympathies, contrary to what Sourdel contends, this hardly explains his decision to adopt Muʿtazilī ideas and initiate the inquisition. Recently some scholars argued that al-Maʾmūn was more of a Jahmī than a Muʿtazilī. See Hinds, "Miḥna"; Van Ess, "Une Lecture"; Van Ess, "Ibn Kullāb." The Jahmī believed that God was the creator of all acts and believed in predestination. See, on this sect, al-Shahrastānī, *al-Milal*, I:97–9; al-Baghdādī, *al-Farq*, 158–9. It is likely that al-Maʾmūn came under Jahmite influence while in Khurāsān. This is hardly surprising, however, since al-Maʾmūn was a syncretist, and, at times, eclectic.

[132] Abū al-Fidāʾ (*al-Mukhtaṣar*, I:328) reports that al-Riḍā's nomination to the caliphate aroused considerable popular opposition in Baghdād.

and al-Ma'mūn started his year-long march to conquer Baghdād and oust the rebel caliph. In 204/819, al-Ma'mūn and his soldiers took off their green clothing and dressed in black again.[133]

The series of events that followed led to the *miḥna* (inquisition) – al-Ma'mūn's confrontation with a considerable number of jurists, judges, and the transmitters of the Prophet's *Sunna*. In 210/825, al-Ma'mūn had Ibrāhīm b. Muḥammad, known as Ibn ᶜĀ'isha, killed and crucified for a suspected plot to overthrow the caliph. Ibn ᶜĀ'isha was the great-grandson of the man in whose name the ᶜAbbāsid revolution started. This was the first ᶜAbbāsid to be crucified,[134] and it further emphasized al-Ma'mūn's intellectual, and political, distance from the ᶜAbbāsid elite. A year later, al-Ma'mūn publicly disavowed the caliph Muᶜāwiya, and proclaimed ᶜAlī's superiority to Muᶜāwiya.[135] A little over a year later, in 212/827, al-Ma'mūn's intellectual wanderings led him to publicly adopt the Muᶜtazilī position of the createdness of the Qur'ān.[136] Al-Ma'mūn did, in fact, have close associations with prominent Muᶜtazilī scholars.[137] Both al-Ma'mūn's teacher, Abū al-Hudhayl al-ᶜAllāf (d. 228/842), and his chief judge and close advisor, Aḥmad b. Abī Du'ād (d. 240/854), were Muᶜtazilī scholars.[138] However, many of al-Ma'mūn's views did not necessarily correspond to the Muᶜtazilī creed. Rather, his views seem to have been syncretistic and to fall somewhere between Shīᶜī and Muᶜtazilī ideas.[139] Reportedly, al-Ma'mūn had even declared himself a Murji'ī on occasion.[140]

The doctrine of the createdness of the Qur'ān maintained that the Qur'ān was neither eternal nor coexistent with God. Rather, it was created by God in response to the circumstances and context of the Prophet.[141] There are clear political connotations to this doctrine. If the

[133] It is very likely that al-Riḍā was poisoned to death, but there is disagreement in the sources on whether it was al-Ma'mūn himself who ordered al-Riḍā's death, or whether it was another member of the ᶜAbbāsid family. See al-Yaᶜqūbī, *Ta'rīkh*, II:453–4; Ibn al-ᶜImād, *Shadharāt*, II:6, 9; Ibn al-Athīr, *al-Kāmil*, V:448; Ibn Khallikān, *Wafayāt*, III:270; al-Masᶜūdī, *Murūj*, II:347; Ibn al-Jawzī, *al-Muntaẓam*, X:120.

[134] Al-Masᶜūdī, *Murūj*, II:352–3; al-Yaᶜqūbī, *Ta'rīkh*, II:459; Ibn al-Athīr, *al-Kāmil*, V:475.

[135] Ibn al-ᶜImād, *Shadharāt*, II:25.

[136] Ibn al-ᶜImād (ibid., 27) notes that this proclamation, coupled with the one from the previous year, repulsed people. This, of course, could be after-the-fact Sunnī apologetics.

[137] Ibn al-Jawzī, *Manāqib*, 386.

[138] See al-Dīnawarī, *al-Akhbār*, 396; Kennedy, *Prophet*, 164; Nawas, "Reexamination," 616. Kennedy draws attention to the fact that Muᶜtazilī thought had become the creed of the Sāmarrā elite that surrounded the caliph. The ᶜAbbāsid caliph al-Muᶜtaṣim later declared Sāmarrā the capital of his empire: Kennedy, *Prophet*, 163–4.

[139] Ibn al-ᶜImād (*Shadharāt*, II:39) calls him a Muᶜtazilī/Shīᶜī. Also see Nawas, "Reexamination," 616–19.

[140] Nawas, "Reexamination," 617.

[141] Al-Bayhaqī, *Risāla*, 86–7.

Qurʾān is circumstantial, then a just ruler may limit its rulings to its specific context. Arguably, the ruler would have the power to override some of its contextual rulings, and legislate as he saw fit.[142] Nonetheless, it would be dangerous to read too much into this aspect of the Muʿtazilī doctrine. The Muʿtazila also argued in favor of a right to rebellion against an unjust ruler,[143] and this would have been problematic for al-Maʾmūn, who insisted on an absolute right to obedience.[144] Furthermore, the doctrine of the createdness of the Qurʾān was widely debated at the time, and was not exclusively held by the Muʿtazila.[145]

THE INQUISITION AND THE CLASH WITH JURISTS

In 218/833, al-Maʾmūn instituted the *miḥna* under which he proclaimed the createdness of the Qurʾān as the formal doctrine of the state. He ordered that judges, jurists, *ḥadīth* specialists, and public officials be tested, and if they failed to accept the formal doctrine they, depending on the person in question, would be dismissed, banned from teaching or issuing legal opinions, tortured, or killed.[146] According to orders reportedly drafted by al-Maʾmūn, he was protecting religion from the ignorant innovators who had corrupted it. This purportedly referred to the proponents of the uncreatedness of the Qurʾān. Yet the *miḥna* had little to do with the doctrine of the createdness or uncreatedness of the Qurʾān. It was more about the role of institutions than about theological dogma. Al-Maʾmūn attacked those who claimed that they represented the true orthodoxy, and considered themselves the guardians of the truth. The rhetorical attacks were directed at the jurists and their emerging institutions. Al-Maʾmūn contended that these pretenders (the jurists) claimed that whoever opposed them was an impious heretic (*thumma aẓharū . . . annahum ahl al-ḥaqq wa al-dīn wa al-jamāʿa wa anna man siwāhum ahl al-bāṭil wa al-kufr*).[147] His edicts also contained personal attacks directed at many jurists accusing them of corruption and hypocrisy. Al-Maʾmūn accused many jurists of ignorance, dishonesty, and unbecoming conduct.[148] This is hardly

142 Kennedy, *Prophet*, 163; also see Lapidus, "Separation."

143 See al-Bayhaqī, *Risāla*, 97, where he also accuses the non-Muʿtazila of inventing traditions demanding blind obedience to the ruler.

144 Nawas, "Reexamination," 621.

145 Ibid., 617.

146 Ibn al-Athīr, *al-Kāmil*, VI:3–6; al-Ṭabarī, *Taʾrīkh*, VIII:643–7; al-Atābakī, *al-Nujūm*, II:221; Ibn Kathīr, *al-Bidāya*, X:284–6; Ibn al-Jawzī, *al-Muntaẓam*, XI:15, 20.

147 Al-Ṭabarī, *Taʾrīkh*, VIII:642; al-Atābakī, *al-Nujūm*, II:219; Ibn al-Jawzī, *al-Muntaẓam*, XI:17.

148 Al-Ṭabarī, *Taʾrīkh*, VIII:647; Ibn al-Jawzī, *al-Muntaẓam*, XI:23; Ibn al-Athīr, *al-Kāmil*, VI:5; al-Atābakī, *al-Nujūm*, II:221. Reportedly, al-Maʾmūn told one of the jurists, "Aren't you the one

surprising because the *miḥna* was an attack on the corporate culture of jurists and, more importantly, on the corpus of jurisprudence that they had constructed, and on which they were uniquely qualified to speak.[149] As discussed above, al-Maʾmūn had come to power after a bloody civil war in which he defeated his brother, and shortly thereafter confronted several serious ʿAlid rebellions. He continued to experiment with various bases of legitimacy, and at the same time apparently perceived himself to have the technical competence that jurists possessed over the accumulating corpus, not just of *ḥadīth*, but of principles, rulings, and precedents. The inquisition was al-Maʾmūn's attempt to assert his own theological and legal authority over the assertive and, at times, aggressive juridical culture.

One of the most famous victims of the inquisition was Aḥmad b. Ḥanbal (d. 241/855) who, as discussed later, with the collaboration of *ahl al-ḥadīth*, insisted on an absolute prohibition against armed rebellion. Unlike the Muʿtazila, Ibn Ḥanbal argued that obedience is due to a ruler, just or unjust, unless one is ordered to commit a grave sin. Even then, one ought passively to accept torture or death, but not rebel.[150] But this was hardly sufficient for al-Maʾmūn. He did not merely want passive obedience by the jurists; he wanted inclusion. It is doubtful that al-Maʾmūn desired either to subjugate or replace the culture of jurists. As noted earlier, al-Maʾmūn was fond of demonstrating his juristic prowess. Furthermore, even after the commencement of the inquisition, he continued to surround himself with Muʿtazilī jurists. Rather, he wanted to be recognized as a legal authority by the juristic culture, and to share the interpretive and legislative legitimacy of the jurists. Jurists may recognize regulations and administrative edicts issued by rulers as law, but not necessarily as jurisprudence. The regulations and edicts of *siyāsa* (political

who told *amīr al-muʾminīn* [i.e. al-Maʾmūn] [in the past], you [i.e. the caliph] [have the power to] make things legal or illegal (*alasta al-qāʾil li amīri al-muʾminīna innaka tuḥallilu wa tuḥarrim*)?" It is not clear from the context what is the intended meaning of the statement. Possibly al-Maʾmūn was using this as evidence that the jurist was a hypocrite because he conceded a power to the caliph that the caliph should not have. It is more likely al-Maʾmūn was confronting the jurist with his past admission that the caliph should, in fact, have this power. Since the caliph had now decreed the doctrine of the uncreatedness of the Qurʾān to be illegal, there was no reason that this jurist should not obey.

149 See Nawas, "Reexamination," 619–24; Zaman, *Religion*, 106–18; Crone and Hinds, *God's*, 93–6; Lapidus, "Separation."

150 Ibn Ḥanbal was tortured and imprisoned for his refusal to admit that the Qurʾān was created. There are no reports that he ever got involved in or sympathized with an armed rebellion. See Gibb and Kramers, eds., *Shorter*, 20–1. Ibn Ḥanbal's doctrine of obedience and rejection of armed rebellion was used by some of his supporters to defend him before the political authorities during the inquisition. See Ibn Ḥanbal, *Sira*, 39.

organs) do not carry precedential value unless sanctioned, authenticated, and incorporated by the jurists. These regulations and edicts are treated as positive legal commands that serve a functional purpose for a certain period of time. However, they are not considered to be a part of the normative *Sharīʿa* or the *de jure* law of God.

THE SURVIVAL AND ENTRENCHMENT OF THE JURISTIC CULTURE

Al-Maʾmūn did not live long enough to see the results of the inquisition; he died a few months after it was instituted. But ultimately, it was a complete failure because it was unable to negotiate with or reformulate the nature of the dynamics with the juridical culture.[151] At the time al-Maʾmūn put the *miḥna* into effect, the vast majority of jurists acquiesced and gave the caliph the admission he wanted. Only a few die-hard traditionists or jurists, such as Aḥmad b. Ḥanbal, refused to compromise and suffered the consequences.[152] Reportedly, the jurists who compromised relied on the interpretation of the Qurʾānic verse: "Anyone who, after accepting faith, utters [words of] unbelief, except under compulsion . . . on them will be God's anger and they will receive a dreadful penalty."[153] Therefore, the jurists reasoned, since they were acting under duress, they could give al-Maʾmūn the confession he sought without being liable in the Hereafter.[154] Although this was hardly an example of complex legal analysis, the legal culture of the jurists was sufficiently formed to permit them to rely on the technicalities and loopholes of law in order to respond to a non-legal issue. Al-Maʾmūn confronted the jurists with a theological, perhaps moral, problem, and they responded

[151] The inquisition was officially stopped in 234/857 during the reign of al-Mutawakkil (r. 232/847–247/861). In fact, the doctrine of the creation of the Qurʾān was banned. See Gibb and Kramers, eds., *Shorter*, 377–8.

[152] Ibn al-ʿImād, *Shadharāt*, II:39; al-Atābakī, *al-Nujūm*, II:224; al-Ṭabarī, *Taʾrīkh*, VIII:648; Ibn al-Athīr, *al-Kāmil*, VI:5; Ibn al-Jawzī, *al-Muntaẓam*, XI:24; Ibn Kathīr, *al-Bidāya*, X:286; al-Yaʿqūbī, *Taʾrīkh*, II:468. Ibn Aʿtham (*al-Futūḥ*, IV:454–5) and Ibn al-Wardī (*Taʾrīkh*, I:211–12) claim that after torture all the jurists except Ibn Ḥanbal and another jurist acquiesced. Ibn Ḥanbal was also tortured by the ʿAbbāsid caliph al-Muʿtaṣim (r. 218/833–227/842). For the details of Ibn Ḥanbal's long torment and perseverance during the *miḥna*, see Ibn al-Jawzī, *Manāqib*, 387–430; Ibn Ḥanbal, *Sīra*, 32–47. Reportedly, al-Muʿtaṣim hesitated before torturing Ibn Ḥanbal, and brought a group of jurists to debate him. Among other things, Ibn Ḥanbal was accused of being a heretical innovator (*muḍill mubtadiʿ*): see Ibn Ḥanbal, *Sīra*, 38.

[153] Qurʾān 16:106.

[154] Al-Ṭabarī, *Taʾrīkh*, VIII:648–9; Ibn al-Athīr, *al-Kāmil*, VI:5–6; Ibn Kathīr, *al-Bidāya*, X:286. These sources are careful to point out that the jurists were wrong in their interpretation, and that the cited verse does not excuse the dissimulation in this situation. But see Ibn al-Wardī, *Taʾrīkh*, I:211.

with a legal solution. Al-Maʾmūn, if he had lived longer, would not have joined the ranks of jurists because he was primarily a politician, and while the cultures of law and politics often cooperate, they frequently clash, limiting and restraining each other.

As Crone and Hinds argue, a confrontation between the caliphal authority and the jurists was long in the making before the time of al-Maʾmūn. As the culture of the jurists increasingly claimed the right to interpret the divine will, the juristic and moral authority of the caliphs became increasingly constrained. Significantly, Crone and Hinds contend that the jurist al-Shāfiᶜī played a major role in the development of this confrontation, as he sought to take religious authority from the caliphs and place it in the community at large, and in the *Sunna* of the Prophet. The scholarly concept of the Prophetic *Sunna* threatened to displace caliphal authority, as it, and not the caliph, became the arbiter of law and authority. In the colorful language of these authors, "If al-Maʾmūn had not sensed where things were going, al-Shāfiᶜī spelt this out for him in no uncertain terms: the caliph was a mere executor of the law chosen by the community. But al-Shāfiᶜī's views were simply nails in the caliphal coffin."[155] While conceding that the introduction of the *miḥna* had more to do with problems of legitimacy than with al-Shāfiᶜī's thoughts, the authors argue that the confrontation between the sacred law and caliphal authority had come to a high point.[156] The jurists and the caliphs were rival representatives of God's law, and ultimately, the jurists won. The jurists became the representatives of the divine law and the caliphs its mere executors.[157]

Some scholars such as Muhammad Zaman take issue with this analysis and, basically, argue that other than the interregnum of the *miḥna*, there had been no conflict between the jurists and caliphs. Citing many examples of patronage between the early ᶜAbbāsids and the jurists, Zaman argues that collaboration, and not confrontation, was the earmark of the relationship between the jurists and the caliphs.[158] According to Zaman, there was never a divorce between religion and politics, and the early ᶜAbbāsid caliphs never lost their authority over religious or

[155] Crone and Hinds, *God's*, 93.

[156] Ibid. Supporting Crone and Hinds' argument is the fact that Ibn Ḥanbal's torment is often mentioned as one example, among many, of jurists who were unjustly persecuted by political authorities in Islamic history. See Ibn al-Jawzī, *Manāqib*, 422–3. In fact, suffering and persecution became a sort of *topos* proving the integrity and prominence of a jurist. See Abū Ghuddah, *Ṣafaḥāt*.

[157] Crone and Hinds, *God's*, 110.

[158] Zaman, *Religion*, 118.

legal matters.[159] In fact, they continued to adjudicate cases and cooperate with the jurists to enforce orthodoxy.[160] Importantly, the ʿAbbāsid caliphs came to rely on the jurists to enhance their own legitimacy, and enforced an extensive system of patronage which rewarded the jurists for their cooperation.[161] Significantly, the author argues that the legitimacy of the ʿAbbāsids, when they first came to power was, in fact, problematic. The author asserts that by that time, political quietism had not yet become established doctrine and, therefore, in the mid-second century, many jurists did join the rebellion of al-Nafs al-Zakiyya. Nonetheless, the ʿAbbāsids pursued a policy of severe retribution against jurists who dared join a rebellion, and concurrently they generously rewarded jurists who cooperated with the regime. The result, Zaman argues, was prevalent quietism among what he calls proto-Sunnī jurists. Zaman concedes that there were moments of mutual distrust and conflict but that ultimately quietism became the established doctrine among proto-Sunnī jurists.[162] His analysis stumbles a bit when it comes to the *miḥna,* but basically he argues that it was cooperation and collaboration between the jurists and the caliphs that prevailed after the *miḥna.*

To the extent that Crone and Hinds overstate their case, I believe that Zaman is justified in his criticisms. Zaman produces a convincing body of evidence proving the existence of a system of patronage and collaboration between the jurists and the early ʿAbbāsids. He is also correct in concluding that the argument of some, such as Thomas Nagel, that the *ahl al-sunna* continued to view the ʿAbbāsids with passionate hostility well into the late second and early third century, is implausible.[163] Nonetheless, while Crone and Hinds' claims about a division between religion and politics are perhaps exaggerated, Zaman ignores the particularity of legal culture and its logic. Once a legal culture develops and a cumulative corpus of legal doctrines and precedent is formed, the tendency is to uphold the integrity and independence of that corpus. This is why, for example, while caliphs continued to adjudicate cases after the *miḥna,* the books of jurisprudence do not, for the most part, incorporate or cite the decisions of these caliphs. In the eyes of Sunnī jurists, rulers rarely reached the point of sufficient competence in the technicalities of law, such that the adjudications of these rulers became part of the official corpus of legal culture. It is not a coincidence that other than the four

159 Ibid., 70. 160 Ibid., 106, 118.
161 Ibid., 156–7, 167–9, 185. 162 Ibid., 70–106. 163 Ibid., 192.

Rightly Guided Caliphs and the Umayyad caliph ʿUmar b. ʿAbd al-ʿAzīz, one will rarely find the caliphs cited in legal hornbooks or in the *fatāwā* literature. Whenever a caliph is cited, he is invariably cast in the role of the inquirer, and a jurist is cast in the role of the responder. We already saw several examples of this in the context of the verses on *baghy* and *ḥirāba*. This, of course, does not mean that a ruler, in his lifetime, is denied the right to adjudicate cases or resolve disputes. But he does so as an outsider to the legal field.[164] Very much like any other developed technical field, specialists such as jurists cite and rely on other specialists. This does not mean that they are not influenced by the demands of politics or society; far from it. Rather, the perceived political and social demands are channeled through the structures and linguistic practice of the legal culture, and are often reconstructed, or at times deformed and mutilated, in the process. It is through the particularities, details, and technicalities of the legal practice that jurists often express cooperation or resistance to political or social demands.

More importantly for our purposes, Zaman's arguments about juridical quietism are unpersuasive. I argued earlier that assertions about juristic quietism are hopelessly ambiguous and quite meaningless. As asserted earlier, once a legal culture develops to a point of becoming institutionalized, the natural inclination of juridical culture is towards stability, law, and order. It is the willingness to engage in an armed rebellion that needs to be explained, and not the desire for order and stability. It is extremely difficult to discharge the necessary functions of law or resolve disputes in an orderly fashion if chaos and anarchy are prevalent. Early Muslim jurists, as demonstrated above, did engage in several rebellions as the corporate culture of jurists was developing. Quietism, however, did not prevail after the mid-second century, as Zaman argues. Rather, the terms of the discourse changed to reflect the emerging

[164] Crone and Hinds (*God's*, 109) state:

> But rulers were obeyed as outsiders to the community, not as representatives of it, except (in Islam) in their performance of ritual duties such as leadership of the prayer or conduct of *jihād*, the latter being an activity particularly apt to restore moral continuity between the ruler and his subjects. The state was thus something which sat on top of society, not something which was rooted in it; and given that there was minimal interaction between the two, there was also minimal political development: dynasties came and went, but it was only the dynasties that changed.

This is true to the extent that jurists indulge in the delusion that they represent the community. Whether or not rulers were allowed to be rooted in the community is not the appropriate question. I would argue that rulers were not allowed to be rooted in the legal culture of the jurists.

sophistication of the legal culture. In the tradition of the best jurists, the topic of rebellion became replete with legal distinctions and technical particulars.

QUIETISM, ACTIVISM, AND LEGAL TECHNICALITIES

We shall deal with the technicalities and linguistic practice of the juridical discourse in the following chapters. Before doing so, it is important to elaborate upon the idea of quietism and the transition to a technical discourse. In order to demonstrate the point, I will focus primarily on a couple of examples. We already discussed the example of Aḥmad b. Ḥanbal, who rejected any right to rebellion, but who steadfastly refused to obey the caliph's orders on the creation of the Qur'ān. It is debatable whether his position can be described as quietist.[165] For example, are those who refuse to obey what they believe to be an illegal order, and consequently are arrested and tortured, quietist or activist?[166]

But beyond Ibn Ḥanbal's example, consider the case of Sufyān al-Thawrī (d. 161/778), who is reportedly "known for his strict quietism."[167] Al-Thawrī refused to join the rebellion of al-Nafs al-Zakiyya and is not reported to have joined any other rebellion. Yet historical reports have transformed him into a juristic folk hero of sorts.[168] Al-Thawrī, like many other jurists, saw himself as a doctor whose job was to nurse people to good health. Reports often cast him in the role of the living conscience of society, and the mouthpiece of the truth.[169] He steadfastly refused to accept a judicial position and seems to have made the criticism of caliphs, such as al-Manṣūr and al-Mahdī, a regular habit.[170] For example, he continued to malign the caliph al-Manṣūr until the caliph vowed to have him killed, and in fact sent an agent to Mecca to have him crucified. Al-Thawrī's response was not only to go into hiding but also to swear to disavow the Kaᶜba if al-Manṣūr ever entered Mecca.

165 Al-Atābakī (*al-Nujūm*, II:221), for example, claims that if it had not been for Ibn Ḥanbal's principled stand, many people would have been led astray. One can only guess whether he would have left a larger impact if he had risen in an armed rebellion. Also see Ibn Kathīr, *al-Bidāya*, X:351.

166 ᶜAthāmina, "Ulamā'," contains useful information on contentious dynamics between the jurists and rulers.

167 Zaman, *Religion*, 185.

168 Al-Dhahabī (*Siyar*, VII:241) says he was slightly influenced by Shīᶜī ideas (*wa fīhī tashayyuᶜ yasīr*). On Sufyān al-Thawrī and his reported Shīᶜī sympathies, see al-Iṣfahānī, *Maqātil*, 415–16. Al-Thawrī reportedly sympathized with ᶜĪsā b. Zayd who advocated rebellion against al-Mahdī.

169 Al-Dhahabī, *Siyar*, VII:243.

170 Al-Ṣafadī, *Kitāb*, XV:280. Al-Dhahabī (*Siyar*, VII:242) asserts that he would criticize rulers (*al-mulūk*), but rejected rebellion.

Fortunately for al-Thawrī, al-Manṣūr died shortly thereafter.[171] An oath to disavow the Kaʿba for political reasons is a rather powerful moral and legal precedent.

When al-Mahdī took power, he asked al-Thawrī to accept a judicial position, and informed him that he was free to judge according to the Qurʾān and *Sunna.* Al-Thawrī again refused. When friends asked him why he refused to accept the position when the caliph had given him license to apply the Qurʾān and *Sunna,* he is reported to have scoffed at the pettiness of their intellect, or their naiveté, and escaped to Baṣra,[172] where he continued to attack and malign al-Mahdī.[173] In another report, al-Thawrī entered the presence of al-Mahdī, and addressed him rudely. The caliph's agent chided al-Thawrī: "You address *amīr al-muʾminīn* [the Commander of the Faithful] in this fashion, and you are a [lowly] man from Thawr." Al-Thawrī responded: "A man from Thawr who obeys God is better than a man from your folk who disobeys God."[174] Al-Thawrī is also reported to have mediated a marital dispute between al-Mahdī and his wife. Al-Mahdī, over his wife's objections, wanted to take a second wife. Al-Thawrī's mediation was requested, and he ruled in favor of al-Mahdī's wife. He argued that since al-Mahdī was not an equitable person, he would not treat his wives justly, and therefore he could not take a second wife.[175] Obviously, there is a not-so-subtle condemnation of al-Mahdī's character in this report. In yet another widely cited report, al-Thawrī was brought before al-Mahdī. Al-Thawrī refused to greet al-Mahdī as caliphs are greeted, and instead greeted him as a commoner. Al-Mahdī smiled indulgently, and said: "You keep hiding from us here and there, and you think that if we wished to harm you, we could not. Here, we have caught you now, don't you fear that we will do with you as we please?" Al-Thawrī responded: "You may do with me as you wish, and a powerful Lord [i.e. God], who distinguishes between truth and falsehood, will judge you [as He wishes]." The caliph's agent offered to have al-Thawrī killed, saying: "Oh, Commander of the Faithful, can this ignorant person address you in this [insolent] fashion! Let me strike his head." Al-Mahdī responded: "Be silent, [may God] confound you! Do people like him want anything other than that we would kill them so that their happiness becomes our misery? No, assign him to the

[171] Ibn al-ʿImād, *Shadharāt,* I:250; al-Dhahabī, *Siyar,* VII:251.
[172] Al-Dhahabī, *Siyar,* VII:262. [173] See, for example, ibid., 244, 264.
[174] Ibn Khallikān, *Wafayāt,* II:388. [175] Ibid., 389.

judgeship of Kūfa, and let no one overturn his judgments." Al-Thawrī took the caliph's letter of appointment, discarded it in the Tigris river, and went into hiding until he died.[176]

Clearly, these reports have the earmarks of folk tales; they are constructed exaggerations but with a kernel of truth. Something about al-Thawrī's legacy captured the popular, or perhaps even the juristic, imagination which then reasserted his legacy into symbols of valor and uprightness. Nothing, not even the Kaᶜba or the hope of applying the Qur'ān and *Sunna*, would tempt him to compromise. These could be transformed into powerful and even dangerous legal precedents. From the point of view of juristic culture, can one say that he was a strict quietist, or that his legacy was one of strict quietism? The answer is yes, but only if one is willing to claim that the only form of possible juristic activism is armed rebellion. Jurists could adopt a militant stance, join armed rebellions, be killed, and leave the rest to the popular imagination. Alternatively, they could express dissent and, at times, subversion through the medium of their own legal culture. Take al-Shāfiᶜī for example. As discussed above, he was involved in a rebellion, but then settled in Egypt and proceeded to develop a discourse on rebellion that was expressed through the technical categorizations and distinctions of law. In a fashion, this is quietist. But from a different perspective, he set a discourse in motion that continued to play a dynamic and tension-filled role well into the modern age. Ibn Taymiyya, as we saw, even accused him and those who preceded him or followed in his footsteps of suborning rebellion and spreading *fitna*. One can argue that juristic discourse and culture are an anomaly, and are largely irrelevant to what or how people go about their lives. This could very well be true. But it is the juristic discourse that is often blamed for becoming quietist. To be consistent, one would have to argue that whether jurists are quietist or not is largely irrelevant to the anthropology of society. One cannot focus on juristic culture to prove a point about quietism, but then ignore the relevance of the technicalities and idiosyncrasies of that legal culture.

There is no doubt that early Islamic juristic culture produced many traditions counseling against *fitna* and advocating law and order. Even Jaᶜfar al-Ṣādiq, the sixth Shīᶜī *imām*, rejected the use of force and armed rebellion against those in power.[177] This is hardly surprising considering

[176] Al-Masᶜūdī, *Murūj*, II:255; Ibn al-ᶜImād, *Shadharāt*, I:250–1; Ibn Khallikān, *Wafayāt*, II:390–1; al-Ṣafadī, *Kitāb*, XV:280.

[177] Modarressi, *Crisis*, 8–9. However, as discussed above, there were a large number of ᶜAlid rebellions. For an extensive list, see al-Ḥasanī, *al-Intifāḍāt*.

the scale of rebellions and civil violence in early Islam, and considering the juristic predisposition towards order and stability. The more the corporate identity of the jurists and their culture developed, the more they became vested, not necessarily in the political regime in power, but in the cultural institutions of society, and in the corollary need for stability. Nonetheless, as we have seen, some of the most notable individuals in Islamic history have either supported or sympathized with rebellions. This included Companions of the Prophet and later jurists. For better or worse, their actions became legal precedents that needed to be incorporated, followed or distinguished, and even perhaps discarded. But considering the extent of the rebellions or the opposition to government in which jurists were frequently involved, to paraphrase Crone and Hinds, the rules of law as articulated by jurists "were frequently and indeed intentionally unhelpful to the state."[178] It is exactly this point that explains the rise of *aḥkām al-bughāh* in Islam, and to that we turn next.

[178] Crone and Hinds, *God's*, 91. The authors maintain that it was the rules of the *Sunna* that were unhelpful to the state. I do not share their views on the *Sunna*. It was a raw body of uninterpreted and undeveloped precedents. It is the legal interpretation of the *Sunna*, and not the *Sunna* itself, that was unhelpful to the state.

CHAPTER 4

The rise of the juristic discourse on rebellion: fragmentation

TERROR AND THE JURIDICAL RESPONSE

In the first two centuries of Islam, the jurists witnessed numerous occasions where Muslims fought each other. While it would be inaccurate to assert that the Umayyads or the early ʿAbbāsids were considered illegitimate,[1] there were several rebellions that attracted the sympathy or participation of some of the most notable jurists. Nonetheless, the issue of rebellion could not be approached dogmatically. It was not a simple matter of declaring one party good and the other evil. Jurists had to live and work within the emerging institutions of society. Furthermore, rebellions, which often elicited cruel and swift vengeance by the caliphs, served as reminders of the evils of *fitan*, and also of the ability of the rulers to apply raw power and force when they deemed it necessary. This was taking place at a time when the corporate and institutional identity of the jurists was developing. Of course, the caliphs claimed the power of the sword and God to their side. But jurists wished to claim the power of legality to their own side. They, in other words, would become the authoritative bearers of lawfulness – the lawful invocation of the sword and God.

The *miḥna* was symptomatic of this process. In a sense, whether the jurists won the battle of the inquisition or not depends on how one looks at the matter. In the short term the vast majority gave in to the caliph's demands and admitted whatever the caliph wanted. But they did not do so by yielding their power to define lawfulness or concede the

[1] There is no question that this matter differed from place to place. The Kūfans, for instance, did not recognize the legitimacy of the Umayyads while the rank-and-file Syrians, perhaps, did. Ḥijāz (Mecca and Medina), to a large extent, remained anti-Umayyad. The vast anecdotal anti-Umayyad literature demonstrates the ambiguity surrounding the legitimacy of the Umayyads. In fact, the large number of *ḥadīth* about the obligatory nature of obedience to unjust rulers seems to indicate that these rulers were often looked at as illegitimate, but, nevertheless, had to be obeyed.

terms of the discourse to the caliph. They did so by declaring the accommodation of the caliph to be a temporary exception brought about by unlawful compulsion. Far from being quietist, unprincipled, or opportunistic, it was an inventive and wonderfully technical way to obey and disobey the caliph all at once.[2] This was also precisely why rulers perceived the legal discourses on duress with much suspicion, which at times resulted in repression.[3] Al-Ma'mūn, of course, by instituting the inquisition, entirely missed the point. If the inquisition was instituted to humble and subdue the juristic culture, in the long term it did not produce many concrete results. The juristic culture was too developed by this time to be substantially affected by politically motivated theological dogma. The jurists had developed their own methodology for discovering the divine will, and hence the jurists continued to be the enunciators, on God's behalf, of lawfulness. This should not be seen as a dogmatic one-sided relationship; the jurists did not become God's representatives on earth, with that being the end of the story. Rather, it should be perceived as a reciprocal and dialectical process of accommodation and resistance. Muslim jurists accommodated and

[2] Creative acts of resistance to challenging conditions often make assessments about which side won a particular conflict unhelpful. For instance, it would make little sense to argue that Sunnī Muslims have ultimately won the battle against Shīʿī Muslims because Shīʿī Muslims have had to adopt, at times, the practice of dissimulation (*taqiyya*). In fact, dissimulation by Shīʿī jurists proved to be a highly effective way of resisting the disintegration of the Shīʿī legal culture. Shīʿī jurists insured the survival of Shīʿī law in Sunnī communities by mastering Sunnī law and, at times, pretending to be Sunnī jurists. For a study on the extensiveness of dissimulation, see Stewart, "*Taqiyyah*." For the creative dynamics of this process, see Stewart, *Islamic*.

[3] We have already alluded to the example of Mālik b. Anas and what reportedly befell him because of his opinion regarding divorce obtained under duress. The Ḥanafī school of law, which seems to have been more pragmatic in its approach and perhaps, therefore, more accommodating of the state, adopted the view that the divorce or manumissions of the duressed are legally effective anyway. See al-Azmeh, *Muslim*, 188, who argues that the Ḥanafī legal tradition is oriented towards the idea of a strong state while the Shāfiʿī legal tradition is more pietistic and bookish. Also see Hinds, "Miḥna," 5–6, for the relationship between the *miḥna* and Ḥanafism. The clear political connotations of the Ḥanafī discourses on duress are well illustrated in an entry in Shams al-Dīn al-Sarakhsī (d. 483/1090–1), *al-Mabsūṭ*, which notes that many rulers compel people to divorce or free slaves, and this should be tolerated because God tests people with worse calamities than this. However, the entry also notes that this is one of the areas of the law that can change with time and place. Despite the Ḥanafī's indulgence of the rulers' whims on this point, this did not necessarily free them from suspicion or repression. For instance, when the same jurist, Shams al-Dīn al-Sarakhsī, composed his book on duress, the ruler of Transoxania ordered that al-Sarakhsī be brought in for questioning, and attempted to seize the book. Fortunately, one of al-Sarakhsī's students hid the book in a well, and it survived. See al-Sarakhsī, *al-Mabsūṭ*, XXIV:39–40. Nevertheless, al-Sarakhsī was put in prison for ten years because of a *fatwā* he issued on an unrelated matter. See, on his life, Heffening, "al-Sarakhsī" Calder, "al-Sarakhsī." The Shāfiʿī jurist Ibn Kathīr was also persecuted because of his views on divorce pronounced under duress: see Ibn al-ʿImād, *Shadharāt*, VI:232. On the topic of duress in Islamic law, see Abou El Fadl, "Common," esp. 150.

resisted rulers to varying extents, and according to a variety of circumstances.[4]

Nevertheless, I do not wish to overemphasize the point about juristic responsiveness. Jurists do not function under either a strict paradigm of realism or of idealism, and forgo all else. As argued earlier, there is also the specific imperative of juristic culture which imposes its own suppositions and logic, and functions within the mandate of its own authoritative sources and processes. This means that juristic culture is often unresponsive to changing political and social needs or, more often, responsive according to its own terms and language.[5] The earliest juristic discourses on rebellion were formulated mostly as a response to pre-*miḥna* circumstances. After the middle ʿAbbāsid period the racial, political, and religious demographics of the Islamic empire changed with considerable speed. As we discuss later, the fact that the juridical discourses appeared to lag behind, or at times appeared entirely unrelated to any contemporaneous reality, invoked some jurists to complain that the law in this field needed to be altered to better suit the age. Some jurists omitted altogether the chapter on the law of rebellion from their legal hornbooks. Nonetheless, the predominant majority of jurists continued to discourse on the law of rebellion within the constructs set up by the legal culture.

As stated above, the *miḥna* was symptomatic of a dynamic already taking place between the jurists and the state. The *miḥna* itself did not

4 This, for example, is well illustrated in the case of tax farming as a method of collecting state revenue. Muslim jurists, particularly from the Ḥanafī school, accommodated certain forms of tax farming, but uncompromisingly objected to others. See Abou El Fadl, "Tax."

5 Alan Watson ably demonstrates that jurists, to a large extent, speak to other jurists. Consequently, juristic discourse is often unresponsive to social needs or demands. Rather, jurists often respond to the logic of other jurists, and to the constructs of their specific culture. See Watson, "Legal"; Watson, *Failures*, esp. 133–54. No doubt because of the constraints of the juristic culture, failures of the legal imagination do occur quite frequently. Two points need to be emphasized – points which I suspect that Watson would not necessarily disagree with. First, the juristic culture does not always fail to respond to social needs. Often, it does. Second, when the juristic culture does respond, it often does so in a manner that is consistent with its own terms of discourse. What from the perspective of the culture of jurists could be considered a revolutionary change in the law, from a social perspective, could be considered pedantic. A jurist, for example, may argue that a statute of limitations does not start running unless the plaintiff has knowledge of a claim of right, or a jurist may argue that a person has constructive knowledge if a reasonable person would have known of a claim of right. Alternatively, a jurist may specify the harshest penalties for the crime of banditry, but require that the act of banditry be observed by two witnesses who are not victims of the alleged crime, and therefore make it nearly impossible to prove the crime. In response to the spread of banditry, a jurist may then argue that if there are no other witnesses to the crime, the testimony of the victims will be accepted; however, in this situation, a death sentence is not allowed. In all of these examples, a jurist might be responding to a social or political need, but the response is articulated within the confines of a certain legal culture. Whether any of these technical responses is effective very much depends on the specific situation.

produce major revisions in the Islamic discourses on rebellion. Nevertheless, the period that followed produced complicated factors that challenged, and at times, altered the way Muslim jurists addressed the topic of rebellion. Some of the main rebellions were led by extremist theological factions and often resulted in territorial secessions for long periods of time.[6] Ethnicity and extreme religious doctrines mixed together, and from the point of view of the jurists it was difficult to distinguish one from the other. Muslim jurists often applied the generic term Bāṭiniyya to many of these movements.[7] For example, during the reign of al-Muʿtaṣim (r. 218/833–227/842), there was a serious rebellion by Māzyār b. Qārin in Ṭabaristān, which was primarily a revolt against the influence of the Ṭāhirids who provided the main source of military support to the caliph. Māzyār was defeated by the caliph in 224/838–9, and the rebel was flogged to death and crucified.[8] One of al-Muʿtaṣim's commanders, called Afshīn, was accused of conspiring with Māzyār, and after a trial, Afshīn was imprisoned, starved to death, crucified, and burned.[9] Importantly, Afshīn's trial focused on the accusation that he was pretending to be Muslim, and that he never sincerely abandoned his ancestral beliefs.[10] Importantly, Māzyār and Afshīn are cited by some Sunnī sources as examples of individuals who belonged to the Bāṭiniyya sect.[11]

Al-Mutawakkil (r. 232/847–247/861), in an attempt to appease the traditionists, reversed the pro-Muʿtazilī policies of his predecessors. In 237/851–2, he persecuted suspected ʿAlid sympathizers, destroyed the tombs of the descendants of ʿAlī, and ordered that ʿAlī be cursed from the pulpits of mosques.[12] After the death of al-Mutawakkil, a period of

[6] Modarressi (*Crisis*, 19–51) demonstrates the rise of extremist theological (Ghulāt) positions from the time of the death of the Prophet, especially from the beginning of the second/eighth century and onwards. The rapid spread of extremist theological views took place in the third/ninth century. On the Ghulāt and their doctrines, see al-Shahrastānī, *al-Milal*, I:203–22.

[7] See, on the Bāṭiniyya, the article in Gibb and Kramers, eds., *Shorter*, 60–1. Also see al-Shahrastānī, *al-Milal*, I:228–35. The editors of this work note that the terms Bāṭiniyya and Ghulāt are often confused: ibid., 228. Incidentally, a few decades later, accusations of being a *bāṭinī* became common as *topoi* connoting heterodoxy.

[8] Al-Ṭabarī, *Taʾrīkh*, IX:51. One of Māzyār's supporters, al-Durrī, had his limbs amputated and was then killed: ibid., 52. The rebels were not humanistic in their approach either. They committed widespread slaughter and pillaging. See especially an incident where they grabbed a young man as he was praying, and lynched him: ibid., 43.

[9] Ibid., 58.

[10] Ibid., 55–66; Ibn al-Athīr, *al-Kāmil*, VI:62–4; some of the accusations against Afshīn were that he owned heretical books, and that he said Arabs are like dogs.

[11] For example, al-Baghdādī, *al-Farq*, 214–15; this source also says that the Bāṭiniyya movement appeared in the reign of al-Maʾmūn and spread during the reign of al-Muʿtaṣim.

[12] Ibn al-Athīr, *al-Kāmil*, VI:108–9; Kennedy, *Prophet*, 169.

anarchy followed in Sāmarrā, the declared capital of the ᶜAbbāsids at the time, which lasted from 247/861 to 256/870, and which saw the rise and fall of four caliphs.[13] Several rebellions of a somewhat indefinite character followed.[14] For example, a man of Arab origins, born in Iran and known as ᶜAlī b. Muḥammad, tried his hand at being a poet in Sāmarrā, and then a prophet in Baṣra. Having failed at both, he declared that he belonged to the ᶜAlid family, although his exact lineage is not clear. Interestingly, he focused on attracting slaves, and in 255/869 started what is known as the Zanj rebellion which lasted for about ten years. The policies adopted by the Zanj rebellion were very cruel, and relied on guerrilla warfare tactics, and the execution of all captives.[15] In 257/871, he sacked Baṣra, pillaged its buildings, massacred many of its inhabitants, and burned its mosques. Before he was defeated and killed in 270/883, he had declared a capital in Mukhtāra, taken the title of al-Mahdī, and minted coins.[16]

The rebellion of the Zanj had hardly been defeated when a far more serious, and equally indefinite, rebellion commenced, by a federation of Arabs and Nabateans known as the Qarāmiṭa in 278/891.[17] Again, the Qarāmiṭa are described as Bāṭiniyya, *zanādiqa*, and Ismāᶜīlī.[18] The likelihood is that the Qarāmiṭa followed in the footsteps of the Zanj, and at one time even thought of allying themselves to the Zanj.[19] The ideas of their founder were synchronistic, esoteric, and quite heretical.[20] Like the Zanj, the Qarāmiṭa applied extremely cruel guerrilla warfare tactics, and slaughtered mercilessly and indiscriminately. Sunnī sources report wide-scale raping and pillaging by the Qarāmiṭa and, as mentioned earlier, in 317/930 they massacred pilgrims on their way to Mecca, sacked Mecca itself, and removed the Black Stone from the Kaᶜba.[21]

13 Kennedy, *Prophet*, 171.

14 By indefinite, I mean that the rebellions described below were synthetic in nature. They seem to have combined ideas of ethnic or racial equality or superiority with gnostic and esoteric notions from Mazdeism or Manichaeism, with fragments from Hellenistic philosophy.

15 On the Zanj, see Massignon, "Zandj."

16 Al-Ṭabarī, *Taʾrīkh*, IX:206–20, 239–46; Ibn al-Athīr, *al-Kāmil*, VI:206–12, 225–6, 229–33; Ibn al-ᶜImād, *Shadharāt*, II:129–30; Kennedy, *Prophet*, 180–1.

17 See the entry "Ḳarmaṭians" in Gibb and Kramers, eds., *Shorter*, 218–23; Madelung, "Ḳarmaṭī"; al-Ṭabarī, *Taʾrīkh*, IX:342–6; Ibn al-Athīr, *al-Kāmil*, VI:363–6.

18 Al-Shahrastānī, *al-Milal*, I:228–9; al-Baghdādī, *al-Farq*, 218–19; Ibn al-ᶜImād, *Shadharāt*, II:171–2. The Qarāmiṭa were, in fact, a branch of the Ismāᶜīlī movement: see Kennedy, *Prophet*, 287–92; Madelung, "Fāṭimids," 21–54; Moosa, *Extremist*, 15. For more on the *zanādiqa*, see Chokr, *Zandaqa*.

19 Al-Ṭabarī, *Taʾrīkh*, X:346; Ibn al-Athīr, *al-Kāmil*, VI:366.

20 Al-Ṭabarī, *Taʾrīkh*, X:345; Ibn al-Athīr, *al-Kāmil*, VI:365.

21 Al-Shahrastānī, *al-Milal*, I:228–9; al-Baghdādī, *al-Farq*, 218–19; Ibn al-ᶜImād, *Shadharāt*, II:171–2.

They continued to be a serious threat until the late fourth/tenth century.[22]

The earmark of these rebellions in the third/ninth–early fourth/tenth centuries was the widespread use of terror tactics. Although these were used by the Khawārij as well, the Zanj and the Qarāmiṭa were not rooted in juridical and historical precedent. ᶜAlī had dealt with the Khawārij, and there was a wealth of historical precedent available to the jurists in discoursing on the Khawārij. Furthermore, the use of esoteric and gnostic theology by the Zanj and the Qarāmiṭa made their categorization, from a juristic point of view, quite problematic. Nevertheless, not all precedents set in the third/ninth century were of such a nature as to motivate Muslim jurists to react by declaring all rebellions and all rebels evil and beyond the pale of law. The realities of the third/ninth century were complex, and did not afford Muslim jurists the luxury of reacting to a one-sided unitary historical precedent. Some rebellions seemed to enjoy widespread popular support. Additionally, at times, the conduct of government forces or forces allied to the government were no less terroristic in nature.

For example, in 250/864–5 a major ᶜAlid rebellion led by Yaḥyā b. ᶜUmar took place in Kūfa. The rebellion was joined by, among others, the bedouins and Zaydīs of the city, and received wide popular support in Baghdād as well. According to the sources, this was the first ᶜAlid rebellion to receive wide support by the Baghdādīs.[23] Yaḥyā was eventually defeated and killed that same year. Nonetheless, when the ᶜAbbāsids tried to display his head in Sāmarrā, there was sufficient popular discontent for the head to be promptly brought down. Another attempt was made to do the same in Baghdād, which failed due to popular discontent as well. Finally, the head of the ᶜAlid was put to rest and buried. Many of the men taken prisoner in the rebellion were pardoned and released.[24] In

[22] Kennedy, *Prophet*, 290–2. Another group which followed equally indiscriminate and ruthless methods of slaughter appeared in the fifth/eleventh century. They were known as the Assassins, and belonged to the Nizārī Ismāᶜīlī branch. They were a secret society and became infamous for their use of assassinations as a primary method of fighting their opponents. They were particularly notorious for strangling their victims to death, and hence became known as the Khunnāq. As we will see, Muslim jurists discussed how the Khunnāq should be treated. On the Assassins, see the article in Gibb and Kramers, eds., *Shorter*, 48–9; Burman, *Assassins*, esp. 26–7; Hodgson, *Order*, esp. 82–4; Lewis, *Assassins*, esp. 38–96. Reportedly, some of the early Khawārij and Shīᶜī Ghulāt used strangulation as a primary method of assassination: see al-Ashᶜarī, *Maqālāt*, II:157.

[23] Al-Ṭabarī, *Taʾrīkh*, IX:135; Ibn al-Athīr, *al-Kāmil*, VI:157.

[24] Al-Ṭabarī, *Taʾrīkh*, IX:136; Ibn al-Athīr, *al-Kāmil*, VI:157. Some of the released prisoners joined another ᶜAlid rebellion about a year later. Each of the repeat offenders was flogged 500 lashes: see al-Ṭabarī, *Taʾrīkh*, IX:166.

251/865, another ᶜAlid rebellion in Kūfa met a different fate. Al-Ḥusayn b. Muḥammad, the rebel, was initially supported by the tribe of Banū Asad and Kūfan Zaydīs, who apparently were wool manufacturers. The rebellion was initially successful in Kūfa and enjoyed considerable support until Muzāḥim b. Khāqān launched a counter-attack. Muzāḥim b. Khāqān (d. 253/867) was one of the military commanders supporting the caliph al-Mustaᶜīn (r. 248/862–252/866), and later fought against the Turks in the siege of Baghdād in 252/865. Muzāḥim, after a short battle, defeated the ᶜAlid rebel, but when he entered Kūfa, its hostile inhabitants pelted him with stones. Muzāḥim took swift and decisive revenge. He bombarded Kūfa with flame throwers, burning most of the marketplaces and many of the homes. He imprisoned all the ᶜAlids in the city, and took the slave girls of the ᶜAlid rebel. He also took a free woman who apparently worked as a servant for the ᶜAlid rebel and had her auctioned off in front of the mosque. The rival caliph, al-Muᶜtazz (r. 252/866–255/869), apparently, was so impressed by Muzāḥim's performance that he wrote to Muzāḥim offering him ample rewards if he would join him.[25]

The conduct of rebels and those who fought rebels is a legally material element. The conduct is not material just because it is precedent. More importantly, the matter of conduct helps inform the culture of jurists as to what acceptable conduct should be. In other words, the conduct of rebels and the treatment of rebels may assist a jurist in constructing a normative argument. The normative argument would be focused on what the conduct or treatment of rebels should be. The normative argument of a jurist takes into account what took place in actuality, but also responds to this actuality with a judgment; it either approves or disapproves of the reported conduct. Although the reported conduct might materially differ from what the juridical culture normatively argues, that does not necessarily motivate the juridical culture to alter or reform its discourses in the immediate future. The juridical culture often responds to events well after the fact. In fact, because of the specificity, and often the conservatism, of juridical culture, jurists will more often than not respond to reality only after it has become persistent, pervasive, and dominant. This, at times, means that juridical culture will revise or reform its argument after it has become apparent that there is a considerable gap between the constructed normative argument and the social and political reality.

[25] Al-Ṭabarī, *Taʾrīkh*, IX:166. Al-Muᶜtazz was picked as the rival caliph by the Turkish forces, and he was the one who laid siege to Baghdād. He defeated al-Mustaᶜīn and sent him into exile. Before long, he was assassinated by the same Turkish forces who brought him to power.

Consequently there is quite frequently a "lag-time" between the social and political circumstances and a juridical reformation. I elaborate upon this point below.

Beyond the issue of conduct, the third/ninth century presented Muslim jurists with a very different problem – one that related more to the area of constitutional than criminal law. The problem was: Who is a rebel? This issue did not present itself for the first time in the third or fourth century. As discussed earlier, this issue existed from the time of the conflict between ʿAlī and his opponents, and there is hardly any period in Islamic history that was not plagued by rebellions. However, the nature of the question has changed. Before the third century, rebellions sought to represent and lead the entire Muslim *umma*. Even if the rebellion originated from the periphery, it sought to reach the center and lead all Muslims. They were not partial rebellions, but totalistic rebellions. Ibn al-Zubayr, al-Ashʿath, or al-Nafs al-Zakiyya did not seek a secession; rather, in principle, they sought a full-scale revolution that would represent Islam and Muslims everywhere. In contrast, many of the rebellions of the third century and onwards sought to carve out a part of the *umma* and establish a local or partial rule. In other words, many of the later rebellions were secessionist movements and not revolutions. The goal was not to unite all Muslims under a single and just rule, but to divide Muslims through achieving a degree of regional autonomy.[26]

[26] Riḍwān al-Sayyid (*al-Umma*, 122) argues that a rebel in Islamic thought was expected to bring his call (*daʿwa*) from the periphery to the center in order to unite the nation under one message. A *bāghī* was one who rebelled in the periphery and did not seek to extend his *ʿaṣabiyya* (tribalism or nationalism) beyond the periphery. He would be tolerated because his *ʿaṣabiyya* is still a part of the *umma*. But because he did not seek to unite the full nation under a single call, he would be considered an outsider (*mutamarrid*). See also his introduction to al-Sayyid, ed., *al-Asad*, 5–35. I must admit that I find his argument hopelessly vague. It is possible that he is arguing that the jurists expected a dissenter to seek to represent the *jamāʿa*, and that if a dissenter sought to represent regional or local interests without aspiring to represent the full *umma*, he was considered to be a deviator who would be tolerated but not endorsed. If this is, in fact, his argument, he does not explain what happens to a rebel who claims to represent the full *umma*. Furthermore, al-Sayyid seems to base his argument on the genre of literature known as the mirror of princes (*naṣīḥat al-mulūk*). This literary genre gives advice to rulers on how to preserve and protect politics and religion. As a methodological matter, it is dangerous to draw conclusions on the legal status of rebels based on this genre of literature. In fact, as discussed later, many jurists argued that those who rebel in the periphery for tribal reasons (*ʿaṣabiyya*) are not to be considered rebels. Rather, they are considered bandits and treated as such. It is possible, however, that al-Sayyid is not talking about the law of the jurists but about the conduct of the government, i.e. the law in administrative practice. The caliph would never tolerate a rebel who wanted to capture Baghdād, for example, and depose him, but could ignore, or even under certain conditions endorse, a rebel in a peripheral territory who would offer nominal symbolic homage to him. If, in fact, this is al-Sayyid's argument, I agree with him.

In the third/ninth century, the duly deputized governor of Egypt, Aḥmad b. Ṭūlūn (d. 270/884), declared his virtual independence from his bosses in Iraq and threatened to capture Syria as well. Ibn Ṭūlūn never stopped formally acknowledging the ᶜAbbāsids as the legitimate caliphs, and is reported to have continued to pay them tribute in return for recognition. However, for all practical purposes he formed an independent dynasty, which was destroyed by the ᶜAbbāsids in 292/905.[27] Ibn Ṭūlūn was not willing to completely sever his formal connection with the ᶜAbbāsids; however, several other rebels did establish independent states. For example, around the mid-third century, al-Ḥasan b. Zayd, after a series of rebellions, succeeded in establishing a Zaydī state to the south of the Caspian Sea, Iran. Meanwhile, al-Qāsim al-Rassī, who first rebelled during the reign of al-Ma'mūn, succeeded in establishing an independent Zaydī state in Ṣaᶜda, Yemen.[28] Furthermore, by the end of the third century, the Fāṭimids, a branch of the Ismāᶜīlīs, established an independent state in North Africa, and in 297/909 the Fāṭimid ruler al-Mahdī (r. 297/909–322/934) was declared as a rival caliph to the ᶜAbbāsids in Raqqāda in Ifrīqiyā.[29] Of course, this was not an entirely novel situation, for there had been autonomous or semi-autonomous dynasties and principalities since the second/eighth century.[30] Nevertheless, we are not just addressing the historical reality but, more importantly, the impression it has left on jurists. The

Lewis (*Islam*, 318) argues that the Muslim juristic discourses on rebellion had in mind secession, not revolution: Muslim jurists were discoursing on secessionist movements, not revolutionary movements. One suspects that this is similar to what al-Sayyid has in mind as well. However, if the implication of this argument is that secessionary movements were tolerated by the jurists but revolutions were not, this is clearly wrong. If, on the other hand, the implication is that secession was discoursed upon but revolution was not imagined or addressed, that is false as well.

27 See Gibb, "Ṭūlūnids."

28 See Strothmann, "Zaidīya." Also see Bosworth, *New*, 96–8.

29 See Canard, "Fāṭimids." The pro-Shīᶜī Buwayhids (Būyids) entered Baghdād in the fourth/tenth century, and for more than a hundred years exercised tutelage over the ᶜAbbāsid caliphate, but they never eliminated the caliphate. See Cahen, "Buwayhids."

30 The most obvious example is the establishment of the Umayyad dynasty in the Iberian peninsula starting in 138/756. The following are all examples of dynasties that maintained autonomous or semi-autonomous status from the ᶜAbbāsids in the second or third centuries: the apparently Shīᶜī Idrīsids in Morocco (starting in 172/789); the Khārijī Rustamids in western Algeria (s. 161/778); the Khārijī, at first, then Shīᶜī Midrārids in south-eastern Morocco (s. 208/823); the Sunnī Aghlābids in Ifrīqiyā (s. 184/800); the Sunnī Ziyādids in Yemen (s. 203/818); the apparently Sunnī Yaᶜfūrids in Yemen (s. 232/847); the apparently Sunnī Shirwānid Shahs in Armenia, Azerbaijān (s. 183/799); the Sunnī Hāshimids of Darband (s. 255/869); the apparently Shīᶜī Justānids in Daylam (s. 175/791); and the Sunnī Sājids in Azerbaijān (s. 276/889). See Bosworth, *New*, 11–13, 25–6, 27–8, 29–30, 31–2, 99, 100, 140–2, 143–4, 145, 147.

existence of autonomous or semi-autonomous principalities did not affect the discourses on rebellion by jurists living in Egypt, the Shām, Irāq, or Arabia under the ʿAbbāsids until well after the third/ninth century. And even when it did affect them, it did not necessarily lead to a radical or revolutionary reformulation of the law. Rather, the law was revised in subtle and conservatively measured ways. There are two main reasons for this. First, the declared autonomous principalities were on the peripheries of the ʿAbbāsid caliphate, and therefore, for the most part could be ignored, at least until the third/ninth century. Second, even the events of that century, for the most part, are not reflected in the discourses of Muslim jurists until much later because of, as argued above, the tendency of the law to have a delayed response to social and political events. This second point needs further elaboration.

THE NOTION OF DELAYED LEGAL RESPONSE

I have argued above that law, at times, is responsive to social and political demands. In fact, law often acts to motivate and shape social realities. Nonetheless, to quote Watson, "Law is [also] very traditional, slow to modify its rules, structure, and mode of creation."[31] Once jurists develop a structure and a set of rules, and build a discourse on these rules, it takes considerable creativity, and sometimes opportunism, to change the rules.[32] Jurists exist within a specific juridical culture in which jurists talk primarily to jurists. As Watson has argued:

> Law . . . despite its practical impact, is above all and primarily the culture of lawyers and especially of the lawmakers – that is, of those lawyers who, whether as legislators, jurists or judges, have control of the accepted mechanisms of legal change. Legal development is determined by their culture; and social, economic, and political factors impinge on legal development only through their consciousness. This consciousness results from the lawmakers' being members of the society and sharing its values and experiences, though of course they are members with a particular standing. Sometimes this consciousness is heightened by extreme pressures from other members of the society, but always the

[31] Watson, *Sources*, 111. I do not completely agree with the proposition that law is inherently traditional or invariably slow.

[32] Watson (*Failures*, 35–59) argues that even legislation, which tends to be the most radical way of changing law, is often non-responsive and slow to change. On opportunism and pragmatism as motivators of legal change, see ibid., 87–101.

lawmakers' response is conditioned by the legal tradition: by their learning, expertise, and knowledge of law, domestic and foreign.[33]

This does not mean that jurists are uninterested in social or political reality.[34] Even if a particular jurist is interested in the circumstances and conditions of the age, to effectuate legal change a jurist has to defy or distinguish already established legal authority. This is often a very risky and contentious process, and it is also often a very protracted and long process.[35] Of course, if there is sufficient political or social pressure, the law might change rather quickly to serve certain dominant interests, and preserve its own legitimacy. However, the legitimacy of a legal culture often depends on its ability to uphold precedent and resist radical change. Even with the existence of political or social pressure, law must also respond to the mandates and pressures imposed by the practice of the legal culture. Frequently, this means that jurists will not disentangle themselves from the weight of precedent, and will not respond immediately to political or social pressures. Therefore, one might find that the social and political realities of a particular age are not addressed until a century or more later. Consequently, the circumstances of the third century might not be addressed until the fourth century or even later. As we will see, jurists writing in the third century did not necessarily reflect the realities of that century. Rather, they were still addressing the law of rebellion that was formulated in response to the second or first century of Islam. This delay between social and political circumstances and the juridical response is directly attributable to the nature of juristic culture, which is often conservative. The juristic culture is conservative because it bases

33 Watson, *Evolution*, 118–19.

34 Alan Watson argues that law has its own standard for existence and that it is largely autonomous and not shaped by social needs: ibid., 115, 119. On the idea of legal revolutions, see ibid., 109–14. I do not go this far. I believe that one can speak of tendencies in the legal culture but not inevitabilities. Legal culture does respond to social and political circumstances, especially if the interests of the influential and powerful are being affected. But legal culture does not always support change and, therefore might resist. I would argue that often there is a considerable delay between the time a social or political need for change arises and when the conservatism of legal culture admits or allows a change. But as argued in the conclusion, law is not autonomous or always conservative or non-responsive. Law is semi-autonomous, and is often responsive and, at times, radical.

35 This is why the most creative and innovative jurists are often the most maligned and criticized. There are many examples of innovative jurists who were heavily criticized or who isolated themselves from society. Examples would include: Abū Isḥāq al-Shāṭibī (d. 790/1388), see Masud, *Islamic*, 103; Abū al-Ḥasan al-Māwardī (d. 450/1058), see Ibn al-ᶜImād, *Shadharāt*, III:286; Muḥammad Ibn Rushd II (d. 595/1198), see al-Dhahabī, *Siyar*, XXI:309; Yaḥyā al-Nawawī (d. 676/1277–8), see Ibn al-ᶜImād, *Shadharāt*, V:354; Aḥmad b. Ḥazm (d. 456/1064), see Ibn al-ᶜImād, *Shadharāt*, III:300; Jalāl al-Dīn al-Suyūṭī (d. 911/1505), see Ibn al-ᶜImād, *Shadharāt*, VIII:53.

itself in the legitimacy of prior authority, and therefore often needs to disentangle itself from the weight of precedent.[36] Importantly, the more developed the juridical culture, the more it labors under the weight of precedents, rules, and prior authority. Therefore, the more developed a juridical culture, the less flexible it is, and the greater the "lag-time" between the social and political realities and the legal response.

THE EMERGENCE OF THE DISCOURSE ON REBELLION: FROM REPORTS TO LAW

Until the mid-second/eighth century there was no jurisprudence on rebellion, but only reports. The reports constitute primitive, undeveloped attempts at jurisprudence; however, they lack the systematic argumentation of jurisprudence. They make a point but do not explore the implications of the point, and they do not categorize or classify acts according to a consistent or coherent scheme. In many ways, reports are raw material that is co-opted and constructed in the service of jurisprudence.[37] By the mid-second century, there were many circulating reports or traditions that were relevant, in one way or another, to the theoretical issue of rebellion. These traditions consisted of two distinct types: reports that related directly to the issue of obedience to those in power, and reports that related only indirectly to the matter. The second type of reports mostly addressed the opinions and purported conduct of the Companions during the civil wars between ᶜAlī and his opponents. We have already mentioned quite a few of these traditions in the context of discussing the debates on the verses on *ḥirāba* and *baghy*. We will now address these two types of reports in the context of examining what may

36 Alan Watson comments that law is "typically backward-looking" and "inherently conservative": Watson, *Evolution*, 119. But as the author notes:

> This does not mean there are not radical lawyers. But except when they are legislators, they are "bad" lawyers – not in an ethical sense, but in the sense that they have to use arguments outside the reach of the accepted mode of legal reasoning. They, therefore, appear to the generality of lawyers to be at the intellectual mercy of traditionalists. *Pointing this out is in no sense to be construed as support for conservative positions.* In fact, precisely because of the force of the legal tradition, legal change is frequently the result of efforts of non-lawyers or of lawyers outside the tradition.
>
> (Ibid., 145, n. 6; emphasis mine)

To a large extent, I concur.

37 This is why, for example, al-Shāfiᶜī told the traditionists, "You are the chemists and we are the doctors (*antum al-ṣayādilatu wa naḥnu al-aṭibbāʾ*)": al-Dhahabī, *Siyar*, x:23. Abū Ḥanīfa reportedly made a similar argument. He argued that one who collects *ḥadīth* but does not study jurisprudence is like a person who collects medicine but does not know how to treat diseases: al-Makkī, *Manāqib*, 350.

be called the obedience and counter-obedience traditions. For our purposes the reports, in either case, are interesting only to the extent that they exhibit early tendencies, and to the extent that they became the raw material that jurists ultimately worked with. Dating these reports or having a sense of when they made their first appearance is an admittedly difficult task.[38] However, for the purposes of this study, one could get a fairly strong sense of which reports appear in the early juristic writings, and which reports seem to appear suddenly in later juristic discourses.

THE TRADITIONS OF OBEDIENCE

Al-Ḥāfiẓ Abū Bakr al-Shaybānī (d. 287/900) quotes an impressive array of reports attributed to the Prophet on the necessity of obeying those in power. A genre of these reports counsels that a Muslim should obey whoever is in power, even if the one in power is a "mutilated Abyssinian slave."[39] The symbolic construct here is not necessarily one of blind obedience but one of non-critical obedience. In other words, one can possibly interpret this genre of reports to simply mean that the physical, racial, or ethnic attributes of a ruler are irrelevant. However, a similar genre of reports goes further, and asserts that the Prophet commanded that Muslims must obey rulers under all circumstances. A typical form for this genre is the following: It is reported that the Prophet said, "Listen and obey, in hardship and in good, in what is pleasant or unpleasant, and prefer them [the rulers] over yourself even if they usurp your wealth or strike your backs."[40] Some reports provide a justification for this methodical imperative of obedience by claiming that the Prophet said: "Who obeys me [the Prophet], he has obeyed God, and who disobeys me, he has disobeyed God. Who obeys the ruler (*al-amīr*), he has obeyed me and who disobeys the ruler, he has disobeyed me."[41] Several traditions

[38] See the engaging study by Cook, "Eschatology." Also see, on the development of *Sunna* and *ḥadīth*, Rahman, *Islamic*, esp. 27–84.

[39] Al-Shaybānī, *Kitāb al-Sunnah*, 29, 445, 491. This version, as well as other versions, are in Ibn Ḥanbal (d. 241/855), *Musnad*, III:143, 215; V:209, 221. Many of the traditions emphasizing obedience can be found in Ibn al-Athīr al-Jazarī (d. 606/1209), *Jāmiʿ*, IV:46–56.

[40] Al-Shaybānī, *Kitāb al-Sunnah*, 478, 479. Ibn Ḥanbal, *Musnad*, II:501, V:402; al-Nawawī, *Sharḥ*, XII:480.

[41] Al-Shaybānī, *Kitāb al-Sunnah*, 492–4. In a different version of this type of *ḥadīth*, the Prophet is reported to have said: "Be steadfast in your obedience to your leaders, and do not contravene them, for obeying them is obeying God, and disobeying them is disobeying God:" ibid., 499; Ibn Ḥanbal, *Musnad*, II:322, 333, 356, 412, 450, 622, 677. A version of this report says that even if the rulers pray sitting down when they are supposed to pray standing up, one should do the same: ibid., 126, 509, 548, 617. Some jurists maintain that this *ḥadīth* only applies to obeying military chiefs (*wujūb al-ṭāʿa li-umarāʾi al-jaysh*).

attributed to the Prophet create a moral distance between the actions of rulers and their followers. As long as Muslims are obedient, they will not be held responsible before God for the indiscretions or injustices of rulers. Rulers are solely liable for their own injustices, Muslims are responsible for a separate religious imperative of obedience.[42]

Nonetheless, these reports must go further. A good legal mind could distinguish these reports, and maintain that they are largely inapposite to a case of rebellion. For example, one could argue that these traditions relate to the duty of obedience, but that they do not relate to the issue of choice of leader. In other words, once we acknowledge a specific person as a ruler, then obedience is due. However, a group that chooses an alternative ruler, a leader of a rebellion for example, owes, pursuant to these traditions, the same unequivocal obedience to the leader of the rebellion. Hence, other reports are needed that more explicitly and specifically prohibit rebellion. One such report states that the Prophet's Companion Abū Dharr al-Ghifārī (d. 32/652) was sleeping in the Medina mosque when the Prophet woke him up and said,

> "Why do I see you asleep here?" Abū Dharr said: "Oh Prophet, I was overcome by sleep." The Prophet asked: "What would you do if you were forced out of it [the mosque of Medina]?" Abū Dharr said: "I would accept the holy blessed land of Shām." The Prophet then inquired: "What would you do if you are forced out of it?" Abū Dharr then puzzled: "What should I do? Should I take my sword and go out striking with it [i.e. rebel]?" The Prophet said: "Shall I tell you what is better and nearer to piety? (The Prophet repeated the phrase twice.) You listen and obey, and go whichever way they lead you."[43]

The report is obviously staged, but the dramatic effects of the story are an integral part of the emotional impact of the message. Despite the emotional place of holy mosques in which one feels sufficiently tranquil and secure to the point of falling asleep, and contrary to the intuitive impulse to resist by force any denial of the right to be in a mosque, it is closer to piety not to use force. Even if one is expelled from the most holy of mosques, one must not rebel. The message of this *ḥadīth* is bolstered by reports that explicitly state that one should not contest or rebel against unjust rulers as long as the rulers permit prayers to be performed. The most a Muslim should do is passively and quietly condemn the injustices

[42] Al-Shaybānī, *Kitāb al-Sunnah*, 485, 496; al-Rāzī (d. 327/938), *ʿIlal*, II:419.

[43] Al-Shaybānī, *Kitāb al-Sunnah*, 497; Ibn Ḥanbal, *Musnad*, V:203. The expression "holy and blessed land of Shām" most probably means Syria. It is quite likely that the report is a pro-Umayyad fabrication justifying Abū Dharr's banishment by Muʿāwiya from Medina and Syria. It is possible, but not probable, that the report refers to the Jerusalem mosque.

and sins being committed, but a Muslim should not rebel (*wa lā yanzaʿanna yadan min al-ṭāʿa*).[44] The message is made abundantly clear in the genre of traditions that states that whoever rebels after the nation (*umma*) or community (*jamāʿa*) has united or agreed on a leader should be killed, whoever he may be.[45] Another report of the same type asserts that the Prophet said: "The blood of a Muslim who attests that there is no God but God and that I am the Prophet of God, may not be shed except for three reasons: 1. adultery, 2. murder, and 3. the abandonment of religion and rebellion against the community (*al-tāriku li dīnihi al-mufāriq li al-jamāʿa*)."[46] Other reports prohibit the cursing, slandering, or even hating of rulers regardless of their merit or lack of merit.[47] The only recourse against unjust rulers is patience.[48] These reports typically command that one steadfastly adheres to the community and not deviate from the *jamāʿa* (plurality or community).

These reports, as strong and clear as they may sound, beg the question: What is the *jamāʿa* to which one must hold steadfastly? It is possible to dilute much of the strength of these reports by debating and reconstructing

[44] Al-Shaybānī, *Kitāb al-Sunnah*, 495. Some reports state that rulers should not be fought as long as they pray: ibid., 501. In another tradition of the same type, the Prophet is reported to have said, "There will be rulers (*umarāʾ*) who will cause the hearts of people to be repulsed and the skin of people to cringe [presumably with disgust or fear]. The Prophet was asked should we fight them? The Prophet said: No, as long as they permit prayer": ibid., 498. The same report is in Ibn Ḥanbal, *Musnad*, VI:31, III:35; al-Rāzī (*ʿIlal*, II:422) reports the same version, but also another one that provides that rulers should be obeyed as long as they pray and fast: ibid., 405.

[45] Al-Shaybānī, *Kitāb al-Sunnah*, 512; al-Nawawī, *Sharḥ*, XII:483–4. For a different version on one who abandons the *jamāʿa* and rebels, see Ibn Ḥanbal, *Musnad*, V:481, 503.

[46] Al-Shaybānī, *Kitāb al-Sunnah*, 30–1, 421. This version of the *ḥadīth* is in Ibn Ḥanbal, *Musnad*, I:477, 535, 556; VI:205. A different version of this *ḥadīth* provides that the blood of a Muslim may not be shed except for adultery, murder, or apostasy: Ibn Ḥanbal, *Musnad*, I:74, 76, 201, VI:69, 206, 233, 243. The caliph ʿUthmān is reported to have cited this *ḥadīth* to his assassins before he was killed, the point being that since he did not commit murder, adultery, or apostasy, assassinating him would be unjust: see ibid., 84–5. Of course, the difference in the two versions is very important. Effectively, the first version permits the killing of a rebel, while the second limits the authorization of killing to an apostate. The theoretical question, however, is how does one distinguish between a rebel and an apostate? In my view, these various versions represent competing trends or needs in early Islam. The complex legal classifications and definitions of rebellion versus apostasy came later.

Several traditions condemn one who abandons the *jamāʿa*, and provide that such a person will die in a state of *jāhiliyya* (a state of ignorance which is commonly associated with the condition of Arabs before Islam): al-Shaybānī, *Kitāb al-Sunnah*, 39–43, 420, 423. A version of these reports creates a nexus between the *jamāʿa* and obedience to the ruler. It states: "Whoever rebels and abandons the community dies a death of ignorance (*man kharaja min al-ṭāʿa wa fāraqa al-jamāʿa māta mītata jāhiliyya*)": ibid., 422, 492. This means that, effectively, the person dies a non-Muslim. A different version provides: "Three types of people God will not care for, one who abandons the *jamāʿa*, disobeys his ruler, or dies a sinner": ibid., 490.

[47] Ibid., 473–6.

[48] Ibid., 509–11; al-Rāzī, *ʿIlal*, II:414.

the definitions of *jamāʿa*. For example, Ibn al-Qayyim (d. 751 / 1350–1) argued that the *jamāʿa* means those who follow the straight path (*al-ḥaqq*) and adhere to the truth. Therefore, the *jamāʿa* could be a single person, and the vast majority of Muslims could be *contra* to the *jamāʿa*. For instance, in the days of the *miḥna*, Ibn al-Qayyim argued, the vast majority of scholars deviated from the truth and Aḥmad b. Ḥanbal persevered on the right path. Hence, he alone became the *jamāʿa*, and the rest of the people deviated from the *jamāʿa*.[49] Of course, Ibn al-Qayyim's argument is not entirely original.[50] The traditionist Muḥammad al-Bukhārī (d. 256/870) much earlier raised the issue of what one should do if there is no *jamāʿa*. Al-Bukhārī then cited a tradition that asserts that in the absence of a *jamāʿa*, one should isolate oneself and abandon all the contentious groups in society.[51] Effectively, Ibn al-Qayyim and others took the reports on the possibility that a *jamāʿa* would not exist, and reconstructed them into a discourse in which the minority, or even one person, would become the *jamāʿa*. Regardless of the merits of these arguments, they demonstrate the power of theological or legal interpretation in distinguishing and reconstructing traditions (raw material) in order to reach certain results.

Later, we will have occasion to discuss the reconstructive activity of Muslim jurists in relation to the traditions on obedience. At this point, it is important to note that the traditions emphasizing the impermissibility of using force against Muslims or the necessity of obedience to those in power were quite widespread in the first two centuries of Islam. Most of the early collections of *ḥadīth* include one version or another of these kinds of reports.[52] Although most of these sources were written

49 Ibn Qayyim al-Jawziyya, *Aʿlām* (Beirut), III:397–8; Ibn Qayyim al-Jawziyya, *Ighātha*, I:97–8.

50 In fact, in order to prove his point, Ibn al-Qayyim cites a whole set of earlier opinions: ibid.

51 Al-Bukhārī, *Ṣaḥīḥ* (Dār Iḥyāʾ al-Turāth al-ʿArabī), IV:225. This tradition is referring to the first civil war, and is advocating non-involvement and neutrality.

52 Al-Bukhārī (d. 256/870), ibid., 221–3 (traditions emphasizing obedience, patience, and the impermissibility of using weapons against fellow Muslims); al-Tirmidhī (d. 297/909), *al-Jāmiʿ*, IV:49, 404–5, 423, 458 (traditions emphasizing obedience, patience, the merits of adhering to the *jamāʿa*, and not rebelling or using weapons against fellow Muslims); al-Nasāʾī (d. 303/915), *Sunan*, IV:90–3 (traditions emphasizing adhering to the *jamāʿa* and obedience); Ibn Māja (d. 273/886–7), *Sunan*, II:847, 860, 954–5 (traditions emphasizing adhering to the *jamāʿa*, obedience, and the impermissibility of using weapons against Muslims); Abū Dāwūd (d. 275/888–9), *Sunan*, IV:92–9 (traditions emphasizing not getting involved in *fitna*); al-Bazzār (d. 292/904–5), *al-Baḥr*, V:173, 329, 334, 386 (traditions emphasizing obedience, adhering to the *jamāʿa*, and not using force against other Muslims); al-Dārimī (d. 255/869), *Sunan*, II:314–15 (traditions emphasizing obedience, patience, and not using weapons against fellow Muslims); Ibn Shuʿba (d. 227/841), *Sunan*, II:192–6 (traditions emphasizing the duty of obedience and adhering to the *jamāʿa*); Muslim b. al-Ḥajjāj (d. 261/875), *al-Jāmiʿ*, I:69, VI:13–25 (traditions emphasizing obedience, adhering to the *jamāʿa*, not rebelling against leaders, patience, and not using weapons against fellow Muslims), Ibn Abī Shayba (d. 235/849), *al-Muṣannaf*, VII:567, 687–8 (traditions

in the third/ninth century, these traditions must have come into circulation much earlier. Considering the scale and nature of the rebellions during the Umayyad period, it is very likely that most of the traditions demanding unquestioning obedience came to existence in the first/seventh century.[53] Furthermore, these traditions seem to have been incorporated in the jurisprudential discourses early on. ᶜAbd Allāh b. Aḥmad (d. 290/902) reported that his father, Aḥmad b. Ḥanbal (d. 241/855), strongly disapproved of those who disobeyed the ruler or who failed to support him.[54] Even earlier, the Ḥanafī judge Abū Yūsuf (d. 183/799) cites many of these traditions, including a tradition attributed to the Prophet, which commands that one should obey every ruler (*amīr*) and pray behind every *imām* without distinction.[55] Another tradition, cited by Abū Yūsuf, alleges that al-Ḥasan al-Baṣrī (d. 110/728) reported that the Prophet said:

> Do not slander the rulers (*al-wulā*), for if they do good, they will be rewarded, and you should be grateful. If they do evil, they will incur the sin [of the deed], and you must show patience. They [the rulers] are God's punishment which God sends upon whomever He wants. Do not meet God's punishment with anger and resistance. Meet God's punishment with acceptance and prayer.[56]

emphasizing obedience and the permissibility of supporting the war efforts of unjust rulers). Most of these traditions are reproduced in Ibn al-Athīr al-Jazarī, *Jāmiᶜ*, IV:46–56. Abū ᶜAwwāna (d. 316/928–9), *Musnad*, IV:420–6, reproduces the same traditions. Interestingly, however, he gives one of the relevant chapters the unusual title "The Duty of Obeying Rulers Even if they do not Follow the Guidance or *Sunnah* of the Prophet, and Even if they Beat the Backs of the People."

53 The nature of the rebellions demanded justification of the harsh measures taken against their initiators. The opponents of the Umayyads, such as Saᶜd b. ᶜUbāda, Abū Dharr, Ḥusayn, and the people of Medina, were morally influential. The obedience traditions were a part of the Umayyad campaign against their opponents. Later, the ᶜAbbāsids used the same traditions against their opponents.

54 Ibn Ḥanbal, *Masāʾil*, 257. One can only guess as to exactly what this position means in light of Aḥmad b. Ḥanbal's position on the *miḥna*. It is possible that the tradition belongs to the time of al-Mutawakkil when Aḥmad was a favorite of the government.

55 Abū Yūsuf, *Kitāb*, 9–10.

56 Ibid., 10. This tradition is nearly identical to the one discussed earlier where Ibn ᶜUmar says that al-Ḥajjāj is God's punishment and should not be resisted. Ironically, al-Ḥasan al-Baṣrī is reported to have harshly criticized and opposed al-Ḥajjāj and the Umayyad caliph ᶜAbd al-Malik: see Gibb and Kramers, eds., *Shorter*, 136. But al-Ḥasan refused to join Ibn al-Ashᶜath's rebellion, arguing that tyrants are God's punishment that must be patiently endured. On al-Ḥasan al-Baṣrī see al-Dhahabī, *Siyar*, IV:563–88, and Ritter, "Ḥasan al-Baṣrī." Reportedly, when al-Ḥasan was asked about al-Ḥajjāj, he said that al-Ḥajjāj was *qāsiṭ ᶜādil*. This is a wonderful play on words. *Qāsiṭ ᶜādil* literally means "pious and just." But these words can be used in a very different sense. The Qurʾān, for example, says that the *qāsiṭūn* (plural form of *qāsiṭ*) will be the firewood of hell (Qurʾān 72:15). Here the word is used in the sense of those who shy or turn away from the right path. Similarly, *ᶜādil* could mean just, but it could also mean those who turn away. The Qurʾān states: "Those who disbelieve *yaᶜdilūn* [i.e. turn away from their Lord]":

Another genre of traditions is even more specific in scope; these traditions condemn the Khawārij or Ḥarūriyya, and counsel Muslims not to get involved in *fitan*. We have already addressed some of the *fitan* traditions, but generally, in their typical form the Prophet is quoted as predicting that there will come a time when civil discord will spread, and Muslims will fight each other. The Prophet then counsels that a pious Muslim should refrain from becoming involved in these compromising situations.[57] Alternatively, a Companion, quite typically Ibn ᶜUmar, would advise other Companions or pious Muslims not to become involved in rebellions, even against someone such as Yazīd b. Muᶜāwiya, who is often considered the epitome of injustice, impiety, and corruption.[58] Some versions of the *fitan* reports specify that the people in Shām (the Umayyads), Ibn al-Zubayr in Mecca, and the Qurrāʾ in Baṣra were all fighting over worldly affairs, and were all engulfed in a *fitna*, therefore, a Muslim must refrain from joining any of the contending parties.[59] The traditions specifically dealing with the Khawārij often assert that the sect had deviated from Islam and that they were the dogs of hellfire.[60] Some reports specify that the Khawārij were to be considered the *bāghiya* (rebellious or deviant) group,[61] and encourage that they be fought and killed.[62] In many versions, the Khawārij are not referred to by name, but are identified by implication. These reports claim that there will come a time when zealots with little understanding of the religion will shed the blood of Muslims. If they are found, the reports assert, they must be killed wherever they may be found.[63] Other reports quote the Prophet as condemning the Rāfiḍa (Shīᶜa), and calling upon all Muslims to fight them.[64] Arguably, because these traditions address specific historical conflicts, they tend to restrict

Qurʾān 6:150. This incident is reported in al-Bazzāzī, *al-Fatāwā*, VI:336. The author, who cites al-Baṣrī's play on words, is quite unhappy about this precedent. He says that those who attempt to imitate this trick by calling the sulṭān of his age (the author died in 827/1423) an *ᶜādil* are *kuffār* (unbelievers) because it is well established that the ruler is not just and this play on words is improper.

57 Al-Bukhārī, *Ṣaḥīḥ* (Dār Iḥyāʾ al-Turāth al-ᶜArabī), IV:221–33; Muslim b. al-Ḥajjāj, *al-Jāmiᶜ*, VIII:208, Abū Dāwūd, *Sunan*, IV:91–4, 96–9; al-Nasāʾī, *Sunan*, IV:92–3; al-Tirmidhī, *al-Jāmiᶜ*, IV:422–5; Ibn Abī Shayba, *al-Muṣannaf*, VIII:590–649; al-Rāzī, *ᶜIlal*, II:411, 413.

58 For example, al-Shaybānī, *Kitāb al-Sunnah*, 498, 500; al-Bukhārī, *Ṣaḥīḥ* (Dār Iḥyāʾ al-Turāth al-ᶜArabī), IV:230.

59 Al-Bukhārī, *Ṣaḥīḥ* (Dār Iḥyāʾal-Turāth al-ᶜArabī), IV:230; Ibn Abī Shayba, *al-Muṣannaf*, VIII:594, 622, 625, 715.

60 Al-Shaybānī, *Kitāb al-Sunnah*, 424; Ibn Ḥanbal, *Musnad*, IV:482.

61 Al-Shaybānī, *Kitāb al-Sunnah*, 427.

62 Ibid., 419–47.

63 Ibid., 424, 427; al-Bukhārī, *Ṣaḥīḥ* (Dār Iḥyāʾ al-Turāth al-ᶜArabī), IV:197; Ibn Shuᶜba, *Sunan*, II:322, 324; al-Dārimī, *Sunan*, II:281; al-Bazzār, *al-Baḥr*, II:187–90, 197.

64 Al-Shaybānī, *Kitāb al-Sunnah*, 460–1; al-Bazzār, *al-Baḥr*, II:139.

the scope of the obedience traditions. In other words, by mentioning specific historical incidents or groups (such as the Khawārij or the rebellion of Ibn al-Zubayr or the Shīᶜa), these traditions become applicable only to these particular sets of facts. For example, if the rebellion of the Khawārij or Ibn al-Zubayr is condemned, that does not necessarily mean that the rebellion of al-Ḥusayn b. ᶜAlī or al-Nafs al-Zakiyya is equally reprehensible. Arguably, one can distinguish these reports on the facts of each case. As discussed later, this in fact was the chosen methodology of some late jurists who argued that regardless of what one might say about Ibn al-Zubayr's rebellion, for example, al-Ḥusayn b. ᶜAlī's rebellion was justified. This gap or loophole, so to speak, is somewhat bridged by traditions that provide that one should not chide or attempt to counsel a ruler (*amīr*) if the result could be the spread of *fitna*.[65] Pursuant to this logic, the prohibition against *fitna* is not limited to particular conflicts that took place in Islamic history, but extends to prohibit any situation that might result in a *fitna*. Likewise, it is not the Khawārij, as a specific historical entity, that is reprehensible, but any other group that follows in its footsteps. This is particularly the case considering that in early legal discourses the word often used for rebels in general was *khawārij* (those who exit or rebel).[66]

THE COUNTER-OBEDIENCE TRADITIONS

The Qur'ān consistently demands the establishment of justice and the removal of oppression. For instance, it states: "Why do you fail to fight in the cause of God, and for the oppressed men, women, and children who pray, 'O Lord, get us out of this city whose people are oppressors, and send us by Your Will an ally and send us an aid.'"[67] In fact, the idea of *fitna* is equated in the Qur'ānic discourse with the existence of injustice and oppression, and not with rebellion or civil war. *Fitna* is often described in the Qur'ān as a pervasive state of oppression by arrogant

[65] Ibn Abī Shayba, *al-Muṣannaf*, VIII:622. These reports, however, provide that one may do so if the ruler commands a person to commit a sin or if one feels compelled to do so; but counseling the ruler should be done in private. On giving counsel to rulers in private, see al-Shaybānī, *Kitāb al-Sunnah*, 507–9.

[66] See, for example, al-ᶜAynī, *ᶜUmda*, XXIV:84, reporting the early opinion that every rebel was called a *khārijī* whether at the time of the Companions or afterwards. The author then contrasts this to the position of the later jurists who distinguished between the *khawārij* and the *bughāh*.

[67] Qur'ān 4:75.

and unjust rulers.[68] While the Qur'ān does not explicitly command insurrection or rebellion against unjust rulers, it does create a powerful symbolic construct that can be easily utilized to justify armed resistance to oppression.[69]

Partly because of the inconsistency between the Qur'ānic symbolism and the obedience traditions, the Muʿtazilī al-Ḥākim al-Bayhaqī (d. 458/1065) accuses non-Muʿtazilī Muslims of having fabricated the traditions that demand that every usurper of power be obeyed, even if he is an Ethiopian slave, and whether he is just or not.[70] One suspects that he is quite right. Nevertheless, an accusation of fabrication was not the chosen methodology of the vast majority of Sunnī jurists. There are many Sunnī jurists who simply ignored the obedience reports. But even more jurists, as we will see, distinguished these reports on technical grounds. Very few, however, declared the reports fabricated. There are a variety of reasons for this, among them the place that *ḥadīth* and *Sunna* achieved in the early juridical culture. More importantly, the inherent conservatism of juridical culture does not usually opt for radical solutions such as declaring a whole body of precedent an invention or fabrication. I do not wish to imply that Sunnī jurists would have necessarily wanted to unequivocally and consistently negate the obedience traditions. In fact, these traditions served an important function when Muslim jurists wished to advocate order and stability. However, a unitary, unwavering reliance on the obedience traditions would have rendered any discourse on rebellion impossible. Significantly, even had jurists wished to emphasize a unitary duty of obedience, they still would have had to distinguish or otherwise deal with the counter-traditions on obedience.

Perhaps the most important and compelling counter-tradition is the practice and conduct of many of the Prophet's Companions and several of the early jurists who took part, supported, or sympathized with a variety of rebellions. We have already discussed this specific heritage. To condemn unequivocally all forms of rebellion, in all circumstances, would raise serious questions as to the credibility of several of the

[68] *Fitna* is also used in the sense of mundane temptations, such as money, ignorance, and disbelief in God. See, for instance, Qur'ān 2:191, 193, 217, 8:25, 28, 39, 73, 29, 10, 64:15.

[69] See Qur'ān 9:12, 23:34, 43:54.

[70] Al-Bayhaqī, *Risāla*, 97. Likewise, al-Jāḥiẓ (d. 255/869), "Risāla fī al-Nābita," 243–4, strongly criticizes those who claimed that slandering or cursing unjust rulers is a *fitna*. He asserts that these "innovating heretics" forbade the criticizing, maligning, or removing of rulers regardless of their injustice.

most honored figures in early Islamic history. In fact, the opponents of rebellion, or the advocates of non-rebellion, focused most of their legal energy on distinguishing, limiting, or explaining away the behavior of the early Companions or jurists. If rebellion was to be declared a sin, some argument had to be found for arguing that the honored forefathers did not commit a sin by rebelling. Even more, the conduct of some of the Companions and jurists was bound to generate counter-traditions that would explain or legitimate their behavior. Again, the counter-traditions represent tendencies or trends in early legal opinions but are not developed systematic positions.

Most counter-traditions appear in the same *ḥadīth* sources that cite the obedience traditions. It is very likely that both types of tradition appeared contemporaneously. The obedience and counter-obedience traditions manifest an unmistakable tension that never becomes fully resolved in the later writings of jurists. This tension is well demonstrated, for example, in a tradition in which al-Ḥasan al-Baṣrī (d. 110/728) reportedly tells al-Ḥajjāj that the Prophet ordered: "[We] respect and honor the rulers (*al-salāṭīn*) because they are God's pride and shadow on this earth if they are just." Al-Ḥajjāj, apparently surprised by this version of the tradition, intimates that he had heard this tradition before, and declares: "[The *ḥadīth*] never said 'if they are just.'" Al-Ḥasan promptly answers, "Yes, it [always] did."[71] In order to get a fuller sense of this tension, we will survey some of these counter-traditions in order to get a sense of the diversity and complexity extant in the sources of the time.

We have already mentioned the tradition which states that one must obey a ruler even if he is an Abyssinian or Ethiopian slave. Some versions of this report add the contingency that such a person should only be obeyed as long as he implements the book of God, and, in some versions, as long as he leads Muslims in accordance with the book of God (*mā aqāma*

[71] See al-Zamakhsharī, *Rabīᶜ*, V:161. (The editor identifies the Ḥasan in the report as Ḥasan b. ᶜAlī who died in 49/669. This cannot be accurate.) Many of the traditions specifying that no obedience is due to an unjust ruler or that a ruler should not be obeyed if he commands a sin are cited in *Kitāb al-Majmūᶜ*, attributed to Zayd b. ᶜAlī (d. 122/740): see al-Ṣarfānī, *Tatimma*, IV:6–11. Nonetheless, it is also very likely that many of the traditions that would have dogmatically supported rebellion against unjust rulers have disappeared or been destroyed. For example, al-Bayhaqī, *Risāla*, 97, states that the Muᶜtazila had narrated traditions in support of their position on rebellion. But it is not clear to which traditions the author is referring. Furthermore, as we noted earlier, several jurists were persecuted because of their positions on the legal effect of duress on acts. This means that various governments had an interest in suppressing certain types of traditions and literature. It would stand to reason that many of these traditions have, in fact, been suppressed or destroyed.

bikum kitābu Allāh or *mā qādakum bi kitābi Allāh*).[72] Other reports make the duty of blind obedience applicable only in the time of the Prophet. Such reports quote the Prophet as saying: "Listen and obey as long as I am with you. After I die, take the book of God, [implement its commands] and make what it makes permissible, permissible, and prohibit what it prohibits."[73] A set of widely cited traditions explicitly states that a ruler should not be obeyed if he commands a sin (*lā ṭāᶜata fī maᶜṣiya*), or that he should be obeyed only to the extent that he commands what is good and just (*innamā al-ṭāᶜatu fī al-maᶜrūf*).[74] This general imperative was put into the form of an interesting narrative which was later heavily cited in juridical sources. According to this narrative, a man from the Anṣār was put in charge of a military expedition, and the Prophet commanded the soldiers under the man's charge to obey him. After leaving on their expedition, the soldiers upset the commander for an unidentified reason. In response, the commander then ordered that a sizable fire be lit, and ordered his soldiers to throw themselves into the fire. When the soldiers hesitated, the commander said, "Didn't the Prophet command you to listen and to obey me?" The soldiers, however, remarked, "We have found refuge in the Prophet from Hellfire," and refused to obey. When the Prophet was told of the incident, he declared, "If they [the soldiers] would have obeyed and walked into the fire, they would have never come out [i.e. they would have burned in hell forever]. Obedience is due only in what is good and just (*innamā al-ṭāᶜatu fī al-maᶜrūf*)."[75] Another version of this report insists that the whole matter started out as a joke. According to this version, the commander ordered the fire lit, and then said, "Don't you have a duty to obey me?" The soldiers said, "Yes." The commander inquired, "So if I tell you to do anything, you will do it?" The soldiers, again, said, "Yes." "Then," the commander asserted, "I order you to jump into the fire." But observing that the soldiers were about to comply with his order, the

72 Al-Shaybānī, *Kitāb al-Sunnah*, 492; Ibn Ḥanbal, *Musnad*, VI:451; Muslim b. al-Ḥajjāj, *al-Jāmiᶜ*, VI:15; Ibn Mājah, *Sunan*, II:955. This is limited somewhat in a tradition in al-Bukhārī, *Ṣaḥīḥ* (Dār Iḥyāʾ al-Turāth al-ᶜArabī), IV:222. In this tradition it is reported that the Prophet said that one should not rebel unless one sees clear acts of disbelief which one can identify as such by clear evidence (*ᶜindakum min Allāhi fīhi burhān*). Building on this, later Muslim jurists argued that one should not rebel as long as the acts of the ruler are legal according to some plausible legal interpretation. If they are not legal under any plausible interpretation, one may rebel. See al-Qasṭalānī, *Irshād*, X:170; al-Nawawī, *al-Majmūᶜ*, XII:468, 471.

73 Ibn Ḥanbal, *Musnad*, II:279.

74 Abū Dāwūd, *Sunan*, IV:94; al-Bazzār, *al-Baḥr*, II:204, 206; Muslim b. al-Ḥajjāj, *al-Jāmiᶜ*, VI:15; Ibn Mājah, *Sunan*, II:956.

75 Muslim b. al-Ḥajjāj, *al-Jāmiᶜ*, VI:16. This version of the report is mentioned in the Zaydī source al-Ṣanᶜānī, *Tatimma*, IV:7.

commander yelled out, "I was just joking with you." When the Prophet was informed of the incident, he said: "If someone orders you to commit a sin [i.e. kill yourselves in this situation], you should not obey."[76]

In another fascinating, but most certainly apocryphal, report, the tensions engendered in the counter-obedience traditions are fully and dramatically displayed. It is reported that Muᶜāwiya's supporter and governor ᶜAmr b. al-ᶜĀṣ was sitting near the Kaᶜba talking to a group of people about the Prophet and his times. Ibn al-ᶜĀṣ explained that the Companions, himself included, were traveling with the Prophet when they stopped to rest. The Prophet called the people to prayer but before they started praying, the Prophet spoke to the Companions and explained that it is incumbent upon every prophet to warn his people about the good and evil that will eventually befall them. The Prophet warned that after he died there would be much chaos and many *fitan* until the heart of every Muslim would be gripped by terror. The Prophet then said that when this takes place, those who would like to escape hellfire and enter heaven, let them die while believing in God and the Hereafter, let them treat others as they would want to be treated, and let them not violate an oath of allegiance they gave to a ruler (*imām*). The Prophet continued, "So, if one comes to challenge him [the *imām*], then strike his neck [i.e. the challenger]." The man listening to the sermon took Ibn al-ᶜĀṣ to the side and said, "By God, did you really hear the Prophet say this?" Ibn al-ᶜĀṣ pointed to his ears and heart and said, "Verily, my ears have heard it and my heart has absorbed it." The man said, "But your cousin Muᶜāwiya commands us to usurp each other's money and commands us to kill each other while God has said . . . [Qur'ānic verse omitted]." Ibn al-ᶜĀṣ fell silent for a while pondering the man's comment then said, "Then obey him [Muᶜāwiya] in what is consistent with God's commands, and disobey him if he orders you to disobey God."[77] In this tradition, an obedience report is confronted and neutralized by a counter-obedience report. Ibn al-ᶜĀṣ, Muᶜāwiya's confidant and supporter, is made to admit that the commands of God come before all else, even before his master and benefactor, Muᶜāwiya.

A different genre of the counter-obedience reports may be called the empowering or enabling traditions. These traditions promote or encourage resistance to rulers in one form or another. A common form

[76] Ibn Māja, *Sunan*, II:956. Later jurists discuss this report, and other obedience and counter-obedience traditions. For example, al-Ghazālī, *Faḍā'iḥ*, 207; Ibn Taymiyya, *Majmūᶜ al-Fatāwā*, XXXV:15.

[77] Muslim b. al-Ḥajjāj, *al-Jāmiᶜ*, VI:18.

of this genre states that the best form of *jihād* (just struggle) is a word of truth spoken before an unjust ruler (*inna min aʿẓami al-jihādi kalimatu ʿadlin ʿinda sulṭānin jāʾir*),[78] or that the Prophet commanded that Muslims speak the truth in whichever context, and not fear the consequences (*wa an naqūla al-ḥaqqa ḥaythumā kunnā lā nakhāfu fī Allāhi lawmata lāʾim*).[79] Another form specifies that the Prophet said that whosoever resists an unjust ruler with his hand, tongue, or heart is a believer. If one fails to resist through one of these means, one is no longer a believer.[80] Other traditions assert that the Prophet warned that if Muslims fail to restrain the unjust (*al-ẓālim*), they will all be overcome by God's vengeance.[81] In a variety of reports, the Prophet is quoted as condemning or disavowing any Muslim who believes, supports, or cooperates with unjust rulers.[82] Importantly, various reports add that the Prophet declared that whoever dies trying to protect his property from a usurper dies a martyr.[83] Of course, a usurper of property could be an unjust ruler, a warring bandit, or even a rebel.

The range of raw materials incorporated into the juristic discourses on rebellion is not limited to the *ḥadīth* of the Prophet. Rather, various reports on specific historical events and incidents were incorporated as well. Because these traditions relate to particular historical contexts, they are more specific and technical in nature, but also ambiguous and vague in meaning. But this is exactly why they lent themselves well to the discourses on rebellion. In one set of traditions, the Prophet is quoted as saying that three types of people will die a pagan's death (*mawt al-jāhiliyya*):

78 Al-Tirmidhī, *al-Jāmiʿ*, IV:409.

79 Ibn Mājah, *Sunan*, II:957. Reports that demand that Muslims enjoin the good and forbid the evil (*al-amru bi al-maʿrūfi wa al-nahyu ʿan al-munkar*) should be included in the counter-obedience type of traditions. In many of these traditions it is reported that the Prophet warned that if Muslims fail to enjoin the good and forbid the evil, they will suffer the fate of previous nations who have been damned by God for failing to discharge this duty. For these kinds of reports, see Ibn Ḥanbal, *Musnad*, V:482, 485; al-Rāzī, *ʿIlal*, II:411, 417, 430. It is not clear from these reports whether the rulers, jurists, or laity, or perhaps all of them, should shoulder the burden of enjoining the good and forbidding the evil. Recently, Michael Cook has written a masterful study on enjoining the good and forbidding the evil: see Cook, *Commanding*.

80 Al-Bazzār, *al-Baḥr*, V:281.

81 Ibid., I:135; Ibn Ḥajar al-ʿAsqalānī, *Fatḥ*, XIV:492. Of similar nature are reports that claim that the Prophet said: "As you are, you will be led," meaning that God permits people to be ruled according to their merits. If people are not diligent in upholding justice, they will be led by the unjust. Likewise, the Qurʾān says: "Thus, we make the unjust rule over each other because of what they [themselves] have earned" (Qurʾān 6:129). This, of course, can be interpreted to mean that if people are led by unjust rulers, they should accept this situation because they deserve to be ruled as such. Alternatively, it could mean that they will continue to be ruled by the unjust unless they resist injustice. Both interpretations are cited by jurists in the context of the law of rebellion. See Ibn Taymiyya, *Majmūʿ al-Fatāwā*, XXXV:20.

82 Al-Tirmidhī, *al-Jāmiʿ*, IV:455.

83 Al-Bazzār, *al-Baḥr*, IV:45; Ibn Mājah, *Sunan*, II:861–2.

(1) Those who depart from the *jamāᶜa* and are not obedient; (2) those who rebel, striking with their sword indiscriminately, not distinguishing between a believer and an unbeliever, and not upholding their promises or covenants; (3) those who fight under a blind flag or blind tribalism (*ᶜaṣabiyya*), or advocate blind tribalism.[84] The first category refers to rebels generally, and the second to the Khawārij specifically. The third category is the most interesting. It is general enough to be a blanket condemnation of any blind loyalty. This is significant, partly because some later jurists argued that the difference between a legitimate rebel and an illegitimate rebel is that the former rebels because of a *taʾwīl* (religious or political interpretation), and the latter rebels because of *ᶜaṣabiyya* (some blind loyalty). More importantly, however, these traditions could be read as a condemnation of Muᶜāwiya and the Umayyads. For example, Mālik b. Anas was reportedly asked about the *ahl al-ᶜaṣabiyya alladhīna kānū bi al-Shām* (the people of blind tribalism that were in Syria); he said that they should have been called to repent, and if they refused they should be fought.[85] From this point of view, the above tradition would be read as upholding ᶜAlī's legitimacy against all who rose against him. The first group identified in the tradition would be ᶜĀʾisha and her party, the second group would be the Khawārij, and the third group would be Muᶜāwiya and the Syrians. Considering that the Syrians eventually took power, the tradition would be derogatory of those who come to power through illegitimate means. In another related tradition, the Prophet reportedly warns that the downfall of his nation will be due to the fact that impetuous youth (in some versions, from Quraysh) will take power. The reports are constructed in such a fashion as to identify the Umayyads as the group meant by the tradition. Some reports claim that the Prophet's Companion Abū Hurayra (d. 58/678) knew the names of every one of these youths, but would only hint at their names without speaking frankly, in fear for his own safety. Other reports explicitly assert that the impetuous youths were Yazīd b. Muᶜāwiya and al-Ḥajjāj.[86]

Other traditions arising from the context of ᶜAlī's conflict with his opponents, instead of being critical of unjust rulers, focus on the moral worth of the rebels or the treatment due to them. These traditions do not necessarily encourage or justify rebellion or challenges to power, but they do insist on a certain degree of tolerance to be afforded to rebels. We have already mentioned the traditions where ᶜAlī commanded that

[84] Ibn Ḥanbal, *Musnad*, II:390, 403, 646; Ibn Ḥajar al-ᶜAsqalānī, *Fatḥ*, XIV:530–1; al-Nawawī, *al-Majmūᶜ*, XII:480, 482.

[85] Saḥnūn, *al-Mudawwana*, I:407.

[86] Al-Bukhārī, *Ṣaḥīḥ* (Dār Iḥyāʾ al-Turāth al-ᶜArabī), IV:222; al-Qasṭalānī, *Irshād*, X:170–1.

rebels should not be pursued or slaughtered. Similar traditions state that in the Battle of Ṣiffīn, whenever ʿAlī captured a rebel, he would take his weapon and take an oath from him not to return to rebellion, and then release him.[87] Importantly, there are various reports asserting that ʿAlī and ʿUmar b. ʿAbd al-ʿAzīz ordered that the rebels would not be attacked unless they initiated the violence.[88] When told that the Khawārij were slandering him, ʿUmar b. ʿAbd al-ʿAzīz reportedly told his governor that if he (the governor) wished to do so, he could slander them back; but ʿUmar b. ʿAbd al-ʿAzīz refused to fight the Khawārij unless the Khawārij fought him first. Similarly, when told that the Khawārij were plotting to kill him, ʿAlī said, "I cannot kill them and they have not killed me [yet]."[89] This is quite similar to a report in which a man was arrested and brought to ʿAlī. ʿAlī was told that the man had adopted the creed of the Khawārij. ʿAlī asked: "What do you want me to do with him?" When it was suggested that the man be executed, ʿAlī refused and said, "I do not kill someone who has not fought me." It was then suggested that the man be imprisoned. Again, ʿAlī refused and proclaimed, "I do not imprison someone who has not committed a crime. Set the man free."[90] Furthermore, there are numerous reports in which ʿAlī confirms that those who rebelled against him were to be considered Muslims and treated as such. When ʿAlī was asked if the rebels in the Battle of the Camel were unbelievers, he said no. He was asked if they were hypocrites, and he said no, because hypocrites rarely mention God. He was then asked, "So what are they?" He responded, "They are our brethren, who have treated us unjustly (*hum ikhwānunā baghū ʿalaynā*)."[91] Exactly the same tradition is reported about the Khawārij.[92]

87 Ibn Abī Shayba, *al-Muṣannaf*, VIII:724–5; also see ibid., 710, 711, 718–19.

88 Ibid., 732.

89 Al-Ṣanʿānī, *al-Muṣannaf*, X:117–18; al-Bayhaqī, *Maʿrifa*, VI:286–7. These reports are widely cited by later jurists. For example, see Ibn al-Humām, *Sharḥ*, VI:93–4; Ibn Qudāma, *al-Mughnī*, X:51–2. Muʿāwiya, reportedly, said, "I will not fight [the rebels] unless I find no other choice": al-Ṣanʿānī, *al-Muṣannaf*, V:462. However, as noted earlier, Sunnī jurists rarely cite or rely on reports about Muʿāwiya's conduct.

90 Ibn ʿAbd al-Barr, *al-Tamhīd* (1982), XXIII:334.

91 Ibn Abī Shayba, *al-Muṣannaf*, VIII:707–8. In a different version, ʿAlī is reported to have said that Muʿāwiya and his party were not unbelievers. Rather, they claimed that "we treated them unjustly, and we claimed that they treated us unjustly, and so, based on our claim, we fought them": see al-Māwardī, *Naṣīḥa*, 462. ʿAmmār b. Yāsir reportedly said that those who rebelled against ʿAlī were to be considered believers, but that they had sinned and acted unjustly: Ibn Abī Shayba, *al-Muṣannaf*, VIII:722. There are conflicting reports on whether dead rebels would go to hell or heaven: ibid., 725, 729.

92 Ibid., 743; Ibn ʿAbd al-Barr, *al-Tamhīd* (1982), XXIII:335–6. The same traditions are cited in the Shīʿī source al-Najafī, *Jawāhir*, XXI:338; however, this source says that those who rebelled against ʿAlī were *kuffār niʿma* (sinners or, literally, ungrateful to the blessings of God) but not *mushrikīn* (polytheists).

We mentioned earlier that several reports claimed that the Companions decided that no liability should be incurred for acts committed during the course of the rebellion. In other words, the contending parties would not be held liable for life and property destroyed during the course of fighting. According to a report attributed to Saʿīd b. al-Musayyab (d. 94/713), one of the prominent jurists of Medina, the reason for the exemption from liability is that "each one of the two [contending] parties sees the other as unjust (*fa-kullu wāḥidatin min al-ṭāʾifatayni tarā al-ukhrā bāghiyah*)."[93] Later jurists explored the implications of this argument, and whether it means that each of the contending parties has a relative moral claim to power or whether it means that the subjective beliefs of each party must be taken into account. Put differently, this report could mean that the two parties contending for power only have a relative claim to power, and hence, if they fight, it is not appropriate to hold one side liable for asserting its claim. Alternatively, the report could mean that although one party is in fact entitled to power, and is ultimately right, the other contending party has a sincerely held subjective belief in the righteousness of its cause. Because of this sincerely held subjective belief, even if the belief is ultimately erroneous, it would not be proper to hold either party liable.

how does this work w/ balancing?

This debate relies heavily on another report which comes by the way of Ibn al-Musayyab's student al-Zuhrī (d. 124/741). The Umayyad Sulaymān b. Hishām reportedly wrote to al-Zuhrī asking about a woman who had left her husband and joined the Khawārij (Ḥarūriyya). She joined the Khawārij in their activities and remarried from among them, but later repented and wanted to rejoin her family. Al-Zuhrī wrote back saying:

> The first *fitna* broke out while many of the companions of the Prophet who fought in [the Battle of] Badr were still alive. They all agreed not to penalize anyone who married (or had intercourse) while relying on an interpretation from the Qurʾān (*bi taʾwīli al-Qurʾān*), not to punish anyone who killed while relying on an interpretation from the Qurʾān, and not to hold anyone liable who destroyed property while relying on an interpretation from the Qurʾān. The only exception was that if the usurped property is found in the possession of the usurper, it must be returned. In my view, the woman should be permitted to

[93] Al-Ṣanʿānī, *al-Muṣannaf*, x:122. This could also be read to mean that each side sees the other as rebels. Nonetheless, by Ibn al-Musayyab's time, the word *bāghiya* had not yet acquired its technical meaning of "rebel." Rather, it was used in a general sense to mean unjust. On Ibn al-Musayyab, see Ibn al-Jawzī, *Ṣifa*, ii:437–40.

return to her [first] husband, and anyone who may have slandered her should be punished.[94]

Effectively, what al-Zuhrī is saying is that the woman's sincerely held belief that it was proper to join the Khawārij exempts her from liability.[95] Interestingly, Sulaymān b. Hāshim, although the son of the former Umayyad caliph ʿAbd al-Malik, at one point had himself joined the Khawārij and fought against the last Umayyad caliph.[96] Al-Zuhrī's father, as we mentioned earlier, had joined Ibn al-Zubayr's rebellion, but al-Zuhrī himself reportedly reconciled with the Umayyads and co-operated with the caliph ʿAbd al-Malik. This could mean that the whole interaction between Sulaymān and al-Zuhrī is apocryphal.[97] Even if it is, this would be largely irrelevant. What is significant is that later Muslim jurists relied heavily on this, and the other reports discussed above, in arguing the law of rebellion in Islam.[98] Importantly, by extending the rule of exemption from liability to the Khawārij, this report represents a significant trend which was later endorsed by many jurists. As discussed later, the status of the Khawārij has remained problematic throughout Islamic history because of the group's extremist views and its bloody methods. If the Khawārij are not to be held liable then, by extension, any other less extreme group would be excused from liability as well. In another report dealing with the Khawārij, this one attributed directly to ʿAlī, it is claimed that ʿAlī said that if the Khawārij rebel against a just

94 Al-Ṣanʿānī, *al-Muṣannaf*, X:120–1; al-ʿAynī, *al-Bināya*, VI:747–8; al-Samarqandī, *Tuḥfa*, III:314; Ibn al-Humām, *Sharḥ*, VI:100.

95 The reference to slander (*qadhf*) is necessary due to the fact that the woman married a second husband. When the woman joined the Khawārij, according to her newly adopted religious creed most Muslims, including her first husband, would be considered unbelievers. Accordingly, she thought that her first marriage was automatically dissolved, and that she was free to remarry. In the opinion of her detractors, she would be considered an adulteress because she wrongly believed that her first marriage was dissolved. In effect, al-Zuhrī is saying that anyone accusing the woman of adultery should be punished because she acted in good faith while basing herself on a religious interpretation.

96 See Kennedy, *Prophet*, 112–15.

97 While it is possible that al-Zuhrī cooperated with the Umayyads, he might have actually made this statement towards the end of the Umayyad dynasty. Around 121 A.H., and especially 123 A.H. when the caliph Hishām died, the deterioration in the empire had become evident. There was widespread disappointment and frustration. It would not be surprising if al-Zuhrī made the above-discussed statement at that time. I have noted the scholarly debate about al-Zuhrī's relationship to the Umayyads earlier.

98 For example, Ibn Ḥajar al-ʿAsqalānī (*Fatḥ*, XIV:312) argues that every rebel with a plausible interpretation (*taʾwīlun sāʾighun fī lisāni al-ʿArab*) does not incur a sin. In a version of this report that probably came into circulation later than the above discussed version, it is the caliph Hishām b. ʿAbd al-Malik who asked al-Zuhrī about the woman. Al-Zuhrī's response was the same: see Abū Yaʿlā, *al-Masāʾil*, II:306–7; al-Nawawī, al-*Majmūʿ*, XIX:210.

ruler, then Muslims should fight them. However, if the Khawārij rebel against an unjust ruler, Muslims should not fight them because in this situation they may have a legitimate cause of action (*fa-lā tuqātilūhum fa-inna lahum maqāl*).[99] Arguably, the reasoning of this report could be extended to less extreme rebels who might rebel against an unjust ruler.

Certainly, I am not contending that any of the reports mentioned above of necessity encourage or support rebellion. Rather, they are susceptible to being interpreted or constructed in such a way that they would render a supposed duty of unquestioning obedience problematic. I have chosen the reports that figure prominently in later discourses on rebellion. If I am correct in asserting that these reports came into circulation in the first half of the second century or earlier, then they were part of the raw material which was used to construct the discourses on rebellion. Of course, it is very likely that early trends and attitudes towards rebellion generated many of these reports in the first place. I am also not discounting entirely the possibility that the Prophet or ᶜAlī, in one form or another, were the originators of some of these reports. It is quite possible that the Prophet made statements on the need to obey God even if it meant disobeying others. Similarly, it is possible that ᶜAlī refused to declare his political opponents unbelievers or shed their blood without limitations. It is also possible that the collective memory of Muslims recalled some exhortations from the Prophet or ᶜAlī on the issue of authority, obedience, and rebellion, which the traditionists later articulated in the form of canonical *ḥadīth* traditions. But even in their canonical form, without the development and systematization of jurists, these traditions, despite their highly structured and formal constructs, are susceptible to an endless array of interpretive and reconstructive activity. Relying on the traditions from ᶜAlī about rebellion, for example, one may argue that ᶜAlī was the just ruler, and that the Umayyads were illegitimate usurpers. Alternatively, one may argue that the Umayyads were the just rulers, and all those who rebelled against them were illegitimate usurpers. In either case, one could still argue that rebellion is not a sin as long as the rebellion relies on a plausible religious interpretation. One can also argue that rebellion is never justified but then argue that it is legal to defend oneself against

[99] Ibn Abī Shayba (*al-Muṣannaf*, VIII:737–8) also adds that ᶜAlī said not to curse the Khawārij. Also see this report in Shīᶜī sources: al-Ḥurr al-ᶜĀmilī, *Wasāʾil*, XI:60; al-Najafī, *Jawāhir*, XXI:333. As discussed later, Muslim jurists built on this tradition. For example, see Ibn Ḥajar al-ᶜAsqalānī, *Fatḥ*, XIV:309: after citing this tradition, he argues that people should not fight those who rebel against an unjust ruler. Even in his book written for the specific purpose of giving advice to rulers, al-Māwardī quotes a version of this report: al-Māwardī, *Naṣīḥa*, 462.

acts of injustice. Hence one can construct an argument that rebellion is illegal unless it is an act of self-defense.

Even the traditions that provide that a ruler should be obeyed only to the extent that he implements the Qur'ān are inherently vague, and can only be given substance within the context of a political, social, or jurisprudential discourse. The rallying call that judgment should be in accordance with the Qur'ān and the command of God was common among the rebels of early Islam.[100] Yet the inherent vagueness of such a call is well demonstrated in an anecdote cited by Muslim jurists. The Qurrā' (eventually called the Khawārij) broke with ᶜAlī and left for Ḥarūrā' because they accused him of having abandoned the law of the Qur'ān when he accepted the possibility of a peaceful settlement with Muᶜāwiya. The Khawārij, who were quite pious but legally unsophisticated, would yell at ᶜAlī, "You have made human beings the supreme judges [sovereigns] over God's religion while God should be the Supreme judge [the Sovereign]." ᶜAlī, frustrated by the polemics, brought a huge Qur'ān and called upon Muslims to gather. He then poked at the Qur'ān with his finger and said: "Oh, Qur'ān speak to the people." The people exclaimed, "What are you asking for? Is it a human being so that it would be able to speak? It is but ink and paper, and we [human beings] speak in accordance with what we recite [understand] from it (*innamā huwa midādun wa waraq wa naḥnu natakallamu bi mā rawaynā minhu*). ᶜAlī then said: "[In this fashion] the book of God judges between me and those people [the Qurrā']." ᶜAlī went on to explain that based on an analogy drawn from Qur'ānic injunctions regarding a marital dispute, and on an analogy drawn from the conduct of the Prophet, his interpretation as to how he should conduct himself with Muᶜāwiya was well supported.[101] Muslim jurists did not cite this example only to demonstrate that ᶜAlī

[100] Crone and Hinds (*God's*, 58–96) demonstrate that a vague call to the judgment of the Qur'ān and *Sunna* was common among many rebels in early Islam. The call to rule or judge according to the book of God had, and still has, a strong emotive appeal. For example, Ibn Ḥazm cites a very interesting incident in which a man agreed to give an oath of allegiance to Muᶜāwiya on the condition that he (Muᶜāwiya) comply with the Qur'ān and the *Sunna* of the Prophet. Muᶜāwiya rejected the qualifying condition, and so the man refused to give him the oath of allegiance: Ibn Ḥazm, *Jamhara*, 401; also see Crone and Hinds, *God's*, 67 n. 59.

[101] Ibn Ḥajar al-ᶜAsqalānī, *Fatḥ*, XIV:303; al-Shawkānī, *Nayl*, VII:166. Another report makes ᶜAlī side-step the issue of who is right or wrong and rely instead on a technicality. A man came to ᶜAlī and asked, "Why do you fight [your opponents] (*ᶜalā mā tuqātilu hā'ulā'*)?" ᶜAlī responded, "[I fight them] over what is right (*ᶜalā al-ḥaqq*)." The man said, "But [your opponents] say, they are right." ᶜAlī responded, "Then I fight them because they violated their oath of allegiance and broke with the *jamāᶜa*": al-Qasṭalānī, *Irshād*, X:196. In a report that perhaps reflects an extreme sense of skepticism, it is claimed that Jubayr b. Nafīr (d. 70/689 or 80/699) asked some people around him: "If two persons emerge, one calling for the book of God (*kitāb Allāh*) [to be implemented], and the other calling for the discretion of the ruler (*sulṭān Allāh*) which one

was more reasonable and knowledgeable than the Khawārij, but also to explore the range of possible legitimate disagreements that might distinguish a rebel from a non-rebel, or distinguish one rebel from another. This example is also relevant to the larger context of ascertaining the proper balance between politics and legality. While Muslim jurists were not willing to argue that all matters that pertain to law are susceptible to only one correct interpretation, they were also not willing dogmatically to champion the cause of politics. Law cannot always yield singular and definitive results, but that does not mean that political expediency should always prevail, or that law, because of its indefiniteness, should abdicate the determination of correctness or legitimacy to politics.[102]

Both the obedience and counter-obedience traditions do not yield any inevitabilities; they merely set trends. The various trends were constructed and reconciled in a fashion that would ultimately make the jurists the ultimate arbiters not only of law and order, but also of the legality of rebellion. At this point, it is useful to give a demonstrative example of this process of reconciling and reconstructing the traditions on obedience. The implication of this example is that the jurists, and not the rulers, are the ones empowered to decide on what is to be considered a legitimate or illegitimate rebellion. The jurist Ibn al-Qayyim, for instance, citing the obedience traditions, conceded that rulers must be obeyed without question, but he also asserted that rulers may only be obeyed if they command that which is good and just (*maᶜrūf*). The tension between the two imperatives is resolved in the following fashion:

> Properly speaking, the rulers (*al-umarāʾ*) are obeyed [only to the extent] that their commands are consistent with the [articulations] of the religious sciences (*al-ᶜilm*). Hence, the duty to obey them [the rulers] derives from the duty to obey the jurists (*fa-ṭāᶜatuhum tabaᶜun li ṭāᶜati al-ᶜulamāʾ*). [This is because] obedience is

would you follow?" The people said: "We would follow the one calling for the book of God." Jubayr said: "Then you will be doomed (*idhan tahlakū*)": al-Rāzī, *ᶜIlal*, II:424–5. Jubayr was a Syrian jurist. Reportedly, he was threatened by Muᶜāwiya because he narrated a tradition in which the Prophet predicts and laments that after he dies, his nation will abandon the Qurʾān: al-Dhahabī, *Siyar*, IV:77. Interestingly, some jurists quoted the Prophet as saying, "If you lay siege to a fortress do not have the inhabitants surrender on the condition of enforcing the judgment of God, for you do not know what is God's judgment. Rather, have them surrender on the condition of enforcing your own judgment": ibid., XVII:190. However, this report did not receive wide circulation, and was not extensively cited by the juristic culture.

[102] For an extreme example, Ibn al-Jawzī claims that ᶜAḍud al-Dawla the Buwayhid (r. 338/949–372/983) was madly in love with a slave girl to the point that she distracted him from administering the affairs of the state. He therefore had the woman drowned so that he would no longer be distracted. Ibn al-Jawzī comments that this is "absolute madness," and that under no possible interpretation can this be considered legal. No claim of public interest can justify the taking of innocent life: Ibn al-Jawzī, *Talbīs*, 186. Also see Ibn al-Jawzī, *al-Shifāʾ*, 55–7.

due only in what is good (*ma*ᶜ*rūf*), and what is required by the religious sciences (*wa mā awjabahu al-*ᶜ*ilm*). Since the duty to obey the jurists is derived from the duty to obey the Prophet, then the duty to obey the rulers is derived from the duty to obey the jurists [who are the experts on the religious sciences]. Furthermore, since Islam is protected and upheld by the rulers and the jurists alike, this means that the laity must follow [and obey] these two [i.e. the rulers and jurists].[103]

If one carefully examines this argument, one finds that Ibn al-Qayyim took parts from the obedience and counter-obedience traditions and reformulated the traditions into an entirely new construct. He argued that the duty to obey the ruler is derivative of the duty to obey jurists, and the duty to obey the jurists is a derivative of the duty to obey the Prophet. Therefore, the jurists are obeyed to the extent that they obey the Prophet, and the rulers are obeyed to the extent that they obey the jurists. Although the last sentence of the quotation gives the impression that rulers and jurists must be equally obeyed by the laity, this impression is superficial. Rulers are to be obeyed if their commands are consistent with the commands of religion, and it is the jurists who study and interpret the commands of religion. Consequently, in the final analysis, it is the jurists that must be obeyed. The traditions on obedience and counter-obedience have been reconstructed in this argument into something entirely different – these traditions now favor the Prophet, then the jurists, then the rulers.[104] A similar process of innovative reconstruction was carried out in the juristic discourses on rebellion with the end result being that the jurists would become the final arbiters of the standards by which a rebellion is measured and treated.

THE DISCOURSE OF REPORTS ON REBELLION AND BANDITRY

In historical practice, as we saw, rebels were often addressed or treated as bandits. The early traditions did not clearly distinguish between rebellion and banditry either. The two categories of *bāghī* and *muḥārib* were not separate and distinct, and many early reports lapsed or confused the two.

[103] Ibn Qayyim al-Jawziyya, *A*ᶜ*lām* (Beirut), 1:10. Of course, there is vast literature on the creative art of reconciling seemingly contradictory *ḥadīth*. Among the better-known works are: al-Ṭaḥāwī, *Sharḥ*; al-Shāfiᶜī, *Ikhtilāf*; Ibn Qutayba, *Ta*ʾ*wīl*.

[104] Al-Ghazālī (*Faḍā*ʾ*iḥ*, 193–4, 206–7) makes a similar argument to Ibn al-Qayyim's. The idea that rulers should consult jurists or that they should not decide anything without the advice of jurists is a common theme in juridical writings. For example, see Ibn al-Jawzī, *al-Shifā*ʾ, 55. In fact, as discussed later, some jurists argued that a ruler should not decide the fate of rebels or bandits without consulting the jurists first.

There were, however, two trends: the first, reflected in the reports above, tended to emphasize amnesty and exemption from liability for rebels, and the second tended to invoke the language and symbolism of the *ḥirāba* verse in the context of addressing rebellion. As noted earlier, in the developed juristic discourses *ḥirāba* became the crime of highway robbery or banditry, and this crime was clearly distinguished from rebellion. However, the early reports did not reflect this distinctive clarity. Many early reports equated *ḥirāba* with the act of waging war against Muslims after having become an apostate. In this context, *ḥirāba* involved the formal renunciation of Islam, and the waging of warfare against Muslims. Other reports did not assume a formal act of apostasy. Rather, these reports referred to general acts of lawlessness in which life and property were destroyed. However, these acts of lawlessness could be committed during the course of a rebellion. This effectively meant that *ḥirāba* would be indistinguishable from rebellion.

Many of the early reports on *ḥirāba* are extremely vague. For example, it is reported that Saᶜīd b. al-Jubayr said: "Whoever wages war is a *muḥārib* (*man ḥāraba fa-huwa muḥārib*). If he destroys a life, he should be killed. If he destroys life and property, he should be crucified because crucifixion is harsher. If he destroys property without destroying life, he should be amputated from opposite ends."[105] The statement "whoever wages war is a *muḥārib*" is very broad, and could possibly apply to a variety of acts and categories of people. It could apply to an apostate, bandit, rebel, or anyone else who uses armed force against society. It should be recalled that Saᶜīd b. al-Jubayr was reportedly executed by al-Ḥajjāj for taking part in the rebellion by al-Ashᶜath.[106] If, in fact, Ibn Jubayr is the source of this report, it would be unlikely that he would say that anyone who wages war against a ruler is to be considered a *muḥārib*. Yet it would be advantageous to the Umayyads to attribute a report to Ibn al-Jubayr in which the clear implication is that whoever wages war against a ruler is to be killed, crucified, or have their limbs amputated.[107]

Other reports, not attributed to Ibn Jubayr, simply state that *ḥirāba* is *shirk* (disbelief or not believing in God),[108] or state that the *muḥārib* is one who fights religion (*al-muḥāribu man ḥāraba al-dīn*). Fighting religion is then

[105] Ibn Abī Shayba, *al-Muṣannaf*, VI:589, VII:603; al-Ṣanᶜānī, *al-Muṣannaf*, X:108–9.

[106] For a dramatic description of his execution, see Ibn al-Jawzī, *Ṣifa*, III:54–8.

[107] Substantially the same report is attributed to al-Ḥasan. He reportedly said, "*man ḥāraba fa-huwa muḥārib*": al-Ṣanᶜānī, *al-Muṣannaf*, X:111. The statement is no less ambiguous than that attributed to Ibn al-Jubayr.

[108] Ibn Abī Shayba, *al-Muṣannaf*, VII:605; al-Ṣanᶜānī, *al-Muṣannaf*, X:106; Abū Dāwūd, *Sunan*, IV:130.

equated with spreading corruption on the earth.[109] These expressions could have a variety of meanings. They could mean that *ḥirāba* only applies to apostates who abandon Islam and then declare war on society, or they could mean that for anyone who rebels against the ruler, even if he claims to be a Muslim, it is as if he has waged war against religion.[110] Several reports refer to the ʿUrayna incident, and give the clear impression that *ḥirāba* refers to an act of apostasy coupled with warfare.[111] However, other reports address *ḥirāba* as a crime involving *qaṭʿ al-ṭarīq*, which literally means to obstruct the road or prevent passage, but usually refers to highway robbery.[112] Nonetheless, this does not necessarily add clarity to the problem. Rebellious groups such as the Khawārij would regularly attack caravans and obstruct passage. In some reports, for example, instructions are given not to attack the Khawārij unless they obstruct passage and terrorize the wayfarer.[113] More precise reports assert that *ḥirāba* involves a thief who commits highway robbery, i.e. a bandit.[114]

Books of *ḥadīth* reflect the ambiguity that surrounded the early discourses on *baghy* and *ḥirāba*. As Ibn Taymiyya noted, they do not contain a chapter on fighting the *bughāh*. Frequently, there is a chapter entitled "Fighting the Khawārij" which often contains a mixture of at times contradictory reports on the early history of the Khawārij and on ʿAlī's conduct towards them. The segment entitled "Fighting the *muḥāribūn*" usually contains the reports on the ʿUrayna incident without further elaboration. Al-Bukhārī does have a section subtitled "What has been reported regarding those who have an interpretation (*mā jāʾa fī al-mutaʾawwilīn*)." Importantly, however, the only reports mentioned under the section pertain to an incident regarding the different readings of the Qurʾān, and incidents during the life of the Prophet and the hypocrites of Medina. But there is no mention of the *bughāh*.[115] The organizational

109 Ibn Abī Shayba, *al-Muṣannaf*, VII:605; al-Ṣanʿānī, *al-Muṣannaf*, X:111–12.

110 As Crone and Hinds in *God's* have demonstrated, Umayyad and early ʿAbbāsid caliphs often thought of themselves as God's representative and shadow on the earth.

111 Al-Ṣanʿānī, *al-Muṣannaf*, X:106–7.

112 Ibn Abī Shayba, *al-Muṣannaf*, VII:602; al-Ṣanʿānī, *al-Muṣannaf*, X:106.

113 Ibn Ḥajar al-ʿAsqalānī, *Fatḥ*, XIV:306; Ibn Abī Shayba, *al-Muṣannaf*, VIII:736; al-Ṣanʿānī, *al-Muṣannaf*, X:117.

114 Al-Ṣanʿānī, *al-Muṣannaf*, X:106.

115 Al-Bukhārī, *Ṣaḥīḥ* (Dār Iḥyāʾ al-Turāth al-ʿArabī), IV:198–9. Al-Ashʿarī (*Maqālāt*, II:171) has a section on the various views regarding whether the *mutaʾawwilūn* (those with a religious interpretation) are considered unbelievers. He mentions the views of the Muʿtazila, Murjiʾa, and Khawārij. His treatment reflects the controversies of the sectarian debates about the Islamicity of the various sects of theology. But it is very different from the treatment of the topic in legal discourses.

structure for these various topics is rather interesting. Reports about the apostates, the heretics (*zanādiqa*), those who break with the *jamāᶜa*, the *muḥāribūn*, those who cause corruption on the earth, and the Khawārij follow each other in a flood of traditions. If one was to speculate about a general organizational heading under which all these topics are subsumed, it might be "the trouble makers."[116]

Although one cannot read too much into the organizational structures of books of *ḥadīth*, the essential point is the lack of clarity as to the concepts or categorizations that surrounded the issue of rebellion in the first two centuries of Islam.[117] Abū al-Ḥasan al-Ashᶜarī (d. 330/941), for example, reporting on the early views on *baghy* and *bughāh*, reflects much of this ambiguity. According to the views that al-Ashᶜarī describes, these terms are used to apply to government or rebel forces, and are used in such a way as to be the functional equivalent of the word "opponent." For instance, the author reports that the Khawārij argued that ᶜAlī had become an unbeliever when he neglected to fight the *bughāh*.[118] *Bughāh* in this context means Muᶜāwiya and those who rebelled against ᶜAlī. Al-Ashᶜarī then reports that various groups disagreed on whether the *bughāh* may be assassinated or killed by stealth (*ikhtalafū fī qatl al-bughāh ghīlatan*). He states that some of the Muᶜtazila, Khawārij, and extreme Shīᶜīs believed that it is permissible to assassinate opponents.[119] Here the word *bughāh* means political opponents or government officials (probably the Umayyads or ᶜAbbāsids). Later, the author discusses the early views on whether one may conduct commercial transactions with *al-qāṭiᶜ al-bāghī* (*wa ikhtalafa al-nāsu fī mubāyaᶜati al-qāṭiᶜ al-bāghī*). As explained earlier, *al-qāṭiᶜ* means someone who obstructs the wayfarer or a highway robber; *al-bāghī* means a rebel or unjust person. Using the two terms together could mean a rebellious bandit or a bandit who is a rebel. Importantly, however, al-Ashᶜarī says that a group of people said that one should not buy or sell from such a person unless he abandons the *fitna*.[120] In this context, it is likely that al-Ashᶜarī is using

[116] For example, al-Bukhārī, *Ṣaḥīḥ* (Dār Iḥyā'al-Turāth al-ᶜArabī), IV:195–9; al-Nasā'ī, *Sunan*, IV:90–128 (who adds the magicians to the fold); Abū Dāwūd, *Sunan*, IV:124–9 (who also lists apostasy and *ḥirāba* under *ḥudūd*); al-Tirmidhī, *al-Jāmiᶜ*, IV:48–50 (places apostasy, *ḥirāba*, and magic under *ḥudūd*).

[117] Authors of *ḥadīth* collections, such as Bukhārī, exercised a considerable degree of creativity in categorizing and organizing the traditions under particular legal headings. Effectively, they helped create and codify the law by deciding on the legal significance of traditions. See Fadel, "Ibn Ḥajar's." However, the organization of *ḥadīth* books presented the categorization of the law in a raw, undeveloped, and contested form.

[118] Al-Ashᶜarī, *Maqālāt*, II:141. [119] Ibid., 157. [120] Ibid., 159–60.

the word to refer to those who attack caravans and commit highway robbery. This could be any common highway robber or rebel who commits highway robbery. Most likely, however, it refers to the Khawārij. Therefore, we find that the word *baghy* has been used, all in one text, to refer to rebels, the state and its officials, and to the rebellious group the Khawārij. This lack of precision in the use of the terminology reflects the fact that legal discourses, at that time, had not yet fully co-opted terms and rendered them into technical terms of art. In fact, the full co-optation of the terms did not take place until well after the fourth/tenth century, and in a few sources, the lapsing and confusing of *ḥirāba* with *baghy* continues up to the ninth/fifteenth century.

THE EARLY JURISTIC EXPOSITIONS ON REBELLION

Early juristic discourses on rebellion are vague and largely unsystematic. At the same time, one cannot claim that these juristic discourses are dogmatic or of a unilateral nature. The complexity found in the traditions discussed above are fully reflected in the early juristic discourses on the topics of rebellion and banditry. The early juristic culture was searching for concepts that would distinguish the treatment of rebels from other elements who violated the law, but that culture was not sufficiently developed to be able to do so with systematic precision.[121]

The *Muwaṭṭa'* of Mālik b. Anas (d. 179/795) does not cover the subjects of *baghy* or *ḥirāba*. There is a report mentioned in it that Saʿīd b. al-Musayyab reported that the caliph ʿUmar b. al-Khaṭṭāb executed six or seven men who killed someone through *ghīla*. As noted earlier, *ghīla* is to kill someone by deception or stealth which, in some situations, could be an assassination. Organizationally, this tradition is placed right before a report on executing someone who uses magic and casts spells.[122] In another narrated version of the *Muwaṭṭa'*, it is reported that Mālik ruled that a man who kills another through *ghīla*, without anger or spite, *must* be killed, and the family of the victim, even if they wish to do so, do not have the right to pardon the offender.[123] Effectively, murder through *ghīla* is considered an aggravated crime which necessitates that the

[121] On the development and processes of early Islamic jurisprudence, see Hasan, *Early*; Guraya, *Origins*; Makdisi, *Rise*, esp. 1–34; Melchert, *Formation*, 1–47; Hallaq, *History*, 1–35; Schacht, *Origins*; Calder, *Studies*. Although I cite Schacht and Calder, I note my disagreement with their methodology and conclusions. See, on Calder, Burton, "Rewriting."

[122] Mālik b. Anas, *al-Muwaṭṭa'*, 487. [123] Ibid., 248.

offender be executed, and that the options of blood money or pardon not be allowed.[124]

Various positions are attributed to Mālik b. Anas by the Mālikī jurists Ibn al-Qāsim (d. 191/806), Ḥammad b. Isḥāq (d. 267/880), his brother Ismāʿīl (d. 282/896), and Saḥnūn (d. 240/854). It is difficult to ascertain whether, in fact, Mālik held any of the views attributed to him. Importantly, however, the various reports, whether attributed to Mālik directly or to one of his students, represent trends in early Mālikī jurisprudence. According to Saḥnūn and Ibn al-Qāsim, Mālik held the view that the Khawārij and Qadariyya should be asked to repent, and if they refused to do so, should be killed.[125] When asked if his view was the same for all such heretics (*ahl al-ahwāʾ* or *ahl al-bidaʿ*), Mālik reportedly said yes.[126] This would presumably mean that the Shīʿa, Muʿtazila, and other groups would also be asked to repent or be killed.[127] But beyond this basic position attributed to Mālik, the consistency of the reports end. Saḥnūn reports that Ibn al-Qāsim said that Mālik asserted that the above-mentioned so-called heretical groups should be asked to repent or be killed only if the ruler (*imām*) is just. This also means, Saḥnūn argues, that if these groups rebel against a just ruler, they are to be fought and asked to repent.[128] No indication is given as to what should take place if the ruler is not considered just. Beyond the issue of the quality or legitimacy of the ruler, the treatment that is supposed to be afforded to the Khawārij and other groups is quite puzzling. Ibn al-Mawwāz (d. 269/882) reports through Ibn al-Qāsim that Mālik held

[124] Al-Ṭabarī (d. 310/923) (*Jāmiʿ*, V:136) reports that Mālik adopted the view that *qatl al-ghīla* (murder through *ghīla*) is a form of *ḥirāba*. According to al-Ṭabarī, this means that if an offender tricks or deceives someone into entering into a private or secluded area and then kills him or her, they have committed the crime of *ḥirāba*. However, one should be skeptical of views attributed by later jurists to the early masters such as Mālik. It is likely that a view would be adopted or advocated by one of the students of Mālik or Abū Ḥanīfa, but then be recalled as the master's position. For reports on Mālik's views on murder through *ghīla*, see Ibn Abī Zayd, *al-Nawādir*, XIV:475.

[125] Saḥnūn, *al-Mudawwana*, I:407.

[126] Ibid.; Ibn ʿAbd al-Barr, *al-Tamhīd* (1982), IV:238. Ibn Abī Zayd (*al-Nawādir*, XIV:540) notes that some of Mālik's students said that the Ibāḍiyya and Qadariyya may be killed. Ibn Abī Zayd comments that he believes, but is not sure, that this was the opinion of Mālik himself.

[127] As mentioned earlier, Mālik was also asked about the followers of blind tribalism in Syria (*ahl al-ʿaṣabiyya al-ladhīna kānū bi al-Shām*). He said they should be asked to repent, or they should be fought: Saḥnūn, *al-Mudawwana*, I:407. Ibn Abī Zayd (*al-Nawādir*, XIV:545) reports that Ibn Ḥabīb (d. 238/853), the author of *al-Wāḍiḥa*, differentiated between the different kinds of Shīʿī belief. Moderate Shīʿīs should be beaten and ostracized until they repent, and extreme Shīʿīs should be killed.

[128] Saḥnūn, *al-Mudawwana*, I:407. Ibn Abī Zayd (*al-Nawādir*, XIV:539–40) notes that Ibn al-Qāṣim said that the Ḥarūriyya may be killed only if the *imām* is just.

that *ahl al-bida*ᶜ should not be fought or killed as long as they accept the authority of the *imām* and do not rebel. Rather, they should be arrested, imprisoned, beaten, boycotted, and socially ostracized until they repent.[129] According to Ibn al-Qāsim, Mālik argued that because the Khawārij rely on a religious interpretation (*ta'wīl*), they should not be held responsible for life or property destroyed.[130] When Saḥnūn inquired of Ibn al-Qāsim about the difference between the *muḥāribūn* and the Khawārij, Ibn al-Qāsim explained that there is a material difference between the two. The *muḥāribūn* violate the law because they are corrupt and sinful, and because they are motivated by selfish interests. On the other hand, the Khawārij fight over a religious interpretation that they believe to be correct (*qātalū ᶜalā dīnin yarawna annahu al-ṣawāb*). Therefore, if the Khawārij repent, they are not to be held liable for life or property that they may have destroyed. However, if property that they may have usurped is in their possession, this property may be retrieved from them. If the *muḥāribūn* repent and surrender before they are seized by the ruler, they are pardoned as far as the rights of the *imām* (*ḥaqq al-imām*) are concerned, but they are not forgiven as far as the rights of people (*ḥuqūq al-nās*) are concerned.[131] At this point, Saḥnūn does not explain what any of this means. The implication, however, is that there is a material difference between those who commit violence because of a religious motivation and those who commit violence because of a desire for private gain. Those who commit violence because of religious motivations are not held liable for life and property destroyed. Those who commit violence because of selfish interests are not forgiven for life and property destroyed. If they repent and surrender before being seized by the ruler only the punishments of God are forgiven but the liability for acts committed against private individuals is not negated.[132]

[129] Ibn Abī Zayd, *al-Nawādir*, XIV:541. Ibn al-Mawwāz wrote the *Mawwāziyya*, which documents Mālik's opinions. See Schacht, "Manuscripts," 247; Sezgin, *Geschichte*, I:472.

[130] Similar opinion is reported through Ibn al-Mawwāz: see Ibn Abī Zayd, *al-Nawādir*, XIV:543.

[131] Saḥnūn, *al-Mudawwana*, I:407. This means that the *ḥudūd* (the punishments specified in the Qur'ān – execution, crucifixion and amputation) would not be applied to them. But victims of the crime would still have the right to demand exaction for the violation of their rights: ibid., IV:430.

[132] Nevertheless, symptomatic of the vagueness that plagued the categories of *ḥirāba* and *bughāh* in early Mālikī thought, Ibn Abī Zayd reports that the early Mālikī jurist Muḥammad held that the wounded and captives of the bandits should not be killed, but must be surrendered to the ruler. This language is typical of the laws applicable to the *bughāh* and not bandits. Ibn Abī Zayd comments that he is not sure if this is Mālik's opinion or Muḥammad's: Ibn Abī Zayd, *al-Nawādir*, XIV:471. Muḥammad is probably Muḥammad al-ᶜUtbī (d. 255/868–9). It could also be Muḥammad b. Saḥnūn (d. 256/869) or Muḥammad b. ᶜĪsā (d. 218/833).

According to Ibn al-Qāsim, Mālik gives the ruler a considerable amount of discretion in dealing with bandits who are motivated by selfish interests. If they terrorize the wayfarer, without usurping property or slaughtering people, the ruler may choose to kill or crucify them or amputate their limbs.[133] Mālik recommended that if bandits are captured before having the opportunity to terrorize or commit any other crime, they are to be whipped and placed in prison until they repent.[134] If, however, bandits kill or usurp property, Mālik recommended that they be killed without amputation or crucifixion.[135] Importantly, Mālik asserted that if a bandit is able to carry on his criminal activity for a long time and become powerful, the ruler does not have discretion and must have him killed, even if the ruler cannot prove that the bandit killed or usurped property.[136] Furthermore, if a bandit usurps property or commits murder and is captured before he repents and surrenders, the bandit must be killed, have his limbs amputated, or be crucified. The ruler cannot pardon him.[137] Fighting bandits or resisting them is to be considered a religious *jihād*.[138]

As a general matter, there are two categories in early Mālikī legal thought: the bandits who are treated according to the *ḥirāba* verse; and the Khawārij, who are an indefinite other. Although the Khawārij, unlike the bandits, are not liable for what they destroy, as long as they continue to adhere to their system of belief, they are to be killed all the same. Therefore, after citing some of the traditions indicating that the Companions agreed to forgive all that had been destroyed in the *fitna*, Saḥnūn cites a tradition which provides that the Khawārij, unless they repent, "should be killed for their *baghy*."[139] This could mean that the Khawārij, and possibly other groups, are to be designated within a special category called the *bughāh*, which is distinguished from the category of *muḥārib*. Nonetheless, this might be a distinction without a substantial difference. Ultimately, it is not clear whether the Khawārij are considered to be morally superior to bandits. For example, Mālik reportedly held that ritual funeral prayers may not be performed on the Khawārij

133 Saḥnūn, *al-Mudawwana*, IV:428.

134 Ibid. Reportedly, in Mālik's time, captured bandits in Medina were sent to Fadak or Khaybar, two suburban districts, and imprisoned there.

135 Ibid., 428–9.

136 Ibid., 430.

137 Ibid. Mālik reportedly also held that those who strangle people, or who give people a drink that renders them unconscious, or who break into homes to steal money are all to be considered *muḥāribūn*: ibid., 431–2.

138 Ibid., 432. For the often conflicting reports by Mālik's students about the views of their master on banditry, see Ibn Abī Zayd, *al-Nawādir*, XIV:462–89.

139 Saḥnūn, *al-Mudawwana*, I:410.

or similar sects. Their funerals may not be attended and their ill may not be visited.[140] Further, Ibn Isḥāq reports that according to Mālik sectarians such as the Khawārij should be killed for the corruption they cause in religion, which is derived from the idea of causing corruption on the earth. The corruption caused by the Khawārij in religion is no less evil than the corruption caused by highway robbers or bandits on the earth. Therefore, those sects are to be given an opportunity to repent, but if they do not, they are to be killed; not for being unbelievers (*kuffār*), but for causing corruption in religion and on the earth.[141] Another report maintains that Mālik argued that the Khawārij and all other innovators in religion (*ahl al-bida*ᶜ) are not to be considered infidels (*kuffār*), but they are to be asked to repent or be killed nonetheless. Reportedly, Mālik considered such groups to be worse than bandits or highway robbers because they cause corruption in religion, and causing corruption in religion is invariably worse than causing corruption on the earth.[142] Even if the opinions attributed to Mālik are in fact his,[143] it is not clear how, according to early Mālikī doctrine, other rebels, who are not Khawārij or who do not belong to a recognizable non-Sunnī sect of Islam, are to be treated.[144]

The Qāḍī Abū ᶜUmar (d. 320/932), a Mālikī jurist who lived well after al-Shāfiᶜī had articulated his doctrine on the *bughāh*, was perhaps aware of the incongruity in the Mālikī discourses.[145] He cited the view that the Khawārij and others must repent or be killed. He, however, insisted that the Mālikī doctrine regarding the *bughāh* is exactly the same as al-Shāfiᶜī's:

[140] Ibid., 407. [141] Ibn ᶜAbd al-Barr, *al-Tamhīd* (1982), XXIII:337. [142] Ibid., IV:238.

[143] For example, this last report is transmitted through Ibn al-Qāṣim. Ibn al-Qāṣim is explaining Mālik's views. One cannot be sure if this is Ibn al-Qāṣim's own view, or if in fact he is accurately conveying Mālik's opinions.

[144] The ambiguity surrounding Mālikī doctrine is compounded by their position on the *zanādiqa* (heretics). Early Mālikīs assert that the *zanādiqa* are the same as the hypocrites of Medina in the Prophet's time. They concede that the Prophet did not kill the *zanādiqa* but argue that he did not do so because he feared that killing them would deter people from becoming Muslims. After the Prophet died, it became necessary to execute the *zanādiqa*. The *zanādiqa* are not to be killed for committing banditry or for causing corruption on the earth. They are to be killed because they are infidels (*kuffār*): Ibn ᶜAbd al-Barr, *al-Tamhīd* (1982), X:154–7. The question then is: what is the difference between the *zanādiqa* who are killed for *kufr*, and *ahl al-bida*ᶜ or *ahl al-ahwā*ʾ who are killed for causing corruption in religion, and bandits who are killed for causing corruption on the earth? There is no clear answer. There are only general concepts or tendencies that do not constitute a systematic or coherent position. Interestingly, the example of the hypocrites of Medina is cited by later jurists primarily from the Shāfiᶜī school as proof that rebels should not be killed if they do not fight. For example, see al-Shīrāzī, *al-Muhadhdhab*, II:283. Ibn al-Mawwāz, on the other hand, claimed that if the hypocrites of Medina had outwardly manifested their hypocrisy, the Prophet would have killed them: Ibn Abī Zayd, *al-Nawādir*, XIV:523.

[145] Abū ᶜUmar presided over the execution of the Ṣūfī master al-Ḥallāj. See Melchert, *Formation*, 173; Ibn al-Athīr, *al-Kāmil*, VII:4–6.

the wounded cannot be killed and the fugitive may not be pursued. He went on to explain that the jurists have agreed that whoever breaks with the *jamā*ᶜ*a*, uses force, terrorizes the wayfarer, and causes corruption on the earth must be killed unless he repents before he is captured. However, Abū ᶜUmar explained, these jurists have considered being defeated in battle and retreating a form of repentance. He therefore implied that while most jurists agree with Mālik's position on repentance (*istitāba*), the main difference is that these jurists considered retreat in battle a kind of repentance. Abū ᶜUmar went on to criticize *ahl al-ḥadīth* for considering the Khawārij and other sects to be unbelievers (*kuffār*). He argued that a person who exercises his *ijtihād* seeking God's approval, but is ultimately wrong, cannot be equated with an unbeliever. The *ahl al-ḥadīth* rely on several traditions from the Prophet which strongly condemn dissenting and waging war against the community. Nonetheless, Abū ᶜUmar noted, these traditions are opposed and contradicted by other traditions which assert that anyone who declares the testament of faith cannot be declared an unbeliever.[146] Abū ᶜUmar went on to argue that Mālik did not prohibit the performing of funeral prayers over the dead from sects such as the Khawārij. Rather, Mālik preferred that the laity, not the jurists, would perform the funeral prayers over such people. However, he argued, the majority of jurists did not object to performing the funeral prayers, and did not agree with Mālik on this point.[147]

Despite Abū ᶜUmar's best efforts at a reconstructive systematization, the early Mālikī doctrine did not become better clarified or more coherent. The Shāfiᶜī doctrine, as we will see, is in reality not at all similar to the early Mālikī position. Furthermore, the idea that the early Mālikī jurists considered a retreat from battle a form of repentance is creative, but completely unfounded. Importantly, it is also not clear why the existence of a religious interpretation is sufficiently material to permit an exemption from liability, but is not material enough ultimately to prevent the execution of a Khārijī. In reality, early Mālikī juristic discourses do not have a doctrine of rebellion, but do have a doctrine of heterodoxy. This does not mean that rebellion was rejected or uniformly condemned; it only means that rebellion was not dealt with as a systematic and coherent issue.[148] Mālik and, perhaps more so his students, were primarily

[146] Ibn ᶜAbd al-Barr, *al-Tamhīd* (1982), XXIII:338–40. [147] Ibid., XXIV:132.

[148] It is very likely that with early Muslim jurists generally, and with Mālik particularly, rebels were dealt with on a case-by-case basis. A rebel such as al-Nafs al-Zakiyya who, as noted earlier, was reportedly supported by Mālik and might offer a greater opportunity for Islamicity or justice would be considered the just one (*al-ᶜādil*) and supported if he was able to offer an orderly and

concerned with condemning those who attack travelers or commit some form of armed robbery. It is also quite probable that Mālik considered the Khawārij and other sectarians to be heretics. Beyond issues of theology, early Mālikī discourses do not deal with the issue of rebels who might not necessarily adhere to heterodox ideas. Nevertheless, as the idea of the special status of *al-muta'awwilūn* (those who have an interpretation) found currency and spread, Ibn al-Qāsim, and later Saḥnūn, integrated the popular notion into Mālikī discourses, but did so in a largely unsystematic fashion. Notably, Ibn Abī Zayd (d. 386/996–7), writing a few years after Abū ᶜUmar, reports the conflicting early opinions of Mālikī jurists discussed above, but also attributes to the Medinese jurist ᶜAbd al-Malik b. al-Mājishūn (d. 212/827) some opinions that resemble the developed determinations concerning the *bughāh*. At this point in his text, Ibn Abī Zayd stops using the labels *ahl al-ahwā'* and the *Khawārij* to describe rebels, and uses terminology typical of *aḥkām al-bughāh*. However, considering the discrepancy between the opinions attributed to Mālikī jurists who were Ibn al-Mājishūn's contemporaries and the views described in Ibn Abī Zayd's text, it is unlikely that Ibn al-Mājishūn actually held the views attributed to him. It is much more likely that Ibn Abī Zayd's writings on the *bughāh* reflect the legal doctrines of his own age, and his own views.[149]

Early Ḥanafī jurists reflect the same type of ambiguity regarding rebels and bandits. Nonetheless, it is clear that a general distinction is made between rebels, bandits, and apostates. Abū Ḥanīfa's student al-Qāḍī Abū Yūsuf (d. 183/799) wrote his *Kitāb al-Kharāj* at the behest of the ᶜAbbāsid caliph Hārūn al-Rashīd, and reportedly he often responded to questions put to him by the caliph. In his book, Abū Yūsuf is keen to point out that the Khawārij were in error, and that they have violated the consensus of the Prophet and the Companions, but he does not extensively focus on the status of the Khawārij.[150] In *Kitāb al-Kharāj*, Abū Yūsuf goes on to respond to a question purportedly put to him by

stable just alternative. This sometimes degenerated into straddling the fence until a winner emerged; hence, Aḥmad b. Ḥanbal's statement, "We support whoever wins (*naḥnu maᶜa man ghalab*)."

[149] This conclusion is bolstered by the fact that it is not clear what exactly Ibn Abī Zayd is attributing to Ibn al-Mājishūn or, to a lesser extent, Ibn Ḥabīb (d. 238/853) of Cordoba. Ibn Abī Zayd cites these two jurists for some rudimentary opinions, but goes on to articulate doctrines similar to the developed doctrines of *aḥkām al-bughāh*, while leaving the authority or basis for his opinions rather vague. As I argue later, it is likely that Ibn Abī Zayd simply borrowed the legal doctrines of his age. See Ibn Abī Zayd, *al-Nawādir*, XIV:547–52.

[150] Abū Yūsuf, *Kitāb*, 59.

the caliph regarding how to conduct warfare against *ahl al-qibla* (fellow Muslims).[151] Abū Yūsuf explains that the authentic reports that have reached him and his fellow Ḥanafī jurists, (*al-ṣaḥīḥu ᶜindanā min al-akhbār*) are that ᶜAlī never fought his opponents without warning them first, and that after defeating them ᶜAlī did not enslave or kill captives, did not kill the wounded or fugitive, and did not confiscate any of his opponents' properties.[152] By contrast, earlier in his book, Abū Yūsuf argues that if people become apostates and wage warfare against Muslims, they may be taken captive and enslaved and their properties confiscated. After defeat, however, the rebels are to be pardoned. However, if the ruler fears that if he pardons the rebels they will reorganize or join another party and rebel again, he may place them in prison until they repent.[153] Other than citing ᶜAlī as his authority, Abū Yūsuf does not explain why Muslims should be treated differently than apostates, and does not elaborate upon the distinction between apostates and rebels. Importantly, he uses the expressions fighting *ahl al-qibla* and *ahl al-baghy* interchangeably. The clear implication is that *ahl al-baghy* are Muslim rebels.[154]

Abū Yūsuf notes two areas of disagreement. He states that some have disagreed with the Ḥanafīs regarding property found in the rebels' war camp. Some have argued that what is found in the war camp, unlike all other properties, may be confiscated. Furthermore, some have said that if the rebels' war camp remains standing, or if the rebels have reinforcements (*idhā kāna lahum fiʾatun yaljaʾūna ilayhā*), then the captive, wounded, and fugitive may be pursued and killed.[155] Significantly, Abū Yūsuf implies that this opinion is a minority position within the Ḥanafī school.[156] He adds that the weaponry and livestock of the rebels may be confiscated and divided. But he reemphasizes that ᶜAlī and his son al-Ḥasan disliked the killing of rebel prisoners, and that they used to release prisoners after taking their weaponry.[157] Abū Yūsuf also adds that the loyalists (*ahl al-ᶜadl*)[158] killed in battle are to be treated as

[151] *Ahl al-qibla* literally means the people who pray towards the Kaᶜba at Mecca. In this context, it is used to refer to Muslims in general.

[152] Ibid., 214. [153] Ibid., 67. [154] Ibid., 191, 214. [155] Ibid., 214.

[156] Notably, however, later on as Ḥanafism became the more popular legal school among Sunnī governments, this became the official position of the Ḥanafī school.

[157] Ibid., 215.

[158] Kraemer, "Apostates," uses the word "loyalists" to refer to *ahl al-ᶜadl*. I think this is an appropriate choice of words in most situations. It is not appropriate when one addresses the jurists who argued that the *bughāh* were an unjust government and the *ahl al-ᶜadl* were the just rebels.

martyrs. Meanwhile, ritual prayers should not be performed on the dead rebels.[159]

In addressing the *bughāh*, Abū Yūsuf does not refer to or cite Abū Ḥanīfa. While referring to some general indefinite debates about the treatment due to rebels, none of the doctrines he addresses seem to be firmly established or well developed. Nonetheless, Abū Yūsuf is actively partaking in constructing a collective memory about ʿAlī's conduct, and then using this conduct as the yardstick of legality. While he mentions the disagreements among jurists concerning how rebels should be treated, he is keen to point out that ʿAlī preferred not to execute or persecute rebels. Abū Yūsuf states that some scholars (*baʿḍ al-mashyakha*) told him that Jaʿfar al-Ṣādiq said that Muḥammad al-Bāqir said that in the Battle of Baṣra ʿAlī would not kill anyone who laid down his weapon or took sanctuary in a home, and that he would not confiscate any of the rebels' personal properties.[160]

When addressing *ḥirāba*, Abū Yūsuf does cite Abū Ḥanīfa but disagrees with him. Abū Yūsuf simply defines the crime as the act of highway piracy with the purpose of killing and stealing property. He goes on to explain that Abū Ḥanīfa had ruled that if a *muḥārib* usurps property, he is to have a hand and a foot amputated from opposite ends but is not to be killed or crucified. If the *muḥārib* commits murder, he is to be executed. If the *muḥārib*, however, usurps property and commits murder, then, according to Abū Ḥanīfa, the ruler has three choices: (1) he may execute the offender, and nothing else; (2) crucify the offender but not amputate his limbs; or (3) amputate the offender's limbs from opposite ends and then crucify or execute him. Abū Yūsuf, however, disagrees with his teacher, and says that in his opinion the penalties should be as follows: if the offender usurps property, he is to have a hand and a foot amputated from opposite ends and nothing else; if he murders, he is to be executed and nothing else, and if he commits murder and usurps property, then he is to be crucified.[161] Effectively, Abū Yūsuf's approach takes all discretion away from the ruler because each crime has a specific punishment.

Apparently, Abū Yūsuf assumed that there is a difference between a bandit and a rebel; the punishments specified in the *ḥirāba* verse apply to bandits, while no specific punishments seem to apply to rebels. Yet it is not clear what distinguishes a rebel from a bandit other than the

159 Ibid., 214–15. 160 Ibid., 215. 161 Ibid.

act of committing highway piracy. This raises the question of whether a rebel who attacks travelers may be treated as a bandit. The ambiguity that surrounds the two categories is emphasized in a passage in which Abū Yūsuf discusses the liability of the rebels. He explains: "Whoever repents from amongst *ahl al-baghy* and follows the ruler, and listens to and obeys him, will not be held liable for blood [spilt] or injuries caused by him during the battle. He will also not be held responsible for destruction of property unless usurped property is found in his possession; if usurped property is found in his possession, it will be returned to its [rightful] owner."[162] But then he goes on to say that the same is applicable to a bandit who commits highway piracy. If he repents before being captured and listens to and obeys the ruler, he will not be held liable for life and property destroyed in the course of his crime.[163] This passage means that bandits and rebels are expected to repent and obey, and by doing so they escape liability. The rebel escapes liability for what he destroyed while the bandit escapes the punishments specified in the Qur'ān. Although Abū Yūsuf cites ᶜAlī's clemency, the question remains: May a rebel be punished at the absolute discretion of the ruler?

The other Ḥanafī jurist who deals with the issue of rebellion and banditry is Muḥammad b. al-Ḥasan al-Shaybānī (d. 189/804) in his *Siyar* from *Kitāb al-Aṣl*. Majid Khadduri has translated Shaybānī's *Siyar*,[164] but whether or not this book was written by al-Shaybānī is open to question. This book is reported to contain Abū Ḥanīfa's views, dictated by Abū Yūsuf to al-Shaybānī. Most copies of *Kitāb al-Aṣl* do not contain the chapter on *Siyar* (this is the chapter that deals with issues relating to the conduct of state).[165] According to Khadduri, the oldest manuscript existing for the chapter on *siyar* is from 638/1240.[166] Importantly, some of the views found in the text translated by Khadduri are too advanced to have been written in al-Shaybānī's lifetime. Many of these views are characteristic of the developed Ḥanafī position in the fourth/tenth century, or even later. Rather, the text translated by Khadduri contains a

[162] Ibid. [163] Ibid. [164] Khadduri, *Islamic Law*.

[165] Ibid., 70. The printed edition of *Kitāb al-Aṣl* does not contain this chapter: al-Shaybānī, *Kitāb al-Aṣl*. Another book attributed to the same author also does not address rebellion or banditry. The only thing mentioned in that source is that Abū Ḥanīfa held that if a man raises his sword against Muslims, they may kill him without being liable. It is not clear whether this applies to fighting a thief or a rebel or both: see al-Shaybānī, *al-Jāmiᶜ*, 513. Abū Yūsuf's *al-Radd* does not report any of Abū Ḥanīfa's views on rebels or rebellion.

[166] Khadduri, *Islamic Law*, 71.

mixture of advanced Ḥanafī legal doctrine and earlier Ḥanafī views.[167] I am not necessarily doubting that al-Shaybānī wrote *Kitāb al-Aṣl* or that there was, in fact, a part of this book that dealt with *siyar*. My argument is that additions have been made to the original text representing late Ḥanafī legal views.[168] Therefore, I have focused on the parts of the text that seem to represent early Ḥanafī doctrine.

The text attributed to al-Shaybānī emphasizes ʿAlī's clemency towards rebels. Prisoners may not be killed or enslaved, and the property of rebels may not be confiscated.[169] The text also attributes to Abū Ḥanīfa the view that if the rebels have a group with which they may take refuge (*fiʾa*), then the rebel prisoners may be killed, the fugitive pursued, and the wounded dispatched.[170] Nonetheless, as noted above, it is doubtful that this had become, by al-Shaybānī's time, settled Ḥanafī doctrine. Rather, the idea that a rebel group that has access to reinforcements or that has a group with which it can take refuge is to be treated more harshly seems to have been one of the competing schools of thought in al-Shaybānī's time. While the text argues that rebels are not to be held liable for life and property destroyed during the course of their rebellion, no sharp distinction is maintained between highway robbers or bandits and rebels.[171] The discussions on highway robbers are intermingled with discussions on rebels.[172] Nonetheless, Abū Ḥanīfa is reported to have maintained that those who fight with a *taʾwīl* (a different religious interpretation) must be treated differently than "marauding adventurers" who commit crimes for private gain.[173] However, in response to the

[167] Al-Sarakhsī (d. 483/1090–1) wrote a commentary on what is purportedly al-Shaybānī's *Siyar*: see al-Sarakhsī, *Sharḥ*. But this work was written by al-Sarakhsī from memory in prison, and it mostly contains his own views. Furthermore, the discrepancies between Khadduri's text and al-Sarakhsī's text are too great for one to be able to conclude that there is any relation between the two sources. According to the *Siyar*, al-Shaybānī made passing reference to fighting the *bughāh*. See al-Sarakhsī, *Sharḥ*, III:1035, IV:1439, V:2263.

[168] Khadduri, throughout his translation, corroborates various points made in the translated text by citing late Ḥanafī sources. The very fact that there is such close correlation between the points made in the translated text and late Ḥanafī sources is a further indication that late Ḥanafī opinions were added to the text Khadduri is translating. Norman Calder contends that *Kitāb al-Aṣl* and other early texts reflect the organic growth of Islamic law. Hence, these books have been authored, edited, redacted, and systematized by various authors. See Calder, *Studies*, 39–66. I agree that one can discern evidence of some editing of early legal texts. However, Calder exaggerates the significance and pervasiveness of this process. Furthermore, his methodology for dating texts is unpersuasive.

[169] Khadduri, *Islamic Law*, 230. [170] Ibid., 232, 243.

[171] Ibid., 234, 247. See also al-Sarakhsī, *Sharḥ*, IV:1439, V:2263.

[172] For example, Khadduri, *Islamic Law*, 149–50. [173] Ibid., 250.

question "Why should the rebels not be held liable for whatever of those things that they have committed [i.e. crimes]?" the text gives a rather technical response: "Because the rulings [of the loyalists] do not apply to them [in rebel territory] and they [the rebels] would be regarded as having been separated [from the Muslims] like the inhabitants of territory of war."[174] According to this logic, rebels are exempted from liability for offenses committed during the course of or after the rebellion because of a jurisdictional point. The rebels' camp during the rebellion, or any territory over which they might have prevailed after the rebellion, is considered to be outside the jurisdiction of the loyalist forces. Therefore, the loyalists do not have jurisdiction over crimes or offenses committed in rebel territory.[175] If rebels, however, commit an infraction before they commence their rebellion, they will be held liable because before the rebellion commences, the rebels remain under the loyalists' jurisdiction.[176] Importantly, it is not the interpretation adopted by the rebels that exempts them from liability, but the notion that rebels have a separate jurisdictional domain from that of loyalists.

This position is entirely consistent with the developed Ḥanafī doctrine of jurisdiction. For example, the Ḥanafīs argue that Islamic laws cannot be applied outside the jurisdiction of Muslim territory.[177] It is difficult, however, to ascertain whether the Ḥanafī theory of jurisdiction had become sufficiently developed as to warrant this argument or whether this portion of al-Shaybānī's text was added later. Nonetheless, the evidence does seem to indicate that issues relating to the jurisdiction of Islamic law were debated between al-Shaybānī and Abū Yūsuf early on.[178] The question then becomes: How does one analyze the fact that rebels are recognized as having a separate jurisdiction, at least during the course of or after the commencement of their rebellion?

One should take note of the fact that al-Shaybānī reportedly maintained that rebels are to be considered Muslims,[179] and yet he argued that funeral prayers may not be performed by loyalists over dead rebels.[180] Furthermore, al-Shaybānī reports that Abū Ḥanīfa held that taxes collected by rebels should not be recollected or reexacted.[181] Furthermore, if loyalists prevail over a territory occupied by rebels, they should affirm the judgments and adjudication of rebels if such adjudications are just or

[174] Ibid., 235. [175] Ibid., 238–9. [176] Ibid., 240.
[177] See Abou El Fadl, "Islamic," 173–4. [178] Ibid.
[179] Khadduri, *Islamic Law*, 253. [180] Ibid., 241. [181] Ibid., 233.

legally supportable, even if only by a minority view.[182] In view of these various indicators mentioned above, one could argue that, although the evidence is mixed, recognizing that rebels have a separate jurisdiction is tantamount to recognizing the legitimacy of the act of rebellion or rebels. In other words, by arguing that rebels are not liable because, during the course of their rebellion, they maintain a separate and distinct jurisdiction, Ḥanafī jurists have effectively granted a degree of legitimacy to the act of rebellion. I think that, although this argument has its merits, it is inaccurate for three reasons: First, if the Ḥanafī doctrine of jurisdiction had become sufficiently established by al-Shaybānī's time, then the jurisdictional argument as it applies to rebels could be nothing more than a technical extension of precedent. In other words, the argument regarding jurisdiction could be a product of Ḥanafī legal culture, and not necessarily an ideologically motivated application of legal principles. Second, al-Shaybānī draws an analogy between the legal jurisdiction of rebels and the legal jurisdiction of unbelievers in the abode of war. This could hardly be a positive association that somehow recognizes the legitimacy of rebellion. Third, recognizing that rebels have a separate jurisdiction, and affirming the rebels' executive tax decisions and their legal adjudications, is quite consistent with the juristic preference for consistency, order, and stability, and not necessarily a radical sanctification of rebellion or rebels.

AL-SHĀFIʿĪ'S DISCOURSE ON THE LAW OF REBELLION

The first systematic exposition on the law of rebellion is that by al-Shāfiʿī (d. 204/819–20). He, however, did not invent the field. It is clear from al-Shāfiʿī's own arguments that he was referring to concepts and ideas that were already circulating in his time. He simply co-opted these ideas and concepts into a systematic discourse on the issue.[183] Like other jurists in his time, he did not focus on whether or when rebellion would

[182] Ibid., 250. Reportedly, the caliph ʿAbd al-Malik b. Marwān affirmed the legal judgments of the rebel ʿAbd Allāh b. al-Zubayr after defeating him. ʿAbd al-Malik asserted that reversing previous judgments and re-litigating cases would be difficult to do. See Wakīʿ (d. 306/918), *Akhbār*, 1:130. As we will see, affirming the judgments or adjudications of rebels became an accepted legal doctrine in the juristic discourses.

[183] There is a considerable amount of work published on al-Shāfiʿī's role in the development of Islamic jurisprudence. Wael Hallaq has challenged the idea that al-Shāfiʿī was the chief architect of Islamic jurisprudence. Al-Shāfiʿī, Hallaq argued, played a very important role in the development of Islamic jurisprudence but his role was not as central as some have assumed. See Hallaq, "Was al-Shafiʿi." I think that Hallaq's points are persuasive.

be justified. Rather, his main focus is on the technical issue of how rebels should be treated or regarded, and in justifying his arguments by grounding them in authoritative Islamic sources or precedents. Most of al-Shāfiʿī's arguments are phrased in terms of a disputation between him and his opponents, and, on occasion, although he concedes that his arguments are without precedent, he still insists that they are more authentically Islamic than the doctrines adopted by his opponents. Furthermore, as we will see, many of the later sources claim that al-Shāfiʿī had completely changed his views on the *bughāh* when he moved to Egypt. This is consistent with the argument that once having removed himself from the political turmoils of his day, he proceeded to develop a legal discourse on rebellion that is largely unhelpful to those in power.

Al-Shāfiʿī starts his exposition by citing the verse on *baghy*. He notes that two things are discernible about the verse: First, the verse does not mention liability for life or property destroyed if two Muslims fight. Second, the verse clearly prefers reconciliation over fighting. Al-Shāfiʿī concedes that it is possible to interpret the verse so as to require liability, at least for death and injuries, but the preferred view is that the verse requires that liability for blood and property be dropped altogether. This, al-Shāfiʿī argues, is due to the *ḥadīth* by al-Zuhrī that the Companions agreed that after the *fitna*, no one would be held liable for life or property destroyed.[184] Al-Shāfiʿī sets this out as the basis on which the rest of his discussion will be structured. The Qur'ānic verse supports reconciliation, and prefers that amnesty be given to all *bāghīs*. Importantly, it affirms that despite his rebellion the *bāghī* remains a Muslim, and is to be treated as such. He is not fought with the purpose of killing or destroying him. Rather, he is fought for the limited purpose of repelling or resisting his aggression.[185]

A *bāghī*, al-Shāfiʿī argues, is one who refuses to obey the just ruler (*al-imām al-ʿādil*), and intends to rebel by fighting him.[186] It is not clear at this point what is meant by the expression "just ruler." It could mean the

[184] Al-Shāfiʿī, *al-Umm*, IV:214. See also al-Bayhaqī, *Maʿrifa*, VI:278–9, who refers to the same argument by al-Shāfiʿī.

[185] Al-Shāfiʿī, *al-Umm*, IV:223. See al-Bayhaqī, *Maʿrifa*, VI:278, discussing al-Shāfiʿī's position. Al-Ṭabarī (d. 310/923) reports that some of the "heretics and ignorant" argued that pursuant to the *baghy* verse, a rebel Muslim may be killed: al-Ṭabarī, *Jāmiʿ*, XXV:82. On the other hand, al-Bayhaqī (*al-Sunan*, VIII:188) reports that some have argued that the *bughāh* should not be fought or killed. The later group criticized al-Shāfiʿī for effectively sanctioning the killing of people such as Muʿāwiya: al-Bayhaqī, *Maʿrifa*, VI:284. According to al-Bayhaqī (d. 458/1065), al-Shāfiʿī's response was that both groups confused killing and fighting (*al-qatl ghayr al-qitāl*). The verse permits the fighting but not the killing of the *bughāh*. Effectively, this means that the *bughāh* may be fought, as a defensive measure, in order to repel their aggression, but it does not permit the execution of the *bughāh*: al-Bayhaqī, *al-Sunan*, VIII:188.

[186] Al-Shāfiʿī, *al-Umm*, IV:216.

ruler who rules justly or it could mean the legitimate or rightful ruler. The former meaning looks to the substantive quality of the ruler's reign. The latter meaning is concerned with how the ruler came to power regardless of how just or unjust his rule might be. This point becomes the subject of extensive debate in later Islamic discourses. Al-Shāfiʿī, however, seems to have used the expression to mean the substantively just ruler. This implies that those who rebel against an unjust ruler are not rebels at all, and in fact later jurists explicitly argue that if the ruler is unjust and the rebels are just, then the ruler is to be considered the *bāghī* and not the rebels. Nonetheless, al-Shāfiʿī does not explicitly argue that those who rebel against the unjust ruler are not to be considered rebels. The reason for this is rather speculative. One notices that the model al-Shāfiʿī had in mind for all his discussions on the *bughāh* is that of the caliph ʿAlī and, to a lesser extent, Abū Bakr. ʿAlī is the model and the source of authority for the vast majority of al-Shāfiʿī's arguments. Al-Shāfiʿī could not have been unaware that the ʿAbbāsid caliphs of his day and age laid claim to a high degree of Islamic authenticity, and claimed to be the rightful and just rulers. In a sense, al-Shāfiʿī was setting ʿAlī as the standard by which the justice of the ruler is to be evaluated. In other words, it is as if al-Shāfiʿī is arguing to the ʿAbbāsids of his age: "If you claim to be the rightful and just rulers, then this is how just rulers treat rebels." In effect, al-Shāfiʿī was setting up a moral and legal standard by which the rulers of his age could be judged. At the same time, the door is left open for the possibility of declaring, if need be, a certain rebellion justified because the ruler is unjust. This is exactly why Ibn Taymiyya, as we saw, accused al-Shāfiʿī and others who followed in his footsteps of opening the door for rebellion and civil discord, and encouraging chaos and anarchy. Speculative as it might be, I believe that this argument is further supported by the structure of al-Shāfiʿī's arguments, which we discuss below.

Al-Shāfiʿī was keen on citing and enlisting, not just the precedent of ʿAlī, but also Abū Bakr, in support of his arguments. Those who rebelled against the caliph Abū Bakr, al-Shāfiʿī argues, were of two distinct types, the apostates and the *bughāh*. The apostates renounced Islam altogether, but the *bughāh*, relying on an erroneous interpretation of the Qur'ān, refused to pay taxes to Abū Bakr. These rebels, al-Shāfiʿī asserts, argued that taxes were paid to the Prophet when he was alive because the Prophet's prayers were a source of security and peace for the believers. The Qur'ān states: "[Oh, Prophet] from their money take alms so that you might purify and sanctify them, and pray for them for your prayers are a source of security for them. God is the One who hears and knows all."[187] After the Prophet died, Abū Bakr was not entitled to collect alms because his prayers were not a source of peace and security. Therefore, the rebels argued they should not be obligated to pay alms to Abū Bakr. Since Abū Bakr was the just ruler, he had every right to demand that alms be paid to him just as they were paid to the Prophet. Abū Bakr gave the rebels every opportunity to recant, but when they refused to do so, they committed an act of rebellion (*khurūj* or *imtināᶜ*). The fact that they committed an act of rebellion meant that the rebels could be fought. But because they relied on a plausible, even if ultimately erroneous, interpretation, this meant that they would not be held liable for any damage caused in the course of their rebellion.[188] Importantly, al-Shāfiᶜī argues, this means that fighting the rebels until they are defeated is permitted. However, nothing beyond fighting them to insure compliance with the law is to be allowed. Unlike bandits or highway robbers, the blood and money of rebels who fight because of an interpretation (*taʾwīl*) remain legally protected and religiously sanctified. Bandits or highway robbers do not rely on an interpretation, and are simply motivated by selfish interests such as financial gain. Therefore, bandits or highway robbers are fully liable for all of their criminal activity.[189] Al-Shāfiᶜī goes on to emphasize his essential point:

> It is not proper to claim that a rebel's blood may be spilled without exception. Rather, one should say that if a rebel refuses to comply with a law that applies to him, or rises and fights while aided by a group of rebels, we may fight him either to protect ourselves or to insure compliance with what is demanded of him. If the rebel is killed during the course of the fight, we are not liable for his blood because it has become legal to kill him under these [limited] circumstances. But if the rebel retreats, or abandons his defiance, or is captured, or is wounded, or becomes ill so that he can no longer fight, it is no longer permissible to kill him. Because of the aforementioned, one cannot say that [as a matter of principle] a rebel's blood may be shed. [This is exactly why] a rebel may not be killed if he stops fighting, or is captured or wounded.[190]

In effect, al-Shāfiᶜī argues that three separate components must exist for a rebel to qualify for the technical category of a *bāghī*. First, the rebel must have an interpretation (*taʾwīl*); second, the rebel must commit an overt act of rebellion (*khurūj*); and third, the rebel must be part of a

[187] Qurʾān 9:103. [188] Al-Shāfiᶜī, *al-Umm*, IV:215–16.
[189] Ibid., 216. [190] Ibid., 223.

larger group of rebels. He must have some power base (referred to as *minʿa, shawka*, or *fiʾa*). Al-Shāfiʿī goes on to elaborate upon the third element by arguing that if one or two rebels rely on an interpretation, and rebel without the support of a more formidable group, they will be liable for any crimes committed. The reason that we require that the rebel act within the context of a large group, al-Shāfiʿī argues, is that when Ibn Muljim assassinated ʿAlī, the caliph did not exempt him from liability. Ibn Muljim did, in fact, rely on an interpretation, but because he acted as an individual, ʿAlī, while on his deathbed, said that Ibn Muljim was not to be exempted from liability.[191] Al-Shāfiʿī is careful to add that ʿAlī's dying wish was that Ibn Muljim not be tortured or mutilated.[192] Nonetheless, al-Shāfiʿī does not explain how much of a group is needed in order for the rebels to qualify as *bughāh*. He only states that one or two individuals, or a small group that can be easily defeated, is to be held fully liable for its criminal activity, while a larger group that cannot be easily subdued should not be held liable.[193]

Al-Shāfiʿī goes on to give greater specificity to his discourse and to address the Khawārij in particular. He argues that if a group, for example, adopts the views of the Khawārij and isolates itself from society, this alone does not make fighting them permissible. In fact, they are not to be prevented from going to the mosque or marketplace, and their testimony is to be accepted in court like any other Muslim. Al-Shāfiʿī argues that the Khawārij, and any other unorthodox group (*ahl al-ahwāʾ*), in terms of their rights and duties, are not to be treated differently from any other Muslim group. However, if these groups believe that all Muslims are infidels and believe that it is permissible to lie in court when litigating against infidels, then their testimony cannot be trusted or relied upon, and should be excluded.[194] Furthermore, if a group commits a crime *before* adopting a system of belief or interpretation (*taʾwīl*), chooses a leader, and rises in rebellion as a group, its members are to be

[191] Ibid., 216.

[192] Ibid., 217. Al-Shāfiʿī, and the vast majority of jurists after him, do not refer to the reports, mentioned earlier, that Ibn Muljim was tortured to death. It is possible that al-Shāfiʿī never heard of the reports about Ibn Muljim's torture. It is also possible that he had heard of these reports, but simply discounted them because he was interested in creating a discourse that would require that rebels be treated in a humane and benevolent fashion. One, of course, cannot discount the possibility that the reports about Ibn Muljim's torture, like the reports about al-ʿUrayna tribe, were invented by the supporters of the Umayyads who wished to justify the often cruel treatment of rebels. It is also possible the Ibn Muljim's torture report was invented by extremist Shīʿī sects (Ghulāt) who seemed to obtain satisfaction from imagining all types of torments that ought to befall the killer of ʿAlī.

[193] Ibid., 218. [194] Ibid., 217.

treated like any other Muslims, and should be held liable for whatever crimes they commit.[195] In other words, the turning point is the crucial moment when one can say that the group has adopted an interpretation, started acting as a cohesive whole, and committed a clear act of rebellion.[196] For example, al-Shāfi^cī argues, ^cAlī treated the Khawārij like any of his subjects. He did not persecute or discriminate against them. When they isolated themselves in a specific locality, ^cAlī appointed a governor to lead them. But when they killed the governor he appointed, ^cAlī demanded that they hand in the murderer. The Khawārij, however, refused, and claimed that the whole group was responsible for the governor's death. Only then did ^cAlī fight and subdue the group.[197]

Al-Shāfi^cī then proceeds to describe the specific rules of engagement, and the details of the treatment due to the rebels. The rebels must be first warned, debated, and given a full chance to repent before being fought.[198] He reiterates that they are to be fought only as long as they continue to fight. The moment they retreat or drop their weapons they may not be fought or killed. Mangonels, flame-throwers, or other weapons of mass destruction may not be used against the rebels unless under circumstances of dire necessity. Dire necessity means that the rebels use these weapons first, or if the rebels occupy a fortress where it becomes difficult to defeat them otherwise. Furthermore, the ruler may not seek the aid of non-believers against Muslim rebels.[199] Importantly, the ruler also may not seek the aid of Muslims who believe that it is permissible to kill a fugitive rebel or a rebel who has surrendered.[200] If "People of protection" (*ahl al-dhimma* – primarily Christians and Jews living in Muslim territory under an agreement of protection) assist Muslim rebels, this does not void their covenant of safe conduct. However, unlike Muslim rebels, they are to be held liable for any life or property they may have destroyed during the course of the rebellion.[201]

195 Ibid.

196 If the rebels disavowed society and isolated themselves – in other words, if they lived in peaceful exclusion, they should not be fought: ibid., 226.

197 Ibid., 217.

198 Ibid., 218, 226. Al-Shāfi^cī argues that the rebels must be warned first because they might mention an injustice that has befallen them or they might complain about a governor who is oppressing them. In this case, the injustice must be redressed and the oppressive governor must be dismissed. He also rejects the argument that fighting Muslim rebels is in any way similar to fighting unbelievers.

199 Ibid., 219, 228–9. Al-Shāfi^cī argues that the aid of unbelievers may be sought against other unbelievers. But the aid of unbelievers may never be sought against fellow Muslims.

200 Ibid., 219. This is a direct rebuke to Ḥanafī jurists who argued that the fugitive may be killed. This becomes an area of considerable debate in later Islamic discourses.

201 Ibid., 221.

Once a Muslim rebel surrenders, he is not to be killed. Al-Shāfiᶜī argues, however, that a rebel may be imprisoned until he gives the just ruler his oath of allegiance, but he also notes that it is preferable that a rebel not be imprisoned at all. It is questionable, al-Shāfiᶜī contends, whether a rebel's wife and children may be imprisoned for any period of time.[202] Even more, if a loyalist kills a fugitive or surrendering rebel, the loyalist will be liable for wrongfully killing the rebel.[203] Furthermore, al-Shāfiᶜī goes beyond the argument that the property of the rebels may not be confiscated. He argues that any property found in the rebel camp may not be divided as spoils of war, and may not be used even temporarily. In addition, weapons and cattle captured from the rebels may not be used against them.[204]

Al-Shāfiᶜī dedicates a large portion of his argument to refuting the claim that if the rebels have a group (*fiʾa*) to which they may retreat or to which they may turn for assistance, then they may be killed or pursued, and that their wounded may then be dispatched. He constructs his refutation on several levels of argument. First, he contends that ᶜAlī never pursued a fugitive or killed a prisoner. He accuses his opponents of making an argument by negative implication. According to al-Shāfiᶜī, his opponents concede that ᶜAlī never gave permission to kill the wounded or fugitive. However, they argue that ᶜAlī, in the Battle of the Camel, did not allow the killing of the wounded or fugitive because ᶜAlī's opponents did not have a group to which they could turn or ask for assistance. By implication, if the people of the Camel had had such a group then ᶜAlī would have permitted the killing of the wounded and fugitive. Al-Shāfiᶜī contends that this argument by negative implication assumes a state of facts that did not exist. Therefore, it is inherently flawed and illogical. Nothing short of a direct command by ᶜAlī permitting the killing of the fugitive or wounded would have sufficed. Second, Abū Bakr and ᶜAlī captured many rebels, yet they never beat or killed a surrendering rebel. In fact, when ᶜAlī fought the rebels of Syria, Muᶜāwiya was, at all times, able to lend assistance to his party. In other words, the rebels of Syria always had a *fiʾa* or group to which they could turn for assistance. Nevertheless, ᶜAlī refused to punish or execute them. Third, al-Shāfiᶜī

202 Ibid., 219.

203 Ibid., 220. Al-Shāfiᶜī argues that the loyalist should be asked to take an oath that he (the loyalist) erroneously thought that the rebel was not surrendering or escaping. If the loyalist takes the oath, he is responsible for the rebel's blood money. If, however, the loyalist refuses to take the oath, he is to be penalized for the wrongful killing.

204 Ibid., 225. Al-Shāfiᶜī argues with his imaginary interlocutor by asserting that it is well established that ᶜAlī refused to confiscate any property found in the rebel camp. Even a pot, in which the loyalist soldiers were cooking, was promptly returned. Then how can one argue that anything found in the rebels' camp may be considered spoils of war?

argues that his opponents conceded that even if a group of rebels intend to fight, and are in the process of sharpening and readying their weapons, it is not permitted to fight them. A mere suspicion or fear of rebellion is not enough to justify waging war against the rebels. How then, al-Shāfiʿī rhetorically asks, can one claim that if the rebels have a group that *might* possibly lend support, it becomes permissible to kill the wounded, prisoner, or fugitive? Even when we know for a fact that the rebels have a group ready and willing to lend support, as in the case of Muʿāwiya and his people, it does not change the fact that fugitives may not be pursued, and prisoners may not be executed.[205]

Not only may the rebels not be executed or fugitives pursued, but a dead rebel may not be crucified, and his head may not be severed and sent to the ruler. The corpse of a rebel must be properly washed and buried without mutilation.[206] Al-Shāfiʿī also takes issue with the argument that funeral prayers may not be performed on a dead rebel. He poses the rhetorical question: What possible reason could there be for not performing the funeral prayers on a rebel? Al-Shāfiʿī's imaginary interlocutor responds that this is a form of punishment for a rebel; a rebel should not be honored in death. Al-Shāfiʿī says: "If that is so, then is it permissible to burn the corpse of a rebel or crucify it or sever the head and send it across the land, for this is surely more degrading?" The interlocutor responds: "No, that would not be allowed." Al-Shāfiʿī then says: "Well, if we confiscate the property of a rebel, that would be a greater deterrence to people so that they may not follow in the footsteps of a rebel. Yet, we do not punish a rebel with anything beyond what is [legally] permitted. We recognize a rebel's testimony and his marriage, and we inherit from him, and we do not withhold from him anything that is permitted to any other Muslim, so how is it that you wish to punish him by proscribing funeral prayers alone?" The interlocutor is unable to respond, and al-Shāfiʿī concludes that a rebel must be treated within the limits of legality, and nothing beyond the confines of the law is permitted or allowed.[207]

[205] Ibid., 224. Al-Shāfiʿī also strongly rejects the position which contended that leniency towards rebels is a discretionary act of kindness. The idea that ʿAlī's leniency was merely a discretionary act implies that his example is merely persuasive, but not mandatory or obligatory. Al-Shāfiʿī contends that ʿAlī's conduct arose out of a firm religious and legal obligation, and is binding on all Muslims who exist after him.

[206] Ibid., 222. This is obviously a direct attack on the common practice during al-Shāfiʿī's time of crucifying dead rebels and sending their heads to the governor or the caliph.

[207] Ibid., 225. Interestingly, al-Shāfiʿī is rather non-committal about the status of dead loyalists. He reports that there are two opinions about the loyalists. Some have argued that they are to be treated as martyrs, while others disagreed. He does not advocate a particular position: ibid., 222.

Significantly, al-Shāfiʿī rejects the Ḥanafī argument that the rebels have a separate jurisdiction, and that loyalists do not have jurisdiction to punish crimes committed in rebel territory. He argues that because the rebels are Muslims, they fall under Muslim jurisdiction, and therefore, if someone commits a crime such as murder or adultery, he or she may be prosecuted by the loyalists for the commission of such a crime.[208] This is consistent with the general Shāfiʿī position that Islamic laws have personal jurisdiction, and hence should apply to Muslims even in non-Muslim territory.[209] Therefore, one should avoid reading too much into this rather technical point of law. Nonetheless, al-Shāfiʿī's argument does imply that the abode or territory of the rebels remains a part of the abode or territory of Islam.[210] Importantly, al-Shāfiʿī argues that the decisions of judges in rebel territory should be treated like the adjudications of any other Muslim judge. They are to be affirmed or overturned on the same bases that apply to any other Muslim judge in loyalist territory.[211] If a judge from rebel territory writes a witnessed letter confirming or claiming certain rights against a man living in loyalist territory, it is recommended that the letter not be accepted because this does not constitute a proper judgment, and because it is feared that the witnesses, living in rebel territory, would be willing to lie in order to wrongfully take property belonging to loyalists.[212] However, if rebel witnesses appear in person, their testimony may be accepted. Yet, al-Shāfiʿī argues, if a judge in rebel territory is known to be just, his letter should be accepted, and given full force.[213] He adds that if a rebel has a claim of right or cause of action against a man in loyalist territory, the rebel's cause or claim must be recognized and given full force. Even if rebels refuse to recognize

[208] Ibid., 227–8. The Ḥanafī interlocutor argues that if a person commits a crime in rebel territory, then he is liable before God on the Final Day. However, loyalists may not prosecute him on this earth because they lack the jurisdiction.

[209] See Abou El Fadl, "Islamic," 173–4.

[210] This does not necessarily mean that al-Shāfiʿī was insisting on the essential unity of all Muslim territory or refusing to recognize the legitimacy of divisions within the abode of Islam. Making such assumptions is reading political theory into what is an inherently technical legal discourse. For example, as noted above, al-Shāfiʿī argues that Islamic Law has universal jurisdiction. This does not mean that he believed that the whole world was unified under the banner of Islam. One should note, however, that later Shāfiʿī jurists explicitly state that rebel territory is part of the abode of Islam. For example, see al-Māwardī, *al-Aḥkām*, 76, who argues that weapons of mass destruction should not be used against rebels because rebel territory remains a part of the abode of Islam.

[211] Al-Shāfiʿī, *al-Umm*, IV:220.

[212] Ibid. This is the equivalent of a judgment rendered by a judge in rebel territory *in absentia*. Since the witnesses signing the claim of right are not available, it is not possible to confront them and take their testimony directly.

[213] Ibid., 220–1, 228.

loyalists' claims of right or causes of action in rebel territory, retaliation in kind is not permitted.[214]

Several of al-Shāfiʿī's points pertain to issues relating to the conduct of state or international law. For example, if the rebels join the loyalists in fighting non-Muslims, they are entitled to an equal share of the spoils.[215] If the rebels sign a peace treaty with unbelievers, the loyalists must honor the treaty and give it full force.[216] Furthermore, if unbelievers take rebels captive and enslave them, loyalist forces must continue to fight the unbelievers until they liberate the Muslim rebels from their hands.[217] If the rebels and the loyalists enter into a treaty and exchange hostages as security, even if the rebels violate the treaty or kill the hostages, the loyalists may not retaliate in kind, and may not kill the hostages under their control.[218] In effect, the rebels' own illegal conduct does not justify illegal retaliatory measures by the loyalists.

Effectively, al-Shāfiʿī makes three elements irrelevant or inapposite to the issue of how rebels should be treated. First, al-Shāfiʿī does not seem to be very concerned with the conduct of the rebels. He is, however, concerned with the conduct of the government and its forces. The behavior of the rebels will not define the limits of legality, and as far as the government is concerned, regardless of how the rebels conduct themselves, the law sets the standards that differentiate between legality and illegality. In relation to the government, the conduct of the rebels is not a legally material factor as long as the rebels rely on an interpretation, and fulfill the condition of *minʿa* or *shawka*.[219] Second, whether the ruler is just or not is largely irrelevant to the problem of how rebels should be treated. As we noted earlier, even if the ruler is just, and even if those who rise against him are considered rebels, the various rules of engagement and treatment, which al-Shāfiʿī outlines, will still apply. A purportedly just ruler is not given discretion to treat rebels as he sees fit, and therefore the issue of the justness or lack thereof of the ruler is made irrelevant to the issue of how rebels are to be treated. Third, the specific substance or content of the interpretation adopted by the rebels is rendered inapposite as well. By arguing that the Khawārij and all unorthodox groups (*ahl al-ahwāʾ*) are entitled to be treated as *bughāh*, al-Shāfiʿī brings them within the purview and dominion of the law. However, he also brings the

214 Ibid., 221.

215 Ibid. However, the just ruler is entitled to the one-fifth (*al-khums*) of the shares reserved as the right of the public treasury.

216 Ibid.

217 Ibid., 222.

218 Ibid.

219 Ibid., 218.

dominion of the law to their opponents by insisting that the Khawārij be treated within the specific confines of the law. As such, al-Shāfiʿī renders the specific content of the interpretation adopted by the rebels irrelevant to the issue of how they are to be treated. It is not clear from al-Shāfiʿī's discourse how far he was willing to take this point. In other words, it is not clear when rebellion ends, and apostasy and heresy begin.

One of al-Shāfiʿī's primary objectives was to make the treatment of rebels more humane. In early Islamic history, rebels were treated by the state basically as bandits, and crucifying or mutilating them was common practice. This early historical practice resulted in a mixed juridical tradition that exhibited conflicting trends. One trend thought of rebels as the equivalent of highway robbers or bandits, while the other trend distinguished rebels, in some form, without clearly delineating the way in which rebels are distinct and separate from common criminals. Two factors contributed to the construction of the discourse on *aḥkām al-bughāh*: (1) the early juridical experience and the precedent set by the Companions of the Prophet and their predecessors did not necessarily demonize rebellion; (2) the jurists were developing a distinct legal culture which aspired to bring the caliphal power under the authority of the *Sharīʿa*. This meant imposing limits on how the caliph might deal with rebels and even bandits. Therefore, al-Shāfiʿī, for example, limits the discretion of the caliph in dealing with bandits, and insists on a strict *tartīb* regime.[220] But he also insists on a relative degree of humaneness in dealing with highway robbers and bandits. For example, he rejects the argument that a bandit may be crucified first and then killed because, he argues, this is a form of torture and torture is prohibited in Islam. A bandit is to be killed first, and then his corpse is to be crucified.[221]

Al-Shāfiʿī's primary loyalty is not even to a just ruler. Rather, it is to the legal order and the rule of law. This meant that even a just ruler could not be given unqualified or unlimited support. In one passage, for example, al-Shāfiʿī argues that the *bughāh* are not to be considered equal to bandits, murderers, or fornicators. All of these are criminals and, legally, are to be treated as such. Rebels are a different category altogether. There is no legal penalty for rebellion, and the rebel is fought only because of the necessity of maintaining order and stability. In other words, fighting a rebel

[220] Ibid., VI:151–2. According to al-Shāfiʿī, if a bandit kills and usurps money, he is to be killed and crucified. If he commits murder alone, he is to be killed, and if he usurps money alone, he is to have limbs amputated from opposite ends. If he terrorizes the wayfarer without killing or taking property, he is to be exiled.

[221] Ibid., 152.

is a necessary evil while punishing a criminal is a legal imperative.[222] It is rather clear that al-Shāfiᶜī's arguments, in certain respects, are somewhat novel and original. At one point, for example, he concedes that the way he is presenting his case is without precedent. He states that after explaining his doctrines on rebellion to some jurists, they commented that many of his arguments and cited evidence are unprecedented. Nonetheless, he argues that his positions on the subject are more Islamically supportable, and more logically consistent, than the arguments of his opponents.[223] It is not that the basic elements of his argument are without precedent; rather, what is original about his thesis is the cohesive and systematic presentation of the case for benevolence towards rebellion. As we argued earlier, his presentation involves a careful construction and ordering of evidence. He distinguishes, and at times ignores, contrary precedent, and then vests his whole argument in the authoritative precedent of the Qur'ānic discourse, and the purported conduct of the Companions ᶜAlī and Abū Bakr. This is not an invention, but it is a creative construction, and it is also how law is argued and formed.

CONCLUSION

We argued earlier that law develops and changes slowly. It took the legal process about two hundred years to produce a coherent and systematic position on rebels and rebellion, and to respond to the early Islamic experience with civil wars, and the constant armed challenges to the Umayyads and early ᶜAbbāsids. Most jurists accepted the legitimacy of the ᶜAbbāsids, but they also reserved the privilege of articulating legality to their own culture – the culture of the jurists. Political legitimacy is not a legal issue, and jurists, as we will see, were willing to concede this point to the rulers. This is exactly why they were willing to recognize the legitimacy of the usurper (*al-mutaghallib*).[224] But beyond legitimacy, the legality of the government's conduct is a legal issue, and this is exactly what caught the attention and interest of the jurists. It would

[222] Ibid., IV:225. [223] Ibid., 223.

[224] For example, al-Muḥāsibī (d. 243/857) and Aḥmad b. Ḥanbal (d. 241/855) accepted the legitimacy of the usurper: see al-Sayyid, *al-Umma*, 111, 140. However, al-Sayyid argues that those who accepted the legitimacy of the usurper belong to a realistic or pragmatic trend that ignored legality in favor of expediency. I think this misses the point. Jurists are not political theoreticians, and their main concern is establishing an ordered and stable process by which society can be managed. This is done by focusing on technical rules, and not by expounding sweeping and abstract theories of legitimacy.

take, however, at least another hundred years before the field of *aḥkām al-bughāh* became firmly established, and a few hundred more before the field was revised and re-argued in order to respond to the Fāṭimid challenge at the end of the third/ninth century, the Buwayhid threat in the fourth/tenth century, and especially the Mongol invasion in the seventh/thirteenth century. Yet, as will be shown, the field is revised in technical increments, and in fairly measured and slow steps.

It is important to note that although *aḥkām al-bughāh* was not uniformly adopted by the third/ninth century,[225] the general legal and moral trend had become swayed in favor of a particular treatment of rebels and rebellion. Al-Muzanī (d. 264/877–8), for instance, reiterates many of al-Shāfiᶜī's arguments, but he is more precise and to the point. He asserts that the verse on *baghy* clearly indicates that the rebels are not liable for life or property destroyed in the course of their rebellion.[226] The *bughāh* are those who refuse to give a right, or to obey the command of the just ruler, and with whom it is not possible for the just ruler to obtain compliance without fighting. However, before being fought, they must be warned and asked about their grievance. If they mention a clear injustice (*maẓlama bayyina*), then the injustice must be redressed. If, however, they complain about a matter susceptible to debate or open to disagreement, they must be commanded to abandon rebellion, and to return to obeying the commands of the just ruler. If the *bughāh* refuse, then they may be fought.[227]

Al-Muzanī argues that if a few individuals or a small group rely on an interpretation and rebel, they will be held liable for all life and property destroyed. If a group that does not have an interpretation kills and usurps property, its members are to be treated as bandits or highway robbers.[228] If, however, a group is of a sufficient number or strength,

[225] For example, early Shīᶜī sources do not yet uniformly adopt the discourses on *bughāh*. Al-Kulaynī (d. 328–9/939), *al-Furūᶜ* v:51–64, vii:245–8, and al-Ṣadūq (d. 381/991–2), *Kitāb*, iv:68–9, mention reports on bandits and highway robbers but do not discuss *baghy* or *bughāh*. Al-Ḥurr al-ᶜĀmilī (d. 1104/1693), *Wasāʾil*, xi:55–69, contains extensive reports on the *bughāh*. Al-Marūzī (d. 294/906), *Ikhtilāf*, 304, 563 addresses the laws of apostasy and the credibility of *ahl al-ahwāʾ*, but does not address the issue of rebellion. It is reported that al-Marūzī was a Shāfiᶜī, but considering personal history and time period, this is highly unlikely. The likelihood is that al-Marūzī, who lived in Nishapur and Egypt, was not associated with any particular legal school. See al-Subkī, *Ṭabaqāt*, ii:252–3; al-Asnawī (a.k.a. Jamāl al-Dīn), *Ṭabaqāt*, ii:195–6. Some Ḥanafī texts written in the fourth/tenth century address the issue of banditry, but not rebellion. For instance, see Abū al-Layth, *ᶜUyūn*, ii:290–5.

[226] Al-Muzanī, *al-Mukhtaṣar*, 255. On al-Muzanī and his text, see Brockopp, "Early"; Calder, *Studies*, 86–104. Again, I note that I disagree with Calder's argument that the text of *al-Umm* was edited and redacted so that the bulk of the material in *al-Umm*, or in the *Mukhtaṣar*, represents the cumulative views of generations after al-Muzanī.

[227] Al-Muzanī, *al-Mukhtaṣar*, 256. [228] Ibid., 257.

and has an interpretation or belief, it is not to be held liable for life or property destroyed.[229] Al-Muzanī reiterates the view that rebels are morally superior to common criminals such as murderers or fornicators. Therefore, as a matter of principle, they are not to be treated as criminals, and they are fought for the limited purpose of repelling their harm. Consequently, the least forceful or destructive means must be pursued, and if it is possible to repel their harm by debate and persuasion alone, then this is the method that should be pursued. If the rebels wish to live in isolation but do not intend to defy the commands of the just ruler or fight him, they should be left alone and not fought.[230]

In all circumstances, the fugitive, wounded, or prisoner may not be killed. A rebel who surrenders cannot be imprisoned after the battle ends, and may be released before the end of battle if he takes an oath of allegiance in favor of the just ruler.[231] Weapons of mass destruction should not be used unless absolutely necessary – for instance, if the rebels use such weapons first. The assistance of unbelievers or those who are willing to pursue the fugitive or kill the prisoner may not be sought against rebels.[232] Funeral prayers should be performed on dead rebels, and it is not permissible to crucify, burn, or otherwise mutilate the bodies of rebels.[233] Al-Muzanī repeats al-Shāfiʿī's arguments regarding the adjudications and judgments of rebel judges.[234] Nonetheless, his discussion on the jurisdiction of the rebels is of a slightly different emphasis. He argues that traveling merchants or prisoners held by rebels are fully liable for offenses committed in rebel territory. In other words, the loyalists have jurisdiction to prosecute such individuals for crimes committed inside rebel territory. Al-Muzanī asserts that since such individuals do not have an interpretation (*taʾwīl*), there is no reason to hold that the loyalists do not have jurisdiction over offenses committed by them outside loyalist territory. Al-Muzanī also argues, however, that the loyalists have jurisdiction to prosecute crimes committed by a rebel against another in rebel territory.[235]

Of course, al-Muzanī is primarily summarizing al-Shāfiʿī's arguments and conclusions.[236] But in doing so, he is also making them more

[229] Ibid., 256. [230] Ibid., 258. [231] Ibid., 256–7. [232] Ibid., 257.
[233] Ibid., 257–8. Their heads may not be severed and sent across the land or displayed.
[234] Ibid., 258. [235] Ibid., 259.
[236] Calder, *Studies*, 86–104, argues that the views and opinions contained in al-Muzanī's text, or for that matter *al-Umm* by al-Shāfiʿī, do not properly belong to the authors. Rather, these views were added by later generations of jurists who creatively constructed the doctrines of the school. Calder believes that most of the early texts were the product of an organic growth by which arguments were cumulatively and gradually formulated, redacted, and reconstructed by generations of jurists. He bases these conclusions on an analysis of the hermeneutics of the text.

accessible and authoritative. It is difficult to assess how much influence al-Muzanī's *Mukhtaṣar* had in propagating al-Shāfiʿī's views, but as we saw earlier, Ibn Taymiyya directed most of his criticism at the widespread use of hornbooks (such as the *Mukhtaṣar*), which in his view, were largely responsible for the propagation of the doctrines of *aḥkām al-bughāh*.[237]

One of the rather interesting indications of the influence of this discourse in the third/ninth century comes from the Muʿtazilī writer al-Jāḥiẓ (d. 255/869). Al-Jāḥiẓ argues that all the groups, except the Muʿtazila, adopted erroneous positions on the matter of fighting the *bughāh*. The Khawārij, he argues, adopted the position that the *bughāh* are to be treated as unbelievers, and therefore, their fugitives, wounded, and prisoners may be killed or enslaved, and their property may be confiscated.[238] Meanwhile, he contends, the Murji'a held that the *bughāh* should not be fought at all. The Muʿtazila, on the other hand, adopted the moderate, and the only correct, position. They argued that one should not seek to slaughter the *bughāh*, and that they are to be fought for the limited purpose of repelling their harm. Their fugitive may not be pursued, and the wounded and prisoner may not be killed. The *bughāh* may not be enslaved and their property may not be confiscated.[239] Al-Jāḥiẓ, however, was being disingenuous.[240] It is clear that by his time, the views that he espoused and claimed as exclusively Muʿtazilī had been adopted and advocated by several jurists. Nonetheless, it is rather telling that al-Jāḥiẓ cites the doctrines that advocate the tolerant treatment of rebels as proof of the superiority of his theological school over others. Clearly, the discourses on rebellion had achieved a rather significant status. They had become a part of the moral framework by which righteousness and legality are measured.

This is not the place to respond to Calder's problematic claims, but in my view Calder's analysis and conclusions are highly speculative, haphazard, and often without foundation. Calder's understanding of legal history, legal text, and the very idea of legal doctrine is very problematic. Most importantly, much of Calder's arguments depends on an unarticulated and unspecified notion of legal doctrinal progress or advancement. As a result, I have not relied on Calder's dating of Muzanī and others. On Calder, see Dutton, "Review."

237 On the role of the *mukhtaṣar* (hornbooks) in the development of Islamic Law, see Fadel, "Social."

238 The Khawārij considered their opponents to be the real *bughāh*.

239 Al-Jāḥiẓ, "Risāla fī al-Ḥakamayn," 380–1.

240 Considering that al-Jāḥiẓ was not a jurist, it is possible that he did not know any better.

CHAPTER 5

The spread of the Islamic law of rebellion from the fourth/tenth to the fifth/eleventh centuries

ADOPTION AND CHANGE IN THE JURISTIC CULTURE

Abū al-Ḥasan al-Ashᶜarī (d. 330/941), the founder of the Ashᶜarī theological school of thought, recites a long list of rebellions in the first two centuries of Islam, and he characterizes some rebels as good, and others as bad.[1] He makes a point of mentioning that many rebellions ended in clemency or pardon, and concludes his recital by emphasizing that ᶜAlī fought those who fought him, but whenever he was asked for a guarantee of safe conduct or amnesty (*al-amān*), he freely granted it.[2] The idea that Muslim rebels should be treated with a degree of tolerance and with clemency was increasingly taking hold in the culture of jurists. Whether this was a reflection of the socio-historical experiences of Muslims after the third/ninth century is doubtful. Rather, it reflects a doctrinal normative allegiance that had taken hold in Muslim juristic culture. Once legal precedent is set, and the legal culture becomes institutionalized and developed, legal doctrines often assume a life of their own. These legal doctrines set their own base of authority and their own doctrinal imperative. Jurists borrow doctrines from each other, and repeat such doctrines simply because they are a part of an established legal discourse within the juristic culture. Nonetheless, changing sociological and political circumstances, cumulatively and eventually, affect juridical discourses and result in incremental modifications to the law. Sociological and political changes also occasionally result in legal revolutions through which the legal doctrines are substantially and materially altered. Such legal revolutions often occur under circumstances of social and political crises that emphasize the fact that a wide gap exists between the social and political realities, and the law. Often, however, these legal revolutions are initiated by political institutions that are outsiders and alien to the juristic

[1] Al-Ashᶜarī, *Maqālāt*, 1:136–65. [2] Ibid., 212.

culture, or by jurists who are exceptionally creative, but they are often not well integrated in the institutional juristic structures.[3] This results in something of a paradox. On the one hand, the substantial modification of the law might be responsive to the social and political circumstances of society. On the other hand, the fact that the juristic revolutions are often initiated or advocated by relative outsiders to the juristic culture limits the effectiveness of such legal changes. Since a developed juristic culture relies on, and is encumbered by, prior authority, advocating changes that are not consistent with prior authority inevitably meets resistance. This is especially the case if the changes are advocated by those who do not comfortably fit within the institutions of the juristic culture.

In this chapter, we will observe a two-pronged phenomenon: first, the continued development and widespread adoption of the doctrines of the Islamic law of rebellion; and second, the advocacy by some jurists of a major rearticulation and reformulation of this law. We will discuss the legal discourses on the law of rebellion through the weakening and fragmentation of the ʿAbbāsid dynasty around the fourth/tenth century, the beginning of the Bāṭinī threat, and the end of the Fāṭimid threat in the fifth/eleventh century. Although the historical circumstances of this period were materially different from the circumstances of the second/eighth and third/ninth centuries, Muslim jurists of the fourth/tenth and fifth/eleventh centuries did not respond to their contemporary reality as much as they responded to paradigms set by the juristic culture. Shāfiʿī jurists consolidated and expanded upon the doctrinal and theoretical foundations of the law of rebellion. They sought to further authenticate the basis of this law by bolstering the evidence of its Islamicity, and by developing its systematic structure. Ḥanbalī jurists borrowed and adopted the Shāfiʿī discourses, but did not contribute to the theoretical or doctrinal development of the law until a few centuries later. Ḥanafī jurists participated in bolstering the authenticity of the law of rebellion, but their doctrines continued to be less tolerant towards rebels. Although Mālikī jurists increasingly acknowledged the existence and spread of the discourse on rebellion, they continued to treat the topic with substantial ambivalence. Significantly, Shīʿī jurists responded to the Sunnī legal discourses on rebellion, but from a decisively different ideological perspective.

[3] On incremental and revolutionary changes in law, see Berman, *Law*, 15, 18–23. The most intellectually satisfying work on law and revolution remains Berman's. However, I am not sure to what extent his methodology can explain developments in the Islamic legal system. In any case, I am using the expression "legal revolution" in a less totalistic and drastic sense.

In all of these cases, lawyers were imitating lawyers, and lawyers were responding to lawyers. This meant that the law could develop along systematic and coherent theoretical categorizations unencumbered by the vagaries of socio-political realities. The distinction between rebellion and banditry would become sharper and clearer. Furthermore, eventually Muslim jurists would break down their analyses into three distinct questions: One, who is a rebel? Two, what is a rebellion? Three, how should rebels be treated? Effectively, by the fifth/eleventh century, the discourses on rebellion became not only firmly established, but even formulaic. Such discourses increasingly assumed a rather objectified and detached tone.

Nonetheless, the cumulative effect of the socio-political changes in the Islamic world after the sixth/twelfth centuries would result in thorough revisions in the law of rebellion. The changes are rather elusive, and if one is not observing the development of the legal discourses over the span of several centuries, such changes could be easily missed. The categorizations and the basic structure of the law remained unchanged. Nonetheless, the definitions and usages of the legal terms were revised and substantially altered. While the external structure of the law appeared unchanged, the substantive interior was slowly altered and restructured to produce materially different results. However, as noted above, this would take place post-sixth/twelfth century. For now, it is important to describe the adoption and consolidation of the law of rebellion. This meant that this field of legal discourse developed from its fairly obscure and vague beginnings to a systematic and permanent field of law.

THE CONSOLIDATION AND SPREAD OF A LEGAL TRADITION: THE SHĀFIʿĪ AND ḤANBALĪ ADVOCACY

Shāfiʿī jurists insisted that, as a general proposition, the ruler must be obeyed. They also accepted the necessity of obeying the usurper of power. However, as argued earlier, this is rather unremarkable. The general legal principle espoused by the jurists was in favor of a system of basic order As argued by al-Ghazālī and others, without a foundation of order the possibility of justice would be denied. Nonetheless, the adherence to this general principle was not as dogmatic or slavish as much contemporary scholarship assumes. Rather, the general principle was permeated with the qualifications and complexities of the doctrines of rebellion. Through these doctrines, Shāfiʿī thought in particular refused to grant the state an absolute, unmitigated right to obedience.

Ibn al-Mundhir (d. 318/930), a Shāfiʿī jurist from Nishapur,[4] provides a fairly detailed discussion of the law of rebellion.[5] For the most part, his exposition is a review of the determinations of the different schools of thought discussed in the last chapter. Most of his discussion, however, is a rehashing of al-Shāfiʿī's discourse on rebellion. Ibn al-Mundhir does not use the expression the just ruler, and does not focus on the necessity of obeying those in power. Rather, he concentrates on the circumstances under which Muslims should support a ruler against possible rebels. Ibn al-Mundhir states that if Muslims give their *bayʿa* (oath of allegiance) to a ruler, and this ruler becomes the legitimate caliph, Muslims should support the ruler against rebels. However, he states that this is so only if the rebels are among those who gave the caliph their allegiance freely and without compulsion. The implication is that if the ruler was not firmly established or if people gave their allegiance to the ruler under compulsion, then Muslims are not obligated to support the ruler against the rebels. Ibn al-Mundhir goes on to assert that if two equally powerful parties fight, then it is a *fitna*, and Muslims should refrain from becoming involved.[6]

Not much is known about Ibn al-Mundhir, and later jurists do not extensively cite his discussions on the law of rebellion. The most notable Shāfiʿī exposition on the law of rebellion emerging from the fourth/tenth and fifth/eleventh centuries, and the one most frequently cited by later jurists, is that of al-Māwardī (d. 450/1058). Al-Māwardī served as a judge in several cities in Irāq before being given the honorific title of *aqḍā al-quḍā* (the most eminent judge) by the ʿAbbāsid caliph al-Qā'im bi-Amriallāh (r. 422/1031–467/1075). Al-Māwardī also often acted as a political emissary and negotiator on behalf of the ʿAbbāsid caliph. Therefore, there is no question that he had a vested interest in the political institutions of his day. As noted earlier, Gibb argued that al-Māwardī wrote his famous book on the ordinances of government in an attempt to assert the authority of the ʿAbbāsid caliphs against the Buwayhid princes who effectively dominated and controlled the ʿAbbāsids. Yet he enjoyed

4 Not much is known about him except his origin. Reportedly, he was a Shāfiʿī, although that is not entirely clear. Some sources assert that Ibn al-Mundhir would attribute to the masters, such as al-Shāfiʿī and Mālik, doctrines which they did not hold: al-Subkī, *Ṭabaqāt*, III:102; Ibn Ḥajar al-ʿAsqalānī, *Lisān*, V:37; Ibn Khallikān, *Wafayāt*, IV:207; al-Ṣafadī, *Kitāb*, I:336.

5 Ibn al-Mundhir (d. 318/930), *al-Ishrāf*, II:385–405. Ibn al-Mundhir appears to use the words Khawārij and *bughāh* interchangeably throughout his text. When he refers to the views of al-Shāfiʿī, he uses the term *bughāh*, but when he refers to the views of Mālik, Abū Ḥanīfa, and al-Awzāʿī, he uses the term Khawārij.

6 Ibid., 402–5.

a close relationship with the Buwayhid ruler of Baghdād, the prince Jalāl al-Dīn (r. 416/1025–434/1042). Nevertheless, al-Māwardī was not simply subservient to his benefactors, and his character and intellectual legacy were complex. He apparently harbored Muᶜtazilī sympathies and adopted some of their views on predestination and other points of creed. Perhaps because of his Muᶜtazilī inclinations and his political role, al-Māwardī also reportedly hid most of his writings during his lifetime, and permitted their publication only on his deathbed. Moreover, his political role was not free of tensions. For example, when the ᶜAbbāsid caliph granted Jalāl al-Dīn the title of "king of kings," al-Māwardī issued a *fatwā* asserting that the title was improper, and that the act of the ᶜAbbāsid caliph was illegal.[7]

Clearly, al-Māwardī had no qualms with the necessity of obeying those in power. But his position was not absolute or dogmatic. For instance, in his book *Naṣīḥat al-Mulūk* (Advice to the Kings), he reiterates al-Shāfiᶜī's view that rebels against unjust rulers should not be fought.[8] Elsewhere, al-Māwardī also cites al-Shāfiᶜī's opinion that only those who oppose the just ruler are to be considered rebels.[9] However, al-Māwardī does not emphasize this point, and does not seem to be primarily concerned with whether the ruler is just or not. Rather, he quotes al-Shāfiᶜī's opinions on this matter without further elaboration. Al-Māwardī's main emphasis is on the treatment due to rebels and not the legitimacy of the ruler. His treatment of the issue of rebellion is very systematic and exhaustive, and even, perhaps, overdeveloped. In fact, some of the finer points of his argument were not adopted by later Shāfiᶜī jurists. But what emerges from his treatment of the topic is a refined and complex discourse that is neither absolute nor dogmatic. Al-Māwardī does not focus his discussions on the right of rebellion against unjust rulers. Rather, he focuses on the categorization of rebellion according to specific criteria and standards. He goes as far as maintaining that if rebels fulfill specific criteria they are not to be considered sinners, but are equivalent to those who adopt

[7] See al-Dhahabī, *Siyar*, XVIII:64–6; Ibn Khallikān, *Wafayāt*, III:282–3; Ibn al-ᶜImād, *Shadharāt*, III:285–7; al-Māwardī, *Adab*, I:37–8; Mikhail, *Politics*, 62–3. Al-Māwardī does not seem to have been physically harmed as a result of this *fatwā*. However, he was vehemently attacked by other jurists who had supported the actions of the caliph. He reportedly defended himself in a wonderfully technical way: he argued that it is improper for Ḥanafī jurists to criticize the legal opinion of a Shāfiᶜī jurist. A Ḥanafī jurist can issue a contrary opinion or simply disagree, but he cannot criticize a *fatwā* issued by a Shāfiᶜī. According to the sources, jurists from the Ḥanafī and Shāfiᶜī schools disagreed on the legality of the caliph's decree. See al-Shahrazūrī, *Adab*, 148–50.

[8] Al-Māwardī, *Naṣīḥa*, 462.

[9] Al-Māwardī, *Kitāb*, 102.

a legitimate school of thought (*madhhab*). In the same way that one may legitimately change from the Shāfiʿī school, for example, to another school of thought, rebels could alter their initial commitment from a loyalist ideology to an oppositional ideology without being branded as iniquitous (*fasaqa*).[10]

Al-Māwardī starts his analysis by invoking the *baghy* Qurʾānic verse. While he notes the ambiguous nature of the verse and the obscure reasons for its revelation, he is able to draw specific conclusions from the verse. He argues that the verse has several clear indications: (1) the rebels are to be considered Muslim and treated as such; (2) reconciliation and peaceful resolution of the conflict is always preferable to fighting; (3) fighting the rebels is permissible if they persist in their defiance; (4) if they repent, the rebels may not be fought; and (5) the fighting parties are not liable for damages incurred. Thus, al-Māwardī argues, the law of rebellion was clearly founded on the Qurʾānic text.[11] By extracting these principles from the Qurʾānic verse, al-Māwardī laid a powerful foundation for his discourse. Importantly, he goes further by arguing that the laws of rebellion were firmly established on the precedent set in the *Sunna* of the Prophet and the Companions. He mentions the traditions attributed to the Prophet concerning the impermissibility of departing from the *jamāʿa*, and the traditions condemning those who use force against fellow Muslims. Interestingly, however, al-Māwardī does not invoke these traditions in the context of discussing the permissibility of rebellion. Rather, he argues that these traditions relate to the issue of whether the rebels may be fought in the first place. Therefore, these traditions are not addressed to the rebels; they are addressed to the loyalists, and they authorize the use of force against rebels if need be.[12] These traditions, according to al-Māwardī, do not necessarily condemn rebels, but simply permit the waging of war against them. Al-Māwardī goes on to conclude that the Qurʾān, the *Sunna* of the Prophet and the Companions, and the consensus of the jurists permit the fighting of rebels.[13] Essentially, he achieves two objectives by this argument, the first theological, and the second legal. From a theological point of view, ʿAlī was right in fighting those who rebelled against him. In this context, al-Māwardī considered Muʿāwiya to have been a rebel, and ʿAlī to have been the

[10] Ibid., 180.
[11] Ibid., 62. Ibn al-Mundhir (*al-Ishrāf*, II:385–6) cites and discusses the same verse but the connection between the verse and the law of rebellion is more ambiguous in his treatment.
[12] Al-Māwardī, *Kitāb*, 63–4. [13] Ibid., 66–7.

legitimate ruler.[14] From the legal point of view, the necessity of sustaining order and stability is maintained.

Since it has been established that fighting rebels is permissible, al-Māwardī argues, it must also be recognized that there are four conditions that must be fulfilled before fighting rebels may be considered lawful. According to al-Māwardī, three of these conditions are agreed upon, while there is disagreement concerning the fourth condition. First, the rebels must be of a sufficient number and strength so that it becomes impossible to obtain their compliance with the law without fighting. At the same time, if the rebels are few in number they cannot be fought. Rather, they are to be treated as any other subject of the state. Second, the rebels must gather in a particular area or locality, so that they become distinct and separate from the rest of the population. Otherwise, they may not be fought. Third, the rebels must adopt an interpretation or ideology that is plausible but not necessarily correct. If they do not have an interpretation, they are to be considered bandits or highway robbers, and should be treated as such. Finally, al-Māwardī asserts that the jurists have disagreed on whether it is necessary that the rebels have a leader whom they follow and obey (*wujūd muṭāᶜ*). Some have argued that as long as the rebels have not chosen a leader, they may not be fought. Al-Māwardī, however, disagrees with this view and maintains that choosing a particular leader is not a valid condition for fighting the rebels.[15] In other words, rebels may be fought even if they have not chosen a leader. If all three conditions have been met, a prima facie case has been established for the permissibility of fighting the rebels. The ruler must then move to the next step, and that is warning and debating the rebels. Fighting must be a last resort, and may be invoked only if the ruler has despaired of achieving a peaceful resolution to the conflict. After all efforts at a peaceful resolution have been exhausted, it becomes permissible to

[14] Ibid., 66, 89, 93. In this context, the author notes that one may not argue that ᶜUthmān refused to fight the rebels, and hence fighting rebels is impermissible. Al-Māwardī simply notes that every age has its appropriate laws, and every *mujtahid* may have a different opinion. The implication is that ᶜUthmān was entitled to his view, and that his view may have been appropriate for his day and age. Al-Māwardī implies that ᶜUthmān's views need not be followed in a subsequent age. Presumably, al-Māwardī is referring to the reports asserting that ᶜUthmān refused to defend himself when he was attacked by a crowd during an uprising.

[15] Ibid., 67–9. The disagreement over whether the rebels must have a leader relates to the issue of what makes a separate community and the role of leadership. Some argued that as long as the rebels have not accepted an alternative leader, they effectively remain part of the community of the loyalists. In other words, groups do not become separate until they establish a different leader and pay allegiance to him. At the heart of this debate is whether a group is in a state of actual rebellion if it has not adopted an alternative leader.

fight the rebels. Al-Māwardī bolsters his argument with various citations of the reported conduct of ʿAlī.[16]

In a segment that exhibits a tendency towards overlegislation, al-Māwardī argues that after exhausting the avenues of a possible peaceful resolution, there are circumstances under which fighting the rebels becomes obligatory, permissible, or disagreed upon. The ruler *must* fight the rebels in one of five conditions: (1) if the rebels assault loyalist women;[17] (2) if they interfere with the state's war efforts against external enemies; (3) if they usurp money or property from the public treasury; (4) if they refuse to pay taxes; and (5) if they attempt to overthrow the ruler by force.[18] In any of these five circumstances, the ruler must wage war against the rebels and bring them back to the fold.[19]

Fighting the rebels is permissible but not mandatory if they conspire, organize, and gather in a location, and exhibit an intent to rebel, but have not yet violated any law or abstained from performing any duty owed to the state. The ruler, nonetheless, may fight them to preempt their rebellion, but it is not obligatory that he do so. In this situation, the rebels have not violated any particular law, but they have renounced the leader, and considered themselves to be in an effective state of rebellion. Al-Māwardī distinguishes between this situation and a situation where a group of people adopt a specific system of belief, live in peaceful isolation from society, and do not exhibit an intent to rebel or overthrow the ruler. He argues that this group may not be fought even if they adopt a system of belief considered objectionable to the loyalists, and that they may not be forced to abandon their system of belief.[20] Finally, the last category that al-Māwardī discusses is that of rebels who gather in a specific location but are otherwise obedient, except for the fact that they refuse to give their alms (*zakāh*) to the ruler. Rather, they insist on distributing them to their sympathizers instead. One can legitimately contend that they *must* be fought or that they *may* be fought. In other words, both views are supportable.[21]

[16] Ibid., 70–3, 75.

[17] The phrasing in the original text indicates that al-Māwardī had in mind a situation where the rebels attack travelers and commit rape, i.e. when their actions resemble the conduct of bandits.

[18] Ibid., 75. Note that al-Māwardī does not say "the just ruler."

[19] In what could have been an oversight, al-Māwardī does not list the murder of a loyalist or a neutral person as one of the circumstances that require the use of force against the rebels. As noted earlier, ʿAlī is presumed to have fought the Khawārij of Nahrawān when they killed ʿAbd Allāh b. Khabbāb (d. 37/657) and claimed responsibility, as a group, for his murder. Ibn al-Mundhir, like other jurists, cites this precedent in arguing that loyalists have a right to fight rebels if they initiate violence: Ibn al-Mundhir, *al-Ishrāf*, II:388.

[20] Al-Māwardī, *Kitāb*, 77, 106–7, 120.

[21] Ibid., 77.

As to the issue of liability, the rebels are liable for life and property destroyed before or after the fighting. Importantly, al-Māwardī argues that the loyalists are liable, as well, for life destroyed before or after the commencement of fighting. As to rebel property destroyed before or after the fighting, as a general matter, the loyalists are to be held liable. If, however, particular individuals, including loyalist soldiers, stand accused of destroying rebel property before or after the fighting, liability will turn on the subjective intent of the offender. If the offenders intended to contribute to weakening and defeating the rebels, they will not be held liable. But if malice and a desire to exact vengeance motivated the offenders, they will be held liable. Nevertheless, neither the loyalists nor the rebels are liable for life or property destroyed during the fighting. Al-Māwardī argues that there are two reasons why the rebels should not be held liable for life or property destroyed in the course of fighting. First, the rebels based themselves on an interpretation, and this distinguishes them from common criminals. Second, they must be encouraged to return to obedience, and if they are to be held liable, this is due to alienate them further and not provide them with a sufficient incentive to end their rebellion.[22]

Al-Māwardī goes on to emphasize that if the rebels are few in number and do not possess a particular force or strength, they are to be treated like any other subjects of the state. If they commingle with the loyalists, as long as they do not break the law, they are not to be persecuted. However, if they break the law, they are to be held responsible for their actions on an equal footing with anyone else. Al-Māwardī cites the example of Ibn Muljim, the man who assassinated ᶜAlī, and argues that although he was motivated by an interpretation, he was punished nonetheless. Importantly, al-Māwardī emphasizes that ᶜAlī, on his deathbed, not only commanded that Ibn Muljim *not* be tortured, but he also urged that Ibn Muljim be treated well and that he be pardoned.[23] Al-Māwardī does not go as far as arguing that every political assassin should be pardoned. Nonetheless, he does insist that political prisoners be treated kindly, and recommends pardon as the pious or religiously preferable course of action, even if the assassin does not technically qualify for *bughāh* treatment.[24]

[22] Ibid., 79–87. Also see Ibn al-Mundhir, *al-Ishrāf*, II:391.

[23] Al-Māwardī, *Kitāb*, 104. Typically, the reports on this incident state that ᶜAlī said that he would decide Ibn Muljim's fate if he (ᶜAlī) lived, but that his son should execute Ibn Muljim if he died. Al-Māwardī's report is rather unusual.

[24] Ibid.

In all circumstances, al-Māwardī insists, it must be remembered that rebels are not fought because of their ideas or systems of belief. God permitted the fighting, and not the killing, of rebels. Killing is merely incidental to the necessity of fighting. Therefore, once the rebellion ends, the permission to fight or kill ends. Al-Māwardī argues that, as a legal matter, the rebellion is considered to have ended in three circumstances: (1) if the rebels renounce the rebellion and declare their willingness to obey the ruler; (2) if the rebels lay down their weapons; and (3) if the rebels are defeated and flee the battlefield. In any of these three situations, the rebellion has ended, and the loyalists no longer have legal cause to fight or kill the rebels.[25] It makes no difference, al-Māwardī contends, whether or not the rebels have a group or camp to which they may return. The moment one of the three situations exists, the fighting must end and the rebels may not be pursued or finished off.[26]

Al-Māwardī then addresses the Khawārij specifically. He explains that the Khawārij believed that all Muslims who did not adhere to the Khārijī creed were infidels, and that the abode of Islam was really an abode of unbelievers. Therefore, the Khawārij permitted the killing and usurpation of the properties of their opponents. If a group appears, al-Māwardī argues, that adopts a similar set of beliefs, they may not be persecuted or fought as long as they live among Muslims and do not commit a specific crime. Furthermore, they are not to be compelled or forced to abandon their beliefs. Rather, the ruler must attempt to debate them and convince them of the error of their ways. Like the Prophet's practice with the hypocrites of Medina, they cannot be prosecuted simply because of their ideas, as long as they outwardly continue to obey the ruler.[27] If this group isolates itself from the rest of society and lives in a specific territory, their area is to be treated as a part of the loyalist territory (*dār ahl al-ᶜadl*), and therefore all laws continue to apply to them without distinction.[28] If a member of the group commits a crime, only the offender, and not the group as a whole, is to be prosecuted for the crime.[29] However, if the group claims collective responsibility for the crime, and protects and

25 Ibid., 109. 26 Ibid., 109–17.
27 Ibid., 120. 28 Ibid., 123.
29 Ibid., 126. Al-Māwardī discusses whether an offender who commits murder must be executed, as in the case of a bandit, or whether the offender is to be treated as any other common criminal. In other words, if a fanatical offender who belongs to a group such as the Khawārij commits murder, does it become imperative to impose the death sentence, or is he to be treated just as any other criminal would be treated? He does not resolve the issue.

gives shelter to the offender, then the whole group may be fought until the offender is captured.[30] The implication of al-Māwardī's argument is that even a fanatical group such as the Khawārij may not be persecuted unless they commit a general act of insurrection, and that ideas alone are not sufficient grounds for commencing warfare against a group adhering to a radical ideology. Individuals belonging to the group are to be held individually responsible for their crimes, and therefore individual acts of violence do not justify a disproportionate violent response by the state. Importantly, like other rebels, the Khawārij, or a group adhering to a similar system of thought, are not liable for life or property destroyed in the course of a general rebellion.[31]

After the digression dealing with fanatical groups such as the Khawārij, al-Māwardī returns to the issue of the treatment of rebels in general. He pays special attention to the rules of conduct of warfare against rebels. Although he repeats many of al-Shāfiʿī's points, his treatment is more exhaustive and systematic.[32] Like al-Shāfiʿī, he maintains that the wounded and fugitives may not be killed and weapons of mass destruction may not be used against rebels. Mangonels and flame-throwers may not be used except for an absolute necessity – for example, if the rebels first use these weapons. Al-Māwardī, however, adds that the rebels may not be attacked without warning or under the cover of darkness. The rebels' homes may not be burned or flooded, and the rebels themselves may not be surrounded and denied food or water. The cattle, war-horses, trees, or crops of the rebels may not be destroyed.[33] Furthermore, the loyalists may not seek the assistance of non-believers, scriptuaries, or those who believe that it is proper to dispatch the wounded and fugitives (as is the case with the Ḥanafīs) against the rebels. If it becomes necessary to use any of these groups against the rebels, the loyalists may do so, but only if certain conditions are met. First, the loyalists must find no other ally against the rebels. Second, the loyalists must obtain an assurance from their allies that they will not kill the wounded or fugitives, and must have a good-faith belief that the allies will, in fact, comply with such an assurance. Third, the loyalists must be capable of restraining their allies from violating the assurance given or committing any other abuses. If they do not have the power to do so, then they may not seek the assistance

[30] Ibid., 127. [31] Ibid., 124.

[32] His treatment is far more systematic than Ibn al-Mundhir's as well. See Ibn al-Mundhir, *al-Ishrāf*, II:389–90.

[33] Al-Māwardī, *Kitāb*, 164–5.

of these allies.[34] Hence, even if it becomes necessary to use such allies, it is imperative that the loyalists be able to ensure compliance with the dictates of legality.

Al-Māwardī reiterates that the property of rebels may not be confiscated. Weapons and supplies captured from them are not to be used against them, and are to be returned to them after the fighting ends. The weapons and supplies, however, may be used in cases of dire necessity. If such weapons and supplies are used or destroyed, adequate compensation must be paid to the rebels.[35] Furthermore, money should not be accepted from the rebels in return for a peace treaty or for releasing rebel prisoners. Attempting to force rebels to ransom their prisoners from the loyalists is improper. Furthermore, even if the loyalists illegally take hostages from the rebels, these hostages may not be killed, even if the rebels kill loyalist hostages.[36]

Al-Māwardī dedicates a considerable amount of attention to the treatment due to rebel prisoners of war. After asserting that rebel prisoners may not be executed or enslaved, he notes that the Ḥanafī position allows for the execution of prisoners as long as the fighting between rebels and loyalists continues. However, he rebuts the Ḥanafī position by citing a report attributed to the Prophet specifying that rebel prisoners may not be killed. It is rather apparent that the Prophet's *ḥadīth* is the product of late circulation since it does not appear in any of the earlier juristic sources.[37] Nonetheless, al-Māwardī further supports his argument by claiming that ʿAlī never executed rebel prisoners, and that Muslims have consistently followed his example ever since (*wa ʿalayhā ʿamila al-Muslimūna baʿdahu*). Al-Māwardī's claim is hardly historical; however, he argues that the treatment of Muslim rebels must materially differ from the treatment afforded to non-Muslim prisoners of war. Therefore, he goes so far as to claim that whoever executes a rebel prisoner either should be put to death or should be liable for the victim's blood money.[38]

Since it is forbidden to execute or enslave rebel prisoners, al-Māwardī asserts, then the only other possibility is imprisonment. Rebel prisoners may be imprisoned as long as the fighting continues. However, if the rebels during the continuation of the fighting give their oath of allegiance

34 Ibid., 158. Also see Ibn al-Mundhir, *al-Ishrāf*, II:397–8.

35 Al-Māwardī, *Kitāb*, 209. Compensation need not be paid to the rebels if the loyalists do not use the weapons and supplies, but they are destroyed or lost anyway through no fault of the loyalists.

36 Ibid., 141, 166–7.

37 Even a jurist from the fourth/tenth century such as Ibn al-Mundhir (*al-Ishrāf*, II:389–90) does not cite this tradition.

38 Al-Māwardī, *Kitāb*, 129–31.

to the ruler, their oath must be accepted, and they must be released immediately. It is not permissible for the ruler to demand hostages or other forms of surety as a condition for their release. The rebels' word must be accepted at face value, and no attempt should be made to investigate possible hidden motives or intentions that they might harbor.[39] If the rebels refuse to give their oath of allegiance to the ruler, they are to be detained until the fighting ends, but then they must be released promptly. Al-Māwardī asserts that the fighting is considered to have ended in three specific situations: (1) if the rebels, as a group, abandon their rebellion and declare their intention to take the oath of allegiance to the ruler; (2) if the rebels, as a group, surrender and lay down their weapons; or (3) if the rebels are defeated and flee the battlefield.[40] If any of these situations exists, al-Māwardī argues, then the fighting must be considered to have come to an end. He however notes that some have argued that, as to the third situation, if the rebels retreat to a standing war camp or have available reinforcements, the prisoners may continue to be detained until the war camp or the reinforcements have been defeated. Significantly, al-Māwardī notes that once the rebel prisoners have been released, they are to be treated as any other subjects of the state, even if they continue to adhere to the system of thought that prompted their rebellion in the first place, and even if they isolate themselves from society.[41]

As noted earlier, al-Māwardī does not focus on the theological or theoretical status of the rebels. He does not systematically or cohesively explain why rebels are entitled to this rather generous treatment. Other than stating that Muslim rebels are not sinners and that they must adhere to a plausible interpretation or cause, he does not produce a systematic justification for the tolerant treatment of Muslim rebels. Furthermore, al-Māwardī does not reproduce earlier opinions which asserted that rebels who are motivated by tribal or partisan justifications are not to be treated as *bughāh*.[42] Therefore, it is not clear who he specifically had in mind when he addressed the category of the *bughāh*. For instance, it is not clear whether he considered certain Buwayhids or Seljuks who might not have

39 Ibid., 132.

40 These conditions are substantially the same as the three conditions under which al-Māwardī argues that a rebellion is considered to have ended, and legal cause no longer exists for killing the rebels.

41 Ibid., 135.

42 However, the Shāfiʿī jurist al-Kiyā al-Harrāsī (d. 504/1110), in his *Aḥkām*, III:382, argues that the prohibition against becoming involved in *fitan* applies to those who fight for tribal and partisan reasons. This implies that those who fight while relying on a *ta'wīl* are considered qualitatively different.

recognized the ʿAbbāsid caliph or might not have given such a caliph their allegiance to be *bughāh*.[43] Nonetheless, it is clear that al-Māwardī sought to give *aḥkām al-bughāh* an expansive reach, and to create an ethical and legal standard that would influence the conduct of warfare between combating Muslims, and a standard under which rulers may be judged. Like al-Shāfiʿī, al-Māwardī was not willing to extend the full protections of *aḥkām al-bughāh* to non-Muslims living in Muslim territories. However, he was not willing to place them outside the scope of these laws either. He, for example, argues that under normal circumstances, if *ahl al-dhimma* assist or join the *bughāh* in rebellion, this will be considered a violation of their covenant (*ʿaqd al-dhimma*). But if these non-Muslims join Muslim rebels, and claim that they did not know that they were not supposed to do so, they should be believed and their covenant remains valid. For instance, if the non-Muslims assert that they thought it was permissible to assist the rebels in the same fashion that it is permissible to join Muslims in fighting bandits, then this is to be considered a valid excuse. In other words, according to al-Māwardī, it is well established that non-Muslims may assist Muslims in fighting bandits. Hence, if the non-Muslims were to claim that fighting with the rebels is not distinguishable from fighting against bandits, this would serve as a valid excuse and the integrity of their covenant with the loyalists would be preserved. Of course, this is not entirely convincing. Logically, one can hardly see a correlation between fighting bandits and fighting the state. But al-Māwardī wished to uphold the view that *ahl al-dhimma* should not be treated harshly simply because they joined a rebellion. In fact, in this situation the rules of conduct that apply to fighting Muslim rebels also apply to fighting *ahl al-dhimma* except that *ahl al-dhimma* would be held liable for life and property destroyed in the course of the rebellion. If the loyalists, however, make it a condition of *ʿaqd al-dhimma* that the *ahl al-dhimma* not fight any Muslim, rebel or otherwise, in that case, assisting or joining a rebellion would be considered an abrogation of the covenant.[44]

The rebels, according to al-Māwardī, remain Muslim despite their rebellion, and in fact, are not sinners. Therefore, al-Māwardī insists that, contrary to the Ḥanafī position, funeral prayers should be performed for dead rebels. He also notes that the jurists have disagreed on whether loyalists killed in battle are martyrs, but he implies that, in fact, they are

[43] Arguably, however, the Seljuks or Buwayhids lacked an interpretation or *taʾwīl*, and therefore should not be treated as *bughāh*.

[44] Al-Māwardī, *Kitāb*, 147–9.

not.[45] Al-Māwardī adds that the testimony of rebels should be accepted in court because the mere fact that they participated in a rebellion does not impeach their credibility. There are, however, two exceptions to this rule. If the rebels believe that all Muslims, other than those who support them, are in reality unbelievers, and believe that it is permissible to kill any Muslim who does not support them, then the testimony of those rebels should not be accepted because this type of belief is sinful and iniquitous. Furthermore, if the rebel adheres to the views of groups such as the Khaṭṭābiyya, his testimony should not be accepted. The Khaṭṭābiyya believed that it was permissible to testify falsely in order to support the claims of one of their own members against their opponents.[46]

Thus far, al-Māwardī deals mostly with rebels in the process of rebellion or whose rebellion ultimately failed. He argues throughout that the territory of the rebels remains a part of the abode of Islam, and that the rebels remain the subjects of the ruler. But he also deals with a situation in which the rebels are temporarily or permanently victorious. In this context, he uses the expression "the abode of rebels" (*dār al-baghy*), juxtaposing it to "the abode of the loyalists" (*dār ahl al-ᶜadl*).[47] Al-Māwardī implies, without ever explicitly conceding as much, that these are two different and separate abodes, but does not treat the two as equals. The abode of the loyalists remains the possessor of legitimacy, while the abode of the rebels is given limited recognition. Following in al-Shāfiᶜī's footsteps, he argues that if the rebels manage to prevail over a specific territory, collect taxes, and implement sanctions against criminals, their legal acts and adjudications must be given full effect if the ruler eventually defeats them.[48] Furthermore, the decisions of judges appointed by rebels in unconquered rebel territory must be given full faith and credit by loyalist judges. Since it has already been established that, contrary to the Ḥanafī position, rebels are not sinners or iniquitous, there is no reason to refuse to give full effect to the adjudications of rebel judges. There are, however, two exceptions. First, if the judge's decision violates the clear consensus of all jurists, then his decision should not be

[45] Ibid., 184. A martyr in Islamic law is not washed before burial. See Kohlberg, "Shahīd." Al-Māwardī states that loyalists killed in battle are to be washed and buried just as is done for the rebels. He therefore implies that loyalists killed in battle are not martyrs.

[46] Al-Māwardī, *Kitāb*, 179–81. See, on the Khaṭṭābiyya, al-Shahrastānī, *al-Milal*, I:210–11; Madelung, "Khaṭṭābiyya."

[47] See, for example, al-Māwardī, *Kitāb*, 213–16.

[48] Ibid., 169. Ibn al-Mundhir (*al-Ishrāf*, II:396–7) briefly addresses this issue but refers to it as the adjudications and legal acts of the Khawārij.

recognized. Second, if the judge appointed by the rebels believes that all other Muslims are unbelievers, his decision may not be recognized regardless of whether it is supportable or not.[49] Additionally, if the rebel judge writes a letter to a loyalist judge, al-Māwardī recommends that the loyalist judge delay in writing a response basically as a sign of disrespect and disregard.[50]

Importantly, peace treaties signed by the leader of the rebels with non-Muslims should not be recognized. The power to enter into treaties with foreign powers is a privilege reserved to the leader of the Islamic community who is the ruler of the loyalists. Nonetheless, any guarantee of safe conduct given by rebels to non-Muslims must be respected and given full effect.[51] Nevertheless, al-Māwardī strongly disagrees with the Ḥanafī jurisdictional argument. He argues that Islamic law has jurisdiction over offenses committed by loyalists or rebels in the abode of the rebels. Like al-Shāfiʿī, al-Māwardī argues that Islamic law has personal jurisdiction over Muslims wherever they may go, even in non-Muslim territory. Therefore, if a Muslim violates God's laws in the abode of unbelievers or in the abode of rebels, jurisdiction is maintained over all such crimes. Significantly, al-Māwardī does not argue that the loyalists have extra-territorial jurisdiction over all offenses committed outside their territory. Rather, his argument is that the laws of Islam and God apply everywhere. Consequently, for example, the obligation to pray and fast applies to Muslims wherever they may go. The issue, al-Māwardī contends, is not whether the ruler maintains control over a specific territory. The relevant issue is that God commands Muslims to observe certain prohibitions and injunctions. The ruler is simply delegated to apply God's commands. Therefore, if the ruler is able to apply the divine commands to any Muslim, he must do so. If, however, the ruler is unable, under certain circumstances, to apply the divine commands, then the application of the commands is deferred until he is able to do so.[52] Consequently, the issue has little to do with the abode of the rebels specifically. The real issue is that Islamic law has universal jurisdiction over all Muslims regardless of the nature of the territory.

It is difficult to evaluate or characterize the nature of al-Māwardī's lengthy discourse. His exhaustively detailed treatment does not seem to

49 Al-Māwardī, *Kitāb*, 174–6. 50 Ibid., 177.
51 Ibid., 203–4, 210–11. 52 Ibid., 213–16.

be inspired by a simple or essentialistic ideological motivation. Significantly, however, one cannot describe al-Māwardī's discourse as either quietist or activist. He does not unequivocally condemn or endorse rebellion against those in power. He recognizes that those who sincerely believe that they have just cause to rebel must not be treated as common criminals. Yet he also upholds the need for law and order by supporting the necessity of putting an end to rebellion. Al-Māwardī's treatment is thoroughly legal and technical. But he is neither unabashedly pragmatic nor idealistic; rather, he combines elements of both pragmatism and idealism. For example, he pragmatically upholds the need to recognize the legal acts of rebels, but he idealistically argues that captured weapons and other war equipment cannot be used, and must be returned to the rebels.[53] Furthermore, he does not concede sovereignty to the rebels, but he does recognize their limited independence. He clearly prefers that they be integrated in society, but rejects the idea of forcible conversion or the instituting of an inquisition against all those who hold Khārijī ideas, for example. Ultimately, al-Māwardī is not writing political theory, but elucidating legal rules that embody competing and conflicting values. Many of his assertions are the product of an adherence to the precedents and doctrines of the Shāfiʿī school. But he also exhibits a genuine concern with the need for stability and order without legitimating the unrestrained slaughter of rebels. Significantly, in works that he wrote in order to render advice to rulers, he repeats the rules discussed above without substantial difference. In other words, al-Māwardī did not revise his discourse in order to cater to the preferences of a separate audience.[54]

Al-Māwardī produced the most exhaustive treatment of the topic of rebellion in his age. Other Shāfiʿī jurists of his time, while repeating many of the doctrines and rules enunciated by al-Māwardī, exhibit different tendencies and preferences. These jurists often addressed the issue of whether rebellion is legal in the first place, which, as has been seen, was largely ignored by al-Māwardī. For instance, Abū Isḥāq al-Shīrāzī (d. 476/1083) states outright that it is illegal to rebel against the ruler

53 The issue of the war equipment of the rebels seems to have been a point of considerable concern for Shāfiʿī jurists. Al-Jawharī (d. 350/961), for example, argues that there was consensus among the Companions that such equipment was not to be treated as spoils of war. It was only after the age of the Companions that people advocated a contrary position. The implication is that people deviated from the correct Islamic position after the age of the Companions: al-Tamīmī, *Nawādir*, 175.

54 Most of the discussion above comes from *al-Ḥāwī*, which is a jurisprudential work written for jurists. In his discussion in works addressed to rulers and administrators, he reproduces the same arguments but in an abridged form. See al-Māwardī, *al-Aḥkām*, 72–7; and his *Naṣīḥa*, 460–3.

(*imām*), and that the *bughāh* are those who rebel, either seeking the overthrow of the ruler or refusing to obey his commands, while basing themselves on an interpretation or cause (*ta'wīl*). He omits the reference to the just ruler (*al-imām al-ᶜādil*), which is probably a recognition of the fact that the use of the term "just" meant the rightful ruler, and not necessarily the ruler who conducts himself justly.[55] As noted earlier, the expression "just ruler" was used by Shāfiᶜī jurists in a very ambiguous sense, but al-Shīrāzī dispenses with the expression altogether because it is largely unhelpful in this context. Like al-Māwardī, despite his assertion that rebellion is unlawful, al-Shīrāzī asserts that rebels who rely on a plausible interpretation or cause are to be considered a form of *mujtahid*, and therefore are not to be treated as common criminals.[56] Otherwise, al-Shīrāzī reproduces most of the rules asserted by al-Māwardī. Rebels are not to be slaughtered, and are not to be held liable for destruction caused in the course of rebellion or fighting. He does mention that some Shāfiᶜī jurists had argued that rebels should be held financially, but not criminally, liable for damages caused during the rebellion. Al-Shīrāzī, however, dismisses this argument as contrary to the consensus.[57] Al-Shīrāzī, like al-Māwardī, distinguishes between rebels and bandits by the fact that rebels have a plausible interpretation or cause. Therefore, al-Shīrāzī states, if a group that does not have a *ta'wīl* prevails over a certain territory, none of their legal acts will be recognized, they will be held responsible for all legal violations committed, and they are to be treated as bandits.[58] This specific point is implicit in al-Māwardī's argument, but al-Shīrāzī makes it explicit, and thus widens the gap between rebels and bandits. Furthermore, al-Shīrāzī's position on rebel prisoners is somewhat different than al-Māwardī's. He agrees that the prisoners should be released if they give their oath of allegiance to the ruler. But after the battle ends, the prisoners who did not give their allegiance to the ruler are to be released only after they promise not to rebel again. He also adds that if the loyalists kill a rebel prisoner, they are responsible for his blood money, which is to be paid to the rebel's

55 Al-Shīrāzī, *al-Muhadhdhab*, II:279. Al-Baghawī (*Sharḥ*, VI:168) uses the expression *al-imām al-ᶜadl*, which means the proper or rightful ruler rather than the just ruler.

56 Al-Shīrāzī, *al-Muhadhdhab*, II:283. Al-Shīrāzī does not state that rebels must reach the rank of *ijtihād* in order for their *ta'wīl* to be considered plausible. Rather, he asserts that rebels are somewhat analogous to *mujtahids*. Later jurists explicitly state that rebels need not be *mujtahids*.

57 Ibid., II:282.

58 Ibid., II:284. Al-Baghawī (*Sharḥ*, VI:170) asserts that the rebels must have a possible or plausible interpretation (*ta'wīl muḥtamal*), some strength or power, and a chosen leader. If one of the three conditions is missing, they are to be treated as bandits, and their testimony or adjudications will not be accepted.

family.[59] In the final analysis, however, although al-Shīrāzī explicitly states that it is unlawful to rebel against any ruler, his position on the treatment of the rebels does not differ from al-Māwardī's in any significant respect.

The Shāfiʿī jurists Imām al-Ḥaramayn al-Juwaynī (d. 478/1085) and Abū Ḥāmid al-Ghazālī (d. 505/1111) are helpful in identifying the assumptions that informed the analysis of the Shāfiʿī jurists of their time. Al-Ghazālī was a student of al-Juwaynī for a period of time, and both jurists were well integrated within the legal institutions of their age. Both of them served as law professors in the Niẓāmiyya school in Nishapur,[60] and their relationship with the Seljuks was largely non-problematic and congenial. However, al-Ghazālī's uncle was executed by the Seljuk sulṭān Barkiyārūq, and some contemporary scholars have suggested that al-Ghazālī fled Baghdād because of his fear of the sulṭān, and because he feared harm from the Assassins (Ismāʿīlīs) of Baghdād.[61] Al-Juwaynī reportedly at one point left the city of Nishapur and headed to Baghdād because of the civil disorder that resulted from the schismatic conflicts between the Ashʿarīs and their opponents, but he returned to Nishapur when stability was restored.[62] Al-Ghazālī, towards the end of his life, adopted Ṣūfī doctrines, and shied away from academic pursuits.[63] Both jurists dealt with the issue of the legality of rebellion, and the treatment of rebels. But their discussion on the topic of the treatment of rebels is not nearly as exhaustive as al-Māwardī's.

Al-Juwaynī, in his theological work *Ghiyāth al-Umam*, indicates that the treatment of rebels is a separate matter from the larger issue of whether rebellions are legal. He asserts that *aḥkām al-bughāh*, which deals with the treatment of rebels, should be sought out in the technical books on law.[64] As to the issue of the legality of rebellion, he asserts that as a general matter, those in power must be obeyed. Individuals from among the laity may enjoin the good and forbid the evil as long as they do not use force and

59 Al-Shīrāzī, *al-Muhadhdhab*, II:281.

60 On the Niẓāmiyya school and its social role and relationship to the juristic culture, see Bowen and Bosworth, "Niẓām"; Makdisi, "Muslim"; Ephart, *Learned*. Ephart argues that schools of law, such as the Niẓāmiyya, were not as important as social networks and shared values in the solidarity and cohesiveness of the juristic culture. I think Ephart overstates his case, but his evidence supports the idea of juristic culture.

61 See Watt, "Al-Ghazālī". Also see Moosa, *Ghazālī*.

62 Ibn al-ʿImād, *Shadharāt*, III:359. On the schismatic conflicts in Nishapur, see Bulliet, *Patricians*.

63 On al-Juwaynī see Ibn Khallikān, *Wafayāt*, III:167–8; al-Dhahabī, *Siyar*, XVIII:468–73; Ibn al-ʿImād, *Shadharāt*, III:358–60. On al-Ghazālī see al-Dhahabī, *Siyar*, XIX:322; Ibn al-ʿImād, *Shadharāt*, IV:10–13.

64 Al-Juwaynī, *Ghiyāth*, 109.

as long as their activity does not lead to the spread of violence and *fitan*.[65] More specifically, armed rebellions by individuals or small groups may not be tolerated or encouraged because this only leads to the spread of violence and lawlessness.[66] Consequently, people should always weigh the harm that results from rebellions against the harm of obeying an unjust ruler; in most cases the harm of rebellion is greater because it leads to the shedding of blood and to the creation of various disasters. The presumption should be in favor of the status quo because a mere suspicion or anticipation that a greater good will result from rebellion is insufficient to justify the violence and harm that one, as a matter of certainty, knows will result.[67] One might argue, al-Juwaynī asserts, that a balancing of evils is improper when it comes to a matter of principle because ᶜAlī did not weigh the good against the evil when he decided to fight Muᶜāwiya. In other words, ᶜAlī fought Muᶜāwiya without regard to the results or possible harms. Al-Juwaynī refutes this argument by claiming many Companions refused to support ᶜAlī specifically because they were concerned with the resulting harm. Furthermore, al-Juwaynī argues, ᶜAlī did not foresee that resorting to war would lead to the amount of destruction that did, in fact, occur. Once ᶜAlī realized the results, he regretted fighting, and attempted to solve the problem peacefully through arbitration.[68] Therefore, if a person who enjoys a considerable amount of strength takes power, it becomes incumbent to recognize and obey

65 Al-Juwaynī, *Kitāb*, 312. Additionally, al-Juwaynī notes that the laity may enjoin the good and forbid the evil only as to grave sins or issues not involving novel issues of law. Al-Ghazālī also argues that individuals may not resort to the use of force while attempting to enjoin the good and forbid the evil because this invariably results in greater harm than good. He adds that if enjoining good and forbidding the evil by speech alone will result in *fitna* and the spread of strife, then individuals must refrain from doing that as well. However, if the anticipated harm will befall the individual enjoining the good and forbidding the evil alone without resulting in a larger harm to society, then it is recommended that the individual resists injustice and sin through the use of speech. Al-Ghazālī emphasizes that the jurists have a duty to enjoin the good and forbid the evil even if the result is that they will be persecuted or harmed. He laments the fact that while the early jurists stood up to injustice and, as a result, were martyred, the jurists of his age are not nearly as upright. These early jurists relied on God and did not fear kings or rulers. The jurists of his day, al-Ghazālī asserts, are silenced by greed, and no longer stand up to unjust kings or rulers: al-Ghazālī, *Iḥyāʾ*, II:243, 357. Interestingly, the Shāfiᶜī jurist al-Kiyā al-Harrāsī (d. 504/1110), in his *Aḥkām*, III:382, argues that fighting the *bughāh* is itself a form of enjoining the good and forbidding the evil. He asserts that this is what ᶜAlī did when he fought those who rebelled against him. As noted below, this is a typically Ḥanafī position which was evidently borrowed by al-Kiyā al-Harrāsī.

66 Al-Juwaynī, *Ghiyāth*, 115.

67 Ibid., 109.

68 Ibid., 111–15. Perhaps al-Juwaynī did not consider ᶜAlī's caliphate to have been firmly established, and that is why he makes this argument. If ᶜAlī's caliphate was firmly established, arguably, there would be no question that he had the right to fight Muᶜāwiya.

him. This is exactly why al-Ḥusayn and al-Ḥasan, ᶜAlī's sons, gave their oath of allegiance to Muᶜāwiya.[69] Al-Juwaynī explains that if a usurper is sinful or iniquitous, some have argued that he is to be recognized, but not as a rightful *imām*. In other words, he is to be given *de facto* but not *de jure* recognition, and therefore, while he is to be recognized as the ruler, he is not to be given the oath of allegiance. Al-Juwaynī does not comment extensively on this position, asserting that while it is open to debate whether a usurper should be given the oath of allegiance, everyone agrees that a usurper must be recognized and obeyed.[70] In effect, al-Juwaynī argues that the prohibition against rebellion and the recognition of a usurper are both a result of necessity, because to argue otherwise is to grant a license to lawlessness. However, al-Juwaynī's position is not absolute. Firstly, to recognize a usurper constitutes, by necessity, a recognition of the fruits of rebellion. This is why al-Juwaynī also argues that if rebels rise against an established ruler and control a certain territory, their legal acts and adjudications must be recognized and not reversed, because to do otherwise is to harm people and to negate order.[71] Secondly, and more importantly, al-Juwaynī argues that if a pious man arises who wishes to enjoin the good and forbid the evil, and who wishes to uphold the best interests of Muslims while possessing enough power to guarantee him a reasonable chance of success, then it is legal for him to rebel and "may God aid him to victory."[72] Consequently, al-Juwaynī's prohibition against rebellion is born out of functional necessity, and not principle. The right of a ruler to stay in power, and the right of a usurper to attain power, is all relative. As a result of this logic rebellion is prohibited not because it is inherently wrongful, but because of its attendant consequences. Therefore, in his *Kitāb al-Irshād* al-Juwaynī argues that if a ruler becomes unjust and oppressive, the possessors of power in society (*ahl al-ḥall wa al-ᶜaqd*, literally, "the people who loosen and bind") may cooperate in resisting and correcting him, even if it means that they would have to resort to the use of force and the waging of war against the ruler.[73] In summary, because rebellion was not considered inherently evil or reprehensible, this, to a large extent, helps to explain why Shāfiᶜī jurists argued that rebels are not sinners, and advocated that rebels be treated with tolerance.

[69] Ibid., 326. [70] Ibid., 326–7.
[71] Ibid., 374. [72] Ibid., 115.
[73] Al-Juwaynī, *Kitāb*, 312.

Not all Shāfiᶜī jurists, however, may be classified within a single trend. For instance, al-Ghazālī is relatively less tolerant of rebels. As will be recalled, al-Ghazālī, the author of the famous statement arguing for the necessity of obeying those in power, is cited by Gibb and others as one of the prime examples of the quietism of Muslim jurists. However, although al-Ghazālī is less tolerant of rebels, his arguments are not absolutist or simply opportunistic. In his apologetic work *Faḍā'iḥ al-Bāṭiniyya* al-Ghazālī argues that a ruler is needed to resolve conflict and establish order and stability. Therefore the *imāma* is established by power and by the general willingness of the populace to obey a particular person in power. It is not necessary that everyone in society be willing to obey a ruler, because even God is not obeyed by all. Rather, it is enough for the ruler to possess the ability to establish order, and for a sufficient number of people to be willing to give him their allegiance. No specific number of people is required, only that the number of those who do give the ruler their allegiance would be sufficient to maintain stability and order.[74] It is also not necessary that the ruler be a *mujtahid* himself, as long as he continues to seek knowledge, and as long as he consults with the jurists regarding every problematic issue that he might confront.[75]

Al-Ghazālī contends that if one looks objectively at the matter, one will clearly conclude that it is the ᶜAbbāsid caliph al-Mustaẓhir bi-Allāh (r. 487/1094–512/1118) who is the rightful ruler of al-Ghazālī's day and age. According to al-Ghazālī, after the caliph al-Muqtadī died, the *fitan* spread everywhere, and it was only al-Mustaẓhir who was able to restore peace and order.[76] But al-Ghazālī goes further and argues that at the beginning of the ᶜAbbāsid caliphate there was general consensus on the right of the ᶜAbbāsids to power. Therefore, anyone who rebels and seeks to displace an ᶜAbbāsid caliph is to be considered a *bāghī*. Al-Ghazālī argues that one of the duties of the caliph is to "purify" the earth from all rebels, even if such rebels are in the Maghrib or in the far end of China.[77] Al-Ghazālī's work is primarily concerned with defending the ᶜAbbāsids against the Bāṭinī (i.e., in this context, Fāṭimid) threat,

74 Al-Ghazālī, *Faḍā'iḥ*, 144, 173–4, 177–8. Al-Ghazālī asserts that the ruler is God's shadow on the earth and that although the people are the ones who give effect to the ruler's power, the people are really the instruments of God. Hence, in reality, it is not the people who choose the ruler, but God chooses him, using the people as His instrumentality.

75 Ibid., 191, 193–4.

76 Ibid., 182, 186–7. Al-Ghazālī also asserts that although the Turks, who were the holders of military power at the time, did not obey al-Mustaẓhir in all affairs, they did support him on most occasions. In fact, he was the only person who could muster their loyalty.

77 Ibid., 178.

and in fact he states that if one rejects the Bāṭinī ruler, the only other possible option is to recognize the legitimacy of al-Mustaẓhir.[78]

Despite al-Ghazālī's political motivations, he is not willing to support rulers without reservation. He argues that a ruler may be obeyed only to the extent that his orders are not contrary to God's commands. He cites the story, discussed earlier, concerning the commander who ordered his soldiers to throw themselves into the fire as proof of the fact that an illegal order should not be obeyed.[79] If the ruler's commands are illegal, or if he does not rely on jurists, and someone more qualified for the position is found, people should weigh the benefits and costs of attempting to overthrow him, and replace him with someone better if they are able to do so.[80] Ultimately, despite all the polemics in favor of the ᶜAbbāsid caliph, al-Ghazālī's argument, like those of his teacher al-Juwaynī, reduces itself to a balancing act between the pros and cons of attempting to overthrow the ruler. Hence, the possibility of disobeying an illegal order or rebellion is not rejected out of hand.

Al-Ghazālī's treatment of the specific topic of rebellion takes place in his juristic work *al-Wajīz fī al-Fiqh*. It is in this work that one gains a fuller understanding of al-Ghazālī's attitude towards rebels, and as stated above, one finds that, compared to other Shāfiᶜī jurists, his attitude is relatively less tolerant. Significantly, al-Ghazālī does not argue against the precedents of the Shāfiᶜī school, but he gives the impression that the law on many points concerning rebels is unsettled and indefinite. He does not explicitly argue for positions that are less accommodating of rebels, but he implicitly leaves many points open to discretion and interpretation. Al-Ghazālī starts his analysis by employing a basic definition of the *bughāh*: it is every group that rebels against the ruler while relying on an interpretation (*ta'wīl*) and enjoying a degree of power (*shawka*), which enables it to resist the ruler. Like other Shāfiᶜī jurists, he does not attempt to clarify how much power is required by law in order for *shawka* to exist. However, he asserts that any *ta'wīl* that is of doubtful validity is to be considered effective for definitional purposes. In other words, if the interpretation of the rebels is groundless and, as a matter of certainty, is known to be erroneous, this is problematic. But if the interpretation is only suspected of being invalid, then it qualifies the rebels to be treated as *bughāh*. Al-Ghazālī notes that there is disagreement as to whether Muᶜāwiya's interpretation was certainly or probably invalid. The implication is that

[78] Ibid., 170, 172. [79] Ibid., 206–8. [80] Ibid., 193.

if Muʿāwiya's interpretation was certainly invalid, then even a groundless interpretation is effective in qualifying rebels for the status of *bughāh*. Interestingly, however, al-Ghazālī asserts that although "we" (the Shāfiʿīs) do not consider the Khawārij to be unbelievers, their interpretation is not to be recognized because it is clearly erroneous.[81]

Al-Ghazālī agrees that the rebels must be warned before being fought, but does not add that they be given a chance to plead an injustice or debated.[82] He does note that both the rebels and loyalists are liable for any destruction that takes place before or after the fighting. As to the destruction incurred during the fighting, al-Ghazālī argues that there is no disagreement that the loyalists are not liable. However, as to the rebels, he argues that there is disagreement as to whether they are to be held liable at all. If they are considered liable, there is disagreement as to whether they are financially or criminally liable, and as to whether they should perform atonement (*kaffāra*).[83] Al-Ghazālī goes on to state that there is no disagreement that if a few individuals have a *ta'wīl* but lack a *shawka*, they are to be held liable. If a group, however, has *shawka* but lacks *ta'wīl*, there is disagreement as to whether they should be held liable.[84]

Again, pursuing this method of indefiniteness, al-Ghazālī states that fugitives should not be pursued if the rebels have been thoroughly defeated. Nonetheless, there is disagreement as to whether the same rule applies if it is feared that they will regroup in the immediate future. Al-Ghazālī claims that there is no disagreement that weapons of mass destruction should not be used if innocent people will be killed, but he claims there is disagreement if only the rebels are affected. The rebel prisoners and their weapons should not be released until the loyalists feel secure that the rebellion has ended. But he notes that if there is a general and indefinite expectation that if released the prisoners might re-ignite the rebellion, there is disagreement on whether this is sufficient to continue detaining the rebels.[85] There is also disagreement, al-Ghazālī asserts, on whether the families of the rebels should be detained. He is somewhat more assertive when he discusses the legal acts of rebels. He argues that if the rebels relied on an interpretation, their testimony should be accepted in court, and that their legal acts and adjudications, if they prevail over a territory, should be recognized. Nonetheless, if the

[81] Al-Ghazālī, *al-Wajīz*, 164. [82] Ibid., 165. [83] Ibid., 164.

[84] Ibid., 165. The idea that even if a group does not have an interpretation it may still be exempted from liability became much more popular after al-Ghazālī's age.

[85] Ibid., 165.

rebels enjoy a *shawka* but lack a *taʾwīl*, their adjudications should not be recognized or given effect.[86]

The fact that al-Ghazālī gives the impression that many areas in the field of rebellion are unsettled could be an indication that he does not find many of the inherited Shāfiʿī doctrines persuasive. Overall, his treatment of the topic is vague and non-committal. Furthermore, his statements on some issues, such as the treatment of prisoners, adopt a tougher and less tolerant stance. Significantly, unlike other Shāfiʿī jurists he does not use the word "loyalists" to refer to the opponents of the rebels. Rather, he often uses the first plural form "we" to refer to loyalists, and the third plural form "they" to refer to rebels. Therefore, he gives the impression that, as a jurist, he identifies himself with the loyalists, rather than maintaining an objective distance from either party. For al-Ghazālī, the "we" probably refers to the supporters of the ʿAbbāsid caliph against any possible contenders. Nonetheless, even if al-Ghazālī was not as supportive of *aḥkām al-bughāh* as other Shāfiʿī jurists, this area of the law had become sufficiently well established that he could not refute or ignore it. Importantly, the fact that al-Ghazālī does not discount altogether the possibility that under certain circumstances a rebellion might be defensible leads one to conclude that, in all probability, he would not have wanted to refute or ignore this area of the law even if he could have done so.

Other Shāfiʿī jurists contemporaneous with al-Ghazālī are not nearly as indefinite or non-committal. For example, Aḥmad al-Qaffāl (d. 507/1113), who taught in the Niẓāmiyya school and was close to the caliph al-Mustaẓhir,[87] also noted some differences of opinion by Shāfiʿī jurists on the issue of rebellion. However, the scope of disagreements reported by him are far more limited than reported by al-Ghazālī, and he unequivocally endorses positions which are tolerant of rebels.[88] Shāfiʿī

86 Ibid., 164.

87 Al-Qaffāl was the head of the Shāfiʿīs in Irāq. He reportedly wrote his main work on jurisprudence, *Ḥulya*, upon the request of the caliph al-Mustaẓhir. See al-Ziriklī, *al-Aʿlām*, V:316.

88 Al-Qaffāl insists, for instance, that a prisoner cannot be executed, and must be released once he gives an oath of allegiance or the fighting ends; whichever comes first: al-Qaffāl, *Ḥulya*, VII:617. Al-Qaffāl also notes that while some Shāfiʿī jurists argued that the rebels are responsible for the blood money of loyalists killed in battle, all Shāfiʿīs agreed that the rebels cannot be physically punished: ibid., 619. Al-Qaffāl was also more tolerant of the Khawārij than al-Ghazālī was. He argues that they are to be treated like regular rebels. If a group adopts Khārijī views but do not rebel, they should not be fought. Interestingly, al-Qaffāl argues that if a rebel claims that he paid his land taxes (*kharāj*), he should not be believed: ibid., 621. It is difficult to understand what he means by this assertion. It could mean that if the rebels prevail over a territory and collect land taxes, these taxes are to be re-collected unless a person can prove that he, in fact, already

jurists such as Muḥammad al-Baghawī (d. 510/1117)[89] lapse the *Sunna* and the law of rebellion together as if there is an exact correlation between the traditions of the *Sunna* and *aḥkām al-bughāh*. For example, he cites a tradition attributed to the Prophet commanding Muslims to kill the Khawārij wherever they may be found. However, he comments that this tradition means that the Khawārij may be fought only if they organize, collect weapons, and assault people.[90] Otherwise, al-Baghawī's treatment of the subject is hardly distinguishable from al-Māwardī's, and he does not allude to substantial differences of opinion on the subject.[91] In the final analysis, al-Ghazālī's discourse on the treatment of rebels is not representative of the views of the Shāfiʿīs of his time. The inherited discourses of the law of rebellion had become a trademark of the school, and al-Ghazālī's ambiguities aside, the doctrines of *aḥkām al-bughāh* were reproduced and repeated as if they were an inherent part of the Islamic legal order.

Shāfiʿī jurists did not simply invent *aḥkām al-bughāh*; they constructed it from the inherited traditions of early Islam. The early rebellions of the Companions, the ʿAlids, and the ʿAbbāsids were the motivating force behind this construction. Since the early centuries of Islam, power was obtained and retained by force. Rebellion and the use of force against those in power was not an anathema, and this fact was reflected in the early discourses of Muslim jurists. Without doubt, the interests of the jurists and the rulers often correlated and overlapped, but this did not mean that the jurists simply became the ideologues of the state. The emerging corporate or institutional culture of the jurists demanded that order and stability be maintained, but once the precedents of the law of rebellion had come to existence, these precedents became an imperative force by themselves. Law often becomes its own justification. In other words, the law was preserved and upheld simply because it had become

paid such taxes. Alternatively, it could mean that the land taxes are to be re-collected in all circumstances. But even then, it is not clear whether the taxes are to be re-collected from all the residents of the territory or from those who had actively joined the rebellion. On the issue of re-collection of taxes from conquered rebel territory, see Modarressi, *Kharāj*, 155–64. Modarressi reviews the various schools of thought on this matter, concluding that the majority of jurists held that taxes should not be re-collected from conquered territory when one is reasonably sure that its inhabitants have paid their taxes to the rebels.

[89] Al-Baghawī spent most of his life and died in Khurāsān. He seems to have lived an apolitical life. See Ibn Khallikān, *Wafayāt*, II:136–7; al-Dhahabī, *Siyar*, XIX:439–43; Ibn al-ʿImād, *Shadharāt*, IV:48.

[90] Al-Baghawī, *Sharḥ*, VI:165.

[91] He argues, for example, that the rebels are not financially or criminally liable for destruction incurred in the course of their rebellion: ibid., 169.

a part of the inherited culture of the jurists. By the fourth/tenth century, the doctrines of the law of rebellion had become sufficiently established, and it had become increasingly difficult to ignore or to challenge their existence. This process was further aided by the fact that the jurists' main loyalty was to the institutions of law, and not necessarily to the state. Importantly, this process was not unique to the Shāfiᶜī school, and even the Ḥanbalī school, despite its dogmatic rejection of the idea of armed rebellion, joined in the process of the acceptance and development of *aḥkām al-bughāh*.

The early adoption of *aḥkām al-bughāh* by Ḥanbalī jurists was imperfect and imprecise. For example, the Ḥanbalī jurist Abū al-Qāsim al-Khiraqī (d. 334/945–6) adopts a very general and imprecise definition of rebellion.[92] He argues that if Muslims accept a particular person as their ruler (*imām*), if a group rebels against him they should be fought. He does not mention the requirements of *ta'wīl* or *shawka*, but his assertions as to how this group should be treated do not differ from al-Shāfiᶜī's in any material respect.[93] Reportedly, the Ḥanbalī jurist Abū Bakr b. Abī Dāwūd (d. 316/929) had argued that the specific number of the rebels is immaterial for the purposes of qualifying them as *bughāh*. Abū Bakr's reported reasoning is interesting because he equates the status of the rebels with that of the just ruler. He argues that the right of the just ruler (*al-imām al-ᶜādil*) to rule does not depend on the number of his supporters.[94] Therefore, even if the just ruler loses many of his supporters, this does not necessarily mean that he has lost his right to stay in power. Similarly, the specific number of rebels is immaterial as long as the rebels distinguish themselves from the loyalists, and follow a chosen ruler.[95] The idea of using the same criteria to evaluate the legitimacy of the ruler and rebels is consistent with Aḥmad b. Ḥanbal's reported position that whoever wins should be recognized as the rightful ruler.[96] Importantly, Abū Bakr's position could be interpreted to mean that the requirement of *shawka* is not a qualifying condition for a group to be treated as *bughāh*.[97]

92 On al-Khiraqī and his work, see Khalid, "*Mukhtasar*," esp. 14–16.

93 al-Khiraqī, *Mukhtaṣar*, 188.

94 The import of this argument is to suggest that ᶜUthmān remained the legitimate caliph despite the popular upheaval against him. In all probability, Abū Bakr was at least partly motivated by a desire to defend ᶜUthmān's legitimacy.

95 Reported in Abū Yaᶜlā, *al-Masā'il*, II:305.

96 Abū Yaᶜlā, *al-Aḥkām*, 22–3.

97 In fact, this is the sense in which Abū Yaᶜlā understands Abū Bakr's position. See Abū Yaᶜlā, *al-Masā'il*, II:305. Abū Yaᶜlā disagrees with Abū Bakr and argues that *shawka* or *minᶜa* is a requirement in order for a group to qualify as *bughāh*. He cites the example of Ibn Muljim, who assassinated ᶜAlī, and asserts that because Ibn Muljim acted without a *shawka*, he was held

Even if this represented an early and ultimately unsuccessful Ḥanbalī trend, by the fifth/eleventh century Ḥanbalī sources adopted nearly verbatim the Shāfiᶜī arguments and positions on the rebellion.[98] Ḥanbalī jurists did not produce the theoretical justification for the adoption of these positions until after the sixth/twelfth century.

THE SYSTEMATIC OBJECTORS AND THE RELUCTANT BORROWERS: THE ḤANAFĪS AND MĀLIKĪS

It is difficult to speak of a comprehensive or cohesive Ḥanafī or Mālikī doctrine on the treatment of rebels in the fourth/tenth and fifth/eleventh centuries. The reason for this is entirely different for each school. In the case of the Ḥanafī school, there is a basic position inherited from the discourses of al-Shaybānī, Abū Yūsuf, and perhaps Abū Ḥanīfa. However, the justifications and elaborations upon this basic position are quite varied. It is likely that the Ḥanafī position in the fourth/tenth and fifth/eleventh centuries is the product of an adherence to precedent, and an adoption or borrowing of some ideas from the Shāfiᶜī school. The Mālikīs, on the other hand, continued to be reluctant in adopting the laws of rebellion, and overall did not distinguish between a rebel and a bandit. In fact, a comprehensive Mālikī doctrine on rebellion did not develop until the sixth/twelfth century.

In principle, Ḥanafī jurists distinguished between bandits and rebels, and in fact a large part of the Ḥanafī discourse focused on the theoretical difference between these two categories. Nonetheless, as we saw above, Shāfiᶜī and Ḥanbalī jurists argued that it is illegal to seek the assistance of Ḥanafīs in fighting rebels because Ḥanafīs believe that it is proper to dispatch the fugitive and wounded. From this fact alone, one is reluctant to generalize about the relationship between the Ḥanafī school and the political structure of the state.[99] Ḥanafī jurists do not simply leave the treatment of rebels to the unmitigated discretion of the state. Further-

liable for his crime. However, Abū Yaᶜlā also adds that Ibn Muljim's interpretation (*ta'wīl*) was inherently implausible. It is not clear whether Abū Yaᶜlā is arguing that Ibn Muljim was held liable because his interpretation was implausible or because he acted without *shawka* or both.

98 For example, see ibid., 305–8; Abū Yaᶜlā, *al-Aḥkām*, 54–6.

99 However, Aziz al-Azmeh (*Muslim*, 188) states, "In all, the Ḥanafī legal tradition seems far more apprised of the idea of a strong state than the more demotically pietistic Shāfiᶜī which appears far more bookish. It was perfectly suited to the Ottoman state." He goes on to say, "But none of this detracts from the essential equivalence of the notions of authority held by the different schools, although the absolute exercise of authority according to the Shāfiᶜī traditions is more minutely regulated by knowledge whose custodians are the *ᶜulamā'*." The assertion made in the last sentence is not supported by evidence.

more, certain trends within the Ḥanafī school adopt positions that can only be unhelpful to the state. Nonetheless, compared to the Shāfiʿīs, the Ḥanafī school is generally less tolerant of rebels. This could be due to the fact that both Abū Yūsuf and al-Shaybānī were judges, and more accepting of ʿAbbāsid legitimacy. Once the precedent was set by the early Ḥanafī jurists, it became self-perpetuating, and difficult to override. Certainly, as discussed below, some of the later Ḥanafī jurists modified aspects of early Ḥanafī doctrine on rebels, and became central to the revisionist trend. Nevertheless, while the Ḥanafī jurists of the fourth/tenth and fifth/eleventh centuries made the theoretical distinction between bandits and rebels sharper and clearer, they also corroborated the idea that rebellion is a sin.

Not all Ḥanafī jurists argued that rebellion is a sin, however. Abū Bakr al-Jaṣṣāṣ (d. 370/980–1), for example, asserts that both bandits and rebels are considered Muslims. He argues, at length, that the *ḥirāba* verse was revealed to address highway robbers, and not apostates or rebels. A material element of the offenses of rebellion and banditry is the existence of a degree of power (*minʿa*). This is why, al-Jaṣṣāṣ maintains, banditry is a crime which can only be committed away from a town or city.[100] Like rebels, bandits organize and gather in a specific territory, and refuse to abide by the commands of the ruler. The moment the bandits organize and gather in a location with the intent of terrorizing the wayfarer, the elements of the crime of *ḥirāba* are complete. Therefore it is not necessary that the bandits rob or kill anyone in order for the crime of *ḥirāba* to exist. In contrast, a person who attacks and robs people in a town or city is to be treated as a common thief, and not a bandit.[101] Importantly, the main distinction between bandits and rebels is that rebels rely on an interpretation (*taʾwīl*), and therefore rebels are fought only for the limited purposes of repelling their harm and self-defense, while bandits are fought in order to punish them for their crimes.[102]

[100] The received Ḥanafī position is that banditry is committed only in the desert away from urban centers.

[101] Al-Jaṣṣāṣ, *Aḥkām*, II:413–14. The author argues for *tartīb* and not *takhyīr* in punishing the bandit. He argues that the ruler has limited discretion in punishing bandits. If the bandits commit the crime of *ḥirāba* and nothing else, they are to be imprisoned. If they commit murder, they must be killed; if they usurp money, their limbs must be amputated from opposite ends. If, however, they kill and usurp money, the ruler has four options. He may amputate their limbs and crucify them; he may amputate their limbs with nothing further; he may crucify them; or he may execute them: ibid., 409–11.

[102] Ibid., 410, III:402.

Like other jurists, al-Jaṣṣāṣ focuses on defending the notion that people should support the ruler in fighting rebels. He concedes that Muᶜāwiya was a *bāghī* against ᶜAlī, but rejects the argument that the precedents of the Prophet and the Companions prohibit supporting the ruler in fighting the rebels. Fighting rebels is a form of enjoining the good and forbidding the evil, and therefore is commendable.[103] The Prophet's traditions prohibiting Muslims from joining *fitna*, al-Jaṣṣāṣ contends, do not apply to fighting rebels because the Prophet intended to prohibit wars of tribalism or of blind partisan causes (*ᶜaṣabiyya*). Significantly, however, al-Jaṣṣāṣ argues that fighting in support of the ruler is, by definition, rightful and proper. He asserts that the group that supports the ruler (*al-imām*) is of necessity the rightful or just group (*al-fi'a al-ᶜādila*), and does not seem concerned with the justness or substantive quality of the ruler's reign. Simply because a ruler is in power, he is to be supported.[104] As noted earlier, like Shāfiᶜī and Ḥanbalī jurists, al-Jaṣṣāṣ was arguing for the need for law and order which is represented by the necessity of supporting the ruler who has established himself in power.

Al-Jaṣṣāṣ goes on to argue that the rebels are not fought for adopting a particular system of belief. In fact, if a group adheres to or adopts rebellious ideas, such as the ideas of the Khawārij, that alone does not grant a license to the loyalists to fight them. The rebels are fought only in self-defense, and hence, if the rebels no longer insist on fighting the loyalists they are not to be fought.[105] It is not clear how much the rebels need to do before it becomes permissible to fight them, but al-Jaṣṣāṣ argues that before the rebels are fought they must be warned and given an opportunity to desist.[106] This, of course, implies that the loyalists do

103 Ibid., III:399–400. The author notes that some have argued that the only weapons that may be used in fighting rebels are sticks and other non-lethal instruments. He calls this argument absurd. Obviously, as noted earlier, whether rebels should be fought was a politically charged issue from early on, and al-Shāfiᶜī, among others, insisted that, in principle, a ruler or a just ruler should be authorized to fight rebels. The issue was initially raised in the context of arguments about whether ᶜAlī acted appropriately when he decided to fight the rebels, and whether people should have supported him against his foes. However, this early, largely dogmatic, problem became relevant to the issue of whether a ruler should be assisted against rebels. The dogmatics of ᶜAlī's conflict quickly became a legal front or camouflage for the practical problem of whether people should support rulers against rebels.

104 Ibid., 400–1. In response to the argument that even ᶜAlī, although the rightful ruler, was not supported by all the Companions, al-Jaṣṣāṣ makes the implausible argument that those Companions did not join ᶜAlī because they saw that he had enough supporters and did not need their assistance.

105 Ibid., 401, 404. 106 Ibid., 401.

not have to wait until they are attacked first. In any case, due to the fact that they rely on an interpretation, the rebels are not held liable for life or property destroyed in the course of the fighting.[107]

All of the above is not unique to the Ḥanafī school; similar arguments have been made by Shāfiʿī or Ḥanbalī jurists. Al-Jaṣṣāṣ, however, discusses several points that became integral to the Ḥanafī discourse. He notes that while all jurists agreed that the property and monies of rebels may not be confiscated, some Ḥanafī jurists held that whatever is found in the rebel war camp is to be considered loot. Other jurists maintained that the rebels' weapons and horses may be used against them, but that after the fighting ends the rebels' money and horses must be returned to them. Al-Jaṣṣāṣ asserts that the truth of the matter is that reports on ʿAlī's conduct are inconsistent on this matter. But he seems to favor the view that none of the rebels' property or money may be confiscated, although the weapons may be temporarily used against the rebels.[108] Furthermore, he asserts that all the earlier authorities from his school (i.e. the authorities that preceded the formation of the Ḥanafī school) held that the fugitive may not be pursued and the captive or wounded may not be dispatched. However, al-Jaṣṣāṣ concedes that late Ḥanafī jurists disagreed with this position, and argued that as long as the rebels have reinforcements or an undefeated party (*fi'a*), fugitives, prisoners, and the wounded may be killed. Al-Jaṣṣāṣ does not explicitly disagree with what he describes as the late Ḥanafī position, although he does imply that he does not find the arguments of the late school persuasive.[109]

As we saw earlier, several jurists held that the testimony and legal acts of rebels should be recognized; however, the Ḥanafī position by the fourth/tenth and fifth/eleventh centuries had become opposed to this view. Neither the legal acts nor the testimony of rebels should be accepted because, according to the Ḥanafīs, rebellion is a sin, and therefore rebels are iniquitous (*fasaqa*). The credibility of sinners is suspect, and hence their testimony and legal acts cannot be recognized. Al-Jaṣṣāṣ himself accepts the view that as a general matter, the judgments and legal acts of the rebels should not be recognized. He qualifies this position in three important respects. First, if the rebels appoint a judge who is loyal to them, his judgments should not be given effect unless they are consistent

[107] Ibid., 402. Al-Jaṣṣāṣ cites an earlier opinion attributed to Abū Yūsuf that maintained that the rebels are not to be held liable if they repent and abandon their rebellion. This opinion, which hinges on a pardon from liability on repentance, does not seem to have survived in the Ḥanafī school.

[108] Ibid. [109] Ibid.

with the views of a loyalist judge. Second, if the rebels appoint a loyalist judge, his decisions should be given full faith and credit. Third, al-Jaṣṣāṣ argues that recognizing the judgments of rebels does not imply that loyalists and rebels are of equal status. Rather, it means that one should not look at who appointed a certain judge, but instead at the character of the judge in question. What is important is that the judge himself be considered of just character, regardless of who appoints him. While al-Jaṣṣāṣ mentions the view that the rebels lack credibility because they are sinners, he does not explicitly endorse this view.[110]

Aside from legal judgments and testimonies, al-Jaṣṣāṣ deals with the question of taxes collected by the rebels. He argues that people who gave their alms (*zakāh*) to rebels should be advised to re-pay their alms because giving them to rebels is not religiously effective. However, he notes that because this matter is between people and God, people should not be forced to repeat their alms. As to other taxes (*ṣadaqāt*), al-Jaṣṣāṣ asserts that the loyalists should not re-collect them either.[111] Al-Jaṣṣāṣ's reasoning is most interesting – he argues that people pay taxes in return for the right of protection from the ruler. Since the ruler failed to protect the inhabitants of a certain territory from the rebels, the right of the ruler to collect such taxes drops, and hence the taxes should not be re-collected.[112]

Some of al-Jaṣṣāṣ's views are not representative of what eventually became the predominant Ḥanafī position. For example, al-Jaṣṣāṣ does not deal with whether funeral prayers should be performed for dead rebels. One suspects that he avoids the issue because he was reluctant to hold that rebels are iniquitous. But it is important to note that al-Jaṣṣāṣ was not a minor figure in the Ḥanafī school of thought. In fact, he was considered the leader of the Ḥanafī school in Baghdād, and although he cooperated with the government of his time, he turned down an offer to become the chief judge of Baghdād.[113] Nonetheless, his views should not be seen as a product of his own personal legacy as much as an indication of the unsettled status of Ḥanafī doctrines at his time. It is clear from al-Jaṣṣāṣ's treatment that there were several competing tendencies within the Ḥanafī school. He supported the general position that law and order should be upheld, but was not a hardliner on the issue of the treatment of rebels. His positions are based on certain trends within the Ḥanafī school

110 Ibid., 403.

111 Normally, *ṣadaqa* means the same as *zakāh*, but sometimes Ḥanafīs use the expression *ṣadaqat al-arḍ* to refer to the *kharāj* (land taxes).

112 Ibid. Al-Samarqandī (Ḥanafī, d. 556/1161: *al-Fiqh*, II:884) makes the same point.

113 Al-Dhahabī, *Siyar*, XVI:340–1; Ibn al-ᶜImād, *Shadharāt*, III:71. Al-Jaṣṣāṣ was also accused of harboring Muᶜtazilī tendencies.

in the fourth/tenth century. The Ḥanafī position on rebellion never became entirely uniform, and the trends that al-Jaṣṣāṣ represents did not completely disappear. However, eventually the predominant Ḥanafī position became less tolerant over the issue of how rebels are to be treated.

The liberal or tolerant trend was still evident more than a century later in the writing of the Ḥanafī judge Abū Qāsim al-Simnānī (d. 499/1105). Al-Simnānī rejects the idea that the ruler should be recognized or not recognized on an ideological basis. He asserts that the Zaydīs and others have argued that a pious man who fulfills the qualifications of the *imāma* may rise against the unjust rulers and enjoin the good and forbid the evil, and declare himself to be the true ruler of Muslims. This leads to chaos and disorder, and therefore it cannot be permissible.[114] Al-Simnānī notes that a ruler in power enjoys a presumption of obedience, which entitles him to resist and fight rebels.[115] Interestingly, however, he argues that if the ruler becomes oppressive and unjust, and usurps property, then it becomes incumbent upon the jurists and Muslims to overthrow him, and he even goes as far as claiming that this has been the consistent practice of Muslims in dealing with corrupt rulers.[116] He goes on to argue that rebels should not be considered unbelievers or hypocrites, and supports a policy of tolerant treatment towards rebels.[117] In the middle of his discourse on rebellion the following passage appears:

> In the final analysis, this whole affair today is hopeless, and if the scholars and those who wrote the books of jurisprudence saw what we see today, they would have known that [all of this] applied to a different age. Today we see the rebels in every town, and every person does what he wishes without anyone uniting the Muslims, and honoring the affairs of this religion.[118]

[114] Al-Simnānī, *Rawḍa*, I:71.

[115] Ibid., II:1215. The expression used by the author is *al-imām al-muftaraḍ al-ṭāʿa*, which means the ruler to whom obedience is due. However, the expression is somewhat ambiguous. It could mean "the ruler who is presumably entitled to obedience," or it could mean "the ruler who enjoys a presumption of obedience." Effectively, it could mean that the ruler is entitled to fight the rebels unless it becomes clear that he is not entitled to obedience, or it could mean that a ruler who is in power is presumed to be entitled to obedience, and hence is empowered to fight the rebels. Furthermore, it is not clear at what point a ruler loses the right to be obeyed.

[116] Ibid., I:152.

[117] For example, while mentioning the Ḥanafī view that as long as the rebels remain a viable threat or have reinforcements, their captives, wounded, and fugitives may be killed, the author asserts that once a rebel lays down his weapon and asks for a guarantee of safety, he should be granted it. He argues that none of the rebels' property may be confiscated, and their weapons may be used only if absolutely necessary. Unlike other Ḥanafī jurists, he also maintains that the heads of rebels may not be severed and sent across the land: ibid., II:1215–18.

[118] Ibid., 1219.

This passage appears to be a sharp departure from the flow of al-Simnānī's narrative,[119] and in light of the author's general position, it is difficult to make sense of its intended purpose. It is possible that al-Simnānī is lamenting the fact that no one fights over religious causes any more. In other words, al-Simnānī, like other jurists, seems to consider tribal or partisan wars to be inherently unjustified and evil. The rebels that he has in mind are those who fight over a religious interpretation or those who fight to enjoin the good and forbid the evil. This reliance on a plausible *ta'wīl* is what entitles the rebels to a tolerant treatment. Therefore, al-Simnānī could be condemning the fact that, in his age, everyone fights over earthly interests that have nothing to do with what he considers to be just causes.[120] Alternatively, al-Simnānī could be lamenting the fact that rulers do not treat rebels as believers and do not observe the rules of conduct that the jurists have explicated on this matter.[121] It is quite likely that he considered the whole discourse of *aḥkām al-bughāh* to be irrelevant to his age, and that the historical developments since the discourse was formed had created a considerable gap between the political and social realities and the legal discourse. Al-Simnānī is lamenting the absence of a government that is capable of establishing law and order. The law of rebellion had assumed the existence of a government which unites Muslims, and which, in turn, is capable of applying the law of rebellion. But in his day, everyone seemed to be a rebel, and there was considerable confusion as to who was legitimate and who was not. Therefore, al-Simnānī is expressing doubt over the relevance or applicability of this whole discourse to his time. Importantly, after making this remark, he continues to elucidate the remainder of the laws of rebellion without further comment or qualification. If this passage was, in fact, authored by al-Simnānī, it is a powerful demonstration of the impact of precedent on the legal mind. Whatever the particular objections al-Simnānī might have had concerning this field of the law, he continued to engage the precedents, picking one precedent over the other, but was unable to restructure or significantly alter the whole discourse.

[119] One cannot exclude the possibility that it was added to the original text by a copyist as a form of critique against the juridical discourse on rebellion.

[120] As we will see, several of the later jurists comment that everyone in their day and age fights over the *dunyā* (earthly interests) and not *dīn* (religious causes).

[121] This possibility is supported by the fact that this passage occurs immediately after al-Simnānī mentions that ᶜAlī was asked about the Khawārij, and he denied that the Khawārij were either unbelievers or hypocrites.

Many of al-Simnānī's arguments were representative of the evolving Ḥanafī doctrines on rebellion.[122] However, the most exhaustive and representative exposition in the fifth/eleventh century is that of the Ḥanafī jurist Abū Bakr al-Sarakhsī (d. 483/1090–1).[123] Like his predecessors, al-Sarakhsī maintained that the main distinction between bandits and rebels is that rebels adopt a *ta'wīl*.[124] Again, in the fashion of earlier Ḥanafī jurists, he does not elaborate upon the notion of a *ta'wīl* or explain what would count as a legally recognizable *ta'wīl*. Importantly, however, al-Sarakhsī assumes that the *ta'wīl* is going to be a religious interpretation concerning God's law.[125] He also implies that, as a legal matter, the *ta'wīl* must be presumed erroneous, and therefore the substantive content of the rebels' ideology or interpretation is irrelevant.[126] As a general matter, al-Sarakhsī argues, Muslims should not become involved in or partake in *fitna*. Nevertheless, when a ruler comes to power and is able to establish order and stability, those who rise against him are the ones who are causing *fitna*. In doing so, they are committing a sin, and fighting these rebels is a form of enjoining the good and forbidding the evil because it is a way to bring an end to the *fitna* that the rebels have caused.[127]

[122] For example, his assertion that funeral prayers should not be held over dead rebels: ibid., 1217. Al-Simnānī distances himself from this position somewhat by stating that his colleagues ruled as such, but he does not explicitly endorse this position.

[123] It is often stated that al-Sarakhsī was the most important Ḥanafī jurist of the fifth/eleventh century, but little is known about his life. He was imprisoned for ten years under the Qarakhānids (382/992–609/1212), reportedly because of some of his legal positions. However, it appears that at some points in his life he did enjoy the patronage of certain rulers. Some reports say that al-Sarakhsī died in prison. See al-Ziriklī, *al-Aʿlām*, V:315; Ibn al-ʿImād, *Shadharāt*, III:367; Heffening, "al-Sarakhsī," 159; Calder, "Al-Sarakhsī."

[124] Interestingly, al-Sarakhsī discusses Abū Ḥanīfa's view that banditry can only be committed outside a town or city. He notes that some late Ḥanafī jurists have argued that Abū Ḥanīfa's opinion was a product of his age and specific context. These late jurists claimed that in Abū Ḥanīfa's time, people used to carry weapons inside a town and, therefore were able to protect themselves from bandits there. However, these jurists argued that by their time people no longer carried weapons while in a town or city, and hence had become vulnerable to banditry committed in urban centers. Consequently, these jurists advocated that banditry be recognized as a crime that could occur inside or outside a city. Al-Sarakhsī mentions this discussion but does not resolve the issue: al-Sarakhsī, *al-Mabsūṭ*, IX:201. On the distinction between bandits and rebels, see al-Samarqandī (d. 539/1144–5), *Tuḥfa*, III:157, who adds that even if the rebels commit highway robbery, they are not to be treated as bandits because they rely on a *ta'wīl*.

[125] He refers to "*bi ta'wīli al-dīni fī al-aḥkām*": al-Sarakhsī, *al-Mabsūṭ*, X:128. Al-Samarqandī (*Tuḥfa*, III:157) defines rebellion in the following way: Rebels disobey certain laws while enjoying a degree of power and force, and while relying on an interpretation, as the Khawārij and others have done. Al-Samarqandī (different from the jurist above), *al-Fiqh*, II:882, seems to limit the definition of rebellion to a case of near or actual secession.

[126] Al-Sarakhsī, *al-Mabsūṭ*, X:128.

[127] Ibid., 124. Al-Sarakhsī is responding to the argument that supporting a ruler against rebels is a form of perpetuating *fitna*. He concedes that Abū Ḥanīfa had advised Muslims not to get

Al-Sarakhsī does not attempt to argue that the prohibition against engaging in *fitna* only applies to tribal or partisan warfare. Rather, he makes the straightforward claim that rebellion is a disruption of stability and order and, therefore, it is *fitna*. Fighting rebels brings an end to disorder and precludes the *fitna*, and hence Muslims should support the ruler against rebels.[128] Importantly, however, al-Sarakhsī adds that because the rebels rely on an interpretation, they and the loyalists are considered equals in terms of the applicability and the treatment of the law (*wa al-taswiya bayn al-fi'atayni al-mutaqātilatayni bi ta'wīli al-dīni fī al-aḥkāmi aṣl*).[129]

Al-Sarakhsī goes on to argue that the point at which it becomes legal to seize or fight rebels is when such rebels organize and gather, and exhibit a firm intent to rebel. He rejects the idea that the ruler must wait until his troops are attacked before it becomes legal for him to respond. However, he also rejects the idea that mere talk of rebellion is sufficient to authorize hostile actions against rebels. The rebels must commit overt acts that clearly indicate an intent to rebel, such as organizing and gathering in a specific location. At that point, the ruler should imprison or fight the rebels before their *fitna* spreads and becomes uncontrollable. Al-Sarakhsī cites the precedents in which ᶜAlī declares that he will not fight the Khawārij until they fight him first, but he argues that this should be read to mean that ᶜAlī refused to fight the rebels until they formed a clear and immediate intent to use force against him.[130] Likewise, al-Sarakhsī concedes that ᶜAlī commanded that the fugitive, captive, or wounded should not be dispatched. He also mentions that ᶜAlī used to take an oath from captives that they would not return to rebellion, and then release them. However, he argues that this only applies if the rebels have been thoroughly defeated and do not have any other reinforcements. He argues that as long as reinforcements remain, it is within the ruler's discretion to imprison, execute, or pardon the fugitive, captive, or wounded. Importantly, unlike al-Simnānī, al-Sarakhsī does not qualify this view in any way. He gives the distinct impression that this is a settled

involved in *fitna*; however, he argues that this does not apply to lending support to a firmly established ruler.

[128] Ibid. The author argues that the Companions who failed to support ᶜAlī did so because they were incapable of fighting. Therefore the precedent of the Companions who refused to support ᶜAlī cannot be cited as evidence that Muslims should not support the ruler against the rebels.

[129] Ibid., 128.

[130] Ibid., 125–6. See also al-Samarqandī, *Tuḥfa*, III:313, who advocates a less exacting standard. He argues that if a group relies on an interpretation and isolates itself from the *jamāᶜa*, the ruler may imprison them until they repent. If they resist, he may fight them.

point of law, and does not cite any other views on the matter.[131] Furthermore, al-Sarakhsī does not show a particular concern with the issue of how long captured rebels may be held. He simply states that rebels may be held until none of their party remains, and then they should be released.[132]

Overall, al-Sarakhsī and other Ḥanafī jurists advocate a harsher policy towards rebels. For instance, al-Sarakhsī asserts that it is recommended that the ruler warn the rebels before attacking them, but this is not mandatory and is to be left to the ruler's discretion. Furthermore, the ruler may use weapons of mass destruction including fire and flooding against the rebels.[133] He also argues that, as a general matter, it is reprehensible to sever any head, including the heads of rebels, and send them across the land. He claims that ʿAlī and Abū Bakr refused to do so, and when told that the Persians and Byzantines followed this practice, Abū Bakr commented, "We are neither Persians nor Byzantines. The Book [Qurʾān] and traditions are sufficient for us [i.e. we follow the Book and traditions]." Nonetheless, al-Sarakhsī notes that some of the late Ḥanafīs permitted the practice because the Prophet did not object to it.[134] By citing the Prophet's supposed precedent in this context, al-Sarakhsī effectively legitimates the already widespread practice of severing the heads of rebels as proof of their defeat.[135]

Al-Sarakhsī adds that the loyalists may not seek the assistance of unbelievers against Muslim rebels, but they may seek the assistance of scriptuaries or protected minorities (*ahl al-dhimma*).[136] Interestingly, however, he argues that if the scriptuaries assist the rebels, this does not constitute an abrogation of their covenant with the loyalists; both the scriptuaries and the rebels remain a part of the abode of Islam. Therefore, as far as liabilities are concerned, the scriptuaries are to be treated on an equal

[131] Al-Sarakhsī, *al-Mabsūṭ*, x:126, 128. Hostages taken from rebels, al-Sarakhsī argues, may not be killed under any circumstances. Also see al-Samarqandī, *Tuḥfa*, III:313. Also see al-Sarakhsī, *Sharḥ*, IV:1439, V:2263.

[132] Al-Sarakhsī, *al-Mabsūṭ*, x:127. Al-Samarqandī (*Tuḥfa*, III:313) asserts that if the rebellion is thoroughly defeated, rebels may be held until they repent, and then they should be released.

[133] Al-Sarakhsī (*al-Mabsūṭ*, x:128) does not qualify this by asserting, for example, that such weapons may be used only if absolutely necessary or only if innocent non-combatants will not be hurt.

[134] Ibid., 131. Al-Sarakhsī does not give any details as to when or how the Prophet supposedly accepted this practice. He does not explain whether this was done in the Prophet's presence, and the Prophet did not object to it. Otherwise, the Prophet's silence is not an endorsement of something that might have never come to his attention. Al-Samarqandī (*Tuḥfa*, III:314) notes that such a practice is reprehensible, but it is permissible if it would demoralize and weaken the rebels.

[135] Al-Sarakhsī does not discuss the equally widespread practice of crucifying (hanging) rebels.

[136] Al-Sarakhsī, *al-Mabsūṭ*, x:133–4.

footing with Muslim rebels.[137] Importantly, although the rebels are considered Muslim, dead rebels may not be prepared for burial by performing the ritual washing, and funeral prayers should not be performed on them either. They, however, are to be buried simply for sanitary reasons (*li imāṭati al-adhā*), and because it was the practice of ʿAlī to bury his dead opponents. Loyalists killed in battle, on the other hand, are martyrs and are to be treated as such.[138] Of course, as we saw earlier, al-Sarakhsī's position on this matter is neither novel nor unprecedented. Nonetheless, his tone and style is quite assertive, and it conveys the impression that this is the only possible position on the matter.

Al-Sarakhsī contends that, at a religious level, the abode of the rebels and the abode of the loyalists are one and the same. Therefore, the property of rebels remains sacrosanct and may not be confiscated. The rebels' weapons may be used against them, but must be returned after the rebellion ends. Horses and livestock should be sold, and the price held in trust until the rebellion ends and then be returned as well.[139] As to matters of liability, al-Sarakhsī contends that since the rebels' interpretation is considered, as a matter of law, to be erroneous, the existence of an interpretation alone is not sufficient to exempt the rebels from liability. However, once the rebellion commences, the existence of an interpretation coupled with the existence of power (*minʿa*) means that the ruler's sovereignty (*wilāyāt al-ilzām*) over the rebels has been interrupted. It should be recalled that according to al-Sarakhsī the rebellion commences once the rebels gather, organize, and evidence a clear intent to rebel. Therefore, according to al-Sarakhsī it is from that point on that the rebels are not to be held liable for offenses committed or for life or property destroyed. If, on the other hand, one or two men rebel while relying on an interpretation, they are to be treated as common thieves because they remain under the ruler's sovereignty.[140] Interestingly, unlike

[137] Ibid., 128. It should be recalled that earlier jurists argued that the scripturaries are to be held liable for property and life destroyed in the course of rebellion. Furthermore, they argued that assisting the rebels does not constitute a violation of the scripturaries' covenant if the scripturaries claimed ignorance of the illegality of their acts.

[138] Ibid., 131. Also see al-Samarqandī, *Tuḥfa*, III:314.

[139] Al-Sarakhsī, *al-Mabsūṭ*, X:126–7. Al-Samarqandī (*Tuḥfa*, III:313) adds that the loyalists do not have to compensate the rebels for any weapons or property used or lost.

[140] Al-Sarakhsī, *al-Mabsūṭ*, X:128, 134. Al-Sarakhsī also argues that if the rebels offer to surrender on condition that they not be held liable for offenses or destruction caused before the commencement of the rebellion, the ruler may not agree to this condition. Everything destroyed before and after the rebellion involves the private rights of people, and the ruler does not have the right to forgive offenses committed against private rights: ibid., 131. Al-Samarqandī (*Tuḥfa*, III:314) asserts that the rebels are liable for everything done before or after the rebellion because, except

other jurists, al-Sarakhsī does not maintain that rebels without *shawka* are to be treated as bandits; rather, they are to be treated as common thieves.[141]

Al-Sarakhsī adopts the Ḥanafī territorial theory of jurisdiction. Therefore, like his predecessors, he argues that the loyalists do not have jurisdiction over crimes committed in rebel territory.[142] However, he argues that since the rebels are considered iniquitous (*fasaqa*), the testimony of their witnesses cannot be accepted by loyalist judges. Presumptively, al-Sarakhsī argues, all residents in rebel territory are considered rebels. Therefore, if a judge from a rebel territory writes to a loyalist judge asserting a claim of right, and such claim is attested by witnesses, the loyalist judge should not recognize such claim. If, however, the loyalist judge has personal knowledge that the witnesses are not affiliated with the rebels, the judge may accept the claim of right under these circumstances. Similarly, if the rebels appoint a judge who is known to be a loyalist, his judgments should be recognized. Al-Sarakhsī adds that it is entirely appropriate for a loyalist to accept a judicial appointment in rebel territory as long as he applies the law of *Sharīᶜa* properly and without bias.[143] In this situation, the loyalty of the appointee is to the *Sharīᶜa*, and not to a particular party. Under any circumstance, if the loyalists eventually conquer the rebel territory, the adjudications of all their judges, loyalists or otherwise, in the interest of finality of judgments, are to be recognized and given full effect, as long as such judgments are well supported in law or deal with novel or unsettled points of law. This is so even if, in the personal opinions of the loyalist judges, such judgments are erroneous.[144] In a rather remarkable passage, al-Sarakhsī supports his argument by citing an example in which he claims that the Umayyads

for the duration of the rebellion, the rebels remain a part of the abode of Islam. The loyalists are liable for all life or property destroyed before or after the rebellion as well. See al-Simnānī, *Rawḍa*, II:1221, who argues that if individuals or small groups who have an interpretation are exempted from liability, this is bound to lead to the spread of lawlessness because, comforted by the fact that they will not be held liable, every minor or insignificant group will invent an interpretation and rebel.

141 Al-Sarakhsī uses the expression *luṣūṣ* and not *quṭṭāᶜ* or *muḥāribūn*. This is significant because the treatment of bandits in Islamic law is far more stringent than that of common thieves. Of course, one cannot exclude the possibility that al-Sarakhsī used the word for thieves rather than bandits out of sloppiness. However, this is unlikely because, as will be shown, other Ḥanafī jurists concurred in his judgment. It is also possible that al-Sarakhsī and the other Ḥanafī jurists considered this to be a case in which the actions of those concerned do not spread terror, and thus do not reach the level of banditry.

142 Al-Sarakhsī, *al-Mabsūṭ*, X:130.

143 Ibid., 130–1. Also see al-Samarqandī, *Tuḥfa*, III:314.

144 Al-Sarakhsī, *al-Mabsūṭ*, X:135.

were the *bughāh*. Despite the fact that the Umayyads were rebels, several notable jurists accepted judicial appointments in their administration. Furthermore, al-Sarakhsī argues that the caliph ᶜUmar b. ᶜAbd al-ᶜAzīz (r. 99/717–101/720), after coming to power, recognized the adjudications and judgments of the judges appointed by the Umayyads.[145] Nonetheless, ᶜUmar b. ᶜAbd al-ᶜAzīz himself was an Umayyad caliph, and therefore this indicates that al-Sarakhsī, at least in this context, is distinguishing between rebels and loyalists purely on ideological grounds. In other words, al-Sarakhsī apparently considered the Umayyads to have been illegitimate rulers, and therefore he brands them as rebels. However, he also seems to have considered, as is popular in many Muslim discourses, the caliph ᶜUmar b. ᶜAbd al-ᶜAzīz to have been a just ruler. Consequently, despite the fact that this caliph was technically a part of the Umayyad dynasty, he is not branded as a rebel.[146] This is significant because, as discussed earlier, al-Sarakhsī argues that if a ruler becomes well established and is able to secure law and order, he is considered the legitimate ruler, and all who rebel against him are to be treated as the *bughāh*. Of course, at the time al-Sarakhsī was writing it was entirely safe to treat the Umayyads as illegitimate, and to speak of ᶜUmar b. ᶜAbd al-ᶜAzīz in favorable terms. Nonetheless, I think this passage points to something more significant than a politically correct recasting of history. Unlike al-Simnānī, al-Sarakhsī does not explicitly state that under certain circumstances it becomes permissible to rebel and overthrow an unjust ruler. In fact, al-Sarakhsī exhibits a clear preference for maintaining the status quo, and order and stability. Nevertheless, as discussed later, like other jurists from the various schools, he was willing to leave open the possibility for a rebel of the moral and religious caliber of ᶜUmar b. ᶜAbd al-ᶜAzīz to be declared the true *imām*, and his opponent the wrongful *bāghī*. Perhaps this is consistent with the fact that al-Sarakhsī himself had suffered political persecution and was imprisoned for a number of years.

By the fifth/eleventh century, the Ḥanafī school had clearly adopted the discourse on rebellion.[147] As we have seen, the doctrines of the schools

[145] Ibid., 130–1.

[146] ᶜUmar b. ᶜAbd al-ᶜAzīz is held in high esteem by Sunnī and non-Sunnī jurists, and many Muslims have claimed that he is a fifth Rightly Guided Caliph. Although he was genealogically an Umayyad, at a moral level he is not treated as such.

[147] Some such as al-Samarqandī (Ḥanafī, d. 556/1161: *al-Fiqh*, II:830–1, 882–4) lapsed banditry with rebellion to a certain extent. Rebels are those who secede, and bandits are those who conspire to attack the wayfarer. He does not mention a *ta'wīl* for rebels, and does not mention the lack of a *ta'wīl* for bandits. Considering the nature of the text, it is possible that this was simply the result of an oversight or lack of knowledge.

remained somewhat unsettled. Nonetheless, overall, the doctrines of the school were less accommodating or tolerant of rebels than the Shāfiʿī and perhaps the Ḥanbalī schools. The idea that rebellion is a sin (*maʿṣiya*) and that rebels are iniquitous had found firm support in the discourses of the Ḥanafī school. Furthermore, the Ḥanafīs were willing to give the ruler greater latitude and discretion in dealing with rebels. The idea that rebels may be pursued and the prisoners executed became well established. This motivated the Shāfiʿīs to go as far as to argue that it is illegal to seek the assistance of Ḥanafīs in fighting rebels. Nonetheless, even the Ḥanafīs refused to equate rebels who are motivated by a cause or interpretation with bandits who are motivated by selfish interests. An ideological offender is not the same as a common criminal. However, the definition of a rebel, other than the twin conditions of *taʾwīl* and *shawka*, remained vague. Consequently, although Ḥanafī jurists, compared to their Shāfiʿī counterparts, clearly catered to the pragmatic interests of the state, they still retained the power of distinction and definition. They retained the power to define and differentiate a rebel from a non-rebel, and to distinguish legitimate rulers from sinful rebels.

Shāfiʿī, Ḥanbalī, and Ḥanafī jurists in the fourth/tenth and fifth/eleventh centuries, for the most part, do not identify specific contemporaneous parties as rebels or non-rebels. Because of the imperative of precedent on legal thinking, they do specifically mention ʿAlī, the Khawārij, and, at times, the Umayyads. These were the early precedents upon which the discourse on rebellion was constructed and, as discussed, the jurists creatively selected and read such precedents in order to delineate general legal principles and specific rules of conduct. Some active jurists such as al-Māwardī and al-Ghazālī identified certain ʿAbbāsid caliphs as the legitimate rulers, and implied that those defying their authority would become the *bughāh*. Nevertheless, the majority of jurists do not indicate, for example, whether the Fāṭimids, Ibn Ṭūlūn of Egypt, or the Seljuks were rebels. Nonetheless, this is hardly surprising. The jurists were interested in constructing normative principles and rules; the application of these principles or rules to specific situations would be decided on a case-by-case basis. These case-by-case considerations would be channeled back to a reformulation and rearticulation of the principles and rules. The complex interplay of precedent, contemporaneous reality, and normative values would ultimately result in reformulations of the legal doctrine. However, as argued earlier, this often resulted in delayed responses to social and political realities. The fact that the discourses on rebellion had become firmly established by the fifth/eleventh century in the Shāfiʿī and Ḥanafī schools is due largely to the fact that jurists from these schools were building upon the precedents set by al-Shāfiʿī, Abū Yūsuf, and al-Shaybānī. The Ḥanbalī school, lacking a precedent of its own, seems to have borrowed most of its doctrines from the Shāfiʿī school. The Mālikī school did have its own traditions and precedents on the issue, but such precedents were ambiguous and conflicting. Nonetheless, it is exactly in this type of situation that a powerful social or political reality might delay or hamper the adoption or borrowing of an already established body of law. Looked at differently, if the traditions or precedents of a school are ambiguous and uncertain, powerful social or political circumstances may perpetuate this ambiguity or uncertainty. As argued below, Mālikī jurists in North Africa, confronting constant rebellions by the Khawārij, Qarāmiṭa, and Berbers, did not develop a consistent doctrine on rebellion; they did, however, develop systematic discourses on bandits. Meanwhile, Mālikī jurists who lived or studied in the eastern part of the Islamic civilization in the fifth/eleventh century did commence the process under which *aḥkām al-bughāh* was borrowed and adopted into Mālikī discourses.

The majority of Mālikī jurists in the fourth/tenth and fifth/eleventh centuries do not mention *aḥkām al-bughāh* and do not address rebellion as a specific legal category. While they do not explicitly state that rebels are to be treated as bandits, they do not conceptually distinguish between bandits and rebels either. It should be recalled that Mālikī discourses in the third/ninth century were ambiguous about the status of the Khawārij and other rebellious groups. Saḥnūn reported that early Mālikī jurists maintained that there was a conceptual distinction between the Khawārij and bandits; the Khawārij fought out of a misguided sense of piety and were motivated by a religious interpretation. Bandits, on the other hand, are common thieves, or worse, who are motivated by selfish interests. Nonetheless, it was argued that the Khawārij and other sectarian groups should repent or be put to death. It was not clear how rebels who might not be sectarian or who adopted ideas not considered heretical should be treated. This basic ambiguity survived into the fourth/tenth century, but even further, some Mālikī jurists refer only to banditry and omit any reference to the Khawārij.[148] Other Mālikī jurists, such as

148 Al-Khushanī (d. 361/971), in his *Uṣūl*, 352, states only that the ruler may choose which penalty to apply in dealing with a bandit, except that if a bandit commits murder, the ruler must execute him. Interestingly, the editor of the work states that a bandit who threatens the security of the community is a *bāghī*. Al-Mālaqī (d. 497/1103), in his *al-Aḥkām*, 189, 349, only addresses banditry and causing corruption on the earth.

Abū al-Qāsim b. al-Jallāb (d. 378/988), give the impression that the law of banditry may, under certain circumstances, be applied to rebels. He, for example, notes that Mālik ruled that the Qadariyya, Ibāḍiyya, and similar groups (*ahl al-ahwāʾ*) should repent or be killed, and then immediately states that those who commit banditry inside or outside a city should be subject to the laws of banditry.[149] The structure of the narrative leaves one with the impression that no distinction is drawn between the above-mentioned groups and bandits. Importantly, Ibn al-Jallāb, in this context, does not specify which crimes constitute banditry, and he does not refer to highway robbery as a specific category.[150] He only states that if a group of people commit banditry, the ruler has the option of either killing, crucifying, severing a hand and foot from opposite ends, or beating, banishing, and imprisoning them.[151] Ultimately, one does not know which specific groups, if any, Ibn al-Jallāb had in mind when he addressed the laws of banditry. Perhaps it is relevant that the author's time was plagued with rebellions by the Qarāmiṭa who, as noted earlier, followed methods of indiscriminate slaughter, pillaging, and plundering reminiscent of the acts of bandits or brigands.[152] The author, however, does not mention the Qarāmiṭa but does mention the much older precedent of the Qadariyya. Presumably, however, the Qarāmiṭa could be included in the broad category of *ahl al-ahwāʾ*.

The most influential Mālikī jurist of the fourth/tenth century is Ibn Abī Zayd al-Qayrawānī (d. 386/996–7), who is credited with playing an influential role in the spread of Mālikism in Ifrīqiyā.[153] Ibn Abī Zayd's treatment of banditry and rebellion raises some challenging issues. Like Ibn al-Jallāb, he grew up during a period of Fāṭimid dominance in Ifrīqiyā. Ibn Abī Zayd was a fairly young man when he experienced the serious rebellion against the Fāṭimids by the Berber Khārijī Abū Yazīd al-Nukkarī (the man on the donkey) from 331/943 to 335/947.

[149] Ibn al-Jallāb, *al-Tafrīʿ*, II:232–3.

[150] In a different context, however, he does state that if a group of Muslims commit highway robbery and cause corruption on the earth, all Muslims should assist the ruler in fighting them and in ridding Muslims of their evil: ibid., 362.

[151] Ibid., 233. The author adds that a bandit may be executed even if he does not commit murder. The ruler may choose to banish him to a town in which he is imprisoned until he repents. If a bandit repents and surrenders before being captured, then the specified punishments for the crime of banditry should not be applied. Nonetheless, he will still be liable for life or property destroyed. This means that the victims of his crimes have the option of demanding retaliation or compensation, or they may forgive him.

[152] See the notes by the editor in ibid., 378.

[153] See Idris, "Ibn Abī Zayd"; Idris, "Deux"; al-Dhahabī, *Siyar*, XVII:10–13. Also see the introduction by the editor to the *Nawādir*: Ibn Abī Zayd, *al-Nawādir*, I:5–43.

Although it is not clear whether Ibn Abī Zayd took part in this rebellion, a large number of Sunnī jurists from Qayrawān aided the Khārijī rebellion against the Ismāʿīlī rulers. Ibn Abī Zayd's teacher and close friend, the Mālikī Abū Isḥāq al-Sabāʿī (d. 356/966), is reported to have played a major role in the rebellion, although he was ultimately betrayed by Abū Yazīd. Ibn Abī Zayd wrote his first book on law, *al-Risāla*, at the request of al-Sabāʿī several years before Abū Yazīd's rebellion. After the rebellion, Ibn Abī Zayd traveled to Medina and Mecca, passing through Egypt where he studied with a large number of Mālikī and Shāfiʿī jurists.

The *Risāla*, written before the rebellion and before Ibn Abī Zayd's travels, says little about rebellion and banditry. This contrasts sharply with Ibn Abī Zayd's work *al-Nawādir wa al-Ziyādāt*, which he wrote late in his life. In *al-Nawādir*, Ibn Abī Zayd sought to collect the opinions of early Mālikī jurists such as Saḥnūn (d. 240/854), al-ʿUtbī (d. 255/868–9), Ibn Ḥabīb (d. 238/853), Ibn al-Mawwāz (d. 269/882), ʿAbd al-Malik b. al-Mājishūn (d. 212/827), and Ibn ʿAbd al-Ḥakam (d. 214/829).[154] In this compendium of Mālikī law, Ibn Abī Zayd's treatment of banditry is not unique. For the most part, he reproduces a large number of divergent opinions by Mālikī scholars, among them several opinions to the effect that the earmark of the crime of banditry is the terrorizing of victims who are unable to defend themselves. Most forms of murder by stealth are considered banditry as well.[155] Ibn Abī Zayd also reports, through al-ʿUtbī and Ibn al-Mawwāz, that Ibn al-Qāsim (d. 191/806) said that if a bandit is motivated by enmity or vengeance instead of pecuniary gain, he is not to be treated as a *muḥārib*.[156] Next, Ibn Abī Zayd addresses the usual Mālikī categories of apostasy, the *zanādiqa*, and the Khawārij. He titles this last chapter "The rule as to the Qadariyya, the Khawārij, and heresy (*ahl al-bidaʿ*)," and, again, the chapter incorporates the usual Mālikī reports we encountered earlier. After this chapter, Ibn Abī Zayd presents a chapter with the rather unusual heading "*Bāb fī qatl ahl al-ʿaṣabiyya wa al-ʿadāwa min al-Muslimīn* (A chapter on killing the people of tribalism and enmity)." Interestingly, the chapter is placed in the section on apostates (*kitāb al-murtaddīn*). After beginning the chapter with a general reference to Saḥnūn, Ibn Abī Zayd writes: "The jurists that we have met informed us . . . (*qāla man laqaynā min al-ʿulamāʾ*)." Having

[154] On Ibn ʿAbd al-Ḥakam's life and works, see the recent work by Brockopp, *Early*, 1–65.

[155] Ibn Abī Zayd, *al-Nawādir*, XIV:462–89. In his *al-Risāla*, 330–1, Ibn Abī Zayd only states that if a bandit kills, he must be killed. Otherwise, the ruler has discretion on the fate of a bandit according to his history of criminality and the degree of danger he poses to society.

[156] Ibn Abī Zayd, *al-Nawādir*, XIV:474.

made this introductory statement, Ibn Abī Zayd proceeds to reproduce a discourse on rebellion that is substantially similar to the doctrines of the Shāfiᶜī school.[157] At several points, Ibn Abī Zayd specifically distinguishes between rebels, bandits, and those who fight out of tribalism (*ahl al-ᶜaṣabiyya*). He contends that those who rebel without an interpretation (*ta'wīl*) are to be considered people of *ᶜaṣabiyya* and therefore are *not* entitled to the protection of *aḥkām al-bughāh*. He goes further and argues that *ahl al-ahwā'* or *al-bidaᶜ*, such as the Khawārij, are to be considered a people with a *ta'wīl*, and hence should be treated as *bughāh*.[158] As such, Ibn Abī Zayd seems to generate four distinct categories: (1) bandits who terrorize people for pecuniary gain; (2) those who commit acts of banditry because of enmity or vengeance; (3) those who fight because of loyalty to a tribe or nationality; and (4) those who fight because of an interpretation. The status of the first and last categories is clear – the former are bandits and the latter are *bughāh*. The status of the second and third categories remains unclear.[159]

It is probable that Ibn Abī Zayd's statement alluding to "jurists that he met" refers to Shāfiᶜī, and perhaps Mālikī, jurists from the east under whom he studied during his travels, and who led him to adopt the discourse on the *bughāh*. However, considering the length and nature of his treatment, one is left wondering about the extent to which the historical context motivated Ibn Abī Zayd's adoption of the discourse. For instance, did he consider the Fāṭimids to be among *ahl al-ahwā'* or *al-bidaᶜ*? Was he partly motivated by the rebellion of Abū Yazīd to declare that the Khawārij were entitled to the treatment of the *bughāh*? Did he consider the Qarāmiṭa to be bandits, *bughāh*, or *ahl ᶜaṣabiyya*? Alternatively, did he adopt the discourse of *aḥkām al-bughāh* through the mechanics of legal borrowing in juristic cultures, and not out of an ideological commitment? If one were to speculate on this issue, one would surmise that, at a minimum, Ibn Abī Zayd must have been motivated by a desire to mitigate the ferocity of the battles waged between the Khawārij, the Fāṭimids, and the Qarāmiṭa, none of whom were Sunnī Muslims. Ibn Abī Zayd lived the second half of his life under the Zīrid governors of the Maghrib who

157 Ibn Abī Zayd also attributes many of the opinions to Ibn Ḥabīb and ᶜAbd al-Malik, but these opinions do not explicitly support Ibn Abī Zayd's positions. Consequently, he interprets these statements so as to make them consistent with *aḥkām al-bughāh*. For instance, see ibid., 549 where Ibn Abī Zayd reports that ᶜAbd al-Malik determined that that rebels should be killed, but Ibn Abī Zayd comments on this by saying, "He [ᶜAbd al-Malik] means, those who rebel without a *ta'wīl*."

158 Ibid., 546–9.

159 Ibid., 547; the passage in which Ibn Abī Zayd makes this clear is missing from some manuscripts.

ruled in the name of the Fāṭimid caliphate. Considering that he became a famous jurist in Qayrawān during his lifetime, he must have reached some kind of rapprochement with the Zīrids, because this would have allowed him to lead a reasonably stable and secure life, and to continue his teaching.[160] This might explain why Ibn Abī Zayd intimates that *aḥkām al-bughāh* apply to an insurrection against any ruler (*imām*), just or rightful or not.[161] Arguably, Ibn Abī Zayd had sufficiently reconciled himself to the Ismāᶜīlī rulers to be willing to focus on the treatment of the rebels rather than the qualitative legitimacy of the rulers.

Considering the influence of Ibn Abī Zayd on the development of the Mālikī school, one would have expected that Mālikī jurists would have uniformly adopted Ibn Abī Zayd's discourse on rebellion, but surprisingly, his work on this subject is not extensively referenced by later jurists. This could be due to the fact that this part of his voluminous book was not widely disseminated, or that his treatment of this subject was edited and exaggerated by later Mālikī jurists. In other words, it is possible that a good part of what is found in the *Nawādir* on the law of rebellion was added several centuries after Ibn Abī Zayd's death.

Even after Ibn Abī Zayd, the status of the law of rebellion remained ambiguous in the Mālikī school. Mālikī jurists of the fifth/eleventh century, particularly those who studied under Shāfiᶜī and Ḥanafī jurists, did integrate the discourse on rebellion, but to a limited extent. The Andalusian judge Abū Walīd al-Bājī (d. 494/1100–1), for instance, studied with several Shāfiᶜī and Ḥanafī jurists including Abū Isḥāq al-Shīrāzī and al-Simnānī in Baghdād, Mosul, Damascus, and Ḥalab.[162] He adheres to Mālikī precedent in the sense that most of his discussion is dedicated to the matter of banditry. Like Ibn Abī Zayd, his discussion on banditry is long and detailed, and cites various opinions on a broad range of issues.[163] He asserts that whoever carries a weapon and terrorizes people without enmity or rancor is a bandit because such a person obstructs free passage and causes corruption on the earth.[164] He also argues that those who obstruct free passage inside or outside a town are bandits even

[160] Ibn Abī Zayd's son was appointed as a judge, and then removed, by the Zīrid al-Muᶜizz b. Badis (r. 406/1016–454/1062).

[161] He does use, at times, the expression *al-imām al-ᶜadl:* to refer to the loyalists, and when he addresses a situation in which there are two warring factions and a neutral ruler who is trying to resolve the conflict. See ibid., 550.

[162] Ibn al-ᶜImād, *Shadharāt*, III:344–5; al-Dhahabī, *Siyar*, XVIII:535–40.

[163] Al-Bājī, *al-Muntaqā*, VII:169–75.

[164] Ibid., 169. If the crime motivated rancor or enmity between certain individuals, then any offense committed is treated as a common crime.

if they do not seek financial gain or the usurpation of property.[165] This is a very broad definition, which dictates that any person or group of persons who terrorize others and render them helpless to resist are to be treated as bandits. Al-Bājī argues that the ruler should have discretion (*takhyīr*) in punishing bandits; however, the ruler should not exercise that discretion according to whim or caprice. Rather, he should consult the jurists about the appropriate punishment due to each case of banditry. Al-Bājī adds that if a bandit does not kill or usurp property, but has a long record of banditry, it is preferred that the ruler beat, banish, and imprison him. However, if the ruler wishes to execute him, or sever his hand and foot from opposite ends, he may do so.[166] Of course, if the crime of banditry could exist despite the fact that the bandit had not killed or usurped money, this has clear political connotations. A political or religious rebel might terrorize the wayfarer and refuse to kill or usurp property, yet apparently be treated as a bandit. Nevertheless, in a rather ambiguous passage, al-Bājī notes that a bandit is distinguishable by the fact that he disobeys the ruler out of pride or power, and not out of a religious conviction or belief.[167] The author does not elaborate or explain what the attendant consequences are if such a person does, in fact, rely on a religious conviction or system of belief. Therefore, although al-Bājī acknowledges that there is a conceptual distinction between those who are motivated by a religious conviction and those who are not, he does not explore the implications of this position.

Perhaps the most noteworthy Mālikī treatment of the subject of rebellion in the fifth/eleventh century is that of the Andalusian judge Ibn ʿAbd al-Barr (d. 463/1071).[168] Ibn ʿAbd al-Barr started out as a follower of the Ẓāhirī school, and although he later switched to the Mālikī school, he was heavily influenced by Shāfiʿī jurisprudence.[169] Ibn ʿAbd al-Barr achieved a synthesis in Mālikī doctrine that clearly reflects Shāfiʿī and Ẓāhirī influences. He was not willing to abandon Mālikī precedents or arguments; however, he also integrated elements of the Shāfiʿī and Ẓāhirī analysis which enabled the Mālikī position to be more systematic and

[165] Ibid. The author adds that, for example, those who declare that they will not allow a group of people to travel to Egypt, Shām, or Mecca are bandits regardless of their motivation for doing so. This same opinion is reported in Ibn Abī Zayd, *al-Nawādir*, XIV:474, but is not explained.

[166] Al-Bājī, *al-Muntaqā*, VII:171–2.

[167] Ibid., 170.

[168] For an overview of the historical context of Ibn ʿAbd al-Barr, al-Bājī, and Ibn Ḥazm (dealt with below) see Urvoy, "ʿUlamāʾ," 850–75.

[169] Ibn al-ʿImād, *Shadharāt*, III:314; al-Dhahabī, *Siyar*, XVIII:153–60; Ibn Khallikān, *Wafayāt*, VII:66.

coherent. Like other Mālikī jurists, he focuses much of his attention on the issue of banditry,[170] but unlike many other Mālikī jurists, he also focuses on the category of rebellion. He argues that if a group rebels against a ruler without a just cause, then a just ruler may fight them.[171] He then repeats the common Shāfiᶜī doctrines of rebellion: The fugitive, captive, and wounded may not be dispatched and rebel property may not be confiscated, and if they rely on an interpretation, the *bughāh* or the Khawārij are not to be held liable for life or property damaged in the course of their rebellion.[172] Importantly, however, he argues that even if the rebels rely on an interpretation, if they terrorize the wayfarer, obstruct passage, and usurp property, they are to be treated as bandits and not as *bughāh*.[173] Therefore, despite their interpretation or religious convictions, if the rebels pursue improper means, they are to be treated as bandits. This is exactly the position implied by the discourses of other Mālikī jurists including Ibn Abī Zayd. However, Ibn ᶜAbd al-Barr makes the argument explicit. Rebels are to be treated with a degree of tolerance unless they pursue methods similar to those pursued by the Qarāmiṭa and such groups. If the method pursued resembles acts of banditry, then it is treated as a crime of banditry.[174]

THE COUNTER-TRADITION OF THE DISSENTERS: THE SHĪᶜĪ AND ẒĀHIRĪ ALTERNATIVE

By the fifth/eleventh century, both the Ẓāhirī and Shīᶜī schools of thought had become fully involved in the juridical debates on rebellion. What distinguishes the discourses of these schools is that they were thoroughly ideological, and that they tended towards the moralistic. While the other schools tended to focus on the treatment due to rebels and, for the most part, were not concerned with the justness of the rebels' cause, the Ẓāhirī and Shīᶜī schools focused on the moral or theological

170 Ibn ᶜAbd al-Barr, *al-Kāfī*, 222–3, 582–6. Essentially, he argues that anyone who terrorizes and obstructs the wayfarer and spreads corruption on the earth is a bandit. Furthermore, if a criminal poisons or sedates his victims, he is to be treated as a bandit.

171 Ibn ᶜAbd al-Barr does not elaborate upon the possibility that the rebels might have a just cause or that the ruler might be unjust. The implication of his argument is that if either of these situations exists, the ruler does not have a right to fight the rebels. As we will see below, the Ẓāhirī jurist Ibn Ḥazm, who was Ibn ᶜAbd al-Barr's friend and close associate, argued that anyone with a just cause should not be treated as a rebel. Conversely, if the ruler is unjust, the ruler is considered to be the rebel.

172 Ibid., 222. 173 Ibid., 583–4.

174 See also Ibn ᶜAbd al-Barr, *al-Tamhīd* (1967), XXIII:334.

worth of the rebels' cause. Put differently, the Ẓāhirī and Shīʿī schools focused on the legitimacy or justness of the ruler contrasted to or in relation to the legitimacy or justness of the cause espoused by the rebels: therefore, much of their discourse focused on a qualitative assessment of the substantive base of the rebels' claims. The above-mentioned appraisal must be qualified, however, in one important respect. As noted earlier, most of the schools discussed above did not entirely abandon the possibility of recognizing the legitimacy of the rebels' cause. Rather, they tended to focus on the technical rules relating to the treatment due to rebels. The Ẓāhirī and Shīʿī schools, at least by the fifth/eleventh century, did not separate the theological and moral question of the rightfulness of the ruler from the largely legal issue of how to treat rebels. This is particularly so in the case of the Ẓāhirī Ibn Ḥazm. As we will see, the Shīʿī position, however, eventually became practically indistinguishable from Sunnī discourses on the subject.

The Ẓāhirī school

The Ẓāhirī school, founded by Dāwūd b. ʿAlī (d. 270/884), has become extinct, and most of its texts did not survive.[175] Nevertheless, the Ẓāhirī doctrine on the issue of rebellion is represented in the writings of the Andalusian Ibn Ḥazm (d. 456/1064).[176] But it is not clear to what extent Ibn Ḥazm's arguments reflect Ẓāhirī doctrines as opposed to his own idiosyncratic positions. Although Ibn Ḥazm attributed many of his arguments to the Ẓāhirī school in general, in all probability these arguments represent Ibn Ḥazm's own views on rebellion and have little to do with the Ẓāhirī school.[177] Ibn Ḥazm's arguments are somewhat conflicting and inconsistent but it is quite clear that he was intolerant of what he considered to be unjust rebels or rulers. Ibn Ḥazm had an unwavering allegiance to his own definition of orthodoxy, and he did not distinguish between the need for law and order and the imperatives of correct belief. However, he was not a stranger to the institutions of the state or the pragmatic processes of government. Like his father, he served as a minister and state administrator under the ʿĀmirids of

[175] See Melchert, *Formation*, 178–90. On the history and doctrines of the Ẓāhirī school, see Goldziher, *Ẓāhirīs*, 3–80, 171–89.

[176] Goldziher, *Ẓāhirīs*, 102–23.

[177] This is especially so in light of the fact that Ibn Ḥazm seems to have developed his own group of loyal followers known as the Ḥazmiyya: see al-Ziriklī, *al-Aʿlām*, IV:254; Goldziher, *Ẓāhirīs*, 156–60.

Valencia. However, early on in his life he abandoned all political positions and dedicated himself to scholarship. He is reported to have been a rather unpleasant and contentious character. He consequently won the animosity of most politicians and jurists, and died in exile.[178] His writings reveal a remarkable willingness to declare the ruler an outlaw and, under certain circumstances, even criminalize a ruler's behavior.

Ibn Ḥazm asserts the general principle that Muslims should obey a rightful ruler, and that rebellion against such a ruler is a sin. As a general matter, the unity of Muslims is imperative, and divisiveness is a sin as well.[179] Ibn Ḥazm, however, qualifies this general principle in several important respects. Whether the rebels are liable for their actions in the Hereafter or on this earth depends on the nature of the system of belief or convictions that inspired the rebellion in the first place. Furthermore, depending on the circumstances, the ruler could be declared an outlaw, or even a bandit, and be treated as a *muḥārib*. Ibn Ḥazm asserts that not all rebels are equal; rather, rebels differ according to the *ta'wīl* they espouse and the reason for their rebellion.[180] If the rebels rely on a plausible religious interpretation, they are to be considered similar to *mujtahids* who exercise an independent judgment regarding a specific point of law. This is so even if the interpretation is against an established consensus, as long as the rebels do not realize that a consensus exists, or clear proof of the existence of such a consensus has not reached them.[181] Furthermore, if the rebels espouse a plausible cause relating to a grievance concerning a specific issue, this *ta'wīl* is legally recognizable as well. Ibn Ḥazm demonstrates this point by arguing that Muʿāwiya, for example, refused to give ʿAlī his pledge of allegiance because ʿAlī had failed to capture and punish ʿUthmān's assassins. Ibn Ḥazm argues that although Muʿāwiya's reasoning was ultimately wrong, this type of interpretation or cause is legally recognizable.[182] Therefore, if rebels espouse these types of interpretations, they will not be held liable in the Hereafter. In fact, because these rebels are well intentioned, even if they are ultimately misguided, they will be rewarded by God in the afterlife.[183] As to issues of liability on

178 Al-Dhahabī, *Siyar*, XVIII:184 98; Ibn al-ʿImād, *Shadharāt*, III:299; Ibn Khallikān, *Wafayāt*, III:325.

179 Ibn Ḥazm, *al-Muḥallā*, XI:354.

180 Ibid., 333, 346. Ibn Ḥazm inconsistently states that rebels are of two distinct types, but later he claims that there are three distinct types. This could be a copyist's error because, substantively, his argument is consistent.

181 Of course, it is quite possible that the rebels would not consider consensus to be binding. Ibn Ḥazm does not deal with this eventuality.

182 Ibid., 335.

183 Ibid., 333.

this earth, the state treasury should pay the blood money for any person killed by the rebels in the course of the rebellion, but the rebels are to be held liable for any property destroyed. In other words, the state is responsible for personal injuries, and the rebels are responsible for injuries to property.[184] Ibn Ḥazm does not explain why the state treasury should pay the blood money of individuals killed, and does not explain why the rebels should be personally responsible for destroyed property. Interestingly, however, Ibn Ḥazm argues that a tradition attributed to al-Zuhrī, which states that the Companions agreed that all life and property destroyed pursuant to an interpretation should be forgiven, is fabricated.[185] Although Ibn Ḥazm challenges the authenticity of this tradition and others, he does not provide an alternative rationalization for his position.[186] He does, however, seem to rely on a non-specific assumption that those who rebel because of non-selfish interests should not be treated as common criminals.

Ibn Ḥazm held a very different view of those who rebel because of what he considered to be an implausible interpretation. He does not provide systematic guidelines for what is to be considered an implausible or unreasonable interpretation. Rather, he asserts that any group that obfuscates or ignores the *Sunna*, or blatantly refuses to recognize the rights of people or God, is to be treated as if it had no *ta'wīl* at all. His list of examples of unreasonable interpretations include: denying that the *imāma* should be confined to Quraysh; denying that an adulterer should be stoned; treating Muslims who sin as infidels; killing Muslim children and women; denying predestination; denying the possibility of intercession; declaring that some of the Companions became apostates; arguing that God does not know the future until it occurs; or refusing to pay the *zakāh*.[187] He argues that groups who adopt such interpretations will not be excused in the Hereafter, and should be held liable for all life and property destroyed during the course of their rebellion.[188] Ibn Ḥazm does not explain whether such groups should be treated as *bughāh* or not,

[184] Ibid., 346. Ibn Ḥazm does not mention the requirement of *shawka*. However, he seems to assume that the rebellion would be instigated by a group. He does not explicitly address the possibility of an individual rebel.

[185] Ibid., 345.

[186] Ibid., 340–1. Ibn Ḥazm argues that the tradition attributed to the Prophet regarding the *bughāh* is fabricated. He also argues that the traditions which assert that ᶜAlī treated the property found in the rebels' war camp as spoils of war are unauthentic as well.

[187] Ibid., 334–5, 343.

[188] Ibid., 347.

but the import of his argument is that such groups are to be treated as common criminals or perhaps apostates.[189]

Ibn Ḥazm distinguishes the two types discussed above from those who rebel for worldly reasons, such as a desire to usurp power or for tribal loyalties. Like other jurists, Ibn Ḥazm's historical examples are derived from the Umayyad period, but they have profound implications well beyond their immediate context. Ibn Ḥazm argues that historical figures such as Yazīd b. Muᶜāwiya, Marwān b. al-Ḥakam, and ᶜAbd al-Malik b. Marwān all rebelled against Ibn al-Zubayr, and Marwān b. Muḥammad rebelled against Yazīd b. al-Walīd for worldly reasons, and because they coveted power. Essentially, these rebellions were political disputes that had little to do with religion.[190] Nevertheless, even when it comes to what Ibn Ḥazm considered to be purely political disputes, he evaluates rebels according to an entirely pietistic and subjective standard. Those he perceived as pious leaders are considered the rightful rulers, and those who fought them are seen as the rebels. Pursuant to this logic, it is Yazīd who is the rebel and not Ibn al-Zubayr, regardless of the fact that it was Ibn al-Zubayr who challenged Umayyad rule and was ultimately defeated. In any case, Ibn Ḥazm argues that this category of rebels are, in fact, *bughāh*, but they are to be held liable for life and property destroyed all the same. Importantly, if the ruler against whom such a group rebelled is also a political opportunist and is equal in moral worth to the rebels he is fighting, both groups, the ruler and the rebels, are to be held liable for life and property destroyed. In other words, if both the ruler and the rebels are fighting over power and worldly interests, both sides are of equal worth, and are morally and legally liable.[191] Ibn Ḥazm adds that in the case of rebels motivated by a simple desire to usurp power, if such a group commits acts of banditry, such as terrorizing the wayfarer or indiscriminately slaughtering people or usurping money, they are no longer to be treated as *bughāh* but must be treated as bandits.[192]

[189] Ibid., 343. Ibn Ḥazm is unclear on this point. He seems to be arguing that if such a group commits acts of banditry and violates the established consensus, then they are to be treated as apostates. Earlier, however, he argues that the Khawārij and similar groups (*ahl al-ahwāʾ*) are *bughāh*, but they are to be held liable anyway. See ibid., 333.

[190] Ibid., 335.

[191] Ibid., 333, 343, 347. However, Ibn Ḥazm indicates that in this situation, those who are killed fighting rebels are martyrs. See ibid., 348. He does not explain why, if both sides are considered of equal moral worth, those who are killed while fighting on the side of the ruler are considered martyrs.

[192] Ibid., 333, 343.

In all of the above, Ibn Ḥazm assumes that the ruler is either superior, or at least equal, in moral value to the rebels. He, however, goes further and argues that if the rebels revolt seeking to enjoin the good and forbid the evil and establish the Qurʾān and *Sunna*, then they are not rebels at all. Rather, whoever opposes them, even if it is the ruler, is the rebel and they are to be considered the just and rightful party. Furthermore, whoever resists an injustice or defends his life or property against an aggressor is not a rebel, even if the aggressor is the ruler. Instead, the aggressor, whether ruler or ruled, is to be considered the outlaw and the rebel. Citing the precedent of the Companions, Ibn Ḥazm argues that Muslims may rightly resist paying unjust taxes even if this means that they may have to resort to force. In this situation, the ruler is the rebel and those who resist are the rightful and just party. Ibn Ḥazm notes that some have argued that an established ruler cannot be considered a rebel, regardless of the reason that motivated a particular group to rebel. He, however, argues that God did not distinguish between a ruler and rebels in moral responsibility. Therefore, an unjust ruler or a ruler who resists enjoining the good or forbidding the evil is to be treated as any other Muslim. Therefore, a ruler may be considered the *bāghī* just like any other element in society.[193] Similarly, any person who causes corruption on the earth and terrorizes people is to be treated as a bandit. If the caliph himself commits these acts, then he should be considered a bandit and treated as such. Ibn Ḥazm also adds that if the caliph orders his soldiers to terrorize people, usurp their property, and commit rape, then the caliph and his soldiers are bandits.[194] At one point, he describes the *mulūk al-ṭawāʾif* of al-Andalus as outright bandits.[195]

Ibn Ḥazm's approach is highly subjective. He assumes that in the majority of situations a just cause can be distinguished from an unjust cause. In order to make this determination, a subjective inquiry into the specific content or substance of the cause espoused by a group is necessary. If the cause is determined to be rightful or just, then those who are leading an insurrection are not to be considered rebels at all, and the ruler and his government may be declared outlaws. Consequently, by definition, one cannot be declared a rebel unless one's cause is unjust or erroneous. But even then there is a fine line between an erroneous cause and an un-Islamic cause. Those whose interpretation violates the *Sunna*, or those who fight out of a desire to usurp political power, are to be held

[193] Ibid., 335–6. [194] Ibid., XII:283.
[195] Barcelo, "Rodes." On *mulūk al-ṭawāʾif*, see Bosworth, *New*, 14–20; Wasserstein, "Mulūk."

liable for life and property destroyed during the course of the fighting. Under certain circumstances, those whose interpretation is not within the scope of a proper *ijtihād* or who rebel for tribal or purely political reasons may be considered bandits. Those whose interpretation is within the proper scope of an *ijtihād* cannot be considered bandits. But Ibn Ḥazm's definition of banditry is very wide and ambiguous. He insists that a *bāghī* and a *muḥārib* are two distinct and different categories.[196] He adds that a bandit is anyone who causes corruption on the earth and terrorizes the wayfarer by killing, stealing, or raping. He contends that this is so, whether the crime is committed in a city or in the desert, in daylight or at night, or in a mosque or the caliph's palace.[197] At this point it sounds as if Ibn Ḥazm is arguing that any crime that renders its victim helpless to resist and has the effect of terrorizing people is banditry. However, he goes on to say that whoever raises a sword intending to terrorize people is a bandit.[198] Nonetheless, he goes even further and argues that those who refuse to pay the *zakāh* may be considered bandits. If a group, while acknowledging that the *zakāh* is a religious obligation, defiantly refuses to pay it, and uses force to resist payment, the group is to be treated as bandits.[199] Ultimately, Ibn Ḥazm does not explain who will make the institutional determination as to whether: (1) a group is espousing a just cause, and therefore its members are not rebels at all; (2) a group is espousing a plausible but erroneous *ijtihād*, and so its members are to be treated as rebels but not considered bandits; (3) a group is coveting political power or espousing an implausible and erroneous cause, and so its members are to be treated as rebels and, possibly, bandits; and (4) what particular institution has the power to declare that the ruler is now to be treated as a rebel, or possibly a bandit.[200]

Clearly, Ibn Ḥazm is not interested in institutions or in the pragmatic application of the law. His discourse is a form of uncompromising moralizing, and although throughout his argument he refers to the far more technical treatments of the other schools, he criticizes these schools

[196] Ibn Ḥazm, *al-Muḥallā*, XII:281. [197] Ibid., 283.

[198] Ibid., 292. Ibn Ḥazm adds that if a person raises a sword because of an enmity or a cause, he is not a bandit.

[199] Ibid., 290. Ibn Ḥazm argues that if the group refuses to acknowledge that the *zakāh* is a religious obligation, then its members are to be treated as apostates.

[200] It is worth noting that Ibn Ḥazm advocates particularly harsh sanctions for bandits. For example, he is one of the very few jurists who asserts that a bandit should not be killed then crucified or crucified then killed. He argues that a bandit should be crucified and left to die a slow and agonizing death: ibid., 296–7.

for their failure to make the proper moral judgments, and for slavish adherence to precedent.[201] But it is also clear that he is not encumbered by earlier opinions or precedents from his own Ẓāhirī school of thought. He seems unrestrained in his attempt to reinvent and reconstruct the discourses on rebellion so that the whole field would become a powerful form of moralizing about the orthodoxy of various rebellious sects and the legitimacy of problematic rulers.

Ibn Ḥazm becomes somewhat technical when he addresses the treatment due to those who qualify as *bughāh*. He argues that as a general matter, rebels should not be slaughtered and should be fought for the limited purpose of removing their harm: the rebel's life is not protected only as long as he continues to fight.[202] He argues that a captive rebel may not be executed under any circumstances.[203] Rebel property, including weapons and horses, remains protected and may not be confiscated or used unless it becomes absolutely necessary to use some of the rebels' weaponry for the limited purpose of self-defense.[204] The wounded and fugitives may be killed, however, if the rebellion continues or if the rebels have reinforcements.[205] If women and children may be hurt, the rightful party may not use fire, mangonels, or flooding, or cut off food or water from the rebels. However, if women or children are not at risk of being hurt, then weapons of mass destruction may be used. Ibn Ḥazm, however, adds that if fire or flooding is used, the rebels must be given an access or a safe pathway to escape death and surrender.[206] He vehemently rejects the Ḥanafī argument that the ruler does not have jurisdiction to punish crimes committed in rebel territory.[207] He also refuses to recognize any legal acts or adjudications performed in rebel territory. When the rightful ruler defeats the rebels, he should recollect all taxes, void all adjudications, and repeat all criminal sanctions enforced by the rebels. The only possible exception is if there is not an established rightful ruler. In this situation, the rebels' legal acts and adjudications may be recognized and enforced.[208] Ibn Ḥazm concludes that once the rebels abandon their

[201] For example, see ibid., XI:336, 357. Ibn Ḥazm was also motivated by sectarian convictions. It was important for Ibn Ḥazm to establish that those who rebelled against ᶜUthmān were unbelievers or bandits. However, he considered those who rebelled against ᶜAlī to be errant Muslims who should be forgiven.

[202] Ibid., 338. [203] Ibid., 336. [204] Ibid., 340–1.

[205] Ibid., 339–40. [206] Ibid., 360. [207] Ibid., 357–8.

[208] Ibid., 352–4.

rebellion and stop fighting, the sanctity of their blood is restored and they become "our brothers [once again]."[209]

Ibn Ḥazm's treatment of the subject of rebellion did not gain general acceptability or become an established doctrine. However, as we will see, many later jurists, particularly from the Mālikī school, gravitated towards a more subjective and ideological position on rebellion. This is particularly so after the Mongol invasion in the seventh/thirteenth century. Nonetheless, these jurists did not necessarily argue that a ruler could be declared a rebel. Rather, they argued that an unjust ruler should not be supported in his attempt to fight rebels.

The Shīᶜa

By the fifth/eleventh century, Shīᶜī jurists had developed a substantial discourse on the *bughāh*.[210] It is not clear to what extent the development of Shīᶜī discourses on the subject was influenced by the rise of the Buwayhids in the fourth/tenth century and their defeat by the Seljuks in the fifth/eleventh century. The Buwayhids are reported to have been Shīᶜīs, particularly of the Zaydī persuasion.[211] It is possible that Shīᶜī jurists responded to the Seljuk challenge by systematizing their discourses on rebellion. Nonetheless, this is unlikely because most of the Shīᶜī discourses, at this stage, were concerned with responding to the Sunnī arguments about the religious status of those who rebelled against ᶜAlī. Furthermore, the majority of Shīᶜī discourses in the fifth/eleventh century focused on addressing the status of those who rebel against the true and infallible *imām*. Therefore, at this point of their development there is a futuristic quality to Shīᶜī discourses on the subject. They address the status of those who rebel against the true *imām* when one eventually exists. At later stages, the Shīᶜī treatment of the subject of rebellion became largely indistinguishable from the Sunnī approach, and Shīᶜī jurists no longer restricted themselves to addressing rebels against the infallible *imām*.

As noted above, the Shīᶜī approach to rebellion was ideological, but was quite different from Ibn Ḥazm's treatment. Ibn Ḥazm scrutinized

209 Ibid., 360.

210 Al-Ṣadūq (d. 381/991–2), in his *Kitāb*, IV:68–9, addresses banditry but does not discuss rebellion. Al-Qāḍī al-Nuᶜmān does address rebellion in his *Daᶜāʾim al-Islām*. I address al-Nuᶜmān below.

211 On this period of Shīᶜī history, see Modarressi, *Crisis*, 96; Momen, *Introduction*, 75–82. Momen argues that although the Buwayhids were Zaydīs, they also had strong Imāmī sympathies.

the content of the rebel's interpretation, and classified rebels according to his assessment of the justness of their cause. The Shīᶜī treatment, for the most part, did not scrutinize the content of the rebel's interpretation. Rather, it focused on whether the *imām* was rightful according to the criteria of Shīᶜī theology. If the *imām* was rightful, then all those who disobeyed him were rebels regardless of the specific content of their interpretation. If the ruler was not rightful, Shīᶜī jurisprudence in the fifth/eleventh century took a rather neutral or non-committal position.

Abū Jaᶜfar al-Ṭūsī (d. 460/1067), one of the most important Shīᶜī jurists of the fifth/eleventh century, emphasized the imperative of obeying the *imām* and the prohibition against dissenting from the *jamāᶜa*.[212] In this context, his discourse is hardly different from that of his Sunnī counterparts who emphasized the need for order and stability. Al-Ṭūsī asserts that anyone who rebels against a just ruler (*imāmᶜādil*), violates his oath of allegiance, and disobeys the ruler's commands is a *bāghī*, and it is permissible for the ruler to fight him.[213] The fact that al-Ṭūsī uses the expression "a just *imām*" gives the impression that, like some of his Sunnī counterparts, he is arguing that only those who rebel against *any* just ruler are to be considered *bughāh*. This impression is reinforced by the fact that al-Ṭūsī asserts that if a group rebels against an unjust ruler, they should not be fought under any circumstances.[214] However, it is unlikely that al-Ṭūsī is arguing that any just ruler should be obeyed, and that those who refuse to do so are rebels.[215] A substantial portion of al-Ṭūsī's arguments are focused on analyzing the status of the Companions who rebelled against ᶜAlī. He argues that although these rebels outwardly remained Muslims, in reality they became unbelievers by rebelling against the true *imām*.[216] He goes on to note that although the Sunnīs have argued that the term *bughāh* does not connote reproach (*laysa bi ismi dhamm*), they are mistaken. He adds that some of the Sunnīs have gone so far as to

[212] Al-Ṭūsī, *al-Mabsūṭ*, VII:263. Al-Ṭūsī studied Shāfiᶜī jurisprudence before studying under the Shīᶜī al-Shaykh al-Mufīd (d. 413/1022). He was no stranger to the ordeal of persecution. His books were burned and he went into hiding and eventually settled in Kūfa. See al-Dhahabī, *Siyar*, XVIII:334–5.

[213] Al-Ṭūsī, *al-Nihāya*, 296. In his *al-Rasāʾil*, 244, he adds that the rebels should not be fought except by the express permission of the ruler. Also see al-Ṭūsī, *al-Mabsūṭ*, VII:263.

[214] Al-Ṭūsī, *al-Nihāya*, 296; al-Ṭūsī, *Tahdhīb*, VI:145.

[215] Madelung, "A Treatise." He argues that the Imāmīs had, at this time, already recognized the possibility of a just ruler other than the infallible *imām*. This proposition would appear to contradict my argument above. However, I am not necessarily challenging Madelung's thesis. I am arguing that at this point in Imāmī jurisprudence, the law of rebellion remained primarily a field for sectarian debate.

[216] Al-Ṭūsī, *al-Mabsūṭ*, VII:264; al-Mufīd (d. 413/1022), in his *Awāʾil*, 42, asserts that the Imāmīs, Zaydīs, and Khawārij agreed that those who rebelled against ᶜAlī are considered unbelievers.

maintain that the *bughāh* are similar to *mujtahids*, and that sedition is similar to juridical disagreements. This is due to the fact that the Sunnīs have maintained that the *bughāh* remain believers because of their reliance on a plausible *taʾwīl*. Al-Ṭūsī argues that the Sunnī position is untenable. *Baghy* is an act of disbelief, and the existence of a plausible *taʾwīl* is irrelevant if the rebellion is against a rightful *imām*.[217] The difference between the Sunnī and Shīʿī approaches is further clarified by Abū al-Qāsim al-Mūsawī al-Sharīf al-Murtaḍā (d. 436/1044–5), who claimed that of all the Muslim sects, the Imāmī Shīʿa alone held that whoever rebels against the just *imām*, it is as if he has rebelled against the Prophet himself. Al-Murtaḍā asserts that obedience to the true *imām* of the age is a great act of religious devotion, and that no prayers or any other religious act will compensate for the sin of disobeying the true *imām*.[218] He then explains that the *imām* must be infallible, and that all of those who believe in the infallibility of the *imām* also believe that the *bughāh* are unbelievers.[219]

Having asserted that the *bughāh* are unbelievers, logically it would seem to follow that the *bughāh* would be treated as apostates or infidels. Surprisingly, however, the Shīʿī discourses on the treatment of rebels are substantially similar to Sunnī doctrines.[220] In order for a group to qualify as *bughāh*, it must have a plausible interpretation or cause, and a degree of power or strength (*minʿa* or *shawka*). If a group rebels without *shawka*, they should be treated as common criminals, but if a group rebels without a plausible *taʾwīl*, they should be treated as bandits.[221] Under all circumstances, as long as an individual or group does not rebel or violate the law, the *imām* should not persecute or fight such an individual or group, even if their system of thought is offensive to the *imām*.[222] If a group which has a *shawka* and a *taʾwīl* does not rebel, but otherwise

[217] Al-Ṭūsī, *al-Mabsūṭ*, VII:264; see also al-Murtaḍā, *al-Intiṣār*, 233.

[218] Al-Murtaḍā, *al-Intiṣār*, 231, 233.

[219] Ibid., 232. Other Shīʿī jurists refer to *al-imām al-ʿadl* (the just *imām*) or to *al-imām al-ḥaqq* (the true *imām*). See al-Ṭarabulusī (d. 481/1088–9), *al-Muhadhdhab*, I:299, 326.

[220] Al-Murtaḍā argues that the *bughāh* should not be treated as apostates. Rebels against the true *imām* are considered unbelievers in the eyes of God in the Hereafter. Nevertheless, on this earth they are treated as sinful Muslims: al-Murtaḍā, *al-Intiṣār*, 232. According to al-Ṭūsī (*al-Mabsūṭ*, VII:278), the *bughāh* are to be treated on this earth as sinful Muslims or unbelievers, depending on the specific legal issue in question.

[221] Al-Ṭūsī, *al-Mabsūṭ*, VII:264, 268.

[222] For support, al-Ṭūsī cites the precedent of the Prophet's conduct with the hypocrites of Medina. He argues that although the Prophet was well aware of their hypocritical beliefs, he did not persecute them. However, he adds that if the rebels malign or slander the *imāms*, they should be killed: ibid., 269–70. Al-Ṭarabulusī (*al-Muhadhdhab*, I:325) states that the loyalists should not initiate the fighting.

violates the law, the *imām* should hold them liable, and should prosecute them for the specific crimes committed.[223]

According to Shīʿī sources, the existence of a *ta'wīl* is what, for the most part, distinguishes a rebel from a bandit. However, they do not elaborate upon what would be recognized as a plausible *ta'wīl*,[224] and, at the same time, these sources adopt a rather broad definition of banditry. This contributes to a blurring of the line between a rebel and a bandit. For example, al-Ṭūsī maintains that a bandit is one who uses weapons to terrorize people in a city or desert, or over land or sea.[225] The primary legal element that distinguishes bandits from others is that bandits spread terror and render their victims helpless by denying them the possibility of rescue.[226] This, of course, could include a rather broad array of criminal activity that is not necessarily limited to an intent to usurp property. In fact, al-Ṭūsī concedes that banditry is not necessarily limited to crimes motivated by a desire to steal or usurp property.[227] Under such a broad definition of banditry, crimes that are of a political nature could be considered a form of banditry. For instance, al-Ṭūsī argues that if a group assassinates a governor or some other official, even if inside a town, this group should be treated as bandits.[228] It is not clear whether al-Ṭūsī is

[223] Al-Ṭūsī, *al-Mabsūṭ*, VII:268. It is not clear whether al-Ṭūsī is arguing that the group should be held collectively liable for the crimes committed by some of its members, or whether only the individual members who committed the crime are to be held liable.

[224] Al-Ḥalabī (d. 447/1055), in his *al-Kāfī*, 34, argues that a recognizable *ta'wīl* is that which claims that something prohibited is allowed or vice versa, or that which would deny a legal obligation, such as the obligation to obey the rightful *imām*, as long as it is supported by some rational argument (*bi al-istidlāl*).

[225] Al-Ṭūsī, *al-Mabsūṭ*, VIII:47, 50. However, in his *al-Nihāya*, 297, the author adds that a bandit is one who intends to usurp money or property. But he also states that a bandit is anyone who terrorizes people in Muslim or non-Muslim territory: ibid., 720. The same is repeated in al-Ṭarabulusī, *al-Muhadhdhab*, X:170. Sallār (d. 448/1056–7), in his *al-Marāsim*, X:111, argues that a bandit is one who uses force in the land of Islam and causes corruption. Al-Ḥalabī (d. 447/1055), *al-Kāfī*, 34, argues that bandits are those who terrorize the wayfarer and cause corruption in *dār al-amn* (the abode of peace and security). Al-Mufīd (*al-Muqniʿ*, X:44) states that bandits are misfits who use weapons in Muslim territory to usurp money. Al-Ḥalabī (d. late fifth/eleventh century), in his *Ishāra*, IX:197, states that bandits are those who cause corruption on the earth and commit highway robbery. Even among jurists writing in the late sixth/twelfth century, the categories of *baghy* and *ḥirāba* are at times confused. For example, see al-Ḥalabī (d. 585/1189), *Ghunya*, IX:153.

[226] Al-Ṭūsī, *al-Mabsūṭ*, VIII:50.

[227] Ibid., 48. Al-Ṭūsī argues that if the bandits committed murder while having formed an intent to usurp property, they must be killed regardless of whether they in fact usurped property or not. The *imām* does not have discretion to pardon them or to impose a lesser penalty. If the bandits did not intend to usurp property but committed murder anyway, the *imām* does have discretion.

[228] Ibid., VII:270. Al-Ṭūsī, however, notes that some jurists have argued that such a group should not be treated as bandits, and therefore the imposition of a criminal sanction against the group is not mandatory.

arguing that assassins of public officials are bandits, even if they have a legally recognizable *ta'wīl*. Put differently, if the group that carried out the assassination has a plausible *ta'wīl*, are its members to be treated as bandits or rebels? The difference, of course, is significant because of the harsh penalties imposed on bandits, and because the rules of engagement that apply to rebels do not apply to bandits.[229]

The rules of engagement that apply to rebels are rather tolerant. If a group, while enjoying *shawka* and a plausible *ta'wīl*, commits a general act of rebellion, the *imām* should warn them, and inquire about their grievances. If they mention an injustice, it should be redressed.[230] The Imāmī Shī^cī rules of conduct of war are similar in certain respects to those of the Ḥanāfī and, in other respects, to Shāfi^cī doctrines. Similar to the Ḥanafī position, a basic distinction is maintained between rebels who have reinforcements (*fi'a*) and those who do not. If the rebels have reinforcements, the wounded and fugitive may be dispatched. However, similar to the Shāfi^cī position, the captive may not be executed. A prisoner is held until the rebels have been thoroughly defeated, or until he repents and takes the oath of allegiance, whichever is first. Rebel property, other than property found in the war camp, may not be confiscated, and under all circumstances rebels cannot be enslaved. Importantly, once the rebels lay down their weapons and surrender, they may not be fought or killed.[231]

Al-Ṭūsī argues that it is not permissible for the just *imām* to use fire or mangonels against rebels. These weapons, al-Ṭūsī contends, kill indiscriminately, and the *imām* is not allowed to kill other than those who fight him. Like his Sunnī counterparts, al-Ṭūsī asserts that these weapons may be used only in cases of necessity. However, he goes further, and does not leave the determination of whether a case of necessity exists to the

[229] See, for example, al-Ḥalabī, *Ishāra*, IX:196.

[230] Al-Ṭūsī, *al-Mabsūṭ*, VII:265; al-Ḥalabī, *al-Kāfī*, 34, 37–8. Al-Ṭarabulusī (*al-Muhadhdhab*, I:325) argues that it is recommended that the *imām* warn the rebels before fighting them, but that if they are aware of the illegality of their actions, the *imām* does not need to warn them.

[231] Al-Ṭūsī, *al-Mabsūṭ*, VII:266–9, 271; al-Ṭūsī, *al-Nihāya*, 296–7; al-Murtaḍā (d. 436/1044–5), *al-Masā'il*, 27; al-Ḥalabī, *al-Kāfī*, 34, 37–8; al-Ḥalabī, *Ishāra*, 190, 196. Al-Ṭarabulusī (*al-Muhadhdhab*, I:325–6) asserts that even in the heat of battle, if a rebel lays down his weapon, asks for safe conduct, and indicates a willingness to obey the true *imām*, he may not be killed. However, in al-Ṭūsī, *Tahdhīb*, VI:144, and his *al-Rasā'il*, 244–5, the author asserts that if the rebels have a *fi'a*, the prisoners may be executed. In *Tahdhīb*, VI:154–5, al-Ṭūsī states that ^cAlī did not enslave the rebels because he wanted to set a precedent which would protect his Shī^ca after him. Nonetheless, when the Qā'im returns, he will kill and enslave the unjust. Modarressi (*Crisis*, 6) describes the Qā'im as "a millenarian figure" who is "a revolutionary leader from the House of the Prophet [who] would rise up, overthrow the unjust government, and establish the rule of justice and truth." Also see Momen, *Introduction*, 165–6.

discretion of the *imām*. He argues that a case of necessity only exists in two distinct situations: (1) the rebels use these weapons first, and so the *imām* is forced to use the same type of weapons in self-defense; (2) the rebels surround the *imām* from every side. In both of these situations, the *imām* may use such weapons to create an opening from which he and his troops can escape.[232] Al-Ṭūsī similarly restricts the discretion of the *imām* over the issue of who may be asked to assist in fighting the rebels. He argues that the killing of the fugitive, captive, or wounded is an injustice and a transgression. Therefore, the *imām* may not seek the aid of any party that will commit such infractions. If it becomes necessary to seek the aid of such a party, the *imām* may do so, but only under two conditions. Al-Ṭūsī reproduces the two conditions found in Shāfiʿī jurisprudence: (1) there is no alternative and no other party that can assist in fighting the rebels; and (2) the *imām* would have sufficient power and force to prevent the killing of the captive, wounded, and fugitive. If either of these conditions does not exist, then the *imām* cannot seek the aid of a party that might violate the rules of engagement.[233] Importantly, al-Ṭūsī argues that *ahl al-dhimma* should not be asked to assist in fighting Muslim rebels because the point of fighting the *bughāh* is to return them to the fold, and not to exterminate them.[234] *Ahl al-dhimma*, however, cannot be trusted to observe this goal. Furthermore, because the rebels are Muslims, under no circumstances may the *imām* agree to a termination of the fighting on the condition that the rebels pay a tribute or surrender hostages.[235]

Despite the fact that the *bughāh* were considered unbelievers for opposing the true *imām*, the rules of conduct of war do not materially differ from the rules advocated by the schools that considered the rebels errant Muslims. In fact, al-Ṭūsī consistently asserts that the rebels continue to enjoy the sanctity and protection afforded by Islam. This is rather powerful evidence of the persuasive moral impact that the discourses

[232] Al-Ṭūsī, *al-Mabsūṭ*, VII:275.

[233] Ibid., 274. It is likely that al-Ṭūsī simply borrowed these two conditions from Shāfiʿī jurisprudence. As we saw earlier, these conditions were adopted as a response to the Ḥanafī claim that the captives, wounded, and fugitives may be dispatched as long as the *bughāh* have a *fi'a*. Al-Ṭūsī himself argues that if a *fi'a* exists, the wounded and fugitive may be killed. Nonetheless, it is likely that al-Ṭūsī has the Ḥanafīs in mind when he insists upon these two conditions.

[234] Ibid., 273–4. The author also adds that if *ahl al-dhimma* support the *bughāh*, their covenant with Muslims is abrogated. However, if *ahl al-dhimma* claim that they were forced or that they, in good faith, believed that it was legal to support the rebels, they are to be believed, and their covenant should not be abrogated.

[235] Ibid., 271–2. Al-Ṭūsī, however, argues that if the rebels ask for a cease-fire, promise to release the prisoners of war held by them, and offer hostages as surety, the hostages may be accepted from them. But if they renege on their promise and execute the prisoners, the hostages may not be killed, and in fact, once the fighting ends the hostages must be released.

on rebellion had achieved by the fifth/eleventh century. The notion that there must be limits imposed on the discretion of a ruler in the conduct of warfare against Muslim rebels had become firmly established. Even the schools that argued that a legitimate ruler should have a near-absolute moral claim to power, or that a rightful ruler is infallible, were not willing to leave the conduct of warfare against Muslim rebels to the ruler's unfettered discretion. At this stage in Shīʿī jurisprudence the *bughāh* are by definition those who rebel against the true *imām*, who has an absolute moral claim to power. The fact that the rebels rely on a plausible *ta'wīl* does not endow them with a relative moral claim, but simply sets them apart from bandits; and saves them from the harsh penalties that apply to the crime of banditry. This means that rebels are a different type of criminal from bandits; however, it does not mean that they are not criminals at all. This is why al-Ṭūsī refuses to exempt the rebels from liability or to recognize the validity of their legal acts.

Al-Ṭūsī argues that if the loyalists destroy life or property before the rebellion commences or after it ends, they should be held liable. This is because until the rebellion actually commences, no crime has been committed. The rebels, however, are liable for life and property destroyed before, during, and after the rebellion. Al-Ṭūsī concedes that many jurists have argued that the rebels should not be held liable for life and property destroyed during the course of their rebellion, and that this rule had become firmly established by *ijmāʿ* (consensus). He, however, denies that an *ijmāʿ* exists on this matter because Shīʿī jurists have never accepted this position. As long as the Shīʿa do not agree with the non-liability rule, all claims to a supposed consensus are unfounded.[236] Moreover, al-Ṭūsī contends that the loyalists have jurisdiction over all crimes committed in rebel territory, and that all legal acts performed by the rebels in such territory are null and void.[237] Taxes or alms collected by the rebels should be re-collected.[238] The testimony of their witnesses should not be accepted in court because the rebels are sinful, and hence are not of just character. Furthermore, their adjudications, regardless of their technical correctness or fairness, are to be abrogated because rebel judges were not properly appointed by the *imām*.[239] Al-Ṭūsī does not fully explain the reasoning behind these rather uncompromising positions. Nonetheless,

236 Ibid., 267.

237 Except that *ḥudūd* (specific criminal sanctions) applied by rebels should not be repeated, out of mercy and compassion for the penalized: ibid., 276, 280.

238 However, in order to alleviate potential hardship, the *imām* may forgive the assessed taxes and alms, and not re-collect them: ibid., 276.

239 Ibid., 277–8.

he asserts that funeral prayers should not be performed for dead rebels because they are *kuffār* (unbelievers).[240] Therefore, rebels are to be treated on this earth as Muslims because as far as the temporal laws are concerned they remain outwardly believers.[241] However, their legal acts lack legitimacy because inwardly, and as far as the Hereafter is concerned, they are unbelievers. This lack of legitimacy is not cured even if the rebels usurp power or gain control over a territory.

All of the discussion above is premised on the assumption that a rightful *imām* would, in fact, exist, and that the rebels would oppose such a rightful ruler. Nonetheless, for the Imāmī Shīᶜīs, this largely remained a hypothetical situation because Shīᶜī jurists continued to live under what they considered unjust and illegitimate rulers. This situation prompted Shīᶜī jurists to deal with two significant issues: (1) should a true believer revolt against an illegitimate ruler; and (2) should a true believer assume an official post under an illegitimate government? Jaᶜfar al-Ṣādiq in the second/eighth century had already forbidden his followers to join any armed rebellion.[242] Therefore, Imāmī Shīᶜītes did not focus on whether one should instigate an armed rebellion; rather, they focused on whether it is permissible to enjoin the good and forbid the evil under an illegitimate government. Al-Ṭūsī, for instance, cites the *ḥadīth* which asserts that the best form of *jihād* is a truthful word uttered before an unjust ruler, and argues that as a general matter, one should enjoin the good and forbid the evil. However, he notes that there are two important qualifications to this general obligation. One should reasonably believe that enjoining the good and forbidding the evil will be effective. Furthermore, a believer does not have an obligation to enjoin the good and forbid the evil if such an activity will result in harm (*mafsada*), such as placing him or others in serious danger. A believer does not need to be certain that such harm will result; it is sufficient that he or she believe that it is probable that such harm would, in fact, occur.[243]

[240] Ibid., 278. Al-Ṭūsī also contends that loyalists killed in battle are martyrs.

[241] Al-Ṭūsī reports that early Shīᶜī jurists had argued that selling weapons to the *bughāh* of al-Shām (Umayyads) is not permitted unless such weapons are going to be used against non-Muslim enemies such as the Byzantines. If one sells weapons, however, to the *bughāh* when they are fighting *ahl al-bayt*, that person becomes an unbeliever. If there is a cease-fire between the *bughāh* and the loyalists, one may sell things such as horse saddles and shields to the *bughāh*. See al-Ṭūsī, *al-Istibṣār*, III:57–8.

[242] See Modarressi, *Crisis*, 7–8.

[243] Al-Ṭūsī, *al-Rasā'il*, 245; al-Ṭūsī, *Tahdhīb*, VI:170; al-Ṭūsī, *al-Nihāya*, 300. Al-Ḥalabī (*Ishāra*, 198) argues that it is sufficient for a believer to suspect that harm will befall him or others in life or property.

As to serving as a public official under an illegitimate government, a believer may, in fact, accept such a position as long as certain conditions are met. The laws that a believer is asked to implement must be consistent with the dictates of *Sharīᶜa*. Furthermore, the believer must serve the *Sharīᶜa*, and not the illegitimate government, while believing that he has been duly delegated by the rightful ruler to do so, even if one does not exist. In other words, the believer should believe that his source of empowerment is a fictitious rightful ruler, and should serve the law of God, and not the unjust rulers in power. If the illegitimate ruler commands the believer to enforce laws that violate the *Sharīᶜa*, then the believer may not acquiesce, and must promptly resign his position. Nonetheless, if the believer is forced by threat of harm to remain in his position and enforce such laws, then dissimulation (*taqiyya*) is permitted. In order to protect himself or others, the believer may remain in his position and enforce the ruler's illegal orders as long as such orders do not include unjustly killing someone. Dissimulation is never permitted if it means enforcing a command to kill an innocent person.[244]

The exposition above is rather cryptic and formulaic, and it creates many points of ambiguity. For instance, considering that there is no single institution that authoritatively defines *Sharīᶜa*, it is not clear how one is to decide whether the ruler's commands are illegal. Furthermore, it is not clear what type of threat of harm would permit one to cooperate in the enforcement of illegal orders. It is also not clear what is meant by a threat to the life of an innocent person. Are individuals who refuse to recognize the rightful *imām* (i.e. Sunnīs) innocent? Does the prohibition apply only to commands that unjustly execute a person, or does it also apply to equally dramatic measures such as long-term imprisonment or the use of torture? We will revisit these issues later.[245] For our purposes at this point, it is not necessary to explore the full implications of the doctrine of dissimulation. What is material is that Shīᶜī jurists, like their Sunnī

244 Al-Ṭūsī, *al-Nihāya*, 301. Al-Mufīd (*Awāʾil*, 118, 120) asserts that assisting or participating in the propagation of injustice or oppression is not permitted. However, assisting illegitimate rulers in lawful and just causes is permitted. He also adds that dissimulation is not permitted if the result will be to place the life of an innocent person at risk, or if dissimulation means that the true religion will be corrupted. In his *al-Muqniᶜ*, IX:15, al-Mufīd adds that a believer may not accept work for unjust rulers unless he intends to use his position to help the true believers (i.e. other Shīᶜīs). Also, he argues that a believer may implement executive orders but may not assist in initiating or creating new executive orders. For a study on the usage of dissimulation, see Stewart, "*Taqiyyah.*"

245 On the legality of living and working under an unjust government and dissimulation, see Madelung, "A Treatise"; Kohlberg, "Some"; Kohlberg, "Development."

counterparts, were willing to participate and partake in the institutions of society, even if these institutions were unjust or so-called illegitimate. Even the duty to enjoin the good and forbid the evil before an unjust or illegitimate authority became qualified by a balancing act. One needs to weigh the costs and benefits of taking an active role, and if the harm outweighs the good, one needs to refrain from needlessly endangering himself or others. However, Shīʿī jurists were not willing to abandon the ideal in its entirety. They implied that those who rise against an unjust or illegitimate ruler are not rebels at all, and they explicitly stated that one should not assist an unjust ruler in fighting or persecuting rebels. This, of course, is consistent with the argument that dissimulation is not permitted if it means killing an innocent person. Arguably, rebels fighting against an unjust or illegitimate ruler are innocent, and a Shīʿī may not take part in their slaughter.

A useful point of comparison to the Imāmī Shīʿī discourses are the discourses of the Ismāʿīlī al-Qāḍī al-Nuʿmān (d. 363/974), who reflects a very different perspective. Al-Nuʿmān was a supporter of the early Fāṭimid dynasty in Egypt, and he served in various capacities under four consecutive Fāṭimid caliphs, al-Mahdī (r. 297/909–322/934), al-Qāʾim (r. 322/934–334/946), al-Manṣūr (r. 334/946–341/953), and al-Muʿizz (r. 341/953–365/975). During the end of al-Qāʾim's reign, al-Nuʿmān was appointed as a judge, but he was also the most influential judicial functionary under the Fāṭimids until his death.[246] In Ismāʿīlī theology, the *imām* is considered divinely guided and infallible. Therefore, he is the final authority for interpreting the law of God. For the Fāṭimid Ismāʿīlīs, after the Qurʾān and *Sunna*, the infallible *imām* was considered the most important source of law. The paradigms of Fāṭimid Ismāʿīlī theology, and the close association of al-Qāḍī al-Nuʿmān with the *imāms* of his age, make al-Nuʿmān's discourse particularly useful for comparative purposes. Reportedly, he consulted contemporary *imāms* on his theological and jurisprudential writings. Furthermore, his main work on law, *Daʿāʾim al-Islām* (Pillars of Islam), became the official Fāṭimid *corpus juris*.[247] Considering the semi-official nature of his work, al-Nuʿmān's exposition on the *bughāh* is of particular interest.

Al-Nuʿmān does deal with the issue of rebellion, but his discussion is rather terse. He does not address whether working with unjust rulers is

246 Fyzee, "Nuʿmān"; Fyzee, "Qadi"; Dachraoui, "al-Nuʿmān."

247 Daftary, *Ismāʿīlīs*, 250, 252–3; Sanders, "Fāṭimid," 158. Reportedly, the caliph al-Muʿizz commissioned the writing of the *Daʿāʾim*: see Walker, "The Ismāʿīlī Daʿwa," 134. It is also reported that al-Muʿizz edited and revised the *Daʿāʾim*: see Poonawala, "al-Qāḍī al-Nuʿmān," 126.

permissible, and also does not address the issue of rebellion against unjust rulers. But he does cite the verse on *baghy* as the relevant verse on the subject, and otherwise focuses on the status of those who rebelled against ᶜAlī. Al-Nuᶜmān argues that those who rebelled against ᶜAlī committed acts of unbelief but were not unbelievers. Although they defied the laws and sanctities of God, they cannot be equated in status to those who never adopted Islam or believed in the Prophet. By the expression "those who rebelled against ᶜAlī," al-Nuᶜmān seems to mean non-Shīᶜīs in general, and not just Muᶜāwiya, ᶜĀ'isha, or the Khawārij. Therefore, he argues, because Sunnīs are not considered unbelievers, it is permissible to marry or inherit from them.[248] Nonetheless, other than the specific historical context of ᶜAlī, it is not clear who al-Nuᶜmān means by the word *bughāh*. He does not define rebellion, and does not engage in a substantive discussion about the justness or unjustness of the rebels. He simply lays out the rules of conduct in dealing with the *bughāh*. At one point he cites reports which assert that the *bughāh* should be fought in the same way unbelievers are fought.[249] However, rather inconsistently, a bit later, he argues that if the *bughāh* have reinforcements, then the wounded, fugitive, and captive may be dispatched. If, however, they do not have reinforcements, the *bughāh* may not be dispatched.[250] Significantly, al-Nuᶜmān does not discuss the concept of *ta'wīl* or *shawka*. However, in one of the extant manuscripts of al-Nuᶜmān's book, it states that if the *bughāh* fight while relying on a *ta'wīl*, they are not liable for life or property destroyed during the course of their rebellion.[251] One cannot exclude the possibility that this passage was a later addition by a copyist who might have wanted to bring al-Nuᶜmān's discourses into greater conformity with Muslim discourses in general. This possibility is supported by the fact that in all of the other manuscripts al-Nuᶜmān argues that the *bughāh* should not be held liable if the identity of an individual who committed a specific offense is not known. In other words, the *bughāh* are not collectively liable for life or property destroyed during the course of the rebellion. However, if the offender responsible for a specific act can be identified, that offender must be held liable.[252] This, of course, is a far more limited exemption from liability than the added passage implies. On issues related to the sanctity of the *bughāh*, al-Nuᶜmān adds that once

[248] Al-Nuᶜmān, *Daᶜā'im*, 1:388. [249] Ibid., 393.
[250] Ibid., 394. [251] Ibid., 395 n. 2. [252] Ibid., 396–7.

the *bughāh* repent and abandon the status of *baghy*, their property must be returned to them.[253] Al-Nuᶜmān's discussion on banditry is equally terse, and does not help in distinguishing a *bāghī* from a bandit. After citing the incident of the ᶜUrayna, he states that bandits are those who attack travelers and usurp their property. Al-Nuᶜmān adopts a position of *takhyīr* but argues that the ruler should punish bandits in proportion to their crime.[254]

In evaluating al-Nuᶜmān's discourse, the pertinent question becomes: Who or what does he mean by the expression *bughāh*? He served a government which espoused a theology consistent with his own beliefs. He is reported to have become an Ismāᶜīlī early in his life, and had risen to a position of prominence in the hierarchy of the *daᶜwa* (the Ismāᶜīlī religious establishment).[255] Furthermore, the caliphs al-Nuᶜmān served did, in fact, confront several serious rebellions.[256] But considering al-Nuᶜmān's background, did he mean to bind the Fāṭimid caliphs by the rules of conduct he enunciated when such caliphs dealt with rebels? Was this discourse intended as a form of restraint on Fāṭimid caliphs or lower-ranking officials, such as governors or military chiefs? It is possible that he did not have in mind rebels against the Fāṭimid caliphs. But then the question is: Did he mean to argue that these are the rules of conduct that apply to Fāṭimids when they fight others (Ibāḍīs and non-Ismāᶜīlī Shīᶜīs of North Africa included)? Alternatively, did he mean to argue that these rules applied to Sunnīs when they fought non-Sunnīs? Al-Nuᶜmān's primary conceptual justification for the rules of conduct enunciated is similar to one of the points argued by the Imāmī jurists. Al-Nuᶜmān reports that the reason ᶜAlī treated the *bughāh* with clemency and mercy was that ᶜAlī knew that his party or followers (Shīᶜa) would be defeated and oppressed by their opponents. He wished to set a precedent so that people would follow his example *when dealing with his party*. Significantly, al-Nuᶜmān then reports that ᶜAlī wished to send a message. If people failed to follow his example in dealing with the Shīᶜa, ᶜAlī wanted Muslims to be able to contrast his example with the behavior of his opponents, and thus Muslims would be able to discern the just from the unjust party.[257] According to this logic, the role of the discourses is

[253] Ibid., 397. [254] Ibid., II:474–5.

[255] Wilferd Madelung argued that al-Nuᶜmān was originally a Sunnī who later became an Ismāᶜīlī: see Madelung, "Sources," 30. However, some scholars have challenged this claim: see Poonawala, "al-Qāḍī al-Nuᶜmān," 136 n. 17.

[256] See Poonawala, "al-Qāḍī al-Nuᶜmān," 119.

[257] Al-Nuᶜmān, *Daᶜāʾim*, I:394.

symbolic and communicative. Those who contrast ᶜAlī's clemency with the vindictiveness of his opponents would know that ᶜAlī was the just party. However, there is a certain tension, in this discourse. The implication of this argument is that the enunciated rules of conduct are primarily for the protection of the Shīᶜa. On the other hand, ᶜAlī's conduct seems to be an independent moral value in itself; it distinguishes between the just and unjust, and between the righteous and errant. This would imply that ᶜAlī's conduct should be emulated and followed by any just party. From this perspective, al-Nuᶜmān's discourse would become binding on Fāṭimid caliphs or any other rulers who claim to be just.

Al-Nuᶜmān does not resolve this tension, and one suspects that the tension, or its resolution, was not central to his concerns. His primary interest was in the theological debates surrounding ᶜAlī and his opponents. His reiteration of certain positive rules of conduct was probably due to the influence of the collective legal culture of the jurists.[258] However, al-Nuᶜmān's legal borrowing is cryptic and unsystematic. In reading al-Nuᶜmān, one is struck with the similarity between his language and that of Sunnī sources. One is also struck by his omission of several elements central to the discourses on rebellion, such as what constitutes a rebellion, the existence of a *ta'wīl* or *shawka*, various rules of engagement, and the validity of the legal acts of rebels. Like the Imāmī Shīᶜīs, al-Nuᶜmān was interested in proving ᶜAlī's high character. But considering the specific nature of Fāṭimid theology, and the institutional role of al-Nuᶜmān, it is doubtful that he sought to limit or restrain the Fāṭimid caliphs. Unlike the Imāmī Shīᶜīs, al-Nuᶜmān did not need to tailor his discussions to the issue of how one should deal with living under an unjust government. In other words, al-Nuᶜmān did not share the legacy and concerns of either the Imāmī or Sunnī jurists. He borrowed parts of the discourses of the jurists from the other legal traditions, but, ultimately, he did not share their purposes.

CONCLUSION: THE SURVIVING LEGACY OF *AḤKĀM AL-BUGHĀH*

As argued earlier, *aḥkām al-bughāh* arose out of the context of the persistent ᶜAlid rebellions in the first two centuries of Islam. We also argued that

[258] Al-Nuᶜmān was well aware of Sunnī jurisprudence, and in fact wrote refutations and critiques of some Sunnī legal doctrines. See Poonawala, "al-Qāḍī al-Nuᶜmān," 139 n. 45. Nevertheless, one of the reasons that the *Daᶜā'im* was written was to reconcile the Ismāᶜīlī and Sunnī schools of law. The point was to gain legitimacy by bringing Ismāᶜīlī law closer to Sunnī law. See Walker, "The Ismāᶜīlī Daᶜwa," 134; Poonawala, "al-Qāḍī al-Nuᶜmān," 129.

Muslim jurists selectively treated historical and textual precedent in order to construct the discourse on rebellion. Muslim jurists insisted that rebels with a cause be treated according to certain tolerant or indulgent guidelines, and that rebels should not be seen as particularly reprehensible or evil. While Muslim jurists were not willing to endorse or legitimate all rebellions without limits, they also were not willing to give rulers unfettered discretion in dealing with rebels. As we noted earlier, there is evidence that the Umayyads and early ᶜAbbāsids attempted to invoke the *ḥirāba* verse in the context of dealing with rebels. Muslim jurists responded by creating a distinction between rebels and bandits, and insisted that the *ḥirāba* verse does not apply to rebels, but applies to bandits. They also invoked the precedent of the Companions who rebelled against ᶜAlī in order to argue that rebels are not necessarily depraved or evil, and that rebellion is not necessarily a crime. In many ways, the discourse on rebellion directly correlates with the discourse on the legitimacy of the usurper. While, for the most part, the legitimacy of the usurper of power was recognized, Muslim jurists refused to de-legitimate all rebels or rebellions. By the fifth/eleventh century, the discourse on *aḥkām al-bughāh* had become firmly established, and clear schools of thought had developed on the issue of how rebels are to be treated. Although the Mālikī school continued to be ambiguous and rather ambivalent, as we will see, it was not too long before the Mālikīs adopted the discourse and started to construct their own specific positions on the matter. Even the Imāmī Shīᶜīs fully adopted the discourse despite the fact that, for them, it had a distinct futuristic and hypothetical quality to it. While the majority of Sunnī jurists focused on how rebels against any ruler should be treated, the Imāmī jurists concentrated on how rebels against a rightful ruler should be treated. Imāmī jurists insisted that rebels against a rightful ruler are not only sinners but unbelievers, and that rebellion against such a ruler is a crime. Remarkably, however, they argued that even if the ruler is rightful, he does not enjoy unfettered discretion in dealing with rebels. The Imāmī jurists also distinguished between a rebel and bandit, although the distinction was rather blurry and unclear. Significantly, if the rebellion is against an unjust or illegitimate ruler, the Imāmī position ends up being substantially similar to the Sunnī position; rebellion, as such, is not a crime.

Although the historical circumstances of the second/eighth century were materially different from those of the fifth/eleventh, the discourse on rebellion had gained an autonomy of its own. One is left with the distinct impression that the Sunnī jurists of the fifth/eleventh century were still responding to the historical conditions of the second/eighth century. For one, most of the precedents cited are from the first to the second century of Islam, and there is very little effort expended in addressing the weakening of the caliphate or the rise of the Fāṭimid dynasty, for example. This is due in part to the fact that the sectarian considerations that sparked these debates in the first place continued to be relevant several centuries later.[259] It is also partly due to the imperatives of legal culture and the hold of legal precedent on juristic discourses. As noted earlier, I am not arguing that law is completely autonomous. I am arguing, however, that the institutions of law and precedent in a legal culture have a force of their own. As we saw, at least one jurist, al-Simnānī, complained that the discourse on rebellion had become disconnected from political reality, yet he was unable or unwilling to ignore a discourse which had become firmly established in his school. Nevertheless, it would be erroneous to claim that Muslim jurists repeated the doctrines of *aḥkām al-bughāh* unthinkingly and without regard to the realities of their day. Legal culture does change and does respond to political and social realities, but it often does so slowly and reluctantly. In fact, as we will see, Muslim jurists ultimately responded to the fragmentation and eventual destruction of the ᶜAbbāsid caliphate in a variety of ways. Furthermore, *aḥkām al-bughāh* became a means by which a moral, religious, and more importantly, a legal ideal was upheld against the pragmatic and undisciplined practices of the state. There is no contradiction between the argument that the discourses on *aḥkām al-bughāh* became established and spread through the force of legal culture and precedent, and the argument that *aḥkām al-bughāh* were upheld as a moral and legal ideal against the practices of the state. As we argued earlier, these discourses arose because of a political and social reality that existed in early Islam. The sectarian disputes that confronted early Muslims generated most of the raw material that was eventually synthesized into the law of rebellion. As discussed earlier, some of the most esteemed Companions engaged in rebellions in early Islam. Furthermore, ᶜAlid rebels, and perhaps rebels such as Ibn al-Zubayr, were seen sympathetically by many early and

[259] It is worth emphasizing that Sunnī jurists sought to condemn the killers of ᶜUthmān and be somewhat tolerant with the people of the Jamal and Ṣiffīn, and this continued to be a consideration in the fourth/tenth century. However, the question is: Was the law of rebellion tailored exclusively to address the sectarian problem, or did the law of rebellion constitute a co-optation of the historical precedent to go beyond the sectarian issue? I have tried to demonstrate in this book that the law of rebellion goes beyond the sectarian issue. The sectarian issue formed the bedrock of the law, but that bedrock was redeployed for symbolic and negotiative purposes by the juristic culture.

late jurists. These historical realities contributed to the dynamics that produced *aḥkām al-bughāh*. As the culture of jurists developed, there was a further institutional incentive to develop and uphold the discourses on rebellion. As discussed earlier, there is no doubt that Sunnī jurists developed a cooperative relationship with the political institutions of the early ʿAbbāsids, but these interests were not necessarily symmetrical or in conformity with each other. Muslim jurists aspired to retain the right to represent and express the divine law, and hold the state accountable to that law. This explains why *aḥkām al-bughāh* were upheld as an ideal against the practices of the state. Nonetheless, this does not explain why the specific structure and terminology of *aḥkām al-bughāh* survived and spread in substantially the same format. The basic distinction between bandits and rebels, and the terminology of *ta'wīl* and *shawka*, as well as the basic expositions on recognizing the legal acts of rebels, continued to be reiterated for well over a thousand years without a radical restructuring or reshaping of the discourse.[260] Responses to historical realities came in the form of technical, but significant, modifications to certain rules rather than in the form of a radical reinvention of the discourse. The remarkable spread and perseverance of *aḥkām al-bughāh*'s terminology and categories is due to the imperative of legal culture and precedent.

Finally, as discussed earlier, the accepted contemporary scholarly and, by now, quite dogmatic view is that Sunnī jurists by the fourth/tenth century had become political quietists. But in light of the discourses on *aḥkām al-bughāh*, this view becomes untenable. It is not possible to describe the juridical positions as either quietist or activist. Sunnī juridical discourses did not consider rebellion a sin, and even the jurists such as the Ḥanafīs who did consider rebellion a sin were not willing to declare rebellion a punishable crime. In fact, as we will see, the idea that rebellion is not a sin or a crime continued to be advocated well after the fifth/eleventh century. Sunnī jurists before and after that century refused to unequivocally condemn or demonize all rebels. As would be expected from an established and institutionalized legal culture, Sunnī jurists upheld the need for stability and order. Even an unjust ruler is better than the anarchy that results from civil wars or rebellions. However, Muslim jurists continued

[260] As Kraemer ("Apostates," 68–9) notes, the distinguishing of rebels from bandits was unusual in ancient legal systems. Yet early Muslim jurists distinguished between ideologically motivated rebellions and acts of brigandage or banditry. The significant question is: Why has this theoretical distinction spread and survived in schools of thought of different political and social contexts? I would argue that the culture of legal borrowing played a major role.

to advocate the humane treatment of rebels and, as argued next, reinterpreted and neutralized the traditions attributed to the Prophet which curse or excommunicate rebels. Importantly, as discussed next, many Sunnī, Zaydī, and Ibāḍī jurists argued that a rebellion could be justified if the anticipated benefits of such a rebellion outweigh the perceived evils.

CHAPTER 6

Rebellion, insurgency, and brigandage: the developed positions and the emergence of trends

The ᶜAbbāsid caliphate was formally extinguished by the Mongols when they sacked Baghdād in 656/1258. Two centuries earlier, the caliphate had fallen under the strong influence of the Seljuk princes who seized Baghdād from the Buwayhids in 447/1055.[1] But, as noted earlier, the ᶜAbbāsid caliphate had become weakened to the point of impotence in the fourth/tenth century. The weakening and eventual extinction of the ᶜAbbāsid caliphate posed a fundamental change in the political structures of the age. The caliphate, as a political and religious symbol, was seriously challenged, and the basis for legitimacy of one dynasty over another had become more problematic.[2] The Sunnī juridical response to these developments was neither uniform nor dogmatic. Sunnī jurists did not lend unrestrained support to whoever happened to be in power, and did not unequivocally condemn rebellion against unjust rulers.

Sunnī juridical doctrines on rebellion underwent major revisions and reconstructions after the fifth/eleventh century. Some of the revisions are likely to have been in response to the imperatives of legal culture, and were not related to the political or social developments of the age. For instance, the Mālikī school fully adopted the discourses on rebellion, and in fact, Mālikī jurists attributed many of their newly adopted positions to the early founders of the Mālikī school. Furthermore, Ḥanbalī jurists further developed the theoretical foundations for *aḥkām al-bughāh* without significantly altering their positive rulings in the field. But other changes are clearly related to political developments of the seventh/thirteenth and

[1] Al-Ẓāhir Baybars set up a shadow caliphate in Cairo in 659/1261. The caliphate in Egypt ended with the Ottoman conquest of Cairo in 923/1517. See Bosworth, *New*, 7–9; Lambton, *State*, 138–9.

[2] Kennedy, *Prophet*, 198–9. The Shīᶜī Fāṭimids set up a caliphate in Egypt in 297/909 which came to an end with the Sunnī Ayyūbid conquest in 567/1171. The Ayyūbids were defeated in Egypt by the Mamlūks in 650/1252, and in Damascus and Aleppo by the Mongols in 658/1260. See Bosworth, *New*, 63, 70–5.

eighth/fourteenth centuries. For example, several jurists argued that the Mongols, even after converting to Islam, should be treated as bandits. In addition, many Shāfiʿī jurists adopted the Ḥanafī position on fighting rebels who had a *fi'a*. Importantly, the development of the legal discourses after the fifth/eleventh century was quite diverse and exhibited a variety of significant trends.

These trends cannot be broken down or understood in terms of traditional legal schools of thought. In other words, not all Shāfiʿīs or Mālikīs, for instance, adopted the same positions. Rather, the various trends crossed school lines and transcended the corporate identity of specific schools. A high degree of commonality continued to exist within each specific school. Jurists, however, exhibited a considerable degree of independence in their treatment of rebellion. Considering the role of legal culture and the power of prior authority on the legal mind, this is a phenomenon that needs to be explained. Put differently, why did jurists not adhere to the prior authority and corporate identity of the schools of thought to which they formally belonged? One must emphasize that for the most part the various jurists did, in fact, adhere to the inherited doctrines of their specific schools of thought. Therefore one will find that on the majority of issues, for example, Shāfiʿī jurists adhered to distinctly Shāfiʿī positions. Nonetheless, when it came to basic attitudes towards obeying and supporting those in power, the traditional boundaries of school doctrines tended to break down. The reason for this development, as explained earlier, is that the doctrines of rebellion in the fourth/tenth and fifth/eleventh centuries were still in response to the political dynamics of the second/eighth and third/ninth centuries. However, especially after the Mongol invasions, the disparity between the inherited legal doctrines and the political realities had become not only undeniable, but shocking. Many jurists reacted to the gap between political reality and legal doctrine by failing to respond at all, and continued to repeat the inherited traditions without further elaboration. Many other jurists were sufficiently disturbed by the disparity to be willing to exercise a degree of initiative and independence. In other words, the evolving gap between the doctrines on rebellion and the political reality resulted in a degree of delegitimation and deconstruction of the moral power of prior authority within each school. The balance between the need to uphold the integrity of a legal culture and the need to stay relevant in society tipped in favor of change. Under these circumstances, some jurists were willing to express views on the need to obey or support a ruler that did not necessarily coincide with the inherited precedent within their particular schools.

Jurists responded to the disparity between the legal doctrine and socio-political realities in a variety of ways. The discourse on rebellion had become firmly established, but it had also become more diverse and complex. This diversity and complexity, as well as a degree of pronounced frustration, is well represented in a *fatwā* issued by the Mālikī jurist Aḥmad al-Wansharīsī (d. 914/1508). In dealing with whether it is lawful to rebel against an unjust ruler, he starts out by complaining that the public or laity (*al-ᶜāmma*) does not listen. He states:

> The public has found it difficult to accept the *fatwā* [in this matter] and refused to abide by it. [But] it is not the fault of the laity, rather it is the fault of that type of people (*dhālika al-ṣinf*) who lend credence to their dissension. They are either non-believers or Khawārij ... [who] permit rebellion against the unjust ruler. But the people of truth (*ahl al-ḥaqq*) who are the [true] people of *Sunna* and tradition said that it is better to persevere in obeying the unjust ruler because sound principles dictate that the greater of two evils must be abandoned.[3]

Al-Wansharīsī's *fatwā* is important not because of what it says, but because of what it fails to state. Obviously he is frustrated by the unwillingness of an undefined public to accept the idea that an unjust ruler should be obeyed. Although he accuses those who legalized rebellion of being unbelievers or seditious individuals, he is clearly referring to individuals who carry a degree of moral weight with the laity, and who are able to persuade them that rebellion is not a sin. The fact that he resorts to invoking the invariably vague notion of *ahl al-sunna* in support of his argument indicates that he was appealing to an assumed orthodoxy on the matter, and it also that he was responding to an unyielding social reality. In other words, he was responding to an existing social dynamic that did not necessarily accept his unequivocal and dogmatic prohibition against rebellion. As such, al-Wansharīsī's frustration is real. It is very likely that he was not responding to unbelievers and Khawārij but also that he was reacting to other jurists who advocated doctrines concerning rebellion that he found divisive and objectionable. In fact, what al-Wansharīsī alludes to but tries to ignore is that by his age, there existed

3 Al-Wansharīsī, *al-Miᶜyār*, v:34–5. The author goes on to argue that even if a ruler demands the payment of unjust taxes, he should be obeyed. Furthermore, he asserts that a ruler enjoys a status equivalent to the Prophet, and should be obeyed just as the Prophet was obeyed. The only difference is that in the case of a corrupt ruler, people should pray to God to guide the ruler away from injustice.

several juridical tendencies on rebellion, some of which were at odds with his own position.[4]

I will describe these various tendencies in turn. I have categorized them in terms of their attitude towards the inherited doctrines of rebellion and towards the necessity of obeying and supporting those in power. Some jurists advocated unequivocal support for those in power, but otherwise did not revise or alter the rules of rebellion in any significant way. Other jurists agreed that those in power should be obeyed, but also expanded the scope and reach of the laws of rebellion in a technical but significant fashion. Some juridical views adopted a neutral stand and refused to support either the rulers or rebels, while other views sanctioned rebellion against unjust rulers without limitation. Under some of these positions, the idea that rebellion against unjust rulers is justified, or at least tolerated, found support. One suspects that it is this diversity in juridical opinion that partly explains the tone of frustration found in al-Wansharīsī's *fatwā*.[5] I have categorized the various views and tendencies into two main categories: the traditional and revisionist trends. For the most part, the traditional trend did not alter or reconstruct the basic framework of *aḥkām al-bughāh*. The revisionist trend modified substantial and essential parts of the discourse.

THE TRADITIONAL TREND

The traditional view inherited the developed doctrines of the law of rebellion, and continued to reiterate them without any substantial change. The basic doctrines of the law of rebellion distinguished between a bandit and a rebel, and held that if a group rebels while adhering to an interpretation and while enjoying an unspecified degree of strength or power, this group qualifies as *bughāh*. As *bughāh*, the group should

[4] Ibn Khaldūn (d. 808/1406) (*al-Muqaddima*, 159–60) asserts that many of the *ʿāmma* (laity) and the *fuqahāʾ* (jurists) advocate or become involved in rebellions. These pious individuals, Ibn Khaldūn argues, do so believing that they are obeying God's command by enjoining the good and forbidding the evil. In reality, all they succeed in accomplishing is destroying themselves and others. Ibn Khaldūn argues that God did not command that people cast themselves unto ruin. God commanded people to resist evil only if they are able to do so effectively. He notes that many people follow in the footsteps of these misguided individuals. He concludes by recommending that if these rebels are insane then they should be treated, and if they are not insane they should be punished. Both al-Wansharīsī and Ibn Khaldūn were frustrated by the social and theological support given to the idea of rebellion.

[5] Interestingly, al-Wansharīsī himself was the subject of persecution in Tilmisān. His house was raided and destroyed, and he escaped to Fez where he eventually died. See al-Ziriklī, *al-Aʿlām*, 1:269; al-Wansharīsī, *al-Miʿyār*, 1:3.

be treated with a certain degree of tolerance, although Sunnī jurists disagreed on the specific treatment to be afforded to rebels. At a minimum, the majority of Sunnī jurists agreed that the rebels are not to be held liable for life and property destroyed during the course of their rebellion, and that, as a general matter, rebels may not be executed and their properties may not be confiscated. Of course, what could be considered traditional to each school differs according to the particular precedents of the school. For example, the traditional Ḥanafī position maintained that the rebels are sinners while the traditional Ḥanbalī view disagreed. Nonetheless, what characterizes what I describe as the traditional trend is its resistance to change or revision. What also characterizes the traditional trend is the insistence on the principle that whoever is in power must be obeyed and supported, and that rebels be treated leniently.

Aḥkām al-bughāh, as argued earlier, originated in the late second/eighth and early third/ninth centuries as a radical doctrine, which was intentionally unhelpful to the state. It was sympathetic and intentionally tolerant of rebels. As argued earlier, it was asserted that *aḥkām al-bughāh* applied to rebels whether the ruler was just or not. The justness of the ruler was rendered an irrelevant consideration, and thus a ruler could not argue that since he was just, he was not bound by *aḥkām al-bughāh.* But the dynamics of the discourses on rebellion had changed materially by the sixth/twelfth century. The traditional doctrines of *aḥkām al-bughāh* had become widely accepted in juridical circles, but the gap between the political realities and the legal discourse had become wide and apparent. Therefore, by the sixth/twelfth century, supporting the traditional inherited doctrines of *aḥkām al-bughāh*, without any material revision, had become an argument in favor of the status quo. In many ways, supporting the traditional doctrines on rebellion became a tacit acceptance of the irrelevance and marginality of the discourse except for its sectarian overtones. The traditional trend, which regurgitates the inherited doctrines without any material revision, tended to focus on the need to obey whoever was in power, just or unjust, and then quickly rehashed the technical rules relating to the treatment of rebels. The emphasis of the traditional trend is on the need to obey whoever is in power, and not necessarily on the treatment of the rebels. As such, it emphasized the illegality of rebellion and not necessarily the broad applicability of *aḥkām al-bughāh.* Unlike the early discourses, the traditional trend was concerned not so much with giving *aḥkām al-bughāh* the broadest application possible; rather, it was primarily concerned with discouraging rebellions.[6] The traditional trend is represented primarily by Ḥanbalī, and some Shāfiᶜī and Ḥanafī, jurists. Most Mālikī jurists can be categorized under the traditional trend as well, but they represent a special case and will be dealt with separately below.

Jurists from within the traditional trend emphasized that regardless of how a ruler comes to power, he or she must be obeyed. The imperative of obedience does not change even if the usurper of power is a child or woman.[7] The only relevant consideration is whether the ruler is able to establish order and stability. If order and stability exists, then rebellion is by necessity forbidden.[8] Whether the ruler is substantively just or unjust is largely irrelevant; rebellion in all circumstances remains illegal.[9] Jurists from this trend conceded that early on in Islamic history, notables such as al-Ḥusayn and Ibn al-Zubayr rebelled against unjust rulers. Of course, these early rebellions pose a serious theological problem for the traditional trend because the jurists did not wish to argue that the likes

[6] I do not want to overstate this point because, as we will see, even the traditional trend expended a considerable amount of energy in defending the theological status of certain rebels.

[7] Ibn Ḥajar al-Haytamī (Shāfiᶜī, d. 974/1566–7), *Fatḥ*, II:295; al-Anṣārī (Shāfiᶜī, d. 926/1520), *Fatḥ*, 155. Al-Qazwīnī (Shāfiᶜī, d. 623/1226), in his *al-ᶜAzīz*, XI:75–6, states that obedience is a functional necessity for unity and stability even if the ruler is unjust.

[8] Ibn Qudāma (Ḥanbalī, d. 620/1223–4), *al-Mughnī*, X:48. Ibn Qudāma (*al-Kāfī*, IV:146) cites the precedent of ᶜAbd al-Malik b. Marwān in support of the argument that a usurper becomes legitimately entitled to power. Al-Zarkashī (Ḥanbalī, d. 772/1370), in his *Sharḥ*, VI:216–17, cites the same precedent, arguing that ᶜAbd al-Malik b. Marwān rebelled against Ibn al-Zubayr and defeated him. Yet ᶜAbd al-Malik b. Marwān became the legitimate ruler. See also al-Buhūtī (Ḥanbalī, d. 1051/1651), *Kashshāf*, VI:158, 160; al-Mardāwī (Ḥanbalī, d. 885/1480–1), *al-Inṣāf*, X:310–11.

[9] Ibn Mufliḥ (Ḥanbalī, d. 763/1361), in his *Kitāb*, VI:159–60, notes that two Ḥanbalī jurists, Ibn al-Jawzī and Ibn ᶜAqīl, permitted rebellion against an unjust ruler. The author, however, rejects this position and argues that rebellion is never permitted, and that impatience and ignorance are the causes of all rebellions. Also see Ibn al-Muqrī (Shāfiᶜī, d. 837/1433), *al-Irshād*, II:295. Ibn Ḥajar al-Haytamī (Shāfiᶜī, d. 974/1566–7) adds that the doors of sedition must be closed. Therefore, regardless of the degree of *ijtihād* or knowledge a rebel may reach, rebellion is never justified: *Fatḥ*, II:294. Al-Qasṭalānī (d. 923/1517), in his *Irshād*, X:170, 220, argues that rebellion is not permitted as long as the ruler's commands or behavior are defensible under any possible interpretation. See also al-Ḥubayshī (d. 1283/1866), *Fatḥ*, 406–7; al-Ghamrāwī, *Anwār*, 253; Ibn Luʾluʾa (Shāfiᶜī, d. 769/1367), *ᶜUmda*, II:302. Al-Ālūsī (Ḥanafī, d. 1270/1853), in his *Rūḥ*, XXVI:151, adds that a rebel commits a grave sin if he rebels without a *taʾwīl* or with a *taʾwīl* that is clearly false. Al-Qurṭubī (Mālikī, d. 671/1273), who does not belong to the traditional trend, claims that *ahl al-ḥadīth* was the only group to outlaw rebellion in all circumstances: al-Qurṭubī, *al-Jāmiᶜ* (1952), VI:157. Also see Ibn ᶜĀbidīn (Ḥanafī, d. 1252/1836–7), *Radd*, VI:411. Al-ᶜĀbidīn belonged to the revisionist trend. He argued, however, that rebellion was prohibited because in his day and age all those who competed over power were motivated by greed, and thus it became impossible to distinguish the just from the unjust. Al-Ḥaṭṭāb (Mālikī, 954/1547), in his *Mawāhib*, VI:277–8, states that while the Muᶜtazila and Khawārij held that it is imperative to rebel against unjust rulers, the people of righteousness (*ahl al-ḥaqq wa humm ahl al-sunna*) held that it is not permissible to do so. However, he goes on to add that Muslims should not aid or cooperate with unjust rulers.

of al-Ḥusayn committed a wrongful act. However, they resolved the theological challenge by distinguishing such precedents. For the most part, these jurists argued that in early Islam rebellion was, in fact, permitted; nevertheless, a subsequent late *ijmāᶜ* (consensus) was reached forbidding all rebellions regardless of the reason. Therefore, while it was permissible for al-Ḥusayn to rebel against Yazīd, this precedent was no longer effective or persuasive.[10] Hence, since the reported consensus, even if the rebels have just cause or even if the specific interpretation adopted by the rebels is religiously correct, rebellion remains forbidden. The traditional trend goes further and argues that, as a legal matter, the ruler is always right (*muḥiqq*) and the rebels are always wrong.[11] A ruler is conclusively presumed to be right, and no inquiry should be made in the qualitative nature of the rebels' interpretations or claims. While these jurists often reiterate the maxim that no ruler should be obeyed if he commands a sin, nevertheless, they also argue that a sinful order should be passively resisted without a resort to arms.[12]

[10] Al-Jamal (Shāfiᶜī), *Ḥāshiya*, v:114; Ibn al-Muqrī, *al-Irshād*, II:295; Ibn Lu'lu'a, *ᶜUmda*, II:302. Al-'Ubbī (d. 828/1424) did not necessarily belong to the traditional trend. However, he reports on the various opinions regarding this debate. Part of the debate is whether the people of Medina rebelled against al-Ḥajjāj because he was iniquitous (*fāsiq*) or an unbeliever (*kāfir*): al-'Ubbī, *Sharḥ*, VI:529, 554, 564. If people rebelled because al-Ḥajjāj was iniquitous, that could mean that rebellion is permitted against any iniquitous ruler. If, however, al-Ḥajjāj was an unbeliever, that could mean that rebellion is permitted only if the ruler effectively becomes a *kāfir*. Most jurists from the traditional trend argued that this debate had become irrelevant after the reported consensus prohibiting rebellion was reached. Ibn Mufliḥ (*Kitāb*, VI:160–1) states that some ignorant Sunnīs went as far as claiming that al-Ḥajjāj was right and al-Ḥusayn was wrong. The author contends that such people make this claim because they seek to antagonize the Shīᶜa. However, he rejects their argument and asserts that al-Ḥusayn was clearly justified in rebelling against al-Ḥajjāj. Nonetheless, al-Ḥusayn's precedent can no longer justify rebellion. Also see al-ᶜAbādī (d. 994/1585), *Ḥāshiya*, XI:330–2, who prohibits rebellion and adds that condemning or cursing Muᶜāwiya or Yazīd is not permissible.

[11] Ibn Qudāma, *al-Kāfī*, IV:154; Ibn Mufliḥ (Ḥanbalī, 884/1479), in his *al-Mubdiᶜ*, IX:159, states that it is irrelevant whether the interpretation adopted by the rebels is right or erroneous; al-Zarkashī (*Sharḥ*, VI:222–5) makes the same point. See also al-Buhūtī, *Kashshāf*, VI:161; Ibn Qāsim (Ḥanbalī, d. 1392/1972–3), *Ḥāshiya*, VII:390, 397. See also al-Shirbīnī (Shāfiᶜī, d. 972/1569–70), *Mughnī*, IV:123.

[12] al-Shawkānī (Zaydī, d. 1250/1834), *al-Sayl*, IV:509, 556; al-Shawkānī, *Nayl*, VII:174. Although the author was not a Sunnī, he could be considered part of the traditional trend. Although he was outwardly Zaydī, al-Shawkānī was actually Wahhābī and Shāfiᶜī. Al-Shawkānī insists that in the vast majority of situations rebellion is not permitted. At one point he argues that as long as an unjust ruler permits Muslims to pray, rebellion is prohibited. At another point he argues that as long as the ruler's commands are not clearly violative of the fundamental principles of religion, rebellion is not permitted: *Nayl*, VII:171–5. Nonetheless, rather inconsistently, he also argues that unjust rulers may be removed if the attempt to remove them would not lead to *fitna* or injustice. Al-Shawkānī is careful to point out that al-Ḥusayn and other ᶜAlids did not commit a wrong by becoming involved in rebellions in early Islam. He however argues that their precedent is not applicable to later ages because the early ᶜAlid rebels were more knowledgeable

Several jurists, especially Shāfiᶜī and Ḥanafī, from the traditional trend continued to repeat the formula that *baghy* is an act of rebellion against the just (*ᶜādil*) ruler. However, this formulaic language did not connote a substantive difference. Typically, after repeating the above-mentioned phrase, these jurists would go on to state that rebellion is prohibited in all or most circumstances. Effectively, the word *ᶜādil* (just) was used as the equivalent of the term *ᶜadl* or rightful. As discussed above, a ruler is rightful whether he or she came to power through usurpation (*bi al-taghallub*), and whether he or she is just or unjust. The Shāfiᶜī jurist al-Shirbīnī (d. 977/1569–70) makes this point abundantly clear. He argues that the rebels are to be considered *bughāh*, even if they are just and the ruler is unjust. He notes that while some jurists state that the *bughāh* are those who rebel against the *ᶜādil* (just), these jurists mean to say the rightful ruler (*ᶜadl*). Therefore, both expressions, *ᶜādil* and *ᶜadl*, mean the rightful ruler, and not the just ruler.[13] Many jurists from the traditional trend omit the words "just" or "rightful" altogether, and simply define *baghy* as an act of rebellion against the ruler or the established ruler (*imām muṭāᶜ* or *man thabatata imāmatuhu*).[14]

Despite the heavy emphasis on the prohibition against rebellion, the traditional trend does not criminalize the act of rebellion. Rather, it often

in religion than anyone who might have come after them: ibid., VII:176. Al-Shawkānī was a judge in Sanaᶜāʾ, Yemen: see al-Ziriklī, *al-Aᶜlām*, VI:298. He expresses conflicting views on the issue of rebellion. On the one hand, he demonstrates a clear preference for order and stability regardless of the perceived injustice. On the other hand, he is unable to logically and systematically distinguish the early precedents set by ᶜAlid rebels.

13 Al-Shirbīnī, *Mughnī*, IV:123. For reasons explained below, al-Shirbīnī himself should be categorized under the revisionist and not the traditional trend. His linguistic assertion that *ᶜādil* and *ᶜadl*, in this context, mean the same thing is true as far as the traditional and revisionist trend is concerned. Al-Dimashqī (Shāfiᶜī, d. 808/1405), *Kifāya*, 492, uses the term *al-ᶜadl*; al-Kāsānī (Ḥanafī, d. 587/1191), in his *Badāʾiᶜ*, VII:140, uses the expression *imām ahl al-ᶜadl*. Al-Marghīnānī (Ḥanafī, d. 593/1196–7), in *al-Hidāya*, II:170, uses the expressions *al-imām* and *al-imām al-ḥaqq* (the rightful ruler) interchangeably. Ibn al-Muqrī, (*al-Irshād*, II:295) uses the word *imām* but explains that it means *imām ahl al-ᶜadl*. Ibn ᶜĀbidīn (*Ḥāshiya*, VI:411) uses the expression *al-imām al-ḥaqq* and *al-imām al-ᶜādil* interchangeably. He explains that both expressions mean whichever ruler has been able to seize power and establish order. Ibn Mufliḥ (*al-Mubdiᶜ*, IX:159) uses *al-imām* and *al-imām al-ᶜādil* interchangeably. Al-ᶜAbādī (Shāfiᶜī, d. 994/1585), in *Ḥāshiya*, XI:330, asserts that *ᶜādil* and *ᶜadl* have the same meaning.

14 Ibn Qudāma, *al-Mughnī*, X:48, 52; Ibn Qudāma, *al-Kāfī*, IV:146; al-Mardāwī, *al-Inṣāf*, X:310; al-Zarkashī, *Sharḥ*, VI:215, 217. Among the jurists that state *imām* without any qualifiers are the following: Abū Shujāᶜ (Shāfiᶜī, d. 593/1196–7), *Matn*, 306–7; al-Anṣārī, *al-Manhaj*, V:113–14; al-Bayḍāwī (Shāfiᶜī, d. 685/1286), *al-Ghāya*, II:919; Abū al-Barakāt (Ḥanbalī, d. 652/1254), *al-Muḥarrar*, in Ibn Mufliḥ (Ḥanbalī, d. 763/1361), *al-Nukat*, II:166; al-Maqdisī (Ḥanbalī, d. 624/1226), *al-ᶜUdda*, 575, 578; al-Buhūtī (Ḥanbalī, d. 1051/1651), *al-Rawḍ*, 517; al-Maqdisī (Ḥanbalī, d. 1033/1623), *Dalīl*, 275; Ibn Mufliḥ, *Kitab*, VI:152; al-Sharqāwī (Shāfiᶜī, 1226/1811), *Ḥāshiya*, IV:273.

repeats that *baghy* is not a term that connotes blame (*laysa bi ismi dhamm*).[15] The rebels must enjoy both a *shawka* and a *ta'wīl*; the *shawka* is simply a damage-control principle. If the *shawka* was not required, the jurists argued, individuals would invent a *ta'wīl* in order to escape from liability for their acts.[16] But it is the existence of a plausible interpretation that substantively distinguishes between rebels and bandits. In fact, several jurists from the traditional trend argued that the reports attributed to the Prophet condemning all rebels as impious or sinners must be understood to apply only to those who rebel without a plausible interpretation. These traditions, they argued, were not intended to condemn rebels who rely on a plausible interpretation or cause.[17] Because the rebels rely on a plausible interpretation or cause, they are to be considered similar to jurists who disagree on particular points of law (*ka al-fuqahā'al-mujtahidīn fī al-furūᶜ*). Hence, the Ḥanbalī Ibn Qudāma (d. 620/1223–4) states: "The *bughāh* . . . are not dissolute (*laysū bi fāsiqīn*), but they are wrong in their interpretations, and the ruler and the loyalists (*al-imām wa ahl al-ᶜ adl*) are right in resisting them. All of them [the ruler and the rebels] are like jurists who disagree on specific points of law."[18] Importantly, however,

[15] Al-Ramlī, *Nihāya*, VII:402; al-Jamal, *Ḥāshiya*, V:113; al-ᶜAynī, *ᶜUmda*, XXIV:90; al-ᶜAbādī, *Ḥāshiya*, XI:330; al-Sharqāwī, *Ḥāshiya*, IV:273; al-Qazwīnī, *al-ᶜAzīz*, XI:70. Al-Ḥubayshī (*Fatḥ*, 406) adopts the unusual position that the notion that *baghy* is a term not connoting blame only applies to the early generations of Islam. He implies that those who rebelled after the early generations were in fact iniquitous or sinners. Interestingly, however, his particular rulings on the treatment of rebels are not different from the rulings of the jurists with whom he disagrees. Al-Qanūjī (Ḥanbalī, d. 1253/1837), in his *al-Rawḍa*, II:480, asserts that rebellion is a grave inequity (*maᶜṣiya ᶜazīma*).

[16] Al-Buhūtī (*Kashshāf*, VI:161) adds that if the rebels number around ten individuals, they lack a *shawka* and should be treated as bandits. Ibn Qudāma (*al-Mughnī*, X:49) states the same. See also Ibn Mufliḥ, *al-Mubdiᶜ*, IX:159. Ibn Qāsim (*Ḥāshiya*, VII:391) asserts that two, three, or ten individuals are to be treated as bandits. Al-Zarkashī (*Sharḥ*, VI:217–18) notes that if the rebels lack a plausible interpretation, they are to be treated as bandits. He also notes that there is disagreement on the status of rebels who have a plausible interpretation but lack a *shawka*. See also al-Mardāwī, *al-Inṣāf*, X:311–12; Ibn Qudāma, *al-Kāfī*, IV:146.

[17] Al-Makkī, *Fayḍ*, II:303; al-Jamal, *Ḥāshiya*, V:113; Ibn Ḥajar al-ᶜAsqalānī, *Fatḥ*, XIV:530. This specific point is often repeated by jurists from the revisionist trend.

[18] Ibn Qudāma, *al-Mughnī*, X:67, 70. See also Abū al-Barakāt, *al-Muḥarrar*, II:166; al-Makkī, *Fayḍ*, II:302, 303; al-Maqdisī, *al-ᶜUdda*, 578; al-Zarkashī, *Sharḥ*, VI:230–1; Ibn Mufliḥ, *al-Mubdiᶜ*, IX:165; al-Buhūtī, *Kashshāf*, VI:165, 166; Ibn Qāsim, *Ḥāshiya*, VII:396. Ibn Mufliḥ (*Kitāb*, VI:157) mentions that some Ḥanbalī jurists considered the *bughāh* sinners, but he refutes this position. Al-Maqbiliyyi (*al-Manār*, II:484) does the same. Ibn Qayyim al-Jawziyya (Ḥanbalī, d. 751/1350–1), in his *Aḥkām*, II:469–70, asserts that if the rebels sincerely believe that they are not committing a sin, they cannot be held liable. Therefore, he implies that the lack of a criminal motive is the primary justification for demanding the existence of a *ta'wīl*. Al-Jamal, a Shāfiᶜī, argues (*Ḥāshiya*, V:114, 115) that some rebels might incur a sin in the Hereafter because of the nature of the belief system they may adopt. But on this earth they are not to be treated as sinners. Al-Ghamrāwī (*Anwār*, 253–4) states that rebels are not sinners. Al-Wazīr (*al-ᶜAwāṣim*, VIII:14) claims that most Sunnīs did not consider rebellion against unjust rulers forbidden or sinful. See also Ibn Ḥajar al-ᶜAsqalānī, *Fatḥ*, XIV:312.

the rebels themselves do not need to be jurists or of an equal degree of learning or knowledge.[19] Furthermore, they do not need to rely on a specifically religious interpretation. In other words, the term *ta'wīl* does not necessarily mean a religious interpretation on a particular point of law. Rather, a *ta'wīl* could be either a disagreement on a legal point or simply a grievance (*maẓlama*). Therefore, a refusal to obey a command which the rebels believe to be illegal or unjust qualifies as a proper *ta'wīl*. If the ruler commands the rebels to pay taxes that they believe to be illegal, this qualifies as a recognizable *ta'wīl* as well.[20] Therefore, the ruler should warn the rebels before fighting them, and if they mention a grievance, the ruler should address it.[21]

Having accepted this basic premise of the discourse on rebellion, the traditional trend goes on to assert that the point in fighting the rebels is to repel their danger and not to destroy them. Furthermore, their legal acts including testimony in court and adjudications may be accepted or

[19] Al-Ramlī, *Nihāya*, VII:402; al-ᶜAbādī, *Ḥāshiya*, XI:330. Al-Qazwīnī (*al-ᶜAzīz*, XI:70) states that because of the *ta'wīl*, *baghy* cannot be considered a crime. Al-Sharqāwī (*Ḥāshiya*, IV:273) adopts an unusual position in implying that the rebels should be qualified to perform *ijtihād*, and that it is this qualification that exempts them from blame.

[20] Ḥanbalī sources assert that if two groups fight for tribal reasons or over power, they are liable to each other for life and property destroyed. However, if one of these groups is fighting pursuant to the commands of the ruler or is fighting to protect the ruler, then, by definition, this group is considered righteous and correct. The other group is treated as *bughāh*: Ibn Qudāma, *al-Mughnī*, X:72–3; Ibn Qudāma, *al-Kāfī*, IV:154. Ibn Qayyim al-Jawziyya (*Aḥkām*, II:470) asserts that those who fight for tribal reasons are not to be treated as rebels because they are not fighting over something that can constitute a legitimate claim of right. See also Abū al-Barakāt, *al-Muḥarrar*, II:167; al-Buhūtī, *al-Rawḍ*, 518; al-Buhūtī, *Kashshāf*, VI:167; Ibn Mufliḥ, *Kitāb*, VI:163; Ibn Mufliḥ, *al-Mubdiᶜ*, IX:170; al-Mardāwī, *al-Inṣāf*, X:325. Al-Baᶜalī (Ḥanbalī, d. 1189/1775), in *al-Rawḍ*, 478–9, indicates that if two factions fight due to ᶜ*aṣabiyya* or a desire for power, they are not *bughāh* and both factions must be held liable.

[21] Al-Makkī (*Fayḍ* II:302) argues that if the rebels attempt to overthrow the ruler or refuse to obey a law that implicates the rights of God or of the people, and which involves criminal or civil liabilities while relying on a plausible justification, this will count as a recognizable *ta'wīl*. Al-Dimashqī (*Kifāya*, 492) argues that the *bughāh* are those who refuse to obey the law or refuse to recognize a right belonging to God or to human beings while relying on a plausible justification. Al-Jamal (*Ḥāshiya*, V:114) mentions a list of acts that qualify as acts of rebellion. The list includes an attempt to overthrow the ruler or a refusal to pay taxes. The interpretation that the rebels rely on must be such that they sincerely believe that their mutiny is justified. Ibn Qudāma (*al-Mughnī*, X:52) states that the *bughāh* are those who refuse to obey the ruler or attempt to overthrow him while relying on a plausible justification. Al-Maqdisī (*al-ᶜUdda*, 575, 578) states that the *bughāh* are those who rebel seeking to overthrow the ruler while relying on a plausible interpretation. Ibn Mufliḥ (*Kitāb*, VI:152) reports that some jurists argued that the *bughāh* must seek to seize power or seek to give power to a person other than the ruler or else they are to be treated as common criminals. Al-Marghinānī (Ḥanafī, d. 593/1196–7), in his *al-Hidāya*, II:170, 172, states that the *bughāh* are those who disobey the ruler and rebel in certain territory while enjoying a plausible interpretation. He also argues that a wrong interpretation is considered the equivalent of a right interpretation if the rebels have a *shawka*. This could be read to mean that if the rebels have a considerable number of followers, no inquiry will be made regarding the correctness of their interpretation.

ratified.[22] Essentially, all the basic components of the discourse of rebellion are repeated without material revision or development. The fugitive, wounded, or captive may not be dispatched;[23] unless for dire necessity, weapons of mass destruction may not be used against rebels; rebel property may not be confiscated; rebels must be released after the fighting ends;[24] rebels are not to be held liable for life or property destroyed in the course of their rebellion;[25] funeral prayers may be performed on dead rebels; and the corpses of rebels may not be mutilated. Ḥanafī jurists continued to argue that rebels who have a *fiʾa* may be pursued and dispatched, and insisted that funeral prayers should not be performed on dead rebels.[26] Most Shāfiʿī and Ḥanbalī jurists continued to respond by arguing that the ruler may not seek the assistance of non-Muslims or Ḥanafīs in fighting rebels unless the ruler is able to restrain them from

22 Al-Ḥubayshī, *Fatḥ*, 407. Ibn Qudāma (*al-Mughnī*, x:69) adds that rebels may control a specific territory for years and that to refuse to recognize their legal acts would create undue hardship on the residents of the territory. See also Ibn Mufliḥ, *al-Mubdiʿ*, ix:165. Ḥanafī jurists continued to argue that the ruler does not have legal jurisdiction over the rebel camp. In fact, al-Kāsānī (*Badāʾiʿ*, vii:141) argues that from the point of view of jurisdiction, the camp of the rebels and the abode of non-believers are equals. However, al-Marghīnānī (Ḥanafī, d. 593/1196–7) argues in his *al-Hidāya*, ii:171 that although the ruler does not have jurisdiction over acts committed in the rebels' camp, he does have jurisdiction over acts committed in territory conquered by rebels. Also see al-Afghānī (Ḥanafī, d. 1326/1908), *Kashf*, i:329.

23 Al-Bayḍāwī (*al-Ghāya*, ii:920) states that the fugitive and captive may not be pursued even if it is feared that the rebels will regroup.

24 Ibn Qudāma (*al-Mughnī*, x:64) reports that there is some disagreement as to whether, if the rebels refuse to exchange prisoners of war, the loyalists may continue to detain captive rebels. Al-Buhūtī, (*Kashshāf*, vi:164–5) argues that if the ruler fears that the rebels will regroup in the *immediate* future, he may continue to detain the rebels until this danger subsides. But al-Mardāwī (*al-Inṣāf*, x:315) notes that there is disagreement on this point. See also Ibn Mufliḥ, *al-Mubdiʿ*, ix:163; al-Ḥubayshī, *Fatḥ*, 408.

25 Ibn Qudāma, *al-Mughnī*, x:61; Ibn Mufliḥ, *al-Mubdiʿ*, ix:164–5. Al-Mardāwī (*al-Inṣāf*, x: 316–17) adopts the unusual position that the rebels should be exempt from financial liability but not from criminal liability. Al-Zamakhsharī (Ḥanafī, 538/1143), in his *Ruʾūs*, 479, misrepresents the Shāfiʿī position by arguing that the Ḥanafīs exempt the rebels from liability but the Shāfiʿīs do not. Of course, this could be a copyist's error, but from the context of the text, I think it is unlikely. Ḥanafī jurists belonging to the traditional trend continued to argue that although the rebels are not liable for life and property destroyed on this earth, they will be held liable in the Hereafter: al-Marghīnānī, *al-Hidāya*, ii:172. Interestingly, some jurists, most notably Shāfiʿīs, from the traditional trend argued that neither the loyalists nor the rebels should be held liable for life or property destroyed if what was destroyed was reasonably related to the rebellion. In all probability, this is a means/ends test – the means pursued must be related to the ends. Life and property destroyed by loyalists and rebels must be incidental or necessary to the rebellion. This position becomes common in the revisionist trend. See al-Makkī, *Fayḍ*, ii:303; al-Ḥubayshī, *Fatḥ*, 408. Al-Jamal (*Ḥāshiya*, v:116) adds that what the rebels did can neither be described as *ḥalāl* or *ḥarām*, but simply as a mistake that should be forgiven.

26 Al-Kāsānī, *Badāʾiʿ*, vii:140–1, 142; al-Ghunaymī, *al-Lubāb*, iv:154–5. See the discussion on this issue in al-Shawkānī, *Nayl*, vii:170; al-Shawkānī, *al-Sayl*, iv:558.

pursuing or dispatching rebels.[27] Some jurists argued that if a loyalist kills a rebel before or after the rebellion, or kills a fugitive, wounded, or captive rebel, the loyalist must be held liable for his transgression.[28]

It is difficult to assess the extent to which the traditional trend was ideologically committed to the doctrines pertaining to the treatment of rebels. There is a question as to the extent this trend repeated these doctrines out of fidelity to precedent and the imperatives of legal culture, and to what extent it promoted this discourse as a means to achieving a moral or social agenda.[29] As noted above, the traditional trend placed a heavy emphasis on the need to obey the ruler, and on condemning rebellion under all circumstances. This trend was not willing to entertain the possibility that, under exceptional circumstances, it might be lawful to rebel or that the ruler might become illegitimate. Although the traditional trend's insistence on preserving the classical doctrines on rebellion cannot be dismissed as simply the product of legal formalism,[30] the fact that there was no serious attempt to amend or change the doctrines on rebellion points to an unmistakable degree of ambivalence about this field of the law. It is quite probable that the jurists of this trend repeated the rules pertaining to the treatment of rebels without an ideological commitment to this area of the law. In other words, it is doubtful that they were citing these rules as a way to criticize the conduct of the state in dealing with rebels or to morally empower rebels against the state. In fact, some jurists, particularly from the Ḥanbalī school, adopted the early Mālikī position that sectarians such as the Murji'a, Qadariyya, and Shīᶜīs should be asked to repent or be killed – not for their *baghy*, but for causing corruption on the earth. In effect, these jurists circumvented the restrictions of the doctrines of rebellion by arguing that if sectarian groups (*ahl al-ahwā'* or *ahl al-bidaᶜ*) rebel initially, they are to be treated as

27 Ibn Qudāma, *al-Mughnī*, X:53–7, 61, 63–6; al-Dimashqī, *Kifāya*, 492–3. However, al-Makkī, a Shāfiᶜī (*Fayḍ*, II:303) adopts the Ḥanafī position on the existence of a *fi'a*.

28 Ibn Qudāma, *al-Kāfī*, IV:150. In *al-Mughnī*, X:60, 64, he also notes that ᶜAlī paid from the public treasury the blood money of rebels killed while retreating. See also al-Maqdisī, *al-ᶜUdda*, 576–7; Ibn Mufliḥ, *al-Mubdiᶜ*, IX:162, 165; al-Buhūtī, *al-Kashshāf*, VI:164. Al-Zarkashī (*Sharḥ*, VI:225) implies that if the loyalists exceed the limits of lawful conduct in dealing with the rebels, they are to be held liable on this earth and in the Hereafter.

29 Part of the moral agenda, of course, was simply sectarian: namely, the need to uphold the credibility of the Companions who rebelled against ᶜAlī and condemn the rebels against ᶜUthmān. This is particularly obvious in the treatment of someone such as al-Sharqāwī (*Ḥāshiya*, IV:282).

30 One option was to simply omit the discourse on the treatment of rebels. The Shāfiᶜī jurist al-Bakrī (*Iᶜāna*, 166–7) did just that. He addresses the laws of banditry but omits the discussion on rebellion. See also al-Jamāᶜīlī (d. 600/1203), *al-ᶜUmda*; ᶜAbd al-Ḥalīm (d. 1088/1677), *al-Ḥāshiya*, I:404–7.

rebels entitled to the protections of *aḥkām al-bughāh*. However, ultimately they may be killed for causing corruption on the earth, and not for the act of rebellion.[31] All of this indicates a certain lack of commitment to the discourses pertaining to the treatment of rebels by jurists from this trend. Adopting the ambiguities associated with the early Mālikī debates on this issue compromises the authoritativeness of the doctrines of rebellion. The question then remains: Why did the jurists of the traditional trend continue to reassert the rules of conduct pertaining to the treatment of rebels who have a *ta'wīl* and *shawka*?

There is no question that part of the answer is that the discourses on rebellion had become firmly rooted in Islamic legal culture, and it would have been quite radical to ignore the inherited doctrines. But one can get a sense of the additional issues that preoccupied the jurists by examining new points of emphasis and focus in the text, or what I have referred to as the linguistic practice of the jurists. It is the points of emphasis or re-emphasis, and the points that are not repeated according to inherited formulaic language, that provide the best insight into the social and political concerns of the jurists. We have already noted that jurists from the traditional trend focused on the need for order and stability, and it is clear that this issue was one of their primary concerns. The other issue that preoccupied them was the distinction between rebels and bandits, and whether the various sects of the Khawārij should be treated as rebels. We have already noted that many of the Khawārij, Qarāmiṭa, and Bāṭiniyya sects pursued tactics similar in nature to those pursued by bandits.[32] They targeted civilians and moving caravans, and adopted non-conventional means of warfare. Furthermore, the Khawārij, Qarāmiṭa, Bāṭiniyya, and similar groups spread terror by pursuing a policy of stealth attacks (*qatl al-ghīla*) and indiscriminate slaughter. This issue became particularly important after the Mongol invasion because of the indiscriminate slaughter committed by the Mongols, and because the Mongols ultimately converted to Islam. Hence, those committing the slaughter

[31] Ibn Mufliḥ, *al-Mubdiᶜ*, IX:160, 169: Mardāwī (*al-Inṣāf*, X:322–4) reports on various positions and argues that the Shīᶜīs are worse than the Khawārij, and that they should be killed. See the discussion on this matter in Ibn Qudāma, *al-Mughnī*, X:58–60, 67, who does not support the idea that the sectarians should be asked to repent or be killed, but he does argue that sectarians are *fasaqa* and that their testimony should not be accepted in court, and funeral prayers should not be performed over their dead. See al-Subkī (Shāfiᶜī, d. 756/1355), *Fatāwā*, II:566–93, which has a lengthy *responsum* on the execution of *ahl al-ahwā'*.

[32] Ibn Ḥajar al-ᶜAsqalānī, *Fatḥ*, XIV:306; al-'Ubbī, *Sharḥ*, VI:556; Ibn Taymiyya, *Majmūᶜ al-Fatāwā*, XXXV:13.

were formally Muslims.[33] Furthermore, perhaps the Mongols desired to achieve certain political objectives but, unlike the Khawārij or Bāṭiniyya, they were not theologically motivated.

The jurists of the traditional trend discuss whether rebels who do not rely on a plausible interpretation or cause should be treated as bandits or whether they should be simply held liable for life and property destroyed.[34] The distinction is significant because bandits are either executed, crucified, have limbs amputated from opposite ends, or banished.[35] Furthermore, bandits may not be forgiven for their transgressions unless they repent and surrender before they are captured, and even then, the victims of their banditry have the right to demand exaction. Rebels who do not qualify for the protections afforded by the status of *baghy*, but who also are not considered bandits, are treated as common criminals not subject to the particularly harsh penalties of banditry. In other words, even if a group does not qualify to be treated as *bughāh*, there is a serious substantive difference as to whether the group is given the status of common criminals or bandits. The question then becomes: If the jurists refuse to recognize the plausibility of a group's interpretation or cause, what is the status of such a group?

Jurists from the traditional trend focus much of their discussion on whether groups such as the Khawārij have a recognizable, plausible

33 This is clearly so in the case of Tamerlane, who became a Muslim and continued to slaughter. Furthermore, Ibn Taymiyya and others speak of Mongol converts to Islam who continued to pillage and plunder.

34 Ibn Qudāma, *al-Mughnī*, X:49; in *al-Kāfī*, IV:146, he states that if the rebels lack either a plausible interpretation or a degree of strength, they are bandits; al-Buhūtī (*al-Rawḍ*, 517) states the same; al-Maqdisī (*Dalīl*, 275) states the same; Ibn Mufliḥ (*Kitāb*, VI:152) states the same; Ibn Mufliḥ (*al-Mubdiᶜ*, IX:159) states the same; al-Buhūtī (*Kashshāf*, VI:161) states the same; Ibn Qāsim (*Ḥāshiya*, VII:391) states the same. Al-Zarkashī (*Sharḥ*, VI:217–18) notes that if the rebels lack a plausible interpretation, they are to be treated as bandits. Al-Mardāwī (*al-Inṣāf*, X:311–12) states that there is disagreement over whether they are to be treated as bandits or common criminals. But he argues that those who lack *shawka* should be treated as bandits. Al-Dimashqī (*Kifāya*, 492) asserts that they are not to be treated as *bughāh*, but they are not to be treated as bandits either. Al-Jamal (*Ḥāshiya*, V:114–15) argues that those who lack a *taʾwīl* or *shawka* are to be held liable for their acts but are not to be treated as bandits. Those who intend to spread terror are to be treated as bandits. See also al-Ḥubayshī, *Fatḥ*, 407, who asserts that rebels should not be treated as bandits even if they lack one of the qualifying conditions for *baghy*. Al-Makkī (*Fayḍ*, II:302) argues that those who do not qualify as *bughāh* should be treated as common criminals and not bandits. Al-Ghamrāwī (*Anwār*, 253) asserts the same. Al-Wazīr (*al-ᶜAwāṣim*, VIII:15) argues that Sunnīs considered those who do not have an interpretation to be bandits, and he adds that Yazīd b. Muᶜāwiya and his like are the real bandits.

35 Al-Subkī (*Fatāwā*, II:581) cites the *ḥirāba* verse in the context of discussing heretical groups and argues that these groups wage war against God and the Prophet by cursing the Companions, but he says that the punishments of the law of banditry do not apply to them.

interpretation or not. Furthermore, if the group is declared not to have a plausible interpretation, what is the group's proper legal status? The material legal elements in the crime of banditry are the spread of terror (*al-ikhāfa* or *al-irᶜāb*), and the fact that bandits render their victims helpless (*ᶜadam luḥūq al-ghawth* or *inᶜidām al-ghawth*).[36] Hence, the material legal question is: What is the status of groups such as the Khawārij whose system of thought justifies the terrorizing and victimizing of people when they are most unable to resist? As we saw earlier, the Mālikī school had dealt with this specific issue and, as we will discuss below, continued to develop it further. The traditional trend, particularly among Ḥanbalī jurists, gravitated towards the Mālikī discourses on this point by extensively citing Mālikī views, but did not necessarily end up adopting positions identical to the Mālikī treatment. As noted below, several legal sources written after the sixth/twelfth century complain about the widespread practice of banditry particularly by what are called the *Aᶜrāb* (bedouins).[37] The traditional trend, however, does not specifically address the practice of these tribes. Rather, it focuses on whether groups such as the Khawārij should be denied the status of *baghy* despite the fact that they might have a plausible interpretation and a degree of strength. Al-Shahrastānī (d. 548/1153) argues that every group that rebelled from the time of the Companions and onwards were simply called the Khawārij.[38] Furthermore, several jurists argue that the Khawārij are *bughāh*, and that there is no material distinction between the Khawārij and any other rebellious group.[39] However, many other jurists argued that

[36] Al-Jamal, *Ḥāshiya*, V:152–3; al-Ḥubayshī, *Fatḥ*, 417; al-Zarkashī, *Sharḥ*, VI:364–5; Ibn Mufliḥ, *Kitāb*, VI:140; Ibn Mufliḥ, *al-Mubdiᶜ*, IX:146; Ibn Qāṣim, *Ḥāshiya*, VII:377; Ibn Qudāma, *al-Mughnī*, X:49–52, 58–60, 62–3; Ibn Qudāma, *al-Kāfī*, IV:168, 170; al-Bayḍāwī, *al-Ghāya*, II:933; al-Ghamrāwī, *Anwār*, 263; Ibn Qayyim al-Jawziyya, *Aḥkām*, II:470. Al-Makkī (*Fayḍ*, II:320) adds that if criminals attack people at home and render them helpless, the criminals are bandits. See al-Zamakhsharī, *Ruʾūs*, 499, who repeats the traditional Ḥanafī position that the crime of banditry cannot be committed in a town because people are not helpless in inhabited areas. Several jurists insisted that bandits must have a pecuniary motive of usurping money from their victims; Abū al-Barakāt, a Ḥanbalī, also adopts the Ḥanafī position that banditry can only be committed in the desert and not in urban centers: *al-Muḥarrar*, II:160. Also see al-Maqdisī, *al-ᶜUdda*, 570. Al-Buhūtī (*al-Rawḍ*, 515) argues that banditry could be committed in the desert, in urban centers, and in the sea. See also al-Buhūtī, *Kashshāf*, VI:150.

[37] Such bandits were often known as *ṣaᶜālīk*, *futtāk*, or *mansar*: see Kraemer, "Apostates," 63. See also Ibn Taymiyya, *al-Siyāsa*, 68; al-Jamal, *Ḥāshiya*, V:117, 153; al-Ramlī, *Nihāya*, VII:405, VIII:4; Ibn ᶜĀbidīn (d. 1252/1836–7), *al-ᶜUqūd* I:148.

[38] Al-Shahrastānī, *al-Milal*, I:132. See also al-Ḥubayshī, *Fatḥ*, 407, who argues that the Khawārij and rebels are the same; al-ᶜAynī (*ᶜUmda*, XXIV:84) mentions the debate over the status of the Khawārij. See also Ibn ᶜĀbidīn, *Radd*, VI:412; Ibn Ḥajar al-ᶜAsqalānī, *Fatḥ*, XIV:308.

[39] Al-Kāsānī, *Badāʾiᶜ*, VII:140. Al-Wazīr (*al-ᶜAwāṣim*, IV:369) claims that most Sunnī jurists did not consider the Khawārij infidels.

even if the Khawārij rely on an interpretation they should not be treated as *bughāh*, and, effectively, should be treated as bandits. This means that if the Khawārij destroy life or property, it is mandatory that they be held liable for their crimes. The ruler does not have discretion to pardon them, and their captives and fugitives may be dispatched. Yet another group of jurists argued that even if the Khawārij are considered rebels, they should be killed for causing corruption on the earth and not for their rebellion.[40]

By focusing on the status of the Khawārij, the traditional trend raises a much larger issue, namely, the status of groups who reject the very logic upon which the order of society is established. It is one thing to tolerate groups that rebel out of zeal for their own rights or because they wish to replace the head of state. In both of these situations, these groups accept the basic logic of law and order, and accept the corollary role of the jurists and their position as the spokespeople for the law of God. They do not necessarily seek to alter the foundation of law and order upon which juridical authority is established and promoted. However, it is quite another matter to tolerate groups that challenge the corporate institutions upon which juridical authority relies. Put differently, bandits or similar groups that pursue policies of indiscriminate slaughter also promote anarchy. This is the reason, for example, that the Ḥanbalī jurist Ibn Mufliḥ (d. 763/1361) argues that even if the Mongols convert to Islam, if they are fought, their wounded, fugitives, and captives may be dispatched, and their property confiscated. The conduct of the Mongols at war qualifies them for the status of bandits.[41] Fundamentally, by reiterating and emphasizing the treatment due to legally recognizable rebels, jurists of the traditional trend emphasized the difference between rebels who accept the legitimacy of Sunnī Muslim society but rebel against the political order, and rebels who accept neither the legitimacy of the political order nor the society it rules.[42] By emphasizing the lenient treatment to be given to rebels, Muslim jurists tacitly condemned groups that pursue indiscriminate slaughter and lawlessness.

[40] Ibn Mufliḥ, *al-Mubdiʿ*, IX:160–1, 169; al-Zarkashī, *Sharḥ*, VI:217–18; Ibn Mufliḥ, *Kitāb*, VI:152, 161; Ibn Qāsim, *Ḥāshiya*, VII:394, 396; al-Buhūtī, *Kashshāf*, VI:161; al-Mardāwī, *al-Inṣāf*, X:312–13, 323–4; al-Bayḍāwī, *al-Ghāya*, II:919; Ibn Qudāma, *al-Kāfī*, IV:146, 153. Al-Jamal (*Ḥāshiya*, V:115) argues that if the Khawārij intend to terrorize the wayfarer, then they should be treated as bandits.

[41] Ibn Mufliḥ, *Kitāb*, VI:162–3; Ibn Taymiyya (*al-Siyāsa*, 68, 71) singles out the bedouins, Turkomans, Kurds, and Mongol soldiers as groups who commit banditry.

[42] This is why the discussion on the status of the Khawārij focuses on "*man yastaḥillu dimāʾa al-muslimīn*" or "*man yukaffiru al-muslimīn*." This is considered the equivalent of causing corruption on the earth.

THE MĀLIKĪ TRADITIONALISTS

Thus far, we have postponed addressing the discourse of the Mālikī jurists on rebellion after the rise of the traditional trend. As discussed earlier, Mālikī jurists were latecomers to the discourses on rebellion, and it is important to trace separately the development of their discourses on the subject, as a school. Eventually, various Mālikī jurists became part of the different trends – traditionalist and revisionist. Nonetheless, before this development took place, Mālikī jurisprudence went through a process of transformation after the fifth/eleventh century through which it accepted the traditional doctrines of *aḥkām al-bughāh*. It is clear that the reason for this transformation is the fact that this field of the law had become universally well established and Mālikī jurists needed either to develop a systematic reason to reject it or to transplant it into their own jurisprudential discourse. While some late Mālikī jurists continued to ignore the whole issue of the *bughāh*,[43] the majority accepted it as part of the general Muslim legal heritage and, as such, fully engaged the discourse. Interestingly, while some jurists adopted positions that had become the trademark of the traditional trend, several other Mālikī jurists led the movement to revise the traditional discourses. In other words, while Mālikī jurists around the sixth/twelfth century were heavily influenced by the inherited doctrines of *aḥkām al-bughāh*, Mālikī jurists around the ninth/fifteenth century in turn influenced the revisionist efforts on the subject.

[43] For instance, Ibn ʿAbd al-Rafīʿ (d. 733/1332), in his *Muʿīn*, II:878–9, addresses banditry but does not address rebellion. He argues that whoever terrorizes the wayfarer is a bandit. The author lived during a turbulent era under the Ḥafṣid dynasty in Tunisia (627/1229–982/1574). He himself apparently supported a rebellion: see ibid., I:37. Ibn ʿĀṣim (d. 829/1425), in his *Tuḥfa*, 280, deals extensively with banditry, arguing that it includes terrorizing the wayfarer, murder by deception or stealth (*ghīla*), and breaking and entering into a home and holding the occupants hostage. He comments that in his age, banditry was widespread in the Maghrib, but he does not address rebellion. Ibn Farḥūn (d. 799/1397), in his *Durra*, 173, passingly mentions the *bughāh*, but deals with banditry on pp. 318–19. Al-Nafrāwī (d. 1125/1713), in *al-Fawākih*, II:217, 222–3, deals extensively with banditry, noting that it is widespread in North Africa, and that bandit groups are powerful and often wreak havoc upon whole territories. Other than commenting that those who fight over political power or out of enmity or rancor are not bandits, he does not deal with rebellion. Al-ʿAdawī (d. 1189/1775), in his *Ḥāshiya*, II:249–55, extensively addresses banditry, noting that it is widespread among the bedouins of Africa, and that such bandits are capable of raiding and destroying wide areas of territory. He does not address rebellion except to state that if a group refuses to pay taxes while having the means to do so, even if they rely on an interpretation, the ruler may imprison them until they comply: ibid., 252. Al-Tasūlī (Madīdash) (a judge in Fez, d. 1258/1842), in his *al-Buhja*, II:347–9, 360–2, 373–4, extensively discusses banditry, noting that in Fez it was widespread and that bandits were respected and glorified, but does not deal with rebellion. See also al-Zarqānī (d. 1122/1710), *Sharḥ*.

As discussed earlier, Ibn Abī Zayd had adopted the law of rebellion and Ibn ᶜAbd al-Barr had achieved a synthesis between the doctrines of rebellion and banditry in the fifth/eleventh century. Nonetheless, the discourses on rebellion continued to occupy an ambiguous position among Mālikī jurists in the sixth/twelfth century. The notable Mālikī jurist and judge Ibn Rushd I (d. 520/1122) provided the nexus between the inherited Mālikī ambivalence towards this discourse and the traditional doctrines widely adopted by the other schools of law. He developed the theoretical justification for the eventual adoption of the doctrines of rebellion, but he also systematized and developed the Mālikī doctrines on banditry. Effectively, he laid the foundation for the adoption into Mālikī discourses of a systematic distinction between rebellion and banditry. Importantly, for the most part Ibn Rushd did not provide the theoretical justification by addressing rebellion directly. Rather, he focused most of his discussion on the conflict between the Companions, and on the rebellion of Muᶜāwiya against ᶜAlī.

Ibn Rushd adopts the traditional Sunnī position that neither ᶜAlī nor those who rebelled against him were morally or religiously blameworthy. He argues that all sides sincerely believed in the justness of their cause, and therefore all sides were acting in good faith. Nonetheless, Ibn Rushd argues that this does not mean that all sides were equally correct or that all their claims were of equal moral or religious worth. Rather, he maintains that ᶜAlī was clearly correct and his opponents were clearly wrong, and no discerning Muslim should believe otherwise. It is improper for a Muslim to adopt a position of moral relativism or neutrality and argue that all the competing parties were equally wrong or equally right. Ultimately, ᶜAlī was the rightful party and the others were mistaken.[44] Nevertheless, Ibn Rushd argues that neither of the contending parties was blameworthy because each of them had acted pursuant to their sincerely held belief. In the Hereafter, those who were ultimately right will be rewarded twice, and those who were wrong will be rewarded once. Those who were wrong are rewarded for acting upon what they sincerely believed to be the just position.[45] Importantly, he argues that

[44] Ibn Rushd I, *al-Bayān*, XVI:360–1, XVII:240–3, 486–8, XVIII:175–7. The Mālikī jurist Ibn al-ᶜArabī (d. 542/1147), in his *Kitāb*, II:593, argues that all the contending parties were partly right but ᶜAlī was closer to being correct than any of the other parties.

[45] Ibn al-ᶜArabī (*Aḥkām*, IV:1717–20) argues that the Companions did not fight over power or worldly affairs. Rather, they fought over a legal dispute. ᶜAlī believed that he should delay pursuing and prosecuting the murderers of ᶜUthmān until he was able to properly establish his power base and order in the empire. The other Companions believed that he should not delay the prosecution of ᶜUthmān's murderers because this should have been a point of first

it was imperative upon each and every Companion to act upon his or her own individual belief. Therefore, it is wrong to adopt a position of neutrality (*iʿtizāl*) and, as a matter of principle, to refuse to take a position on the conflict as a whole.[46] Ibn Rushd adds that as a matter of principle, one cannot obey a command which entails disobeying God, and that one must act upon what one sincerely believes is the divine imperative.[47] Significantly, Ibn Rushd was well aware that there is a certain risk inherent in his argument. The logic of his argument is such that it would support a resort to armed rebellion if one sincerely believes that such is the divine command, or that one's religious convictions require one to reject an illegal temporal command.[48] Ibn Rushd does not deal systematically with this risk, but simply warns that shedding the blood of fellow Muslims is a grave matter, and if it is taken lightly or dealt with negligently, it will result in committing a sin.[49] Therefore, using the example of the Companions, the import of Ibn Rushd's argument is that rebellion is at times justified, or even imperative. But shedding the blood of Muslims without sufficient cause or justification is a sin.

Apart from the specific issue of rebellion, Ibn Rushd deals with the status of what he calls *ahl al-ahwāʾ* (sectarian groups) such as the Qadariyya, Murjiʾa, Muʿtazila, Khawārij, and Rāfiḍa. Ibn Rushd is indecisive as to their status; he reports that there is considerable disagreement as to

priority. Therefore they disagreed over a proper point of *ijtihād*, and the various contending parties cannot be considered blameworthy. However, he maintains that ʿAlī was clearly the rightful ruler and that all the other parties were *bughāh*. He argues that some of the parties such as the people of Shām refused to give ʿAlī their *bayʿa* (oath of allegiance) while others such as *ahl al-Nahrawān* (the Khawārij) sought to overthrow him. All parties opposing ʿAlī should have sought conciliation and reform, but when they rose in arms against him, they became *bughāh*.

46 Ibn Rushd I, *al-Bayān*, XVI:360, XVIII:175–7, 288. Ibn al-ʿArabī (*Aḥkām*, IV:1719) seems to agree that a position of neutrality is not acceptable. He apologizes for Companions who failed to support ʿAlī by arguing that they mistakenly thought that ʿAlī did not need their assistance. He even mentions a report in which Muʿāwiya chides Saʿd b. Abī Waqqāṣ for failing to take an active role in the conflict by either reconciling the contending parties or fighting against the unjust party. Saʿd is reported to have expressed his regrets for not fighting the *bughāh*. The interesting point, of course, is why Ibn Rushd I cited this report. Did he mean to say that Saʿd was expressing his regret for not fighting against Muʿāwiya since Muʿāwiya was considered the *bāghī*, or did he mean to say that Saʿd was apologizing for not supporting ʿUthmān? The context of Ibn Rushd I's discussion leaves one with the impression that he meant the first.

47 Ibn Rushd I, *al-Bayān*, XVI:362, XVIII:188.

48 Ibn al-ʿArabī makes the nexus between the conflict of the Companions of the Prophet and the law of rebellion more explicit. He argues that the reason that the Companions fought is so that Muslims would learn the rules of fighting rebels – that the wounded and fugitives would not be dispatched, women would not be taken captive, and rebel money would not be taken as spoils of war. See Ibn al-ʿArabī, *Kitāb*, II:593–4; his *Aḥkām*, IV:1720, 1722, states the same and adds that the Companions established the principle of non-liability for life and property damaged during the fighting.

49 Ibn Rushd I, *al-Bayān*, XVIII:288.

whether they are to be considered infidels or not.[50] He however counsels that declaring anyone who outwardly professes the faith to be an infidel is a grave matter, and therefore it is safer not to consider them infidels although their theology is clearly reprehensible.[51] The implication of Ibn Rushd's argument is that there are limits to the admissibility of subjective individual systems of belief, even if they are sincerely and honestly held. But it is not clear from his discourse, as well as in Mālikī discourse in general, what distinguishes rebels from sectarians or what are commonly called *ahl al-ahwāʾ*. Importantly, Ibn Rushd argues that sectarians who rebel are to be distinguished from bandits. Rebels who rely on an interpretation or system of conviction (*taʾwīl*) such as *ahl al-ahwāʾ* are not to be treated as bandits.[52]

Ibn Rushd deals extensively with the issue of banditry.[53] He employs a rather broad definition of banditry: Whoever spreads terror and corruption on the earth is a bandit, even if he or she does not usurp money or commit murder.[54] His point is that banditry is a crime that relies on terror and the helplessness of its victims to achieve an illegal objective. For instance, while Ibn Rushd served as a judge, he adjudicated a case involving a group that abducted and raped a woman. Ibn Rushd ruled that they were bandits and should be treated as such. Several jurists disagreed and argued that they should not be considered bandits because they did not usurp money or property. However, Ibn Rushd defended his decision by arguing that rape is worse than the destruction of property, and that the crime of rape deserves the harshest possible penalty. People, he argued, will willingly give away their property but not have their wives or daughters raped. Interestingly, Ibn Rushd also engages in a sharply worded criticism of those who did not support his ruling in the case. He accuses those jurists of ignorance and shortsightedness, and warns people against accepting the views of narrow-minded and ignorant judges and *muftīs* (*wa ḥasbukum min balāʾi ṣuḥbat al-juhhāl wa khuṣūṣan fī al-futyā wa al-qaḍāʾ*).[55]

[50] Ibid., 486–8.

[51] Ibid., XVI:363–5. Ibn Rushd adds that it is reprehensible to sell weapons in Berber territory because this is the territory of *ahl al-ahwāʾ*.

[52] Ibn Rushd I, *al-Muqaddamāt*, III:236.

[53] Ibn Rushd I, *al-Bayān*, XVI:416–18; Ibn Rushd I, *al-Muqaddamāt*, III:227–36.

[54] Ibn Rushd I, *al-Muqaddamāt*, III:227–8. However in his *al-Bayān*, XVI:416, he refers to bandits as robbers.

[55] The case is reported in Ibn al-ʿArabī, *Aḥkām*, II:597. Reportedly, Ibn Rushd also convicted of banditry criminals who entered homes and threatened its inhabitants with weapons as they proceeded to rob them. See ibid., 601–2.

Although Ibn Rushd's definition of banditry is not precise, it is clear that banditry is not limited to acts of armed robbery, and that an element of the crime is that it results in the spread of terror and insecurity.[56] Therefore, because of the particularly heinous nature of the crime, Ibn Rushd argues that the ruler must enjoy considerable discretion in dealing with bandits. He should be able to choose whether to execute, crucify, amputate from opposite ends, or banish bandits. Nonetheless, Ibn Rushd insists that the ruler should not be able to choose the punishment according to his whim, but according to the danger posed by the bandit, and the amount of actual harm the bandit has caused.[57] Ibn Rushd argues, however, that if a bandit committed murder, the bandit must be killed or crucified, and the ruler does not have discretion to choose a more lenient penalty such as amputation or banishment. If the bandit takes money or property, the ruler may not banish him, but must either execute, crucify, or amputate him.[58] Ibn Rushd then engages in a fairly lengthy discussion on whether, if the bandit repents and surrenders before being captured, this exempts him from the criminal penalties of banditry, and whether, even if he or she is exempted from such penalties, the victims retain the right to demand vengeance or compensation.[59] Interestingly, in all circumstances, Ibn Rushd argues, the vast majority of jurists held that if a bandit is killed, crucified, or executed, he or she must be properly buried as a Muslim, and funeral prayers should be performed.[60]

Importantly, after this long exposition on banditry, Ibn Rushd asserts that all that has been stated applies to those who fight for selfish interests (*yakhrujna fisqan wa khulūʿā*), but it does not apply to those who fight while relying on a system of belief, such as *ahl al-ahwāʾ*. Those who rely on an interpretation should not be treated as bandits.[61] Ibn Rushd does not mention the traditional definition of rebellion; he does not talk in terms of an act of rebellion committed while relying on a *shawka* and an interpretation. Rather, his definitional approach is to first identify banditry, and then to argue that those who commit acts of banditry while

[56] Therefore, Ibn al-ʿArabī (ibid., 598) argues that murder by stealth or assassination is a form of banditry.

[57] Ibn Rushd I (*al-Muqaddamāt*, III:230) argues that a bandit who terrorizes society by means other than murder could be far more harmful to society than a bandit who murders someone.

[58] Ibid., 230–1. Ibn Rushd also mentions early Mālikī opinions which held that bandits who have become powerful or who have eluded the law for a long time must be killed and the ruler does not have discretion to select a lesser punishment.

[59] Ibid., 234–6.

[60] Ibid., 233. Ibn Rushd reports the opinion of the early jurist ʿAbd al-Malik b. al-Mājishūn (d. 212/827) that funeral prayers should not be performed on bandits, and that they should not be buried. Rather, they should be left for dogs and wolves to eat their corpses.

[61] Ibid., 236.

relying on an interpretation should not be treated as bandits. Therefore, he seems to assume that rebels would commit acts that would qualify as banditry if it was not for the existence of an interpretation. This is significant in two respects: (1) it eventually led to the conclusion by some Mālikī jurists that rebellion, like banditry, could be committed by an individual, and that an individual could qualify as a *bāghī*; (2) it clearly signaled the acceptance of the legal effect of the existence of a *ta'wīl* in the Mālikī school. This ultimately led to the widespread adoption of the laws of rebellion in the Mālikī school.

Dealing with the treatment of groups that rely on an interpretation, Ibn Rushd reports that there is some disagreement as to whether such a group should be held liable for life and property destroyed. Drawing upon the precedent of the Companions, he asserts that the Companions agreed upon the principle of no liability in these types of situations. He contends, however, that the ruler may choose to execute a rebel prisoner as long as the fighting is still in progress. As to the fate of these individuals after the fighting ends, Ibn Rushd notes that there is disagreement among the early Mālikī authorities on whether they should be asked to repent or be executed, or whether they should be pardoned.[62] Ibn Rushd's discourse on what he calls *ḥarb al-muta'awwilīn* (fighting by those with an interpretation) is short and non-committal. He does not refer to the doctrines developed by the other schools on rebellion, and does not use the word *bughāh* or the terminology of the field of *aḥkām al-bughāh*. Nonetheless, he produces the most systematic Mālikī justification for the idea of treating those who commit an illegal act while relying on an interpretation as separate and distinct from bandits or common criminals. By doing so, he opened the door for a genuine Mālikī contribution to the discourses on rebellion. Mālikī jurists writing only a generation or two after Ibn Rushd readily accepted the distinction between those with an interpretation and those without. For instance, Ibn Rushd's grandson, the judge Abū al-Walīd Ibn Rushd (Averroes) (d. 595/1198), reiterates the distinctions of his grandfather, and adds that whoever rebels while relying on an interpretation cannot be considered to be an unbeliever, and should not be held liable for his acts. He maintains that this principle was established on the basis of the precedent of the Companions.[63]

The prominent Mālikī jurist and judge Ibn al-ʿArabī (d. 542/1147) went even further. He adopted the terminology and categories of the jurists from the non-Mālikī schools, and argued that a *bāghī* is one who

[62] Ibid., 237. [63] Ibn Rushd II: *Bidāya*, II:458.

rebels against a ruler seeking to overthrow him, or who refuses to obey his commands while relying on a plausible interpretation.[64] A rebel should not be pursued or executed, and the fugitives, captives, or wounded may not be dispatched. Pursuant to the example of the Companions, he argues, rebels should not be held liable for life or property destroyed. Ibn al-ᶜArabī went even further in replicating the discourses of non-Mālikī jurists on the subject, and argued that the legal acts and adjudications of rebels should be recognized.[65] Importantly, he traveled extensively in the eastern Arab world and studied with prominent Shāfiᶜī jurists such as al-Ghazālī, and it is likely that his thought was heavily influenced by these experiences.[66] However, Ibn al-ᶜArabī should not be considered a simple borrower of legal doctrine, because he made a genuine contribution to the Mālikī discourses on rebellion – a contribution which is one of the main doctrines of the revisionist trend. Building on the discourses of Ibn Rushd I regarding the duty of Muslims to join the righteous party, he claimed that the Mālikī jurists held that Muslims should always fight on the side of whoever is just, whether it is the ruler or the rebels. If neither party is just, then every Muslim must remain neutral and not support either the ruler or the rebels. If, however, a Muslim's life or property is targeted by the ruler or rebels, then that Muslim has a right to defend himself, and he or she is not considered an outlaw for doing so.[67]

Contrary to Ibn al-ᶜArabī's assertion, this was not the accepted Mālikī position before or during his time. As we have seen, Mālikī discourses on rebellion continued to be rather ambivalent until well into the sixth/twelfth century. Clearly, Ibn al-ᶜArabī did not invent the position advocating not supporting unjust rulers.[68] However, he was giving expression to a position that was increasingly becoming prevalent among

[64] Ibn al-ᶜArabī, *Aḥkām*, IV:1721. [65] Ibid., 1722.

[66] Al-Dhahabī, *Siyar*, XX:197–203; al-Ziriklī, *al-Aᶜlām*, VI:230. Ibn al-ᶜArabī lived in Andalusia in the city of Ishbīliyya. His father was a close companion of Ibn Ḥazm, but Ibn al-ᶜArabī himself vehemently attacked Ibn Ḥazm on numerous occasions. Ibn al-ᶜArabī and his father traveled to Baghdād, Damascus, Jerusalem, Mecca, and Egypt and studied with several notable jurists, among them Shāfiᶜī jurists. He was appointed as a judge in Ishbīliyya but was removed, reportedly because he was too harsh and stern. Ironically, he was also accused of adulating rulers and being too close to those in power.

[67] Ibn al-ᶜArabī, *Aḥkām*, IV:1721.

[68] Ibid. In fact, Ibn al-ᶜArabī asserts that Ibn al-Qāsim reported that Mālik had held that if the ruler is just and is of the caliber of ᶜUmar b. ᶜAbd al-ᶜAzīz, then he should be supported against those who rebel against him. Otherwise, Muslims should not aid a ruler against rebels. However, the historicity of this report is doubtful. It is not widely reported by early Mālikī sources, and it did not have a serious impact on the development of early Mālikī discourses on the issue of rebellion.

what I have called the revisionist trend. By articulating this position within the context of a systematic discourse on rebellion, Ibn al-ᶜArabī facilitated the adoption of this position in the Mālikī revisionist trend.

After the age of Ibn Rushd I and Ibn al-ᶜArabī, Mālikī discourses on rebellion may be seen in terms of a traditional and a revisionist trend. We will address the revisionist trend in the next section. However, as far as the Mālikī traditional trend is concerned, it adopted the terminology and categories of *aḥkām al-bughāh*. It assumed that whoever disobeys or rebels against whoever is in power is a *bāghī*, and it relied on the existence of an interpretation as the main factor distinguishing rebels from bandits.[69] Like the traditional trend of the other Sunnī schools, the traditional trend in the Mālikī school focused on the treatment of rebels, and differentiated between the treatment due to rebels and that due to bandits. In many ways, the Mālikī traditional trend became indistinguishable from the traditional trend of the other Sunnī schools of thought. Both in terms of its basic approach and of its specific conclusions, the Mālikī traditional trend accepted the paradigms of the traditional discourse on rebellion. The legal transplant from the other Sunnī schools to the Mālikī school had become complete. However, as discussed below, Mālikī jurists continued to develop the law of banditry, and reasserted a position similar to the synthesis achieved by Ibn ᶜAbd al-Barr. The Mālikī traditional trend did not explicitly argue, as Ibn ᶜAbd al-Barr did, that if a rebel pursues methods similar in nature to banditry, he or she no longer qualifies for the status of a *bāghī*. This trend, however, did argue, in effect, that means or methods that rely on the use of terror for the propagation of rebellion are, in fact, criminal, and therefore might lead to the disqualification of a rebel from the status of a *bāghī*.

The classic articulation of the law of rebellion from within the Mālikī traditional trend is that of the Egyptian Mālikī jurist Shihāb al-Dīn al-Qarāfī (d. 684/1285). Al-Qarāfī was the most prominent Mālikī jurist in Cairo at a time when the Mālikī school was consistently receding before the spread of the Shāfiᶜī school in Egypt.[70] In his discourse on *baghy*,

[69] See, for example, al-Wansharīsī (d. 914/1508), *al-Miᶜyār*, V:34, XI:129–30, emphasizing the need to obey even an unjust ruler. Al-Wansharīsī asserts that normally doing *duᶜā*ʾ (supplications or prayer asking God for some favor) in support of rulers is not allowed. However, he argues, in his day and age it had become necessary to pray for rulers because sedition and corruption had become widespread: ibid., VI:385.

[70] Al-Qarāfī lived during several late Ayyūbid and early Mamlūkī regimes, a time that included political assassinations and insurrections, and the Mongol pillaging of Baghdād and threatening of Egypt. On the circumstances of al-Qarāfī, see Jackson, *Islamic*, 33–68. Al-Qarāfī's work outlining the functions of the executive and judiciary is his *Kitāb*. Sherman Jackson has persuasively

al-Qarāfī asserts that a *bāghī* is one who, while relying on an interpretation, rebels seeking to overthrow a ruler, refuses to obey the ruler's command, and refuses to discharge a right or demand made upon him by the ruler.[71] He remarks that Mālikī jurists have disagreed over whether the rebels must be of sufficient number – for instance, more than ten individuals – for the ruler to have to employ considerable force in order to resist them.[72] This is a clear reference to the requirement of a *shawka* or degree of strength, but he does not use that specific term. He also notes that there is disagreement as to the status of the Khawārij because they espoused indiscriminate slaughter against all Muslims, and considered most of the Companions unbelievers.[73] Al-Qarāfī, and the other Mālikī jurists from the traditional trend, do not resolve the issues relating to the Khawārij or the requirement of *shawka*, but they go on to state that the rebels must be considered believers, and may not be fought once their rebellion comes to an end.[74] If the rebels are defeated, their wounded and fugitives may not be pursued or killed. But the ruler may kill the wounded and fugitives as long as the rebellion continues or if the rebels continue to enjoy reinforcements.[75] Prisoners of war, however, may not

argued that in this context, al-Qarāfī composed works aiming to set limitations upon the powers of the government and to protect the integrity of the Mālikī juristic culture. see Jackson, *Islamic*, 142–224. I cannot ascertain if similar considerations motivated al-Qarāfī's discourse on rebellion, but considering his political position in Egypt, his fidelity to the Mālikī school, and the internal violence he witnessed in his time, it is not surprising that he would co-opt this discourse. Al-Qarāfī had a strong incentive to prove the worthiness of the Mālikī school compared to the Shāfiʿī school, and to attempt to limit the use of force by the state against its foes. I should note that Jackson uses the concept of juristic culture in his analysis; however, by juristic culture he seems to mean adherence to the precedent of the *madhhab*. My use of juristic culture has more to do with discursive techniques, terms of art, and selectivity of precedents all in the context of a historical and theological reality that induces jurists to write about a topic in the first place.

71 Al-Qarāfī, *al-Dhakhīra*, XII:5. See al-Gharnāṭī (d. 741/1340), *Qawānīn*, 368; Ibn Farḥūn (d. 799/1397), *Tabṣira*, II:191. Khalīl (*Mukhtaṣar*, 282) reproduces the same definition but adds that the *ʿadl* has a right to fight them. It is not clear whether *ʿadl* in this context means just ruler or rightful ruler. Al-Ābī al-Azharī (a contemporary commentator on Khalīl), in his *Jawāhir*, 277, adds that the rebels are those who disobey the ruler concerning a command that does not involve disobeying God.

72 Al-Qarāfī, *al-Dhakhīra*, XII:5.

73 Ibid., 6; al-Gharnāṭī (*al-Qawanīn*, 369) states that the Khawārij are *bughāh*.

74 Al-Qarāfī, *al-Dhakhīrā*, XII:6. Ibn Farḥūn (*Tabṣira*, II:191), citing a Ḥanbalī jurist, argues that there is a distinction between the *bughāh* and *ahl al-bidaʿ* (sectarians). He asserts that sectarians must repent or be killed; but he does not systematically distinguish rebels from sectarians other than by implying that sectarians adopt heretical beliefs. The idea that sectarian groups should repent or be killed, as we saw earlier, finds support in several Mālikī and Ḥanbalī sources.

75 Al-Qarāfī, *al-Dhakhīra*, XII:7. Interestingly, al-Qarāfī cites the *ḥadīth* attributed to the Prophet that states that the law of God with regard to rebels is that the fugitives, wounded, and captives may not be killed. But the version which he cites now adds "unless it is feared that they will return [to rebellion] (*in lam yaʾman rujūʿahum*)." This is obviously a late addition to the report. See also Ibn Farḥūn, *Tabṣira*, II:191; al-Gharnāṭī, *al-Qawānīn*, 369; Khalīl, *Mukhtaṣar*, 282.

be killed, and even if the rebels kill loyalist hostages, the loyalists cannot reciprocate in kind.[76] Al-Qarāfī argues that the ruler may use weapons of mass destruction such as flame-throwers, flooding, and mangonels against the rebels unless there is a reasonable chance that innocents may be harmed in the process; then weapons of mass destruction may not be used. He defines innocents as anyone residing in the targeted areas who might not share the views of the rebels or loyalists. Nonetheless, other Mālikī jurists were even less accepting of the permissibility of using weapons of mass destruction.[77] The corpses of rebels may not be mutilated, and their heads may not be severed and sent across the lands, or be placed on display by being raised on spears.[78] Al-Qarāfī adds that killed loyalists are to be treated as martyrs, and loyalists should not perform funeral prayers on killed rebels. Nevertheless, the families and compatriots of rebels should be given an opportunity to perform funeral prayers for the killed rebels, and then the corpses should be properly buried.[79] Importantly, the Mālikī traditional trend repeats what had become the earmark of the field of *aḥkām al-bughāh*: As long as the rebels have an interpretation or cause on which they rely, they are not to be held liable for anything destroyed during the course of their rebellion. Loyalists and rebels are liable, however, for anything destroyed before or after the rebellion. Al-Qarāfī and others add that those who fight out of tribal reasons (*ʿaṣabiyya*) and not a principled cause or interpretation are liable for their actions.[80] Furthermore, Mālikī jurists continued to disagree over whether the legal acts and adjudications of the rebels should be recognized and given effect.[81]

The Mālikī discourses of the traditional trend are redundant; they adopt the terminology and categories of the traditional trend in general, and add very little to the inherited positions. While Mālikī jurists, such as al-Qarāfī, were to an extent responding to specific historical contexts, the

[76] Al-Qarāfī, *al-Dhakhīra*, XII:9, 11, 12. Al-Gharnāṭī (*al-Qawānīn*, 369) and Ibn Farḥūn (*Tabṣira*, II:191) add that although the prisoner may not be killed, he should be punished and imprisoned until he repents.

[77] Al-Qarāfī, *al-Dhakhīra*, XII:8. Ibn Farḥūn (*Tabṣira*, II:191) states that the *ʿadl* specifically may use weapons of mass destruction. It is not clear whether he means the rightful ruler or just ruler, but in this context, it is likely that al-Qarāfī means the rightful ruler. Al-Gharnāṭī (*al-Qawānīn*, 369) argues that the ruler may not use weapons of mass destruction and may not cut down trees or burn rebel homes.

[78] Al-Qarāfī, *al-Dhakhīra*, XII:12; Khalīl, *Mukhtaṣar*, 282; al-Ābī, *Jawāhir*, 277.

[79] Al-Qarāfī, *al-Dhakhīra*, XII:12.

[80] Ibid., 10; Khalīl, *Mukhtaṣar*, 282; al-Gharnāṭī, *al-Qawānīn*, 369.

[81] Al-Qarāfī, *al-Dhakhīra*, XII:10; Khalīl, *Mukhtaṣar*, 282; al-Ābī, *Jawāhir*, 277; al-Gharnāṭī, *al-Qawānīn*, 369.

style and tone of the discourses clearly demonstrate that these determinations were the product of legal borrowing from the other Sunnī schools. In other words, after Ibn Rushd I provided the ideological grounding, the adoption of *aḥkām al-bughāh* into Mālikī discourses was largely in response to legal culture, and in response to the pervasiveness of these doctrines in Islamic legal culture. But as discussed earlier, Mālikī jurists, in response to a pervasive historical reality, had developed an extensive discourse on the law of banditry, and it is in this field that the Mālikī school made a genuine contribution. As noted earlier, Mālikī jurists argued that the essential components of the crime of banditry are that it relies on the element of terror and that it renders its victims helpless. Therefore, those who commit highway robbery or terrorize the wayfarer are bandits. But, even more, it is irrelevant whether the armed robbery is committed in a town or in the desert, or whether it is committed inside a house or on a street. Furthermore, an assassin who kills stealthily, a murderer who strangles his victim, or a criminal who uses a narcotic to drug his victim before robbing him are all treated as bandits. Importantly, in order for the elements of the crime of banditry to exist, the criminal does not need to have an intent to commit robbery. In other words, an intent to usurp property or gain possession of property is not a constitutive element of the crime of banditry. Rather, it is sufficient that the criminal commit acts that, by definition, rely on the helplessness of the victim, and have the effect of spreading terror. Mālikī jurists often exemplify this point by stating that if persons or groups, for whatever reason, decide to use the threat of harm in order to prevent people from traveling from one point to another, such persons or groups are bandits.[82] Therefore, if people avoid traveling through a particular road out of fear of being harmed by a certain group, then the group is to be treated as bandits. For the crime of banditry to exist, it is sufficient that the group had taken concrete steps to terrorize people such that people would have a realistic fear of harm, and such that due to this fear, people would comply with the demands of the bandits. Consequently, Mālikī jurists often stated that those who use the threat of harm or terrorize their victims in order to commit rape are bandits as well.[83]

[82] This position is at times attributed to Ibn al-Mawwāz, al-ᶜUtbī, Ibn al-Qāsim, and, ultimately, Mālik: see Ibn Abī Zayd, *al-Nawādir*, XIV:474.

[83] Al-Qarāfī, *al-Dhakhīra*, XII:10, 123–5; Ibn Farḥūn, *Tabṣira*, II:184–5, 189; Ibn ᶜĀṣim, *Tuḥfa*, 280; al-Nafrāwī, *al-Fawākih*, II:217, 222; al-Ābī, *Jawāhir*, 294; al-Gharnāṭī, *al-Qawānīn*, 367; Khalīl, *Mukhtaṣar*, 290; al-Juᶜalī, *Sirāj*, II:227–8.

Mālikī jurists continued to give the ruler broad discretion in dealing with bandits.[84] However, the ruler does not have discretion to pardon the bandits for their crimes unless they repent before they are captured.[85] Even then, these jurists continued to repeat that the repentance of bandits does not affect the right of the victims to demand retaliation or compensation. Mālikī jurists limited the discretion of the ruler somewhat by demanding that he should not punish according to whim and that he should consult the jurists regarding the appropriate penalty in each situation.[86] Al-Qarāfī, for example, argues that there should be proportionality between the crime committed or the threat posed and the penalty imposed. He argues that if a bandit commits murder, he or she must be killed and a lesser penalty should not be permitted. If the bandit commits murder, usurps property, and terrorizes people, the bandit should be crucified and then killed, but he or she should not suffer amputation from opposite ends. If the bandit is not particularly dangerous and has not committed murder, then it is preferable for the ruler to beat, imprison, or exile the bandit.[87] Nonetheless, the main emphasis in Mālikī discourses is on flexibility in dealing with the crime of banditry. Mālikī jurists emphasized that the penalty should be in proportion to the actual threat of harm that the bandit poses, and not necessarily in direct correlation to the specific offense committed.[88]

[84] For example, al-Tasūlī (*al-Bahja*, II:348–9, 360–2) argues that the ruler must be given wide discretion not only in punishing bandits but in punishing groups that might give indirect support to bandits. He also argues that considering that the crime of banditry is particularly destructive and that it is very widespread, the rules of evidence should be liberalized so that the crime of banditry may be more readily proven. Wide discretion is also given to judges in dealing with banditry: see al-Wansharīsī, *al-Miᶜyār*, II:285–6.

[85] However, some late Mālikī jurists state that when a member of a group of bandits was executed in North Africa, his group would retaliate by wreaking havoc in the land. In this situation, they argued, it is permissible for the ruler not to execute bandits because the evil of such a punishment outweighs its benefits. See, for instance, al-ᶜAdawī, *Ḥāshiya*, II:254; al-Nafrāwī, *al-Fawākih*, II:223.

[86] Ibn Farḥūn, *Tabṣira*, II:187; al-Gharnāṭī, *al-Qawānīn*, 368; al-Qarāfī, *al-Dhakhīra*, XII:126.

[87] Al-Qarāfī, *al-Dhakhīra*, XII:126; al-Wansharīsī, *al-Miᶜyār*, II:285–6. Interestingly, al-ʾUbbī (*Sharḥ*, VI:97) says that the custom in Tunisia was to exile bandits out of the jurisdiction of the governorship in which the crime was committed or to banish bandits on boats – meaning that they would be exiled overseas. He also reports that the Mālikī judge Muḥammad b. ᶜAbd al-Salām (d. 749/1348) related that a bandit was banished from Tunisia to the east. The jurists of the east protested that banishing such a person to the east was improper because he was bound to cause corruption. Tunisian jurists responded that such an action was justified because it was not known, to a degree of certainty, that such a person would once again commit banditry.

[88] Ibn Farḥūn, *Tabṣira*, II:187–8; al-Nafrāwī, *al-Fawākih*, II:222; al-Ābī, *Jawāhir*, 295; al-Juᶜalī, *Sirāj*, II:228; al-ᶜAdawī, *Ḥāshiya*, II:254; al-Tasūlī, *al-Bahja*, II:360–1.

The question remains, however, as to the status of rebels who might rely on an interpretation but otherwise pursue methods that resemble those pursued by bandits. If rebels, for instance, kill by stealth or terrorize the wayfarer, are they still treated as *bughāh* or as bandits? The answer is provided in a two-part response. Mālikī jurists often stated that rebels may not be treated as bandits. Furthermore, if the bandits act out of competition for power, enmity, or rancor (*imra, ʿadāwa,* or *thāʾira*), they are not to be treated as bandits. If a group of people is motivated by a specific enmity or a desire to seek revenge against a person or a group, they may not be treated as bandits. Similarly, if people commit acts of banditry because they seek to overthrow the ruler or come to power, they may not be treated as bandits. In these circumstances, those individuals are to be treated as common criminals who are held liable for their acts under the regular criminal penalties of *Sharīʿa.*[89] Therefore, if rebels who might otherwise qualify as *bughāh* commit acts of banditry, they are not to be treated as bandits, but as common criminals. This position is a development from the synthesis achieved by Ibn ʿAbd al-Barr between the laws of rebellion and banditry. But unlike Ibn ʿAbd al-Barr's synthesis, the late Mālikī position protects rebels who in good faith rely on an interpretation and commit acts of banditry from being treated as bandits. At the same time, rebels who pursue tactics oriented towards the spread of terror are denied the liberal treatment of *aḥkām al-bughāh.* The Mālikī position is somewhat similar to that adopted by jurists from the other schools which maintained that rebels are exempt from liability for life and property destroyed, as long as the destruction was reasonably related to the act of rebellion. Arguably, acts of banditry could be declared to be unrelated to a reasonable propagation of a rebellion. In other words, arguably, certain acts could, by definition, be excluded from the protection afforded by the status of *baghy*. In fact, several non-Mālikī jurists explicitly adopt this position. For instance, the Shāfiʿī jurist al-Shirbīnī (d. 977/1569–70) adopts the position that an act of rape is not protected under the laws of rebellion because, by definition, rape is not an acceptable means of propagating rebellion (*lā taʿalluqa lahu bi al-qitāl*).[90] In this situation, despite the existence of an interpretation, a person who commits rape is treated as a common criminal.[91]

[89] Al-Qarāfī, *al-Dhakhīra*, XII:123; al-Nafrāwī, *al-Fawākih*, II:222; al-Gharnāṭī, *al-Qawānīn*, 367, 368–9; Ibn ʿĀṣim, *Tuḥfa*, 280; Ibn Farḥūn, *Tabṣira*, II:185–6. However, al-Khirshī (d. 1101/1689–90), in his *Sharḥ*, VIII:103–4, argues that if a person commits acts of banditry for the purpose of usurping power, he or she is to be treated as a *bāghī*.

[90] Al-Shirbīnī, *Mughnī*, IV:125–6. Al-Shirbīnī notes that several jurists have adopted this position.

[91] I will address the crime of rape later.

Mālikī and non-Mālikī jurists of the traditional trend ended up preserving the technical rules of the laws of rebellion. These rules primarily focused on the treatment due to those who rebel while relying on an interpretation. Initially, due to specific historical circumstances in the early Islamic polity, these discourses developed as a moral, and perhaps legal, restraint on the discretion of rulers in dealing with dissent and rebellion. The corporate legal culture of the jurists was not willing to concede unfettered discretion to rulers in dealing with rebels. Furthermore, many jurists insisted on retaining the power to differentiate between a rebel and a legitimate ruler. The traditional trend arose out of the fact that a wide discrepancy had developed between the advocated ideals of *aḥkām al-bughāh* and the political reality. Many jurists had developed a vested interest in the political institutions of the day. More importantly, after the weakening of the ʿAbbāsid empire rebellions, insurrections, and secessions had become very widespread, and at times the situation presented a state of anarchy. Nevertheless, the traditional trend continued to repeat the inherited doctrines of *aḥkām al-bughāh.* This was largely due to the power of legal precedent and the influence of legal culture on the legal mind. Substantively, the traditional trend focused on the duty of obedience to those in power – this became its primary focus. Otherwise, the main contribution of the traditional trend was to limit the scope of the laws of rebellion in order to exclude certain actions from its coverage. The discourses on rebellion were too entrenched in Muslim legal culture to be abandoned or eradicated altogether. Nonetheless, the traditional trend argued that either certain groups, such as the Khawārij, or certain acts, such as rape, are not to be protected under the rules of *aḥkām al-bughāh.*

AL-WANSHARĪSĪ'S *RESPONSA* AND THE POSSIBLE IMPACT OF THE TRADITIONAL TREND

It is difficult to assess to what extent *aḥkām al-bughāh* impacted the day-to-day dynamics of Islamic law and politics. This issue needs a far more exhaustive study, and cumulative investigations focused on specific historical periods and geographic areas. However, it would be useful to introduce some evidence of how certain jurists, particularly Mālikī, from the traditional trend dealt with the general issue of dissent. Several *responsa* preserved in the works of the Mālikī jurist al-Wansharīsī (d. 914/1508) deal with what he calls "the misguided groups and secessionist rebels" (*al-ṭawāʾif al-ḍālla wa al-bughāt al-munshaqqīn*). These *reponsa*, however, do not deal with the treatment of rebels in the course of rebellion. Rather, they deal with groups that have separated or seceded from the general Muslim community but have not resorted to armed rebellion. We have already mentioned al-Wansharīsī's *responsa* regarding the illegality of rebelling against unjust rulers. However, in the *responsa* discussed below, al-Wansharīsī reproduces the opinions of jurists regarding a sect from the Khawārij known as Wahbī Ibāḍīs, and similar sectarian factions. According to the text, the groups addressed were not seditious Sunnī rebels, but sectarian groups accused of propagating heretical beliefs. Of course, one cannot exclude the possibility that the accusation of sectarianism was leveled against otherwise "orthodox" political opponents[92] or, alternatively, that opposition to political regimes was expressed in terms of "unorthodox" theological beliefs.[93] The *responsa* record the opinions of jurists from the fourth/tenth to the tenth/sixteenth centuries.[94] Therefore, one must be careful not to assume that the *responsa* represent the developed Mālikī position on all points addressed.

Al-Wansharīsī lived in Tilmisān (Tlemcen) in western Algeria during the Spanish reconquest of Andalusia. His father was a notable judge in the principality, and al-Wansharīsī himself was a respected jurist and teacher. In 874/1469, for reasons that are not entirely clear, he displeased the sulṭān Abū ʿAbd Allāh al-Thābitī (Muḥammad VI from the Ziyānid line of rulers, r. 873/1469–910/1504).[95] The sulṭān ordered that his home be ransacked and demolished, and al-Wansharīsī promptly escaped to Fez where he occupied himself with teaching and writing. His writings often reflect an agonizing concern with the external threat posed by the Christian reconquest, and the instability posed by the constantly warring principalities of North Africa. Furthermore, like other Mālikī scholars of his place and time, he was also preoccupied with the heresy of the Bāṭinī creed, which he considered threatening to Sunnī Islam.[96]

In the first set of *responsa*, Mālikī jurists are asked about a group, reportedly from the Ibaḍī sect, which lived in the Maghrib in the midst of

[92] This suspicion is supported by the fact that the description of the theological belief system of these groups is very ambiguous. They are described as Ibāḍīs (Khawārij), as Rāfiḍīs (Shīʿīs), as Imāmīs (Shīʿīs), and as *ahl shaṭāra* (people of corruption): see al-Wansharīsī, *al-Miʿyār*, II:445, 449, VII:218–19.

[93] This suspicion is supported by the fact that there are constant references in the *responsa* to the fact that these groups attracted and misled the laity or that such groups tended to be popular among the laity.

[94] Fierro, "Heresy," refers to similar *responsa* by other Andalusian Mālikī jurists.

[95] See Bel, "Tlemcen"; Marcais, "ʿAbd al-Wādids."

[96] *Alf*, 4–5; Ibn Maryam, *al-Bustān*, 53–4; Sirkīs, *Muʿjam*, II:1923–4; al-Ḥajwī, *al-Fikr*, II:313; Ibn al-Qāḍī, *Durra*, I:91–2; Ibn al-Qāḍī, *Jidhwa*, I:156–7.

Sunnī Muslims. They lived in certain territories in which they built their own mosques. Furthermore, according to the unidentified questioners, they intermarried with Mālikī women because by marrying such women, they sought to gain legitimacy and acceptance in the Sunnī community. Those seeking the *responsa* inquired about three distinct issues. First, if the territories come under the control of Sunnī governors, may the mosques be torn down? Second, may they be beaten and forced to adopt the Mālikī school of thought? Third, should their marriages to Mālikī women be nullified?[97]

Al-Wansharīsī reports that Mālikī jurists disagreed on whether the mosques should be torn down. Relying on the incident of the Ḍirār mosque at the time of the Prophet, some jurists argued that these mosques should be torn down.[98] This would have the effect of demoralizing and undermining the influence of these groups (*fīhi dhillatun lahum*).[99] Other jurists argued that, on principle, the mosques should not be torn down, but that they should come under Sunnī control and the followers of the deviant sect be denied access to such mosques. Some added that if the mosques have become a symbol for the power of these sects or have become irrevocably associated in the minds of people with a deviant sect, then it is permissible to tear them down.[100] Several jurists argued that the decision hinges on whether the mosques were built for the specific purpose of serving these groups or whether they were initially built for proper purposes, but later on these groups gained control of them. In this context, al-Wansharīsī relates a *responsum* in which a man built a mosque in Andalusia, but after the mosque was built, a deviant group (*ahl al-sharr*) and unveiled women (*mutabarrijātu al-nisāʾ*) started frequenting it and gained control of it. The man who built the mosque asked whether it should be torn down.[101] Several Mālikī jurists argued that if it was initially built for appropriate purposes, it should not be torn down. They added that if the location of the mosque was such that it would benefit the public, it should not be torn down, but that the deviant group should

[97] Al-Wansharīsī, *al-Miʿyār*, II:445–6, X:149–50.

[98] The incident of the Ḍirār mosque is documented in the Qurʾān 9:107. Reportedly, at the time the Prophet was in Medina, a group of hypocrites built a mosque in which they met and prayed. The Prophet reportedly perceived the mosque as a source of dissension and division and tore it down. On this incident see Lecker, "Ḍirār," who argues that the incident is historical.

[99] Al-Wansharīsī, *al-Miʿyār*, II:447, X:14, 151.

[100] Ibid., II:446, 447, X:150–3. In another *responsum*, al-Wansharīsī reports on the status of a mosque that was created as a trust (*maḥbas*) for indigent Ibāḍīs. Mālikī jurists disagreed on whether the trust should be nullified or restructured so that the objects of the trust would accrue to the benefit of indigent Sunnīs. See ibid., VII:362–3.

[101] Ibid., VII:218.

be prevented from accessing it. If the location of the mosque, however, lent itself to being exploited by the deviant group, then it should be torn down. Some Mālikī jurists disagreed, and argued that the focus should be on preventing the deviant group from gaining access to the mosque, but under no circumstances should the mosque be demolished.[102]

Al-Wansharīsī also reports on an incident that took place during the time of the Shāfiʿī jurist Jalāl al-Dīn al-Suyūṭī (d. 911 / 1505). A group from the Khawārij used to pray in a separate mosque close to the Prophet's mosque in Medina. Al-Suyūṭī ruled that the mosque should be closed, and that the group should be forced to pray with the rest of the Muslim community in the main mosque in Medina. Later on, the same group separated itself from the community and built a prayer area in which they met and prayed, but they did not rebel and did not openly defy the authority of the governor. The governor of Medina consulted with the jurists regarding this affair, and reportedly all the Shāfiʿī, Mālikī, and Ḥanafī jurists in Medina agreed that the prayer area should be demolished, and that the group should be forced to pray with the rest of the community.[103]

The matter of whether dissenting groups should be allowed to maintain their own mosques involves the much larger issue of the role of mosques as communal places of worship. In principle, mosques are communal places of worship in which the whole community has an interest and right to worship. Theoretically, mosques belong to God and should be accessible to the whole community. This, however, raises the question: Who has the right to define the community, and who has the right to define orthopraxy in such mosques? Forcing the various theological and political schools of thought to worship together is a tacit acceptance of both diversity and the need for unity. A balance needs to be struck between the idea of accessibility of all mosques to the whole community, and the attendant institutional reality that full accessibility will also mean an inevitable compromise of diversity. Accessibility of mosques to all trends

[102] Ibid., VII:219–20. The Mālikī jurist Ibn Farḥūn argued that the decision of whether or not to tear down the mosque hinges on the purposes for which it was built in the first place. See ibid., II:447. Ibn Farḥūn's argument relates to the following Qur'ānic verse: "A mosque whose foundation was laid from the first day on piety is more worthy of thy standing forth [in it for prayer]." See Qur'ān 9:108–9.

[103] Al-Wansharīsī, *al-Miʿyār*, II:448. See Ibn Kathīr, *al-Bidāya*, XI:163, for the incident of Masjid of Barāthī in 313/925. A group described as Rāfiḍa built a mosque where they met to curse the Companions, corresponded with the Qarāmiṭa between Kūfa and Baghdād, and called for the removal of the caliph al-Muqtadir. Al-Muqtadir consulted the jurists who, citing the Ḍirār incident, recommended tearing down the mosque. Reportedly, the caliph had the heretics beaten and tore down their mosque.

and schools of thought will require a certain degree of voluntary or involuntary consensus building and, hence, a compromise of diversity. On the other hand, permitting dissenting groups to maintain their own separate places of worship by necessity means accepting the idea of diversity, but also the idea that mosques do not need to be accessible to all. Permitting various groups to maintain separate places of worship constitutes a tacit acceptance of both the idea of diversity and the idea of inaccessibility of places of worship. But even more, allowing separate groups to maintain separate places of worship concedes that consensus building is not possible, and ultimately may constitute not just an acceptance of diversity, but also the acceptance of fragmentation.

The extent to which these considerations motivated the discourses of jurists needs a more extensive study. Nonetheless, it is important to note that in the precedent of the group in Medina, unlike the group in Maghrib, there is no suggestion that the dissenting group should be punished or forced to abandon its beliefs. Rather, the emphasis is on denying the group its institutional separateness or autonomy. There is no discussion in the Mālikī Andalusian *responsa* regarding the unveiled women frequenting a certain mosque, or whether the group should be compelled to abandon its beliefs. Furthermore, there is no elaboration upon the belief system of this group. However, there is reference to the fact that the group lived in the mountains, and that the unveiled women of that mountain were not a novel social phenomenon. The Mālikī judge of Cordoba, Muḥammad b. al-Salīm (d. 367/977), held that this group should be prevented from accessing the specific mosque in question, but did not recommend any other measures.[104]

However, the Mālikī *responsa*, dealing with Ibaḍī groups addressed at length whether or not these groups should be punished and forced to abandon their system of belief. The Mālikī jurist Abū al-Ḥasan al-Lakhmī (d. 478/1085) argued that groups such as the Ibaḍīs are a great threat to religion. They cause considerable corruption by attracting and misguiding the laity, and in fact are worse than the Christians and Jews. People know that the Christians and Jews are not Muslims, he argues, and so people are not in danger of being deceived by the followers of these religions. However, the Ibāḍīs claim that they are Muslim and quote the Qur᾿ān and *ḥadīth*, and hence people are easily deceived and misled by them. Therefore the Ibāḍīs should not be left to intermingle with people, and should be imprisoned and beaten until they repent.

[104] Al-Wansharīsī, *al-Mi῾yār*, VII:219–20.

Even if they repent, as long as they have associates that have not yet been captured, they should not be released from prison. If all of their associates have been captured and they have repented, then they may be released. If, however, they did not repent, al-Lakhmī notes that there is disagreement as to whether or not they should be killed.[105] Al-Lakhmī lived before the development of the Mālikī traditional trend, and therefore, it is not clear whether his opinions represent a specific historical trend in Mālikī jurisprudence. Nevertheless, al-Wansharīsī gives the impression that the notion that groups such as the Ibāḍīs should be beaten and forced to abandon their beliefs was not an anomaly in his time.[106] Furthermore, he reports on a set of *responsa* that deal with the limitations of proper educational and social interactions with such groups. Al-Wansharīsī mentions *responsa* regarding the permissibility of teaching the Khawārij and their children the Qur'ān and the art of writing. Some Mālikī jurists argued that one should not teach the Khawārij writing or the sciences, such as mathematics, in territory which is under their own control because this is bound to strengthen them. However, in all circumstances, teaching the Khawārij the Qur'ān is permissible. Other jurists argued that if the territory is under the Sunnī ruler's control, it is preferable not to teach them either the Qur'ān or writing and the sciences. Literacy or knowledge is bound to strengthen the Khawārij and aid their ability to convert others to their way of thought.[107]

The dichotomy between the Mālikīs and the Ibāḍī Khawārij is further emphasized in the *responsa* dealing with the marriage of an Ibāḍī to a Mālikī. Al-Wansharīsī reports that the Mālikī jurist Abū Qāsim al-Sayūrī had held that after a territory, dominated by the Ibāḍīs, had come under Mālikī control, the marriage of an Ibāḍī to a Mālikī should be abrogated.[108] However, the reasoning behind this view is not clear. As noted above, it was argued that the Ibāḍīs used to marry Mālikī women in order to gain legitimacy with Sunnīs, and it is possible that al-Sayūrī's opinion is justified by a pragmatic social and political consideration aimed at combating Ibāḍī legitimacy. Nonetheless, al-Wansharīsī mentions a lengthy discussion blaming rulers for being too lax in accepting the testimony of Ibāḍī witnesses in issues relating to marriage and divorce. According to al-Wansharīsī, the testimony of Ibāḍī witnesses is problematic because the Ibāḍī law of marriage and divorce is inconsistent

[105] Ibid., II:446–7, X:150–1, XI:168–9. [106] Ibid., II:447–8, XI:168.
[107] Ibid., VIII:237. [108] Ibid., II:446, XI:168.

with Mālikī law in a variety of important respects.[109] Therefore, al-Wansharīsī implies that the marriage of an Ibāḍī to a Mālikī should be abrogated because Mālikī law is irreconcilable with Ibāḍī law. Furthermore, al-Wansharīsī quotes a discussion by al-Lakhmī in which he argues that all the legal acts performed by Ibāḍīs during a time in which they controlled a certain territory are null and void. Al-Lakhmī contends that the Ibāḍīs, in the *responsa* mentioned above, were not usurpers (*mutaghallibūn*), so one cannot claim that they acquired a degree of legal autonomy from the legitimate ruler. Further, they were not deputized (*lam yufawwaḍ ilayhim*) by the legitimate ruler as his agents, and therefore their legal acts, including marriages, cannot be recognized.[110] It is not clear which of these factors is the most material to the idea of abrogating the marriage of an Ibāḍī to a Mālikī. Importantly, however, none of the rationales cited above maintains that such a marriage should be abrogated because the Ibāḍīs are considered infidels.

As cautioned above, I am unable in this book to adequately analyze the diverse historical contexts of the *responsa* on rebels and heretics, or the complex dynamics that negotiated the determinations of insurrection or heresy.[111] As noted, this will require a series of studies. Consequently, I have resisted the temptation to read too much into the *responsa* preserved in al-Wansharīsī. However, I suspect that although the traditional trend transplanted the legal discourses on rebellion into Mālikī jurisprudence, the social and political dynamics of the Mālikī school, particularly in the Maghrib, functioned in a far more complex fashion than the dogmatic positions on rebellion would lead us to believe. Mālikī legal discourses in the Maghrib, particularly after the sixth/twelfth century, exhibited a certain exclusionary attitude that sometimes bordered on xenophobia.[112] Importantly, however, despite the complex social and political reality and the tendency of the Mālikī school towards exclusion and rejection of the "other," a traditional trend did develop in Mālikī jurisprudence. As argued above, largely in response to the influence of legal culture after the sixth/twelfth century, the Mālikī jurists joined their Sunnī counterparts in adopting and propagating the law of rebellion in Islam.

[109] Ibid., II:448–9.

[110] Ibid., II:449. Al-Wansharīsī also mentions the opinions of various Mālikī jurists that the testimony of sectarians (*ahl al-ahwāʾ wa al-bidaʿ*), as a general matter, should not be accepted: see ibid., II:451.

[111] See Fierro, "Heresy," which analyzes several *responsa* on heresy including the legal determinations of Ibn Sahl. Al-Subkī (*Fatāwā*, II:570–1) discusses the execution of someone from *ahl al-ahwāʾ* who was cursing some of the Companions in Damascus in 755/1354.

[112] See Abou El Fadl, "Islamic," 153–7.

THE REVISIONIST TREND

Jurists of the revisionist trend often express skepticism about both rulers and rebels of their day and age. Najm al-Dīn al-Ṭarsawī (d. 758/1356–7), for example, somberly notes that there is no just ruler in the world in his day,[113] while Fakhr al-Dīn al-Zaylaʿī (d. 743/1343) maintains that in his age, government is a function of raw power, and it is impossible to distinguish the just from the unjust because everyone fights over worldly affairs.[114] This is not just commentary expressing disillusion with the political affairs of their age. Rather, it is commentary about the role and utility of the discourses on rebellion. These observations are often made in the context of the discussions on *aḥkām al-bughāh*, and therefore connote a certain degree of dissatisfaction with the traditional discourses on rebellion. As discussed earlier, *aḥkām al-bughāh* continued to be propagated by the power and force of legal culture, but a substantial disparity developed between the initial critical purposes of this field of law and the *pro forma* repetition of the doctrines. Muslim jurists of the post-sixth/twelfth centuries responded to the circumstances that developed in the fourth/tenth century by emphasizing the need for order and stability, and the need to avoid rebellion. But Muslim jurists continued to repeat the traditional doctrines of *aḥkām al-bughāh* as an established part of Islamic law without substantial revisions. The main area of development was in limiting the range of means recognizable as a legitimate method of rebellion, and hence protected by the law of rebellion. This does not mean that the discourses on rebellion had ceased being a method of criticizing the practices of rulers against rebels. In fact, I have argued that largely because of the field of *aḥkām al-bughāh*, one cannot describe the attitude of Muslim jurists, even from the traditional trend, as quietist. Rather, the attitude of the jurists from the traditional trend was thoroughly legalistic. Even if the ruler was unjust, it was illegal to rebel; but it was also illegal to mistreat rebels or to suppress rebellion outside the bounds permitted by the law. Furthermore, as we saw, the jurist Ibn Mufliḥ (d. 763/1361) used the traditional discourses on rebellion and banditry to argue, for instance, that the Mongols, even if they converted to Islam, should be considered the equivalent of bandits, and treated as such.[115] But the emphasis of the traditional trend had been on advocating the impermissibility of rebellion,

113 Al-Ṭarsawī, *Tuḥfa*, 121.

114 Al-Zaylaʿī, *Tabyīn*, III:294. See also al-ʿAynī (d. 855/1451), *al-Bināya*, VI:735, who laments that it was impossible to differentiate the just from the unjust in his day.

115 Ibn Mufliḥ, *Kitāb*, VI:162.

and otherwise, on preserving the doctrines of rebellion as inherited from the cumulative legacies of legal culture.

Nevertheless, a large number of jurists, especially after the sixth/twelfth century, reoriented and redirected the discourses on rebellion in substantive and considerable ways. They effectively reasserted the discourses on rebellion as a means of moral and legal criticism against objectionable power dynamics and as a means of defiance against unjust rulers. Importantly, the revisionist jurists did not reject the majority of the inherited discourses on rebellion. In fact, for the most part they restated the same rules of conduct, but they also instituted substantive changes that redirected the focus of the discourses. Furthermore, the revisionist jurists did not reject the imperative of law and order. Rather, as we will see below, they continued to state that as a matter of principle rulers should be obeyed and rebellion should be avoided. In fact, the Shāfiʿī jurist Ibn Jamāʿa (d. 733/1332–3), often cited as the epitome of juridical pragmatism and quietism, was among the jurists of the revisionist trend. However, while the jurists of the revisionist trend insisted on the need for order and stability, they also expanded the scope of *aḥkām al-bughāh* in significant ways and refused to lend support to unjust rulers.

Ibn Taymiyya as a revisionist

Most of the jurists of the revisionist trend tended to be from the Shāfiʿī, Ḥanafī, and Mālikī schools of thought. However, one of the most notable critics of the traditional discourses on rebellion, and one of the most notable revisionists, was the Ḥanbalī jurist Ibn Taymiyya (d. 728/1327–8). It is doubtful that Ibn Taymiyya would have described himself as a revisionist[116] since, as discussed earlier, he accused the Kūfans and al-Shāfiʿī of inventing the discourses on *aḥkām al-bughāh*, and tended to be rather hostile to the whole field. Nonetheless, besides being an avid critic of the discourses of the traditional trend, Ibn Taymiyya ended up replicating, to a large extent, the reconstructive efforts of the revisionist trend.

Ibn Taymiyya's main objection to *aḥkām al-bughāh* as a field is that it equates and confuses political and religious wars. Religious wars are the fighting or resisting of sectarians, such as the Khawārij. By their nature, they are just and permissible in order to protect religion from

[116] Of course, the terms "traditional" and "revisionist" are interpretive categorizations that I have adopted. Muslim jurists speak of *aḥkām al-bughāh* as if it is a unitary field that has not experienced development or change.

corruption. Political wars are contests over power and worldly affairs, and so are a *fitna* and therefore impermissible. Ibn Taymiyya contends that the Kūfan jurists and al-Shāfiᶜī, and most other jurists since then, have confused the two types of war and erroneously equated fighting groups such as the Khawārij with fighting rebels. The reason for this confusion, Ibn Taymiyya argues, is that these jurists misunderstood or mischaracterized the battles that took place between the Companions at the time of ᶜAlī. They treated conflicts over power as equivalent to conflicts over religion, and hence did not distinguish between fighting the Khawārij and fighting rebels.[117] The two cannot be equated because while fighting the Khawārij is a praiseworthy act, fighting rebels is simply a part of an unlawful *fitna*. The wars between the Companions was a *fitna* that should have been avoided. Ibn Taymiyya concedes that in the wars between the Companions, the various contending parties had relied on a plausible cause or interpretation, and therefore all the parties will go to heaven, and no side is blameworthy. But he insists that most of the Companions refused to get involved in the civil war, that it would have been better not to fight for or against ᶜAlī, and that even ᶜAlī himself eventually regretted his decision to become involved in these wars.[118]

Importantly, Ibn Taymiyya accepts the notion that if they rely on a plausible interpretation or cause, rebels are similar in status to *mujtahids*.[119] For the most part, he also accepts the traditional rules pertaining to the treatment of rebels, and that those who rely on a plausible *ta'wīl* should not be held liable for property or life destroyed during the course of their rebellion.[120] He maintains that even the Khawārij should not be considered unbelievers, and that the laws of rebellion should be extended to them as well.[121] However, he challenges the traditional discourses on rebellion from a different perspective; his main objection is to the notion of the permissibility of rebellion or the permissibility of fighting rebels in the first place. Ibn Taymiyya contends that there is clear

[117] Ibn Taymiyya, *Majmūᶜ al-Fatāwā*, IV:450–2; Ibn Taymiyya, *al-Fatāwā*, III:443; Ibn Taymiyya, *Minhāj*, II:233.

[118] Ibn Taymiyya, *Majmūᶜ al-Fatāwā*, IV:431–3, 441–2; Ibn Taymiyya, *al-Fatāwā*, III:444–5, 458; Ibn Taymiyya, *Minhāj*, II:243. Ibn Taymiyya's student Ibn Qayyim al-Jawziyya (d. 751/1350–1), in his *Aḥkām*, II:469–70, argued that if the rebels rely on a *ta'wīl*, they should not be held liable. But if two groups fight for tribal reasons (*ᶜaṣabiyya*), they should be held liable to each other.

[119] Ibn Taymiyya, *al-Fatāwā*, III:457–8.

[120] Ibn Taymiyya, *Majmūᶜ al-Fatāwā*, IV:452; Ibn Taymiyya, *al-Fatāwā*, III:514–15; Ibn Taymiyya, *Minhāj*, II:232. Ibn Taymiyya argues that rebels are not held liable because they believed in good faith in the legality of their actions: *Minhāj*, II:246. He also compares the *bughāh* to those who enjoin the good and forbid the evil because of the mistaken belief in the justness of their cause. Ibn Taymiyya, *al-Fatāwa*, XIV:171–3.

[121] Ibn Taymiyya, *Majmūᶜ al-Rasā'il*, II:378–9.

evidence in the scriptural sources that the Khawārij, if they rebelled, must be fought, and that the masses should aid a ruler against the Khawārij. He argues, however, that al-Shāfiᶜī and the Kufān jurists erroneously equated the Khawārij and other rebels, and by doing so gave support to *fitna*. By equating the Khawārij and other rebels, these jurists effectively created an obligation upon the masses to support a ruler against all rebels. Ibn Taymiyya argues that these jurists went as far as presuming that any ruler is to be considered the just ruler, and that anyone who rises in an armed insurrection against such a ruler is to be presumed a rebel. Therefore these jurists created an obligation upon all people to support the presumed just ruler against anyone who might rebel against him. Ibn Taymiyya asserts that this is a form of reprehensible tribalism (*ᶜaṣabiyya*), presumably because the ruler is supported whether he is just or not.[122] According to Ibn Taymiyya, God did not command the fighting of rebels; rather, He decreed reconciliation between the contending parties, and enjoined that one abstain from becoming involved in *fitna*. By requiring that people support rulers against rebels, these jurists effectively required people to become involved in reprehensible *fitan*. Ibn Taymiyya concludes that people should not obey rulers if it means disobeying God, and therefore people should not obey rulers if such rulers command them to fight rebels or become involved in a *fitna*.[123]

Having condemned the idea of blindly supporting rulers against rebels, Ibn Taymiyya goes on to condemn the idea of rebellion itself. He contends that *aḥkām al-bughāh* has incited *fitna* by lending support to the idea of rebellion. Throughout the ages, he argues, many jurists and religious people have risen in armed insurrection, believing in the correctness of their interpretation or cause. These people sought to enjoin the good and forbid the evil, or to establish justice, but all they ever achieved was to spread *fitna* and bloodshed. Invariably, they caused more harm than good by rebelling, and they realized at the end that their efforts, even if well intentioned, were entirely misguided and in vain.[124] Ibn Taymiyya argues that the reason for this repeated pattern of behavior is shortsightedness and lack of patience. People by their very nature gravitate towards insisting upon demanding their rights and rejecting injustice. Therefore, when a ruler commits injustice and deprives people of their rights, people

[122] Ibn Taymiyya, *Majmūᶜ al-Fatāwā*, IV:440–1, 452; Ibn Taymiyya, *al-Fatāwā*, III:443; Ibn Taymiyya, *Minhāj*, II:232. Ibn Taymiyya argues that this is also similar to being blindly loyal to a certain group, teacher, or school of thought. All such forms of blind loyalty are reprehensible.

[123] Ibn Taymiyya, *Majmūᶜ al-Fatāwā*, IV:442–3.

[124] Ibn Taymiyya, *Minhāj*, II:241, 243–4.

tend to rebel, but in doing so, they fail to consider the public good, and the widespread corruption that results from such rebellions.[125] In order to demonstrate the point, Ibn Taymiyya engages in lengthy discussions on the early rebellions in Islam, attempting to prove that all such rebellions were misguided and resulted in more harm than good. Among the rebellions or conflicts that he discusses are the following: the war between al-Amīn and al-Ma'mūn; the rebellions by Ṭalḥa, al-Zubayr, and ʿĀ' isha; al-Ḥusayn b. ʿAlī; Ibn al-Zubayr; Muḥammad and Ibrāhīm b. ʿAbd Allāh; Ibn al-Ashʿath; Ibn al-Muhallab and ʿAbd Allāh b. ʿAlī; Zayd b. ʿAlī; and Ibn Muslim.[126] Ibn Taymiyya's point is that all of these political conflicts resulted in immeasurable evil, and therefore should not be emulated in any form. Ibn Taymiyya also engages in a lengthy defense of Muʿāwiya and Yazīd, insisting that it is not appropriate to curse or condemn either of them. Particularly in the case of Yazīd, Ibn Taymiyya's ultimate justification for refusing to condemn or curse him is that if the door of cursing unjust rulers is opened, it will prove difficult to close.[127] According to Ibn Taymiyya, the best response to unjust rulers is patience.[128]

Ibn Taymiyya's objection to rebellion is functional; it is based on a balance of evils. But he does not seem to be willing to concede that, under certain circumstances, a balance-of-evils analysis might support an armed insurrection. According to Ibn Taymiyya, history has proved that armed insurrections never yield positive results. Nonetheless, he does not support the idea of blind obedience to those in power. As noted above, he insists that one should never obey a ruler's sinful command, and should not support rulers against rebels. He advocates non-violent resistance to illegal commands, and seems to accept that in certain circumstances one may use violence in self-defense. In response to the question of whether one may defend oneself in a *fitna*, he simply notes that there is a difference of opinion on the matter.[129] As to whether one should affirmatively enjoin the good and forbid the evil through non-violent means, again Ibn Taymiyya employs a balance-of-evil analysis. He argues that, for example, a sulṭān (absolute ruler) may convert to Islam but continue to drink alcohol and commit other sins. One should

[125] Ibid., 244.

[126] Ibn Taymiyya, *Majmūʿ al-Fatāwā*, IV:450–2; Ibn Taymiyya, *Minhāj*, II:239–43, 245–6.

[127] Ibn Taymiyya, *Majmūʿ al-Fatāwā*, IV:507–8; Ibn Taymiyya, *Minhāj*, II:253–4; Ibn Taymiyya, *al-Fatāwā*, III:455.

[128] Ibn Taymiyya, *Majmūʿ al-Fatāwā*, XXXV:21, IV:443; Ibn Taymiyya, *Minhāj*, II:241–2; Ibn Taymiyya, *al-Siyāsa*, 139.

[129] Ibn Taymiyya, *al-Siyāsa*, 77.

attempt to prevent such a ruler from committing such sins. But if there is a risk that upon being told to refrain from drinking, the ruler will abandon Islam altogether and become an apostate, then such a ruler should be left alone, and one should not attempt to reform him. Nonetheless, this does not mean that one should obey a ruler's sinful commands.[130] Rather, Ibn Taymiyya argues, Muslims should focus on keeping their own private consciences pure and promoting incremental non-violent reforms as circumstances might permit. In this context, Ibn Taymiyya argues that there are Muslims who insist on the ideal of a just caliphate and reject anything less. On the other hand, there are those who unequivocally accept kingship, and completely abandon the ideal of a just caliphate. Both sides, Ibn Taymiyya argues, are wrong. One should not completely reject the political reality of kingship, and one should not forget the ideal of the caliphate. Rather, one should work within the prevailing reality, as long as one does not legitimate what is wrong, and one should strive to achieve the ideal through incremental steps.[131]

Ibn Taymiyya does not espouse neutrality towards political conflicts. Rather, he advocates disengagement from all violent political conflicts; Muslims should not support rulers and should not support rebels either. Although he in principle affirms the paradigms and rules of conduct of *aḥkām al-bughāh* such as non-liability because of the existence of a *ta'wīl* and the prohibition against executing rebels, this is not Ibn Taymiyya's main focus. It is likely that he affirms such paradigms and rules of conduct more out of deference to the inherited legal precedents than from conviction. Despite the fact that he is a virulent critic of *aḥkām al-bughāh*, he is unable to entirely abandon the inherited positions of the legal culture that he criticizes. Ibn Taymiyya himself did not lead a politically quiet life. He served as a law professor in Damascus on several occasions, but lived most of his life between Damascus and Cairo. He consistently adopted theological and legal positions that got him into considerable trouble with the authorities in Damascus and Egypt. In one incident, he refused to issue a *fatwā* that would have permitted Sulṭān al-Nāṣir (r. 693/1293–694/1294, 698/1299–708/1309, 709/1310–741/1341) to seek revenge against, and exterminate, some of his political foes, and as a result, Ibn Taymiyya was imprisoned. In fact, he was imprisoned several times in Alexandria and Damascus, and he eventually died in prison in Damascus. Nonetheless, he was extremely active in supporting the war efforts against the Mongols and was present, in his capacity as an official

[130] Ibn Taymiyya, *Majmūᶜ al-Fatāwā*, XXXV:21, 32. [131] Ibid., 27–32.

preacher, at the victory over the Mongols in Shaghab (699/1299). Importantly, in 704/1305 he took part in the fighting against the Ismāᶜīlīs and Nuṣayrīs in Jabal Kasrawān in Syria, and he made a habit throughout his life of attacking groups that he considered innovators in religion, such as the Ṣūfīs, Khawārij, Rāfiḍa, Qadariyya, Muᶜtazila, and Ashᶜariyya.[132]

Ibn Taymiyya's personal history disproves any suspicion that his deconstruction of, or lack of commitment to, *aḥkām al-bughāh* was the result of a desire to appease the political authorities of his age. However, his history does help in contextualizing and understanding Ibn Taymiyya's system of priorities. He was preoccupied with the external threat posed to Islam by the Mongols, and with the internal threat posed by what he considered to be heretical theologies. Confronted by these threats, he insisted upon the imperative of unity among Muslims. But he also insisted upon the ideal of the state as the protector of order and stability, and guarantor of correct religion or orthodoxy. This is evident from his consistent exhortations that the state must refrain from engaging in battles with political foes, but must relentlessly combat unorthodox groups such as the Khawārij. In his *responsa*, Ibn Taymiyya insists that the Fāṭimids of Egypt, and the Nuṣayriyya, Ismāᶜīliyya, Qarāmiṭa, Bāṭiniyya, Karrāmiyya, and al-Muḥrima cannot be considered rebels, but must be fought and treated as heretics.[133] Other than the problem of heretical groups, it is clear from the *responsa* literature that Ibn Taymiyya's time was plagued by a considerable amount of feuding and civil strife between tribes. When asked about infighting between such groups, Ibn Taymiyya does not focus on the technicalities of *aḥkām al-bughāh*. Instead, he consistently emphasizes that all fighting between Muslims, regardless of the reason, is a *fitna*, and is strictly prohibited.[134] In his book *al-Siyāsa al-Sharᶜiyyah* he argues that all types of tribal feuding are by definition not an acceptable *ta'wīl*, and hence do not qualify under *aḥkām al-bughāh*.[135]

Ibn Taymiyya's system of priorities is also evident in his unequivocal condemnation of banditry and brigandage. He gives the impression that

[132] Ben Cheneb, "Ibn Taimīya"; Laoust, "Ibn Taymiyya"; Ibn al-ᶜImād, *Shadharāt*, VI:80–6; al-Ziriklī, *al-Aᶜlām*, I:144. See Ibn Rajab, *al-Dhayl*, IV:320–35, which provides many details about his persecution.

[133] Ibn Taymiyya, *al-Fatāwā*, III:487, 513–15. Ibn Taymiyya is asked about two groups that refuse to obey the ruler and constantly fight with each other. These groups do not pray and do not observe the laws of Islam. Furthermore, they take each other's prisoners captive and sell the captives to non-Muslims. Ibn Taymiyya responds that the state must fight both groups and teach them the laws of Islam: see ibid., III:472–3.

[134] Ibid., III:442, 460, 463.

[135] Ibn Taymiyya, *al-Siyāsa*, 70. He cites the fighting between the tribes of Qays and Yaman as examples of prohibited tribal feuding. In *al-Fatāwā*, III:463, he condemns feuding and vengeance killings.

banditry was widely practiced in Egypt, Syria, and Arabia by bedouins, and what he refers to as *fasaqat al-jund* (mercenary or outlaw soldiers). He describes bandits as those who seek to terrorize people and pillage and rape, and he insists that the state must fight and destroy such groups.[136] But he does not concede much discretion to the state in dealing with such groups. Therefore he argues that such groups must be held jointly and severally liable for the acts of their individuals. If a member of a group commits murder, the group must be executed; if a member usurps property, the group must have limbs amputated from opposite ends; and if they raise weapons without killing or usurping property then the ruler has discretion to either imprison or exile them according to what the public interest dictates.[137] Ibn Taymiyya alludes to the political connotations of the crime of banditry by asserting that most often this crime is committed by soldiers or tribes that resist the authority of the state. Such groups take refuge in the mountains and form alliances to attack travelers, often between Syria and Iraq, and call this *al-nahīḍa* (which could mean the support, resilience, resistance, or rebellion).[138] Although Ibn Taymiyya states that bandits do not fight over religion or politics but simply over material gains,[139] this statement is ambiguous. It could mean that if groups pursue terror-filled tactics such as those employed by bandits, they are not to be considered rebels. Alternatively, it could mean that if a group has religious or political motives, it is not to be treated under the laws of banditry, even if the group pursues methods similar in nature to those pursued by bandits. It is not clear which of these two meanings Ibn Taymiyya intends, but it is likely that he means the former rather than the latter. Ibn Taymiyya is primarily concerned with the impact that stealthy and terror-filled means of attack have on society. He emphasizes that the methods pursued by bandits have the effect of causing public corruption and spreading insecurity and lawlessness. Furthermore, we have already demonstrated that he was not sympathetic enough to the moral claims of political rebels to strive to protect them regardless of the means pursued. Additionally, he notes that there is support for the view that a political assassin should be treated as a bandit because of the public corruption (*al-fasād al-ʿāmm*) that such a person creates.[140]

In summary, Ibn Taymiyya opposes rebellion, not out of an unreserved fidelity to those in power, but out of fidelity to the ideal of order

[136] Ibn Taymiyya, *al-Siyāsa*, 75; Ibn Taymiyya, *al-Fatāwā*, III:525.
[137] Ibn Taymiyya, *al-Siyāsa*, 70–1.
[138] Ibid., 71, 75. [139] Ibid., 75. [140] Ibid., 74.

and stability. Even then, he is unwilling to argue that people should support rulers regardless of the rulers' conduct. For Ibn Taymiyya, all forms of violent conflict between Muslims are reprehensible and forbidden. But this imperative takes second place to the importance of insuring orthodoxy and sound religion. Ibn Taymiyya clearly expected the state to play an active role in fighting heresy, and destroying groups that destabilize society, such as bandits. Significantly, he does not hesitate to label soldiers, who might otherwise be helpful to the state, as bandits if their behavior destabilizes society and spreads terror. As far as the law of rebellion is concerned, Ibn Taymiyya was a revisionist, not because he consciously attempted to reform or develop the traditional discourses on the subject. Rather, he was a revisionist because he attempted to deconstruct the field, and stress what he considered its unprincipled and lawless tendencies. According to Ibn Taymiyya, the field tends to simultaneously encourage rebellion and lend support to rulers against rebels regardless of the substantive claims of the rulers or the rebels. The jurists equated the Khawārij with all other rebels because they did not wish to become entangled in the substantive claims made by specific rebellious groups. Therefore they argued that any plausible interpretation is sufficient to qualify a group as *bughāh*. Ibn Taymiyya found this to be reprehensible because he was more of a moralist, and less of a jurist than he perhaps realized.[141] His system of priorities emphasized correct belief and religion first, then order and stability, and finally the technicalities of the inherited legal discourses. In many ways, Ibn Taymiyya tried to rise above the technicalities of the law of rebellion, and to emphasize the perceived substantive needs of religion and society. It is rather ironic that through constant tribulations Ibn Taymiyya was the one who repeatedly found himself accused of heresy and incitement against rulers. But it is exactly his attempts to construct paradigms beyond political expediency that made him a problematic political figure. By challenging the legal presumption that rulers, whether just or unjust, should be supported against rebels, he was, in fact, instituting a significant legal change in the discourses on rebellion and taking a thoroughly political position. Importantly, he shared more with the early jurists who constructed the discourses on rebellion than he was willing to admit. The early jurists

[141] This statement is bound to generate some controversy, but I believe it is warranted. Over many legal issues, Ibn Taymiyya would, so to speak, cut to the chase and do away with the legal technicalities in favor of what he considered to be desirable normative values. Furthermore, often he did not hesitate to break away from Ḥanbalī legal precedent. This issue needs a separate book.

responded to absolute moral claims of power by rulers by granting rebels a competing moral claim. The discourses on rebellion rendered moral claims to power relative, and simply a matter of interpretation (*ta'wīl*). Furthermore, any ruler, just or unjust, was declared bound by the rules limiting the discretion of rulers in dealing with rebels. In other words, the early juridical discourses limited and qualified the support given to rulers against rebels. Ibn Taymiyya might have been right in suspecting that *aḥkām al-bughāh* encouraged rebellions, but he was wrong in assuming that the early jurists intended to give rulers unqualified and uncritical support. Like Ibn Taymiyya, the early jurists sought to qualify the support given to rulers but through a different methodology. They reacted with a belief in the ideal of the technicalities of the law as a restraining element. With the benefit of many centuries past, Ibn Taymiyya sought to rise above the technicalities, and to emphasize the substantive ideal of qualified support to rulers. Ultimately, he differed from the jurists he criticized in method and not in purpose.

Ibn Taymiyya's criticisms were directed at the doctrines and ideas of the inherited discourses on rebellion. His revisionist program was based on a polemical deconstruction of the logic and paradigms of the discourses of the traditional trend. Although Ibn Taymiyya does not acknowledge it, many of his contemporaries revised the inherited doctrines on rebellion in substantial and significant ways. Nonetheless, unlike Ibn Taymiyya, they did not attempt to deconstruct or criticize the inherited doctrines. Rather, they instituted the revisions subtly, and at times even claimed historical authenticity in support of such revisions. Often, the jurists gave the distinct impression that novel legal doctrines were settled and well-established points of law. A reader who did not trace the historical progression of the discourses would hardly realize the existence of revisions or developments in the law. Unlike Ibn Taymiyya, the revisionist jurists emphasized the technicalities and details of the law of rebellion, but reformed its doctrines so as to offer symbolic and moral resistance to unjust rulers. As I argue below, besides insisting on a certain minimum standard of behavior in dealing with rebels, these jurists refused to unequivocally condemn rebellion or lend unmitigated support to rulers. This should be understood in the context of the power dynamics taking place between the jurists and the state. By rehabilitating the law of rebellion, they legitimated the moral function of the law and the legal institution that they represented. In other words, by insisting that the law did not simply support rulers, wrong or right, these jurists legitimated and defended the integrity of the legal discourses.

The revisionist discourse

The jurists of the revisionist trend start their analysis by reaffirming the general rule: Rulers should be obeyed and rebellion is impermissible. Some jurists specify that whether the ruler is a usurper, just, or unjust, he must be obeyed in order for stability and order to be achieved.[142] Many jurists repeat the formula that a ruler cannot be obeyed if it entails disobeying God,[143] and some go on to explain that there is a difference between a sin (*maᶜṣiya*) and hardship, or something reprehensible (*makrūh*). Commanding a sin means ordering something that is clearly, and without doubt, contrary to the laws of God. *Makrūh*, however, is a command that entails doing something that is reprehensible or disfavored. These jurists note that there is some disagreement as to whether a ruler should be disobeyed if he commands a sin or commands something reprehensible. The majority of the jurists, however, state that as long as the ruler's command does not clearly entail committing an obvious sin, the ruler should be obeyed.[144] Rebellion means refusing to obey the command of the lawful ruler or rising in an insurrection attempting to overthrow and resist such a ruler or his agents. Having established these familiar grounds, the jurists of the revisionist trend go on to reiterate that rebellion, as long as it is based on a plausible interpretation or cause, is not a sin, and that the word *baghy* does not entail blame or censure.[145] They also reiterate that all the *ḥadīth* attributed to the Prophet that

[142] Al-Ṣāwī (d. 1241/1825–6), *Bulgha*, II:414; al-Zaylaᶜī (d. 743/1343), *Tabyīn*, III:234; Ibn ᶜĀbidīn (d. 1252/1836–7), *Radd*, VI:411, 414; al-Nawawī (d. 676/1277–8), *al-Majmūᶜ*, XIX:190, 198; al-Nawawī, *Rawḍa*, VII:266–7; al-Ramlī (d. 1004/1595–6), *Ghāya*, 405; al-Shirbīnī (d. 977/1569–70), *Mughnī*, IV:123, 132; al-Anṣārī (d. 926/1520), *Fatḥ*, 155; al-Ramlī (d. 1004/1595–6), *Nihāya*, VII:409; Ibn Jamāᶜa (d. 733/1332–3), *Taḥrīr*, 55, 61–2. Al-Jamal (*Ḥāshiya*, V:113, 121) adds that a usurper's claim to power is recognized only if the person overthrown by the usurper did not have a better claim to power, i.e. through a proper delegation or contract.

[143] Al-Ṣāwī, *Bulgha*, II:414–15; Ibn ᶜĀbidīn, *Radd*, VI:414; al-Ramlī, *Ghāya*, 407.

[144] Al-Khirshī (1101/1689–90), *Sharḥ*, VIII:60; al-Dusūqī (1201/1786–7), *Ḥāshiya*, IV:298; Ibn ᶜĀbidīn, *Radd*, VI:416; al-Jamal, *Ḥāshiya*, V:114; al-Nawawī, *Sharḥ*, XII:464–5, 468; Ibn Ḥajar al-Haytamī (d. 974/1566–7), in his *Fatḥ*, II:294–5, also challenges the idea that the Muslim nation needs to be ruled by a single *imām*. He argues that not since the days of the Companions has a single ruler ruled over all Muslim territory. See the discussion on *maᶜṣiya* and the limits of obedience in al-Kāndahlawī, *Awjaz*, VIII:214–15.

[145] Al-Ṣāwī, *Bulgha*, II:414–15; al-Nawawī, *Rawḍa*, VII:270–1; Ibn Ḥajar al-Haytamī, *Fatḥ*, II:294; al-Shirbīnī, *Mughnī*, IV:124; al-Anṣārī, *Fatḥ*, 153; al-Ramlī, *Nihāya*, VII:402; Ibn al-Muqrī (d. 837/1433), *Kitāb*, III:371; Ibn al-Muqrī, *Ikhlāṣ*, IV:127; Ibn Jamāᶜa, *Taḥrīr*, 240. Al-Jamal (*Ḥāshiya*, V:113, 116) adds that what the rebels destroy during the course of their rebellion cannot be described as allowed or not allowed. It is merely a mistake that should be forgiven. See also al-Shirbīnī, *Mughnī*, IV:125.

condemn or curse rebels only apply to those who rebel without a plausible interpretation or cause. As long as rebels act in good faith while believing in the justness of their cause, they are not blameworthy or accursed, and the *ḥadīth* of the Prophet does not apply to them.[146] Furthermore, these jurists go on to lay out in great detail the rules pertaining to the proper treatment of rebels. They repeat many of the inherited discussions about how rebels are to be fought and how they are to be treated once the fighting ends. Rebels are not to be held liable for life and property destroyed during the course of their rebellion, and since rebels are not considered iniquitous (*fasaqa*), their adjudications and testimony should be accepted and validated.[147]

Thus far, the discourses of the revisionist trend appear identical to the traditional inherited doctrines. However, these jurists introduce several significant new elements to the discussion. Several jurists, particularly from the Ḥanafī school, assert that not only is there no material distinction between the Khawārij and the *bughāh*, but also that, as a matter of principle, *takfīr* (the act of calling a Muslim an unbeliever) must be avoided. They note that *ahl al-ḥadīth* did, in fact, call the Khawārij unbelievers, but they claim that no one has approved of the position adopted by *ahl al-ḥadīth*. Typically, these jurists comment that "while it is true that many sectarians (*ahl al-madhāhib*) accuse others of disbelief, the jurists do not do so (*al-fuqahā'u lā yukaffirūn*)." They also add that, in this context, "only the opinions of the jurists matter (*lā*ᶜ*ibrata bi ghayri al-fuqahā'*)."[148] These statements are significant because they are made in the context of

146 Ibn al-Humām (d. 681/1282), *Sharḥ*, VI:97; Ibn ᶜĀbidīn, *Radd*, VI:416; al-Nawawī, *Rawḍa*, VII:271; al-Jamal, *Ḥāshiya*, V:113; al-Ramlī, *Fatāwā*, IV:19; al-Ramlī, *Ghāya*, 405; al-Ramlī, *Nihāya*, VII:402, 403–4; Ibn Ḥajar al-Haytamī, *Fatḥ*, II:294; al-Shirbīnī, *Mughnī*, IV:124; Ibn al-Muqrī, *Kitāb*, III:371. See also al-Wazīr (d. 840/1436), *al-*ᶜ*Awāṣim*, VIII:12–13, which argues that the majority of Sunnī jurists did not consider rebellion against an unjust ruler a sin.

147 Al-Ṣāwī, *Bulgha*, II:415; al-Khirshī, *Sharḥ*, VIII:61; al-Dusūqī, *Ḥāshiya*, IV:300; al-ᶜAynī, *al-Bināya*, VI:750–1; al-Nawawī, *al-Majmū*ᶜ, XIX:210–11, 214–15; al-Nawawī, *Rawḍa*, VII: 273–4; al-Jamal, *Ḥāshiya*, V:115; al-Ramlī, *Ghāya*, 406; al-Ramlī, *Nihāya*, VII:403–4; Ibn Ḥajar al-Haytamī, *Fatḥ*, II:296–7; al-Shirbīnī, *Mughnī*, IV:124; al-Anṣāri, *Fatḥ*, V:153–4; Ibn al-Muqrī, *Kitāb*, III:372; Ibn Jamāᶜa, *Taḥrīr*, 241. Several of the above-cited jurists also note that the rebels' adjudications should be accepted out of concern for the public interest. Some Ḥanafī jurists continued to hold that the rebels are liable in the Hereafter, but not on this earth, for life and property destroyed: for example, see al-ᶜAynī, *al-Bināya*, VI:747; al-Ṭarsawī, *Tuḥfa*, 131. Other Ḥanafī jurists continued to state that the rebels are iniquitous: for example, see Ibn al-Humām, *Sharḥ*, VI:100, 102; Ibn ᶜĀbidīn, *Radd*, VI:420–1.

148 Ibn al-Humām, *Sharḥ*, VI:93–4; Ibn ᶜĀbidīn, *Radd*, VI:413; al-ᶜAynī, *al-Bināya*, VI:735–6, 748; Ibn Nujaym al-Miṣrī (d. 970/1562), *al-Baḥr*, V:235. Also see al-Wazīr, *al-*ᶜ*Awāṣim*, IV:369, which argues that the Sunnī jurists do not consider the Khawārij unbelievers, and VIII:10–11, which argues the same regarding the Muᶜtazila.

discussing the requirement of a *ta'wīl*.[149] Their import is that one may not discount the validity of an interpretation or cause in order to accuse a group of rebels of being unbelievers. Hence, the requirement that the interpretation or cause be plausible becomes minimalist in nature. Even sectarian groups (*mubtadiᶜa*) may not be accused of disbelief in the context of applying the law of rebellion.[150] Of course, the accusation of disbelief or *takfīr* is a powerful rhetorical device that could be used against rebels; however, the statement that jurists, in the context of the law of rebellion, do not practice *takfīr* is a powerful symbolic counterbalance. Stated in the unequivocal fashion quoted above, it tends to strengthen the idea that rebels may not be accused of being unbelievers.

Nonetheless, the jurists of the revisionist trend go beyond this rhetorical point, and argue that if a group possesses a degree of strength (*shawka*), but does not have an interpretation or cause (*ta'wīl*), the group is not to be held liable for life or property destroyed during the course of its rebellion. If a group which lacks an interpretation or cause commits acts of banditry, its members are to be treated as bandits. But if the group rises in rebellion and does not commit acts of banditry, it is not to be held liable, even if it lacks a plausible interpretation or cause. The jurists justify this position on the grounds of the public interest in achieving reconciliation and social peace. However, the effect of this ruling is to deemphasize the importance of a *ta'wīl*, because even if a *ta'wīl* is missing the group might still not be held liable. But the jurists of the revisionist trend do not completely compromise the centrality of the existence of an interpretation or cause. They argue that if a group lacks a plausible interpretation or cause, its testimony and adjudications should not be accepted, and, other than the issue of liability, the group is not to be afforded the treatment given to rebels.[151] Significantly, Mālikī jurists of

[149] However, in the context of discussing *zandaqa* and apostasy, al-Qanūjī (*al-Rawḍa*, II:421–2, 431) asserts that before jurists proclaim someone an unbeliever, the evidence against such a person must be clearer than the sun itself. He adds that the Bāṭiniyya and the Bohras of India should not be killed as heretics or apostates. But see the discussion in al-Subkī, *Fatāwā*, II:566–93, who, as noted above, mentions the execution of a Rāfiḍī in Damascus because he cursed the Companions and refused to pray with the *jamāᶜa* (congregation) in the Umawī mosque.

[150] For instance, see al-Ramlī, *Nihāya*, VII:403–4. But some revisionist jurists, however, argued that the Khawārij should be treated as bandits: see, for example, Ibn al-Muqrī, *Ikhlāṣ*, IV:128; al-Nawawī, *Rawḍa*, VII:272. But see Ibn Ḥajar al-Haytamī, *Fatḥ*, II:296, al-Anṣāri, *Fatḥ*, V:153, and al-Shirbīnī, *Mughnī*, IV:124, for a refutation of this view. See, on al-Rawāfiḍ, the *fatwā* in Ibn ᶜĀbidīn, *al-ᶜUqūd*, I:103–7, which argues that the Rawāfiḍ (Shīᶜa) are both *bughāh* and *kuffār* at the same time.

[151] Al-Jamal, *Ḥāshiya*, V:116–7; al-Shirbīnī, *Mughnī*, IV:126; al-Ramlī, *Ghāya*, 406; al-Ramlī, *Nihāya*, VII:405; al-Ramlī, *Fatāwā*, IV:19–20; al-Anṣāri, *Fatḥ*, V:153; Ibn al-Muqrī, *Ikhlāṣ*, IV:126, 128; Ibn al-Muqrī, *Kitāb*, III:372–3; Ibn Ḥajar al-Haytamī, *Fatḥ*, II:295; al-Nawawī, *Rawḍa*, VII:

the revisionist trend go further and argue that if a group rebels against an unjust ruler, it will be presumed to have a plausible interpretation or cause (*al-khāriju ʿalā ghayri al-ʿādili ka al-mutaʾawwil*). Therefore, if the ruler is deemed unjust no inquiry should be made into the existence of a plausible interpretation or cause. By definition, if the ruler is unjust the rebels are deemed to have a plausible interpretation or cause.[152] The effect of these concepts is to reduce the need to make substantive inquiries into the plausibility of the rebels' interpretation or cause. Even rebels who might lack an interpretation or cause are afforded some protection.

Beyond modifications to the concept of *taʾwīl*, the jurists of the revisionist trend go beyond the traditional paradigms by reinserting an inquiry into the substantive quality of those in power. This inquiry is not intended to assess the basis for the legitimacy of power, or question whether those in power are legitimate. The majority of jurists had held that power could be attained by *de facto* usurpation.[153] Rather, the substantive inquiry is directed specifically at the issue of rebellion. These discourses reflect what might be called a "moral or evaluative aspect" and a "positive or procedural aspect." The moral or evaluative aspect relates to whether those who commit an insurrection are outlaws in the first place. The moral or evaluative aspect also relates to whether the ruler has a right to fight or resist those who commit an insurrection against him. The positive or procedural aspect relates to whether Muslims should assist the rebels or assist the ruler. It also relates to the treatment of those who commit an insurrection regardless of how they are classified at the moral level.

At the moral or evaluative level, many jurists make a distinction between rebels who, in self-defense, resist the illegal orders of an unjust ruler (sometimes referred to as *imtināʿ*), and those who rise in rebellion seeking to overthrow the ruler (sometimes referred to as *khurūj*). An example of the first (i.e. *imtināʿ*) is when a ruler demands unjust taxes. Upon the refusal of the group to pay, the ruler seeks to exact the taxes by force, and

275, 276. But Ibn Jamāʿa (*Taḥrīr*, 240, 243) argues that the same analysis applies to rebels who lack a *taʾwīl* or a *shawka*.

152 Al-Ṣāwī, *Bulgha*, II:415; al-Khirshī, *Sharḥ*, VIII:61; al-Dusūqī, *Ḥāshiya*, IV:300.

153 However, al-Jamal (*Ḥāshiya*, V:121) argues that if a ruler came to power through a contract or designation, he cannot be removed by usurpation. Al-Shirbīnī (*Mughnī*, IV:132) states the same. Al-Ṣāwī (*Bulgha*, II:414) argues that a usurper is recognized only when the majority of people obey him. Al-Ramlī (*Ghāya*, 407) states that only a usurper who fulfills the proper conditions will be recognized. But it is not clear to what conditions is he referring. It is possible he is referring to the condition of *shawka* (sufficient power or strength) or the eight conditions of *imāma* such as piety and knowledge: see al-Ramlī, *Nihāyat*, VII:409.

the group defends its property. In this case, the jurists assert that those who resist are not rebels at all. They are entirely within their rights.[154] This is to be distinguished from a situation where a group actively seeks to overthrow the ruler and directly assume power. In the first situation, the group seeks only to defend itself and its property from an affirmative duty placed upon it. In the second situation, a group is not responding to a specific injustice inflicted upon it, but actively seeking to replace the ruler in power. In the first situation, the group of people resisting an injustice inflicted upon them are not *bughāh* because they are acting within their rights. On the other hand, those who seek to overthrow the ruler are *bughāh* because they are not fighting in self-defense, but rather, over a desire for power. Some jurists add that if the ruler is unjust it is illegal to seek to overthrow him, but it is also illegal for him to fight the rebels. Consequently, whether the rebels are resisting in self-defense or actively seeking to overthrow the ruler, if the ruler is unjust it is not lawful for him to fight the insurrection. Other jurists argue that if the rebels are seeking to overthrow the ruler, even if he is unjust, he has a right to resist the rebels.[155] In other words, most of the jurists agree that if the cause of the rebellion is an injustice inflicted upon a particular group, then the ruler does not have the right to fight the rebels. But if the rebellion is a conflict over power, and not a response to an injustice, the jurists disagree on whether an unjust ruler has a right to fight the rebels.

At the procedural or positive level, if the ruler is unjust and a rebellion actively seeks to overthrow the ruler, Muslims should not assist the rebels, but should not assist the ruler either. Muslims should not assist an unjust ruler against rebels because the possibility exists that it is his injustice that caused the rebellion in the first place. At the same time, Muslims should not assist the rebels because it is unlawful for them to rebel (*fa-lā yajūzu lahu qitālahum li iḥtimāli an yakūna khurūjuhumᶜalayhi li ẓulmihi wa in*

[154] Ibn al-Humām, *Sharḥ*, VI:96; Ibn Nujaym al-Miṣrī, *al-Baḥr*, V:235; Ibn ᶜĀbidīn, *Radd*, VI:411–12, 416; al-Ramlī, *Nihāya*, VII:402; al-Ṣāwī, *Bulgha*, II:414–15; al-Dusūqī, *Ḥāshiya*, IV:299; II:205. Al-ᶜAynī (*al-Bināya*, VI:735) argues that if the rebels are resisting an injustice, they are not *bughāh*. But he asserts that Muslims should not assist the ruler or the rebels. Al-Zaylaᶜī (*Tabyīn*, III:294) argues the same, as does Al-Ṭarsawī (*Tuḥfa*, 119, 121, 123, 126). Also see the discussion in al-Ḥalabī (d. 956/1549), *Multaqā*, 379, and al-Ṣāwī, *Bulgha*, I:370; al-Khirshī, *Sharḥ*, III:150. Al-Dusūqī (*Ḥāshiya*, II:205) also argues that if a *dhimmī* leaves the abode of Islam because of an injustice inflicted upon him, this will not constitute an abrogation of his covenant with Muslims. Al-Ḥaṭṭāb (*Mawāhib*, VI:279) asserts that if *ahl al-dhimma* rebel against an unjust ruler, that does not constitute an abrogation of their covenant.

[155] Al-Ṣāwī, *Bulgha*, II:414–15; al-Khirshī, *Sharḥ*, VIII:60; al-Dusūqī, *Ḥāshiya*, IV:299; Ibn Ḥajar al-ᶜAsqalānī, *Fatḥ*, XIV:309 and see also the citations below.

kāna lā yajūzu lahum al-khurūju ʿalayhi).[156] In the words of the Mālikī jurist al-Khirshī, "If the *imām* is unjust leave him to the demands made upon him. God punishes one oppressor by another, and then destroys both of them together (*daʿhu wa mā yurādu minhu. Yantaqimu Allāhu min al-ẓālimi bi ẓālimin thumma yantaqimu min kilayhimā*)."[157] However, in the case of a group that resists in self-defense Muslims should assist such a group only if doing so will not result in a greater social harm than good.[158]

Some jurists, however, adopt a position similar to that taken by Ibn Ḥazm, and argue that if a people rebels against a ruler because of his injustice, even if they are seeking to overthrow him, they are not to be considered *bughāh*. In other words, these jurists deny the distinction between resisting in self-defense and attempting to overthrow the ruler. In either case, they argue, if the motivating factor for the rebellion is the injustice of the ruler, then the rebellious group is considered just, and the rebellion justifiable.[159] But this, again, means that Muslims should not

[156] Al-Ṣāwī, *Bulgha*, II:414–15; al-Khirshī, *Sharḥ*, VII:60; al-Dusūqī, *Ḥāshiya*, IV:299. Ibn Ḥajar al-ʿAsqalānī (*Fatḥ*, XIV:309) states that if someone rebels against an unjust ruler, he is excused and it is not permissible to fight the rebel. Al-Zaylaʿī (*Tabyīn*, III:294) argues that if a group resists in self-defense, Muslims should not assist the ruler or the rebels. But if a group seeks to affirmatively overthrow an unjust ruler, then Muslims should either assist the ruler or remain neutral, but should not take part in the rebellion. *Al-Fatāwā al-ʿĀlamgīriyya*, II:284, asserts that if the cause of the rebellion is an injustice inflicted by the ruler on the rebels or on someone else, Muslims should not assist the rebels or the ruler. If, however, the rebels are competing for power, Muslims should assist the ruler. Al-Ṭarsawī (*Tuḥfa*, 119–21, 123, 126) argues for a three-way division: (1) If an injustice has been committed against the rebels, Muslims should not assist the ruler or the rebels. (2) If two somewhat equally culpable or meritorious parties fight for power, Muslims should not get involved and should not support either side. (3) If there is a well-established ruler who has enforced stability and order, and a group tries to overthrow him (but the group has not suffered an injustice), Muslims should assist the ruler against the rebels. Al-Qurṭubī (*al-Jāmiʿ* [1952], VI:157) reports that *ahl al-ḥadīth* held that a person has a right to self-defense but not against the ruler. The right to self-defense cannot be asserted against an injustice inflicted by the ruler.

[157] Al-Khirshī, *Sharḥ*, VIII:60. Al-Shinqīṭī (d. 1322/1904) (see *Tabyīn*, IV:471–2) survived under the patronage of governors in Saudi Arabia and Egypt. Nevertheless, he states that if the ruler is not just, people should not come to his aid during a rebellion. It is not permissible to help an unjust ruler defeat an insurrection. Al-Ḥaṭṭāb (*Mawāhib*, VI:277) notes that it is unlawful to fight rebels if the cause of the rebellion is the injustice of the ruler. He reports that the caliph al-Maʾmūn asked the Egyptian judge Ḥārith Ibn Miskīn about the legality of fighting some rebels in Egypt; Ibn Miskīn responded by saying that it is unlawful to fight rebels if the caliph is a tyrant. He also reports that Mālik said the same to the caliph al-Rashīd.

[158] Ibn ʿĀbidīn, *Radd*, VI:416. Al-ʿAynī (*al-Bināya*, VI:736) reports that (Fakhr al-Dīn) al-Rāzī held that in this case Muslims have a duty to support the rebels regardless of the consequences. Ibn al-Humām (*Sharḥ*, VI:96) argues that in this case Muslims should assist the rebels only if it is clear that an injustice has been committed against such rebels. Ibn Nujaym al-Miṣrī (*al-Baḥr*, V:235–6) argues the same, and adds that if it is clear that an injustice was inflicted upon the rebels *or others*, Muslims should assist the rebels against the ruler.

[159] Al-Wazīr (*al-ʿAwāṣim*, VIII:19) claims that the Sunnīs in general held that one who rebels against an unjust ruler is not a *bāghī*.

assist the ruler, and should assist the rebels only if the benefits outweigh the harm. It is important to note that, under this analysis, this does not necessarily mean that the group committing an insurrection is entitled or has a right to rebel. It only means that if a group rebels and the ruler is unjust, then they, at a moral level, cannot be considered rebels. At the positive or procedural level, whether the jurists distinguished between resisting in self-defense or committing an outright rebellion, and whether the ruler had a right to fight the rebels or not, in all circumstances the ruler remains bound to afford the treatment of *aḥkām al-bughāh* to those whom he fights.

All of the above mentioned specifically relates to whether or not a ruler has a right to fight rebels, and to the moral classification of rebels once a rebellion occurs as a *de facto* matter. It also relates to whether or not Muslims should assist the rebels or the ruler, and what treatment is due to those who rebel. It does not, however, directly address whether rebellion is permitted in the first place. Of course, the notion that a group resisting an injustice inflicted upon it is not breaking the law implicitly endorses a right to what one might call defensive rebellion. But this, arguably, means that rebellion is permitted only when a ruler attempts to assault or usurp the property of certain people, and, as a result, they resist.[160] It does not address the larger issue of when it is permissible to forcibly remove an unjust ruler. In response to this specific issue, many jurists advocated what is effectively a balancing act. Rebels should balance the chance of success and weigh it against the potential harm that will result from the rebellion. If the potential harm to society is grave, and the chances of success are limited, then rebellion is prohibited. However, if the chances of success are reasonably good, and the harm to society is limited, then rebellion is permitted.[161]

[160] However, I argue below that distinguishing between defensive and aggressive rebellions is, at a practical level, untenable. This distinction should be appreciated as a symbolic construct.

[161] Ibn ᶜĀbidīn, *Radd*, VI:415. Al-Dusūqī (*Ḥāshiya*, IV:299) argues that if a just person rebels, seeking to overthrow an unjust ruler, then rebellion becomes permissible and Muslims should assist the just rebel. Al-Wazīr (*al-ᶜAwāṣim*, VIII:75, 165) argues that the Sunnīs, like the Shīᶜīs, in principle permitted rebelling against unjust rulers. But, he argues, both Sunnīs and Shīᶜīs limited the permissibility to occasions when the good outweighs the harm. Al-ʾUbbī (*Sharḥ*, VI:529) argues that rebelling and attempting to overthrow a corrupt ruler is permissible only if there is reasonable certainty that the rebellion will succeed. Al-Rāzī (*al-Tafsīr*, XXVIII:109) asserts that it is possible for the ruler to be the *bāghī*. In that case, he may be resisted by proper advice or stronger means as long as a *fitna* does not result. Al-Shirbīnī (*Mughnī*, IV:123) notes that some have argued that if the ruler came to power through usurpation, then it is permissible to rebel against him if he is unjust. But if he came to power through a contract, it is not permissible to rebel against him. Ibn Mufliḥ *Kitāb*, VI:160) reports that al-Nawawī held that an unjust ruler may be removed by force only if the attempt to remove him does not result in a greater harm. See also the discussion on when rebellion is permissible in al-Nawawī, *Sharḥ*, XII:470–1;

The significance of the fact that some jurists effectively permitted rebellion after a balancing act should not be overestimated. Nor should it be taken as an indication of either radicalism or activism on the part of these jurists. Advocating outright rebellion runs the risk of undermining the stability of the legal order that ultimately supports the corporate legal culture of the jurists. In many ways it does not constitute a negotiation between the political and legal orders, but rather an outright declaration of war by the legal order against the political order. That is why even the jurists who advocated a balancing act hedged their analysis with repeated warnings against the evils of *fitna* and chaos. It is clear that these jurists sought a way to achieve greater justice in the political order, but worried about the untamed zeal of political idealists and opportunists. Therefore explicit permission to rebel was given grudgingly and with much reserve. The majority of the jurists of the revisionist trend negotiated, through creative acts, with the political order, instead of declaring an open state of war. It is the symbolism of these creative acts, and the subtleties and details of the legal discourses, that was most material to the negotiating process.

THE LINGUISTIC PRACTICE AND THE SYMBOLISMS OF REBELLION AND TERROR

As argued earlier, a large gap remained between the way the political order dealt with rebels and the dictates of the law of rebellion.[162] Furthermore, from the writings of Ibn Taymiyya, one suspects that both rulers and rebels used the paradigms of *aḥkām al-bughāh* to support their own interests. Rulers cited these paradigms to argue that Muslims must support the ruler against rebels, and rebels cited them to justify rebellion. Jurists of the traditional trend continued to repeat the inherited doctrine without substantial change. In doing so, they validated the legitimacy and integrity of this body of law, specifically, and the *Sharīʿa*, generally. Jurists of the revisionist trend, however, responded differently. They affirmed the doctrines of *aḥkām al-bughāh*, and continued to demand conciliation and lenient treatment towards rebels. But they also deemphasized, but did not completely undermine, the centrality of the *ta'wīl*. They argued that *takfīr* (ruling that a Muslim is an infidel) is not appropriate in this context. They also argued that even a group without a plausible *ta'wīl* cannot be held liable for life and property destroyed during the course of rebellion. Some went further and asserted that if the ruler is unjust,

Kāndahlawī, *Awjaz*, VIII:215; Ibn Ḥajar al-ʿAsqalānī, *Fatḥ*, XIV:498; al-ʾUbbī, *Sharḥ*, VI:554, 563–5.

[162] Al-Zaylaʿī (*Tabyīn*, III:293) hints at this fact by asserting that this body of law is rarely applied.

the rebels will be presumed to have a valid *ta'wīl*. More importantly, however, the jurists of the revisionist trend argued that if the rebellion is in response to an injustice, then the rebels are not *bughāh* at all. This, in effect, constituted an admission that *aḥkām al-bughāh* was ineffective, at the pragmatic administrative level, because ultimately this law was not going to be applied by rulers. Therefore the conduct of a group responding to an injustice was decriminalized or made a non-issue. By declaring such a group not to be *bughāh*, the jurists were making a rhetorical, and not a legal, point. It should be remembered that the status of *bughāh* is a preferred or special status, and therefore rebels would want to qualify as *bughāh* in order to avoid liability for crimes and other possible harsh treatment. But the revisionist jurists argued that the group that resists an injustice has not committed an infraction in the first place, and does not need to qualify for any status at all. At the symbolic and rhetorical level, this meant two things: (1) the ruler does not have a right to even fight the rebels; (2) Muslims, at a minimum, should not assist the ruler against the rebels. The power of this largely symbolic point can be appreciated when one considers the inherently subjective and relative standard set by the jurists. It is difficult, if not impossible, to evaluate whether a rebellion is undertaken to resist an injustice or to overthrow the ruler. Evaluating whether a group is rebelling in response to an affirmative duty placed upon it, or whether it is aggressively seeking to overthrow the ruler, is untenable. The procedural difficulties in making this type of evaluation are insurmountable. Furthermore, it is difficult to imagine that a judge would declare that in a specific case the ruler did not have a right to fight or resist a certain rebellion.

The early response of *aḥkām al-bughāh* was to widen the scope of the application of the law by objectifying the inquiry into rebellion. Whether a ruler is just or unjust, he is bound to afford rebels a certain preferred treatment. All the rebels need in order to qualify is a degree of strength and a plausible interpretation or cause. The early purposes of the law had become frustrated. The jurists of the revisionist trend responded by affirming the initial purposes, but they also added a subjective inquiry: Who is the real cause of the rebellion? By introducing this inquiry, these jurists retained a symbolic and largely rhetorical power, the power of definition. Theoretically, if the cause of the rebellion is the injustice of the ruler, Muslims are under no obligation to assist the ruler.[163] The act of discoursive negotiation is evident in the fact that these jurists also

[163] Of course, earlier Shīʿī, and some Sunnī, jurists had argued that Muslims should not assist an unjust ruler in fighting or persecuting rebels. However, the revisionist trend adopted and systematized this position in Sunnī discourses, and developed its symbolic and rhetorical significance.

emphasized the duty of obedience to rulers, whether just or not, and emphasized the general impermissibility of rebellion. In other words, the jurists of the revisionist trend did not seek to declare war on the political order, but sought to bargain and negotiate with the political order by further mitigating its moral claims against rebels. They glumly noted that their day and age had become so corrupt that it had become very difficult to distinguish a just from an unjust party; everyone fought over worldly affairs.[164] This implied a tacit condemnation of rebellion because it expressed a degree of cynicism about advocates of just causes – people are motivated by material gain and power rather than principle. However, this cynicism is balanced by condemnations of the corruption and injustice of rulers, and assertions that such rulers often oppress people.[165] Concurrently, the jurists declared those who rebel because they suffer an injustice to be just.

The negotiative aspects of this discourse can be understood only by looking beyond the juridical generalizations and focusing on the details and subtleties. In other words, it is the reservations, exceptions, and qualifications to the general principles that are the most telling as to the purposes and objects of the legal discourse. As the typically insightful jurist al-Wazīr noted, only those who scrutinize the particularities of the Sunnī juristic discourses will understand its purposes (*wa in ẓanna dhālika man lam yabḥath min ẓawāhiri baʿḍi iṭlāqihim fa-qad naṣṣū ʿalā bayāni murādihim wa khaṣṣū ʿumūma alfāẓihim*).[166] Muslim jurists, in principle, supported those in power, but did so with reservations.[167] The symbolic and negotiative nature of this discourse is further evident in the debates among late revisionist jurists on whether rulers (sulṭāns) and lords (*al-umarāʾ*) can commit the crime of banditry. The bulk of these debates deal with situations in which a warlord, or perhaps landlord, exacts unjust levies (*mukūs*) on people. Although such a person does not commit highway robbery, he does terrorize and prey on the helplessness of people. The question is: Is such a person a usurper (*ghāṣib*) or bandit? The problem is aggravated if such a person has a general authorization (*taqrīr*) from the sulṭān to collect

[164] Al-Ṭarsawī, *Tuḥfa*, 121; al-Khirshī, *Sharḥ*, VIII:60; *al-Fatāwā al-ʿĀlamgīriyya*, VI:336; Ibn ʿĀbidīn, *Radd*, VI:411; al-ʿAynī, *al-Bināya*, VI:735; al-Zaylaʿī, *Tabyīn*, III:294. Al-Ṣāwī (*Bulgha*, II:414) notes that rebellion is the most destructive offense.

[165] For instance, see al-Ṭarsawī, *Tuḥfa*, 121; al-Khirshī, *Sharḥ*, VIII:60; *al-Fatāwā al-ʿĀlamgīriyya*, VI:336.

[166] Al-Wazīr, *al-ʿAwāṣim*, VIII:75; he also notes that by particularizing their general statements, Sunnī jurists did not give unjust rulers unqualified support.

[167] This fact is acknowledged in ibid., 172–4, where, in part, he argues that Sunnī jurists did not accept the authority of unjust rulers by choice (*ikhtiyār*), but by necessity (*iḍṭirār*). Al-Wazīr states: "*Wa man lam yufarriq bayna ḥālay al-ikhtiyār wa al-iḍṭirār fa-qad jahila al-maʿqūl wa al-manqūl.*"

taxes, because if he does possess such an authorization it becomes very difficult to resist or oppose him. The jurists raise the issue of whether such a person is a usurper or bandit, but do not unequivocally resolve it.[168] However, some jurists specifically state that a sulṭān who exacts unjust taxes is a usurper and not a bandit. Their proffered rationale for this position is most interesting. They argue that a sulṭān is not a bandit because it is possible to seek the aid of the jurists (*ʿulamāʾ*) against him. The jurists can and should restrain him by offering him proper advice.[169] But the implication of this argument is that if a sulṭān ignores the jurists and refuses to yield to their advice, then he may be considered a bandit. The jurists also add that it is illegal for anyone to assist the ruler or his agents in collecting unjust taxes.[170]

Of course, it is rather unlikely that jurists will declare a ruler to be a bandit.[171] Nonetheless, the discourse is part of the jurists' symbolic arsenal in dealing with those in power. It is not clear what exact role the symbolism constructed by the revisionist trend played in Islamic social or political history. This is an issue that needs a more exhaustive study. However, it is clear that the jurists themselves were concerned about the practical implications of their discourses. They were interested in who and what their legal discourses supported or encouraged. For instance, several jurists noted that the discourses on rebellion should not, in their day and age, be understood to excuse the behavior of bedouins, mercenary soldiers, and groups of brigandage such as the *mansar*. They insisted that such groups terrorize the wayfarer and commit acts of banditry, and thus should be treated as bandits. These jurists were concerned about the practical implications of their discourses, and they wished to ensure that such discourses would not lend support to certain groups perceived as violent and lawless. Importantly, these jurists stress that groups such as the *mansar* are motivated only by material gain, and not by political ends.[172] Therefore they are denied the status of *bughāh*, not necessarily because of their particularly indiscriminate or violent methods but because, in

168 Al-Ṣāwī, *Bulgha*, II:435; al-Khirshī, *Sharḥ*, VIII:104; al-Dusūqī, *Ḥāshiya*, IV:348; Ibn ᶜĀbidīn, *al-ʿUqūd*, II:283. On the issue of unjust taxes, see Abou El Fadl, "Tax," 22–3.

169 Al-Khirshī, *Sharḥ*, VIII:104; al-Dusūqī, *Ḥāshiya*, IV:348. The authors also state that *jabābirati ʿumarāʾi miṣr* or *ẓalamati miṣr* are bandits. Also see al-Juᶜalī, *Sirāj*, II:228. I also noted earlier that Ibn Ḥazm declared the rulers of the *ṭawāʾif* to be bandits.

170 For a more complete discussion on aiding unjust taxes, see Abou El Fadl, "Tax," 22–3, 26 and the citations contained therein.

171 According to some, it is possible to declare that a ruler is a *bāghī*: see al-Rāzī, *al-Tafsīr*, XXVIII:109.

172 Al-Jamal, *Ḥāshiya*, V:117, 153; al-Ramlī, *Nihāya*, VII:405, VIII:4. Al-Ṣāwī (*Bulgha*, II:435) states that groups of his time that raped women in Egypt were bandits.

the estimation of the jurists, these groups were committing simple acts of banditry and not rebellion.

It is not clear whether, according to the jurists of the revisionist trend, it is the means or the ends that distinguish a rebel from a bandit. If it is the means then, even if a group that commits indiscriminate acts of terror or slaughter has a plausible interpretation or cause, its members will be treated as bandits. In other words, by definition, the commission of certain acts will result in a group being dealt with as bandits. However, if it is the ends that are material, then regardless of the means pursued, a group that otherwise qualifies for the status of rebels will not be treated as bandits. To put the issue differently: What if a group of rebels abduct and murder, or attack the unsuspecting at their homes, or otherwise terrorize people? The jurists of the revisionist trend are divided on this issue. Some specifically state that if rebels terrorize the wayfarer or commit certain crimes such as rape, they are no longer to be treated as rebels, but must be treated as bandits.[173] Other jurists, however, assert that if the primary motivation of a group of rebels is not to spread terror but is to propagate a rebellion, then they cannot be treated as bandits. In other words, even if the means pursued by rebels resemble acts of banditry, as long as the rebels are motivated by an interpretation or cause, such rebels shall not be treated as bandits.[174] Yet another group of jurists adopted a position similar to the approach taken by the traditional trend. They argued that if acts of banditry are motivated by enmity or a contest over power and government, the offenders are not to be treated as bandits but are to be held liable for their crimes under the regular criminal laws.[175]

173 Al-Ramlī, *Ghāya*, 405; al-Ramlī, *Nihāya*, VII:403; Ibn Ḥajar al-Haytamī, *Fatḥ*, II:296; al-Jamal, *Ḥāshiya*, V:115; Ibn al-Muqrī, *Ikhlāṣ*, IV:128. Ibn ᶜĀbidīn (*Radd*, VII:188) does not deal with the issue directly, but asserts that financial gain is not a necessary element in the crime of banditry. An intent to terrorize, however, is a sufficient element. Ibn Ḥajar al-Haytamī (*Fatḥ*, II:314) asserts that if the people of one village attack another, killing and robbing them, the attackers are bandits. Ibn al-Muqrī (*Kitāb*, III:429) asserts the same.

174 Al-Shirbīnī (*Mughnī*, IV:124) also implies that it is the motivation of the actor that distinguishes rebellion from banditry; also see al-Anṣāri, *Fatḥ*, V:153. Al-Khirshī (*Sharḥ*, VIII:103) states that those who commit acts of banditry but do so because of a contest over government are not bandits.

175 Al-Nawawī (*Rawḍa*, VII:364–5) argues that the material issue is the helplessness of the victims. He argues that if a group of mercenary soldiers (*ᶜaskar*) raids a helpless village, then the soldiers are bandits. But if the village is not helpless, either because of an internal power or external assistance, the soldiers are considered plunderous looters (i.e. dealt with as thieves [*muntahibūn*]). Al-Ṣāwī (*Bulgha*, II:435–6) mentions rape, killing by stealth, using a drug to murder or rob someone, or armed robbery as crimes of banditry. Al-Dusūqī (*Ḥāshiya*, IV:348–9) lists the same. Arguably, if the motivation for these crimes is rancor, enmity, or power, they are considered regular crimes and not brigandage. It is not clear whether rape is treated as a regular crime even if committed because of rancor, enmity, or power.

Importantly, however, many revisionist jurists, mostly Shāfiʿī, accepted the same reform adopted by several jurists from the traditional trend. As discussed earlier, it had become well established in the discourses on rebellion that rebels and loyalists are liable for any life or property destroyed before or after the rebellion.[176] However, several revisionist jurists adopted a limitation that relates to the way the rebellion itself is conducted.[177] They argued that groups that qualify for the status of *bughāh* will not be held liable for life and property destroyed in the course of rebellion if such destruction was necessarily related to the rebellion (*ḍarūrat al-ḥarb*). Therefore, if the acts committed were unrelated to the ends of the rebellion, such acts are not protected.[178] Hence, rape, for example, is not protected because it is not directly related to the act of rebellion.[179] Most jurists applied the same restriction to loyalist forces as well. Pursuant to this position, loyalists are not liable for life or property destroyed if their acts were necessarily related to the goal of resisting a rebellion. If the behavior of the loyalists was *ultra vires*, or not necessarily related to the specific goal of defeating the rebellion, then the loyalists will be held liable for such excesses.[180] Therefore, wanton or vengeful destruction of property would be held liable.[181] Of course, whether something is necessarily related to the propagation or the resisting of a rebellion is a vague standard. But it indicates a desire to limit the range of acts that fall under the protection of *aḥkām al-bughāh*. It indicates a real concern with the pragmatic consequences that might result from the discourses of the jurists.[182] At the same time, it confirms the symbolic and negotiative nature of these discourses because it is the jurists who would decide what is necessarily related or unrelated to a rebellion.

176 Although some jurists had held that the loyalists are not liable for property destroyed before the commencement of the rebellion, if such destruction was necessary to weaken the rebels. See, for instance, al-Nawawī, *Rawḍa*, VII:275, citing the opinion of al-Māwardī.

177 As discussed earlier, this limitation had also been adopted by some jurists from the traditional trend.

178 Ibn Jamāʿa, *Taḥrīr*, 246; al-Nawawī, *Rawḍa*, VII:276; Ibn Ḥajar al-Haytamī, *Fatḥ*, II:295, 297; al-Jamal, *Ḥāshiya*, V:116–17; al-Shirbīnī, *Mughnī*, IV:125; al-Anṣāri, *Fatḥ*, V:153; al-Ramlī, *Nihāya*, VII:405.

179 Al-Shirbīnī, *Mughnī*, IV:126; al-Nawawī, *Rawḍa*, VII:276.

180 Al-Jamal, *Ḥāshiya*, V:116–17; Ibn Ḥajar al-Haytamī, *Fatḥ*, II:297; al-Shirbīnī, *Mughnī*, IV:125.

181 Al-Ramlī, *Nihāya*, VII:405.

182 The concern with the pragmatic consequences of their discourse is also evident in the discussions on the requirement of *shawka*. The jurists often state that a *shawka* must exist, otherwise every person or isolated individuals will invent an interpretation or cause. Such individuals will then rebel and claim that they are entitled to the benefits of *aḥkām al-bughāh*. If this is allowed to take place, disorder and anarchy will prevail. For example, see al-Shirbīnī, *Mughnī*, IV:126; Ibn al-Muqrī, *Ikhlāṣ*, IV:126; Ibn al-Muqrī, *Kitāb*, III:371; al-Ramlī, *Nihāya*, VII:405.

CONCLUSION

The discourses on rebellion had become firmly established by the sixth/twelfth century in the Sunnī juristic culture, and even jurists such as Ibn Taymiyya who criticized the inherited legacy could not abandon its paradigms or specific regulations. Both the revisionist and traditionalist jurists accepted and repeated the formulas of inherited discourses on rebellion. Importantly, both trends developed some aspects of the discourses as well. The traditionalists focused on the regulatory aspects, and therefore emphasized the distinction between rebellion and banditry. They focused on the particular acts that would or would not be protected under the law of rebellion. But this betrayed a certain fidelity to the integrity and systematization of the juristic discourses themselves. It is doubtful whether the traditionalists had any illusions about these discourses being applied as positive law, and it is also doubtful whether the jurists thought that the political reality would honor the subtle distinctions of the juristic discourse. To the extent that the traditionalists engaged and negotiated with the political system, they did so by emphasizing the duty of obedience, and reiterating the inherited discourses. One cannot dismiss this as irrelevant because, after all, it did legitimate and affirm the validity and integrity of the legal culture. However, the response of the traditionalists is not as creative or negotiative as the response of the revisionists.

Responding to the same reality that confronted the traditionalists, the revisionists focused on the symbolic aspects of the discourses. The revisionists did reiterate all the technical regulatory aspects of the inherited discourses, but their emphasis was on reintroducing subjective ideological elements into the inquiry. They distinguished between rebels who are responding to an injustice and those who are attempting to overthrow the ruler. They also bolstered the notion that a ruler might not be entitled to the support of Muslims against his opponents. Furthermore, under certain circumstances, if a ruler is not a bandit, he could be a criminal usurper. Ultimately, both revisionists and traditionalists did not simply respond to the internal logic of the legal culture, but also to the political and social implications of their discourses. The traditionalists responded by somewhat undercutting the tendency of the discourses to encourage or support rebellion. But they did not entirely abandon the ideals constructed by the discourses on rebellion. The revisionist response was to bolster the critical content of the discourses. Ultimately, one cannot describe either the traditionalist or revisionist trends as quietist or activist.

Rather, they were both technical and symbolic, pragmatic, and idealistic. Most of all, they were thoroughly complex and legalistic.

From a sociological perspective, it is difficult to establish how the revisionist approach began. It is also difficult to ascertain why a particular jurist adopted the revisionist approach while another adopted the traditionalist. The jurists of the revisionist trend came from diverse backgrounds and vocations. Most served as law professors, judges, or administrators. Their dynamics with those in power seem to be multi-faceted and varied. The Ḥanafī jurist Badr al-Dīn al-ᶜAynī (d. 855/1451), for example, served in various teaching and administrative positions in Egypt. He was also fired from several official positions and suffered persecution as well. Eventually, he developed a close relationship to the Mamlūk ruler Abū al-Naṣr Barsbay (r. 825/1422–841/1438) and was appointed the chief Ḥanafī judge of Egypt.[183] The Shāfiᶜī Abū Zakariyyā al-Anṣārī (d. 926/1520) reluctantly accepted the position of chief judge of Egypt, but was later removed when he criticized the injustices of Qāyit Bay Sayf al-Dīn (r. 872/1468–901/1496).[184] On the other hand, the Shāfiᶜī Ibn al-Muqrī (d. 837/1433), who lived and died in Yemen, was mostly a teacher. However, he reportedly coveted a judicial position, but was never appointed.[185] One notices, however, that a large number of the revisionist jurists came from Egypt, and thus one cannot exclude the possibility of the emergence of a localized juristic culture which might have then spread to other localities.[186] This is especially so because from 648/1249 the Sunnī jurists of Egypt might have felt alienated from their Ismāᶜīlī overlords.[187] However, a more exhaustive study of the lives and socio-political dynamics of each jurist and his circumstances might yield greater insight into the rise of the revisionist trend, and might be able to correlate the collective experiences of each trend and, perhaps, each jurist and his adopted position.

[183] Ibn al-ᶜImād, *Shadharāt*, VII:286; al-Ziriklī, *al-Aᶜlām*, VII:163.

[184] Al-Ziriklī, *al-Aᶜlām*, III:46.

[185] Ibn al-ᶜImād, *Shadharāt*, VII:220–1. Reportedly, Ibn al-Muqrī was also appointed a governor: see al-Ziriklī, *al-Aᶜlām*, I:310–1.

[186] For example, the Ḥanafī al-Zaylaᶜī taught and died in Egypt: see al-Ziriklī, *al-Aᶜlām*, IV:210; Ibn Ḥajar al-Haytamī studied in Egypt but died in Mecca: see ibid., I:234; the Shāfiᶜī Shams al-Dīn al-Ramlī taught and died in Egypt: see ibid., VI:7; the Mālikī al-ᶜAdawī lived and died in Egypt, ibid., IV:260; the Mālikī al-Dusūqī lived and died in Egypt: see ibid., VI:17; the Mālikī al-Ṣāwī lived in Egypt but died in Medina: see ibid., I:246.

[187] The Ottomans replaced the Fāṭimids in 923/1517. But for a variety of reasons I do not believe that this is an adequate explanation.

CHAPTER 7

The developed non-Sunnī positions

The main focus of this chapter will be on the Imāmī Shīʿī discourses on rebellion. However, for the sake of comprehensiveness, we will also comment on the Zaydī and Ibāḍī positions. Our purpose is to provide an overview of the treatment of the subject in these schools of thought, and draw comparisons to the Sunnī tradition. The Ibāḍīs were the more moderate descendants of the Khawārij, although the history of the sect can be traced back to the first century of Islam. The Zaydiyya is a Shīʿī sect which is distinguished from the Jaʿfarīs (later, the Imāmī Shīʿīs), partly by its recognition of Zayd b. ʿAlī who led a rebellion against the Umayyads in 122/740. Both Zaydīs and Ibāḍīs had been involved in a series of rebellions throughout Islamic history, but they also succeeded in establishing independent states.[1] Particularly in the case of the Ibāḍīs, but certainly for the Zaydīs as well, issues such as who is a rebel, when is rebellion permitted, and how should opponents be treated are integral to the theology of the sect. Therefore it would be very useful to study the theology of the sects in conjunction with the doctrines of rebellion from the point of view of a historical progression. However, this would be outside the scope of this study. We are interested in examining the extent to which Sunnī symbolism and juristic categorizations are similar to or different from the discourses of these sects. As argued below, at a minimum, the developed doctrines of the Imāmīs, Zaydīs, and Ibāḍīs are similar in several important respects to Sunnī doctrines, which is further evidence of the impact of the inherited legal culture.

THE IMĀMĪ SHĪʿĪ SCHOOL

As argued earlier, the Imāmī approach to the issue of rebellion was for the most part ideological. It tended to focus on rebellion in a hypothetical

[1] On the Zaydīs, see Gibb and Kramers, eds., *Shorter*, 651–3; al-Shahrastānī, *al-Milal*, 1:179–89; al-Baghdādī, *al-Farq*, 16. On the Ibāḍīs, see Gibb and Kramers, eds., *Shorter*, 143–5; al-Shahrastānī, *al-Milal*, 1:156–9; al-Baghdādī, *al-Farq*, 70.

sense – those who will rebel against the true, awaited *imām* when such a ruler appears. Therefore, several sources emphasized that those who disobey the true ruler are unbelievers, and even if they are not treated as such on this earth, they will be considered unbelievers in the Hereafter. The concept of rebellion was focused upon disobedience to the infallible *imām* when one exists. In the meanwhile, armed rebellion against illegitimate rulers was outlawed because it was perceived as ineffective and harmful, but Imāmī jurists also prohibited assisting unjust rulers against rebels. Nonetheless, by limiting their discourses to the problem of disobeying the infallible ruler, Imāmī doctrines continued to be of limited applicability. The rules of conduct dictating how rebels should be treated would apply only if an infallible ruler exists. However, these discourses played a powerful symbolic role since they implied that rebels against any ruler, in the absence of the *imām*, are not *bughāh* at all. Nevertheless, because of their futuristic and hypothetical quality, the power of this symbolism is somewhat compromised. Starting probably from the fifth/eleventh century and especially after the sixth/twelfth century, Imāmī jurists, particularly from Irāq, used the expression "a just ruler" (*imām ᶜādil*) instead of "the just ruler" (*al-imām al-ᶜādil*), connoting a shift from the idea of the infallible, awaited ruler to an acceptance of the *de facto* temporary authority of a just authority.[2]

Several late Imāmī jurists such as Shams al-Dīn al-ᶜĀmilī (d. 786/1384) and Muḥammad Bāqir al-Najafī (d. 1266/1850) continued to define *baghy* as an act of rebellion against the awaited, infallible ruler. Accordingly, in contrast to Sunnī views, they insisted that the word *baghy* does connote blame (*ism dhamm*), and that the *bughāh* cannot be considered equal in status to jurists who exercise an independent opinion on a matter (*mujtahidūn*).[3] Proclaiming the error of Sunnī views, ᶜAbd Allāh al-Suyūrī (d. 826/1422) argued that since the ruler is infallible, the *bughāh* should be considered unbelievers or, at a minimum, hypocrites (*munāfiqūn*).[4] Furthermore, according to some jurists such as al-Najafī,

[2] On the ambiguity of the term "just ruler" in Imāmī discourses and the development of the term, see Sachedina, *Just*, 100–5. On Imāmī political thought and attitude towards authority, see Lambton, *State*, 219–41; Momen, *Introduction*, 191–3. On Imāmī views on *jihād* in the absence of the *imām*, see Kohlberg, "Development." Kohlberg focuses on the theological connotations of the debates on the *bughāh*. He seems to assume that the debates on *bughāh* are relevant only to the status of those who rebelled against ᶜAlī.

[3] Al-Najafī, *Jawāhir*, XXI:322–3; al-ᶜĀmilī, *al-Lumᶜa*, II:407.

[4] Al-Suyūrī, *Kanz*, I:386–8. The author also argues that the Qur'ānic verse on *baghy* does not, as is often assumed by jurists, refer to rebels. Rather, it refers to situations where two Muslim parties quarrel. The Qur'ānic verses that address hypocrites and unbelievers are the ones more relevant to rebellion.

the primary reason for the restrictions on the conduct of warfare against rebels was for the benefit of the Shīʿa. ʿAlī knew that his party would ultimately be oppressed and persecuted and he wanted to set a precedent that would protect the Shīʿa. By not slaughtering or taking his opponents captive, Sunnīs would feel obligated to follow his example when dealing with the Shīʿa. Hence, ʿAlī's conduct did not arise out of binding principle, but was a utilitarian necessity produced by the need for dissimulation (*taqiyya*). However, when the infallible ruler (*al-Qāʾim*) appears, dissimulation is no longer needed. The Qā'im will not be bound by ʿAlī's precedent, and may dispose of his opponents in whichever way he deems fit at the time.[5] From this perspective, the discourse on the *bughāh* plays a limited symbolic role. The rules of conduct are designed to obligate and embarrass Sunnīs dealing with Shīʿī opponents, but the Qā'im ultimately has the discretion not to follow the rules. Ironically, the *bughāh* are defined as those who rebel against *the* just ruler. This creates a definite tension in the discourses. On the one hand, only those who rebel against the just ruler are the *bughāh*. On the other hand, the opponents of the Shīʿīs are bound by *aḥkām al-bughāh* in dealing with Shīʿīs who, in the final analysis, are not *bughāh* at all, but rather, are the just party.[6] This creates a question as to the relevance of *aḥkām al-bughāh*. If, in the final analysis, the just ruler is not bound by *aḥkām al-bughāh*, then arguably the rules of conduct do not yield a religiously binding imperative.[7] These rules of conduct exist for

5 Al-Najafī, *Jawāhir*, XXI:335–8. The author argues that the Qā'im may slaughter or take his opponents captive because he will know that his Shīʿa will not be defeated after him. He adds that in the period before the appearance of the Qā'im (*zaman al-hudna*) opponents are treated as Muslims, but after his appearance opponents will be treated as unbelievers. The author concedes that ʿAlī did not call his opponents unbelievers, but he seems to argue that ʿAlī did so only out of the need for dissimulation. See also al-Ḥurr al-ʿĀmilī, *Wasāʾil*, XI:56–7, 59. However, al-ʿĀmilī (*al-Lumʿa*, II:408–9) seems to disagree with the idea that ʿAlī's conduct is not binding on all.

6 For instance, al-Najafī (*Jawāhir*, XXI:332) asserts that al-Shāfiʿī admitted that Sunnīs learned *aḥkām al-bughāh* only from ʿAlī. Also see al-Suyūrī, *Kanz*, I:386. This ambiguity is also reflected in the doctrine that ʿAlī was the one who had a *taʾwīl*, and Muʿāwiya, as the *bāghī*, lacked a reasonable *taʾwīl*. See al-Ḥurr al-ʿĀmilī, *Wasāʾil*, XI:17; Ibn al-Murtaḍā (al-Kāshānī), *Tafsīr*, V:50. Al-Najafī (*Jawāhir*, XXI:333–4) argues that there is no evidence that the rebels must have a *taʾwīl*. At most, the rebels must not have a well-founded legitimate grievance, because if they do the grievance should be redressed. Nonetheless, by definition the rebels cannot be considered to have a valid interpretation.

The above points add ambiguity and confusion to the field. In the discourses on rebellion, rebels are the ones who are presumed to need an interpretation. This interpretation distinguishes rebels from common criminals or bandits. The argument that ʿAlī is the one who had an interpretation, while Muʿāwiya did not, furthers a rhetorical point but does not aid the legal distinction between rebels and others.

7 As discussed below, post-fifth/eleventh-century jurists argued that a fallible just ruler could exist. Such a ruler would be bound by the law of rebellion.

the utilitarian purpose of protecting the Shīʿa, a group which ultimately cannot be described as the *bughāh*. Nonetheless, despite the ambiguity, the essential point these jurists were making was that those who rebel against illegitimate rulers cannot be considered outlaws, and at the same time the benefit of ʿAlī's conduct was claimed for the protection of the Shīʿa.

Since at least the fifth/eleventh century, a large number of Imāmī jurists did not define *baghy* as an act of rebellion against *the* just ruler but against *a* just ruler (*man kharaja ʿalā imāmin ʿādil*).[8] Therefore, if a group refuses to obey or attempts to overthrow a just ruler while relying on an interpretation or cause, they are the *bughāh*. Importantly, many of these jurists avoid stating that the *bughāh* are unbelievers.[9] The *bughāh* are not fought until they pose an imminent threat of an armed insurrection, and when they are fought, the wounded, captive, and fugitive are not dispatched unless the rebels have reinforcements (*fiʾa*). Rebel prisoners are released once the danger from the rebellion subsides. The personal property of the rebels may not be confiscated, but there is disagreement as to the fate of their horses and weapons. However, Imāmī sources insist that the rebels, unlike the loyalists, are in fact liable for life and property destroyed during the course of the rebellion.[10]

The expression "a just ruler" is vague, but it connotes a significant shift in the discourse. The expression is broad enough to apply to various structures of authority that could exist before the appearance of the Qāʾim.[11] Hence, at a symbolic level, the Imāmī discourses on rebellion register a powerful point. A just ruler does have the right to resist rebels, but must follow the precedent set by ʿAlī. However, those who rebel against an unjust ruler have not committed an infraction; rebellion is

[8] Al-Rāwandī (d. 573/1177), *Fiqh*, I:363–4; Fakhr al-Muḥaqqiqīn (d. 771/1369), *Īḍāḥ*, I:396; al-Muḥaqqiq (d. 676/1277), *Sharāʾiʿ*, II:336; Ibn Ḥamza (d. after 566/1171), *al-Wasīla*, IX:162; al-Ḥillī (d. 598/1201), *al-Sarāʾir*, IX:183.

[9] For instance, see the following sources: al-Rāwandī, *Fiqh*, I:363–4; Fakhr al-Muḥaqqiqīn, *Īḍāḥ*, I:396–7; al-Muḥaqqiq, *Sharāʾiʿ*, II:336–8; al-Kāshānī, *Tafsīr*, V:50–1. Furthermore, these sources do not mention that the Qāʾim is not bound by the rules of conduct in the field of rebellion.

[10] Fakhr al-Muḥaqqiqīn, *Īḍāḥ*, I:396–7; al-Muḥaqqiq, *Sharāʾiʿ*, II:336–8; al-Ḥillī (d. 841/1437), *al-Muhadhdhab*, II:300–1; al-Ḥalabī (d. 585/1189), *Ghunya*, IX:151–3; Ibn Ḥamza, *al-Wasīla*, IX:164; al-Ḥillī, *al-Sarāʾir*, IX:183–6; al-Ḥalabī (d. late fifth/eleventh century), *Ishāra*, IX:190, 196; al-Hudhalī (d. 689/1290), *al-Jāmiʿ*, IX:238; al-Ḥillī (d. 726/1325), *Qawāʿid*, IX:267–8. See also Mughniyya, *Fiqh*, II:279–80; al-Amīnī, *al-Ghadīr*, I:325, X:304.

[11] Some have argued that the sole purpose of the Imāmī jurists in using the expression "a just ruler" or other descriptive equivalents was *taqiyya* (dissimulation) in order to avoid a confrontation with the illegitimate authority under which they lived. By diluting the term "just *imām*," Shīʿī jurists could avoid explicit condemnation of those *de facto* in power. See Calder, "Structure." But this point is challenged by the fact that Imāmī jurists argued that a Muslim may not assist an unjust ruler against rebels.

an infraction only if committed against a just ruler. Yet Imāmī jurists often state that if enjoining the good and forbidding the evil requires killing or injury, the permission of the *imām* is required. That practically closes the gate to rebelling against an unjust ruler. But the rationale for this prohibition is functional or utilitarian. The *imām*'s deputy (*nāʾib al-ghayba*) may authorize a rebellion, but only if certain conditions are met.[12] Among the conditions are the avoidance of *fitna* and harm. However, in most circumstances, rebellion results in *fitna* and greater harm than good, and in many circumstances rebelling is as if one is casting oneself unto ruin (i.e. a form of suicide). Therefore one should not enjoin the good or forbid the evil against an unjust ruler unless there is a greater probability that doing so would be effective and would not endanger the enjoiner's safety or the safety of others. If a person or group reasonably believes that enjoining the good and forbidding the evil will either be ineffective, or will endanger their own safety or the safety of others, then they should refrain from doing so.[13]

In the opinion of most jurists, resistance to unjust or, in the discourse of some, illegitimate rulers should be largely passive. A Muslim should not support or aid unjust rulers in any material way. Working with unjust rulers might be a pragmatic necessity, but one should not engage in such conduct unless one knows, to a degree of certainty, that doing so will not entail committing an injustice. A Shīʿī must believe that he is applying the law of God by the authorization of the rightful ruler, and not the unjust ruler in power. Therefore, a Shīʿī's loyalty or commitment is not to the unjust ruler, and his service is not for the benefit of unjust rulers. In working with unjust rulers, a Shīʿī may, in fact, assist such a ruler in applying the *Sharīʿa*, even if it is Sunnī law, but the Shīʿī must engage

[12] Frequently, Imāmī jurists do not explicitly address rebellion but refer only to the duty to enjoin the good and forbid the evil. Enjoining the good and forbidding the evil could be through a variety of means including armed force. However, most Imāmī jurists do not approve of armed force if the result is a greater harm than good.

[13] Ibn al-Murtaḍā (d. 1091/1680), *al-Maḥajja*, IV:111–13; al-Suyūrī, *Kanz*, I:397, 407; al-Muḥaqqiq, *Sharāʾiʿ*, II:342; Fakhr al-Muḥaqqiqīn, *Īḍāḥ*, I:398; Ibn Ḥamza, *al-Wasīla*, IX:165; al-Ḥillī, *al-Sarāʾir*, IX:190; al-Ḥalabī, *Ishāra*, IX:198; al-Hudhalī, *al-Jāmiʿ*, IX:239; al-Ḥillī, *Qawāʿid*, IX:268. Al-Najafī (*Jawāhir*, XXI:367–8, 371, 384–5) adds that in his time the conditions for rebellion were very difficult if not impossible to fulfill (at p. 385). Al-Ḥurr al-ʿĀmilī (*Wasāʾil*, XI:400–6, 409–11, 425, 464, 472, 482–3, 492, 497) records numerous conflicting traditions on rebellion and enjoining the good and forbidding the evil. Many traditions assert the futility of rebellion, and some claim that the best way to resist an unjust ruler is through dissimulation. In one set of traditions, dissimulation is described as a form of *jihād*. Mughniyya (*Fiqh*, II:283–4) argues that dissimulation and abandoning the duty to enjoin the good and forbid the evil is permissible only if the *furūʿ* (branches of religion) are involved. If, however, the *uṣūl* (foundations of religion) are threatened, then *jihād* and the sacrifice of life and property become necessary.

in a legal fiction – he must believe that he is authorized by the rightful ruler. A Shīʿī may not commit injustice unless forced by the threat of serious harm. In situations of duress, a Shīʿī may practice dissimulation; however, under no circumstances may a Shīʿī help an unjust ruler kill the innocent. As discussed earlier, Imāmī jurists stress that dissimulation is not permitted if it entails murder.[14] Furthermore, a Shīʿī may not assist an unjust ruler in resisting an insurrection or fighting rebels.[15]

Concretely, passive resistance to an unjust ruler is expressed through non-cooperation and non-support. There is a pragmatic acceptance of the necessity of upholding the *de facto* structures of society and order. But this concession is not given without reservations or limitations. Not only is an unjust ruler not granted *de jure* recognition, but even more, one cannot cooperate with all the endeavors of an unjust ruler regardless of the consequences. Of course, Imāmī discourses arise from a specific theological framework which shapes its differentiation between legitimate and illegitimate authority. Nonetheless, at the procedural and symbolic level, the Imāmī response to injustice, however that injustice is defined, is similar to certain Sunnī responses in important respects. At the procedural level, Muslims may not assist an unjust ruler in committing injustice. At the symbolic level, the Imāmī discourse ends up making a point similar to the one made by the Sunnī revisionist school. Rebellion, in principle, is prohibited because of the social harm that it produces. However, this prohibition is only a default position; in the absence of countervailing circumstances, rebellion is prohibited. But this does not mean that rebellion can never be justified. Ultimately, obedience to an unjust authority is a pragmatic necessity, but it is not an ideal situation. As the Zaydī jurist al-Wazīr argues, the fact that the authority of an unjust ruler is recognized as a matter of necessity is evidence that such an authority is illegitimate. Therefore, for example, as al-Wazīr notes, the fact that under conditions of necessity a person may drink alcohol is evidence that the consumption of alcohol, under normal circumstances, is prohibited.[16] This basic logic is accepted by Sunnīs and non-Sunnīs alike.[17] Consequently, depending on the circumstances, rebellion might be justified. However, like the

14 Al-Ḥillī, *al-Muhadhdhab*, II:327; al-Muḥaqqiq, *Sharāʾiʿ*, II:344–5; Fakhr al-Muḥaqqiqīn, *Īḍāḥ*, I:399; al-ʿĀmilī, *al-Lumʿa*, II:420; al-Suyūrī, *Kanz*, I:394; al-Ḥillī, *al-Sarāʾir*, IX:191; al-Hudhalī, *al-Jāmiʿ*, IX:240; al-Ḥillī, *Qawāʿid*, IX:268–9. Al-Najafī (*Jawāhir*, XXI:390–3, 407–10) adds that if threatened by death, a Shīʿī may kill a Sunnī because a thousand Sunnīs are not worth the life of one Shīʿī. This view is atypical.

15 Al-Ḥillī, *al-Sarāʾir*, IX:184; al-Hudhalī, *al-Jāmiʿ*, IX:238.

16 Al-Wazīr, *al-ʿAwāṣim*, VIII:163–4.

17 See ibid., 14–18, 75, 163–4.

Sunnī revisionist trend, the explicit discourse of the jurists did not focus on the circumstances under which rebellion might be justified. Rather, the discourse focused on the status of rebels. As to the status of rebels, the symbolic component in Imāmī discourses was more pronounced than in the discourses of their Sunnī counterparts. If the ruler is just, those who rebel against him are *bughāh*, but they are entitled to preferred treatment. If the ruler is not just, those who rebel against him have not committed an infraction, and the ruler cannot be assisted in fighting the rebels. As discussed above, the expression "a just ruler" is ambiguous, and therefore, arguably, any illegitimate ruler is also an unjust ruler.[18] Accordingly, it is possible that anyone who rebels against any illegitimate ruler, whether the ruler is just or not, is not a *bāghī* and has not committed an infraction. But by using the construction "a just ruler," instead of "the just ruler," the Imāmī discourses become purposely ambiguous, and such discourses no longer speak simply in terms of the legitimacy or illegitimacy of the temporal rulers. Rather, the Imāmī discourses become more pertinent, as a political and moral commentary, upon the contemporaneous reality under which the Imāmī jurists lived.

Another area of considerable ambiguity, however, rich with symbolic content, is the Imāmī discourses on banditry. Imāmī jurists do not directly address the distinction between rebellion and banditry. However, their discourses implicitly assume that there is a difference between bandits and rebels, and that a significant part of the difference is the existence of a *taʾwīl*. The Imāmī definition of banditry, however, is quite broad. Banditry is the causing of corruption on the earth by terrorizing people through the use of the threat of material harm. The crime of banditry can be committed on land or sea, in a town or desert, and in the abode of Islam or in the abode of non-Muslims, whether or not the victims or the offenders are Muslim.[19] The focal point of the crime is the existence of terror. There is disagreement among the jurists, however, on whether an intent to terrorize is one of the elements of the crime. Some argue that if the effect of the criminal activity is to spread terror, then banditry exists whether or not the criminal intended to terrorize.[20] Significantly, the resulting terror must be general in effect. In other words, if a person

[18] Madelung ("Treatise") argues that after the fifth/eleventh century not every illegitimate ruler was considered unjust. I think his argument is persuasive.

[19] Al-Najafī, *Jawāhir*, XLI:564–5; al-Ṭarabulusī, *al-Muhadhdhab*, X:170; al-ʿĀmilī, *al-Lumʿa*, IX:290; Fakhr al-Muḥaqqiqīn, *Iḍāḥ*, IV:542; al-Muḥaqqiq, *Sharāʾiʿ*, IV:180.

[20] Al-Najafī, *Jawāhir*, XLI:566; al-ʿĀmilī, *al-Lumʿa*, IX:290; al-Muḥaqqiq, *Sharāʾiʿ*, IV:180; al-Ḥillī, *al-Sarāʾir*, X:272. Al-Ḥillī (*Qawāʿid*, X:431) adds that the bandits must have a degree of strength (*shawka*).

terrorizes another because of an individual or private enmity or rancor, this is not banditry. However, if the terror is indiscriminate or general in impact, even if the victims of the terror constitute a specific group, then the elements of banditry exist.[21] Some jurists add that a person cannot be convicted of banditry unless the criminal is a person of disrepute (*min ahl al-rība*). This is a limiting factor; a person must already be known as a criminal before being convicted of banditry, but there is significant disagreement among the jurists surrounding this element.[22] Under the Imāmī definition of banditry, highway robbery or armed robbery is only one form of banditry.[23] An arsonist who burns people's homes or businesses, or a person who seeks to take Muslims captive or commit rape is a bandit as well.[24] Importantly, the definition of banditry is broad enough to apply to rebels who employ methods of terror or to unjust rulers who might terrorize the populace. Nevertheless, the resolution to this issue, perhaps wisely, is left ambiguous.[25]

THE ZAYDĪ SCHOOL

Zaydī jurists differentiate between a person who sins due to defiance and one who sins due to a mistaken belief. The former is described as *fāsiq taṣrīḥ* (iniquitous by defiance) and the later as *fāsiq ta'wīl* (iniquitous by interpretation). The iniquitous by defiance does not have a recognizable justification for sinning. The iniquitous by interpretation mistakenly believes that he is serving God or doing what is permitted by God. The iniquitous by defiance commits a much more grievous sin than the iniquitous by interpretation.[26] An unjust ruler is placed in the category of the iniquitous by defiance, while a *bāghī* is placed in the category of the iniquitous by interpretation.[27] A *bāghī* is someone who rebels against

[21] Al-Najafī, *Jawāhir*, XLI:569.
[22] Ibid., 567; al-ᶜĀmilī, *al-Lumᶜa*, IX:291; Fakhr al-Muḥaqqiqīn, *Īḍāḥ*, IV:543; al-Muḥaqqiq, *Sharā'iᶜ*, IV:180; al-Ḥillī, *al-Muhadhdhab*, V:122; al-Suyūrī, *Kanz*, II:351; al-Rāwandī, *Fiqh*, II:387.
[23] Al-Najafī, *Jawāhir*, XLI:588; al-Suyūrī, *Kanz*, II:351.
[24] Al-Najafī, *Jawāhir*, XLI:566, 570. Fraud, conversion, and theft are not crimes of banditry unless accompanied by the threat of harm and terror. See ibid., 596.
[25] There is wide disagreement among Imāmī jurists concerning the amount of discretion the *imām* has in punishing the crime of banditry. Some argue for strict proportionality between the crime and punishment while others argue that the *imām*, with some limitations, may choose the punishment that best serves the public interest. See ibid., 573–97; al-ᶜĀmilī, *al-Lumᶜa*, IX:294–302; Fakhr al-Muḥaqqiqīn, *Īḍāḥ*, IV:543–4; al-Muḥaqqiq, *Sharā'iᶜ*, IV:180–2; al-Ḥillī, *al-Muhadhdhab*, V:123–6; al-Suyūrī, *Kanz*, II:351–2; al-Rāwandī, *Fiqh*, II:387.
[26] Ibn al-Murtaḍā, *Kitāb*, VI:415. [27] Ibid.

the just ruler while claiming to be right concerning an issue or a set of issues, and while alleging that the ruler is wrong.[28] Therefore, Zaydī jurists explicitly state that an unjust ruler cannot be considered a *bāghī* although he is considered a sinner.[29] At the same time, those who rebel against an unjust ruler cannot be considered *bughāh* because they have not committed an infraction in the first place.[30] By definition, *baghy*, which is considered a sin, can only be committed against a just ruler. This approach has the advantage of definitional clarity. *Baghy* is a technical category which applies only to those who rebel against a just ruler. An unjust ruler cannot be called a *bāghī*, but his sin is more grievous than the sin committed by the *bughāh*.[31]

Zaydī jurists argue that although the *bughāh* are sinners, they are not considered unbelievers.[32] Rebels against a just ruler are sinners because such a ruler is entitled to obedience.[33] At the same time, if the rebels believe in good faith that they are right and possess a degree of strength (*shawka*), then they are entitled to be treated as *bughāh* and not as common criminals or bandits.[34] Zaydī jurists do not emphasize that the *bughāh* must have a plausible interpretation, but only that they refuse to obey a just ruler while believing in the justness of their cause, and that the ruler's command is wrong.[35] If a group qualifies as *bughāh*, they become entitled to a particular form of treatment. The treatment of the *bughāh* according to the Zaydī position is similar in many respects to the Sunnī position. If the *bughāh* criticize the ruler, they may not be persecuted, but if they refuse to discharge an obligation or rise in armed rebellion, they may be fought. However, they should be warned first, since fighting is only a last resort.[36] The wounded, fugitive, and captive may not be killed unless the rebels have reinforcements (*fi'a*). Flooding, fire, and other means of indiscriminate slaughter may not be used unless for an absolute necessity. The ruler may not solicit the assistance of Muslims who would indiscriminately slaughter the rebels, and once the rebels surrender and the fighting ends, the rebels may not be executed, and the prisoners must be released.[37] Zaydī jurists are divided on the issue of the rebels' liability. It appears that the majority has held that the ruler, at his discretion, may

28 Ibid.; al-Ṣanᶜānī (d. 1331/1912), *Kitāb*, IV:331.
29 Ibn al-Murtaḍā, *Kitāb*, VI:415.
30 Al-Wazīr, *al-ᶜAwāṣim*, VIII:14.
31 Ibn al-Murtaḍā, *Kitāb*, VI:415.
32 Ibid., 419; al-Ṣanᶜānī, *Tatimma*, IV:261–2.
33 Ibn al-Murtaḍā, *Kitāb*, VI:387–8.
34 Ibid., 415.
35 Ibid.; al-Ṣanᶜānī, *Kitāb*, IV:331.
36 Ibn al-Murtaḍā, *Kitāb*, VI:387–8, 416, 423; al-Ṣanᶜānī, *Kitāb*, IV:307.
37 Ibn al-Murtaḍā, *Kitāb*, VI:417–19, 420–1; al-Ṣanᶜānī, *Kitāb*, IV:331–3.

hold the rebels liable for life and property destroyed during the course of the rebellion. However, rebels are held financially, and not criminally, liable, and only to the extent of the collective damage that they may have caused.[38] Furthermore, any property that may have been usurped by the rebels must be returned to its rightful owner. However, if the owner is not known, the property is to be given to the public treasury. Property belonging to the rebels, other than property found in the war camp, may not be confiscated.[39] Significantly, funeral prayers should not be performed on dead rebels. Nonetheless, despite the fact that rebels are considered iniquitous, their adjudications and testimony are accepted as long as they are not clearly erroneous or unsupportable.[40]

Zaydī jurists clearly consider a rebellion against a just ruler as fundamentally unjustified. They seem to use the expressions "just ruler" and "rightful ruler" as equivalents, but there is considerable ambiguity surrounding both expressions. According to Zaydī theology, a rightful ruler must be from the family of the Prophet (*ahl al-bayt*) and possess the requisite amount of learning and piety. The ambiguity remains, however, because it is possible for several rightful *imāms* to exist at the same time.[41] Furthermore, obedience is due to an *imām* only if he is pious and just, otherwise the *imām* loses his right to obedience.[42] Regardless of the problems of definition, if the ruler is considered just, those who rebel against him are entitled to the treatment outlined above, because the rebels proclaim an honest disagreement over what is right or wrong. However, those who commit an armed insurrection without an interpretation or claim of right may be subject to execution. In fact, the main distinction between rebels and bandits is the existence of such an interpretation. Nonetheless, the nature of this interpretation or claim is not clear. Zaydī jurists state that the *bughāh* fight out of religiosity (*tadayyunan*) while bandits fight out of greed.[43] Furthermore, those who fight out of a raw desire for power are said not to be *bughāh*.[44] Hence, arguably, the *bughāh* in Zaydī thought are those who rebel because of a perceived injustice or because they mistakenly believe that rebellion is part of the obligation to enjoin the good and forbid the evil. However, having argued that *baghy* can only be committed against an unjust ruler, Zaydī jurists, like the Imāmī jurists,

[38] Ibn al-Murtaḍā, *Kitāb*, VI:416, 421–2. [39] Ibid., 420–2; al-Ṣanᶜānī, *Kitāb*, IV:332–4.
[40] Ibn al-Murtaḍā, *Kitāb*, VI:422–3.
[41] Gibb and Kramers, eds., *Shorter*, 652. See also al-Ṣanᶜānī, *Tatimma*, IV:19.
[42] Al-Ṣanᶜānī, *Tatimma*, IV:6.
[43] Ibid., 22. [44] Ibid., 9.

do not conceive of the just ruler as having a relative claim to power. The *bughāh* are treated with a degree of deference, not because their interpretation or cause is plausible and could ultimately be correct, but because they cannot be equated with those who are motivated by selfish interests. This leaves a high degree of uncertainty as to how to distinguish between those who are motivated by selfish interests and those who are not. For instance, the just ruler may decide to treat certain groups as bandits and not rebels. Hence, some Zaydī authorities state: "The oppressors who usurp villages, towns, and provinces may be treated as bandits. [This is because] they cause corruption on the earth, and usurp money when no one can assist [the victims] . . . Therefore, they deserve to be treated as bandits if the *imām* prevails over them."[45] Conceptually, this quotation does not apply to the *bughāh* because it addresses those who victimize the innocent and usurp their money. Practically, however, it is possible that a ruler would refuse to recognize a certain secessionist group as *bughāh*, accuse them of victimizing the innocent and of not having an interpretation, and treat them as bandits. Nevertheless, the ambiguity that exists in the distinction between the legal category of *bughāh* and other categories is, arguably, a part of the dynamics of the negotiative process. If a presumed just ruler wrongfully accuses certain rebels, for instance, of being bandits and not *bughāh*, and the jurists happen to disagree, the jurists may declare the ruler unjust.[46]

Much of the attention of Zaydī jurists is focused on the issue of how one is to deal with unjust rulers. Zaydī jurists start out with the general principle: if the ruler is unjust, rebellion is not only permissible but obligatory. In fact, some jurists emphasize that one of the main differences between the Zaydī and Imāmī schools is that the Imāmīs prohibited rebellion against unjust rulers until the Qā'im appears, while the Zaydīs demanded immediate rebellion against injustice.[47] Despite the declared general principle, Zaydī jurists place the same limitations and restrictions on rebellion set by jurists from other schools. Rebellion, or enjoining the good and forbidding the evil, should be exercised only if it is potentially effective, the good outweighs the evil, and the risk of *fitna* is not very high. Accordingly, obeying an unjust ruler might be necessary if rebellion will produce undue civil strife.[48] Some Zaydī jurists caution against foolishly

[45] Ibn al-Murtaḍā, *Kitāb*, VI:202.

[46] Ibid., 387–8, argues that if a person violates his oath of allegiance to a just ruler then he has sinned unless the just ruler has breached his obligations. The issue of breach of obligations leaves room for negotiation.

[47] Ibid., I:40–1. [48] Al-Wazīr, *al-ʿAwāṣim*, VIII:75, 163–7.

engaging in rebellions because, according to them, since the Umayyad and ᶜAbbāsid eras, and up to the eleventh/seventeenth century, one can readily observe the amount of chaos and hardship that has resulted from rebellions. Therefore, the best response to injustice is often patience.[49] These jurists argue that it is exactly because of the drastic results of rebellion that the Prophet's traditions often emphasize the duty of obedience and patience. These traditions should be interpreted to mean that unless rebellion has a reasonable chance of success and will not result in greater harm than good, one should obey and be patient. However, if a person subjectively but honestly believes that the conditions are appropriate and then rebels, seeking to enjoin the good and forbid the evil, he is not blameworthy.[50]

There is not much discussion in Zaydī sources on what forms of rebellion against unjust rulers are permitted. For example, are acts of brigandage a legitimate form of rebellion? Interestingly, however, there is a discussion regarding assassinating unjust rulers and their aides. The majority of Zaydī jurists apparently had held that assassinations are not subject to a utilitarian balancing analysis. Rather, assassinations are simply prohibited, but the assassin is liable only for the blood money, and may not be physically punished.[51] Other than violent forms of resistance, Zaydī jurists also address the amount of cooperation permissible between Muslims and unjust rulers. Muslims may engage in *jihād* with unjust rulers against non-Muslim enemies. Muslims, however, should not trust or support unjust rulers or assist unjust rulers in propagating injustice.[52] Arguably, this means that Muslims may not assist an unjust ruler in fighting those who rebel against him. Even more, if an unjust ruler is ultimately defeated, he may possibly be treated as a bandit. Both unjust rulers and bandits are considered iniquitous by defiance (not by interpretation). As the passage quoted above indicates, the just ruler may treat oppressors who cause corruption on the earth and usurp people's money as bandits. The category of oppressors who cause corruption on the earth and usurp people's money might be broad enough to encompass unjust rulers.

THE IBĀḌĪ SCHOOL

Like the Zaydī school, the Ibāḍī school's discourse on rebellion is infused with theological paradigms which differentiate between piety and

[49] Al-Ṣanᶜānī, *Tatimma*, IV:8–9. [50] Ibid., 9, 19.
[51] Ibn al-Murtaḍā, *Kitāb*, VI:423. [52] Al-Ṣanᶜānī, *Kitāb*, IV:306; Ibn al-Murtaḍā, *Kitāb*, VI:396.

sinfulness, and belief and disbelief. However, unlike the Zaydīs and Imāmīs, the Ibāḍīs supported the idea of rebellion against ᶜAlī. Much of their theology focuses on the legitimacy of rebellion, and on resistance to rebellion. According to Ibāḍī theology, ᶜAlī committed a grievous error when he failed to fight Muᶜāwiya, who is seen as a rebel against ᶜAlī. Because of this presumed grievous error, it became incumbent on every Muslim to reject ᶜAlī's caliphate and rebel against him. Muslims who continued to support either ᶜAlī or Muᶜāwiya have committed a major sin. Hence, the failure to uphold the truth, whether it is in resisting rebellion or in failing to rebel, is a grievous sin. Unlike other sects of the Khawārij, the Ibāḍīs held that their opponents are not polytheists (*mushrikūn*), but *kuffār*. In this context, *kuffār* does not necessarily mean unbelievers; rather, it means not true or genuine Muslims.[53] Therefore, the Ibāḍīs held that it is legal to intermarry with and inherit from their opponents, and that their opponents may not be killed or enslaved and their properties may not be taken as booty.[54]

The history of the Ibāḍiyya goes back to ᶜAbd Allāh b. Ibāḍ al-Murrī al-Tamīmī, who dissociated himself from the more extreme Khawārij in the first century of Islam. The early Ibāḍīs oscillated between policies of cooperation with and rebellion against the Umayyads and ᶜAbbāsids. Nevertheless, they managed to establish independent principalities, notably in Oman by al-Julandā b. Masᶜūd b. Jaᶜfar b. al-Julandā (d. 131/748), and western Algeria by ᶜAbd al-Raḥmān b. Rustam (d. 161/778).[55] Although the Rustamids were defeated by the Fāṭimids in 296/909, from the second Rustamid ruler, ᶜAbd al-Wahhāb b. ᶜAbd al-Raḥmān (r. 171/788–208/824), emerged the most important Ibāḍī sect, the Wahbiyya. Furthermore, the Yaᶜrubids (1034/1625–1156/1743) and the Āl Bū Saᶜīds (1167/1754–present) established Ibāḍī rule in Oman.[56] Throughout their history, the Ibāḍīs dealt with conflicts with external, non-Ibāḍī enemies as well as internal rebellions. As recently as 1333/1913, the Ibāḍī jurists led a rebellion against what

53 Ibāḍī sources refer to their opponents as *ahl al-tawḥīd* or *ahl al-qibla* (people of faith or people who face towards Mecca in prayer), therefore indicating that such opponents are not considered unbelievers. These expressions may indicate that non-Ibāḍī Muslims share the *qibla* (direction of prayer) and the belief in God, but are not righteous Muslims.

54 Al-Shahrastānī, *al-Milal*, I:156–9; al-Baghdādī, *al-Farq*, 70; al-Kindī (d. 557/1162), *al-Muṣannaf*, XI:103, 250, 264; al-Saᶜdī, *Qāmūs*, VIII:106, IX:297–301.

55 For more on the early Ibāḍī movement, see Wilkinson, "Early," 125–44.

56 Zanzibār was ruled by the Āl Bū Saᶜīd from 1256/1840 to 1383/1964. See Bosworth, *New*, 27–8, 111, 113–15, 137; Gibb and Kramers, eds., *Shorter*, 143–5; Wilkinson, *Imamite*, esp. 12–14. See also al-Ziriklī, *al-Aᶜlām*, IV:144.

they regarded as the corrupt rule of the Bū Saᶜīds. Therefore, Ibāḍī discourses deal with rebellion against non-Ibāḍī and Ibāḍī rulers, and their discourses are replete with references to the actual practices of Ibāḍī rulers throughout history. Most of the available texts were written by Wahbī Ibāḍī jurists, and tend to cite the practices of Ibāḍī *imāms* in Oman and South Arabia.

In Ibāḍī thought, only a rightful and just ruler is entitled to obedience. A rightful ruler must follow the Wahbī Ibāḍī sect, although a ruler may be just but not rightful.[57] If a ruler is just, even if not rightful, rebellion might not be obligatory.[58] A rightful ruler must be pious and knowledgeable, but does not need to belong to a particular family or tribe and, in principle, rule by succession or usurpation is not recognized.[59] The ruler is picked by the jurists with the general acquiescence or approval of Muslims.[60] If the jurists are not confident about the qualifications of a candidate, they may contract the rulership to him on the condition that he does not decide certain issues without consultation with a council of jurists. If he fails to abide by the condition, he may be removed from office.[61] Furthermore, the jurists may contract rulership to someone for a one-year probationary period after which a more permanent arrangement is considered.[62] If any rightful ruler becomes unjust or commits a major sin, unless he repents he may be removed from office, even by force if necessary.[63] It is obligatory upon every Muslim to investigate the merits or demerits of a ruler, and to reach a decision as to any competing claims.[64] Importantly, the consensus of the majority of the notables or jurists that a ruler should be removed is strong and persuasive evidence of the necessity of such removal, but it does not necessarily establish the fact conclusively. The extent to which the jurists' opinions are binding depends on the issue under consideration, but

[57] Al-Kindī, *al-Muṣannaf*, X:55, 57, 97; al-Saᶜdī, *Qāmūs*, VIII:101, IX:253, 279; al-Tamīmī (d. 1223/1808), *Kitāb*, XIV:476.

[58] Al-Tamīmī, *Kitāb*, XIV:311, 341; al-Kindī, *al-Muṣannaf*, X:60; al-Rustāqī, *Manhaj*, VIII:76.

[59] Al-Kindī (*al-Muṣannaf*, X:60, 63, 78–9) states that it is preferred that the ruler be a pure Qurayshī; al-Tamīmī, *Kitāb*, XIV:358; al-Rustāqī, *Manhaj*, VIII:44–5.

[60] Al-Kindī, *al-Muṣannaf*, X:10, 60, 98; al-Saᶜdī, *Qāmūs*, IX:264; al-Rustāqī, *Manhaj*, VIII:44, 50.

[61] Al-Kindī, *al-Muṣannaf*, X:69–70; al-Rustāqī, *Manhaj*, VIII:45–7, 59.

[62] Al-Rustāqī, *Manhaj*, VIII:51.

[63] Al-Kindī, *al-Muṣannaf*, X:126, 193, 207–8, 215, 218; al-Saᶜdī, *Qāmūs*, VIII:103–4.

[64] Al-Kindī, *al-Muṣannaf*, X:194–5; al-Rustāqī, *Manhaj*, VIII:99–101; al-Saᶜdī, *Qāmūs*, VIII:115–16, IX:53. However, al-Saᶜdī (*Qāmūs*, IX:264, 332) argues that the consensus of the jurists on the appointment or removal of a ruler is binding on everyone. But see *Qāmūs*, IX:281, for the views of the Nazwāniyyūn. The author seems to contradict himself in ibid., IX:287, 291, 335, 350–1.

ultimately each individual must decide for himself whether to join a certain rebellion.[65]

Ibāḍī discourses on rebellion are extensive, and they combine elements of idealism and pragmatism in a complex mosaic. They focus not only on whether one should rebel against an unjust ruler, but also on the mechanics by which the justice or injustice of a ruler is ascertained. Furthermore, rebellion is not conceived of simply as an armed insurrection, but ranges in scope from the act of disavowing a certain ruler to non-cooperation and dissimulation, and ultimately to an armed challenge to power. We have already noted that according to Ibāḍī thought, only a rightful and just ruler is entitled to obedience, but Ibāḍī jurists deal with the mechanics by which a claim is made that such a ruler is no longer rightful or just. In order to understand Ibāḍī discourses, one should keep in mind that the Ibāḍī concept of *baghy* is very broad. Ibāḍī jurists employ the term to mean the act of committing an injustice or exceeding the bounds. Therefore, anyone who commits an injustice or sin could be a *bāghī*.[66] Furthermore, *baghy* is not a constant or static category; someone could start out at the beginning of a conflict just, and end up being a *bāghī*, or alternatively, one could start out a *bāghī*, but end up just. Which category one fits in depends on the type of claim made, and the behavior of the contending parties.[67]

Truth in all worldly and religious affairs is singular and absolute; however, people imperfectly understand such truth according to the evidence and intellect that they possess. Hence as to all competing claims, there is a singular truth, but people may disagree because of the fact that they are limited in their ability to seek or understand such truth.[68] As a matter of principle, in most disputed issues a rightful ruler is entitled to a presumption of good faith. As long as a matter is open to interpretation, a rightful ruler is entitled to the benefit of the doubt, and hence he should not be disobeyed or resisted.[69] Beyond this general principle, Ibāḍī jurists divide all disputes into three main categories. The first are

[65] Al-Tamīmī, *Kitāb*, XIV:343–4. The author also argues that generally a person should follow the guidance of the jurists. But if a person engages in a *fitna*, he will be excused if the jurists are in disagreement on the matter: ibid., 716–17. See al-Saᶜdī, *Qāmūs*, IX:259, 332; al-Rustāqī, *Manhaj*, VIII:83.

[66] For example, see the broad usage of the term *baghy* in al-Tamīmī, *Kitāb*, XIV:397–8, 433–7, 753–4; al-Kindī, *al-Muṣannaf*, XI:117; al-Rustāqī, *Manhaj*, VIII:24.

[67] Al-Tamīmī, *Kitāb*, XIV:585, 663–4, 673–4, 712; al-Kindī, *al-Muṣannaf*, X:194–5, 198.

[68] Al-Tamīmī, *Kitāb*, XIV:585, 685; al-Saᶜdī, *Qāmūs*, VIII:115–16, IX:241, 254–5, 323–4; al-Rustāqī, *Manhaj*, VIII:99–101.

[69] Al-Tamīmī, *Kitāb*, XIV:722–35; al-Kindī, *al-Muṣannaf*, X:219; al-Saᶜdī, *Qāmūs*, IX:253, 312, 320, 326, 330–2; al-Rustāqī, *Manhaj*, VIII:70, 79.

called disputes of opinion (*ikhtilāf al-raʾy*). Disputes of opinion relate to what is lawful or unlawful, but is not clearly covered by the Qurʾān, the *Sunna*, or consensus of the jurists. Over disputes of opinion, disagreement is legitimate, and one does not need to disavow (*barāʾa*) one side or the other.[70] The ruler is entitled to a degree of deference over such disputes, and consequently disputes of opinion do not create an unwavering obligation to rebel.[71] The second type of disputes is disputes of competing claims (*ikhtilāf daʿāwī*). Disputes of claims (as opposed to disputes of opinion) relate to issues in which the law is not in question, but the facts are in dispute. These are disputes in which if all the parties agree on the facts or the intentions of the people involved, the law would clearly settle the matter.[72] For example, whether someone stole or usurped certain property is a dispute of claims. A dispute as to whether a rebellious group is motivated by blind tribalism or religious zeal is a matter of intent and fact, and therefore is a dispute of competing claims as well. If the jurists are in disagreement as to who is right or wrong, a Muslim has the right to disavow whichever party he does not believe. Conversely, a Muslim has the right to ally himself (*yatawallā*) to whichever party he happens to believe. A Muslim should not join either of the disputing parties unless he affirmatively believes in the justice and truthfulness of one of the sides.[73] If he does not know who is right or wrong, he has an obligation to inquire and investigate in order to reach a decision. Significantly, a Muslim should not rely on the statements made by the ruler or his army, but should ask credible Muslims who are not biased.[74] If he is unable to ascertain the true from the false, then it is permissible to abstain from judgment (*wuqūf*) until such time as he is able to decide.[75] However, it is not permissible for a Muslim to abstain or exercise neutrality as a way of life or as a permanent condition (*lā yanṣibu al-shakka dīnā*). Therefore, in the words of one Ibāḍī jurist: "A person must distinguish between the people of the truth and the people of error. It is a binding obligation upon him to investigate and differentiate between them. The righteousness of truth is not affected by the prevalence of error."[76] Abstaining

70 Al-Saʿdī, *Qāmūs*, IX:254–6.
71 Al-Kindī, *al-Muṣannaf*, X:219; al-Rustāqī, *Manhaj*, VIII:70, 79.
72 Al-Saʿdī, *Qāmūs*, IX:257–8, 262.
73 Al-Tamīmī, *Kitāb*, XIV:341. Al-Saʿdī (*Qāmūs*, IX:257–8, 326, 350–1) adds that if Muslims are uncertain about who is right or wrong then the original presumption in favor of the ruler stays in effect until such time as it is rebutted. In other words, in a case of uncertainty, the ruler remains entitled to rule. See also al-Rustāqī, *Manhaj*, VIII:79.
74 Al-Rustāqī, *Manhaj*, VIII:99–101.
75 Al-Saʿdī, *Qāmūs*, VIII:109, 112–16, 118, IX:5–7, 43–5.
76 Al-Saʿdī, *Qāmūs*, VIII:115.

from judgment should only be a temporary state produced by a lack of information, created by a specific context in a particular dispute.[77] Importantly, as to disputes of claims, the consensus of the jurists could settle a particular dispute, and such a resolution is considered binding on all.[78]

The third form of disputes are disputes of heresy (*ikhtilāf al-bida*ᶜ). These are disputes involving issues that are clearly settled in religion, and are not a proper subject for disagreement.[79] For example, the prohibitions against drinking alcohol, eating pork, or taking Muslims as booty in war are clearly established in religion. As to this category, the ruler is not entitled to deference, and even the consensus of all the jurists may not alter the law. For instance, it is argued that if all the jurists in the world argued that it is proper to enslave Muslims or to drink alcohol, that would not alter the law. Furthermore, if all the jurists agreed that the party of *bida*ᶜ is correct, that would be ineffective and irrelevant.[80] Therefore, if a ruler murders an innocent person, he would clearly abdicate his right to rule, and would even be liable for the murder, whether he personally committed the murder or ordered someone else to execute it.[81] If the ruler denies that he committed the murder, that would be a dispute of claims because it relates to an issue of fact. But if it is established that he did commit the murder, there should be no question that he is liable and that he has abdicated his right to rule. In disputes of heresy, every Muslim must disavow what is wrong, and if he does not, he is liable in the Hereafter. Furthermore, in this category of disputes, whoever is wrong is the *bāghī*, regardless of his official position. Even if the facts are in dispute, if it becomes widely believed that the ruler has committed major sins, has become unjust or ineffective, or is unwilling to apply the law, then he must be removed.[82]

All disputes, except the disputes of heresy, are a form of *fitna*. That, however, does not mean that either side to the dispute is a *bāghī*. One becomes a *bāghī* when one exceeds the bounds of what is legitimate in a dispute.[83] While the ruler is entitled to the benefit of the doubt,

[77] Ibid., IX:46, 53, adds that when people disagree and accuse each other of being wrong, investigating the truth becomes a binding duty (*farḍ*). If a person does not investigate because he is too preoccupied with making a living and feeding his children, that person is not blameworthy as long as he had formed an intent to investigate, but never had the opportunity to give force to such an intent.

[78] Al-Tamīmī, *Kitāb*, XIV:716; al-Saᶜdī, *Qāmūs*, VIII:109, IX:264.

[79] Al-Saᶜdī, *Qāmūs*, IX:258–9, 282. See al-Warjalānī, *al-ᶜAdl*, II:109.

[80] Al-Saᶜdī, *Qāmūs*, IX:241, 259, 264.

[81] Al-Kindī, *al-Muṣannaf*, X:218.

[82] Al-Tamīmī, *Kitāb*, XIV:341–2; al-Kindī, *al-Muṣannaf*, X:215; al-Saᶜdī, *Qāmūs*, VIII:109, IX:303.

[83] Al-Kindī, *al-Muṣannaf*, X:194–5; al-Tamīmī, *Kitāb*, XIV:615, 628, 663–4, 666, 712.

every Muslim, including the jurists, must support what they believe to be just.[84] The benefit of doubt granted to the ruler is not permanent or absolute.[85] The jurists, or presumably a judge, could hold in the final analysis that either side to a dispute was correct. In that case, the group that violated the ruler's commands would not be held liable. Furthermore, as explained below, in certain matters, the ruler or his agents may be held liable for attempting to enforce illegal commands. As to most issues, at the procedural level, if a group, in a matter involving a dispute of opinion or claims, has a grievance against the legitimate ruler, they may adhere to their opinions and may even speak against the ruler; that in itself will not make them *bughāh*.[86] The group should present its evidence and give the ruler an opportunity to respond, but since the ruler is entitled to the benefit of the doubt they should not resort to force. If the group insists on disobeying the law or seeks to remove the ruler by force, the group becomes the *bughāh*.[87] Moreover, if the ruler admits his errors and repents, yet the group refuses to accept his repentance, the group becomes the *bughāh* as well. However, if the ruler refuses to reform and insists on injustice, it might become legitimate to use force against him.[88] Nevertheless, it is not clear whether the ruler's repentance is accepted in the case of murder or rape.[89]

Effectively, in Ibāḍī thought, armed rebellion against a legitimate ruler is permitted if the ruler commits major sins or if the jurists agree that he is no longer fit to rule. Furthermore, if there is general agreement that the ruler is consistently unjust, that might legitimate rebellion as well.[90] In these situations the rebels are not *bughāh* because they have not exceeded the bounds. In disputes involving competing claims or opinions

[84] Alternatively, if they do not know who is right or wrong, they may abstain: see al-Kindī, *al-Muṣannaf*, X:194; al-Tamīmī (*Kitāb*, XIV:684–5, 689) argues that it is a major sin to fight on someone's side out of blind loyalty.

[85] Al-Saʿdī (*Qāmūs*, VIII:101, IX:335) argues that even if the ruler was appointed through a consensus, it is not permissible to claim that the ruler is correct and every rebel is wrong. See al-Rustāqī, *Manhaj*, VIII:52, 79, 99–100.

[86] Al-Tamīmī, *Kitāb*, XIV:336–7.

[87] Al-Kindī, *al-Muṣannaf*, X:196, 198, XI:216.

[88] Al-Tamīmī, *Kitāb*, XIV:341–2; al-Kindī, *al-Muṣannaf*, X:215.

[89] Al-Kindī (*al-Muṣannaf*, X:217) asserts that the ruler abdicates his right to rule the minute he commits a capital crime.

[90] Al-Rustāqī, *Manhaj*, VIII:54; al-Kindī, *al-Muṣannaf*, X:193. Al-Saʿdī (*Qāmūs*, IX:303, 314, 319) raises doubts as to whether a consensus on the removal of a ruler could ever exist. Therefore, if a sizable group knows of the ruler's injustice, it should rebel and should not wait until the populace shares its views. Al-Tamīmī (*Kitāb*, XIV:343–4) asserts that the existence of a general consensus that a ruler should be removed is evidence against him. Al-Rustāqī (*Manhaj*, VIII:83) argues that if the notables agree that the ruler has committed what warrants his removal, that is to be taken as evidence against the ruler even if the populace does not concur.

a Muslim is not a *bāghī* and does not commit a sin by supporting one side or another as long as force is not used. In fact, every Muslim must investigate and make an affirmative determination as to who is right or wrong.[91] Some claims are by definition illegitimate, and not recognized; for instance, disputes involving family honor or tribalism and disputes in which the rebels are advocating heresy. Otherwise, in disputes of claims or opinions, the *bāghī* is whoever unjustly resorts to force or exceeds the proper limits of conduct. Of course, differentiating between when one is a *bāghī* and when not involves the drawing of subtle, and perhaps haphazard, distinctions. It is not clear, for example, when one might decide that a ruler's injustice has become widespread and well known, and therefore armed rebellion is permissible. It is also not clear what the proper balance is between the presumption of good faith conceded to legitimate rulers and the imperative of resisting sin and injustice.

Regardless of the nature of the claims made against him, the legitimate ruler is bound by several rules of conduct. He must strive to settle disputes peacefully, and must warn his opponents before resorting to force.[92] The ruler may not fight the *bughāh* unless they resort to arms or insist on not complying with the law – for instance, if they refuse to pay taxes.[93] Interestingly, when debating or warning the rebels, a ruler should not call upon such rebels to obey him, but must call upon them to submit to the law of God. In other words, the emphasis of the ruler should not be on allegiance to him personally, but on submission to the institution of *Sharīʿa*.[94] If his opponents continue to refuse, he may fight them but only to bring them to the fold and not to slaughter them. The laws regulating the treatment of rebels is similar to the non-Ibāḍī schools. The ruler is under an obligation to instruct his army as to the rules of engagement, and the limitations on the conduct of warfare. If the ruler's army violates the rules, the public treasury must compensate the victims. If the ruler does not properly instruct his army, he might be held personally liable.[95] Furthermore, the ruler may not seek the assistance of a group that might violate the rules of conduct because of a preexisting enmity towards

91 Al-Saʿdī, *Qāmūs*, IX:320.

92 Al-Rustāqī (*Manhaj*, VIII:37) asserts that if there is clear evidence that a group of people gave their oath of allegiance to a challenger, the just ruler may imprison the challenger and his followers until they repent. After repenting, they must be released.

93 Al-Tamīmī, *Kitāb*, XIV:383, 570; al-Kindī, *al-Muṣannaf*, XI:118, 215, 220–2; al-Rustāqī, *Manhaj*, VIII:13, 24, 97–8.

94 Al-Kindī, *al-Muṣannaf*, XI:220; al-Rustāqī, *Manhaj*, VIII:97, 99.

95 Al-Tamīmī, *Kitāb*, XIV:385–6, 390–1, 598–600: the ruler and his soldiers are liable for committing acts of injustice. However, not all the soldiers are collectively liable; it is possible for a group of soldiers to be liable while the other groups are not. See also al-Kindī, *al-Muṣannaf*, XI:234.

the rebels. In the opinion of the majority of jurists, the wounded and fugitives may not be dispatched unless the rebels have reinforcements (*fiʾa*). Some argue that in no circumstances may the wounded be dispatched.[96] Furthermore, there is disagreement among the Ibāḍī jurists as to whether captives may be killed during the continuation of the fighting.[97] The ruler may not use weapons of indiscriminate destruction unless for an absolute necessity.[98] However, there is disagreement as to whether fire may be used against the rebels, and as to whether the rebels may be denied food or water.[99] Nonetheless, torture, mutilation, or needless destruction of property or trees is not permitted.[100] Furthermore, rebels may not be enslaved, and their property may not be confiscated. In the opinion of some, rebels' weapons and horses may be sold, but the money from such a sale should be returned to them.[101] After the fighting ends, prisoners may not be executed, and must be released. However, in the view of some Ibāḍī jurists, the leader of the rebels may be executed if he is responsible for murders.[102]

The above-mentioned rules of conduct apply to fighting any *bughāh*, whether the opponents are Ibāḍīs or not, and regardless of the reason for the fighting. Therefore the same rules apply even if the Ibāḍī ruler is fighting Sunnīs.[103] If the ruler himself exceeds the proper bounds he may be considered a *bāghī*, and will be held liable for his violations. The same rules of conduct apply to rebels as well. Consequently, if either party

[96] Al-Tamīmī, *Kitāb*, XIV:381, 383; al-Rustāqī, *Manhaj*, VIII:113–15; al-Kindī, *al-Muṣannaf*, XI:98, 102, 243. Several jurists argue that the wounded who are too weak to fight should not be killed, even if the rebels have reinforcements.

[97] Al-Rustāqī (*Manhaj*, VIII:114) asserts that the ruler should consult the jurists as to the fate of rebels captured while the fighting is continuing.

[98] Al-Kindī (*al-Muṣannaf*, XI:228) argues that if arrows or rocks are used, and women and children are killed, the loyalists must pay the blood money.

[99] Al-Rustāqī, *Manhaj*, VIII:97, 119. Al-Kindī (*al-Muṣannaf*, XI:224–6, 239, 241–2) adds that water may be denied rebels during a siege but not if they have livestock with them. Food or water may not be denied to rebels if they have women and children with them. The use of fire or flooding is not permitted. The author cites an incident in Ibāḍī history where rebels' homes were burned, so the ruler paid them compensation.

[100] Al-Tamīmī (*Kitāb*, XIV:384–5, 421) adds that the people of Ḥaḍramūt cut down the trees of rebels. See also al-Kindī, *al-Muṣannaf*, XI:236; al-Rustāqī, *Manhaj*, VIII:120–1.

[101] Al-Tamīmī, *Kitāb*, XIV:383; al-Kindī, *al-Muṣannaf*, XI:230–2.

[102] Al-Kindī, *al-Muṣannaf*, XI:229, 245, 247–9, 251: a minority view maintains that if certain rebels are seen killing people, the ruler has discretion in killing them. However, al-Kindī asserts that there is consensus that rebels who rely on an interpretation may not be held liable for life or property. Al-Rustāqī (*Manhaj*, VIII:114–16) adds that when the *imām* Ghassān b. ᶜAbd Allāh captured the rebel leader ᶜĪssā b. Jaᶜfar, the *imām* consulted the jurists. The jurists advised that the matter was to be left to his discretion. However, the *imām* decided not to kill him, in order to avoid the possibility of committing a sin.

[103] The ᶜAbbāsids and Umayyads are considered *bughāh*. See al-Rustāqī, *Manhaj*, VIII:73–4.

violates the prescribed rules of conduct, they are liable for their excesses. Importantly, the majority of Ibāḍī jurists argue that if the rebels are motivated by piety and not greed, they are not to be held liable for life or property destroyed in the fighting. The rebels need not have an interpretation, but must be motivated by considerations of right and wrong which arise from a religious conviction.[104] Those who fight for family honor or tribal reasons are not exempt from liability.[105] Rather, it must be ascertained that the rebels were motivated by matters of conscience and piety. Whether the rebels were ultimately right or wrong is not relevant because it is the subjective intent of the parties that is considered material. If the rebels believed, in good faith, in the legality of their behavior, they should not be held liable for the life and property destroyed in the fighting. However, like the jurists of the other schools, the Ibāḍī jurists disagreed as to whether rebels who commit acts of banditry or rape may be considered to be people of piety. The majority view is that the terrorizing of the wayfarer or raping and pillaging is irrebuttably presumed to be contrary to piety.[106] Therefore, if a group commits acts of banditry they may be treated as common criminals, and may be held liable for life and property destroyed during the course of fighting.[107] Arguably, however, the accusation of banditry is equally applicable to unjust rulers. Unjust rulers who terrorize people and attack without warning may be fought as bandits.[108]

The Ibāḍī doctrines on the rules of conduct are, for the most part, limiting or control factors. Ibāḍī jurists negotiated and balanced two

[104] Al-Tamīmī, *Kitāb*, XIV:393; al-Kindī, *al-Muṣannaf*, XI:251–2.

[105] Al-Tamīmī, *Kitāb*, XIV:664, 698; al-Kindī, *al-Muṣannaf*, XI:119–20.

[106] Al-Kindī (*al-Muṣannaf*, XI:118, 223, 249) argues that those who commit acts of banditry should not be fought as rebels, and should be treated as bandits; al-Tamīmī (*Kitāb*, XIV:542, 557–8) argues that if a *bāghī* seeks to assault or rape a woman, he may be killed; al-Rustāqī (*Manhaj*, VIII:237) argues that arson is an act of banditry, but it is not clear if an arsonist is a bandit even if he relies on an interpretation.

[107] In certain contexts, al-Tamīmī (*Kitāb*, XIV:622) distinguishes between common bandits and religiously motivated bandits. Religiously motivated bandits may not be fought without warning. Some Ibāḍī jurists adopted the view that bandits should not be held liable for life or physical injuries inflicted during the time in which they are resisting arrest. The logic for this minority view is reciprocity. The ruler is not liable for life or injuries inflicted upon the bandits during fighting, so they should not be held liable either. Bandits, however, are liable for acts of banditry: see ibid., 612, 614. Al-Kindī (*al-Muṣannaf*, XI:240–1) reports that the Qarāmiṭa were fought as non-Muslims because they burned the homes of Muslims and indiscriminately killed Muslims. Since the Qarāmiṭa employed means similar to those used by bandits, it became permissible to kill their captives and fugitives, and to burn their homes. See also al-Rustāqī, *Manhaj*, VIII:37, 127. Many Ibāḍī jurists argued that a Muslim, even a bandit, may not be crucified. Crucifixion was reserved for non-Muslim bandits. See al-Tamīmī, *Kitāb*, XIV:612; al-Kindī, *al-Muṣannaf*, XI:274; al-Rustāqī, *Manhaj*, VIII:126.

[108] See al-Rustāqī, *Manhaj*, VIII:107; al-Kindī, *al-Muṣannaf*, XI:223, 263; al-Tamīmī, *Kitāb*, XIV: 617–18.

competing values. On the one hand, a legitimate ruler is entitled to obedience so that law and order may be upheld. On the other hand, Ibāḍī jurists were not willing to grant a legitimate ruler an absolute right to obedience, and were concerned with substantive issues of justice. Therefore, as noted above, the ruler should not call upon rebels to obey him, but call upon them to obey the law of God. This is not simply a rhetorical point because it is ultimately the law of God that reigns supreme. Consequently, as to disputes of heresy, the ruler is not entitled to obedience, nevertheless, as Ibāḍī discourses themselves demonstrate, it is very difficult to systematically distinguish between disputes of heresy and disputes of opinion. It is virtually impossible to depoliticize or objectify disputes of heresy.[109] Moreover, even as to disputes of opinion or claims, the ruler is entitled to a presumption in his favor; however, this presumption is not irrebuttable or absolute. Therefore Ibāḍī jurists argue that particularly in disputes involving life and physical integrity, Muslims should act according to their consciences. Muslims should resist what they sincerely believe to be an injustice.[110] As a general matter, they should obey rulers and judges, and in most situations, it is the rulers and judges who are directly responsible for any illegal commands that they may have issued. Therefore, in most situations Muslims are not liable for executing the orders of a duly authorized ruler or judge. Nonetheless, even obedience to legitimate rulers and judges does not necessarily insulate Muslims from responsibility. In issues involving life and physical integrity, they must rely on their consciences, and therefore, if someone obeys an order from a superior which he should have known is illegal, he might be held liable for executing the illegal order.[111] On the other hand, if a Muslim resists what he believes to be an illegal order, he does so at his own risk. If it is subsequently decided that the order was, in fact, legal, and that the Muslim did not have a right to resist, such a Muslim will be held liable on this earth, although he might not be blameworthy in the Hereafter because he relied on a sincere belief.[112] On the other hand, if it is subsequently held that the order was illegal and resistance was justified, the resisting

[109] See al-Saᶜdī, *Qāmūs*, IX:291, 319, 350–1; al-Warjalānī (*al-ᶜAdl*, II:46–7) argues that the dispute over the rulership of the caliph ᶜUthmān was one of religion and heresy, not a dispute of opinions or claims. To say the least, this is debatable.

[110] Al-Tamīmī, *Kitāb*, XIV:717; al-Kindī, *al-Muṣannaf*, XI:267; al-Rustāqī, *Manhaj*, VIII:40–1, 79.

[111] Al-Tamīmī (*Kitāb*, XIV:598–600, 716–17) adds that the ruler and his soldiers are liable for issuing and executing illegal orders.

[112] Ibid., XIV:585, asserts that in the Hereafter, one who relied on what one may reasonably rely on is not liable. On this earth, however, right or wrong is judged according to objective evidence which could be erroneous.

person will not be held liable for violating an illegal command.[113] In essence, Ibāḍī jurists attempted to strike a balance between the need for order and stability and the imperative of substantive justice. Nonetheless, since a Muslim acting on good conscience did so at his or her own risk, Ibāḍī jurists mitigated the nature of this dynamic by adopting the rules limiting the conduct of warfare against rebels. This conceptually guarded against rebellion becoming a zero–sum game. Rebels are afforded certain protections even if, in the final analysis, it is held that they did not have a right to rebel.

As noted above, Ibāḍī jurists insist that an illegitimate ruler should not be obeyed and must be removed. In fact, this is what Ibāḍī jurists often cite as one of the main distinguishing factors between them and other schools of thought.[114] Despite the Ibāḍī ideological commitment to the rejection of illegitimate rulers, Ibāḍī jurists, like the jurists from other schools, engage in a balancing dynamic. An illegitimate ruler is one who came to power through usurpation and force, or one who was appointed by iniquitous people, or a ruler who insists on committing major sins including widespread injustice.[115] Nonetheless, some Ibāḍī jurists argue that even if a ruler came to power through usurpation, it might not be necessary to remove him if his subsequent policies were just.[116] However, even as to unjust rulers, Ibāḍī jurists do not impose an absolute duty to rebel. Rebellion is obligatory only if there is a reasonable chance of success, and only if the risks to the rebels and society are not prohibitively high. One should not rebel if rebellion effectively constitutes casting oneself into ruin. In all circumstances, one should balance the harm to oneself and others with the expected benefit.[117] Some Ibāḍī jurists assert that the preconditions for legitimating armed rebellion rarely exist. Therefore, armed rebellion in most circumstances is not justified.[118] Most jurists, however, argue that it is permissible to assassinate unjust rulers as long as notice and warning is first provided to the oppressors. Some Ibāḍī jurists add that an unjust ruler may be assassinated only if he is responsible for the murder of people. Most Ibāḍī jurists assert that it is

[113] Ibid., XIV:714, argues that if one relies on the advice of credible witnesses in supporting what turns out to be the wrong party, one is held liable on this earth but not in the Hereafter.

[114] See ibid., XIV:311, 341; al-Kindī, *al-Muṣannaf*, X:215; al-Saᶜdī, *Qāmūs*, IX:279; al-Warjalānī, *al-ᶜAdl*, II:49; al-Rustāqī, *Manhaj*, VIII:76.

[115] Al-Kindī, *al-Muṣannaf*, X:60, 73, 75–6; al-Rustāqī, *Manhaj*, VIII:45.

[116] Al-Kindī, *al-Muṣannaf*, X:97.

[117] Al-Tamīmī, *Kitāb*, XIV:343, 763; al-Kindī, *al-Muṣannaf*, X:51–2, XI:267; al-Saᶜdī, *Qāmūs*, VIII:104; al-Rustāqī, *Manhaj*, VIII:78, 112.

[118] Al-Warjalānī, *al-ᶜAdl*, II:49–51.

not permissible to assassinate the rank and file in the unjust ruler's army or police. Therefore, murder by stealth would not be allowed if directed at the ruler's soldiers.[119] Some Ibāḍī jurists argue that if a particular soldier has killed someone, that soldier may be assassinated.[120]

If the use of force against unjust rulers is not possible, Muslims should exercise a variety of forms of non-cooperation.[121] As far as possible, Muslims should resist accepting government posts. They should avoid accepting judicial positions or even testifying in court. They should try to avoid paying taxes to the government and avoid providing other forms of support to the ruler's army.[122] Nonetheless, all of these are not absolute prohibitions; they must be weighed in light of competing interests and values. For instance, Muslims may assist an unjust ruler in waging *jihād* against non-Muslims, or even assist him in defending against an assault by another unjust ruler if their own homes or the homes of others are threatened.[123] Furthermore, they may assist an unjust ruler in implementing certain laws if such laws are just, and they may accept official positions as long as they exercise great caution lest they commit an injustice. If threatened or forced, Muslims may practice all forms of dissimulation in order to avoid harm.[124] They may refrain from criticizing the ruler's injustice, or may carry out illegal commands. A Muslim has greater discretion in exercising dissimulation with regard to disputes of opinion or claims. Dissimulation in matters where there is difference of opinion or disagreement is not as serious as dissimulation in matters considered essential for Islam. Dissimulation in matters that are central to the core of Islam or in issues that are clearly established in law is not proper unless under extreme forms of duress.[125] However, under no circumstances may a Muslim practice dissimulation if it involves murder or serious physical injury, such as rape, to another person.[126]

The Ibāḍī discourse, like the Imāmī and Zaydī discourse, engages in a negotiative dynamic with power. These discourses start out with general

[119] Al-Rustāqī, *Manhaj*, VIII:107–9. Some jurists argue that if warning is provided, the ruler or the soldiers may be assassinated: see al-Kindī, *al-Muṣannaf*, X:278.

[120] Al-Kindī, *al-Muṣannaf*, XI:264–9.

[121] See al-Tamīmī, *Kitāb*, XIV:339–440; al-Kindī (*al-Muṣannaf*, X:296–303) details many forms of non-cooperation.

[122] Al-Tamīmī, *Kitāb*, XIV:340; al-Warjalānī, *al-ᶜAdl*, II:50.

[123] Al-Warjalānī, *al-ᶜAdl*, II:53; al-Kindī (*al-Muṣannaf*, XI:75–6) adds that Muslims may assist an unjust ruler to fight a more unjust ruler. If Muslims do not know who is more unjust, they should not assist either side. See also al-Rustāqī, *Manhaj*, VIII:104.

[124] Al-Tamīmī, *Kitāb*, XIV:337–8; al-Kindī, *al-Muṣannaf*, X:273, 285–92.

[125] Al-Warjalānī, *al-ᶜAdl*, II:49, 51–4.

[126] Ibid., 55.

statements which uphold certain ideals – the ideals of order, stability, and substantive justice. The ideals are weighed and balanced, and from this balancing process certain conditions, exceptions, and limitations are articulated. The discourse is negotiative because it does not uphold a certain ideal as absolute and unmitigated. There are absolute moral values, such as not assisting in the murder of an innocent person, but these moral values constitute the outer limits or external parameters of the discourse. Within the outer limits there is considerable room for negotiation and the weighing of competing considerations. The discourses are not dogmatic because they are not absolute, and they are negotiative because they are legalistic. Law is often forced to weigh competing considerations, and strike a balance between conflicting demands. Even the outer limits are difficult to define. As noted above, it is difficult to distinguish a dispute of heresy from a dispute of opinion. If one claims that there is a consensus that a certain ruler is just, and another challenges this consensus, does this become a dispute of heresy or opinion? In practice, even an attempt to define the outer limits is negotiative because it is forced to deal with challenges, objections, and qualifications.[127] Besides being negotiative, these discourses are also symbolic because they are designed to embarrass, shame, educate, and praise. They identify certain conduct as acceptable, and other conduct as reprehensible. For example, when Ibāḍī jurists contend that the cutting down of the rebels' trees, the burning of the rebels' homes, and the pursuing of the fugitives are not among the practices of Muslims or is not what Muslims normally do,[128] they are not making a sociological observation. They are arguing that such conduct is not what a good Muslim should be comfortable with. Moreover, these jurists are not stating a rule prohibiting the conduct in question: rather, they are raising a question as to the acceptability of such conduct. The symbolic aspect of the discourse acts as a moral commentary on how power dynamics are negotiated.

CONCLUSION: LEGAL BORROWING AND THE NEGOTIATIVE PROCESS

Ibāḍī, Imāmī, and Zaydī discourses affirm a high ideal: a legitimate ruler should be just, and only a legitimate ruler is owed obedience. Therefore

[127] See the discussion in al-Saʿdī, *Qāmūs*, IX:260–2, 291, 319, 350–1. The author discusses various political conflicts in Oman and Yemen, and whether they were disputes involving conflicting claims and opinions or disputes of *bidaʿ*. He observes that these disputes are problematic because a consensus on the appointment or removal of a certain ruler will never exist.

[128] Al-Rustāqī, *Manhaj*, VIII:120; al-Kindī, *al-Muṣannaf*, XI:237, 243.

those who rebel against a just ruler are iniquitous because they violate their duty of obedience. Nonetheless, this forces a competing claim, and a truism. An unjust ruler could not be legitimate, and therefore is not owed obedience, and those who rebel against him are not committing an error. Like the Sunnī jurists, the Ibāḍī, Imāmī, and Zaydī jurists realized that drawing the line between legitimacy and illegitimacy or between justice and injustice is a subtle and difficult matter. Consequently, they imposed rules of conduct that mitigate and limit the consequences of rebellion. Such rebellion could be a miscalculation or misjudgment as to the merits or chances of success, and such misjudgments should not result in absolute and draconian measures. Significantly, the Sunnī, Ibāḍī, Imāmī, and Zaydī schools ended up articulating similar rules of conduct. This is partly due to the similarities in the dynamics surrounding the juridical culture of these various schools. However, one suspects that legal borrowing played a central role in the pervasiveness of the language and categories of *aḥkām al-bughāh*.[129] For instance, the Ibāḍī school, on ideological grounds, does not refer to the precedent of ᶜAlī in constructing its rules of conduct. As discussed earlier, all the other schools agree that it is ᶜAlī's precedent that shaped the discourses of rebellion. Despite the fact that the Ibāḍī jurists do not cite ᶜAlī or his practices, they end up articulating the same rules of conduct prevalent in the other schools. Yet Ibāḍī jurists insist that their doctrines are based on precedents set by their own *imāms*. It is pointless to accuse any school of intentionally fabricating or projecting traditions in order to reach certain results. Nonetheless, the similarities between the Ibāḍīs and the other schools point to the pervasiveness of legal culture and legal borrowing, and to the creative, constructive, and selective process that incorporates and legitimates such borrowing.

[129] On the dynamics and interactions between the Shīᶜī and Sunnī legal cultures, see Stewart, *Islamic*. The author emphasizes the process of resistance and borrowing between the Shīᶜī and Sunnī legal systems.

CHAPTER 8

Negotiating rebellion in Islamic law

REBELLION AND THE LINGUISTIC PRACTICE OF MUSLIM JURISTS

Technique is the art of the jurist. Technique is the specialized method by which the jurist expresses normative values, instrumentalist objectives, and functionalist goals. The methodology of the jurist is the product of a juristic culture which develops and legitimates a specialized method of discourse. The juristic culture itself reflects the cumulative institutional experiences and commitments of innumerable collaborators preserved in specialized books, continually reinforced, and revived in the minds of the practitioners within that culture. The juristic culture is defined, somewhat, by unitary or uniform institutional and ideological commitments, but most of all it is defined by a specialized code, namely, a technical language. The technique of the jurist relies on language as its primary tool by which power is asserted, legitimated, or challenged. Language is the main tool by which a jurist attempts to negotiate reality, produce domains of truth, and frustrate claims of truth or reality. Because of the centrality of language, it is imperative to examine the linguistic practice of the jurists. A meaningful understanding of the law, its functions or purposes must be based on a study of the details, or what some have called the microdiscourses, of the linguistic practice.[1] It is primarily through the medium of language that juristic culture defines, perpetuates, and reforms itself. As John Conley and William O'Barr argue, "First and foremost, the details of legal discourse matter because language is the essential mechanism through which the power of the law is realized, exercised, reproduced, and occasionally challenged and subverted."[2] Most importantly, the details of the linguistic practice are essential to understanding the creative

[1] Conley and O'Barr, *Just*, 106. See also Danet, "Language"; Levi and Walker, eds., *Language*; Morrill and Facciola, "Power." Also see the excellent study by Fallers, *Law*.

[2] Conley and O'Barr, *Just*, 129.

act by which juristic culture responds to socio-political challenges and negotiates power dynamics.

The fact that Islamic law is divine in origin should not conceal the fact that it creatively responds to the socio-political dynamics of society placed within a specific historical context. Islamic law is influenced by the economic infrastructure, pressured by political demands, impacted by social considerations, and shaped and channeled by the text, but it is ultimately not fully determined by any of them.[3] Law, and this is certainly true of Islamic law, is also molded by a corporate identity, and a common culture produced by and for the jurists. In this sense, law generally, and Islamic law specifically, is not autonomous but semi-autonomous.[4] Islamic law is influenced by theological imperatives and socio-political demands, but it is articulated, constructed, and asserted by jurists who belong to a common, although not uniform, culture. This juristic culture constructs its own rituals, habits, paradigms, and symbolism, and its own domains of truth. It also defines its own rules for acceptability, inclusion, and exclusion. This does not mean that all legal doctrines are the product of the legal culture, or that they exist to serve the interests of the members of that culture. It does mean, however, that within specific historical contexts, legal culture expresses, promotes, challenges, and undermines socio-political demands. At times legal culture transmits and supports certain socio-political demands, but it also frustrates, dilutes, and makes it possible to thwart them.

Law responds and acts sometimes through inertia.[5] Once formed, legal culture does not necessarily respond efficiently to the demands placed upon it. Legal culture, with its inherited doctrines and truths, could become a habit that is difficult to alter or change. This is the influence of the accumulated precedents and rules of exclusion. This inertia gives law its stability, predictability, and appearance of immutability. In many ways, by failing to respond, law validates its own legitimacy and, at times, the legitimacy of the social and political institutions of society. However, it is dangerous to read too much into legal inertia, or to assume that the failure of the legal system to respond necessarily means that the juristic

[3] This statement was inspired by Abel (*Politics*, 523), who states, "[Law] is 'relatively autonomous,' influenced by economic infrastructure, pressured by political forces, and shaped by the social system, but not fully determined by any of them."

[4] On the idea of relative or semi-autonomous law, see Balbus, "Commodity."

[5] This position is represented by Alan Watson, *Society*. See the critique of this position in Abel, "Law." On law and social change, and on the gap between law and society, see Ogburn, *Social*; Ogburn, *On Culture*; Sumner, *Folkways*; Barber and Inkeles, eds., *Stability*. Levi (*Introduction*) argues that the common law responds slowly to changing social values.

culture is legitimating the existing social or political institutions. At times, the legal system does not change because of the convenience of habit. Furthermore, the failure of the legal system to alter its inherited doctrines could be a form of protest against the dominant social or political practice. By insisting on a certain doctrinal ideal, the juristic culture could protest the dominant social or political practices.

The legal system often does eventually respond to socio-political realities and the dynamics of the juristic culture with a creative act. This creative act reexamines the inherited doctrines or paradigms, and selectively and imaginatively reconstructs the discourse or parts of the discourse. The creative act is not necessarily instrumentalist or functional; it does not necessarily aim at concrete and tangible results. It does not always aim to accomplish immediate changes in the way people go about their daily lives or in the way people resolve conflicts. Rather, the purposes of the creative process are negotiative, symbolic, clarifying, and at times intentionally obfuscating. It often legitimates, aspires, educates, and protests. Importantly, the creative process is expressed primarily through the subtleties of language, and hence, unless one focuses on the details of the juridical linguistic practice, one would not be able to notice, much less appraise, the dynamics of the legal discourse. In fact, all claims about the nature or purpose of a legal system are highly suspect unless grounded in a thorough understanding of the microlinguistic practices of the legal culture.[6]

It is exactly because of the failure to examine the details of the linguistic practices of Muslim legal discourses that most contemporary commentators have adopted an erroneous view of the role of Muslim jurists. The traditional or accepted scholarly view tends to see Muslim jurists as conservative legitimists who simply rationalized the existing political order. According to this accepted scholarly view, Muslim jurists moved from the realm of political idealism to the absolute realm of political realism; they emptied the contract of the caliphate of all moral content, and left only the factor of power operative in the juridical discourses. Therefore Muslim jurists insisted upon an unchanged obligation of submission to the ruler. They sanctioned the authority of the usurper of power, and made obedience a moral and legal, as well as religious, obligation. Ultimately, according to the accepted scholarly view, Muslim jurists condemned all forms of civil strife, and fostered the belief that rebellion is the most heinous of all crimes. However, the accepted scholarly view

[6] Paraphrased from Conley and O'Barr, *Just*, 130.

achieves a very partial understanding of juristic discourse because it fails to focus on the details of the legal discourse – the linguistic practice – and analyze it in terms of the dynamics of power, legal culture, and legitimation. It fails to examine the microdiscourses of the law, to look beyond its stated instrumental goals, and instead to search for the creative process and its symbolic content. Consequently, the accepted view results in a starkly monochromatic or bipolar understanding of the juristic discourses: rulers must be either just or unjust; unjust rulers must either be obeyed or disobeyed; rebellion is either permitted or prohibited; and Muslim jurists were either activists or quietists.

Quite to the contrary, the dynamics engendered in the juristic discourses on rebellion and banditry reveal a far more complex process. Much earlier than the discourses of al-Ghazālī and Ibn Jamāᶜa, Muslim jurists accepted the functional necessity of obeying those in power. In principle, those in power should be obeyed. But that, in itself, is not remarkable for two reasons. First, legal systems, particularly premodern systems, often demanded an absolute duty of obedience, and mandated harsh penalties for rebels. At least from the point of view of normative legal injunctions, rebels were often seen as traitors, and normative law commonly showed little tolerance for those who defied the political order.[7] Second, and more importantly, as discussed earlier, legal culture

[7] Article 2(1) of the Qing Code lists the plotting of rebellion as one of the ten great wrongs. Under article 255, no distinction is made between rebellion and treason. Article 254 provides that principals and accessories to the crimes of high treason and of plotting a rebellion will be put to death by slicing. Male relatives of the perpetrator who are over sixteen years of age will be beheaded, and female relatives will be given to officers as slaves. Interestingly, article 210 provides that a military officer who is unkind to people, violates the rules, and pushes honorable people so far that they rebel will be beheaded. See also articles 2(9), 333, 334, 337(2): Jones, trans., *Great*, 35, 36, 67, 204, 237–9, 315.

See Todd, *Shape*, 141 n. 21 (treason punished by death, confiscation of property, and prohibition of burial within Athenian sovereignty). However, MacDowell (*Law*, 176–7) argues that treason by attempting to overthrow the government was differentiated from an act of treason, which consisted of cooperating with a foreign power. On Roman law and political crimes see Schisas, *Offences*, 3–15; MacMullen, *Enemies*, 218; Jolowicz, *Historical*, 325–6.

Maimonides in the *Mishneh Torah* dedicates a chapter to rebels. In this chapter, the punishments of execution by strangulation and flagellation are mandated for rebellious elders who defy or resist the rulings of the Supreme Court, and advocate contrary opinions to the positions of the Supreme Court: see Maimonides, *Code*, 138–50. The justification for the punishments is "in order that strife may not increase in Israel" (ibid., 144). Maimonides does not address armed rebellion – however, by implication, it is doubtful that it would be tolerated. Also see Cohen, *Jewish*, 1:69–70 n. 28.

See Drew, trans., *Lombard* (the Edict of Laws issued by King Rothair in 643: Law One specifies that a person who conspires or gives counsel against the life of the king shall be killed and his property confiscated; Law Six provides that anyone who revolts while on a campaign or who raises a revolt in any part of the army shall be killed). See also Schild, "History," 130 (treason in the Frankish period and the Middle Ages included breaches of the loyalty owed the king

inclines towards order and stability, and a context in which conflicts may be peacefully resolved. However, this propensity or inclination is not absolute because it functions within the power dynamics of the legal culture and the state. In other words, the emphasis on order and stability is only one of the negotiative powers at the disposal of a legal culture. If a juridical culture emphasizes a singular and unwavering obligation to obey and submit to a political order, it compromises its own negotiative power and may compromise its own legitimacy.

From the context of persistent early ᶜAlid rebellions, Muslim jurists argued that a just ruler should be obeyed, but that those who rebel are not dissolute or evil. Muslim jurists co-opted the early theological discourses concerning the conflicts between the Companions of the Prophet in order to legitimate the construction of *aḥkām al-bughāh*. Pursuant to this discourse, they asserted that rebels are entitled to certain benevolent

Treason was later extended to include conspiracy and rebellion against the national sovereign and the city councils. It was punishable by hanging, drowning, beheading, burning, breaking on the wheel, or quartering).

The *Constitutio Criminalis Carolina* promulgated by the Holy Roman Emperor Charles V in 1532 prescribed the death penalty for treason. High treason, which included the assassination or attempted murder of a sovereign, was punished by quartering. The Prussian General Law Code of 1794 punished lesser forms of treason by decapitation. High treason was punished by "dragging the perpetrator to the scaffold wrapped in an oxhide as well as broken with the wheel from the bottom up." See Evans, *Rituals*, 29–31, 134.

See Bursell, *Liturgy, Order*, 201 n. 25 (those executed for high treason may not be admitted to Christian burial); Staire, *Institutions* (laws and customs of Scotland as collected and published by Stair in 1681: open rebellion and bearing arms against the king is treason, pp. 955–6; the penalty for treason is forfeiture of life, lands, and goods, p. 640).

Under the *Glanvill*, the crime of *lèse-majesté* included: the killing or betrayal of the king or the kingdom or army, the breach of the king's peace, homicide, arson, robbery, rape and certain types of falsifications (e.g. falsifying the royal charter). All such crimes are punishable by death or the cutting off of limbs: de Glanvill, *Treatise*, 3, 176–7. Also see Hudson, *Formation*, 161. On the trial of those accused of sedition or plotting against the king in England, see de Glanvill, *Treatise*, 171–3. For an earlier time period, see White, *Legal*, 115–16, which addresses the procedure after the Norman invasion of England in 1066.

Gatrell (*Hanging*, 281) notes that until the 1790s, an aggravated punishment applied to traitors in England. Such punishment often included hanging and disembowelment. Acording to Taswell-Langmead (*English*, 573–84) the crime of treason at the time of Edward III (r. 1327–77) was vague and ambiguous. Any breach of allegiance to the king was treason which could lead to, among other things, forfeiture of life and property. The statute 25 Edw. III, st. 5, c. 2 (1352) was passed to clarify the ambiguities. Under the statute levying war against the king, either directly against his person or constructively against his government, is treason. Hence, every insurrection which in the judgment of law is intended against the king, either to dethrone or imprison him, or to oblige him to alter his measures of government, or to remove evil counselors – although not conducted with military array – has been held to be a levying of war. However, the beneficiaries of the limitation of the ambiguities of the 1352 statute were the mesne lords: see Bellamy, *Tudor*, 87. On 25 Edw. c. 2, also see Blackstone, *Commentaries*, IV:74–5, and Plucknett, *Concise*, 443. On King Richard II, Edward III's successor, and the attempt to expand the treason laws to cover any opposition to the king, see Smith, *Constitutional*, 203.

forms of treatment. The traditions regarding ᶜAlī's conduct were co-opted in support of the various technical rules of conduct enunciated by the jurists. There is no doubt that the collective memory of Muslims recalled that ᶜAlī treated rebels with a certain degree of benevolence. I am not claiming that Muslim jurists invented the traditions describing ᶜAlī's conduct. However, as we saw, there were various competing traditions and trends regarding the conduct of Abū Bakr, ᶜUthmān, and Muᶜāwiya. Even more, there were competing traditions regarding the Prophet's conduct towards the people of ᶜUrayna, ᶜAlī's treatment of rebels, and the fate of people such as ᶜAlī's assassin, Ibn Muljim. The creative juridical act comes in constructing what is remembered and how it is remembered, and on the doctrinal impact that such a memory will exercise on the legal discourses.[8] For instance, as we saw, there were several conflicting positions represented in the traditions of the Prophet with regard to obedience to authority. Some traditions emphasized obedience to God and the duty to reject any illegal command by a ruler. Other traditions emphasized the obligation to obey the ruler, and even called for the execution of any rebels. In the context of *aḥkām al-bughāh*, Muslim jurists reconstructed and synthesized these traditions by arguing that the traditions condemning rebellion apply only to those who rebel without a plausible interpretation or cause. Furthermore, only those who rebel without a plausible interpretation or cause may be prosecuted or executed.

Muslim jurists insisted that the articulated rules of *aḥkām al-bughāh* are binding whether a ruler is just or unjust. If the rebels relied on a plausible interpretation or cause, they were not to be equated with common criminals.[9] Muslim jurists responded to the political challenges posed

[8] Norman Calder has emphasized the creative, dialectical, and redactive process by which Islamic law has developed. I agree that the process is creative and often dialectical. But I think Calder exaggerates the role of redactiveness and invention in Islamic legal history. See Calder, *Studies*, esp. 19, 198–222, 244–7.

[9] Decriminalizing rebellion or subversion is unusual in legal systems. Often, rebellion is equated to an act of treason and dealt with as a serious crime. See citations above, and also Holland, *Elements*, 382 (acts tending to the subversion of the government, such as the assassination of princes, rebellion and similar acts of high treason are described as criminal offenses; furthermore, riots and other offenses against public order and tranquillity and resistance or disobedience to lawful authority are criminal as well); Geldart, *Introduction*, 181–2 (under the Treason Act of 1352, high treason includes imagining the king's death, levying war against the king in his realm, and adhering to the king's enemies in his realm, giving them aid or comfort in the realm or elsewhere); McLynn, *Crime*, 336–7 (under the 1795 Treasonable Practices Act introduced by William Pitt, inciting hatred or contempt toward the king, constitution, or government was an act of treason punishable by death). On seditious speech and its relation to "compassing the king's death," see Bellamy, *Law*, 119–20.

by the early ᶜAlid rebellions and rebellions of people such as Ibn al-Zubayr with legalities. As discussed, within the context of a juridical culture, that is hardly surprising. However, legalities are not irrelevant or merely pedantic; the practice of legalities is the language of jurists, and like all discourses it aims to express and challenge, transmit, and undermine. Like all discourses, legalities have an undeniable symbolic quality. Whether the state would give effect to or implement the injunctions of the jurists or not, it could not deny the jurists the power to embarrass, shame, and castigate. *Aḥkām al-bughāh* would stand as a technical and symbolic commentary on the dynamics of power and the practices of the state.

Confronted by an absolute claim to power, Muslim jurists responded by a creative and negotiative act. They constructed the doctrines of rebellion and created an interpretive process that legitimated and authenticated these doctrines. The jurists refused to completely withdraw support from the state which, in turn, legitimated and supported their institutional roles as judges and teachers. However, their main loyalty was to the legal order, and not necessarily to the political order. If rebels were denied any legitimacy or demonized, that would politicize the legal order, and give it the appearance of impartiality. Because of the fact that their loyalty was primarily to the legal order, and not the political system, Muslim jurists argued that rebellion could be the result of a plausible interpretation or cause, but an interpretation that was considered as a matter of law to be in error. This played the dual function of preserving the appearance of impartiality of the legal order, and hence its legitimacy, and acting to temper the legitimacy of the political order against its foes.

Treason and its relation to rebellion and disloyalty towards the sovereign is typically vague. A nineteenth-century legal historian summed up the vagueness of the crime of treason by stating: "Treason is a crime which has a vague circumference and more than one centre" (Maitland and Pollock, *History*, II:503). In English law, treason was often seen as a betrayal or violation of allegiance to a superior. See Plucknett, *Concise*, 536. For example, Blackstone, *Commentaries*, IV:75, states, "Treason is indeed a general appellation, made use of by the law, to denote not only offences against the king and government, but also that accumulation of guilt which arises whenever a superior reposes a confidence in a subject or inferior . . . and the inferior so abuses that confidence . . . as to destroy the life of any such his superior or lord." See also Sharpe, *Judicial*, 27 (under sixteenth-century English law the murder of a master by his servant was an act of treason punishable by death); Walker and Walker, *English*, 66–7. On the history of the crime of treason in English law, the categories which the crime covered, and the relation of treason to the religious turmoils in England, see Maitland, *Constitutional*, II:148, 227, 229, 514. The Commons in the parliament of 1429–30 successfully petitioned for the law of treason to be extended to include arson. See Bellamy, *Law*, 131. In the German legal tradition of the Middle Ages, treason was not limited to political crimes, but also covered treachery and betrayal; see Schild, "History," 129. On the law of treason in Italy, France, and England, see Cuttler, *Law*; Lowe, "Political," 184–203; Smith, *Treason*; Bellamy, *Tudor*.

This creative response by the juristic culture was negotiative because it engaged in and bargained with the doctrinal sources of Islam and the institutions of power.

The negotiative and creative dynamics of the discourses on rebellion are also demonstrated in the juristic debates on banditry, and the liability of the rebels. As discussed earlier, the Qur'ānic verse on causing corruption on the earth and fighting God and His Prophet played a prominent role in the discourses on rebellion. There is evidence that the Umayyads and early ʿAbbāsids attempted to invoke this verse against rebels, and hence justify mutilating and crucifying them. Muslim jurists insisted that the *ḥirāba* verse was unrelated to rebellion, and that it applied to the crime of banditry. They argued that bandits terrorize people and victimize the helpless, and that is what is meant by the Qur'ānic expression "those who fight God and His Prophet and cause corruption on the earth." Rebels who rely on a plausible interpretation or cause do not necessarily cause corruption on earth, or fight God and His Prophet. This, of course, is a legal construct or fiction, but it is as much of a fiction as claiming that rebels do, in fact, cause corruption or fight God and His Prophet. It depends on how one defines concepts such as causing corruption on the earth, and fighting God or the Prophet.

Often, definitions require redefinitions. The same negotiative and creative process that produces a definition, through an interactive and perhaps dialectical dynamic, will often produce a redefinition. Various demands are placed on definition, and if a definition is to remain viable and dynamic, often it will have to interact with and respond to these demands. One such demand is that of legitimacy; in order for a definition to remain persuasive, it is often forced to respond to a need for legitimacy produced by social, cultural, or political dynamics or, importantly, by the dynamics of the legal culture. One suspects that the extent of the redefinition will be in proportion to the intensity of the demands. However, socio-political demands must still be filtered through the prism of legal culture which generates its own logic and demands. As discussed earlier, legal culture does not always respond efficiently or immediately. How fast or to what extent a legal culture responds depends on a variety of factors including the institutional structure, the cohesiveness and the age of the culture. Importantly, one of the factors is to what extent the redefinition can be rooted in the established discourses within that legal culture.

The challenge produced to the discourses of the jurists was the increased dynastic and tribal fighting that accompanied the weakening of the ʿAbbāsid empire, and the conduct of various historical groups who relied on banditry as a means of propagating their ends. Historical and legal sources indicate that there was considerable social turmoil caused by groups such as the Qarāmiṭa. Muslim jurists responded by a creative refinement and redefinition. They debated whether rebels who pursued indiscriminate and terrorizing methods may be qualified as *bughāh*. Furthermore, many jurists excluded certain acts of terror, such as rape, murder by stealth, and the poisoning of water sources, from the coverage of *aḥkām al-bughāh*, and treated such crimes as acts of corruption on the earth. Consequently, if rebels committed such acts, they would be held liable under the law of banditry or the common law of crimes. Additionally, many jurists reconstructed the rules of liability under the law of rebellion. Under this reconstruction, rebels are not liable for life and property damaged in the course of the rebellion if such destruction was incidental and necessary to the rebellion. Hence, certain conduct, such as rape, could be considered unrelated or unnecessary to the rebellion, and excluded from the coverage of *aḥkām al-bughāh*. Ultimately, these juristic creative acts responded to some of the rhetorical consequences of *aḥkām al-bughāh*, and simultaneously defended the legitimacy of the discourses on rebellion. If the juristic discourses persistently legitimated or excused problematic social and political practices, the legitimacy of the juristic doctrines could itself be rendered problematic. By excluding certain particularly offensive conduct from the protection of *aḥkām al-bughāh*, Muslim jurists upheld the credibility and legitimacy of this field of law.

By the sixth/twelfth century the juridical discourses on rebellion had become widely and firmly established in the juristic culture. As discussed earlier, even the reluctant borrowers such as the Mālikīs and Imāmīs eventually fully adopted the symbolism, linguistic practices, and technicalities of the field. Significantly, one finds the same linguistic practice or substantial fragments of it in Ismāʿīlī, Ibāḍī, and Zaydī juristic discourses. These various schools have diverse theological paradigms, and yet one finds that their linguistic practice was quite similar to that of the Sunnī tradition. This is powerful evidence of the impact and influence of legal culture, and predominance of legal borrowing. Moreover, the discourses on rebellion engaged the non-Sunnī schools in the definitional dynamics of identifying and categorizing who are the *bughāh* and, consequently, into their own symbolic and negotiative processes.

As the doctrines of *aḥkām al-bughāh* became firmly established, the linguistic practices and formulas of the field were consistently repeated in

Sunnī and non-Sunnī discourses. Often, the consistent repetition of legal formulas is the product of an inherited practice and habit in a legal culture, and therefore it is difficult to assess the negotiative and symbolic quality of the discourses after they have become widespread and common. Nevertheless, as argued earlier, often a juridical culture responds to social or political realities long after those realities have come into existence. Therefore, some of the reforms limiting the non-liability of rebels were not fully asserted until the sixth/twelfth century. There is considerable evidence that even after the discourses on rebellion had become firmly established, the legitimating, negotiative, and symbolic dynamics of these discourses continued. Importantly, far from simply legitimating or sanctioning the realities of power, Muslim jurists continued to engage, negotiate, undermine, and thwart power.

While many of the early discourses on rebellion focused on what one might call the depoliticization of the doctrines of rebellion, the Sunnī revisionist trend repoliticized substantial aspects of the discourse. By depoliticization, I do not mean that the discourses on rebellion were apolitical or not intended to engage and negotiate with the political. Rather, depoliticization, in this context, means that early Muslim jurists focused on the technicalities of the treatment to be afforded to rebels. These technicalities were formalized and objectified so as to give the appearance of impartiality. This was embodied in the notion that whether the ruler is just or unjust the interpretation of the rebels, as a legal matter, is presumed to be erroneous, and whether the ruler is just or unjust he is bound by rules of conduct enunciated in *aḥkām al-bughāh*. Regardless of the substantive quality of the rebels the ruler is presumed to be right, and regardless of the substantive quality of the ruler he is bound by the law. This construct was hardly apolitical, but it attempted to move the focus away from the ideological to the legal and technical. The Sunnī revisionist trend, however, reintroduced several ideological and unabashedly symbolic elements into the discourse.

The revisionist trend reformulated a variety of doctrines. Some jurists, particularly Mālikī, argued that those who rebel against an unjust ruler are conclusively presumed to have an interpretation or cause. Others argued that rebels should not be held liable even if they do not rely on an interpretation or cause. The main emphasis of the revisionist trend was not on justifying rebellion, but on withdrawing support from unjust rulers. Therefore, it was argued, Muslims should not assist unjust rulers in fighting rebels. Importantly, a right of self-defense, of sorts, was recognized by arguing that those who are responding to an injustice inflicted upon them are not rebels at all. As argued earlier, the process of defining who is legitimately responding to an inflicted injustice, as opposed to aggressively waging an unjustified rebellion, involves its own negotiative and symbolic dynamic. Furthermore and remarkably, both the Sunnī revisionist trend and the non-Sunnī schools turned the ominous accusation of banditry against those in power. Pursuant to this logic, it is possible for the ruler or his agents to act as the equivalent of bandits if they terrorize and victimize. Whether the jurists had the enforcement mechanism to punish the rulers or his agents for acts of banditry was largely irrelevant. The point was largely symbolic – it was a form of denunciation and disapprobation, and of rhetorical threat. It is somewhat ironic, but entirely logical, that the discourse concerning the causing of corruption on earth and the fighting of God and His Prophet was turned on its head and employed against the state.

The intellectual history revealed by examining the linguistic practice of the jurists, and placing this practice within the power dynamics of the juristic culture, is rich and multilayered. It defies extreme or essentialist characterizations. As Richard Abel observes, "extreme positions . . . quickly founder on uncomfortable facts."[10] One of the uncomfortable facts challenging any simplistic or essentialist characterization of the Islamic juristic culture and its relation to political power is found in the linguistic practices of *aḥkām al-bughāh*. One suspects that if particular linguistic practices are examined in the context of specific historical incidents, one will gain greater insight into the microdynamics of the juristic culture and its relation to power. This is bound to yield more accurate generalizations about the role played by the Islamic discourses on rebellion. At the doctrinal level, the Muslim juridical debates suggest a complex process that is inadequately explained by the contemporary scholarly discourses on quietism versus activism. For example, even as to the ultimate question of whether one should rebel against an unjust government, Muslim jurists gave a complex but succinct response summarized in the expression "it depends." The question as to whether one should rebel against an unjust government is so simplistic, general, and vague that it would only warrant either a highly dogmatic or a highly conditional response. Muslim jurists, for the most part, responded by arguing that on the one hand, rulers carry the burden of protecting Islam, but on the other hand, one cannot obey a superior if it means disobeying God. On the one hand, order and stability are necessary, but on the other

[10] Abel, *Politics*, 523.

hand, God commanded justice, and God's law must reign supreme. On the one hand, one should avoid pointless violence, but on the other hand, if the rebels have a reasonable chance of success, then perhaps rebellion would be justified. This results in a balance-of-evils test in which the good is weighed against the harm. This could be pragmatic and utilitarian, but it is also the same test that provided a *de facto* acceptance of the authority of the usurper and the unjust. In other words, it is a double-edged sword which, theoretically, may be used for or against the state. Importantly, it is a functional and pragmatic test placed in the context of the principled parameters of *aḥkām al-bughāh.* The same process can be observed in the non-Sunnī discourses on rebellion. It is suggestive that the Shīᶜī and Ibāḍī juristic discourses, despite the fact that they arise from very different theological paradigms, resorted to a substantially similar balancing test. According to Shīᶜī and Ibāḍī discourses, rebellion against injustice is not an absolute value – as an imperative it must yield to the pragmatic considerations of social and personal harm weighed against the anticipated benefits. I am not arguing that the linguistic practices of the non-Sunnī schools are identical to the Sunnī discourses, and I am not arguing that the balancing test is value-neutral. I am arguing that the Sunnī and non-Sunnī juridical cultures responded in similar ways because of the similarities in the paradigms of the juristic culture. This point is well illustrated by a report mentioned earlier in this study and which is often cited in Sunnī, Shīᶜī, and Ibāḍī discourses. According to this report, a military commander ordered some of his troops to jump into a fire. The troops refused to carry out the order. Upon hearing about the incident, the Prophet informed the troops that they exercised proper judgment, and, in fact, if they had complied with the order, God would have punished them with hellfire. What is the import of this tradition? Arguably, it means that one should not obey an illegal command. However, one could slightly vary the details of the report, and end up with a conditional response. One can assume that the Prophet is dead, and that the commander, whose probity and piety are in contention, orders some of his troops to jump into a swamp. Should the troops obey? Should they fight the commander's loyalists, and attempt to take command? Effectively, the response given by Muslim jurists to this hypothetical situation is that the questions as posed are too vague, and one would have to answer such questions with the phrase "it depends."

Within the discourses on rebellion, not all concepts or ideas were rendered subject to a balancing or pragmatic test. The parameters of *aḥkām al-bughāh* were asserted as absolutes. For instance, it was argued that rebels may not be tortured or mutilated, and that they may not be executed after the fighting ends. Nonetheless, within the absolutist parameters there remained a substantial creative and negotiative power retained by the jurists, and that is the power of definition. This power was asserted well into the modern age, but was not necessarily asserted precisely or clearly. It was often suggestive, confounding, and obfuscating.

THE LAW OF REBELLION IN THE MODERN AGE

The Ḥanafī jurist Ibn ᶜĀbidīn (d. 1252/1836–7) dealt with the Wahhābī rebellions against the Ottoman empire in the nineteenth century.[11] He describes the Wahhābīs as the Khawārij of the modern age, and strongly condemns the fact that the Wahhābīs claimed to be the true representatives of Islam, and that they called their opponents unbelievers. He also condemns the fact that the Wahhābīs slaughtered many Muslims, and attacked the jurists of Islam. Clearly, Ibn ᶜĀbidīn strongly disapproved of the movement and its practices. Notably, by comparing them to the Khawārij and emphasizing their indiscriminate means of slaughter, Ibn ᶜĀbidīn implies that the Wahhābīs should not be treated as *bughāh*. Yet, as a matter of principle and precedent, he was unwilling to make this categorization explicit. In fact, he was careful to note that the majority of jurists considered the Khawārij *bughāh*. Nevertheless, he does not explicitly describe the Wahhābīs as *bughāh*. Rather, he only rejoices at the fact that they were defeated by Muḥammad ᶜAlī Pashā (d. 1265/1849) in 1234/1818, and describes their defeat as a blessing from God.[12] Similarly, the Mālikī jurist al-Ṣāwī (d. 1241/1825–6), who lived in Egypt and died in Medina, accuses the Wahhābīs of being no better than the historical Khawārij. Like the Khawārij, al-Ṣāwī contends, the Wahhābīs espouse corrupt interpretations of the Qur'ān and *Sunna* (*yuḥarrifūna ta'wīl al-kitāb wa al-sunna*) in order to legitimate the indiscriminate slaughter of Muslims. Al-Ṣāwī calls the Wahhābīs the "party of the Devil" (*ḥizb al-shayṭān*), and prays to God to destroy them.[13] The impression the reader is left with is that the Wahhābīs do not deserve to be treated as *bughāh*. These cases tested the applicability of the discourses on rebellion to a

[11] Followers of the puritanical teachings of Muḥammad Ibn ᶜAbd al-Wahhāb (d. 1206/1792). Many of his teachings still pervade Saudi Arabia today. See Gibb and Kramers, eds., *Shorter*, 618–21.

[12] Ibn ᶜĀbidīn, *Ḥāshiya*, VI:413. Interestingly, Ibn ᶜĀbidīn does not comment on the fact that ᶜAbd Allāh, the leader of the Wahhābīs at the time, was captured and beheaded in Constantinople in 1818.

[13] Al-Ṣāwī, *Ḥāshiya*, III:307–8.

specific historical context. However, while sustaining the integrity and cohesiveness of the doctrines of rebellion, one suspects that Ibn ʿĀbidīn and al-Ṣāwī were intentionally ambiguous about the applicability of the doctrines to a problematic contemporaneous case.

A different example demonstrating the dynamics and subtleties of the juristic discourse on the permissibility of rebellion and the definition of *bughāh* is found in the *responsa* of the Mālikī jurist al-Shaykh ʿUlaysh (d. 1299/1882). In this example, the technicalities and particulars of the law replace the need for clear definitions by providing for clear results. In various *responsa* dealing with the theoretical and historical aspects of the discourse on the *bughāh*, ʿUlaysh repeats many of the inherited doctrines on rebellion. He reiterates that those who fight while relying on an interpretation are not to be held liable for life or property destroyed during the course of rebellion. Furthermore, he states that rebels, including groups such as the Khawārij, may not be mutilated, and funeral prayers should be performed on their dead. ʿUlaysh's language and tone are technical and detached; he conveys the impression that the doctrines of rebellion are immutable and absolute. Therefore, he suggests, al-Ḥusayn, the Prophet's grandson, despite his virtues, was the *bāghī* in relation to Yazīd because Yazīd was the ruler in power. Nevertheless, reciting many of Yazīd's indiscretions, he argues that Yazīd was iniquitous while al-Ḥusayn was pious. He contends that the conflict between al-Ḥusayn and Yazīd was one that involved competing interpretations, although al-Ḥusayn was the more pious party.[14] This, however, does not seem to alter the fact that al-Ḥusayn is categorized as a rebel, and Yazīd as a ruler.

ʿUlaysh's construct is solid, technical, and unequivocal. Nevertheless, this construct does not deny him the negotiative power that may be found in the details of the juristic linguistic practice. In a separate *responsum*, ʿAbd al-Qādir b. Muḥyī al-Dīn al-Jazā'irī (d. 1300/1883), a leader of the Algerian resistance, presented ʿUlaysh with an issue involving the practical application of the discourses on rebellion. ʿAbd al-Qādir explained that after the French invaded Algeria, ʿAbd al-Qādir had led the resistance against the French. However, he was betrayed by Sulṭān ʿAbd al-Raḥmān b. Hishām (r. 1238/1822–1276/1859), who signed a treaty with the French, and cut off ʿAbd al-Qādir's supply of food and weapons. ʿAbd al-Qādir's main concern is to solicit ʿUlaysh's support against the sulṭān. ʿAbd al-Qādir asks: Despite the fact that the sulṭān is a Muslim ruler, is it permissible to fight him because of his cooperation

14 ʿUlaysh, *Fatḥ*, 1:350–3.

with the French? ᶜUlaysh responds by asserting that all jurists have agreed that Muslims have a right to defend their life and property, and that no one, including a ruler, may deny Muslims such a right. ᶜUlaysh suggests that it is the sulṭān who is behaving like a *bāghī* because he is transgressing the bounds of acceptable Islamic conduct. While it is true that a ruler is entitled to obedience, he cannot be obeyed if he commands a sin, and the sulṭān commanded a sin when he ordered Muslims to stop fighting the French. Therefore, ᶜUlaysh concludes, ᶜAbd al-Qādir may fight the sulṭān, and in fact, if the sulṭān attempts to send an army to attack ᶜAbd al-Qādir, it becomes mandatory upon ᶜAbd al-Qādir and his troops to defend themselves and fight the sulṭān. Even more, those who die resisting the sulṭān are martyrs.[15]

Clearly, ᶜUlaysh was not willing to concede any degree of credibility to the sulṭān's appeasement of the French, and his sympathies towards ᶜAbd al-Qādir are apparent. ᶜUlaysh did not wish to describe ᶜAbd al-Qādir as a *bāghī* or a rebel because of the implicit reprobation that this might entail. He was also not willing to unequivocally categorize the sulṭān as *bāghī* because this might constitute an implicit approbation of the sulṭān. Arguably, if the sulṭān is the *bāghī*, then his conflict with ᶜAbd al-Qādir is a matter of competing interpretations and different points of view, and it should be remembered that in the juristic discourses, the word *baghy* does not connote censure or blame. ᶜUlaysh obfuscates the issue of definitions, and proceeds to reach a result through the application of the details. He affirms the general principle that rulers should be obeyed, but the principle is largely inapposite. ᶜAbd al-Qādir, ᶜUlaysh concludes, is acting in self-defense. Even if the sulṭān is only disabling ᶜAbd al-Qādir from defending himself against the French, that is sufficient to legitimate fighting the sulṭān. Of course, ᶜUlaysh did not invent this discursive dynamic, because the idea that those who act in self-defense against an unjust ruler are not *bughāh* was already firmly established in the Sunnī revisionist trend. ᶜUlaysh's contribution was in employing the doctrinal details in order to negotiate a specific result within the parameters of the inherited discourses of the juristic culture. ᶜUlaysh himself, who served for a long time as a professor at al-Azhar University in Egypt, died in prison after being accused of supporting ᶜUrābī's rebellion against the French in 1299/1882.[16]

[15] Ibid., 387–92.

[16] See al-Ziriklī, *al-Aᶜlām*, VI:19–20. After fighting the French for fifteen years, ᶜAbd al-Qādir, partly due to the sulṭān's cooperation with the French, was defeated. After surrendering, ᶜAbd al-Qādir was given a pension by the French, and died in exile in Damascus. See ibid., IV:45–6.

The dynamics of a legal process produce an enormous amount of factual and discursive detail. The details produced respond to a vast array of considerations, but such details impact upon these considerations imperfectly, and in a complex and highly varied fashion. The enormity of the factual detail often does not yield to abstract generalizations. In fact, there is a sufficient amount of factual detail in the discourses on *aḥkām al-bughāh* to discourage generalized abstractions. This, however, does not mean that one should eschew all generalizations, but only that generalizations must be analyzed in light of the historical dynamics of law and society. As Abel states, "Historical interpretation must complement and often displace sociological generalizations."[17] Analyzing the details of the intellectual history of *aḥkām al-bughāh*, one finds a dynamic creative and negotiative process, but can one generalize from this analysis that such a process is inherent and inevitable? For instance, will the creative and negotiative process necessarily continue in the discourses on rebellion in the contemporary age? Arguably, there is a rupture between the juristic culture of precolonial and postcolonial Islam sufficient to make any generalizations about the former not necessarily applicable to the latter.[18] Even the dynamics played out in the late Ottoman period and in the age of colonialism might not be relevant to the age of nation states. Arguably, the Muslim juristic culture in the age of nation states is capable of less independence, and therefore its negotiative and creative power is heavily constrained.

I do agree that the dynamics of Islamic law in the contemporary age are considerably different than the dynamics of the premodern age. But while I do think that Islamic law in the modern age has not exhibited much creativity or originality, it is premature to come to any conclusions about the role that *aḥkām al-bughāh* will play. At the symbolic and ideological level, the juristic discourses on *aḥkām al-bughāh* are extremely relevant to the contemporary age in various ways. For example, the notion that even violent rebels are *mujtahids* of sorts, or that people have a right to self-defense against a perceived unjust ruler might aid in reconstructing Islamic theories of government, and might challenge absolutist conceptions of power. Furthermore, the idea that rebels should not be executed or mutilated might limit the pragmatism and opportunism of politics. *Aḥkām al-bughāh* might set moral and legal limits on power conflicts, and

[17] Abel, *Politics*, 545.

[18] See Sonn, "Irregular," 130–3. I should note that I find the analysis of the author unpersuasive at many levels. Most importantly, she bases her analysis on the assumption that rebellion has been unequivocally condemned throughout Islamic history. This assumption is not justified.

temper the legitimacy of the savagery that a government may visit upon its opponents. Even more, as discussed earlier, Muslim jurists often cited "causing terror or terrorizing" as one of the elements of the crime of banditry. This has an obvious relevance to contemporary discourses on terrorism.[19] Of course, there is the very real risk that a government would accuse its opponents of committing the crime of *ḥirāba* (terror) and corruption on earth, and treat them as such. However, the premodern juristic discourses on *ḥirāba* and *baghy* are material in developing a coherent and systematic distinction between terrorism and rebellion. Finally, the conceptualization of certain forms of sexual assault as a crime of terror or as a form of terrorism is significant for the gender dynamics within a Muslim society at the rhetorical, symbolic, and functional levels. For instance, the notable jurist and reformer Rashīd Riḍā (d. 1354/1935) argued that rape or abduction for the purposes of obtaining a ransom is a form of *ḥirāba*, and should be treated as such.[20]

In the contemporary age, Islamic law is bound to go through its own definitional processes which will be influenced by the inherited legacy of Islamic law, and by the power dynamics of its present context. For better or worse, these processes will result, and have resulted, in a renegotiation and selective reconstruction of Islamic law. For example, both Saudi Arabia and Sudan, which claim to apply Islamic law as a whole, adopted the laws of banditry and apostasy into their legal systems but omitted, without comment, *aḥkām al-bughāh*.[21] The Egyptian Criminal Code does use the term *bughāh*; article 101 describes those who conspire or plot to overthrow the government as *bughāh*, but otherwise no substantive aspect of *aḥkām al-bughāh* is adopted.[22] In short, *aḥkām al-bughāh* has been excluded from the legal systems of all Arabic-speaking Muslim countries, while the law of banditry and the language of causing corruption on earth has been incorporated by some legal systems.

The juristic discourses of contemporary Muslim commentators are mixed, but are no less selective and reconstructive. For example, Āyatullāh Khumaynī (d. 1409/1989), in his *Taḥrīr al-Wasīla*, deals at length with the duty to enjoin the good and forbid the evil against an unjust ruler. Effectively, he advocates a balancing test in which the risk

[19] Kraemer ("Apostates," 63) has already noted this point.

[20] Riḍā, *Tafsīr*, V:299–300.

[21] See Aḥmad, *Uṣūl*, 188–234; Lawyers Committee, *Beset*, 62–3.

[22] Article 101 provides that if a person joins the *bughāh* but repents before being captured, and turns in his/her co-conspirators to the police, then that person will be pardoned. See al-Jamīlī, *Aḥkām*, I:308–9; Muṣṭafā, *Sharḥ*, 48–50; Asʿad, *Qānūn*, 161–91.

of harm is weighed against the importance of the religious interests at stake. The greater the religious interest, the more one should be willing to sacrifice oneself and endure harm.[23] He also deals with the technicalities of the law of banditry. His conception of banditry is very traditional; it is the terrorizing of the wayfarer for the purposes of usurping money.[24] Interestingly, however, he does not mention or deal with *aḥkām al-bughāh*. One should not infer too much from this silence, but it is reasonable to suggest that the omission was a reconstructive act.[25] Other writers who also reconstruct by partial omission include the ideologue of the Muslim Brotherhood Sayyid Quṭb, who was executed in Egypt in 1387/1966. Quṭb does deal with *ḥirāba* and *baghy*; however, he asserts that *ḥirāba* is the crime of armed rebellion against a just ruler who faithfully implements the *Sharīʿa*. *Ḥirāba*, according to Quṭb, is the crime of resisting the application of the law of God, or fighting those who seek to apply the law of God. He does not mention highway robbery or terrorizing the wayfarer, but focuses on the idea that those who fight a genuine and true just ruler deserve the harsh penalties proscribed in the *ḥirāba* verse.[26] Commenting on the *baghy* verse, Quṭb does not mention many of the details of *aḥkām al-bughāh*. He only mentions that the *bughāh*'s wounded, captives, and fugitives should not be killed. However, he seems to consider *baghy* to be the act of two groups of Muslims having a quarrel and fighting with each other.[27] In other words, according to Quṭb, rebellion against a just ruler is treated as a crime of corruption on the earth and not *baghy*. This reverses the doctrines of the classical tradition. Considering that Quṭb was a member of the Muslim Brotherhood and a rebel against the Egyptian government, it would seem that it would have been in his interest to avail himself of the protections of the classical doctrines of *aḥkām al-bughāh*. Nonetheless, it is probable that Quṭb perceived his political opponents, i.e. the Egyptian government and its agents, to be engaged in the crime of corruption on the earth and in fighting God and His Prophet. It was very unlikely that the Egyptian government would have felt compelled or embarrassed by the doctrines of *aḥkām al-bughāh*. Therefore it would have been more effective to assert, as Quṭb did, that those who fight the application of God's law, or fight those who seek

[23] al-Khumaynī, *Taḥrīr*, I:405–10. [24] Ibid., II:443–5.

[25] The reasons for the omission may be theological more than political. However, this omission is interesting in light of the fact that by May 1979 the revolutionary tribunal had executed 200 people for causing corruption on the earth. See Kraemer, "Apostates," 71.

[26] Quṭb, *Fī Ẓilāl*, II:878–9. [27] Ibid., VI:3343–4.

to apply God's law, are the most heinous criminals. This is a powerful condemnation of all those who oppose the imposition of Islamic law. It is a symbolic, but effective, undermining of the legitimacy of proponents of secularization. It is somewhat ironic that Quṭb was executed after being accused of involvement in a variety of terrorist conspiracies including a charge of plotting to assassinate President Nasser of Egypt.

The discourse of Rashīd Riḍā, one of the main reformers in the modern age, exhibits a dynamic similar to that of Quṭb, but Riḍā's discourse is more sophisticated. He broadly defines *ḥirāba*, arguing that besides including highway robbery, rape, and similar crimes, it also includes those who resist the application of *Sharīʿa* (Islamic law).[28] Riḍā emphasizes that the constitutive elements of the crime of *ḥirāba* must be subject to reconsideration and redefinition in light of modern needs and interests.[29] *Ḥirāba*, according to Riḍā, focuses on the act of causing corruption on the earth, and therefore it includes those who form groups in order to resist the application of *Sharīʿa*.[30] Riḍā, however, transforms this discourse into a justification for the overthrow of unjust rulers. He argues that it is obligatory to overthrow rulers who cause corruption on the earth by oppressing people. Such rulers lack legitimacy and should be removed by force, if possible. Furthermore, he approvingly cites as an example the overthrow of the Ottoman ruler Sulṭān ʿAbd al-Ḥamīd II in 1293/1876.[31] The subtleties of Riḍā's discourse become more apparent when one notices that he remarks, rather casually, that some have claimed that the Khawārij, and those who rebelled against ʿAlī were *muḥāribūn* (bandits). Such a claim, Riḍā argues, is erroneous because those rebels relied on an interpretation (*taʾwīl*).[32] The sum total of Riḍā's discourse is that tyrants should be overthrown, rebels who seek to fight the law of God are bandits, but rebels who rely on an interpretation are not bandits. This provides Riḍā with considerable room to negotiate his discourses in response to his own context. Importantly, his argument that unjust rulers could be considered the equivalent of bandits derives its legitimacy from the discourses of the revisionist trend.

Several contemporary Muslim jurists, who had the benefit of a French education, negotiated and reconstructed the classical discourses of *aḥkām al-bughāh* towards a very different result. Among those jurists was judge

[28] Riḍā, *Tafsīr*, V:295. [29] Ibid., 297. [30] Ibid., 296.
[31] Ibid., IV:367–8. [32] Ibid., V:303–4.

ᶜAbd al-Qādir ᶜŪdah, who was one of the leaders of the Muslim Brotherhood in Egypt in the 1950s, and who was executed in 1374/1954. ᶜŪdah, and several others, argued that *aḥkām al-bughāh* is the equivalent of the doctrine of political crimes in Europe. Pursuant to this doctrine, those who commit political crimes are not to be treated as common criminals, they may not be executed or tortured, and their property may not be confiscated. ᶜŪdah, and others, defined political crimes as the non-violent or violent opposition to a government, as long as the motivation is political and the target of the crime is governmental. In other words, attacking a police station might qualify as a political crime, but attacking a movie theater would not. Importantly, they argued that *aḥkām al-bughāh* should apply whether the ruler is just or not. The approach of these jurists tended to be very technical and detached, conveying the impression of objectivity.[33] Nonetheless, their dynamic is negotiative and reconstructive. They conceded that *baghy* is a crime, but it is a crime that calls for a preferential and humane treatment. Essentially, this discourse reconstructed *aḥkām al-bughāh* in order to co-opt a particular humanitarian European tradition.[34] In many ways it Islamized the European, particularly French, doctrine of political crimes.

It is not surprising that modern jurists occupying a semi-official capacity, such as the members of the Saudi Permanent Council for Scientific Research and Legal Opinions (*al-Lajna al-Dāʾima li al-Buḥūth al-ᶜIlmiyya wa al-Iftāʾ* – *Lajna*, for short), have resisted adopting either the doctrine of political crimes or *aḥkām al-bughāh*. For instance, the jurists affiliated with this body have issued a set of *responsa* heavily emphasizing the duty of obedience to the government of Saudi Arabia and, in this context, repeatedly quoted the traditions attributed to the Prophet mandating the killing of rebels. Even more, they often assert that obedience to rulers is indistinguishable from obedience to God and His Prophet. Unless rulers command something that is a clear and undisputed sin, they must be obeyed.[35] In one such *responsum*, Ibn Fawzān, a prominent member of the *Lajna*, wrote that contemporary groups that rebel against established Muslim rulers are *bughāh* that should be killed. God and the Prophet have

[33] See ᶜŪdah, *al-Tashrīᶜ*, I:100–9, II:671–705; Sanad, *Naẓariyāt*, chap. 3 *et seq.*; Abū al-Faḍl, "Jarīma," 69.

[34] On political crimes in Western and Islamic law, see Abou El Fadl, "Political Crime." On political crimes in European law see Ingraham, *Political*.

[35] Al-Fawzān, *al-Muntaqā*, I:366–9, 386–8; *Fatāwā al-Lajna*, IV:332; Ibn Bāz (a.k.a. Bin Bāz, hereinafter Bin Bāz), *Majmūᶜ*, IV:89–96, V:248–9.

commanded that the *bughāh* and the Khawārij be fought without pause.[36] Hence, the author intimates that Islamic law mandates the execution of the *bughāh*, which as we saw is far from the truth. When asked if it is ever permissible to rebel against unjust rulers, Ibn Fawzān answered that as a general matter rebellion is a *fitna*, and even if the ruler is a *kāfir* Muslims should avoid shedding blood.[37]

The former head of the *Lajna*, Bin Bāz (d. 1421/1999), authored *responsa* in which he condemned the hijacking of airplanes, the taking of hostages in an embassy,[38] and the explosion of a bomb in Medina in 1989. Bin Bāz did not refer to the *ḥirāba* verse or the law of banditry (terrorism). Rather, he indicated that the individuals involved were rebels, and asked the government to deal with them appropriately. He implored the government to apply the *ḥadd* punishment, thus indicating that execution is the appropriate measure.[39] In 1979 the full body of the *Lajna*, headed by Bin Bāz, issued a *responsum* regarding an incident in which a rebellious group occupied the *ḥaram* (the area around the Kaʿba) in Mecca for a few days.[40] The *Lajna* called the rebellion a *fitna* and corruption based on a false interpretation (*taʾwīl bāṭil*), but it did not use the words *baghy* or *ḥirāba*. The predominant focus of the *responsum* was not on the prohibition of shedding blood in the *ḥaram*, but on the evils and corruptions of rebellion. Again, the *Lajna* extensively quoted the traditions calling for the killing of rebellious and seditious groups and, ultimately, the jurists thanked the government for dealing firmly and wisely with the incident.[41] Notably, over sixty members of the rebellion were tortured and executed after the rebellion ended. I believe it is reasonable

[36] Ibn Fawzān, *al-Muntaqā*, I:368. The *Lajna* issued a *responsum* stating that rebellion might be permitted if there is a clear and unequivocal *kufr* (acts that are indisputably acts of disbelief): see *Fatāwā al-Lajna*, IV:332.

[37] Ibn Fawzān, *al-Muntaqā*, I:387–8.

[38] The *responsum* was issued in 1973 before the Iranian hostage crisis.

[39] Bin Bāz, *Majmūʿ*, I:276–81; V:248–9. Bin Bāz does not explain what he means by the *ḥadd* punishments in this context, but he quotes traditions attributed to the Prophet calling for the killing of rebels.

[40] Normally, *responsa* are signed by four jurists from the *Lajna*. This particular *responsum* was signed by all sixteen members. The facts of this event are not clear. Some reports indicated that the rebellion commenced outside the *ḥaram*, but the rebels retreated into the *ḥaram* thinking that they would have a safe haven in that area. They were mistaken; they were all slaughtered. Other reports claim that the rebellion commenced in the *ḥaram* area. The jurists state in the beginning of the *responsum* that they volunteered to issue the *fatwā* as a matter of conscience and religious duty. On this incident see Dekmejian, *Islam*, 134–7; Ochesenwald, "Saudi Arabia," 103–15, esp. 104–5.

[41] These are two *responsa* basically saying the same thing. Bin Bāz, *Majmūʿ*, IV:89–92 and 92–7.

to assume that the jurists of the *Lajna* were aware of the Islamic law of rebellion, but intentionally avoided any reference to it.

This brief survey of some of the contemporary dynamics of *aḥkām al-bughāh* is not intended to be exhaustive. A separate, extensive, and fairly long, study on the contemporary discourses is needed. Rather, this survey is intended to demonstrate tendencies and potentialities. Furthermore, this survey suggests that in the same fashion that Islamic law was creatively constructed in the past, it will be constructed in the present. How creative or profound this construction will be depends on many variables including social, political, and economic factors, and it will also depend on the structural nature of the contemporary Islamic juristic culture. The contemporary juristic culture is materially different from that of the past.[42] But as Conley and O'Barr noted, "When we look into the past, we find the antecedents of some of the most significant socio-legal issues in our own world."[43] The premodern juristic culture weighed the moral and ethical with the political and pragmatic, and weighed the symbolic and educative with the practical and technical, and achieved a rich and creative discourse. Contemporary articulations of Islamic law often derive legitimacy from the juridical traditions of the past. Indeed, to the extent that the premodern Islamic discourses constitute part of the cumulative legal heritage, if through the power dynamics of society these discourses are revived in the modern mind, they will exert a certain degree of influence on how rebels are perceived and treated in the contemporary age. To the extent that we can learn from the past, the idea of aspiring to limit the discretion of the state in dealing with its opponents, even those who are violent, seems to be eminently reasonable.

[42] See, on this issue, Abou El Fadl, *Speaking*.

[43] Conley and O'Barr, *Just*, 128.

Works cited

ARABIC SOURCES

al-ʿAbādī, Aḥmad b. Qāsim. *Ḥāshiya ʿalā Tuḥfat al-Muḥtāj*. Beirut: Dār al-Kutub al-ʿIlmiyya, 1996.

ʿAbd al-Ḥalīm, Ibn Ḥamza b. Bir Qadam. *al-Ḥāshiya ʿalā al-Ghurar wa al-Durar*. N.p.: Dār al-Ṭibāʿa al-ʿĀmira, 1270 AH.

al-Ābī, Ṣāliḥ ʿAbd al-Samīʿ al-Azharī. *Jawāhir al-Iklīl Sharḥ Mukhtaṣar al-ʿAllāma al-Shaykh Khalīl*. Beirut: al-Maktaba al-Thaqāfiyya, 1347 AH.

Abū ʿAwwāna, Yaʿqūb b. Isḥāq al-Asfarāʾinī. *Musnad Abī ʿAwwāna*. Edited by Ayman b. ʿĀrif al-Dimashqī. Beirut: Dār al-Maʿrifa, 1998.

Abū al-Barakāt, Muḥammad. *al-Muḥarrar fī al-Fiqh*. Edited by Muḥammad Ḥāmid al-Fiqī. In Ibn Mufliḥ, *al-Nukat*.

Abū Dāwūd, Sulaymān b. al-Ashʿath al-Sijistānī al-Azdī. *Sunan*. Cairo: Dār al-Ḥadīth, 1988.

Abū al-Faḍl, Midḥat. "Jarīmat al-Baghy fī al-Fiqh al-Islāmī." *al-Muḥāmī* (April–May–June, 1982): 69–79.

Abū al-Fidāʾ, ʿImād al-Dīn b. Shāhinshāh Ayyūb. *al-Mukhtaṣar fī Akhbār al-Bashar*. Edited by Maḥmūd Dayyūb. Beirut: Dār al-Kutub al-ʿIlmiyya, 1997.

Abū Ghuddah, ʿAbd al-Fattāḥ. *Ṣafaḥāt min Ṣabr al-ʿUlamāʾ*. Beirut: Maktab al-Mutbūʿāt al-Islāmiyya, 1997.

Abū Ḥayyān al-Andalusī, Athīr al-Dīn Muḥammad b. Yūsuf. *Tafsīr al-Nahr al-Mādd min al-Baḥr al-Muḥīṭ*. Beirut: Dār al-Jinān, 1987.

Abū al-Layth, Naṣr b. Muḥammad b. Ibrahīm al-Samarqandī. *ʿUyūn al-Masāʾil*. Edited by Ṣalāḥ al-Dīn al-Nāhī. Baghdad: Maṭbaʿat Asʿad, 1967.

Abū Mikhnaf, Lūṭ b. Yaḥyā b. Saʿīd al-Ghāmidī al-Azdī al-Kūfī. *Nuṣūṣ min Taʾrīkh Abī Mikhnaf*. Edited by Kāmil Sulaymān al-Jubūrī. Beirut: Dār al-Maḥajja al-Bayḍāʾ, 1999.

Abū Shujāʿ, al-Qāḍī Aḥmad b. al-Ḥusayn b. Aḥmad al-Iṣfahānī. *Matn al-Ghāya wa al-Taqrīb*. Edited by Mājid al-Ḥamawī. Beirut: Dār Ibn Ḥazm, 1994.

Abū Yaʿlā, Muḥammad b. al-Ḥusayn al-Farrāʾ. *al-Aḥkām al-Sulṭāniyya*. Edited by Muḥammad Ḥāmid al-Fiqī. Beirut: Dār al-Kutub al-ʿIlmiyya, 1983.

al-Masāʾil al-Fiqhiyya min Kitāb al-Riwāyatayn wa al-Wajhayn. Edited by ʿAbd al-Karīm b. Muḥammad al-Laḥḥām. Cairo: Maktabat al-Maʿārif, n.d.

Abū Yūsuf, Ya^{c}qūb b. Ibrāhīm. *Kitāb al-Kharāj*. Beirut: Dār al-Ma^{c}rifa, n.d.
al-Radd ^{c}alā Siyar al-Awzā^{c}ī. Edited Abū al-Wafā' al-Afghānī. Beirut: Dār al-Kutub al-^{c}Ilmiyya, n.d.
Abū Zahra, Muḥammad. *al-Jarīma wa al-^{c}Uqūba fī al-Fiqh al-Islāmī: al-^{c}Uqūba*. Cairo: Dār al-Fikr al-^{c}Arabī, n.d.
Uṣūl al-Fiqh. Cairo: Dār al-Fikr al-^{c}Arabī, n.d.
al-^{c}Adawī, ^{c}Alī al-Ṣa^{c}īdī. *Ḥāshiya ^{c}alā Kifāyat al-Ṭālib al-Rabbānī li-Risālat Ibn Abī Zayd al-Qayrawānī*. Cairo: Sharikat Maktabat wa Maṭba^{c}at Muṣṭafā al-Bābī al-Ḥalabī, 1938.
al-Afghānī, ^{c}Abd al-Ḥakīm. *Kashf al-Ḥaqā'iq Sharḥ Kanz al-Daqā'iq*. Karachi: Idārat al-Qur'ān wa al-^{c}Ulūm al-Islāmiyya, 1987.
Aḥmad, Hilālī. *Uṣūl al-Tashrī^{c}al-Jinā'ī al-Islāmī ma^{c}a Ishārah ilā Taṭbīqātihi fī al-Mamlaka al-^{c}Arabiyya al-Su^{c}ūdiyya*. Cairo: n.p., 1995.
Akhbār Majmū^{c}a. Edited by Ibrāhīm al-Abyārī. Beirut: Dār al-Kutub al-Islāmiyya, 1981.
Alf Sannah min al-Wafayāt. Edited by Muḥammad Ḥajjī. Ribat, Morocco: Maṭbū^{c}āt Dār al-Maghrib li al-Ta'līf wa al-Tarjamah wa al-Nashr, 1976.
al-Ālūsī, Shihāb al-Dīn Maḥmūd b. ^{c}Abd Allāh. *Rūḥ al-Ma^{c}ānī fī Tafsīr al-Qur'ān al-^{c}Aẓīm wa al-Sab^{c}al-Mathānī*. Beirut: Dār Iḥyā' al-Turāth al-^{c}Arabī, 1985.
Amḥazūn, Muḥammad. *Taḥqīq Mawāqif al-Ṣaḥāba fī al-Fitnah*. Riyadh: Maktabat al-Kawthar, 1994.
al-Āmidī, Sayf al-Dīn ^{c}Alī b. Muḥammad. *al-Iḥkām fī Uṣūl al-Aḥkām*. 2nd ed., Beirut: al-Maktab al-Islāmī, 1402 AH.
al-^{c}Āmilī, Shams al-Dīn Muḥammad b. al-Makkī. *Ghāyat al-Murād fī Sharḥ Nukat al-Irshād*. Qum: Markaz al-Abḥāth wa al-Dirāsāt al-Islāmiyya, 1414 AH.
al-Lum^{c}a al Dimashqiyya. Edited by Muḥammad Kalantar. Najaf: Maṭba^{c}at al-Ādāb, 1386 AH.
al-Amīnī, ^{c}Abd al-Ḥusayn Aḥmad al-Najafī. *al-Ghadīr fī al-Kitāb wa al-Sunnah wa al-Adab*. Beirut: Dār al-Kitāb al-^{c}Arabī, 1983.
al-Anṣārī, Zakariyyā b. Muḥammad. *Fatḥ al-Wahhāb bi-Sharḥ Minhāj al-Ṭullāb*. Cairo: Muṣṭafā al-Bābī al-Ḥalabī, 1948.
Al-Manhaj. In *Ḥāshiyat al-Jamal ^{c}alā Sharḥ al-Manhaj*, by Sulaymān al-Jamal. Beirut: Dār Iḥyā' al-Turāth al-^{c}Arabī, n.d.
As^{c}ad, Aḥmad. *Qānūn al-^{c}Uqūbāt al-Miṣrī*. Cairo: n.p., 1964.
al-Asadī, Sayf b. ^{c}Umar al-Ḍabbī. *al-Fitnah wa Waq^{c}at al-Jamal*. Edited by Aḥmad Rātib ^{c}Armūsh. Beirut: Dār al-Nafā'is, 1993.
al-Ash^{c}arī, Abū al-Ḥasan ^{c}Alī b. Ismā^{c}īl. *Maqālāt al-Islāmiyyīn wa Ikhtilāf al Muṣallīn*. Edited by Muḥammad Muḥyī al-Dīn ^{c}Abd al-Ḥamīd. Beirut: al-Maktaba al-^{c}Aṣriyya, 1990.
al-Asnawī, ^{c}Abd al-Raḥīm (a.k.a. Jamāl al-Dīn). *Ṭabaqāt al-Shāfi^{c}iyya*. Edited by Kamāl al-Ḥūt. Beirut: Dār al-Kutub al-^{c}Ilmiyya, 1987.
al-Atābakī, Jamāl al-Dīn Abū al-Maḥāsin Yūsuf b. Taghrī Birdī. *al-Nujūm al-Ẓāhira fī Mulūk Miṣr wa al-Qāhira*. Cairo: al-Mu'assasa al-Miṣriyya al-^{c}Āmma, 1963.
al-^{c}Aynī, Abū Muḥammad Maḥmūd b. Aḥmad. *al-Bināya fī Sharḥ al-Hidāya*. Beirut: Dār al-Fikr, 1990.

ʿUmdat al-Qārī Sharḥ Ṣaḥīḥ al-Bukhārī. Beirut: Dār al-Fikr, n.d.
al-Baʿalī, Aḥmad b. ʿAbd Allāh b. Aḥmad. *al-Rawḍ al-Nadī Sharḥ Kāfī al-Mubtadī*. Cairo: al-Maṭbaʿa al-Salafiyya, 1960.
al-Baghawī, Abū Muḥammad al-Ḥusayn b. Masʿūd. *Sharḥ al-Sunna*. Edited by Muʿawwaḍ al-Laḥḥām. Beirut: Dār al-Fikr, 1994.
al-Baghdādī, ʿAbd al-Qāhir b. Ṭāhir b. Muḥammad. *al-Farq bayn al-Firaq*. Beirut: Dār al-Kutub al-ʿIlmiyya, n.d.
Bahnasī, Aḥmad Fatḥī. *Madkhal al-Fiqh al-Jināʾī al-Islāmī*. Cairo: Dār al-Shurūq, 1980.
al-Bājī, Abū al-Walīd Sulaymān b. Khalaf al-Andalusī. *al-Muntaqā Sharḥ Muwaṭṭaʾ al-Imām Mālik*. Beirut: Dār al-Kitāb al-ʿArabī, 1983.
al-Bakrī, al-Sayyid. *Iʿānat al-Ṭālibīn*. Beirut: Dār Iḥyāʾ al-Turāth al-ʿArabī, n.d.
al-Bayḍāwī, Abū Saʿīd ʿAbd Allāh b. ʿUmar b. Muḥammad al-Shīrāzī. *Anwār al-Tanzīl wa Asrār al-Taʾwīl*. Beirut: Muʾassasat Shaʿbān, n.d.
al-Ghāya al-Quṣwā fī Dirāyat al-Fatwā. Edited by ʿAlī Muḥyī al-Dīn al-Qasrī. Baghdad: n.p., n.d.
al-Bayhaqī, Abū Bakr Aḥmad b. al-Ḥusayn b. ʿAlī. *Maʿrifat al-Sunan wa al-Āthār*. Edited by Sayyid Kasrawī Ḥusayn. Beirut: Dār al-Kutub al-ʿIlmiyya, 1991.
al-Sunan al-Kubrā. Beirut: Dār al-Maʿrifa, n.d.
al-Bayhaqī al-Jishumī, al-Ḥākim Abū Saʿd al-Muḥassin b. Muḥammad b. Karāmah. *Risālat Iblīs ilā Ikhwānihi al-Manāḥīs*. Edited by Ḥusayn al-Mudarrisī al-Ṭabāṭabāʾī. Qum: n.p., 1986.
al-Bazzār, Abū Bakr Aḥmad b. ʿAbd al-Khāliq al-ʿAtakī. *al-Baḥr al-Zakhkhār*. Edited by Maḥfūẓ al-Raḥmān Zayn Allāh. Medina: Maktabat al-ʿUlūm wa al-Ḥikam, 1988.
al-Bazzāzī, Muḥammad b. Muḥammad b. Shihāb al-Kardarī. *al-Fatāwā al-Bazzāziyya*. Printed in the margins of *al-Fatāwā al-ʿĀlamgīriyya*.
Bin Bāz, ʿAbd al-ʿAzīz b. ʿAbd Allāh. *Majmūʿ Fatāwā wa Maqālāt Mutanawwiʿa*. Edited by Muḥammad b. Saʿd al-Shuwīʿar. Riyadh: n.p., 1990.
al-Buhūtī, Manṣūr b. Yūnus b. Idrīs. *Kashshāf al-Qināʿ ʿan Matn al-Iqnāʿ*. Edited by Hilāl Muṣilḥī Muṣṭafā Hilāl. Beirut: Dār al-Fikr, 1982.
al-Rawḍ al-Murbiʿ Sharḥ Zād al-Mustaqniʿ. Edited by Muḥammad ʿAbd al-Raḥmān ʿAwaḍ. Beirut: Dār al-Kitāb al-ʿArabī, 1986.
al-Bukhārī, Abū ʿAbd Allāh Muḥammad b. Ismāʿīl. *Ṣaḥīḥ al-Bukhārī*. Cairo: Dār Iḥyāʾal-Kutub al-ʿArabiyya, n.d.
Ṣaḥīḥ al-Bukhārī. Cairo: Dār Iḥyāʾ al-Turāth al-ʿArabī, n.d.
al-Dardīr, Abū al-Barakāt Aḥmad b. Muḥammad. *al-Sharḥ al-Ṣaghīr*. Printed in the margins of al-Ṣāwī, *Bulgha*.
al-Dārimī, Abū Muḥammad ʿAbd Allāh b.ʿAbd al-Raḥmān. *Sunan*. Edited by Fawāz Zamrālī and Khālid al-ʿAlamī. Beirut: Dār al-Kitāb al-ʿArabī, 1987.
al-Dhahabī, Shams al-Dīn Muḥammad b. Aḥmad. *Siyar Aʿlām al-Nubalāʾ*. Beirut: Muʾassasat al-Risāla, 1996.
al-Dimashqī, Taqī al-Dīn Abū Bakr b. Muḥammad al-Ḥusaynī al-Ḥiṣnī. *Kifāyat al-Akhyār fī Ḥall Ghāyat al-Ikhtiṣār*. Edited by ʿAlī ʿAbd al-Ḥamīd al-Balṭajī and Muḥammad Wahbī Sulaymān. Beirut: Dār al-Khayr, 1991.

al-Dīnawarī, Abū Ḥanīfa Aḥmad b. Dāwūd. *al-Akhbār al-Ṭiwāl*. Edited by Ḥasan al-Zayn. Beirut: Dār al-Fikr, 1988.

al-Dusūqī, Shams al-Dīn Muḥammad b. Aḥmad b. ᶜArafa. *Ḥāshiyat al-Dusūqī ᶜalā al-Sharḥ al-Kabīr*. Beirut: Dār Iḥyāʾ al-Kitāb al-ᶜArabī, n.d.

Fakhr al-Muḥaqqiqīn, Abū Ṭālib Muḥammad b. al-Ḥasan b. Yūsuf al-Ḥillī. *Īḍāḥ al-Fawāʾid fī Sharḥ Ishkālāt al-Qawāᶜid*. Qum: Muʾassasat Ismāᶜīliyān, n.d.

al-Fatāwā al-ᶜĀlamgīriyya = al-Fatāwā al-Hindiyya. Cairo, 1274 AH.; reprint, Beirut: Dār Iḥyāʾ al-Turāth al-ᶜArabī, 1986.

Fatāwā al-Lajna al-Dāʾima li al-Buḥūth al-ᶜIlmiyya wa al-Iftāʾ. Edited by Aḥmad b. ᶜAbd al-Razzāq al-Dawīsh. Riyadh: Dār ᶜĀlam al-Kutub, 1991.

al-Fawzān, Ṣāliḥ b. Fawzān b. ᶜAbd Allāh (a.k.a Ibn Fawzān). *al-Muntaqā min Fatāwā Faḍīlat al-Shaykh*. Edited by ᶜĀdil b. ᶜAlī al-Farīdān. Riyadh: Maktabat al-Ghurabāʾ al-Athariyya, 1997.

al-Ghamrāwī, Muḥammad al-Zuhrī. *Anwār al-Masālik Sharḥ ᶜUmdat al-Sālik wa ᶜUddat al-Nāsik*. Cairo: Sharikat Maktabat wa Maṭbaᶜat Muṣṭafā al-Bābī al-Ḥalabī, 1948.

al-Gharnāṭī, Abū al-Qāsim Muḥammad b. Aḥmad b. Juzayy al-Kalbī. *Qawānīn al-Aḥkām al-Sharᶜiyyah wa Masāʾil al-Furūᶜ al-Fiqhiyya*. Edited by ᶜAbd al-Raḥmān Ḥasan Maḥmūd. Cairo: ᶜĀlam al-Fikr, 1985.

al-Ghazālī, Abū Ḥāmid Muḥammad b. Muḥammad. *Faḍāʾiḥ al-Bāṭiniyya*. Edited by Nādī Faraj Darwīsh. Cairo: al-Maktab al-Thaqāfī, n.d.

Iḥyāʾ ᶜUlūm al-Dīn. Beirut: Dār al-Maᶜrifa, n.d.

al-Mustaṣfā min ᶜIlm al-Uṣūl. Baghdad: Maktabat al-Muthanna, 1322 AH.

al-Wajīz fī al-Fiqh Madhhab al-Imām al-Shāfiᶜī. Cairo: Maṭbaᶜat al-Ādāb, 1317 AH.

al-Ghunaymī, ᶜAbd al-Ghanī al-Dimashqī. *al-Lubāb fī Sharḥ al-Kitāb*. Edited by Muḥammad Muḥyī al-Dīn ᶜAbd al-Ḥamīd. Cairo: Maṭbaᶜat al-Madanī, 1963.

al-Ḥajwī, Muḥammad al-Ḥasan al-Thaᶜālabī al-Fāsī. *al-Fikr al-Sāmī fī Taʾrīkh al-Fiqh al-Islāmī*. Edited by Ayman Ṣāliḥ Shaᶜbān. Beirut: Dār al-Kutub al-ᶜIlmiyya, 1995.

al-Ḥalabī, Abū al-Ṣalāḥ Taqī al-Dīn b. Najm al-Dīn ᶜAbd Allah. *al-Kāfī fī al-Fiqh*. In Murwārīd, ed., *Mawsūᶜa*, vol. IX.

al-Ḥalabī, ᶜAlāʾ al-Dīn Abū al-Ḥasan ᶜAlī b. Abī al-Faḍl al-Ḥasan b. Abī al-Majd. *Ishārat al-Sabaq ilā Maᶜrifat al-Ḥaqq*. In Murwārīd, ed., *Mawsūᶜa*, vol. IX.

al-Ḥalabī, Ḥamza b. ᶜAlī b. Zuhra al-Ḥusaynī. *Ghunyat al-Nuzūᶜ ilā ᶜIlm al-Usūl wa al-Furūᶜ*. In Murwārīd, ed., *Mawsūᶜa*, vol. IX.

al-Ḥalabī, Ibrāhīm b. Muḥammad b. Ibrāhīm. *Multaqā al-Abḥur*. Edited by Wahba Sulaymān al-Albānī. Beirut: Muʾassasat al-Risāla, 1989.

al-Ḥasanī, Hāshim Maᶜrūf. *Al-Intifāḍāt al-Shīᶜiyya ᶜAbr al-Tārīkh*. Beirut: Dār al-Kutub al-Shaᶜbiyya, n.d.

al-Ḥaṭṭāb, Abū ᶜAbd Allāh Muḥammad b. ᶜAbd al-Raḥmān al-Ṭarābulsī. *Mawāhib al-Jalīl li-Sharḥ Mukhtaṣar Khalīl*. Tripoli: Maktabat al-Najāḥ, 1911.

al-Ḥillī, Abū Manṣūr Muḥammad b. Idrīs al-ᶜIjlī. *Al-Sarāʾir al-Ḥāwī li Taḥrīr al-Fatāwī.* In Murwārīd, ed., *Mawsūᶜa*, vol. IX.

al-Ḥillī, Jamāl al-Dīn Abū al-ᶜAbbās Aḥmad b. Muḥammad b. Fahd. *al-Muhadhdhab al-Bāriᶜ fī Sharḥ al-Mukhtaṣar al-Nāfiᶜ*. Edited by Mujtabā al-ᶜArāqī. Qum: Mu'assasat al-Nashr al-Islāmīya, 1407 AH.

al-Ḥillī, Jamāl al-Dīn Abū Manṣūr al-Ḥasan b. Sadīd al-Dīn Yūsuf b. al-Muṭahhar. *Qawāᶜid al-Aḥkām fī Masāʾil al-Ḥalāl wa al-Ḥarām.* In Murwārīd, ed., *Mawsūᶜa*, vol. IX.

al-Hindī, ᶜAlāʾ al-Dīn ᶜAlī al-Mutaqī b. Ḥusām al-Dīn. *Kanz al-ᶜUmmāl fī Sunan al-Aqwāl wa al-Afᶜāl.* Beirut: Mu'assasat al-Risāla, 1985.

al-Ḥubayshī, Muḥammad b. ᶜAlī b. Muḥsin. *Fatḥ al-Mannān Sharḥ Zubad Ibn Raslān.* Beirut: Mu'assasat al-Kutub al-Thaqāfiyya, 1988.

al-Hudhalī, Yaḥyā b. al-Ḥasan b. Saᶜīd. *al-Jāmiᶜ li al-Sharāʾiᶜ*. In Murwārīd, ed., *Mawsūᶜa*, vol. IX.

al-Ḥurr al-ᶜĀmilī, Muḥammad b. al-Ḥasan. *Wasāʾil al-Shīᶜa ilā Taḥṣīl Masāʾil al-Sharīᶜa.* Edited by ᶜAbd al-Raḥīm al-Rabbānī al-Shīrāzī. Beirut: Dār Iḥyāʾ al-Turāth al-ᶜArabī, n.d.

Ibn ᶜAbd al-Barr, Abū ᶜUmar Yūsuf b. ᶜAbd Allāh b. Muḥammad al-Namirī. *Kitāb al-Kāfī fī Fiqh Ahl al-Madīnah al-Mālikī.* Edited by Muḥammad Muḥammad Aḥyad Wild Mādīk. Riyadh: Maktabat al-Riyāḍ al-Ḥadītha, 1980.

al-Tamhīd li mā fī al-Muwaṭṭaʾ min al-Maᶜānī wa al-Asānīd. Edited by Muṣṭafā b. Aḥmad al-ᶜAlawī et al. Morocco: Maṭbaᶜat al-Faḍāla, 1982.

al-Tamhīd li mā fī al-Muwaṭṭaʾ min al-Maᶜānī wa al-Asānīd. Edited by Muṣṭafā b. Aḥmad al-ᶜAlawī and Muḥammad ᶜAbd al-Kabīr al-Bakrī. N.p.: Dar al-Ḥadīth al-Ḥasaniyya, 1967.

Ibn ᶜAbd al-Rafīᶜ, Abū Isḥāq Ibrāhīm b. Ḥasan. *Muᶜīn al-Ḥukkām ᶜalā al-Qaḍāyā wa al-Aḥkām.* Edited by Muḥammad b. Qāsim b. ᶜIyāḍ. Beirut: Dār al-Gharb al-Islāmī, 1989.

Ibn Abī al-Ḥadīd, ᶜIzz al-Dīn ᶜAbd al-Ḥamīd b. Hibat Allāh al-Madāʾinī. *Sharḥ Nahj al-Balāgha.* Beirut: Dār al-Jīl, 1987.

Ibn Abī Shayba, ᶜAbd Allāh b. Muḥammad al-ᶜAbsī. *al-Muṣannaf fī al-Aḥādīth wa al-Āthār.* Edited by Saᶜīd Muḥammad al-Laḥḥām. Beirut: Dār al-Fikr, 1989.

Ibn Abī Zayd, ᶜAbd Allāh b. ᶜAbd al-Raḥmān al-Qayrawānī. *al-Nawādir wa al-Ziyādāt ᶜalā mā fī al-Mudawwana min Ghayrihā min al-Ummahāt.* Edited by Muḥammad Ḥajjī. Beirut: Dār al-Gharb al-Islāmī, 1999.

al-Risāla. Cairo: Muṣṭafā al-Bābī al-Ḥalabī, n.d.

Ibn ᶜĀbidīn, Muḥammad Amīn b. ᶜUmar al-Dimashqī. *Ḥāshiyat Radd al-Muḥtār ᶜalā al-Durr al-Mukhtār.* Edited by ᶜĀdil Aḥmad Muᶜawwaḍ. Beirut: Dār al-Kutub al-ᶜIlmiyya, 1994.

al-ᶜUqūd al-Durriyya fī Tanqīḥ al-Fatāwā al-Ḥāmīdiyya. Cairo: n.p., 1337 AH.

Ibn al-ᶜArabī, Abū Bakr Muḥammad b. ᶜAbd Allāh. *Aḥkām al-Qurʾān.* Edited by ᶜAlī Muḥammad al-Bajāwī. Beirut: Dār al-Jīl, 1987.

Kitāb al-Qabas fī Sharḥ Muwaṭṭaʾ Mālik b. Anas. Edited by Muḥammad ᶜAbd Allah Walad Karīm. Beirut: Dār al-Gharb al-Islāmī, 1992.

Ibn ᶜArabī, Muḥyī al-Dīn Muḥammad b. ᶜAlī (attrib.). *Tafsīr al-Qurʾān al-Karīm*. Edited by Muṣṭafā Ghālib. Beirut: Dār al-Andalūs, n.d.

Ibn ᶜĀṣim, Abū Bakr Muḥammad b. Muḥammad. *Tuḥfat al-Ḥukkām*. Cairo: Maṭbaᶜat al-Istiqāma, n.d.

Ibn Aᶜtham, Abū Muḥammad Aḥmad al-Kūfī. *al-Futūḥ*. Beirut: Dār al-Kutub al-ᶜIlmiyya, 1986.

Ibn al-Athīr, Abū al-Ḥasan ᶜAlī b. Muḥammad b. ᶜAbd al-Karīm. *al-Kāmil fī al-Taʾrīkh*. Edited by Abū al-Fidāʾ ᶜAbd Allāh al-Qāḍī. Beirut: Dār al-Kutub al-ᶜIlmiyya, 1987.

Ibn al-Athīr al-Jazarī, Majd al-Dīn Abū al-Saᶜādāt al-Shaybānī. *Jāmiᶜ al-Uṣūl fī Aḥādīth al-Rasūl*. Beirut: Dār al-Kutub al-ᶜIlmiyya, 1998.

Ibn Farḥūn, Abū Isḥāq Ibrāhīm b. ᶜAlī al-Yaᶜmurī. *Durrat al-Ghawwāṣ fī Muḥāḍarat al-Khawāṣṣ*. Edited by Muḥammad Abū al-Ajfān and ᶜUthmān Baṭīkh. Beirut: Muʾassasat al-Risāla, 1985.

Tabṣirat al-Ḥukkām fī Uṣūl al-Qaḍāyā wa Manāhij al-Aḥkām. Beirut: Dār al-Kutub al-ᶜIlmiyya, n.d.

Ibn Ḥajar al-ᶜAsqalānī, Aḥmad b. ᶜAlī. *Fatḥ al-Bārī bi Sharḥ Ṣaḥīḥ al-Bukhārī*. Beirut: Dār al-Fikr, 1993.

Lisān al-Mīzān. Edited by ᶜĀdil Aḥmad ᶜAbd al-Mawjūd and ᶜAlī Muḥammad Muᶜawwaḍ. Beirut: Dār al-Kutub al-ᶜIlmiyya, 1996.

Fatḥ al-Jawād Sharḥ al-Irshād. Cairo: Muṣṭafā al-Bābī al-Ḥalabī, 1971.

Ibn Ḥammād, Abū ᶜAbd Allāh Nuᶜaym al-Marwazī. *Kitāb al-Fitan*. Edited by Suhayl Zakkār. Beirut: Dār al-Fikr, 1993.

Ibn Ḥamza, ᶜImād al-Dīn Muḥammad b. ᶜAlī al-Ṭūsī. *al-Wasīla ilā Nayl al-Faḍīla*. In Murwārīd, ed., *Mawsūᶜa*, vol. IX.

Ibn Ḥanbal, ᶜAbd Allah b. Aḥmad. *Masāʾil al-Imām Aḥmad b. Ḥanbal*. Edited by Zuhayr al-Shāwīsh. Beirut: al-Maktab al-Islāmī, 1988.

Ibn Ḥanbal, Aḥmad. *Musnad*. Beirut: al-Maktab al-Islāmī, 1993.

Ibn Ḥanbal, Ṣāliḥ b. Aḥmad. *Sīrat al-Imām Aḥmad b. Ḥanbal*. Edited by Muḥammad al-Zaghlī. Beirut: al-Maktab al-Islāmī, 1997.

Ibn Ḥazm, Abū Muḥammad ᶜAlī b. Aḥmad b. Saᶜīd. *Jamharat Ansāb al-ᶜArab*. Edited by E. Levi-Provençal. Cairo: Dār al-Maᶜārif, 1948.

al-Muḥallā bi al-Āthār. Edited by ᶜAbd al-Ghaffār Sulaymān al-Bandārī. Beirut: Dār al-Kutub al-ᶜIlmiyya, n.d.

Ibn al-Humām, Kamāl al-Dīn Muḥammad b. ᶜAbd al-Wāḥid al-Sīwāsī. *Sharḥ Fatḥ al-Qadīr*. Edited by ᶜAbd al-Razzāq Ghālib al-Mahdī. Beirut: Dār al-Kutub al-ᶜIlmiyya, 1995.

Ibn al-ᶜImād, Abū al-Falāḥ ᶜAbd al-Ḥayy. *Shadharāt al-Dhahab fī Akhbār man Dhahab*. Beirut: Dār al-Kutub al-ᶜIlmiyya, n.d.

Ibn al-Jallāb, Abū al-Qāsim ᶜUbayd Allāh b. al-Ḥusayn b. al-Ḥasan al-Baṣrī. *Al-Tafrīᶜ*. Edited by Ḥusayn b. Sālim al-Dahmānī. Beirut: Dār al-Gharb al-Islāmī, 1987.

Ibn Jamāʿa, Badr al-Dīn Muḥammad b. Ibrāhīm. *Taḥrīr al-Aḥkām fī Tadbīr Ahl al-Islām*. Edited by Fu'ād ʿAbd al-Munʿim Aḥmad. Qatar: al-Shu'ūn al-Dīniyya, 1985.

Ibn al-Jawzī, Abū al-Faraj ʿAbd al-Raḥmān b. Muḥammad al-Baghdādī. *Manāqib al-Imām Aḥmad b. Ḥanbal*. Edited by ʿAbd Allāh b. ʿAbd al-Muḥsin al-Turkī. Cairo: Maktabat al-Khānjī, 1979.

al-Muntaẓam fī Taʾrīkh al-Umam wa al-Mulūk. Edited by Muḥammad ʿAbd al-Qādir ʿAṭā and Muṣṭafā ʿAbd al-Qādir ʿAṭā. Beirut: Dār al-Kutub al-ʿIlmiyya, 1992.

al-Shifāʾ fī Mawāʿiẓ al-Mulūk wa al-Khulafāʾ. Edited by Fu'ād ʿAbd al-Munʿim Aḥmad. Alexandria: Dār al-Daʿwa, n.d.

Ṣifat al-Ṣafwa. Edited by ʿAbd al-Raḥmān al-Lādqī and Ḥayāh Shīḥā al-Lādqī. Beirut: Dār al-Maʿrifa, 1995.

Sīrat wa Manāqib ʿUmar b. ʿAbd al-ʿAzīz al-Khalīfa al-Zāhid. Edited by Naʿīm Zarzūr. Beirut: Dār al-Kutub al-ʿIlmiyya, 1984.

Talbīs Iblīs. Jedda: Dār al-Madanī, 1983.

Zād al-Masīr fī ʿIlm al-Tafsīr. Beirut: al-Maktab al-Islāmī, 1965.

Ibn Kathīr, Abū al-Fidā' Ismāʿīl b. ʿUmar al-Dimashqī. *al-Bidāya wa al-Nihāya*. Edited by Aḥmad Abū Mulḥim et al. Beirut: Dār al-Kitāb, 1985.

al-Nihāya fī al-Fitan wa al-Malāḥim. Edited by Muḥammad Aḥmad ʿAbd al-ʿAzīz. N.p.: Dār al-Ḥadīth, n.d.

Tafsīr al-Qurʾān al-ʿAẓīm. Beirut: Dār al-Khayr, 1990.

Ibn Khaldūn, Abū Zayd ʿAbd al-Raḥmān b. Muḥammad. *al-Muqaddima*. Beirut: Dār Iḥyā' al-Turāth al-ʿArabī, n.d.

Ibn Khallikān, Abū al-ʿAbbās Shams al-Dīn Aḥmad b. Muḥammad b. Abī Bakr. *Wafayāt al-Aʿyān wa Anbāʾ Abnāʾ al-Zamān*. Edited by Iḥsān ʿAbbās. Beirut: Dār Ṣādir, n.d.

Ibn Khayyāṭ, Abū ʿUmar Khalīfa al-ʿUṣfurī. *Taʾrīkh Ibn Khayyāṭ*. Najaf: Maṭbaʿat al-Ādāb, 1967.

Ibn Lu'lu'a, Aḥmad b. al-Naqīb al-Miṣrī. *ʿUmdat al-Sālik*. Printed with al-Makkī, *Fayḍ*.

Ibn Māja, Abū ʿAbd Allāh Muḥammad b. Yazīd. *Sunan*. Beirut: Dār Iḥyā' al-Kutub al-ʿArabiyya, n.d.

Ibn Manẓūr, Abu al-Faḍl Muḥammad. *Lisān al-ʿArab*. Cairo: Dār al-Maʿārif, n.d.

Ibn Maryam, Abū ʿAbd Allāh Muḥammad b. Muḥammad b. Aḥmad. *al-Bustān fī Dhikr al-Awliyāʾ wa al-ʿUlamāʾ bi Tilimsān*. N.p.: al-Maṭbaʿah al-Thaʿālibiyya, 1908.

Ibn Mufliḥ, Burhān al-Dīn Ibrāhīm b. Muḥammad al-Rāmīnī al-Dimashqī. *al-Mubdiʿ fī Sharḥ al-Muqniʿ*. Beirut: al-Maktab al-Islāmī, 1980.

Ibn Mufliḥ, Shams al-Dīn Muḥammad al-Maqdisī al-Ṣāliḥī. *Kitāb al-Furūʿ*. Beirut: ʿĀlam al-Kutub, 1985.

al-Nukat wa al-Fawāʾid al-Saniyya. Edited by Muḥammad Ḥāmid al-Fiqī. Beirut: Dār al-Kitāb al-ᶜArabī, n.d.
Ibn al-Mundhir, Muḥammad b. Ibrāhīm al-Naysābūrī. *al-Ishrāf ᶜalā Madhāhib Ahl al-ᶜIlm*. Edited by Muḥammad Najīb Sirāj al-Dīn. Doha, Qatar: Dār al-Thaqāfa, 1986.
Ibn al-Muqrī, Sharaf al-Dīn Ismāᶜīl b. Abī Bakr. *Ikhlāṣ al-Nāwī*. Edited by ᶜAbd al-ᶜAzīz ᶜAṭiyya qalaṭ. Cairo: Lajnat Iḥyāʾ al-Turāth al-Islāmī, 1989.
al-Irshād. In Ibn Ḥajar al-ᶜAsqalānī, *Fatḥ*
Kitāb al-Tamshiyya bi Sharḥ Irshād al-Ghāwī fī Masālik al-Ḥāwī. Cairo: Dār al-Hudā, n.d.
Ibn al-Murtaḍā, Aḥmad b. Yaḥyā. *Kitāb al-Baḥr al-Zakhkhār al-Jāmiᶜ li Madhāhib ᶜUlamāʾ al-Amṣār*. Cairo: Dār al-Kitāb al-Islāmī, n.d.
Ibn al-Murtaḍā, Muḥammad (a.k.a. Muḥsin al-Kāshānī). *al-Maḥajja al-Bayḍāʾ fī Tahdhīb al-Iḥyāʾ*. Beirut: Muʾassasat al-Aᶜlamī li al-Maṭbūᶜāt, 1983.
Tafsīr al-Ṣāfī. Beirut: Muʾassasat al-Aᶜlamī, 1982.
Ibn Nujaym al-Miṣrī, Zayn al-Dīn b. Ibrāhīm b. Muḥammad. *al-Baḥr al-Rāʾiq Sharḥ Kanz al-Daqāʾiq*. Edited by Zakariyyā ᶜUmayrāt. Beirut: Dār al-Kutub al-ᶜIlmiyya, 1997.
Ibn al-Qāḍī, Abū al-ᶜAbbās Aḥmad b. Muḥammad al-Miknāsī. *Durrat al-Ḥijāl fī Asmāʾ al-Rijāl*. Edited byMuḥammad al-Aḥmadī Abū al-Nūr. Cairo: Dār al-Turāth, 1970.
Jidhwat al-Iqtibās fī Dhikr man Ḥalla min al-Aᶜlām Madīnat Fās. Ribat, Morocco: Dār al-Manṣūr li al-Ṭabāᶜa wa al-Wirāqa, 1973.
Ibn Qāsim, ᶜAbd al-Raḥmān b. Muḥammad al-ᶜĀṣimī al-Najdī. *Ḥāshiyat al-Rawḍ al-Murbiᶜ Sharḥ Zād al-Mustaqniᶜ*. Riyadh: n.p., 1410 AH.
Ibn Qayyim al-Jawziyya, Shams al-Dīn Abū ᶜAbd Allāh Muḥammad b. Abī Bakr. *Aḥkām Ahl al-Dhimma*. Edited by Ṣubḥī Ṣāliḥ. Beirut: Dār al-ᶜIlm li al-Malāyīn, 1983.
Aᶜlām al-Muwaqqiᶜīn ᶜan Rabb al-ᶜĀlamīn. Edited by Ṭāhā ᶜAbd al-Raʾūf Saᶜd. Beirut: Dār al-Jīl, n.d.
Aᶜlām al-Muwaqqiᶜīn ᶜan Rabb al-ᶜĀlamīn. Edited ᶜAbd al-Raḥmān al-Wakīl. Cairo: Maktabat Ibn Taymiyya, n.d.
Ighāthat al-Lahfān min Maṣāʾid al-Shayṭān. Edited by Ḥassāb ᶜAbd al-Mannān and ᶜIṣām al-Ḥurastānī. Beirut: Muʾassasat al-Risāla, 1994.
Ibn Qudāma, Muwaffaq al-Dīn Abū Muḥammad ᶜAbd Allāh b. Aḥmad b. Muḥammad al-Maqdisī. *al-Kāfī fī Fiqh al-Imām Aḥmad b. Ḥanbal*. Edited by Zuhīr al-Shāwīsh. Beirut: al-Maktab al-Islāmī, 1982.
al-Mughnī. Beirut: Dār al-Kutub al-ᶜIlmiyya, n.d.
Ibn Qutayba, Abū Muḥammad ᶜAbd Allāh b. Muslim (attrib.). *al-Imāma wa al-Siyāsa*. Cairo: Muṣṭafā al-Bābī al-Ḥalabī, 1969.
al-Maᶜārif. Edited by Tharwat ᶜUkāsha. Cairo: Dār al-Maᶜārif, 1981.
Taʾwīl Mukhtalaf al-Ḥadīth. Cairo: Muṣṭafā al-Bābī al-Ḥalabī, n.d.
Ibn Rajab, Abū al-Faraj ᶜAbd al-Raḥmān b. Shihāb al-Dīn. *al-Dhayl ᶜalā Ṭabaqāt al-Ḥanābila*. Edited by Abū Ḥāzim b. Ḥasan and Abū Zahrāʾ ᶜAlī Bahjat. Beirut: Dār al-Kutub al-ᶜIlmiyya, 1997.

Ibn Rushd I, Abū al-Walīd Muḥammad b. Aḥmad al-Qurṭubī. *al-Bayān wa al-Sharḥ wa al-Taḥṣīl wa al-Sharḥ wa al-Tawjīh wa al-Ta^{c}līl fī al-Masā'il al-Mustakhraja*. Edited by Muḥammad Ḥajji. Beirut: Dār al-Gharb al-Islāmī, 1988.

al-Muqaddamāt al-Mumahhidat. Edited by Muḥammad Ḥajjī. Beirut: Dār al-Gharb al-Islāmī, 1988.

Ibn Rushd II, Abū al-Walīd Muḥammad b. Aḥmad b. Muḥammad b. Aḥmad al-Qurṭubī. *Bidāyat al-Mujtahid wa Nihāyat al-Muqtaṣid*. Edited by ^{c}Alī Muḥammad Mu^{c}awwaḍ and ^{c}Ādil Aḥmad ^{c}Abd al-Mawjūd. Beirut: Dār al-Kutub al-^{c}Ilmiyya, 1996.

Ibn Sa^{c}d, Abū ^{c}Abd Allāh Muḥammad. *al-Ṭabaqāt al-Kubrā*. Beirut: Dār Ṣādir, 1985.

Ibn Sahl, Aḥmad al-Rāzī. *Akhbār Fakhkh wa Khabar Yaḥyā b. ^{c}Abd Allāh wa Akhīh Idrīs b. ^{c}Abd Allāh*. Edited by Māhir Jarrār. Beirut: Dār al-Gharb, 1995.

Ibn Shu^{c}ba, Sa^{c}īd b. Manṣūr al-Khurasānī. *Sunan*. Edited by Ḥabīb al-Raḥmān al-A^{c}ẓamī. Beirut: Dār al-Kutub al-^{c}Ilmiyya, n.d.

Ibn Ṭāwūs, Raḍī al-Dīn Abū al-Qāsim ^{c}Alī b. Mūsā al-Ḥasanī al-Ḥusaynī. *al-Malāḥim wa al-Fitan*. Beirut: Mu'assasat al-A^{c}lamī, 1988.

Ibn Taymiyya, Abū al-^{c}Abbās Taqī al-Dīn Aḥmad. *al-Fatāwā al-Kubrā*. Edited by Muḥammad ^{c}Abd al-Qawī ^{c}Aṭā and Muṣṭafā ^{c}Abd al-Qawī ^{c}Aṭā. Cairo: Dār al-Rayyān li al-Turāth, 1988.

Majmū^{c}al-Fatāwā. Edited by Muḥammad b. ^{c}Abd al-Raḥmān b. Qāsim. Riyadh: n.p., n.d.

Majmū^{c}al-Rasā'il wa al-Masā'il. Beirut: Dār al-Kutub al-^{c}Ilmiyya, 1983.

Minhāj al-Sunna al-Nabawiyya. Beirut: al-Maktaba al-^{c}Ilmiyya, n.d.

al-Siyāsa al-Shar^{c}iyyah fī Iṣlāḥ al-Rā^{c}ī wa al-Ra^{c}īyya. Beirut: Dār al-Āfāq, 1983.

Ibn al-Wardī, Zayn al-Dīn ^{c}Umar b. Muẓaffar. *Ta'rīkh Ibn al-Wardī*. Beirut: Dār al-Kutub al-^{c}Ilmiyya, 1996.

al-Iṣfahānī, Abū al-Faraj. *Maqātil al-Ṭālibīyyīn*. Edited by Sayyid Aḥmad Ṣaqr. Beirut: Dār al-Ma^{c}rifa, n.d.

al-Jāḥiẓ, Abū ^{c}Uthmān ^{c}Amr b. Baḥr. "Risāla fī al-Ḥakamayn wa Taṣwīb Amīr al-Mu'minīn ^{c}Alī b. Abī Ṭālib fī Fi^{c}lih." In *Rasā'il al-Jāḥiẓ: al-Rasā'il al-Siyāsiyya*. Edited by ^{c}Alī Abū Mulḥim. Beirut: Dār al-Hilāl, 1987.

"Risāla fī al-Nābita." In *Rasā'il al-Jāḥiẓ: al-Rasā'il al-Kalāmiyya*. Edited by ^{c}Alī Abū Mulḥim. Beirut: Dār al-Hilāl, 1987.

Ja^{c}īṭ, Hishām. *al-Fitnah*. Beirut: Dār al-Ṭalī^{c}a, 1989.

al-Jamā^{c}īlī, ^{c}Abd al-Ghanī b. ^{c}Abd al-Wāḥid al-Maqdisī. *Al-^{c}Umda fī al-Aḥkam fī Ma^{c}ālim al-Ḥalāl wa al-Ḥarām*. Edited by Muṣṭafā ^{c}Abd al-Qādir ^{c}Aṭā'. Beirut: Dār al-Kutub al-^{c}Ilmiyya, 1986.

al-Jamal, Sulaymān. *Ḥāshiyat al-Jamal ^{c}alā Sharḥ al-Manhaj*. Beirut: Dār Iḥyā' al-Turāth al-^{c}Arabī, n.d.

al-Jamīlī, Khālid Rashīd. *Aḥkām al-Bughāh wa al-Muḥāribīn fī al-Sharī^{c}a al-Islāmīyya wa al-Qānūn*. Baghdad: Dār al-Ḥurriyya, 1977.

al-Jarrāḥī, Ismā^{c}īl b. Muḥammad b. ^{c}Abd al-Hādī. *Kashf al-Khafā' wa Muzīl al-Ilbās*. Beirut: Mu'assasat al-Risāla, 1983.

al-Jaṣṣāṣ, Abū Bakr Aḥmad b. ᶜAlī al-Rāzī. *Aḥkām al-Qurʾān*. Beirut: Dār al-Kitāb al-ᶜArabī, 1986.
al-Juᶜalī, ᶜUthmān b. Ḥusayn Barrī. *Sirāj al-Sālik Sharḥ Ashal al-Masālik*. Cairo: Sharikat Maktabat Muṣṭafā al-Bābī al-Ḥalabī, n.d.
al-Juwaynī, Abū al-Maᶜālī ᶜAbd al-Malik b. ᶜAbd Allāh Imām al-Ḥaramayn. *Ghiyāth al-Umam fī Iltiyāth al-Qulam*. Edited by ᶜAbd al-ᶜAẓīm al-Dīb. Qatar: al-Maktaba al-Kubrā, 1401 AH.
Kitāb al-Irshād ilā Qawāṭiᶜ al-Adilla fī Uṣūl al-Iᶜtiqād. Edited by Asᶜad Tamīm. Beirut: Muʾassasat al-Kutub al-Thaqāfiyya, 1992.
al-Kāndahlawī, Muḥammad Zakariyyā. *Awjaz al-Masālik ilā Muwaṭṭaʾ Mālik*. Beirut: Dār al-Fikr, 1989.
al-Kāsānī, ᶜAlāʾ al-Dīn Abū Bakr b. Masᶜūd. *Kitāb Badāʾiᶜ al-Ṣanāʾiᶜ fī Tartīb al-Sharāʾiᶜ*. Beirut: Dār al-Kutub al-ᶜIlmiyya, 1986.
Khalīl b. Isḥāq. *Mukhtaṣar Khalīl*. Edited by Aḥmad Naṣr. Cairo: al-Maktaba al-Mālikiyya, 1981.
al-Khiraqī, Abū al-Qāsim ᶜUmar b. al-Ḥusayn. *Mukhtaṣar al-Khiraqī ᶜalā Madhhab al-Imām Aḥmad b. Ḥanbal*. Damascus: Dār al-Salam, 1378 AH.
al-Khirshī (a.k.a. al-Khurashī), Abū ᶜAbd Allāh Muḥammad. *Sharḥ Mukhtaṣar Sayyidī Khalīl*. Beirut: Dār Ṣādir, n.d.
al-Khumaynī, Rūḥ Allāh b. Muṣṭafā al-Mūsawī. *Taḥrīr al-Wasīla*. Tehran: Manshūrāt Maktabat al-Iᶜtimād, n.d.
al-Khushanī, Muḥammad b. al-Ḥārith. *Uṣūl al-Futyā fī al-Fiqh ᶜalā Madhhab al-Imām Mālik*. Edited by Muḥammad al-Majdūb et al. N.p.: Dār al-ᶜArabiyya li al-Kitāb, 1985.
al-Kindī, Abū Bakr Aḥmad b. ᶜAbd Allah b. Mūsā. *al-Muṣannaf*. Cairo: ᶜĪsā al-Bābī al-Ḥalabī, n.d.
al-Kiyā al-Harrāsī, ᶜImād al-Dīn b. Muḥammad al-Ṭabarī. *Aḥkām al-Qurʾān*. Beirut: Dār al-Kutub al-ᶜIlmiyya, 1985.
al-Kulaynī, Abū Jaᶜfar Muḥammad b. Yaᶜqūb b. Isḥāq al-Rāzī. *al-Furūᶜ min al-Kāfī*. Edited by ᶜAlī Akbar al-Ghaffārī. Tehran: Dār al-Kutub al-Islāmiyya, 1397 AH.
al-Maḥmaṣānī, Ṣubḥī. *Falsafat al-Tashrīᶜ fī al-Islām: Muqaddima fī Dirāsat al-Sharīᶜah al-Islāmiyya ᶜalā Ḍūʾ Madhāhibihā al-Mukhtalifa wa ᶜalā Ḍūʾ al-Qawānīn al-Ḥadītha*, 3rd ed. Beirut: Dār al-ᶜIlm li al-Malāyīn, 1961.
al-Majlisī, Muḥammad Bāqir. *Malādh al-Akhyār fī Fahm Tahdhīb al-Akhbār*. Edited by Mahdī al-Rajāʾī. Qum: Maktabat al-Marᶜashī, 1407 AH.
al-Makkī, al-Muwaffaq b. Aḥmad. *Manāqib Abī Ḥanīfa*. Beirut: Dār al-Kitāb al-ᶜArabī, 1981.
al-Makkī, ᶜUmar Barakāt al-Biqāᶜī. *Fayḍ al-Ilāh al-Mālik Sharḥ ᶜUmdat al-Sālik*. Cairo: Maṭbaᶜat al-Istiqāma, 1955.
al-Mālaqī, Abū al-Muṭarrif ᶜAbd al-Raḥmān b. Qāsim al-Shaᶜbī. *al-Aḥkām*. Edited by al-Ṣādiq al-Ḥalawī. Beirut: Dār al-Gharb al-Islāmī, 1992.
al-Mālaqī, Abū al-Qāsim b. Riḍwān. *al-Shuhub al-Lāmiᶜa fī al-Siyāsa al-Nāfiᶜa*. Edited by ᶜAlī Sāmī al-Nashshār. Morocco: Dār al-Thaqāfa, 1984.

Mālik b. Anas, Abū ᶜAbd Allāh. *al-Muwaṭṭaʾ*, narrated by Abū Muṣᶜab al-Zuhrī. Edited by Bashshār ᶜAwwād Maᶜrūf and Maḥmūd Muḥammad Khalīl. Beirut: Muʾassasat al-Risāla, 1993.

al-Muwaṭṭaʾ, narrated by Yaḥyā b. Yaḥyā al-Laythī. Beirut: Dār al-Kutub al-ᶜIlmiyya, n.d.

al-Maqbiliyyi, Ṣāliḥ b. Mahdī. *al-Manār fī al-Mukhtār min Jawāhir al-Baḥr al-Zakhkhār*. Beirut: Muʾassasat al-Risāla, 1988.

al-Maqdisī, Bahāʾ al-Dīn ᶜAbd al-Raḥmān b. Ibrāhīm. *al-ᶜUdda Sharḥ al-ᶜUmda*. Beirut: n.p., n.d.

al-Maqdisī, Marᶜī b. Yūsuf al-Karmī. *Dalīl al-Ṭālib*. Damascus: al-Maktab al-Islāmī, n.d.

al-Mardāwī, ᶜAlāʾ al-Dīn Abū al-Ḥasan ᶜAlī b. Sulaymān. *al-Inṣāf fī Maᶜrifat al-Rājiḥ min al-Khilāf*. Beirut: Dār Iḥyāʾ al-Turāth al-ᶜArabī, n.d.

al-Marghīnānī, Abū al-Ḥasan ᶜAlī b. Abī Bakr. *al-Hidāya Sharḥ Bidāyat al-Mubtadī*. Cairo: Muṣṭafā al-Bābī al-Ḥalabī, n.d.

al-Marūzī, Abū ᶜAbd Allāh Muḥammad b. Naṣr. *Ikhtilāf al-Fuqahāʾ*. Edited by Muḥammad Ṭāhir Ḥakīm. Riyadh: Dār Aḍwāʾ al-Salaf, 2000.

al-Masᶜūdī, Abū al-Ḥasan ᶜAlī b. al-Ḥusayn b. ᶜAlī. *Murūj al-Dhahab wa Maᶜādin al-Jawhar*. Edited by Muḥammad Muḥyī al-Dīn ᶜAbd al-Ḥamīd. Cairo: Kitāb al-Taḥrīr, 1966.

al-Māwardī, Abū al-Ḥasan ᶜAlī b. Muḥammad b. Ḥabīb. *Adab al-Qāḍī*. Edited by Muḥyī Hilāl al-Sarḥān. Baghdad: Maṭbaᶜat al-Irshād, 1971.

al-Aḥkām al-Sulṭāniyya wa al-Wilāyāt al-Dīniyya. Beirut: Dār al-Kutub al-ᶜIlmiyya, 1985.

al-Ḥāwī al-Kabīr Sharḥ Mukhtaṣar al-Muzanī. Edited by ᶜAlī Muᶜawwaḍ and ᶜĀdil ᶜAbd al-Mawjūd. Beirut: Dār al-Kutub al-ᶜIlmiyya, 1994.

Kitāb Qitāl Ahl al-Baghy min al-Ḥāwī al-Kabīr. Edited by Ibrāhīm b. ᶜAlī Ṣandaqjī. Cairo: Maṭbaᶜat al-Madanī, 1987.

Naṣīḥat al-Mulūk. Edited by Muḥammad Jāsim al-Ḥayrathī. Baghdad: Dār al-Shuʾūn al-Thaqāfiyya al-ᶜĀmma, 1986.

al-Nukat wa al-ᶜUyūn. Beirut: Dār al-Kutub al-ᶜIlmiyya, 1992.

al-Mufīd, Muḥammad b. Muḥammad b. al-Nuᶜmān (Ibn al-Muᶜallim) al-ᶜUkbarī. *Awāʾil al-Maqālāt*. Edited by Ibrāhīm al-Anṣārī. N.p.: al-Muʾtamar al-ᶜĀlamī, 1413 AH.

al-Muqniᶜ fī al-Uṣūl wa al-Furūᶜ. In Murwārīd, ed., *Mawsūᶜa*, vol. X.

Mughniyya, Muḥammad Jawād. *Fiqh al-Imām Jaᶜfar al-Ṣādiq*. Qum: Intishārāt Quds Muḥammadī, n.d.

al-Muḥaqqiq, Abū al-Qāsim Najm al-Dīn Jaᶜfar b. al-Ḥasan al-Ḥillī. *Sharāʾiᶜ al-Islām fī Masāʾil al-Ḥalāl wa al-Ḥarām*. Edited by ᶜAbd al-Ḥusayn Muḥammad ᶜAlī. Beirut: Dār al-Aḍwāʾ, n.d.

Muqātil, Ibn Sulaymān. "Tafsīr al-Qurʾān." Manuscript. Vol. 74/II. Saray Ahmet III Library.

al-Muqrī, Abū ᶜAmr ᶜUthmān b. Saᶜīd al-Dānī. *al-Sunan al-Wāridah fī al-Fitan wa Ghawāʾilihā wa al-Sāᶜah wa Ashrāṭihā*. Edited by Riḍāʾ Allāh b. Muḥammad Idrīs al-Mabārkafūrī. Riyadh: Dār al-ᶜĀṣimah, 1995.

Murwārīd, Alī Aṣghar, ed. *Mawsūʿat Silsilat al-Yanābīʿal-Fiqhiyya.* Beirut: Dār al-Turāth and al-Dār al-Islāmiyya, 1990.

al-Murtaḍā al-Mūsawī, Abū al-Qāsim ʿAlī b. al-Ḥusayn al-Sharīf *Al-Intiṣār.* Edited by Muḥammad Riḍā al-Sayyid Ḥasan al-Kharsān. Beirut: Dār al-Aḍwāʾ, 1985.

al-Masāʾil al-Nāṣiriyāt. In Murwārīd, ed., *Mawsūʿa*, vol. IX.

Muslim b. al-Ḥajjāj, Abū al-Ḥusayn al-Qushayrī al-Naysābūrī. *al-Jāmiʿ al-Ṣaḥīḥ.* Beirut: Dār al-Maʿrifa, n.d.

Muṣṭafā, Maḥmūd. *Sharḥ Qānūn al-ʿUqūbāt: al-Qism al-ʿĀmm.* Cairo: n.p., 1964.

al-Muzanī, Abū Ibrāhīm Ismāʿīl b. Yaḥyā. *al-Mukhtaṣar.* Printed as the final volume of al-Shāfiʿī, *al-Umm.*

al-Nafrāwī, Aḥmad b. Ghānim b. Sālim. *al-Fawākih al-Dawānī ʿalā Risālat Ibn Abī Zayd al-Qayrawānī.* Beirut: Dār al-Fikr, n.d.

al-Najafī, Muḥammad Ḥasan. *Jawāhir al-Kalām fī Sharḥ Sharāʾiʿ al-Islām.* Tehran: Dār al-Kutub al-Islāmiyya, 1377 AH.

al-Nasafī, ʿAbd Allāh b. Aḥmad. *Tafsīr al-Nasafī: Madārik al-Tanzīl wa Ḥaqāʾiq al-Taʾwīl.* Edited by Marwān Muḥammad al-Shiʿār. Beirut: Dar al-Nafāʾis, 1996.

al-Nasāʾī, Abū ʿAbd Allāh al-Raḥmān Aḥmad b. Shuʿayb b. ʿAlī . *Kitāb Khaṣāʾiṣ Amīr al-Muʾminīn ʿAlī b. Abī Ṭālib.* Beirut: Dār Kitāb al-ʿArabī, 1996.

Sunan. Beirut: Dār al-Qalam, n.d.

Tafsīr al-Nasāʾī. Edited by Ṣabrī b. ʿAbd al-Khāliq al-Shāfiʿī and Sayyid b. ʿAbbās al-Julaymī. Beirut: Muʾassasat al-Kutub al-Thaqāfiyya, 1990.

al-Nawawī, Muḥyī al-Dīn Yaḥyā b. Sharaf. *al-Majmūʿ Sharḥ al-Muhadhdhab.* Beirut: Dār al-Fikr, n.d.

Rawḍat al-Ṭālibīn. Edited by ʿĀdil Aḥmad ʿAbd al-Mawjūd and ʿAlī Muḥammad Maʿriḍ. Beirut: Dār al-Kutub al-ʿIlmiyya, 1992.

Sharḥ Ṣaḥīḥ Muslim. Edited by Khalīl al-Mīs. Beirut: Dār al-Qalam, n.d.

al-Nuʿmān, al-Qāḍī Abū Ḥanīfa b. Muḥammad b. Manṣūr al-Tamīmī. *Daʿāʾim al-Islām wa Dhikr al-Ḥalāl wa al-Ḥarām wa al-Qaḍāyā wa al-Aḥkām.* Edited by ʿĀṣif b. ʿAlī Aṣghar al-Fayḍī. Cairo: Dār al-Maʿrifa, n.d.

al-Qaffāl, Sayf al-Dīn Abū Bakr Muḥammad b. Aḥmad al-Shāshī. *Ḥulyat al-ʿUlamāʾ fī Maʿrifat Madhāhib al-Fuqahāʾ.* Edited by Yāsīn Aḥmad Ibrāhīm. Mecca: Dār al-Bāz, 1988.

al-Qanūjī, Abū al-Ṭayyib Ṣiddīq b. Ḥasan b.ʿAlī al-Ḥusayn al-Bukhārī. *al-Rawḍa al-Nadiyya Sharḥ al-Durar al-Bahiyya.* Edited by ʿAbd Allāh b. Ibrāhīm al-Anṣārī. Beirut: al-Maktaba al-ʿAṣriyya, n.d.

al-Qarāfī, Shihāb al-Dīn Aḥmad b. Idrīs. *al-Dhakhīra.* Beirut: Dār al-Gharb al-Islāmī, 1994.

Kitāb al-Iḥkām fī Tamyīz al-Fatāwā ʿan al-Aḥkām wa Taṣarrufāt al-Qāḍī wa al-Imām. Edited by ʿAbd al-Fattāḥ Abū Ghuddah. Aleppo: Maktabat al-Maṭbūʿāt al-Islāmiyya, 1967.

Sharḥ Tanqīḥ al-Fuṣūl fī Ikhtiṣār al-Maḥṣūl fī al-Uṣūl. Edited by Ṭāha ʿAbd al-Raʾūf Saʿīd. Cairo: Dār al-Fikr, n.d.

al-Qasṭalānī, Abū al-ᶜAbbās Shihāb al-Dīn. *Irshād al-Sārī Sharḥ Ṣaḥīḥ al-Bukhārī.* Cairo: Dār al-Fikr, 1304 AH.

al-Qazwīnī, Abū al-Qāsim ᶜAbd al-Karīm b. Muḥammad al-Rafᶜī. *al-ᶜAzīz Sharḥ al-Wajīz (a.k.a al-Sharḥ al-Kabīr).* Beirut: Dār al-Kutub al-ᶜIlmiyya, 1997.

al-Qurṭubī, Abū ᶜAbd Allah Muḥammad b. Aḥmad al-Anṣārī. *al-Jāmiᶜli Aḥkām al-Qurʾān.* Beirut: Dār al-Fikr, 1987.

al-Jāmiᶜ li Aḥkām al-Qurʾān. Cairo: n.p., 1952.

Quṭb, Sayyid. *Fī Ẓilāl al-Qurʾān.* Cairo: Dār al-Shurūq, 1987.

al-Ramlī, Shams al-Dīn Muḥammad b. Aḥmad al-Anṣārī. *Fatāwā al-Ramlī.* Printed in the margins of *al-Fatāwā al-Kubrā al-Fiqhiyya* by Ibn Ḥajar al-Haytamī. Beirut: Dār al-Kutub al-ᶜIlmiyya, 1983.

Ghāyat al-Bayān Sharḥ Zubad Ibn Raslān. Cairo: Maṭbaᶜat Muṣṭafā al-Bābī al-Ḥalabī, n.d.

Nihāyat al-Muḥtāj ilā Sharḥ al-Minhāj fī al-Fiqh ᶜalā Madhhab al-Imām al-Shāfiᶜī. Cairo: Muṣṭafā al-Bābī al-Ḥalabī, 1968.

al-Rāwandī, Quṭb al-Dīn Saᶜīd b. Hibat Allāh. *Fiqh al-Qurʾān.* Edited by Aḥmad al-Ḥusaynī. Qum: Maktabat al-Marᶜashī, 1405 AH.

al-Rāzī, Fakhr al-Dīn Muḥammad b. ᶜUmar. *ᶜIlal al-Ḥadīth.* Beirut: Dār al-Maᶜrifa, 1985.

al-Maḥṣūl fī ᶜIlm Uṣūl al-Fiqh. Edited by Ṭāha Jābir al-ᶜAlwānī, 2nd ed. Beirut: Mu'assasat al-Risāla, 1992.

al-Tafsīr al-Kabīr = Mafātīḥ al-Ghayb. Beirut: Dār al-Kutub al-ᶜIlmiyya, 1990.

al-Rāzī, Muḥammad b. Abī Bakr. *Unmūdhaj Jalīl fī Asʾilah wa Ajwibah min Gharāʾib Āyī al-Tanzīl.* Edited by Muḥammad Riḍwān al-Dāya. Beirut: Dār al-Fikr, 1990.

Riḍā, Muḥammad Rashīd. *Tafsīr al-Manār.* Cairo: al-Miṣriyya al-ᶜĀmma li'l-Kitāb, 1972.

al-Rustāqī, Khamīs b. Saᶜīd b. ᶜAlī b. Masᶜūd al-Shaqṣī. *Manhaj al-Ṭālibīn wa Balāgh al-Rāghibīn.* Edited by Sālim b. Ḥamad b. Sulaymān b. al-Ḥārithī. Cairo: ᶜĪsā al-Bābī al-Ḥalabī, 1983.

Al-Saᶜdī, Jamīl b. Khamīs. *Qāmūs al-Sharīᶜa al-Ḥāwī li Ṭuruqihā al-Wasīᶜa.* Oman: Wizārat al-Turāth, 1983.

al-Ṣadūq, Abū Jaᶜfar Muḥammad b. ᶜAlī b. Bābawayh al-Qummī. *Kitāb man lā Yaḥḍuruhu al-Faqīh.* Edited by ᶜAlī Akbar al-Ghaffārī. Qum: Mu'assasat al-Nashr al-Islāmī, n.d.

al-Ṣafadī, Ṣalāḥ al-Dīn Khalīl b. Aybak. *Kitāb al-Wāfī bi al-Wafiyyāt.* Edited by Bernd Radtke. Beirut: Dār Ṣādir, 1991.

Saḥnūn, ᶜAbd al-Salām b. Saᶜīd al-Tanūkhī. *al-Mudawwana al-Kubrā.* Beirut: Dār al-Fikr, 1986.

Sallār, Abū Yaᶜlā Ḥamza b. ᶜAbd al-ᶜAzīz al-Daylamī. *al-Marāsim al-ᶜAlawiyya.* In Murwārīd, ed., *Mawsūᶜa*, vol. x.

al-Samarqandī, ᶜAlā' al-Dīn Muḥammad. *Tuḥfat al-Fuqahāʾ.* Beirut: Dār al-Kutub al-ᶜIlmiyya, 1984.

al-Samarqandī, Nāṣir al-Dīn Abū al-Qāsim Muḥammad b. Yūsuf al-Ḥasanī. *al-Fiqh al-Nāfiʿ*. Edited by Ibrāhīm b. Muḥammad b. Ibrāhīm al-ʿAbbūd. Riyadh: Maktabat al-ʿUbaykān, 2000.

Sanad, Najātī Sayyid. *Naẓariyyat al-Jarīma al-Siyāsiyya fī al-Qawānīn al-Waḍʿiyya al-Muqārana wa fī al-Sharīʿa al-Islāmiyya*. Cairo: Top Guy, n.d.

al-Ṣanʿānī, Abū Bakr ʿAbd al-Razzāq b. Hammām. *al-Muṣannaf*. Edited by Ḥabīb al-Raḥmān al-Aʿẓamī. Riyadh: al-Majlis al-ʿIlmī, n.d.

Tafsīr al-Qurʾān al-ʿAzīz. Beirut: Dār al-Maʿrifa, 1991.

al-Ṣanʿānī, Aḥmad b. Ibrāhīm al-Ḥasanī al-Yamanī. *Tatimmat al-Rawḍ al-Naḍīr Sharḥ Majmūʿal-Fiqh al-Kabīr* (The *Tatimmat* is the completion of *Kitāb al-Rawḍ al-Naḍīr* printed at the end of *al-Rawḍ*). In al-Ṣanʿānī, *Kitāb*.

al-Ṣanʿānī, Sharaf al-Dīn al-Ḥusayn b. Aḥmad al-Sayyāghī. *Kitāb al-Rawḍ al-Naḍīr Sharḥ Majmūʿal-Fiqh al-Kabīr*. Beirut: Dār al-Jīl, n.d.

al-Sarakhsī, Abū Bakr Muḥammad b. Aḥmad b. Sahl Shams al-Dīn. *al-Mabsūṭ*. Beirut: Dār al-Maʿrifa, 1986.

Sharḥ Kitāb al-Siyar al-Kabīr. Cairo: Maṭbaʿat Sharikat al-Iʿlānāt al-Sharqiyya, 1971.

al-Ṣāwī, Aḥmad b. Muḥammad. *Bulghat al-Sālik li Aqrab al-Masālik ilā Madhhab al-Imām Mālik ʿalā al-Sharḥ al-Ṣaghīr*. Cairo: Muṣṭafā al-Bābī al-Ḥalabī, 1954.

Ḥāshiyat al-ʿAllāma al-Ṣāwīʿalā Tafsīr al-Jalālayn. Beirut: Dār Iḥyāʾ al-Turāth al-ʿArabī, n.d.

al-Sayyid, Riḍwān, ed. *al-Asad wa al-Ghawwāṣ*. Beirut: Dār al-Ṭalīʿa, 1992.

Mafāhīm al-Jamāʿāt fī al-Islām. Beirut: Dār al-Tanwīr, 1983.

al-Umma wa al-Jamāʿa wa al-Sulṭah: Dirāsāt fī al-Fikr al-Sīyāsī al-ʿArabī al-Islāmī. Beirut: Dār Iqraʾ, 1984.

al-Shāfiʿī, Muḥammad b. Idrīs. *Ikhtilāf al-Ḥadīth*. Printed in the margins of Muḥammad b.Idrīs al-Shāfiʿī, *al-Umm*, vol. VII. Cairo: Maṭbaʿat Būlāq, 1325 AH.

al-Umm. Edited by Muḥammad Zuharī al-Najjār. Beirut: Dār al-Maʿrifa, n.d.

al-Shahrastānī, Abū al-Fatḥ Muḥammad b. ʿAbd al-Karīm. *al-Milal wa al-Niḥal*. Edited by Amīr ʿAlī Muhannā and ʿAlī Ḥasan Fāʿūr. Beirut: Dār al-Maʿrifa, 1992.

al-Shahrazūrī, Abū ʿAm, ʿUthmān b. ʿAbd al-Raḥmān b. Ṣalāh. *Adab al-Muftī wa al-Mustaftī*. Edited by Muwaffaq b. ʿAbd Allāh b. ʿAbd al-Qādir. Cairo: Maktabat al-ʿUlūm wa al-Ḥikam, 1986.

al-Shaljī, ʿAbbūd. *Mawsūʿat al-ʿAdhāb*. Beirut: al-Dār al-ʿArabiyya li al-Mawsūʿāt, 1998.

Shaltūt, Maḥmūd. *al-Islām: ʿAqīda wa Sharīʿah*, 17th ed. Cairo: Dār al-Shurūq, 1991.

al-Sharqāwī, ʿAbd Allāh b. Ḥijāzī b. Ibrāhīm. *Ḥāshiyat al-Sharqāwīʿalā Tuḥfat al-Ṭullāb*. Dār al-Kutub al-ʿIlmiyya, 1997.

al-Shāṭibī, Abū Iṣḥāq Ibrāhīm b. Mūsā. *al-Muwāfaqāt fī Uṣūl al-Sharīʿah*. Beirut: Dār al-Kutub al-ʿIlmiyya, n.d.

al-Shawkānī, Muḥammad b. ʿAlī b. Muḥammad. *Nayl al-Awṭār Sharḥ Muntaqā al-Akhbār*. Cairo: Dār al-Ḥadīth, n.d.

al-Sayl al-Jarrār ʿalā Ḥadāʾiq al-Azhār. Edited by Maḥmūd Ibrahīm Zāyid. Beirut: Dār al-Kitāb al-ʿIlmiyya, 1995.

al-Shaybānī, ʿAbd al-Qādir b. ʿUmar and Ibrāhīm b. Muḥammad b. Ḍuwayyān. *al-Muʿtamad fī Fiqh al-Imām Aḥmad*. Edited by ʿAlī ʿAbd al-Ḥamīd al-Balṭajī and Muḥammad Wahbī Sulaymān. Beirut: Dār al-Khayr, 1991.

Al-Shaybānī, Abū ʿAbd Allāh Muḥammad b. al-Ḥasan. *Al-Jāmiʿ al-Ṣaghīr*. Beirut: ʿĀlam al-Kutub, 1986.

Kitāb al-Aṣl al-Maʿrūf bi al-Mabsūṭ. Edited by Abū al-Wafāʾ al-Afghānī. Beirut: ʿĀlam al-Kutub, 1990.

al-Shaybānī, Abū Bakr al-Ḍaḥḥāk b. Makhlad. *Kitāb al-Sunnah*. Edited by Muḥammad Nāṣir al-Dīn al-Albānī. Beirut: al-Maktab al-Islāmī, 1993.

al-Shiblī, Badr al-Dīn Abū ʿAbd Allāh ʿUmar b. ʿAbd Allāh al-Ḥanafī. *Iḥkām al-Marjān fī Aḥkām al-Jānn*. Beirut: Dār al-Qalam, 1988.

al-Shinqīṭī, Muḥammad al-Shaybānī b. Muḥammad b. Aḥmad al-Mūrītānī. *Tabyīn al-Masālik Sharḥ Tadrīb al-Sālik ilā Aqrab al-Masālik*. Beirut: Dār al-Gharb al-Islāmī, 1995.

al-Shīrāzī, Abū Isḥāq Ibrāhīm b. ʿAlī. *al-Muhadhdhab fī Fiqh al-Imām al-Shāfiʿī*. Cairo: Muṣṭafā al-Bābī al-Ḥalabī, n.d.

al-Shirbīnī, Muḥammad al-Khaṭīb. *Mughnī al-Muḥtāj ilā Maʿrifat Maʿānī Alfāẓ al-Minhāj*. Cairo: Muṣṭafā al-Bābī al-Ḥalabī, 1958.

al-Simnānī, Abū al-Qāsim ʿAlī b. Muḥammad b. Aḥmad al-Raḥbī. *Rawḍat al-Quḍāh wa Ṭarīq al-Najāh*. Edited by Ṣalāḥ al-Dīn al-Nāhī. Beirut: Muʾassasat al-Risāla, 1984.

Sirkīs, Yūsuf Ilyān. *Muʿjam al-Maṭbūʿāt al-ʿArabiyya wa al-Muʿarraba*. Cairo: Yūsuf Ilyān Sirkīs wa Awlāduhu, 1931.

al-Subkī, Tāj al-Dīn ʿAlī. *Ṭabaqāt al-Shāfiʿiyya al-Kubrā*. Edited by Maḥmūd al-Ṭanāḥī and ʿAbd al-Fattāḥ al-Muḥammad al-Ḥulw. Cairo: ʿĪsā al-Bābī al-Ḥalabī, 1383 AH.

al-Subkī, Taqī al-Dīn Abū al-Ḥasan ʿAlī b. ʿAbd al-Kāfī. *Fatāwā al-Subkī*. Beirut: Dār al-Maʿrifa, n.d.

al-Suddī, Abū Muḥammad Ismāʿīl b. ʿAbd al-Raḥmān. *Tafsīr al-Suddī al-Kabīr*. Edited by Muḥammad ʿAṭā Yūsuf. Riyadh: Dār al-Wafāʾ, 1993.

al-Suyūrī, Jamāl al-Dīn al-Miqdād b. ʿAbd Allāh. *Kanz al-ʿIrfān fī Fiqh al-Qurʾān*. Edited by Muḥammad Bāqir al-Bihbūdī. Tehran: al-Maktaba al-Murtaḍawiyya, n.d.

al-Tanqīḥ al-Rāʾiʿ li Mukhtaṣar al-Sharāʾiʿ. Edited by al-Sayyid ʿAbd al-Laṭīf al-Kūhkamarrī. Qum: Maktabat al-Marʿashī, 1404 AH.

al-Suyūṭī, Jalāl al-Dīn. *al-Durr al-Manthūr fī al-Tafsīr bi al-Maʾthūr*. Cairo: Maṭbaʿat al-Anwār al-Muḥammadiyya, n.d.

Ikhtilāf al-Madhāhib. Edited by ʿAbd al-Qayyūm Muḥammad al-Basṭāwī. Cairo: Dār al-Iʿtiṣām, 1404 AH.

al-Ṭabarī, Abū Jaʿfar Muḥammad b. Jarīr. *Jāmiʿ al-Bayān fī Tafsīr al-Qurʾān*. Beirut: Dār al-Maʿrifa, 1989.

Taʾrīkh al-Umam wa al-Mulūk. Beirut: Mūʾassasat ʿIzz al-Dīn, 1987.

al-Ṭabāṭabā'ī, al-Sayyid Muḥammad Ḥusayn. *al-Mīzān fī Tafsīr al-Qur'ān*. Qum: Maṭba'at Ismā'īliyān, 1412 AH.

al-Ṭabrīsī, Abū 'Alī al-Faḍl b. al-Ḥasan. *Majma'* al-Bayān fī Tafsīr al-Qur'ān. Beirut: Dār Maktabat al-Ḥayāt, n.d.

al-Ṭaḥāwī, Abū Ja'far Aḥmad b. Muḥammad b. Salāma. *Sharḥ Mushkil al-Ḥadīth*. Edited by Shu'ayb al-Arna'ūṭ. Beirut: Mu'assasat al-Risāla, 1994.

al-Ṭaḥṭāwī, Aḥmad. *Ḥāshiyat al-Ṭaḥṭāwī 'alā al-Durr al-Mukhtār*. Beirut: Dār al-Ma'rifa, 1975.

al-Tamīmī, Ḍiyā' al-Dīn 'Abd al-'Azīz. *Kitāb al-Nīl wa Shifā' al-'Alīl*. Jedda: Maktabat al-Irshād, 1985. (The commentary by Muḥammad b. Yūsuf Aṭṭafayyīsh, *Sharḥ Kitāb al-Nīl* is in the margins.)

al-Tamīmī, Muḥammad b. al-Ḥasan al-Jawharī. *Nawādir al-Fuqahā'*. Edited by Muḥammad Faḍl 'Abd al-'Azīz al-Murād. Damascus: Dār al-Qalam, 1993.

al-Ṭarabulusī, al-Qāḍī 'Abd al-'Azīz Ibn al-Barrāj. *al-Muhadhdhab*. Edited by Ja'far al-Subḥānī. Qum: Mu'assasat al-Nashr al-Islāmī, 1409 AH.

al-Ṭarsawī, Najm al-Dīn b. 'Alī. *Tuḥfat al-Turk fī mā Yajib 'an Yu'mal fī al-Mulk*. Edited by Riḍwān al-Sayyid. Beirut: Dār al-Ṭalī'a, 1992.

al-Tasūlī (Madīdash), Abū al-Ḥasan 'Alī b. 'Abd al-Salām. *al-Buhja fī Sharḥ al-Tuḥfa*. Beirut: Dār al-Fikr, n.d.

al-Tha'ālibī, 'Abd al-Raḥmān b. Muḥammad b. Makhlūf. *al-Jawāhir al-Ḥisān fī Tafsīr al-Qur'ān*. Beirut: Mu'assasat al-A'lamī li al-Maṭbū'āt, n.d.

al-Thawrī, Abū 'Abd Allāh Sufyān b. Sa'īd b. Masrūq. *Tafsīr Sufyān al-Thawrī*. Beirut: Dār al-Kutub al-'Ilmiyya, 1983.

al-Tirmidhī, Abū 'Īsā Muḥammad b. Sūra. *al-Jāmi' al-Ṣaḥīḥ*. Edited by Kamāl al-Ḥūt. Cairo: Dār al-Ḥadīth, 1987.

al-Ṭūsī, Abū Ja'far Muḥammad b. al-Ḥasan b. 'Alī. *al-Istibṣār fī mā Ikhtalafa min al-Akhbār*. Edited by Ḥasan al-Mūsawī al-Kharsān. Tehran: Dār al-Kutub al-Islamīyya, 1390 AH.

al-Mabsūṭ fī Fiqh al-Imāmiyya. Edited by Muḥammad Taqī al-Kashafī. Tehran: al-Maktabah al-Murtaḍawiyya, 1387 AH.

al-Nihāya fī Mujarrad al-Fiqh wa al-Fatāwā. Qum: Intishārāt Quds Muḥammadī, n.d.

al-Rasā'il al-'Ashr. Qum: Mu'assasat al-Nashr al-Islāmī, n.d.

Tahdhīb al-Aḥkām. Edited by Ḥasan al-Mūsawī al-Kharsān. Beirut: Dār al-Aḍwā', 1985.

al-Tustarī, Nūr Allāh al-Ḥusaynī al-Mar'ashī. *Iḥqāq al-Ḥaqq wa Izhāq al-Bāṭil*. Qum: Maktabat al-Mar'ashī, 1404 AH.

al-'Ubbī, Muḥammad b. Khalīfa al-Wishtānī. *Sharḥ Ṣaḥīḥ Muslim*. Beirut: Dār al-Kutub al-'Ilmiyya, 1994.

'Ūdah, 'Abd al-Qādir. *al-Tashrī' al-Jinā'ī al-Islāmī*. Beirut: Dār al-Kitāb al-'Arabī, n.d.

'Ulaysh, Abū 'Abd Allāh Muḥammad b. Aḥmad. *Fatḥ al-'Alī al-Mālik fī al-Fatwā 'alā Madhhab al-Imām Mālik*. Cairo: Muṣṭafā al-Bābī al-Ḥalabī, 1958.

Wakīʿ, Muḥammad b. Khalaf b. Ḥayyān. *Akhbār al-Quḍāh*. Beirut: ʿĀlam al-Kutub, n.d.

al-Wansharīsī, Aḥmad b. Yaḥyā. *Al-Miʿyār al-Muʿrib*. Edited by Muḥammad Ḥajjī. Beirut: Dār al-Gharb al-Islāmī, 1981.

al-Warjalānī, Abū Yaʿqūb Yūsuf b. Ibrāhīm. *al-ʿAdl wa al-Inṣāf fī Maʿrifat Uṣūl al-Fiqh wa al-Ikhtilāf*. Oman: Wizārat al-Turāth, 1983.

al-Wazīr, Muḥammad b. Ibrāhīm al-Yamānī. *al-ʿAwāṣim wa al-Qawāṣim fī al-Dhabb ʿan Sunnat Abī al-Qāsim*. Beirut: Muʾassasat al-Risāla, 1992.

al-Yamanī, Abū Muḥammad. *ʿAqāʾid al-Thalātha wa al-Sabʿīna Firqa*. Edited by Muḥammad b. ʿAbd Allāh Zarbāb al-Ghāmidi. Medina: Maktabat al-ʿUlūm wa al-Ḥikam, 1414 AH.

al-Yaʿqūbī, Aḥmad b. Isḥāq b. Jaʿfar b. Wāḍiḥ. *Taʾrīkh al-Yaʿqūbī*. Beirut: Dār Ṣādir, n.d.

al-Zamakhsharī, Abū al-Qāsim Maḥmūd b. ʿUmar al-Khawārizmī. *al-Kashshāf*. Beirut: Dār al-Maʿrifa, n.d.

Rabīʿ al-Abrār fī Nuṣūṣ al-Akhbār. Edited by ʿAbd al-Amīr Muhannā. Beirut: Muʾassasat al-Aʿlamī, 1992.

Ruʾūs al-Masāʾil. Edited by ʿAbd Allāh Nazīr Aḥmad. Beirut: Dār al-Bashāʾir al-Islāmiyya, n.d.

al-Zarkashī, Shams al-Dīn Muḥammad b. ʿAbd Allāh. *Sharḥ al-Zarkashī ʿalā Mukhtaṣar al-Khiraqī fī al-Fiqh ʿalā Madhhab al-Imām Aḥmad b. Ḥanbal*. Edited by ʿAbd Allāh b. ʿAbd al-Raḥmān b. ʿAbd Allāh b. al-Jibrīn. Riyadh: al-ʿUbaykān, n.d.

al-Zarqānī, Muḥammad b. ʿAbd al-Bāqī b. Yūsuf. *Sharḥ al-Zarqānī ʿalā Muwaṭṭaʾ al-Imām Mālik*. Beirut: Dār al-Kutub al-ʿIlmiyya, 1990.

al-Zaylaʿī, Fakhr al-Dīn ʿUthmān b. ʿAlī. *Tabyīn al-Ḥaqāʾiq Sharḥ Kanz al-Daqāʾiq*. Medina: Dār al-Kitāb al-Islāmiyya, n.d.

al-Ziriklī, Khayr al-Dīn. *al-Aʿlām*. Beirut: Dār al-ʿIlm li al-Malāyīn, 1989.

NON-ARABIC SOURCES

Note: Articles from the following sources shall be referenced as indicated:

EI1 = *Encyclopedia of Islam*, 1st edition. Edited by M. T. Houtsma et al., 9 vols. Leiden: E. J. Brill, 1913–36.

EI2 = *Encyclopaedia of Islam*, 2nd edition. Edited by H. A. R. Gibb et al., 8 vols. and supplement to date. Leiden: E. J. Brill, 1960–.

Abel, Richard. "Law as Lag: Inertia as a Social Theory of Law." *Michigan Law Review* 80 (March, 1982): 785–809.

Politics by Other Means: Law in the Struggle against Apartheid, 1980–1994. New York: Routledge, 1995.

"Redirecting Social Studies of Law." *Law and Society* 14 (Spring, 1980): 803–26.

Abou El Fadl, Khaled. "*Ahkam al-Bughat*: Irregular Warfare and the Law of Rebellion in Islam." In *Cross, Crescent, and Sword: The Justification and Limitation of War in Western and Islamic Traditions*. Edited by James Turner Johnson and John Kelsay. Westport, CT: Greenwood Press, 1990.

"The Common and Islamic Law of Duress." *Arab Law Quarterly* 6, no. 2 (1991): 121–59.
"Islamic Law and Muslim Minorities: The Juristic Discourse on Muslim Minorities from the Second/Eighth to the Eleventh/Seventeenth Centuries." *Islamic Law and Society* 1, no. 2 (1994): 141–87.
"Political Crime in Islamic Jurisprudence and Western Legal History." *Journal of International Law and Policy* 4, no. 1 (Winter, 1998): 1–28.
Speaking in God's Name: Islamic Law, Authority, and Women. Oxford: Oneworld Press, 2001.
"Tax Farming in Islamic Law: A Search for a Concept." *Islamic Studies* 31, no. 1 (Spring 1992): 5–32.
Abou El Fadl, Khaled and Alan Watson. "Fox Hunting, Pheasant Shooting, and Comparative Law." *The American Journal of Comparative Law* 48, no. 1 (2000): 1–37.
ʿAlī, ʿAbdullah Yūsuf, trans. *The Meaning of The Holy Qurʾān.* Beltsville, MD: Amana Publications, 1995.
Anderson, J. N. D. *Law Reform in the Muslim World.* London: Athlone Press, 1976.
Arzt, Donna E. "Heroes or Heretics: Religious Dissidents under Islamic Law." *Wisconsin International Law Journal* 14 (Spring 1996): 349–421.
ʿAthāmina, K. "The Ulamā' in the Opposition: The 'Stick and Carrot' Policy in Early Islam." *The Islamic Quarterly* 36 (1992): 153–78.
Austin, John. *Lectures on Jurisprudence*, 5th ed. London: John Murray, 1885.
The Province of Jurisprudence Determined. New York: Noonday Press, 1954.
al-Azami, Muhammad M. *On Schacht's Origins of Muhammadan Jurisprudence.* New York: John Wiley & Sons, Inc., 1985.
al-Azmeh, Aziz. "Islamic Legal Theory and the Appropriation of Reality." In *Islamic Law: Social and Historical Contexts.* Edited by Aziz al-Azmeh. London: Routledge, 1988.
Muslim Kingship: Power and the Sacred in Muslim, Christian and Pagan Polities. London: I. B. Tauris, 1997.
Balbus, Isaac D. "Commodity Form and Legal Form: An Essay on the Relative Autonomy of the Law." *Law and Society Review* 11 (Winter, 1977): 571–87.
Barber, Bernard, and Alex Inkeles, eds. *Stability and Social Change.* Boston: Little, Brown & Co., 1971.
Barcelo, Miquel. "Rodes que giren dins el foc de l'infern'o per que servia la moneda dels taifes?" *Gaceta Numismatica* 105–6 (1992): 15–24.
Barkey, Karen. *Bandits and Bureaucrats: The Ottoman Route to State Centralization.* Ithaca: Cornell University Press, 1994.
Bauman, Richard A. *Crime and Punishment in Ancient Rome.* London: Routledge, 1996.
Bel, A. "Tlemcen," *EI1*, VIII:801.
Bellamy, John G. *The Law of Treason in England in the Later Middle Ages.* Cambridge: Cambridge University Press, 1970.
The Tudor Law of Treason. London: Routledge & Kegan Paul, 1979.

Ben Cheneb, Mohammad. "Ibn Taimīya," *EI1*, III:421.
Bentham, Jeremy. *Of Laws in General.* New York: Athlone Press, 1970.
The Limits of Jurisprudence Defined. New York: Columbia University Press, 1945.
Bercher, L. "L'apostasie, le blaspheme et la rebellion en droit Musulman malekite." *Revue Tunisienne* (1923): 115–30.
Berman, Harold J. *Law and Revolution: The Formation of the Western Legal Tradition.* Cambridge: Harvard University Press, 1983.
Bianqus, Thierry. "Autonomous Egypt from Ibn Ṭūlūn to Kāfūr, 868–969." In *The Cambridge History of Egypt: Volume One, Islamic Egypt 640–1517*. Edited by Carl F. Petry. Cambridge: Cambridge University Press, 1998.
Blackstone, William. *Commentaries on the Laws of England.* Chicago: University of Chicago Press, 1979.
Blankinship, Khalid Yahya. *The End of the Jihād State: The Reign of Hishām Ibn ʿAbd al-Malik and the Collapse of the Umayyads.* Albany: State University of New York Press, 1994.
Bosworth, Clifford Edmund. *The New Islamic Dynasties.* New York: Columbia University Press, 1996.
Bowen, H. and C. E. Bosworth. "Niẓām al-Mulk" *EI2*, VIII:69.
Brockopp, Jonathan E. "Early Islamic Jurisprudence in Egypt: Two Scholars and their *Mukhtaṣars.*" *International Journal of Middle East Studies* 30, no. 2 (1998): 167–82.
Early Mālikī Law: Ibn ʿAbd al-Ḥakam and his Major Compendium of Jurisprudence. Leiden: E. J. Brill, 2000.
Bulliet, Richard W. *The Patricians of Nishapur: A Study in Medieval Islamic Social History.* Cambridge: Harvard University Press, 1972.
Burman, Edward. *The Assassins: Holy Killers of Islam.* London: Aquarian Press, 1987.
Bursell, Rupert D. H. *Liturgy, Order and the Law.* Oxford: Clarendon Press, 1996.
Burton, John. "Rewriting the Timetable of Early Islam." *Journal of the American Oriental Society* 115 (1995): 453–62.
Cahen, Claude. "Buwayhids." *EI2*, I:1350.
Calder, Norman. "Al-Sarakhsī." *EI2*, IX:35.
"The Structure of Authority in Imāmī Shīʿī Jurisprudence." Ph.D. thesis, University of London, School of Oriental and African Studies, 1980.
Studies in Early Muslim Jurisprudence. Oxford: Clarendon Press, 1993.
Canard, M. "Fāṭimids." *EI2*, II:850.
Chokr, Melhem. *Zandaqa et Zindiqs en Islam au Second Siècle de l'Hégire.* Damascus: Institut Français de Damas, 1993.
Christenson, Ron. *Political Trials: Gordian Knots in the Law*, 2nd ed. New Brunswick and London: Transaction, 1999.
Cohen, Boaz. *Jewish and Roman Law: A Comparative Study.* New York: Jewish Theological Seminary of America, 1966.
Cohen, Morris Raphael. *The Faith of a Liberal.* New Brunswick: Transaction, 1993.

Law and Social Order: Essays in Legal Philosophy. New Brunswick: Transaction Books, 1982.

Reason and Law: Studies in Juristic Philosophy. Glencoe, IL.: Free Press, 1950.

Conley, John, and William O' Barr. *Just Words: Law, Language and Power.* Chicago: University of Chicago Press, 1998.

Cook, Michael. "Activism and Quietism in Islam: The Case of the Early Murji'a." In *Islam and Power.* Edited by Alexander S. Cudsi and Ali E. Hillal Dessouki. Baltimore: Johns Hopkins University Press, 1981.

Commanding Right and Forbidding Wrong in Islamic Thought. Cambridge: Cambridge University Press, 2000.

"Eschatology and the Dating of Traditions." *Princeton Papers in Near Eastern Studies* 1 (1992): 23–47.

Coulson, N. J. *A History of Islamic Law.* Edinburgh: Edinburgh University Press, 1964.

Crone, Patricia. *Slaves on Horses: The Evolution of the Islamic Polity.* Cambridge: Cambridge University Press, 1980.

"Were the Qays and Yemen of the Umayyad Period Political Parties?" *Der Islam* 71, no. 1 (1994): 1–57.

Crone, Patricia, and Martin Hinds. *God's Caliph: Religious Authority in the First Centuries of Islam.* Cambridge: University of Cambridge Oriental Publications, 1986.

Cross, Rupert, and J. W. Harris. *Precedent in English Law*, 4th ed. Oxford: Clarendon Press, 1991.

Cuttler, S. H. *The Law of Treason and Treason Trials in Later Medieval France.* Cambridge: Cambridge University Press, 1981.

Dachraoui, F. "al-Nuᶜmān." *EI2*, VIII:117.

Daftary, Farhad. *The Ismāᶜīlīs: Their History and Doctrines.* Cambridge: Cambridge University Press, 1990.

Danet, Brenda. "Language in the Legal Process." *Law and Society Review* 14 (1980): 445–64.

De Glanvill, Ranulf. *The Treatise on the Laws and Customs of the Realm of England Commonly Called Glanvill.* Edited and translated by G. D. G. Hall. Oxford: Clarendon Press, 1993.

Dekmejian, R. Hrair. *Islam in Revolution: Fundamentalism in the Arab World*, 2nd ed. Syracuse: Syracuse University Press, 1995.

D'Entreves, A. P. *Natural Law.* London: Hutchinson, 1951.

Downer, L. J., trans. *Leges Henrici Primi.* Oxford: Clarendon Press, 1972.

Drew, Katherine Fisher, trans. *The Lombard Laws.* Philadelphia: University of Pennsylvania Press, 1973.

Duri, A. A. *The Rise of Historical Writing among the Arabs.* Translated by Lawrence J. Conrad. Princeton: Princeton University Press, 1983.

Dutton, Yasin. *The Origins of Islamic Law: The Qur'ān, the Muwaṭṭa' and Madinan ᶜAmal.* Surrey: Curzon Press, 1999.

"Review of Calder's *Studies in Early Muslim Jurisprudence.*" *Journal of Islamic Studies* 5 (1994): 102–8.

Ehrlich, Eugen. *Fundamental Principles of the Sociology of Law.* Translated by Walter L. Moll. Cambridge: Harvard University Press, 1936.

El Awa, Mohamed S. *Punishment in Islamic Law.* Indianapolis: American Trust Publications, 1993.

Enayat, Hamid. *Modern Islamic Political Thought.* Austin: University of Texas Press, 1982.

Ephart, Daphna. *A Learned Society in a Period of Transition: The Sunnī ᶜUlamāʾ of Eleventh-Century Baghdad.* Albany: State University of New York Press, 2000.

Evans, Richard J. *Rituals of Retribution: Capital Punishment in Germany 1600–1987.* Oxford: Oxford University Press, 1996.

Fadel, Hossam Mohammad. "Adjudication in the Maliki Madhhab: A Study of Legal Process in Medieval Islamic Law." Ph.D. thesis, University of Chicago, 1995.

"Ibn Ḥajar's *Hady al-Sārī:* A Medieval Interpretation of the Structure of al-Bukhārī's *al-Jāmiᶜ al-Ṣaḥīḥ:* Introduction and Translation." *Journal of Near Eastern Studies* 54, no. 3 (1995): 161–97.

"The Social Logic of *Taqlīd* and the Rise of the *Mukhataṣar* [sic]." *Islamic Law and Society* 3, no. 2 (1996): 193–233.

Fallers, Lloyd A. *Law without Precedent: Legal Ideas in Action in the Courts of Colonial Busoga.* Chicago: University of Chicago Press, 1969.

Fierro, Maria Isabel. "Heresy in al-Andalus." In *The Legacy of Muslim Spain.* Edited by Salma Khadra Jayyusi. Leiden: E. J. Brill, 1992: 895–904.

Finnis, John. *Natural Law and Natural Rights.* Oxford: Oxford University Press, 1980.

Finnis, John, Joseph Boyle, and Germain Grisez. *Nuclear Deterrence, Morality and Realism.* Oxford: Oxford University Press, 1987.

Frank, Jerome. *Law and the Modern Mind.* New York: Tudor Publishing Co., 1930.

Friedrich, Carl Joachim. *The Philosophy of Law in Historical Perspective*, 2nd ed. Chicago: University of Chicago Press, 1963.

Fuller, Lon. *The Morality of Law.* New Haven: Yale University Press, 1964.

Fyzee, A. "Nuᶜmān." *EI1*, VI:953.

"Qadi an-Nuᶜman: The Fatimid Jurist and Author." *Journal of Royal Asiatic Society* (1934): 1–32.

Gatrell, V. A. C. *The Hanging Tree: Execution and the English People 1770–1868.* Oxford: Oxford University Press, 1994.

Geldart, William. *Introduction to English Law.* Revised by David Yardley. Oxford: Oxford University Press, 1995.

Gibb, Hamilton A. R. "ᶜAbd Allāh b. al-Zubayr," *EI2*, I:54.

"Constitutional Organization." In *Origin and Development of Islamic Law*, vol. 1 of *Law in the Middle East.* Edited by Majid Khadduri and Herbert J. Liebesny. Washington, DC: Middle East Institute, 1955.

"al-Māwardī's Theory of the Caliphate." In *Studies on the Civilization of Islam.* Princeton: Princeton University Press, 1962. Originally published in *Islamic Culture* 11 (1937): 291–302.

"Ṭūlūnids." *EI1*, VIII:834.

Gibb, H. A. R. and J. H. Kramers, eds. *Shorter Encyclopedia of Islam*. Leiden: E. J. Brill, 1991.

Goldziher, Ignaz. *The Ẓāhirīs: Their Doctrine and their History*. Translated by Wolfgang Behn. Leiden: E. J. Brill, 1971.

Gray, John Chipman. *The Nature and Sources of the Law*, 2nd ed. Boston: Beacon Press, 1963.

Guraya, Muhammad Yusuf. *Origins of Islamic Jurisprudence*. Delhi: Noor Publishing House, 1992.

Hallaq, Wael B. *A History of Islamic Legal Theories*. Cambridge: Cambridge University Press, 1997.

"Model *Shurūṭ* Works and the Dialectic of Doctrine and Practice." *Islamic Law and Society* 2, no. 2 (June, 1995): 109–34.

"Was the Gate of Ijtihad Closed?" In *Law and Legal Theory in Classical and Medieval Islam*. Brookfield, VT: Variorum, 1994. Originally published in *International Journal of Middle East Studies* 16 (1984): 3–41.

"Was al-Shafiʿi the Master Architect of Islamic Jurisprudence?" *International Journal of Middle East Studies* 25, no. 4 (1993): 587–605.

Hamidullah, Muhammad. *The Muslim Conduct of State*, 7th ed. Lahore: S. Muhammad Ashraf, 1977.

Hart, H. L. A. *The Concept of Law*. Oxford: Oxford University Press, 1961.

Hasan, Ahmad. *The Early Development of Islamic Jurisprudence*. Islamabad: Islamic Research Institute, 1970.

Hawting, G. R. *The First Dynasty: The Umayyad Caliphate AD 661–750*. London: Croom Helm, 1986.

"Al-Mukhtār b. Abī ʿUbayd." *EI2*, VII:521.

"Saʿd." *EI2*, VIII:696.

"The Significance of the Slogan *Lā Ḥukm illā Lillāh* and the References to the *Ḥudūd* in the Traditions about the *Fitna* and the Murder of ʿUthmān." *Bulletin of the School of Oriental and African Studies* 41 (1978): 452–463.

Heffening, Willi. "Al-Sarakhsī." *EI1*, VII:159.

Hinds, M. "Miḥna." *E2*, VII:2.

"The Murder of the Caliph ʿUthmān." *International Journal of Middle East Studies* 3 (1972): 450–69.

Hodgson, Marshall G. S. *The Classical Age of Islam*, Vol. 1 of *The Venture of Islam: Conscience and History in a World Civilization*. Chicago: University of Chicago Press, 1974.

"Djaʿfar al-Ṣādiḳ." *EI2*, II:374.

The Order of Assassins: The Struggle of the Early Nizārī Ismāʿīlī against the Islamic World. New York: AMS Press, 1955.

Holland, Thomas Erskine. *The Elements of Jurisprudence*, 13th ed. Oxford: Clarendon Press, 1924.

Hudson, John. *The Formation of the English Common Law*. New York: Longman, 1996.

Ibrahim, Mahmood. "Religious Inquisition as Social Policy: The Persecution of the *Zandiqa* in the Early Abbasid Caliphate." *Arab Studies Quarterly* 16, no. 2 (1994): 53–72.

Idris, H. R. "Deux juristes kairouanais del' epoque zīrīde: Ibn Abī Zayd et al-Qābisī." *Annales de l'Institut des Etudes Orientales* (1954): 121–98.

"Ibn Abī Zayd al-Ḳayrawānī." *EI2*, III:695.

Ingraham, Barton L. *Political Crime in Europe: A Comparative Study of France, Germany and England.* Berkeley: University of California Press, 1979.

Jackson, B. S. *Theft in Early Jewish Law.* Oxford: Clarendon Press, 1972.

Jackson, Sherman A. *Islamic Law and the State: The Constitutional Jurisprudence of Shihāb al-Dīn al-Qarāfī.* Leiden: E. J. Brill, 1996.

Johansen, Baber. *The Islamic Law on Land Tax and Rent.* London: Croom Helm, 1988.

Jolowicz, H. F. *Historical Introduction to the Study of Roman Law*, 2nd ed. Cambridge: Cambridge University Press, 1952.

Jones, William C., trans. *The Great Qing Code.* Oxford: Clarendon Press, 1994.

Juynboll, G. H. A. "The Qurrā' in Early Islamic History." *Journal of the Economic and Social History of the Orient* 16 (1973):113–29.

"The Qur'ān Reciters on the Battlefield and Concomitant Issues." *Zeitschrift der deutschen morgenlandischen Gesellschaft* 125 (1975): 11–27.

Kamali, Mohammad Hashim. *Freedom of Expression in Islam.* Kuala Lumpur: Berita Publishing, 1994.

Principles of Islamic Jurisprudence. Cambridge: Islamic Texts Society, 1991.

Kelly, J. M. *A Short History of Western Legal Theory.* Oxford: Oxford University Press, 1992.

Kelsen, Hans. *Pure Theory of Law.* Translated by M. Knight, 2nd ed. Berkeley and Los Angeles: University of California Press, 1967.

Kennedy, Hugh. *The Prophet and the Age of the Caliphates.* London: Longman, 1986.

Khadduri, Majid. *Islamic Conception of Justice.* Baltimore: Johns Hopkins University Press, 1984.

War and Peace in the Law of Islam. Baltimore: Johns Hopkins University Press, 1955.

Khadduri, Majid, trans. *The Islamic Law of Nations: Shaybānī's Siyar.* Baltimore: Johns Hopkins University Press, 1966.

Khalid, Anas. "The *Mukhtaṣar* of al-Khiraqī: A Tenth Century Work on Islamic Jurisprudence." Ph.D. thesis, New York University, 1992.

Kirchheimer, Otto. "Legality and Legitimacy." In *The Rule of Law under Siege: Selected Essays of Franz L. Neumann and Otto Kirchheimer.* Edited by William E. Scheuerman. Berkeley and Los Angeles: University of California Press, 1996.

Political Justice: The Use of Legal Procedure for Political Ends. Princeton: Princeton University Press, 1961.

Kohlberg, Etan. "The Development of the 'Imāmī Shīʿī Doctrine of Jihād." *Zeitschrift der deutschen morgenlandischen Gesellschaft* 126 (1976): 64–86.

"Shahīd." *EI2*, IX:203.

"Some Notes on the Imāmī–Shīʿī Views on Taqiyya." *Journal of the American Oriental Society* 95 (1975): 395–402.

Kraemer, Joel L. "Apostates, Rebels and Brigands." *Israel Oriental Studies* 10 (1980): 35–73.

Lambton, Ann K. S. "Changing Concepts of Authority in the Late Ninth/Fifteenth and Early Tenth/Sixteenth Centuries." In *Islam and Power*. Edited by Alexander S. Cudsi and Ali E. Hillal Dessouki. Baltimore: Johns Hopkins University Press, 1981.

State and Government in Medieval Islam: An Introduction to the Study of Islamic Political Theory: The Jurists. Oxford: Oxford University Press, 1981.

Laoust, Henri. "Ibn Taymiyya." *EI2*, III:951.

La Politique de Ġazālī. Paris: P. Geuthner, 1970.

Lapidus, Ira M. "The Separation of State and Religion in the Development of Early Islamic Societies." *International Journal of Middle East Studies* 6 (1975): 363–85.

Lassner, Jacob. *Islamic Revolution and Historical Memory.* New Haven: American Oriental Society, 1986.

The Shaping of ʿAbbāsid Rule. Princeton: Princeton University Press, 1980.

Laven, Peter. "Banditry and Lawlessness on the Venetian *Terraferma* in the Later *Cinquecento*." In *Crime, Society and the Law in Renaissance Italy.* Edited by Trevor Dean and K. J. P. Lowe. Cambridge: Cambridge University Press, 1994.

Lawyers Committee for Human Rights. *Beset by Contradictions: Islamization, Legal Reform and Human Rights in Sudan.* New York: Lawyers Committee for Human Rights, 1996.

Lecker, Michael. "Biographical Notes on Ibn Shihāb al-Zuhrī." *Journal of Semitic Studies* 41 (1996): 21–63.

"The Ḍirār Mosque (9 AH)." In *Muslims, Jews and Pagans: Studies on Early Islamic Medina.* Leiden: E. J. Brill, 1995.

Levi, E. H. *Introduction to Legal Reasoning.* Chicago: University of Chicago Press, 1948.

Levi, Judith N. and Anne G. Walker, eds. *Language in the Judicial Process.* New York: Plenum Press, 1990.

Lewis, Bernard. *The Assassins: A Radical Sect in Islam.* Oxford: Oxford University Press, 1967.

Islam in History: Ideas, People and Events in the Middle East, 2nd ed. Chicago: Open Court, 1993.

The Political Language of Islam. Chicago: University of Chicago Press, 1988.

Llewellyn, Karl N. *The Bramble Bush: on our Law and its Study.* New York: Oceana Publications, 1951.

The Common Law Tradition. Boston: Beacon Press, 1960.

Lowe, Kate. "The Political Crime of Conspiracy in Fifteenth and Sixteenth Century France." In *Crime, Society and the Law in Renaissance Italy.* Edited by Trevor Dean and K. J. P. Lowe. Cambridge: Cambridge University Press, 1994.

MacCormick, Neil. *Legal Reasoning and Legal Theory*, rev. ed. Oxford: Clarendon Press, 1994.

MacDowell, Douglas M. *The Law in Classical Athens.* Ithaca: Cornell University Press, 1978.

MacMullen, Ramsey. *Enemies of the Roman Order: Treason, Unrest and Alienation in the Roman Empire.* London: Routledge, 1992.
Madelung, Wilferd. "The Fāṭimids and the Qarmaṭīs of Baḥrayn." In*Mediaeval Isma^cili History and Thought.* Edited by Farhad Daftary. Cambridge: Cambridge University Press, 1996.
"Ḳarmaṭī." *EI2*, IV:660.
"Khaṭṭābiyya." *EI2*, IV:1132.
"The Sources of Ismā^cīlī Law." *Journal of Near Eastern Studies* 35 (1976): 29–40.
The Succession to Muḥammad: A Study of the Early Caliphate. Cambridge: Cambridge University Press, 1997.
"A Treatise of the Sharīf al-Murtaḍā on the Legality of Working for the Government (*Mas'ala fī 'l-^cAmal ma^ca 'l-Sulṭān*)." *Bulletin of the School of Oriental and African Studies* 43 (1980): 18–31.
Mahmasani, Subhi. *The Philosophy of Jurisprudence in Islam.* Translated by Farhat J. Ziadeh. Selangor Dorul Ehsan: Penerbitan Hizbi, 1987.
Maimonides, Moses. *The Code of Maimonides: The Book of Judges.* Translated by Abraham M. Hershman. New Haven: Yale University Press, 1977.
Maitland, F. W. *The Constitutional History of England.* Cambridge: Cambridge University Press, 1946.
Maitland, F. and F. Pollock. *The History of English Law before the Time of Edward I.* Cambridge: Cambridge University Press, 1895.
Makdisi, George. "Muslim Institutions of Learning in Eleventh-Century Baghdad." *Bulletin of the School of Oriental and African Studies* 24 (1961): 1–15.
The Rise of Colleges: Institutions of Learning in Islam and the West. Edinburgh: Edinburgh University Press, 1981.
Marcais, G. "^cAbd al-Wādids." *EI2*, I:91.
Margoliouth, D. S. "Karrāmīya." *EI1*, IV:773.
Marin-Guzman, Roberto. *Popular Dimensions of the ^cAbbasid Revolution: A Case Study of Medieval Islamic Social History.* Cambridge: Fulbright-Laspau, 1990.
Marlow, Louise. *Hierarchy and Egalitarianism in Islamic Thought.* Cambridge: Cambridge University Press, 1997.
Massignon, L. "Zandj." *EI1*, VIII:1213.
Masud, Muhammad Khalid. *Islamic Legal Philosophy: A Study of Abu Ishaq al-Shatibi Life and Thought.* New Delhi: International Islamic Publishers, 1989.
McLynn, Frank. *Crime and Punishment in Eighteenth-Century England.* Oxford: Oxford University Press, 1991.
Melchert, Christopher. *The Formation of the Sunni Schools of Law: 9th–10th Centuries C.E.* Leiden: E. J. Brill, 1997.
Mikhail, Hanna. *Politics and Revelation: Māwardī and After.* Edinburgh: Edinburgh University Press, 1995.
Modarressi, Hossein. *Crisis and Consolidation in the Formative Period of Shi^cite Islam.* Princeton: Darwin Press, 1993.
Kharāj in Islamic Law. London: Anchor Press Ltd, 1983.

Momen, Moojan. *An Introduction to Shīᶜī Islam*. New Haven: Yale University Press, 1985.

Moosa, Ebrahim. *Ghazālī of Tus: The Life and Times of a Sufi Mystic*. Oxford: Oneworld, 2001.

Moosa, Matti Moosa. *Extremist Shiites: The Ghulat Sects*. Syracuse, NY: Syracuse University Press, 1988.

Morrill, Calvin and Peter C. Facciola. "The Power of Language in Adjudication and Mediation: Institutional Contexts as Predictors of Social Evaluation." *Law and Social Inquiry* 17 (1992): 191–212.

Murphy, Jeffrie G. and Jules L. Coleman. *Philosophy of Law: An Introduction to Jurisprudence*, rev. ed. Boulder: Westview Press, 1990.

Nagel, T. "Ḳurrāʾ." *EI2*, V:499.

Nawas, John A. "A Reexamination of Three Current Explanations for al-Ma'mun's Introduction of the Miḥna." *International Journal of Middle East Studies* 26, no. 4 (1994): 615–29.

Ochesenwald, William. "Saudi Arabia." In *The Politics of Islamic Revivalism: Diversity and Unity*. Edited by Shireen Hunter. Bloomington: Indiana University Press, 1988.

Ogburn, William Fielding. *On Culture and Social Change: Selected Papers*. Edited by Otis Dudley. Chicago: University of Chicago Press, 1964.

Social Change with Respect to Culture and Original Nature. Gloucester, MA.: P. Smith, 1964.

Peters, Rudolph. *Islam and Colonialism: The Doctrine of Jihad in Modern History*. The Hague: Mouton Publishers, 1979.

Peters, Rudolph and Gert J. De Vries. "Apostasy in Islam." *Die Welt des Islams* 17, nos. 1–4 (1976–7): 1–25.

Plucknett, Theodore F. T. *A Concise History of the Common Law*, 5th ed. New York: Little, Brown & Co., 1956.

Poonawala, Ismail K. "Al-Qāḍī al-Nuᶜmān and Ismāᶜīlī Jurisprudence." In *Mediaeval Ismaᶜili History and Thought*. Edited by Farhad Daftary. Cambridge: Cambridge University Press, 1996.

Pound, Roscoe. *An Introduction to the Philosophy of Law*. New Haven: Yale University Press, 1952.

Social Control through Law. New Brunswick: Transaction Publishers, 1997.

Rahman, Fazlur. *Islamic Methodology in History*. Islamabad: Islamic Research Institute, 1965.

Islamic Methodology in History. Delhi: Adam Publishers, 1994.

"The Law of Rebellion in Islam." In *Islam in the Modern World: 1983 Paine Lectures in Religion*. Edited by Jill Raitt. Columbia, MO: University of Missouri–Columbia, n.d.

Reckendorf, H. "ᶜAmmār." *EI1*, I:332; *EI2*, I:448.

Ritter, H. "Ḥasan al-Baṣrī." *EI2*, III:247.

Rommen, Heinrich A. *The Natural Law: A Study in Legal and Social History and Philosophy*. Translated by Thomas R. Hanley. Indianapolis: Liberty Fund, Inc., 1998.

Rosenthal, E. I. J. *Political Thought in Medieval Islam: An Introductory Outline.* Cambridge: Cambridge University Press, 1962.

Ross, Alf. *On Law and Justice.* London: Stevens Publishers, 1958.

Rubinacci, R. "Azāriḳa." *EI2*, 1:810.

Sachedina, Abdulaziz. *The Just Ruler in Shīʿite Islam.* Oxford: Oxford University Press, 1988.

Sanders, Paula A. "The Fāṭimid State, 969–1171." In *The Cambridge History of Egypt: Volume One, Islamic Egypt, 640–1517.* Edited by Carl F. Petry. Cambridge: Cambridge University Press, 1998.

Schacht, Joseph. *An Introduction to Islamic Law.* Oxford: Clarendon Press, 1964.

The Origins of Muhammadan Jurisprudence. Oxford: Clarendon Press, 1950.

"On Some Manuscripts in Kairouan and Tunis." *Arabica* 14 (1967): 225–58.

Schild, Wolfgang. "History of Criminal Law and Procedure." In *Criminal Justice through the Ages.* Translated by John Fosberry. Rothenburg: Mittelalterliches Kriminalmuseum, 1981.

Schisas, Pandias M. *Offenses against the State in Roman Law.* London: University of London Press, 1926.

Schwartz, David Aaron. "International Terrorism and Islamic Law." *Columbia Journal of Transnational Law* 29 (Summer 1991): 629–52.

Seligsohn, M. "ʿĀʾisha." *EI1*, 1:216.

Selznick, Philip. *The Moral Commonwealth: Social Theory and the Promise of Community.* Berkeley: University of California Press, 1992.

Selznick, Philip, and Philippe Nonet. *Law and Society in Transition: Toward Responsive Law*, 1st ed. New York: Harper & Row, 1978.

Selznick, Philip, Philippe Nonet, and Howard M. Vollmer. *Law, Society and Industrial Justice.* New York: Russell Sage Foundation, 1969.

Sezgin, Fouad. *Geschichte des arabischen Schrifttums.* Leiden: E. J. Brill, 1967.

Shaban, M. A. *Islamic History: A New Interpretation I.* Cambridge: Cambridge University Press, 1971.

Islamic History: A New Interpretation II. Cambridge: Cambridge University Press, 1976.

Sharon, Moshe. *Black Banners from the East: The Establishment of the ʿAbbasid State – Incubation of a Revolt.* Jerusalem: The Hebrew University, 1983.

Revolt: The Social and Military Aspects of the ʿAbbāsid Revolution. Jerusalem: The Hebrew University, 1990.

Sharpe, J. A. *Judicial Punishment in England.* London: Faber & Faber, 1990.

Smith, Goldwin. *A Constitutional and Legal History of England.* New York: Dorset Press, 1990.

Smith, Lacey Baldwin. *Treason in Tudor England: Politics and Paranoia.* Princeton: Princeton University Press, 1986.

Sonn, Tamara. "Irregular Warfare and Terrorism in Islam: Asking the Right Questions." In *Cross, Crescent, and Sword: The Justification and Limitation of War in Western and Islamic Tradition.* Edited by James Turner Johnson and John Kelsay. Westport, CT: Greenwood Press, 1990.

Sourdel, Dominique. "La politique religieuse du calife ᶜabbaside al-Ma'mun." *Revue des etudes islamiques* 30 (1962): 27–48.

Spellberg, D. A. *Politics, Gender, and the Islamic Past: The Legacy of ᶜĀ'isha Bint Abī Bakr.* New York: Columbia University Press, 1994.

Staire, James Viscount. *The Institutions of the Law of Scotland.* Edited by David M. Walker. Edinburgh: University of Edinburgh Press, 1981.

Stewart, Devin J. *Islamic Legal Orthodoxy: Twelver Shiite Responses to the Sunni Legal System.* Salt Lake City: University of Utah Press, 1998.

"*Taqiyyah* as Performance: The Travels of Bahā' al-Dīn al-ᶜĀmilī in the Ottoman Empire (991–93/1583–85)." *Princeton Papers: Interdisciplinary Journal of Middle Eastern Studies* 4 (Spring, 1996): 1–70.

Strothmann, R. "Zaidıya."*EI1*, VIII:1196.

Sumner, William Graham. *Folkways: A Study of Sociological Importance of Usages, Manners, Customs, Mores and Morals.* New York: Dover Publications, 1959.

Taswell-Langmead, Thomas Pitt. *English Constitutional History from the Teutonic Conquest to the Present Time.* Edited by Theodore F. T. Plucknett, 10th ed. London: Houghton Miflin Co., 1946.

Todd, S. C. *The Shape of Athenian Law.* Oxford: Clarendon Press, 1995.

Udovitch, Abraham L. *Partnership and Profit in Medieval Islam.* Princeton: Princeton University Press, 1970.

Urvoy, Dominique. "The ᶜUlamā' of al-Andalus." In *The Legacy of Muslim Spain.* Edited by Salma Khadra Jayyusi. Leiden: E. J. Brill, 1992.

Vadet, J. C. "Ibn Masᶜūd." *EI2*, III:873.

Vaglieri, L. Veccia. "ᶜAbd Allāh ibn ᶜUmar." *EI2*, I:53.

"al-Ashᶜarī." *EI2*, I:695.

Van Ess, Joseph. "Ibn Kullāb et la Miḥna." *Arabica* 38 (1990): 173–233.

"Une Lecture a rebours de l'histoire du muᶜtazilisme," parts 1 and 2. *Revue des études islamiques* 46 (1978): 163–240; 47 (1979): 19–69.

Walker, Paul E. "The Ismāᶜīlī Daᶜwa and the Fāṭimid Caliphate." In *The Cambridge History of Egypt: Volume One, Islamic Egypt, 640–1517.* Edited by Carl F. Petry. Cambridge: Cambridge University Press, 1998.

Walker, R. J. and M. G. Walker. *The English Legal System*, 2nd ed. London: Butterworth, 1970.

Wasserstein, D. J. "Mulūk al-Tawā'if in Muslim Spain." *EI2*, VII:552.

Watson, Alan. *The Evolution of Law.* Baltimore: Johns Hopkins University Press, 1985.

Failures of the Legal Imagination. Philadelphia: University of Pennsylvania Press, 1988.

"Legal Change: Sources of Law and Legal Culture." *University of Pennsylvania Law Review* 131 (1983): 1121–57.

Legal Transplants. Charlottesville: University of Virginia Press, 1974.

The Nature of Law. Edinburgh: Edinburgh University Press, 1977.

Society and Legal Change. Edinburgh: Scottish Academic Press, 1977.

Sources of Law, Legal Change, and Ambiguity. Philadelphia: University of Pennsylvania, 1984.
Watt, Montgomery. "ʿĀʾisha Bint Abī Bakr." *EI2*, I:307.
The Formative Period of Islamic Thought. Edinburgh: Edinburgh University Press, 1973.
"Al-Ghazālī," *EI2*, II:1038.
Islamic Political Thought. Edinburgh: Edinburgh University Press, 1968.
White, Edward J. *Legal Antiquities: A Collection of Essays upon Ancient Laws and Customs.* London: Thomas Law Book Co., 1913.
Wilkinson, J. C. "The Early Development of the Ibāḍī Movement in Baṣra." In *Studies on the First Century of Islamic Society.* Edited by G. H. A. Juynboll. Carbondale: Southern Illinois University Press, 1982.
The Imamite Tradition of Oman. Cambridge: Cambridge University Press, 1987.
Zaman, Muhammad Qasim. *Religion and Politics under the Early Abbasids: The Emergence of the Proto-Sunni Elite.* Leiden: E. J. Brill, 1997.
Zettersteen, K. V. "ʿAbd Allāh ibn ʿUmar." *EI1*, I:28.
"Saʿd." *EI1*, VII:29.
Zwemer, S. M. *The Law of Apostasy in Islam.* London: Marsall Brothers, 1924.

Index of names

Index of subjects

LaVergne, TN USA
28 January 2010
171379LV00003B/34/A

9 780521 030571